Lecture Notes in Computer S

Lecture Notes in Artificial Intelligence 15203

Founding Editor

Jörg Siekmann

Series Editors

Randy Goebel, *University of Alberta, Edmonton, Canada*
Wolfgang Wahlster, *DFKI, Berlin, Germany*
Zhi-Hua Zhou, *Nanjing University, Nanjing, China*

The series Lecture Notes in Artificial Intelligence (LNAI) was established in 1988 as a topical subseries of LNCS devoted to artificial intelligence.

The series publishes state-of-the-art research results at a high level. As with the LNCS mother series, the mission of the series is to serve the international R & D community by providing an invaluable service, mainly focused on the publication of conference and workshop proceedings and postproceedings.

Yang Gao	Chang'an University, China
Xing Liu	Northwestern Polytechnical University, China
Jiyu Cheng	Shandong University, China
Yanfeng Lv	Chinese Academy of Sciences, China
Liang Zhao	Henan University of Technology, China
Anzhu Gao	Shanghai Jiao Tong University, China
Yixing Gao	Jilin University, China
Laihao Yang	Xi'an Jiaotong University, China
Yuquan Leng	South University of Science and Technology, China
Honghao Lv	Zhejiang University, China
Weiliang Zuo	Xi'an Jiaotong University, China

Contents – Part III

Emerging Techniques for Intelligent Robots in Unstructured Environment

Three-Dimensional Path Planning Algorithm of UAV Based on Thermal Gradient 3
   Yunlong Wang, Shaoke Wan, Rongcan Qiu, Yuanyang Fang, and Xiaohu Li

Multi-layer Semantic Map Based Navigation for Mobile Robots in Agriculture Environment 16
   Wei Chen, Xuan Zhao, and Huiliang Shang

A General Collision-Free Scheme for Redundant Manipulators 31
   Zongwu Xie, Wandong Sun, Baoshi Cao, Yang Liu, Zhengpu Wang, Hong Liu, and Boyu Ma

Design and Analysis of a Flexible Parallel Robot for Rope-Driven Upper Limb Rehabilitation 45
   Zaixiang Pang, Xiaomeng Deng, Linan Gong, and Nan Wang

A Practical Method for Orchard Robots to Navigate Along Row Medians Using Tree Trunk Maps 60
   Anmin Huang, Enbo Liu, Changguo Xu, Wei Tang, Renyuan Zhang, and Xuebing Yuan

Recursive Neural Network: Small Target Detection in Remote Sensing Images 73
   Changlin Yu, Juchao Zhang, Zhongyu Sun, Zaixiang Pang, Changxian Xu, and Zhongbo Sun

Mobile Robot Path Planning Method Based on Weight Coefficient Improved A* Algorithm 85
   Tao Qin, Hao Chu, Jia Wang, Peng Ren, Min Fu, and Xi Wu

Wolf Pack Algorithm: An Overview 96
   Wei Xu, Yueming Wang, Peng Xu, Tianqi Qiu, Tong Yan, and Zhirui Wang

A Discrete Time-Varying Zeroing Neural Dynamics for Solving Equality
Constrained Optimization 111
   Jie Zhou, Qiaowen Shi, Ruicong Wang, Chao Mou,
   Dimitrios K. Gerontiti, and Yang Shi

Workspace Analysis Based on a Serial-Parallel Hybrid Robot:
Representing Robot Capabilities 123
   Xinze Tian, Baoshi Cao, Le Qi, Xueai Li, Yang Liu, Kui Sun, Fenglei Ni,
   and Zongwu Xie

Path Planning and Gait Switching for Quadruped Robots in Perceptually
Complex Environments 138
   Weijun Tian, Kuiyue Zhou, Jian Song, Xu Li, Zhu Chen, Ziteng Shen,
   Ruizhi Wang, Lei Jiang, and Qian Cong

Real-Time Obstacle Avoidance and Pathfinding for Robot Manipulators
Based on Deep Reinforcement Learning 154
   Jun Hu, Jianliang Mao, Xin Zhou, and Chuanlin Zhang

A Novel Building Construction Inspection Method Based on Naive Bayes
Model by Fusing BIM and Lidar Point Cloud 167
   Boyu Jiang, Liting Fan, Yang Zhang, Yu Han, and Zhongjiang Cheng

Development and Implementation of a Six-Legged Skiing Robot
for Cross-Country Skiing Techniques 185
   Liangyu Wang, Yunpeng Yin, Limin Yang, Feng Gao, and Xianbao Chen

Soft Actuators and Sensors

Design of the Pole-Climbing Robot Based on Yoshimura Origami Actuator 201
   Shilong Liu, Gangqiang Tang, Kangning Tan, Xiaofeng Yu, Dong Mei,
   Shunan An, and Yanjie Wang

A Soft Pneumatic Gripper Integrated Strain and Piezoresistive Sensors
for Grasping Detection 211
   Xin Zhao, Jianfeng Wang, Gangqiang Tang, Dong Mei, Chun Zhao,
   and Yanjie Wang

Drift-Free Ionotronic Sensing 223
   Canhui Yang

Design and Analysis of an Exoskeleton Robotic Actuator for Lumbar
Spine Assisted Rehabilitation 235
   Lisheng Wang, Linsen Xu, Zhihuan Wang, Liangzhi Ye, and Huan Mei

Variable Stiffness Performance Analysis of Layer Jamming Actuator
Based on Bionic Adhesive Flaps 249
   Liangzhi Ye, Linsen Xu, Zhihuan Wang, Lisheng Wang, and Huan Mei

Research on End-Effector Decoupling Control Strategy Based on Dual
Force Sensors 261
   Ying Zhong, Han Chen, Chin-Yin Chen, Junjie Dai, Yuncai Zhao, and Chi Zhang

MLP-Depth: An Improved Visuo-Tactile 3D Reconstruction Method
Applied to TIRgel Sensor 275
   Shixin Zhang, Yuhao Sun, Funchun Sun, Huaping Liu, Yiyong Yang, and Bin Fang

Design and Performance Testing of Electro-fluidic Soft Actuator 286
   Yuze Ye, Qingsong He, Lin Xie, Changli Yang, and Shouyi Ni

A Flexible Sensor Based on PVC Gel for Detections of Robotic Grasping 299
   Qiyun Zhong, Qingsong He, Lin Xie, and Ziyan Shi

A Soft Amphibious Robot with Buoyancy Control and Underwater
Manipulation Capabilities 311
   Yang Yang, Haozhe Zheng, Yuan Xie, Pei Jiang, and Yingtian Li

Deep Learning Network Based Time Series Prediction Model
for Cyanobacterial Concentration Using a Many-Objective Algorithm 325
   Bao Liu and Jiaxin Li

Research and Application of Key Technology of "One-Click Opening
and Closing" of Hydropower Station Gate Based on Intelligent Portal Crane ... 336
   Hailong Zhang, Jin Yang, Hui Zeng, Xiaoxiang Wei, Wu Zhou, Wen Liu, Haiwei Lei, and Jun Chen

Superior Performances of a Novel Soft Electroactive Actuator Based
on High-Purity Single-Walled Carbon Nanotubes 352
   Guangyao Hu, Weixing Feng, Nan Zhang, Longlong Wang, Dewen Niu, and Jie Ru

A Sound Absorber Based on IPMC Electro-Mechanical Conversion
Mechanism 360
   Tao Wang, Yachao Zhang, Bo Li, Ying Hu, Alvo Aabloo, and Longfei Chang

Advanced Intelligent and Flexible Sensor Technologies for Robotics

Design of a Wearable EEG Signal Acquisition System for Brain-Computer Interaction 373
    Fei Fei, Yiqi Wu, Ruonan Yang, Lizhi Mao, and Qianru Zhang

Enhancing Robotic Hand Control with Electronic Slime-Based Flexible Finger Joint Motion Sensor 388
    Yu Feng, Hui Sun, Meng Chen, Xiaodong Yu, Cong Wu, Guanglie Zhang, and Wen Jung Li

A Biocompatible Strain Sensor Based on Ni-GaIn and SA-Doped PAAM for Implantable Bioelectronics 400
    Mingxi Tu, Jiawen Liang, Hongji Guo, Tianming Zhao, and Haibo Yu

Advancing Human-Machine Interaction Using Intelligent Wearable Acoustic Sensors in Noisy Environments 409
    Hui Sun, Xiaomeng Yang, Cong Wu, Yu Feng, Meng Chen, Guanglie Zhang, and Wen Jung Li

A Fast Online Adapting Algorithm for SEMG-Based Gesture Recognition in Non-Ideal Conditions 422
    Shengli Zhou, Chuan Liu, Meibo Lv, Ruixing Yu, and Kuiying Yin

Author Index 435

Emerging Techniques for Intelligent Robots in Unstructured Environment

Three-Dimensional Path Planning Algorithm of UAV Based on Thermal Gradient

Yunlong Wang, Shaoke Wan, Rongcan Qiu, Yuanyang Fang, and Xiaohu Li(✉)

Department of Mechanical Engineering, Xi'an Jiaotong University, Xi'an 710049, China
li.xiaohu@xjtu.edu.cn

Abstract. Three-dimensional path planning is one of the key technologies for UAVs to achieve autonomous movement. Due to the influence of environmental diversity, currently commonly used algorithms have certain limitations. This paper proposes a three-dimensional planning algorithm for UAVs based on thermal gradients. This algorithm uses the idea of solving the heat transfer path in the steady-state thermal potential field to analogize the UAV's flight path, and regards the UAV's optimal path as a stable The path with the fastest temperature drop in the state thermal potential field, the key navigation points planned according to the principle of the fastest drop in thermal gradient, and the trajectory after path planning were optimized, and a safe and feasible trajectory was successfully planned in the three-dimensional environment. The transformed thermal potential field contains global environmental information, and combined with the principle of the fastest temperature gradient descent search, it can overcome the blindness in the path planning process. There are no local minima in the thermal potential field, which allows the method to efficiently handle scenes with complex obstacles. The simulation and comparison results show that the algorithm has faster convergence speed compared to commonly used UAV path planning algorithms and is widely applicable to various three-dimensional environments.

Keywords: Thermal Gradient · Three-dimensional Space · UAV Path Planning

1 Introduction

With the development of current science and technology, UAVs are widely used in various environments due to their high mobility and other characteristics, and three-dimensional path planning has become a new research focus. The path planning problem can be described as follows: given a robot and its working environment, considering the geometric constraints and robot motion constraints in the space, plan a safe and feasible path based on the starting position and target position. Good path planning technology can not only significantly improve the flight efficiency of UAVs, but also effectively reduce the collision and wear of UAVs and improve their safety. Therefore, UAV path planning has important application value [1].

In the past few decades, researchers have proposed a variety of UAV three-dimensional path planning algorithms, including the heuristic-based Dijkstra [2] algorithm, the A* algorithm [3], and the swarm intelligence bionic-based algorithm ant colony algorithm [4], genetic algorithm [5], particle swarm algorithm [6] and artificial potential field method [7]. Dijkstra's algorithm uses the breadth-first idea to find the optimal solution, but this method does not use target point information and requires a large amount of calculation. The A* algorithm adds a heuristic function to the Dijkstra algorithm framework to guide nodes to expand in the target direction and improve computing efficiency. It is one of the most commonly used search algorithms. The swarm intelligence algorithm has several shortcomings such as unsatisfactory algorithm convergence speed, complex design, large memory consumption, and is not suitable for low-cost robots [8]. Although the artificial potential field method is widely used in dealing with dynamic or unknown environments, its common local minimum problem causes mobile robots to oscillate near obstacles or get stuck [9]. Many scholars have found that analogizing the path planning problem of mobile robots to solving the heat transfer path problem in a thermal potential field can effectively solve the local minimum problem existing in the potential field method. Researchers have proposed a variety of path planning methods based on the principle of thermal potential field. Inspired by the principles of steady-state heat transfer, Wang et al. [10] pioneered a novel path-planning approach grounded in thermal-potential theory. This method avoids local minima inherently as steady-state heat conduction aligns with the characteristics of harmonic potentials, which is a point previously demonstrated by Connolly et al. [11]. Saudi [12] and others continue to improve the numerical method for solving the thermal potential field. In 2017, Golan [13] et al. used the finite difference method to achieve online navigation of mobile robots in temperature gradient solution. J.C. Ryu [14] and others introduced the topology optimization method in the thermal potential field and verified the feasibility of this method in a variety of environments and conditions. Baotong Li [15] proposed a computational framework for the growth simulation concept, which realizes path planning through the process of continuous growth of materials, but it is only applicable to static environments. Xiaohu Li [16, 17] and others proposed an innovative online navigation approach leveraging thermal compliance, guaranteeing optimal routes in dynamic and unknown environment. However, this algorithm is only applicable to two-dimensional mobile robots, and UAVs in three-dimensional space require a path planning algorithm with faster convergence speed to cope with their own ever-changing states and complex obstacle environments.

Therefore, there are some defects in path planning of UAVs in three-dimensional environments, such as causing UAVs to get stuck in traps at local minimum points and being unable to handle more complex environments. This paper proposes a three-dimensional path planning algorithm for UAVs based on thermal gradients, which can essentially solve the problem of local minimum points. According to the mapping rules, the path planning problem of the mobile robot is converted into a thermal potential field to find optimal heat transfer path problem. Then, combined with the principle of the fastest temperature gradient descent search, proposed method can overcome the blindness in the path planning process, find the optimal UAV path.

2 Thermal Gradient Model

2.1 Problem Analogy

In the realm of thermodynamics, the interplay between a heat source and a heat sink elucidates a fundamental principle: the tendency of heat to flow from regions of higher temperature to those of lower temperature until equilibrium is attained. Analogously, in the domain of path planning, the quest for an optimal trajectory from an initial point to a final destination mirrors this dynamic. Here, the aim is to navigate through the space efficiently, much like heat seeking its equilibrium, while considering various constraints such as safety, avoidance of obstacles, and minimizing distance traveled. In both contexts, the underlying objective revolves around achieving an optimal outcome with the least expenditure of resources. Just as heat diffuses along the path of least resistance between a source and a sink, a path planner endeavors to chart a course that minimizes obstacles and maximizes efficiency, ensuring a swift and safe journey from start to finish. This parallel underscores the common thread of optimization, where the goal is to achieve the desired objective—be it thermal equilibrium or path traversal—with minimal energy expenditure and time delay, thus optimizing the overall process [16, 17].

To apply the heat conduction heat transfer path identification method to the problem of three-dimensional path planning for UAVs, it is essential to establish a direct analogy between key physical parameters in both problem domains. Here, we model the starting point and the target point as analogs to heat source and heat sink, respectively. The open areas within the UAV's configuration space are designated as the heat conduction domain, while regions occupied by obstacles are delineated as non-heat conductive areas. This analogy relationship is summarized in Table 1 [17].

Table 1. Analogy relationship table

UAV path planning	Identification of heat transfer paths
Start point	Heat source
Target point	Heat sink
Free space	Heat transfer domain
Obstacle space	Non-thermal conductive area
Raster map	Finite element mesh
Optimal motion path	Optimal heat transfer path

2.2 Mapping Relations

Before using thermodynamic methods to solve the UAV path planning problem, it is indispensable to construct the corresponding mapping relationship. In a three-dimensional complex environment, the goal of the path planning algorithm is not only to find a collision-free path, but also to meet optimality indicators such as the shortest path length or the least energy consumption. In a three-dimensional steady-state thermal environment, heat flow will also flow from the heat source to the heat sink along an optimal heat transfer path, and will not pass into the area where the thermal conductivity is zero. Judging from indicators such as optimality and security, the requirements of the two paths are very similar. Although one dimension is added to the three-dimensional space, no additional physical quantity is added to the thermal potential field. The three-dimensional space is modeled through the unit decomposition method, and the resulting raster map can correspond to the finite element grid.

As shown in Fig. 1, the three-dimensional configuration space of the UAV is composed of four parts: the starting point, the target point, the free area, and the obstacle area of the UAV:

$$C = \left(C_O^1 + C_O^2 + \cdots\right) + C_S + C_G + C_F \tag{1}$$

where C is mobile robot configuration space. C_O^i is the obstacle area. C_s and C_g are the starting point and the target point of the mobile robot. C_F is mobile robot's free space.

The UAV configuration space C is mapped to the entire heat conduction finite element analysis domain H according to the following correspondence [16].

$$C \rightarrow H : \begin{cases} C_S \rightarrow H_S \\ C_G \rightarrow H_G \\ C_F \rightarrow H_F \\ C_O \rightarrow H_O \end{cases} \tag{2}$$

Similarly, the entire thermal analysis domain includes four parts:

$$H = \left(H_O^1 + H_O^2 + \cdots\right) + H_S + H_G + H_F \tag{3}$$

where H is thermal analysis area. H_o^i is non-heat conducting region. H_S and H_G are heat source and heat sink in thermal analysis areas. H_F is heat conduction region.

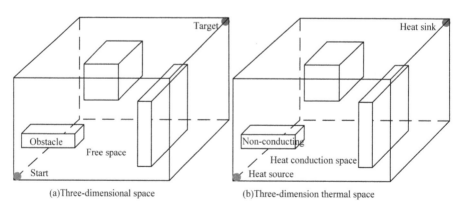

Fig. 1. Three-dimensional configuration space of UAV and converted thermal analysis domain

3 Three-Dimensional Path Planning Algorithm Based on Thermal Gradient

The search based on thermal gradient is to find the path with the fastest temperature drop in the three-dimensional space. To determine this path, the temperature field of the entire thermal analysis domain must be obtained by numerically solving the thermal conduction differential equation. For the three-dimensional steady-state heat conduction problem, the simplified differential equation is as shown in Eq. (4):

$$\frac{\partial}{\partial x}\left(k_x \frac{\partial \mathbf{T}(x,y,z)}{\partial x}\right) + \frac{\partial}{\partial y}\left(k_y \frac{\partial \mathbf{T}(x,y,z)}{\partial y}\right) + \frac{\partial}{\partial z}\left(k_z \frac{\partial \mathbf{T}(x,y,z)}{\partial z}\right) + Q = 0 \quad (4)$$

where $\mathbf{T}$ is temperature field. k_x, k_y and k_z are thermal conductivity of the material along the x, y and z directions. Q is heat per unit volume of the heat source.

Materials with the same properties have the same thermal conductivity:

$$K_x = K_y = K_z = \lambda_0 \quad (5)$$

The temperature field $\mathbf{T}(x, y, z)$ within the unit is expressed as:

$$\mathbf{T} = [\mathbf{N}]\{T_e\} \quad (6)$$

where $[\mathbf{N}]$ is shape function. $\{T_e\}$ is the node degree of freedom.

The temperature is gradient expressed as:

$$\begin{aligned} \{T_x, T_y, T_z\}^\mathrm{T} &= [\mathbf{B}]\{T_e\} \\ [\mathbf{B}] &= \left\{\frac{\partial}{\partial X}, \frac{\partial}{\partial Y}, \frac{\partial}{\partial Z}\right\}^\mathrm{T} [\mathbf{N}] \end{aligned} \quad (7)$$

where $[\mathbf{B}]$ is derivative matrix of the shape functions.

Its heat conduction matrix is defined as follows:

$$\begin{aligned} \mathbf{K} &= \mathbf{K}_1 + \mathbf{K}_2 \\ &= \sum_e \int_{\Omega^e} \mathbf{B}^\mathrm{T} \lambda_0 \mathbf{B} d\Omega + \sum_e \int_{\Omega^e} \beta [\mathbf{N}]^\mathrm{T} [\mathbf{N}] dS \end{aligned} \quad (8)$$

where e is the number of units; Ω^e is the area occupied by the unit; $\mathbf{K}_1$ is the volume integral part, representing the heat conduction within the material; $\mathbf{K}_2$ is the surface integral part, representing the heat conduction and boundary condition contributions at the surface or boundary.

For the thermal conductivity domain of the thermal analysis domain, its interior is regarded as a low thermal conductivity material, and the positive thermal conductivity assigned to this type of unit is 1; in order to prevent large numerical errors in subsequent calculations, nodes covered by non-thermal conductive areas are assigned a far A positive number less than 1. By assembling the overall stiffness matrix of the entire thermal analysis domain, the temperature field $\mathbf{T}$ can be solved.

$$\mathbf{K} \cdot \mathbf{T} = \mathbf{F} \quad (9)$$

where **F** is the thermal load that determined by heat sink and heat source.

After obtaining the temperature field of the overall thermal analysis domain, the unit temperature covered by the obstacle is regarded as infinite to prevent the path planning algorithm based on thermal gradient from planning the obstacle nodes into a feasible path. Starting from the starting point, the heat source, the thermal gradient between this cell and its adjacent cells is calculated. According to Eq. (10), determine the node with the fastest temperature gradient drop and add it to the path point, and repeat this process until the heat sink.

$$J_{best\_grad} = \min(\frac{\mathbf{T}_{x+i,y+j,z+k} - \mathbf{T}_{x,y,z}}{L_{i,j,k}})$$

$$\text{s.t.} \quad i, j, k \in \{-step, 0, step\} \quad |i| + |j| + |k| \neq 0 \tag{10}$$

$$L_{i,j,k} = \sqrt[3]{\frac{i^2 + j^2 + k^2}{3}}$$

where $\mathbf{T}_{x,y,z}$ is the temperature of coordinates (x, y, z) in the corresponding three-dimensional steady-state temperature field.

Since changes in the temperature field are often nonlinear, unreasonable step size design will lead to searching for the wrong optimal direction. It is worth noting that in some narrow channel areas, there are cases where the temperature gradient in the nearby area does not change significantly. A large step-length "look-ahead step" is introduced here to improve the algorithm's optimization capability. In addition, the step size in the diagonal direction is $\sqrt{2}$ times the unit step size, which also needs to be multiplied by an appropriate coefficient to eliminate the impact of nonlinear changes in the temperature field. The objective function form of Eq. (10) can be rewritten as follows:

$$J_{best\_grad} = \min(\alpha_1 \frac{\mathbf{T}_{x+i,y+j,z+k} - \mathbf{T}_{x,y,z}}{L_{i,j,k}} + \alpha_2 \frac{\mathbf{T}_{x+2i,y+2j,z+2k} - \mathbf{T}_{x,y,z}}{L_{2i,2j,2k}}) \tag{11}$$

where α_1 and α_2 are the weight coefficient, setting to a positive number less than 1.

Based on the above principles, the three-dimensional path planning algorithm based on thermal gradient proposed in this article includes the following 2 basic steps:

1) According to the corresponding relationship, the global path planning problem in the three-dimensional environment is converted into a design to find the path with the fastest temperature drop in the thermal analysis domain. Discretize the thermal analysis domain into a finite element mesh. Define all boundary constraints, thermal loads, and material thermal conductivity properties for each zone.
2) Define the starting point and end point as the heat source and heat sink. Thermal conductivity coefficients are assigned according to the thermal conductivity properties of different areas, and the temperature field is solved through the finite element method. After obtaining the temperature field of the overall thermal analysis domain, start from the starting point, which is the heat source, and search for the adjacent nodes with the largest thermal gradient according to the optimization model. Repeat the above steps until the end point to obtain the movement path of the drone. The pseudo code is shown in Table 2.

Table 2. Pseudo code of three-dimensional path planning algorithm based on thermal gradient

Algorithm
1: **Input**: Map; Start; Goal; Grid_size;
2: **Output**: path
3: **Function**: Initialize (Map, Start, Goal, Grid_size)
4:    Heat_source = Start; Heat_sink = Goal; Heat_space = Map;
5: **Function** Main ( )
6:    Initialize (Map, Start, Goal, Grid_size);
7:    $K = K_{Conductor} + K_{Insultor}$; $T = K^{-1}F$;
8:    $x = Start\_x$; $y = Start\_y$; $path[Loop] = Start$;
9: **loop**:
10:    best_grad = 0;
11:    **for** $i = -step : step$
12:      **for** $j = -step : step$
13:        $temp\_grad = (T(x,y,z) - T(x+i, y+j, z+k))\sqrt{((i^2+j^2+k^2)/2)}$;
14:        **if** $temp\_grad > best\_grad$ **do**
15:            $best\_grad = temp\_grad$; $x_{next} = i$; $y_{next} = j$; $z_{next} = k$;
16:    $(x, y, z) = (x+i, y+j, z+k)$;
17:    **if** $(x, y, z) = Goal$ **do**
18:        $path[Loop] = (x, y, z)$; **terminate**(success);
19:    $Loop = Loop + 1$; $path[Loop] = (x, y, z)$;
20: **end loop**

4 Experimental Comparison

In this article, a series of three-dimensional environments are designed to verify the aforementioned three-dimensional path planning algorithm based on thermal gradients, and the Minimum snap trajectory optimization algorithm is used on the planned trajectory to smooth the trajectory and facilitate the execution of the drone. The simulation experiment environment is: MATLAB R2016b, Windows 10, CPU: Inter(R) Core(TM) i5-9400F CPU @ 2.90 Ghz, RAM: 8 GB. The motion planning framework of the UAV system refers to the MEAM620 project of the University of Pennsylvania [19]. In the entire framework, it is only necessary to write the path planning algorithm and trajectory planning algorithm proposed in this article as sub-functions to replace the algorithms in the source file. The PID tracking control algorithm is provided in the motion planning framework. The parameters of the simulated quadcopter UAV are shown in Table 3.

Table 3. Parameter table of quad-rotor UAV

Parameter	M/kg	L/m	I_{xx}/kg·m^{-2}	I_{yy}/kg·m^{-2}	I_{zz}/kg·m^{-2}
Value	0.030	0.046	1.43×10^{-5}	1.43×10^{-5}	2.89×10^{-5}

Case 1: A three-dimensional space with obstacles scattered at different heights

Set the simulation environment to a three-dimensional space with a length of 8 m, a width of 4 m, a height of 4 m, and a unit side length of 0.2 m. In this space, set the starting position and target position, use the algorithm proposed in this article to plan the path of the UAV, and optimize the path at the same time. Use the PID control method for trajectory tracking. Figure 2 UAV movement process shows the quad-rotor UAV. The movement process of the UAV. Figure 3 show the position and speed curves of the UAV. The blue curve is the final trajectory obtained by the UAV three-dimensional planning algorithm based on thermal gradient and the planning generation algorithm based on Minimum snap. The red curve is the final trajectory of the UAV. The trajectory tracked by the machine PID control algorithm. The A* algorithm [3] and the RRT-bias [20] algorithm were selected to compare with the algorithm in this paper. The final data results are shown in Table 4.

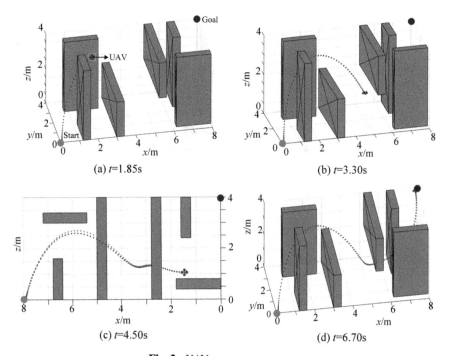

Fig. 2. UAV movement process

As can be seen from Table 4, in an unstructured environment with sparse obstacles, the gradient method takes 0.353 s to plan the global motion trajectory of the UAV, and the planned global path length is 15.154 m, which is very close to the optimal solution of 14.767 m. It can be seen in Fig. 2 that the UAV reached the target point in 6.70 s and was able to avoid obstacles during the movement; Fig. 3 position and speed curves illustrate that the speed curve is continuous without sudden changes during the movement of the UAV. Moreover, the planning curve and the tracking curve have a high degree of overlap, indicating that the tracking effect is good. This example illustrates that the proposed three-dimensional method based on thermal gradient and the trajectory

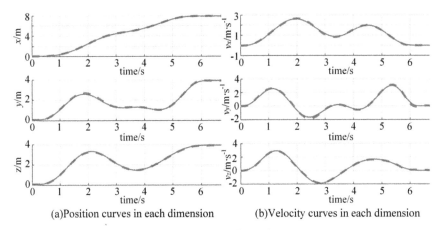

Fig. 3. Position and speed curve

Table 4. Algorithm data comparison of Case 1

	A*	RRT-bias	Thermal gradient
Time/s	0.865	0.172	0.353
Length/m	14.767	19.231	15.154

planning algorithm based on Minimum snap can effectively solve the path planning problem of obstacles in three-dimensional space, and the planned trajectory meets the requirements of smoothness, safety and collision-free.

Case 2: Three-dimensional space with narrow passages

In this example, the thermal gradient algorithm is used to deal with the path planning problem in an environmental space with narrow passages. Figure 4(a) intuitively shows the obstacle configuration in this environment. The size of the map is 19 m × 5 m × 5 m, and the entire three-dimensional space is discretized into a 95 × 25 × 25 three-dimensional grid map with a unit side length of 0.2 m. There are three 1 m × 5 m × 5 m obstacles of 1 m × 1 m × 1m in the space. There is only one narrow channel on each obstacle that allows the drone to pass. The volume of the narrow channel is. The starting point coordinates of the drone are (0, 5, 5), and the target point coordinates are (19, 5, 5). The path planning results and UAV motion process are shown in Fig. 4, the position and speed curves are shown in Fig. 5, the trajectories of A* Algorithm and RRT-bias Algorithm are shown in Fig. 6, and Table 5 shows the algorithm comparison results.

After mapping the three-dimensional space into a thermal potential field, a safe and collision-free path can be quickly found in the three-dimensional thermal analysis domain based on the principle of finding the path with the fastest thermal gradient descent. This also proves that the thermal potential field has no local pole. Due to the characteristics of small points, the planned path passes through the center of the narrow passage, which improves the safety of the path. As can be seen from Table 5, the search algorithm based on thermal gradient only takes 1.533 s to plan the global path, and

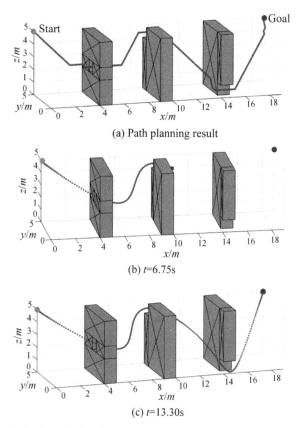

(a) Path planning result

(b) t=6.75s

(c) t=13.30s

Fig. 4. Path planning results and UAV movement process

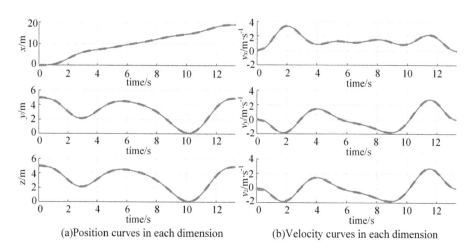

(a) Position curves in each dimension   (b) Velocity curves in each dimension

Fig. 5. Position and velocity graph

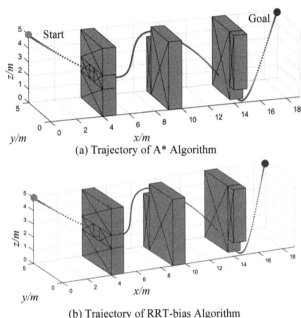

Fig. 6. Trajectories of A* Algorithm and RRT-bias Algorithm

Table 5. Algorithm data comparison of Case 2

	A*	RRT-bias	Thermal gradient
Time/s	5.481	12.354	1.533
Length/m	28.175	29.125	28.175

the algorithm convergence time is 12% of the RRT-bias algorithm and 30% of the A* algorithm. The planning method based on the RRT class has a slow convergence speed in an environment with narrow channels, and it takes 12.354 s to plan the global path. The UAV reached the target point in 13.30 s and was able to pass through the narrow passage safely and stably during the movement. The position and speed curves in Fig. 5 also show that the UAV's speed did not produce oscillation mutations. The trajectory planning algorithm based on Minimum snap Plan safe and smooth trajectories in 3D space with narrow passages.

It can be seen from the above results that the planning algorithm based on thermal gradient fundamentally avoids the blindness of the search. The security, rapidity of the algorithm and the characteristics of the thermal potential field without local minimum points still exist. Combining the above characteristics, this method It can effectively handle global path planning problems in three-dimensional space. The trajectory planning algorithm based on Minimum Snap can plan a safe, smooth trajectory that conforms to the dynamic model of the UAV. The speed of the UAV is stable without sudden changes during tracking the trajectory, which shows that the proposed method is suitable for UAV trajectory planning problems and has wide adaptability.

5 Conclusion

After establishing a three-dimensional heat transfer model based on the mapping rules between the path planning problem and the problem of finding the optimal heat transfer path in the thermal potential field, based on the key navigation points planned by the three-dimensional path planning algorithm based on thermal gradients, differential flatness is used The method converts the high-dimensional planning problem of UAV into a low-dimensional flat space and combines the optimization criteria of polynomial curve and Minimum snap to realize the trajectory planning of UAV in three-dimensional space. The simulation results show that the proposed method The blindness of the search is eliminated, and the algorithm converges quickly. In complex environments, the algorithm convergence time is 12% of the RRT-bias algorithm and 30% of the A* algorithm. It can plan safe, smooth and consistent dynamics trajectory for the drone. According to the trajectory of the model, the speed of the UAV is stable without sudden changes during the trajectory tracking process, and can be widely used in non-structured three-dimensional environments.

References

1. Xu, X.: Research on Location and Path Planning Algorithm for Outdoor Mobile Robots. Beijing University of Posts and Telecommunications (2021)
2. Dijkstra, E.W.: A note on two problems in connexion with graphs. Numer. Math. **1**(1), 269–271 (1959)
3. Heuristics, P.J.: Intelligent search strategies for computer problem solving (1984)
4. Miao, C., Chen, G., Yan, C., et al.: Path planning optimization of indoor mobile robot based on adaptive ant colony algorithm. Comput. Ind. Eng. **156**, 107230 (2021)
5. Lamini, C., Benhlima, S., Elbekri, A.: Genetic algorithm based approach for autonomous mobile robot path planning. Procedia Comput. Sci. **127**, 180–189 (2018)
6. Dai, H.P., Chen, D.D., Zheng, Z.S.: Effects of random values for particle swarm optimization algorithm. Algorithms **11**(2), 23 (2018)
7. Song, Q., Liu, L.: Mobile robot path planning based on dynamic fuzzy artificial potential field method. Int. J. Hybrid Inf. Technol. **5**(4), 85–94 (2012)
8. Patle, B.K., Pandey, A., Parhi, D.R.K., et al.: A review: on path planning strategies for navigation of mobile robot. Def. Technol. **15**(4), 582–606 (2019)
9. Koren, Y., Borenstein, J.: Potential field methods and their inherent limitations for mobile robot navigation. In: ICRA, vol. 2, pp. 1398–1404 (1991)
10. Wang, Y., Chirikjian, G.S.: A new potential field method for robot path planning. In: Proceedings of the IEEE International Conference on Robotics and Automation, pp. 977–982. IEEE (2000)
11. Connolly, C.I., Burns, J.B., Weiss, R.: Path planning using Laplace's equation. In: Proceedings of the IEEE International Conference on Robotics and Automation, pp. 2102–2106. IEEE (1990)
12. Saudi, A., Sulaiman, J.: Path planning for indoor mobile robot using Half-Sweep SOR via nine-point Laplacian (HSSOR9L). IOSR J. Math. **3**(2), 01–07 (2012)

13. Golan, Y., Edelman, S., Shapiro, A., et al.: Online robot navigation using continuously updated artificial temperature gradients. IEEE Robot. Autom. Lett. **2**(3), 1280–1287 (2017)
14. Ryu, J.C., Park, F.C., Kim, Y.Y.: Mobile robot path planning algorithm by equivalent conduction heat flow topology optimization. Struct. Multidiscip. Optim. **45**(5), 703–715 (2012)
15. Li, B., Liu, H., Su, W.: Topology optimization techniques for mobile robot path planning. Appl. Soft Comput. **78**, 528–544 (2019)
16. Wan, S., Wang, Y., Qi, P., Fang, Y., Li, X.: Online navigation method for mobile robot based on thermal compliance. IEEE Trans. Ind. Electron. https://doi.org/10.1109/TIE.2024.3360608
17. Li, X., Zhao, G., Li, B.: Generating optimal path by level set approach for a mobile robot moving in static/dynamic environments. Appl. Math. Model. **85**, 210–230 (2020)
18. Dbouk, T.: A review about the engineering design of optimal heat transfer systems using topology optimization. Appl. Therm. Eng. **112**, 841–854 (2017)
19. MEAM 620: Robotics. https://alliance.seas.upenn.edu/~meam620/wiki/
20. Urmson, C, Simmons, R.: Approaches for heuristically biasing RRT growth. In: Proceedings of the International Conference on Intelligent Robots and Systems, pp. 1178–1183. IEEE (2003)

Multi-layer Semantic Map Based Navigation for Mobile Robots in Agriculture Environment

Wei Chen[1], Xuan Zhao[2], and Huiliang Shang[3](✉)

[1] School of Information and Software Engineering, University of Electronic Science and Technology of China, Chengdu, China
[2] Yiwu Research Institute, Fudan University, Shanghai, China
zhaox@fudan.edu.cn
[3] School of Information Science and Technology, Fudan University, Shanghai, China
shanghl@fudan.edu.cn

Abstract. Autonomous navigation has significant applications in agricultural environments. Based on the characteristics of agricultural environments, navigation is required to have a high level of intelligence, which necessitates making intelligent anthropomorphic decisions by comprehensively considering the actual environment. Traditional navigation methods often rely on the use of radar and cameras, which can lead to issues with adaptability and accuracy in practical applications. Agricultural environments often have many dynamic factors and environmental noise, and because they cannot distinguish between pedestrians and other dynamic obstacles, there may be potential resource wastage in path planning. This paper proposes an integrated semantic information layered cost map navigation system, which integrates different semantic information for different environments and provides it for use by the layered cost map. This enables it to make anthropomorphic decisions by comprehensively considering complex and variable environmental factors and the system's own characteristics. The use of layered cost maps is also conducive to the design of multi-agent collaborative systems.

Keywords: Costmap · Semantic information · Agriculture Environment

1 Introduction

Agricultural robots have the potential to revolutionize farming by enhancing productivity, reducing labor costs, and increasing the precision of agricultural practices. Robots equipped with advanced sensors and AI can also gather and analyze data to optimize crop management, leading to better resource utilization and higher yields. For example, they can detect and treat diseases or pests early, reducing the need for chemical interventions and promoting sustainable farming practices. In regions facing labor shortages, agricultural robots can fill the gap, ensuring that critical farming tasks are completed on time. Efficient navigation is crucial for these robots to operate autonomously in complex agricultural environments, which are often unstructured and dynamic. Traditional navigation systems, primarily designed for urban or indoor settings, struggle to adapt to the unique challenges posed by agricultural fields, such as varying terrain, dense vegetation, and unpredictable obstacles. In agricultural environments, robots must not only navigate efficiently but also interact intelligently with their surroundings. This requires a deep understanding of the environment, which can be achieved through semantic mapping. Semantic maps provide a richer representation by categorizing different elements of the environment, allowing robots to make informed decisions. However, existing semantic mapping approaches often lack the necessary granularity and multi-layered perspective required for complex agricultural tasks.

The primary objective of this research is to develop a multi-layer semantic map-based navigation system tailored for mobile robots operating in agricultural environments. This system aims to enhance the robots' ability to navigate, perceive, and interact with the environment more effectively. By integrating multiple layers of semantic information, such as terrain types, crop distributions, and obstacle locations, the proposed navigation system seeks to improve the robustness and efficiency of robotic operations in agriculture.

This paper establishes relationships between different semantic levels using multi-level semantic mapping. By connecting semantic information at various levels, it achieves a mapping relationship that allows for the transmission of semantic information across these levels, which uses the layers that are called transfer layers, recording the mapping relationships between different levels [5]. This method offers the following advantages in agricultural navigation systems:

- **Intelligent Path Planning:** The system uses layered cost maps for smarter path planning, synthesizing environmental conditions and robot modules for better decision-making.
- **Environmental Adaptability:** The modular design allows for different module selections based on needs. By integrating multi-source data, the system adapts well to various environments.

2 Related Works

2.1 Existing Navigation Methods

Mobile robots use various navigation technologies in agricultural environments, including GPS, MU, visual, LiDAR, SLAM, and wireless beacon navigation. Each has advantages and limitations. GPS offers high accuracy and wide coverage but can be affected by obstacles and requires good reception. INS is not affected by external factors but accumulates errors over time and needs a stable system. Visual navigation can acquire rich environmental information and perform real-time target recognition and tracking, but is sensitive to environmental changes and requires substantial computational support. LiDAR enables precise measurement of environmental information, obstacle avoidance, and is suitable for complex environments, but has high equipment costs and requires integration and installation. SLAM allows for positioning and map construction in unknown environments, enabling real-time localization and map updates, but demands high computational resources and accuracy is affected by map construction and sensor errors. Wireless beacon navigation provides precise positioning and navigation with stable signals, but requires pre-installation of devices and has limited signal coverage. The choice of navigation technology depends on specific scenarios and requirements. This paper aims to integrate the advantages of these technologies to address a wider range of application scenarios using semantic mapping and layered cost mapping methods [6].

2.2 Semantic Mapping Approaches

Semantic mapping is a technique used to assign semantic labels (e.g., floor, wall, furniture) to the points in a robot's environment. This approach goes beyond traditional occupancy grid-based mapping and provides a more meaningful representation of the environment. Semantic mapping is particularly useful for enabling robots to understand and interact with their environment in a more human-like manner [9].

It typically involves the use of sensor data (e.g., LiDAR, RGB-D) and machine learning algorithms to classify the observed points into different semantic categories. The mapping process involves the creation of a semantic grid or point cloud, where each cell or point is associated with a specific semantic label.

With the advantages that semantic mapping provides a rich representation of the environment, which can be used for various tasks such as object recognition, scene understanding, and path planning and it enables robots to interpret the environment in a more human-like manner, which is beneficial for tasks requiring interaction with the environment or human-robot collaboration, it also has limitation that semantic mapping can be computationally expensive, especially when using high-resolution sensors or large datasets, and the performance of semantic mapping algorithms can be affected by variations in the environment, such as changes in lighting conditions or the presence of occlusions.

2.3 Layered Costmap Approaches

The approach of stratified cost mapping serves to quantify the traversal expenses at particular locations or along certain segments within a given environment. Widely implemented in robotic pathfinding, this strategy is instrumental in formulating obstacle-avoiding routes. It involves the development of a series of cost layers, each representing a unique environmental attribute, such as stationary barriers, transient impediments, or the irregularity of the ground. The formation of each layer is commonly facilitated by distinct sensing mechanisms or computational techniques. The composite cost at specific points is determined by integrating the costs contributed by each layer.

It has the advantages that layered costmap approaches allow for the integration of diverse sensor data and algorithms, providing a comprehensive representation of the environment for navigation tasks, [5] and they enable robots to adapt to different environmental conditions and requirements by adjusting the weights or adding/removing costmap layers.While the limitation is that the generation of multiple costmap layers can be computationally demanding, especially for complex environments or robots with limited computational resources. The accuracy and effectiveness of layered costmap approaches depend on the quality and reliability of the underlying sensor data and algorithms.

2.4 Semantic Mapping

Integrating semantic labeling into the navigation of mobile robots in agricultural environments involves combining the process of creating environmental maps with assigning meaningful tags or semantics to the mapped features. This integration can provide a more nuanced understanding for navigation controls, enhancing the robot's adaptability and operational capabilities within the respective environment. In agricultural settings, this technology enables the robot arm to recognize and process targets detected during navigation while the vehicle is in motion, adopting different strategies for different objects. For example, it can move aside branches with fruit, avoid immovable obstacles like beams, and disregard harmless leaves. Consequently, this technology can be applied to autonomous driving and harvesting tasks.We typically achieve the desired results through the following steps:

The first is positioning and mapping. Through lidar and depth camera, the robot has a preliminary understanding of the surrounding environment. At this time, the corresponding algorithm is used to convert the 2D map into a 3D map [4].

$$X = (u - c_x) \cdot \frac{d}{f_x}$$
$$Y = (v - c_y) \cdot \frac{d}{f_y}$$
$$Z = d$$

Thereafter, the machine learning algorithm is used to divide the features in the mapped area, such as we can divide the elements in the tomato garden into tomatoes, branches, leaves, etc. The segmented semantics are then marked, such as "leaf", "fruit", etc. Based on the semantic information obtained before, the robot uses this information to make decisions and plan the path, and such a path can avoid many unnecessary losses. With the movement of the robot, the navigation will feedback the collected information and update the original costmap, so that the robot can better adapt to the changes of the environment to obtain a more robust and reliable system.

3 System Architecture

The system integrates modules such as perception, SLAM, and semantic processing, and the functions of each module are shown below:

Perception System: This system consists of sensors and data processing units. It collects environmental data using LiDAR, cameras, ultrasonic sensors, infrared sensors, etc., and preprocesses it with noise reduction, calibration, and data fusion.

SLAM Integration: The SLAM (Simultaneous Localization and Mapping) system fuses data from various sensors for real-time robot positioning and environmental mapping. It performs semantic mapping during the map construction process, identifying and labeling areas and objects like fruits, branches, and pedestrians.

Semantic Processing Module: This module employs deep learning models, such as CNNs (Convolutional Neural Networks), for semantic segmentation of images or point cloud data. It uses hierarchical semantic labeling to upgrade low-level perceptual data to higher-level semantic information, like recognizing object shapes to identifying specific object categories.

Decision and Planning Module: Divided into behavior planning and decision-making, this module plans the robot's actions based on the semantic map for tasks like obstacle avoidance, path planning, and task execution. It also adapts to environmental changes and task requirements by selecting appropriate paths and prioritizing tasks.

Communication, Control, and Software Layers: These systems manage communication, robot control, and software operations, providing the necessary infrastructure for the navigation system.

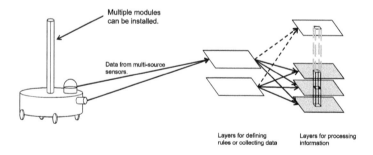

Fig. 1. Overall Design

4 Multi-layer Semantic Mapping

Multi-layer semantic mapping is a method that correlates and integrates semantic information across various levels, commonly utilized in domains such as natural language processing, information retrieval, and knowledge graph construction. This framework can be depicted as a hierarchical system where each layer serves as an abstraction and extension of the layer beneath it. This layered approach allows the mapping process to handle semantic information at various levels, thereby better accommodating complex data and application scenarios [5].

As shown in the figure below, we assign different information to colors for different layers for the system to use.

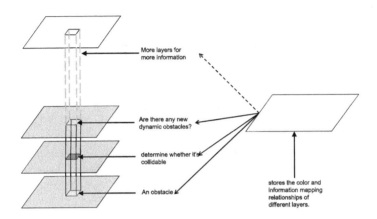

Fig. 2. Mapping Rules

4.1 Different Layers

In the navigation system, we set up different layers to classify different semantic information. Here are some of the basics: Standard Layers

Static Map Layer: In order to perform global planning, the robot needs a map that reaches beyond its sensors to know where walls and other static obstacles are. The static map can be generated with a SLAM algorithm a priorior can be created from an architectural diagram.Such layers are generally unchanged, but in the hierarchical cost graph allows the robot to update the static map layer without losing the information of the remaining layers.

Obstacles Layer: Based on high-precision sensors such as lidar and RGB-D cameras, the corresponding data is collected and stored on a two-dimensional grid, along with real-time environmental cognition and map update.

Voxels Layer: This layer has the same function as the Obstacles Layer, but tracks the sensor data in three-dimensions.The three dimensional voxel grid, introduced in Marder Eppstein et al. allows for more intelligent clearing of obstacles to reflect the multiple heights at which they can be seen.Voxels Layer Usually implemented in the form of a three-dimensional array, each voxel unit stores information about its spatial location, such as whether it is occupied, occupation probability, distance, and so on. This approach allows the robot to process complex three-dimensional spatial information in a relatively simple and efficient manner. However, because voxel representations may require large amounts of memory and computational resources, the resolution and precision need to be weighed in practice to accommodate the computational power of the robot.

Inflation Layer: The Inflation Layer (Expansion layer) is a technology used in robot navigation and path planning, especially when dealing with cost maps (costmap). It is a virtual layer used to create an additional "buffer" around known obstacles to ensure that the robot not only avoids actual obstacles, but also maintains a safe distance to avoid being too close to them.

Terrain layer: we created a terrain layer, which records the robot navigation in the process of use will encounter terrain type, including flat fields, rolling hills, irregular orchard, etc., at the same time planning the robot path planning may be covered because of terrain, so as to improve the stability and security of the robot.

Forbidden area layer: the forbidden area should be smaller than the inflation area, which covers the area that must not be touched by the robot movement. This area is especially reflected by pedestrians and beam. Based on the detected position of the pedestrians and the beam and the motion parameters of the pedestrian, the best path is planned further away from both.

Alert area layer: The alert area will be larger than the inflation area, which covers the areas where the robot collides during motion that will not be risky but should be avoided, such as branches and leaves, etc. This area will have less weight in path planning, making it easier for robots to drive in risk-free, open environments.

Obstacle type layer: Different warning areas and prohibited areas should be set for different obstacles, such as pedestrians having large prohibited areas and smaller warning areas (because pedestrians will spontaneously avoid the robot route); branches will have smaller prohibited areas and larger warning areas (because branches are allowed to be removed and driven directly if necessary). The obstacle type layer stores the information of the warning area and the forbidden area of different obstacle types to plan a safer path for the robot.

4.2 Integration

Regarding the integration of semantic information and traditional maps, the focus lies mainly in the following aspects: Data Collection and Preprocessing: Initially, collect map information from the agricultural environment, including field layouts, roads, and obstacles. Concurrently, utilize sensors (such as depth cameras, LiDAR, etc.) to collect information on crop growth, pests, and diseases. Preprocess the collected data, such as noise removal and calibration, to ensure data quality. Map Semanticization: Semanticize the traditional map data through annotation, assigning semantic tags to each map element, such as crops, roads, and obstacles. Construction of Semantic Maps: Integrate the map elements with semantic tags to build a map that contains both geographic location information and rich semantic information. This map will support more intelligent decision-making for agricultural navigation robots. Robot Navigation Algorithms: Develop navigation algorithms for agricultural robots that are integrated with semantic maps. These algorithms need to understand the semantic information on the map so that the robot can effectively plan paths and avoid obstacles based on this information. System Integration and Testing: Integrate the navigation algorithms with the agricultural robot hardware system and conduct field tests. Optimize the algorithms during testing to improve the performance of the navigation robots in actual agricultural environments.

5 Navigation Algorithm

We utilize an integrated semantic information layered cost map to provide data support for navigation algorithms. Based on the information provided by the cost map, navigation can more fully consider the system's own conditions and the surrounding environment to plan a better route.

```
Data: System Information, Rule Definition Layer
Input: Sensor Sources
1 for LayerID != Max do
2     for Position in Map do
3         UpDate Data[LayerID][Position] ;
          /* From Sensor Sources And System Information, Store
             corresponding block information using colors.        */
4         Position++
5     end
6     LayerID++
7 end
8 for LayerID != Max do
9     for Position in Map do
10        Detect Color[LayerID][Position] ;
          /* Detect area's color and respond                       */
11        Position++
12    end
13    LayerID++
14 end
   // For example, we process the forbidden area layer
15 for Position in Map do
16    if Color == red then
17        area.PositionID = 1;
          // Mark the area as a restricted zone.
18    end
19 end
   /* After processing all layers, we have the map with semantic
      information. We use this map for path planning algorithm, like A*
      and so on.                                                   */
```

5.1 Description of the Algorithm

This paper proposes an algorithm using multi-layer semantic mapping for path planning and obstacle avoidance. By introducing the custom layer such as terrain layer into the hierarchical cost graph, it realizes the more efficient and convenient use of navigation path planning for agricultural robots. Based on this algorithm, the robot can use a robotic arm to help adjust its walking path, just as a person can choose to handle an obstacle. In the process of robot navigation path planning, the first for grid map topology processing, and complete the path planning between point and point, then when the robot arrived at each point, it will be set the corresponding behavior logic, in the experimental robot will enter both sides of planting crops, and planning the path of the inspection channel. In the process, the hanging branches and leaves that can be removed will not stop the robot, while the fruit will be treated more gently.

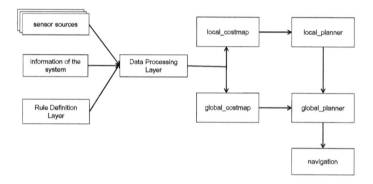

Fig. 3. Navigate Process

5.2 Integration of Layered Costmaps

This paper presents an agricultural robot navigation system based on hierarchical cost mapping and semantic information, which enhances the accuracy and intelligence of the robot's path planning in complex environments. Below are the components of the system and some of its advantages.

System Components:

Sensor Data Synchronization: The navigation system is equipped with various sensors, including LIDAR, cameras, and sonar, which collect data synchronously. This data is integrated to form a comprehensive environmental model.

Semantic Recognition and Cost Map Construction: Semantic segmentation is performed on the integrated data from earlier stages, classifying the point cloud data in the environment based on semantics, such as paths, fruit trees, and branches in an orchard. Multiple cost maps are created according to the classification results, each containing different semantic information.

Path Selection and Strategy Optimization: The navigation system calculates the optimal path using the hierarchical cost map integrated with semantic information. During the decision-making process, the algorithm considers the weights of each cost map and their corresponding semantic data to determine a path that is both safe and efficient.

System Advantages: The navigation system updates the cost map and semantic information in real-time according to environmental changes, such as the appearance of new static obstacles or the movement of dynamic obstacles, which gives the system strong environmental adaptability. Additionally, when performing path planning, the system takes into account factors such as its own mechanical arm, resulting in a more human-like decision-making model. Compared to conventional methods, the integration of semantic data makes the robot's decision-making more efficient and rapid, with a more human-like approach to obstacle handling.

6 Implementation

The experimental platform adopts a modular agricultural robot design and redundant collaborative control algorithm. The hardware architecture of the manipulator system as a whole adopts the configuration of a Cartesian manipulator, with redundant degrees of freedom on specific coordinate axes. The transmission mode is steel cable and pull-line mode, characterized by large working space, high speed, and high precision. The execution part includes a lifting platform and a manipulator, which are used to adjust the height and extension length of the manipulator, respectively. The system chassis adopts a track-type chassis with independent steering for four wheels, which can carry the manipulator to achieve mobile functions. On the experimental platform, a navigation algorithm based on layered cost maps with integrated semantic information in agricultural environments is mounted [7].

Fig. 4. Experimental Results

Sensor Integration: [8]

1. LiDAR: Provides accurate distance measurements through laser ranging, laying the foundation for a three-dimensional point cloud representation of the environment.
2. (Depth) Cameras: Capture visual and depth information, capable of recognizing road signs, traffic signals, pedestrians, etc., and transforming the 2D maps obtained from LiDAR into 3D maps.
3. Inertial Measurement Unit (IMU): Offers data on vehicle dynamics parameters, delivering precise information on motion and orientation.
4. Odometry: Estimates changes in the robot's position over time using data from motion sensors.

Data Collection and Processing: Synchronizes data collection from multiple sensors based on an aligned timeline. The collected data undergoes preprocessing such as noise reduction and filtering to enhance data quality. Key features are then extracted, and data from different sensors are integrated to obtain more comprehensive environmental information.

Semantic Segmentation and Vectorization Processing: Employs deep learning models for semantic segmentation of images, identifying various objects and scene elements. These extracted map elements are converted into a vectorized representation for easier machine understanding and utilization [10].

Perspective Transformation and 3D Processing: Achieves perspective transformation from the camera's front view to a bird's-eye view based on the camera's internal and external parameters. The collected two-dimensional data is then transformed into three dimensions using depth map data to create high-precision maps. These maps are evaluated and optimized using metrics such as Mean Average Precision (mAP).

7 Experimental Setup and Results

As shown in the Fig below, there are three types of signal points represented by red, black, and green colors. The red points determine the main path of the system's operation. When no green points are detected, the system sequentially traverses all the red points. Upon arrival at each red point, the system will first go to the detected green point and then return, at which time the green point will be marked as visited and removed from the system. Once all the green points in the cost map have been traversed, the system will consider that it has completed the sequential inspection and return to the original black point.

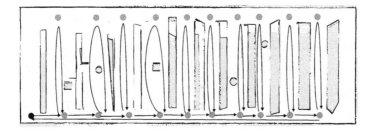

Fig. 5. Global Path Planning

In the simulation of an agricultural environment on both sides of the cart as shown in the Fig, hanging vines and fruits are set up. The obstacles are divided into two types: fruits that cannot be directly crossed and branches that can be moved aside. The cart navigates through this environment and tests its response to different obstacles.

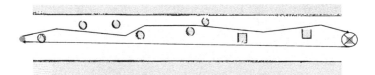

Fig. 6. Local Path Planning

The cart can identify and avoid obstacles that require a safe distance to be maintained, such as fruits and pedestrians, and can also navigate over obstacles like branches that can be pushed aside.

As shown in the Fig, the robot operates in an agricultural environment, and the mechanical arm can recognize and process the surrounding environment to some extent.

Fig. 7. Object Detection

8 Discussion

8.1 Strengths and Limitations

As an agricultural navigation system, it incorporates semantic information processing on the basis of the original layered cost map, which can make path planning more flexible and efficient. Considering this, the system will be widely applicable to environments with many obstacles. Based on its effective distinction between whether obstacles can be processed by a robotic arm and whether they need to be avoided, intelligent agricultural robots will achieve an effect that is more in line with human action patterns. In addition, the layered cost map introduced by this system can provide better social and environmental adaptability. It dynamically updates specific layers according to environmental changes, instead of the entire cost map, which improves efficiency and reduces the consumption of computing resources. At the same time, due to the use of layered cost maps, the system has good adaptability and scalability, allowing developers to add or remove specific layers as needed to customize the navigation system for different agricultural application scenarios.

However, the system has certain limitations. For example, computational complexity, although the layered cost map provides flexibility, it may also increase computational complexity, especially in agricultural work environments that require real-time response. Therefore, to achieve optimal performance, the layered cost map may require fine-tuning of multiple parameters, which may require professional knowledge and a large number of experiments, posing a greater challenge in parameter tuning. At the same time, the current system only considers its implementation in a single robot system and does not plan jointly for multiple robots. In the future, it may consider setting up a local area network server for centralized planning of the system.

In summary, the development of agricultural robot navigation systems should focus on communication technology, system optimization, and user experience to achieve more efficient, intelligent, and automated agricultural operations.

8.2 Comparison

In the agricultural environment, GNSS, INS, and MV each have their applications and limitations as previously mentioned.

This system uses a semantic information-based layered cost map for navigation, employing multi-sensor information fusion technology to enhance the accuracy of LiDAR. It combines the advantages of sensors such as GNSS, INS, and MV, creating data redundancy or complementary characteristics. For SLAM mapping, the system adopts TextSLAM: Visual SLAM with Semantic Planar Text Features, effectively improving accuracy [2,3].

In summary, the development of agricultural robot navigation systems should focus on communication technology, system optimization, and user experience to achieve more efficient, intelligent, and automated agricultural operations.

8.3 Future Research Directions

Agricultural robots for mobile navigation should focus on enhancing communication technology. With this in mind, we propose some future development ideas and plans for the agricultural robot navigation system:

Set up a local server to transmit the navigation data of robots within a certain range into the server. Allocate work tasks and plan routes to develop multi-agricultural machinery cooperative operation technology, which improves the overall efficiency of agricultural machinery operations. Construct a remote monitoring platform on the server to realize real-time monitoring and management of agricultural machinery operations, enhancing the transparency and controllability of the work, making it convenient for personnel to make corrections and adjustments [1].

Based on the aforementioned design, a user interface (UI) that is more aligned with actual needs is developed [11]. Research is conducted into more natural and intuitive human-computer interaction methods to enhance the convenience and user experience of the agricultural robot navigation system. At the same time, the path planning is presented in a more intuitive and effective manner, opting for path designs that may not be the shortest but are optimal, thereby reducing resource waste during the operation process.agricultural operations.

8.4 Expanding the Capabilities

Precision Agriculture Implementation: Utilizing multi-layer semantic mapping technology, we conduct a meticulous analysis and processing of the agricultural environment, including precise identification of crop types, growth conditions, and soil status. With this information, we implement targeted fertilization, irrigation strategies, and pest and disease control measures.

Intelligent Driving Path Planning for Agricultural Robots: Based on multi-layer semantic mapping, the navigation system can carry out detailed path planning and obstacle avoidance, thereby achieving more efficient autonomous driving operations and enhancing the safety of the work. In addition, through semantic mapping technology, agricultural robots can also perform tasks such as crop identification, pollination, harvesting, tilling, and weeding, further improving the level of intelligence and automation in agricultural operations.

Optimization of Agricultural Management: Applying multi-layer semantic mapping to monitor the growth conditions of crops helps to identify and diagnose issues promptly, providing data support and decision analysis for agricultural management. This assists agricultural managers in gaining a more accurate understanding of on-site conditions and facilitates reasonable work planning and resource allocation, thereby improving production efficiency and resource utilization efficiency. It also enables the possibility of coordinated operations among multiple machines.

8.5 Conclusion

This paper presents the implementation of a mobile robot navigation system in agricultural environments based on multi-layer semantic mapping. It integrates multi-source sensing technology, positioning techniques, and path planning algorithms to develop an intelligent navigation system suitable for complex agricultural work environments.

Semantic information processing is combined with layered cost maps to enhance the accuracy and adaptability of path planning.

Custom layers such as terrain, obstacle types, and alert areas are introduced to better meet agricultural requirements.

Anthropomorphic decision-making based on the system's own factors is employed to achieve more intelligent path planning.

The system has been implemented and tested in an agricultural environment, proving its optimization of agricultural work efficiency.

References

1. Cui, J., Li, L., Guo, P., Liu, K., Huang, J.: Design and experimental research of M2M2A system for multi-robot intelligent collaborative operation. Robot **39**(4), 415–422 (2017). https://doi.org/10.13973/j.cnki.robot.2017.0415
2. Li, B., Zou, D., Huang, Y., Niu, X., Pei, L., Yu, W.: TextSLAM: visual SLAM with semantic planar text features (2023)
3. Li, B., Zou, D., Sartori, D., Pei, L., Yu, W.: TextSLAM: visual SLAM with planar text features. In: IEEE International Conference on Robotics and Automation (ICRA) (2020)
4. Li, H., et al.: DFA3D: 3D deformable attention for 2D-to-3D feature lifting. In: Proceedings of the IEEE/CVF International Conference on Computer Vision (2023)
5. Lu, D.V., Hershberger, D., Smart, W.D.: Layered costmaps for context-sensitive navigation, pp. 709–715 (2014)
6. Man, Z., Yuhan, J., Shichao, L., Ruyue, C., Hongzhen, X., Zhenqian, Z.: Research progress of agricultural machinery navigation technology. Nongye Jixie Xuebao/Trans. Chin. Soc. Agricult. Mach. **51**(4), 1–18 (2020)
7. Pan, Y., Wei, J., Islam, K.R.A., Chen, X., Wang, H., Shang, H.: Design analysis and redundant collaborative control of a new modular agricultural robot. J. Mechanical Eng., 1–14
8. Wang, W., Huang, P., Yang, Z.: Indoor positioning method based on UWB odometer and RGB-D fusion. Comput. Sci. **47**, 334–338 (2020)
9. Yu, C., et al.: DS-SLAM: a semantic visual SLAM towards dynamic environments. arXiv preprint arXiv:1809.08379 (2018)
10. Yu, Z.: Research and application of text vectorization based on deep learning, Ph.D. thesis, East China Normal University (2016)
11. Yuan, L.: **42**, 67 (2020)

A General Collision-Free Scheme for Redundant Manipulators

Zongwu Xie, Wandong Sun, Baoshi Cao(✉), Yang Liu, Zhengpu Wang, Hong Liu, and Boyu Ma(✉)

State Key Laboratory of Robotics and Systems, Harbin Institute of Technology, Harbin 150080, China
cbs@hit.edu.cn, boyu.ma@stu.hit.edu.cn

Abstract. Considering manipulation tasks of redundant manipulators in complex environments, this article presents a general scheme that integrates model-based obstacle avoidance, Cartesian space trajectory tracking, and joint physical limit avoidance. Based on the minimum velocity norm scheme, the proposed scheme combines the escape velocity-based obstacle avoidance with Gilbert-Johnson-Keerthi (GJK) algorithm-based critical point detection, empowering the manipulator with model-based obstacle avoidance capabilities. Additionally, a multi-critical point restriction set is proposed, improving the success rate of obstacle avoidance in extreme situations. Moreover, the scheme introduces sampling time to joint physical constraints, ensuring that the physical limits of joints are not violated at the next sampling time. Finally, comparative experiments and simulations are conducted to verify the feasibility and the potential of practical application of the proposed scheme.

Keywords: Redundant manipulators · GJK algorithm · obstacle avoidance · quadratic program

1 Introduction

1.1 Related Work

In recent years, manipulators have reshaped automation industries, playing an irreplaceable role in industry [1], medical [2], service [3], space exploration [4] and other fields [5]. The redundant manipulator has extra degrees of freedom (DOF) than required while performing the desired task giving it the ability to perform subtasks such as obstacle avoidance, singularity avoidance.

Motion planning refers to generating a path from the starting point to the end point for the manipulator, ensuring that the manipulator avoids obstacles during movement, reaches a predetermined position, and meets physical constraints such as velocity and acceleration. It can be roughly divided into sampling-based methods [6] and optimization-based methods [7].

Z. Xie, W. Sun and B. Ma—These authors contributed equally.

The sampling method finds a feasible path from the starting point to the end point by randomly sampling in the configuration space, and various optimization goals including collision avoidance can be set during the planning process. Representative algorithms include rapidly expanding random trees (RRT) [8] and probabilistic path planning (PRM) [9]. The sampling method has the advantages of strong applicability, high computational efficiency, simple and easy to implement algorithm, and asymptotic completeness, and is suitable for high-dimensional spaces and complex environments. However, the real-time performance of the sampling method is poor, making it difficult to manage dynamic obstacles. Moreover, due to its randomness, the results are hard to replicate.

The optimization-based method formulates the motion planning problem as an optimization problem, aiming to find the optimal path that satisfies given constraints. Representative methods include the minimum velocity norm (MVN) scheme [10], the minimum acceleration norm (MAN) scheme [11], and the minimum jerk norm (MJN) scheme [12], where obstacle avoidance is expressed as an inequality escape velocity, escape acceleration, and escape jerk constraints to avoid collisions. Based on diverse and mature solution methods, the real-time performance of planning can be guaranteed. However, each time integration leads to more violations of the obstacle avoidance limit. Moreover, when dealing with non-convex objectives and constraints, optimization methods may require additional work to ensure optimal results.

In terms of collision detection, Madhevan et al. [9] assumes the manipulator as links and the obstacle as a point, and the shortest distance and critical point from the point to the connecting rod are calculated. Although this proved to be fast and effective, due to the irregular shape of the actual manipulator and obstacles, how to solve it considering the complex environment requires further exploration. Gilbert et al. [13] proposes a model-based nearest distance detection method for convex sets, providing the possibility for precise collision detection.

1.2 Contribution and Structure of This Article

To solve the above problems, this article proposes a general scheme at the joint-velocity level that integrates model-based obstacle avoidance, Cartesian trajectory tracking, and joint limit avoidance from an optimization perspective. Based on the MVN scheme, the goal of optimization is set as the norm of velocity. At the same time, a method based on escape velocity is used for obstacle avoidance, and a model based GJK algorithm is introduced for critical point detection, giving the manipulator arm the ability to finely avoid obstacles in complex spaces. Innovatively, this article proposes a multi-critical point restriction set, improving obstacle avoidance success rate in extreme situations. In addition, we introduce the sampling time into the physical limit, ensuring that the physical limit at the next sampling time will not be violated. Subsequently, a general scheme integrating all the above is proposed and reformulated into a unified quadratic programming framework that can be solved by any method. Finally, rigorous experiments and simulations are conducted to verify the feasibility and practical application potential of the proposed scheme.

2 Model-Based Obstacle Avoidance

In this section, we first introduce the critical point and critical link detection method based on the Convex Hull Algorithm and GJK algorithm, and then constructed the collision-free planning constraints of the entire manipulator at the velocity level based on the detection results.

2.1 Model-Based Critical Point Detection

The preliminary work in constructing the obstacle avoidance inequality is to perform critical point and critical link detection. For a redundant manipulator with n joints and u obstacles in the workspace, there are $u \times n$ sets of critical point pairs between all links of the manipulator and obstacles. The following is an example of the calculation process of link L_1 and obstacle O_1. The remaining critical points can be obtained through loop iteration.

A necessary condition for collision points detection based on models is an approximate model of the manipulator link, which is assumed to be known. However, most models are not directly suitable for GJK calculations because the GJK algorithm requires a convex hull shape. Therefore, we first calculate the convex hull L_{1c} and O_{1c} for link L_1 and obstacle O_1. We used the open-source 3D processing library VTK [14] to export the vertices and calculate the convex hull through the Graham Scan algorithm [15]. This is a preprocessing process and only needs to be calculated once and stored before the first planning.

After obtaining the convex hull, use the GJK algorithm to calculate the critical point of link L_1 and obstacle O_1. The GJK algorithm is an algorithm for calculating the shortest distance between two convex shapes. It is mainly used in real-time applications, because of its high computational efficiency and good stability. The core idea of the GJK algorithm is to use Support Function and Minkowski Difference to iteratively approximate the shortest distance between two convex shapes. The following is a brief introduction to the GJK algorithm.

First use the support function to find the furthest point of the shape in a certain direction. For a convex hull L_{1c} and O_{1c}, the support function is defined as:

$$\text{supporrt}(L_{1c}, \boldsymbol{d}) = \underset{\boldsymbol{\theta}(t)}{\arg\max}(\boldsymbol{l}_{1c} \cdot \boldsymbol{d}) \tag{1}$$

$$\text{supporrt}(O_{1c}, \boldsymbol{d}) = \underset{\boldsymbol{\theta}(t)}{\arg\max}(\boldsymbol{o}_{1c} \cdot \boldsymbol{d}) \tag{2}$$

where $\boldsymbol{d} \in \mathbb{R}^{3 \times 1}$ is a direction vector. The support points of the Minkowski difference in direction d can be calculated as:

$$p_i = \text{supporrt}(L_{1c}, \boldsymbol{d}) - \text{supporrt}(O_{1c}, \boldsymbol{d}) \tag{3}$$

where i is the number of iterations. Then describe the Minkowski difference, the Minkowski difference of two convex shapes L_{1c} and O_{1c} is defined as the set of differences between the midpoints of L_{1c} and O_{1c}:

$$L_{1c} \ominus O_{1c} = \{l_{1c} - o_{1c} | l_{1c} \in L_{1c}, o_{1c} \in O_{1c}\} \tag{4}$$

The GJK algorithm uses the Minkowski difference to convert the collision problem of two shapes into a problem containing the origin. Subsequently, starting from the support function of the Minkowski difference, the GJK algorithm gradually approximates the Minkowski difference by constructing a simple shape such as a point, line segment, triangle, or tetrahedron. If the new support point p_i fails to get closer to the origin, stop the iteration. The algorithm checks whether the shape contains the origin, gradually adjusting the shape's vertices until it finds the closest distance to the origin or confirms that the two shapes intersect. Pseudocodes of the GJK algorithm shown in Algorithm 1.

Algorithm 1 GJK Algorithm

Input: Convex hulls A and B
Output: Whether there is a collision, the nearest distance N_L, the nearest point pair C_A and C_B

1:   $d \leftarrow$ arbitrary non-zero vector
2:   $p_0 \leftarrow$ Support (A, d) − Support (B, −d)
3:   **if** $\text{dot}(p_0, p_0) == 0$:
4:     return True
5:   **end**
6:   Simplex $\leftarrow \{p_0\}$
7:   $d \leftarrow p_0$
8:   **while** True:
9:     $p \leftarrow$ Support (A, d) − Support (B, −d)
10:     **if** $\text{dot}(p, p) \leq 0$:
11:       calculate nearest length N_L and nearest point pair C_A and C_B
12:       return False, N_L and C_A and C_B
13:     **end**
14:     add new support points to the simplex
15:     **if** shape contains the origin
16:       return True
17:     **end**
18:   **end**

By iterating over n links and u obstacles, we can finally get $u \times n$ critical points $C_{un} \in \mathbb{R}^{3\times1}$ on each link and $C_{un} \in \mathbb{R}^{3\times1}$ on each obstacle and $u \times n$ closest distances $d_{un} \in \mathbb{R}$ based on actual shape. The critical point on the entire manipulator and all obstacles can be described as:

$$C_m, C_o = \operatorname{argmin}(d_{un}) \tag{5}$$

where $C_m \in \mathbb{R}^{3\times 1}$ represents the critical point on the manipulator, $C_o \in \mathbb{R}^{3\times 1}$ represents the critical point on all obstacles.

2.2 Obstacle Avoidance Limits

The next step is to construct collision-free planning constraints, using C_m and C_o for demonstration calculations.

First define the safety distance D, which represents the maximum allowed distance from any point on the manipulator to the obstacle. Position-level obstacle avoidance can be described as:

$$\|C_m - C_o\|_2 \geq D \tag{6}$$

what it means is that the distance to the nearest point is beyond the defined maximum safe distance. Define $\mathfrak{D}$ to describe the relationship between the closest distance and the safe distance, which can be described as:

$$\mathfrak{D} = \|C_m - C_o\|_2 - D \tag{7}$$

When $\mathfrak{D} > 0$, the manipulator is in a collision risk-free state; when $\mathfrak{D} < 0$, there is a collision risk. Derive both sides of (5) and describe (5) using $\mathfrak{D}$ as the speed level:

$$\frac{d\|C_m - C_o\|_2}{dt} \geq -\frac{\mathfrak{D}}{T} \tag{8}$$

where T represents the sampling time. (7) limits the approach speed between collision points when $\mathfrak{D} > 0$, ensuring that this group of collision points will never enter a safe distance at the next sampling time. When $\mathfrak{D} < 0$, it drives the nearest point away, ensuring that the group collision point is outside the safe distance at the next sampling time. The left side of the equation can be calculated as:

$$\begin{aligned}\frac{d(C_m - C_{o2})}{dt} &= \frac{d}{dt}\sqrt{(C_m - C_o)^T(C_m - C_o)} \\ &= \frac{\left((\dot{C}_m - \dot{C}_o)^T(C_m - C_o) + (C_m - C_o)^T(\dot{C}_m - \dot{C}_o)\right)}{2\sqrt{(C_m - C_o)^T(C_m - C_o)}} \\ &= \frac{(\dot{C}_m - \dot{C}_o)(C_m - C_o)^T}{\sqrt{(C_m - C_o)^T(C_m - C_o)}}\end{aligned} \tag{9}$$

Considering the case of static obstacles, where $\dot{C}_o = 0$:

$$\frac{(\dot{C}_m - \dot{C}_o)(C_m - C_o)^T}{\sqrt{(C_m - C_o)^T(C_m - C_o)}} = \frac{(\dot{C}_m)(C_m - C_o)^T}{\sqrt{(C_m - C_o)^T(C_m - C_o)}}$$

$$= u_{om}^T \dot{C}_m \tag{10}$$

where $\boldsymbol{u}_{om} = \dfrac{(\boldsymbol{C}_m - \boldsymbol{C}_o)^T}{\sqrt{(\boldsymbol{C}_m - \boldsymbol{C}_o)^T (\boldsymbol{C}_m - \boldsymbol{C}_o)}} \in \mathbb{R}^{3 \times 1}$, is the unit vector pointing from $\boldsymbol{C}_o$ to $\boldsymbol{C}_m$. At this point, the actual shape obstacle avoidance (8) at the speed level can be expressed as:

$$-\boldsymbol{u}_{om} \dot{\boldsymbol{C}}_m \leq \frac{\mathcal{D}}{T} \tag{11}$$

Use the Jacobian to represent the speed of critical point:

$$\dot{\boldsymbol{C}}_m = \boldsymbol{J}_m(\boldsymbol{q}) \dot{\boldsymbol{q}} \tag{12}$$

where $\boldsymbol{J}_m(\boldsymbol{q})$ represents the Jacobian of $\boldsymbol{C}_m$. Finally, the actual shape obstacle avoidance at the velocity level can be described as:

$$\boldsymbol{J}_c \dot{\boldsymbol{q}} \leq \frac{\mathcal{D}}{T} \tag{13}$$

$$\boldsymbol{J}_c = -\boldsymbol{u}_{om} \boldsymbol{J}_m(\boldsymbol{q}) \tag{14}$$

Then, the restrictions are applied to all $u \times n$ groups of $\boldsymbol{C}_{un}$ and $\mathcal{C}_{un}$.

Remark1: (11) limits the obstacle avoidance based on the actual shape of the manipulator, and the collision point at the previous moment will never enter the nearest safe distance. However, when only the speed limit of the nearest point group is imposed and considering the actual shape, the collision point locations may not be continuous. In detail, the collision point at the previous sampling time may be very different from the collision point at the next sampling time, even if the closest distance between the two sets of points is very close. The sudden change of the critical point will bring about a sudden change of velocity constrains. What is even more fatal is that there is a situation where the nearest point oscillates back and forth near two sets of points that are far apart, resulting in failure to avoid obstacles and large velocity fluctuations. Therefore, for most cases, it is more feasible to limit the approaching speed of $u \times n$ groups of critical points.

3 A General Motion Planning Scheme

In this section, we discuss goals and constraints of manipulator tasks. Subsequently, a general scheme at velocity level for manipulator manipulation is proposed. Then we briefly introduce some available solution methods.

3.1 Kinematic Model

Considering Cartesian trajectory tracking of a redundant manipulator, the forward kinematics can be expressed as:

$$\boldsymbol{x}(t) = f(\boldsymbol{q}(t)) \tag{15}$$

where $\boldsymbol{x}(t)$ represents the Cartesian trajectory desired to be tracked, usually executed by an end effector and $\boldsymbol{x}(t) \in \mathbb{R}^{m \times 1}$, m represents the dimension of the task. $\boldsymbol{q}(t) \in \mathbb{R}^{n \times 1}$,

n represents the DOF of the redundant manipulator. $f(\cdot)$ represents the homogeneous transformation from Cartesian space to joint space, this is usually a complex non-linear and non-convex constraint. A common solution is to differentiate (12) with respect to time and formulate the problem to velocity level, it can be described as:

$$\dot{x}(t) = J(q(t))\dot{q}(t), \tag{16}$$

where $J(q(t)) \in \mathbb{R}^{m \times n}$ represents the Jacobian matrix from Cartesian space to joint space and solved the non-linear problem.

3.2 Physical Limitations

The manipulator must always follow physical limits that cannot be violated during manipulation. Define the physical limitations of the manipulator's joints as follows:

$$Q_{min} \leq q(t) \leq Q_{max} \tag{17}$$

$$V_{min} \leq \dot{q}(t) \leq V_{max} \tag{18}$$

Where $Q \in \mathbb{R}^{n \times 1}$ and $V \in \mathbb{R}^{n \times 1}$ represent the physical limits of the joint. According to (14), the limit unified to the velocity level can be expressed as:

$$V_{min}(t) \leq \dot{q}(t) \leq V_{max}(t) \tag{19}$$

$$V_{min}(t) = \max\left\{\frac{Q_{min} - q(t)}{T}, V_{min}\right\} \tag{20}$$

$$V_{max}(t) = \min\left\{\frac{Q_{max} - q(t)}{T}, V_{max}\right\} \tag{21}$$

Through restriction (15), it is guaranteed that the manipulator is within the joint position limits of the next sampling time and will not exceed the limit.

3.3 Scheme Design

In this part, A universal manipulation scheme that integrates actual shape-based obstacle avoidance, position tracking and joint physical limit avoidance is proposed and unified into the form of quadratic planning. At the same time, the canonical expression makes arbitrary solution methods feasible.

The quadratic programming of any problem can be expressed as:

$$\begin{aligned} \min_{x} \quad & \frac{1}{2} x H x^{\mathrm{T}} + f x \#(22) \\ \text{s.t.} \quad & A_{eq} x = b_{eq} \# \\ & b_{min} \leq A_{\lim} x \leq b_{max} \# \end{aligned} \tag{22}$$

The various goals are unified below. First, the optimization objective is defined as the norm of the joint velocity:

$$\min_{\dot{q}} \frac{1}{2}\dot{q}\dot{q}^T \tag{23}$$

where $H = I \in \mathbb{R}^{n\times n}$, f is an empty matrix. The norm of joint speed is used as an optimization goal, which helps to ensure the continuity of solution results and reduce unnecessary energy waste. Then, the Cartesian position tracking of the redundant manipulator is expressed as:

$$J\dot{q} = \dot{x}(t) \tag{24}$$

To improve tracking accuracy, an error feedback mechanism is introduced:

$$\dot{r}(t) = \dot{x}(t) + K_p(x(t) - f(q)) \tag{25}$$

where $\dot{r}(t) \in \mathbb{R}^{3\times 1}$ represents the corrected expected speed after introducing position feedback compensation. This is done by introducing the difference between the desired position and the actual position and affecting the desired velocity through the hyperparameter K_p. The Cartesian position tracking described so far as an equality constraint can be expressed as:

$$J\dot{q} = \dot{r}(t) \tag{26}$$

Subsequently, the joint physical limits and obstacle avoidance are expressed as inequality constraints:

$$A_{\lim} = \left(I, J_C^1, J_C^2, J_C^3 \cdots J_C^{u\times n}\right)^T \tag{27}$$

where $A_{\lim} \in \mathbb{R}^{(n+u\times n)\times n}$, the first component $I \in \mathbb{R}^{n\times n}$ is used to derive the joint velocity $\dot{q}$, $J_C^i \in \mathbb{R}$ is used to derive the approach speed between $u \times n$ collision points and obstacles. The upper and lower bounds can be expressed as:

$$b_{\max} = \left(V_{\max}(t), \frac{\mathfrak{D}^1}{T}, \frac{\mathfrak{D}^2}{T}, \frac{\mathfrak{D}^3}{T} \cdots \frac{\mathfrak{D}^{u\times n}}{T}\right)^T \tag{28}$$

$$b_{\min} = (V_{\min}, -\inf, -\inf, -\inf \cdots -\inf)^T \tag{29}$$

It is worth pointing out that due to the constraints on joint velocity and position, the optimization problem still has a clear lower bound even the lower bound for obstacle avoidance is set to negative infinity. At this point, the general manipulation scheme that unifies actual shape-based obstacle avoidance, Cartesian trajectory tracking, and joint physical limit avoidance can be expressed as:

$$\begin{aligned}\min_{\dot{q}} \quad & \frac{1}{2}\dot{q}\dot{q}^T \#\\ \text{s.t.} \quad & J\dot{q} = \dot{r}(t)\#\\ & b_{\min} \leq A_{\lim} x \leq b_{\max} \# \end{aligned} \tag{30}$$

Remark 2: (24) is formulated as a unified quadratic programming form. Mature quadratic programming solving methods such as Interior Point Method [16], Simplex Method [17], and Lagrange Dual Method [18] can be used for real-time solution.

4 Experimental Results and Discussion

In this section, we conducted experiments and simulations to verify the feasibility of the proposed scheme and conducted discussions to further clarify the advantages.

4.1 Experiment Methodology

This part provides a brief introduction to the experimental condition settings. we use a Franka Emika Panda manipulator, the goal of Cartesian tracking is set to the robot grasping coordinate system, and the physical limits of the manipulator are set as $q^+ =$ [2.7437, 1.7837, 2.9007, −0.1518, 2.8065, 4.5169, 3.0159] rad, $q^- =$ [−2.7437, − 1.7837, −2.9007, 3.0421, −2.8065, 0.5445, −3.0159] rad, $\dot{q}^+ =$ [2.62, 2.62, 2.62, 2.62, 5.26, 4.18, 5.26] rad/s, $\dot{q}^- = -\dot{q}^+$. The sampling time is set to 0.01s, which is proven to be less than a single computation time, hyperparameter $D = 0.01$ m, $K_p = 50$.

The obstacle is fixed at [0.33, −0.06, 0] m, with the total height of 0.885 m. The manipulator tracks a rectangular trajectory and a heart-shaped trajectory. For rectangular trajectories, the initial joint angles are set at $q_0^r =$ [0.471, 0.128, 0.000, −1.73, 0.000, 1.936, −0.190] rad. For heart-shaped trajectories, the initial joint angles are set at $q_0^h =$ [0.314, −0.319, 0.000, −1.748, 5.181, 1.924, 0.495] rad.

4.2 Results and Discussion

Figure 1 shows the simulation results of tracking a rectangular trajectory while obstacle avoidance is not performed. At the same time, the maximum joint velocity is limited to 0.1 rad/s. Figure 1(a) shows the joint velocities of the tracking process. The joint velocities at starting point and end point are both 0 and keep continuous. At the same time, there are no violations of joint velocity limits. Figure 1(b) shows that tracking error is at 10^{-4} m level. Figure 1(c) shows the joint angles of the tracking process. Figure 1(d) directly shows the position of the end effector. Figure 1(e) intuitively shows the tracking process. The manipulator collides with the obstacle.

Figure 2 shows the experiment and simulation results when tracking a rectangular trajectory with collision detection. Figure 2(a) shows the joint angles of the tracking process, joint angles are within limits and keep continuous. Figure 2(b) shows that when considering obstacle avoidance, the manipulator avoids collision successful. Figure 2(c) shows that tracking error is at 10^{-4} m level, demonstrating the strong trajectory tracking capability of the proposed general scheme. Figure 2(d) directly shows the position of the end effector. Figure 2(e) and Fig. 2(f) show the trajectory tracking process in simulation and experiment. The manipulator avoids obstacles while tracking the end trajectory. The consistency between them demonstrates the feasibility of the proposed general scheme in real manipulation tasks.

Figure 3 shows the experiment and simulation results when tracking a heart-shaped trajectory with collision detection. The joint angles in Fig. 2(a) do not exceed physical limits and are continuous. Figure 3(b) shows that the manipulator successfully avoided collision. Figure 3(c) shows that the tracking error of the proposed scheme is close to 0. Figure 3(d) directly shows the position of the end effector. Figure 3(e) and Fig. 3(f) show the trajectory tracking process in simulation and experiment. The manipulator avoids the model-based obstacle while accurately tracking the heart-shaped trajectory.

Through three comparative experiments and simulations, it can be found that the proposed solution can accurately track the Cartesian trajectory while performing model-based obstacle avoidance planning. Additionally, the physical limits of joints are also well considered. Furthermore, simulation and experiment maintain a high degree of consistency, demonstrating the potential of this solution in practical applications.

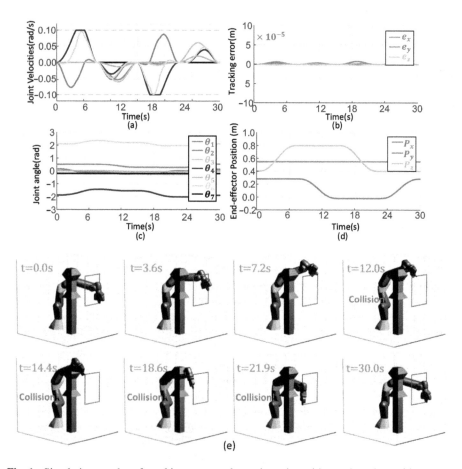

Fig. 1. Simulation results of tracking rectangular trajectories without obstacle avoidance. (a) Profile of manipulator joint velocities. (b) Profile of the tracking error. (e) Motion process of simulation tracking.

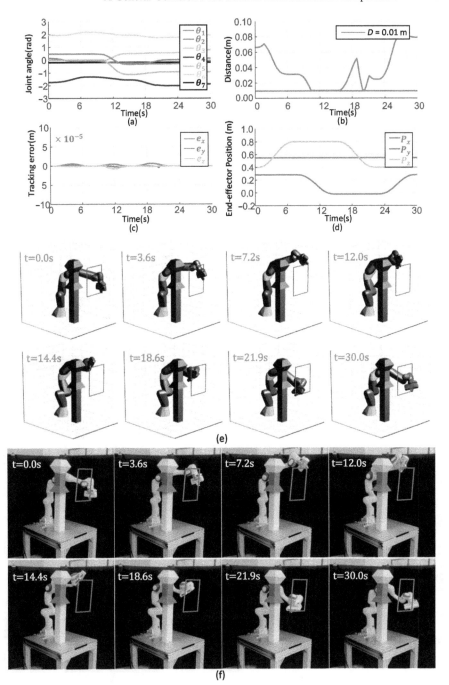

Fig. 2. Simulation and experimental results of tracking rectangular trajectories. (a) Profile of manipulator joint angles. (b) The actual closest distance between the obstacle and the manipulator. (c) Profile of the tracking error. (d) Profile of the end-effector position. (e) Motion process of simulation tracking (f) Motion process of experiment tracking.

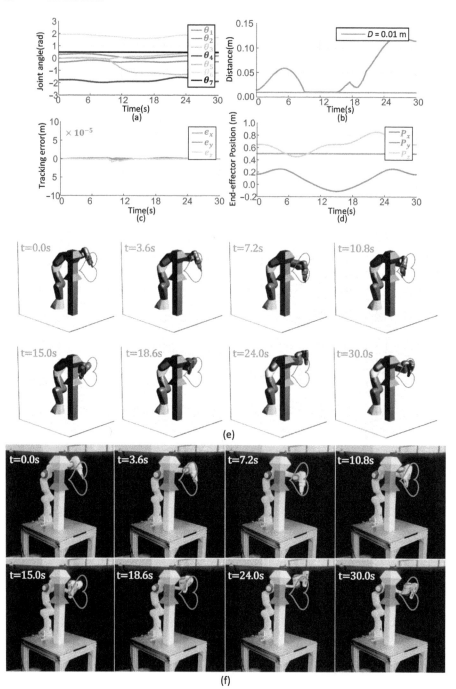

Fig. 3. Simulation and experimental results of tracking heart-shaped trajectories. (a) Profile of manipulator joint angles. (b) The actual closest distance between the obstacle and the manipulator. (c) Profile of the tracking error. (d) Profile of the end-effector position. (e) Motion process of simulation tracking (f) Motion process of experiment tracking

5 Conclusion

In this article, we propose a general scheme that integrates model-based obstacle avoidance, Cartesian trajectory tracking, and joint physical limit limitations, providing a general solution for the precise operation of redundant manipulators in complex environments. The obstacle avoidance algorithm that combines the escape velocity and the GJK algorithm gives the manipulator a sophisticated model-based obstacle avoidance method. Moreover, the proposed multi-critical point restriction improves the obstacle avoidance success rate in extreme situations. Additionally, the introduction of the sampling time strictly guarantees that joint physical limits will not be violated. Finally, comparative experiments and simulations were conducted to verify the feasibility of the proposed solution, as well as the consistency between the simulations and experiments, demonstrating its potential for practical application. Future work includes integrating task-based goals, giving the manipulator more possibilities in a variety of tasks.

References

1. Ghodsian, N., et al.: Toward designing an integration architecture for a mobile manipulator in production systems: industry 4.0. Procedia CIRP **109**, 443–448 (2022)
2. Bouteraa, Y., Abdallah, I.B., Ghommam, J.: Task-space region-reaching control for medical robot manipulator. Comput. Electr. Eng. **67**, 629–645 (2018)
3. Stückler, J., Schwarz, M., Behnke, S.: Mobile manipulation, tool use, and intuitive interaction for cognitive service robot Cosero. Front. Robot. AI **3** (2016)
4. Papadopoulos, E., Aghili, F., Ma, O., Lampariello, R.: Robotic manipulation and capture in space: a survey. Front. Robot. AI **8** (2021)
5. Abdelmaksoud, S.I., Al-Mola, M.H., Abro, G.E.M., Asirvadam, V.S.: In-depth review of advanced control strategies and cutting-edge trends in robot manipulators: analyzing the latest developments and techniques. IEEE Access **1** (2024)
6. Noreen, I., Khan, A., Habib, Z.: Optimal path planning using RRT* based approaches: a survey and future directions. Int. J. Adv. Comput. Sci. Appl. **7** (2016)
7. Sandakalum, T., Ang, M.H.: Motion planning for mobile manipulators—a systematic review. Machines **10**, 97 (2022)
8. Kingston, Z., Moll, M., Kavraki, L.E.: Sampling-based methods for motion planning with constraints. Annu. Rev. Control Robot. Auton. Syst. **1**, 159–185 (2018)
9. Madhevan, B., Sreekumar, M.: Identification of probabilistic approaches and map-based navigation in motion planning for mobile robots. Sadhana SāDhanā **43** (2018)
10. Zhang, Y., Wang, J.: Obstacle avoidance for kinematically redundant manipulators using a dual neural network. IEEE Trans. Syst. Man Cybern. Part B Cybern. **34**, 752–759 (2004)
11. Guo, D., Zhang, Y.: Acceleration-Level Inequality-Based MAN scheme for obstacle avoidance of redundant robot manipulators. IEEE Trans. Ind. Electron. **61**, 6903–6914 (2014)
12. Chen, D., Zhang, Y.: Minimum jerk norm scheme applied to obstacle avoidance of redundant robot arm with jerk bounded and feedback control. IET Control Theory Appl. **10**, 1896–1903 (2016)
13. Gilbert, E.G., Johnson, D.W., Keerthi, S.S.: A fast procedure for computing the distance between complex objects in three-dimensional space. IEEE J. Robot. Autom. **4**, 193–203 (1988)
14. Hanwell, M.D., Martin, K.M., Chaudhary, A., Avila, L.S.: The visualization toolkit (VTK): rewriting the rendering code for modern graphics cards. SoftwareX **1–2**, 9–12 (2015)

15. Kong, X., Everett, H., Toussaint, G.: The Graham scan triangulates simple polygons. Pattern Recognit. Lett. **11**, 713–716 (1990)
16. Roos, C., Terlaky, T., Vial, J.-P.: Interior point methods for linear optimization (2005)
17. Nelder, J.A., Mead, R.: A simplex method for function minimization. Comput. J. **7**, 308–313 (1965)
18. Tai, X.C., Wu, C.: Augmented Lagrangian method, dual methods and split Bregman iteration for ROF model. In: Tai, XC., Mørken, K., Lysaker, M., Lie, KA. (eds.) SSVM 2009. LNCS, vol. 5567, pp. 502–513. Springer, Heidelberg (2009). https://doi.org/10.1007/978-3-642-02256-2_42

Design and Analysis of a Flexible Parallel Robot for Rope-Driven Upper Limb Rehabilitation

Zaixiang Pang[1], Xiaomeng Deng[1], Linan Gong[2(✉)], and Nan Wang[3]

[1] School of Computer Science and Engineering, Changchun University of Technology, Changchun, China
pangzaixiang@ccut.edu.cn

[2] School of Mechanical and Electrical Engineering, Changchun Vocational Institute of Technology, Changchun, China
gonglinan2019@163.com

[3] Jilin Weimiao Medical Technology Co., Ltd., Changchun, China

Abstract. The traditional motion vice and rigid structure of the human upper limb complex joints between the forms of movement present significant challenges to ensuring consistency and addressing other problems. This paper proposes a 6-degrees-of-freedom cable-driven upper limb rehabilitation flexible parallel robot. The robot combines a flexible parallel mechanism with the advantages of light mass, good flexibility, and the ability to realize complex force position control. First, this paper examines the anatomy of human upper limb skeletal muscles. Second, a three-dimensional motion capture system is employed to obtain experimental data and to analyze the range of motion of the human upper limb. Finally, the structural design of the shoulder joint, elbow joint, and wrist joint is completed.

Keywords: Upper limb rehabilitation robot · Flexible parallel · Rope drive · Structural design

1 Introduction

Stroke is a persistent neurological deficit of the brain caused by acute cerebrovascular disease [1, 2]. Empirical studies have demonstrated that targeted rehabilitation training can facilitate functional reorganization of the brain in patients with motor dysfunction, thereby restoring the original function [3–6]. Currently, the number of rehabilitation physicians is far from sufficient to meet the needs of patients. Each patient has a different degree of disability and requires multiple repetitions of training on a daily basis. This limits the number of patients that physicians can serve, resulting in inefficient rehabilitation. However, hiring specialized physicians on a long-term basis increases the cost of medical care, which places a financial burden on families and leads many ordinary families to forego treatment.

The development of artificial intelligence has led to the creation of rehabilitation robots that can complete repetitive rehabilitation training tasks instead of physicians. These robots provide a novel approach to upper limb hemiplegic rehabilitation training, enhancing the quality of rehabilitation while simultaneously increasing productivity [7–10]. Currently, the structural design of rope-driven exoskeleton-based upper limb rehabilitation robots is a highly active area of research. Numerous domestic and international research and medical institutions are developing various rope-driven exoskeleton type upper limb rehabilitation robots. For example, ADEN-7 rehabilitation robot [11], Dampace rehabilitation robot [12], CAREX rehabilitation robot [13] and Armeo Power rehabilitation robot [14]. In comparison to traditional rehabilitation training methods, rehabilitation robots demonstrate superior rehabilitation outcomes, a broader range of rehabilitation modalities, and a more personalized rehabilitation experience. To ensure optimal integration, rehabilitation robots must be tailored to patients of varying sizes, with the robot's rotational axes aligning with the patient's joint axes. Concurrently, the installation of multiple motors and sensors at the end of the robot necessitates the augmentation of the rotational inertia of the robot. This approach is not conducive to the precise control of the robot and hinders the promotion of rehabilitation robots.

The traditional motion vice and rigid structure, as well as the human upper limb interarticular movement form, present difficulties in maintaining consistency and addressing other issues. This paper proposes a flexible parallel mechanism that offers advantages in terms of light mass, good flexibility, and the ability to achieve complex force position control. A 6-degree-of-freedom rope-driven upper limb rehabilitation flexible parallel robot is presented. The robot is designed to enhance the quality of late rehabilitation for stroke patients. This paper commences with an analysis of the anatomical structure of the human upper limb. This is followed by an investigation into the main bone and muscle composition of each joint of the upper limb. The motion acquisition of each joint is accomplished by a three-dimensional motion capture system to obtain motion data. By utilizing this data to clarify the design requirements of the robot, its components were designed to obtain the desired overall structure.

The main contributions of this paper are as follows: (1) A shoulder joint mechanism combining motor and gear drive is proposed. The objective is to design a gravity compensation device that will reduce the torque requirement of the shoulder joint flexion and extension drive motor. It is essential that the torque magnitude will not change with the adjustment of the length of the large arm, in order to meet the rehabilitation training requirements of different patients. (2) A novel elbow joint limiting device is proposed that can flexibly change the limiting angle. The adjustment of the elbow flexion/extension limit angle is achieved by changing the mounting position of the limit pin. (3) A novel rope-driven, compression spring-supported flexible parallel wrist rehabilitation mechanism is proposed. The fixed and moving platforms of the mechanism are connected by three ropes and compression springs. The springs are used to simulate the carpal bone and ligament complex, supporting and restricting the movement of the movable platform corresponding to the metacarpal bone. The moving platform simulates the end of the metacarpal, and the fixed platform simulates the end of the radius and ulna. Three cords are employed to simulate muscles and drive the parallel mechanism.

The remainder of the paper is organized as follows: In Sect. 2, the anatomical and kinematic characteristics of the human upper limbs are analyzed based on human anatomy. Movement data of the upper limbs is collected to obtain the movement of each joint and its range. In Sect. 3, the modular design and modeling of the upper limb rehabilitation robot are completed. Finally, Sect. 4 presents the conclusion.

2 Human Upper Limb Anatomy Analysis and Data Acquisition

2.1 Anatomical Analysis of the Human Upper Limb

In daily activities, the human upper limb plays a vital role. As illustrated in Fig. 1, the human upper limb is a highly complex locomotor system. In this system, external loads are primarily borne by the bones, which maintain the fundamental morphological characteristics of the system. Muscles and ligaments are attached to the bones separately. The muscles are responsible for driving the movement of the bones, while the ligaments connect the individual bones. This limits the range of motion of the bones to ensure that the parts remain within a safe range of motion. The upper limb is flexible and can move in seven degrees of freedom, as illustrated in Fig. 2.

The elbow joint is the most prominent joint connecting the upper arm to the forearm. It is primarily a gliding joint and relies on the relative motion between the cartilages to achieve movement of the joint. Flexion and extension of the upper extremity are dependent on this joint, including flexion/extension and pronation/pronation of the forearm. These two degrees of freedom are of critical importance in daily activities. The maximum flexion/extension angle of the elbow is 135°, while the range of forearm pronation/pronation is greatest at 90°. Both have very important roles and should be retained. However, when the forearm internal/external rotation is fixed, the shoulder joint internal/external rotation angle does not change much. Concurrently, the redundancy of the degrees of freedom of the kinematic mechanism has permitted the shoulder joint to be analyzed with internal/external rotation in mind. For the sake of convenient control and structural stability, the forearms can be fixed together with internal/external rotation for movement. Consequently, the maximum angle range of shoulder internal/external rotation has been designed to be 110°, so that the elbow flexion/extension is equivalent to a single joint kinematic vice.

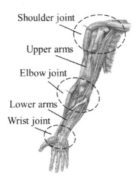

Fig. 1. Physiological structure of the human upper limb.

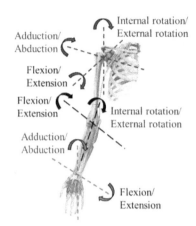

Fig. 2. Distribution of degrees of freedom of the human upper limb.

2.2 Upper Limb Motion Data Acquisition and Analysis

The human upper limb exhibits high flexibility and complex forms of movement. To design an upper limb rehabilitation robot with optimal rehabilitation efficacy, the range of motion of the human upper limb must be quantified. In this study, 20 research subjects (10 males and 10 females) were selected for the collection and analysis of upper limb movement data. The research subjects were all university students and teachers and provided informed consent. The physical parameters of the study subjects are presented in Table 1.

Table 1. Table of physical parameters of the study subjects.

Gender	Maximum height	Minimum height	Average height	Maximum weight	Minimum weight	Average weight
Men	192 cm	167 cm	175.56 cm	95 kg	55 kg	71.25 kg
Women	172 cm	157 cm	162.65 cm	63 kg	41 kg	51.25 kg

This paper is based on the Qualisys Motion Analysis 3D motion capture system to complete the experimental data acquisition. Figure 3 illustrates the six degrees of freedom motion for acquisition. The black dashed line indicates the limit angle of the motion range. The red dotted line indicates the initial position of that degree of freedom measurement. The orange dot indicates the center of rotation of the joint.

First, marker points were installed on the hand, small arm, large arm, wrist, elbow, shoulder, head, and torso of the research subject, as illustrated in Fig. 4. Second, the research subject was seated in a fixed position and completed six single-degree-of-freedom movements of the upper limbs to the best of his or her ability. Finally, four daily movements of drinking water, touching the head, shoulder, and back were completed. In total, there were ten groups of movements, each of which lasted eight seconds.

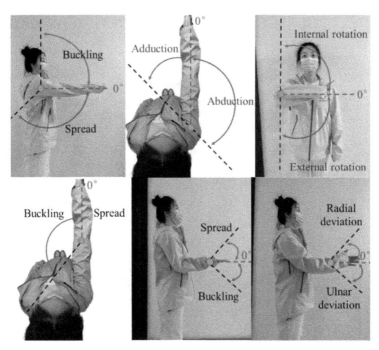

Fig. 3. Schematic diagram of the degree of freedom of movement of the human upper limb.

Fig. 4. Installation of marking points.

The motion information of the marked points is collected and recorded by the 3D motion acquisition and analysis software. The selected data are finally displayed in the form of graphs. Figure 5 illustrates the hand movement of the research subject engaged in the drinking action.

The trajectories of the upper limb end when completing the drinking maneuver can be observed to vary among the 20 subjects. These differences are primarily attributed to the varying lengths of the upper limbs and the individualized movement habits of the subjects. However, it is evident that these trajectories exhibit a consistent movement trend. This indicates that there is a specific movement pattern of the human upper limb

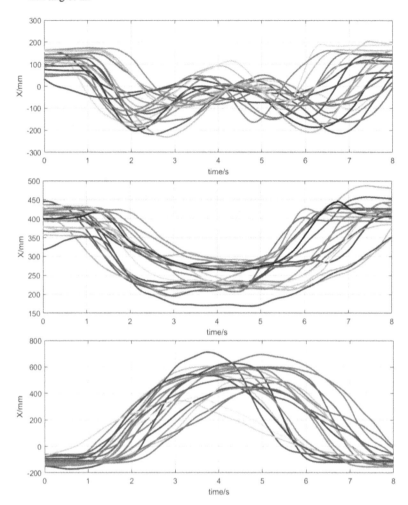

Fig. 5. Recordings of hand movements for water-drinking maneuvers in 20 study participants.

when different individuals complete the same movement. The data were processed to exclude any obvious noise data, and the movement angles of each joint of the upper limb were obtained, as shown in Table 2.

3 Structural Design of Upper Limb Rehabilitation Robot

3.1 Structural Design of Robot Shoulder Joints

The bones, muscles, and ligaments of the human upper extremity were anatomically analyzed. It was discovered that the shoulder joint is not only flexible but also connects the entire upper extremity to the torso. Therefore, it must be strong enough to withstand large loads. Since the shoulder joint rehabilitation device is close to the support part of the robot, direct motor drive is used. This method does not add much to the rotational

Table 2. Range of motion of each joint of the human upper limb in degrees of freedom.

joint	form of motion	Range of motion of the human body
shoulder joint	adduction	0°–50°
	abduction	0°–130°
	flexion	0°–90°
	extension	0°–135°
	internal rotation	0°–60°
	external rotation	0°–60°
elbow joint	flexion	0°–145°
	extension	0°
wrist joint	adduction	0°–20°
	abduction	0°–30°
	flexion	0°–75°
	extension	0°–75°

inertia of the robot end. The shoulder rehabilitation unit is required to carry the combined load of the entire robot arm and the patient's upper limb. If a rope drive or a flexible drive is used for this part, complex tensioning devices must be installed. To achieve precise control, the elongation of the rope must be considered. Therefore, an efficient transmission method of motor plus gear is employed in the shoulder joint rehabilitation part.

In shoulder rehabilitation devices, the motor that drives the shoulder flexion/extension has the highest torque requirement. This is particularly evident when performing shoulder flexion, where the robot must overcome gravity in conjunction with the patient's upper limb to complete the task. However, there are fewer motors available that meet both the power and torque requirements of the shoulder joint. Consequently, the majority of commercially available motors that can meet the power and torque requirements are not optimal in terms of size and weight. For this reason, a gravity compensation device is designed in this paper to reduce the torque requirement of the shoulder flexion-extension drive motor.

As illustrated in Fig. 6, the primary shoulder joint flexion/extension (q_1) is linked to the robot body via an L-shaped shoulder load-bearing member. The servomotor output shaft is connected to the input shaft of the helical tooth planetary reducer. The output end of the helical tooth planetary gearbox is equipped with a crossed roller bearing. The outer ring of the crossed roller bearing is connected to the shoulder load-bearing member, while the inner ring is connected to a gravity compensation disk. The starting end of the rope is fixed to the gravity compensation disk. The necessity of ensuring that the tension spring and the gravity compensation disk are co-planar is addressed by changing the direction of force to the axial direction of the servomotor via the use of longitudinal and transverse fixed pulleys. This design increases the diameter of the gravity compensation disk, optimizes the effective working length of the tension spring, and makes the layout more compact. Additionally, the external dimensions of the device are reduced, component interference is minimized, and the effective working space of the robot is expanded. By increasing the diameter of the gravity compensation disk, the torque requirements of the motor and reducer can be reduced while the effective working length of the tension spring is increased. However, this also increases the length of the shoulder load-bearing member in the axial direction of the motor, thereby increasing the rotational inertia of the shoulder joint rehabilitation device. To address this issue, this paper proposes the addition of a dynamic pulley to the pulley block. Connecting the tension spring and the dynamic pulley ensures that the effective length of the tension spring only needs to reach half of the effective rotational circumference of the gravity compensation disk. Consequently, the force arm is significantly shortened, and the rotational inertia of the rehabilitation component of the shoulder joint is reduced.

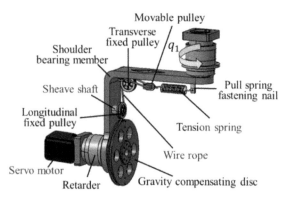

Fig. 6. Structure of the shoulder flexion/extension part of the robot.

The larger, more flexible movements of the human upper extremity originate primarily from shoulder internal/external rotation. Therefore, it is critical to ensure safety and comfort when this degree of freedom is used for rehabilitation. The shoulder joint internal/external rotation (q_2) part is shown in Fig. 7. One of the U-shaped fixation pieces is connected to the gravity compensation disk for shoulder flexion/extension to reduce the rotational inertia of the system. To meet the rehabilitation needs of most patients, the large arm needs to be longer. This results in the overall center of the device being biased towards the end of the robot. In this paper, the servomotor and reducer are fixed to the rear end of the U-shaped fixture. This brings the center of the large arm rehabilitation device closer to the axis of the shoulder flexion/extension motors, which facilitates later control.

The slide is affixed to the front of the U-shaped fixture in a direction opposite to that of the servomotor mounting. Its function is to connect the gearbox with shoulder joint rotation in/out and the slide with a self-locking mechanism. This design allows the robot arm length to be adjusted, while the output shaft of the gearbox transmits torque to the gears via a telescopic universal drive shaft. This design ensures that the amount of torque remains constant regardless of the adjustment of the arm length, thereby meeting the rehabilitation requirements of different patients.

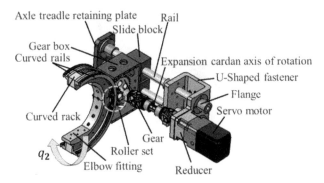

Fig. 7. Structural diagram of the shoulder joint of a robot with internal/external rotation.

The gears are meshed with the curved rack to achieve the internal/external rotation of the arm. The two ends of the curved rack and pinion are toothless zones, preventing the gears from meshing properly when they come into contact with the two ends. This has the effect of hard limit protection, preventing secondary injury to the patient. In order to prevent discomfort to the user due to momentary impacts during training, cushioning pads at both ends of the curved rack are to be considered in future research in order to minimize such impacts. Both sides of the gearbox are fitted with pulley sets, each consisting of four pulleys. The pulleys serve to constrain the curved guide rail and ensure that the circumferential movement of the curved guide rail and the rack is carried out smoothly. The pulleys are constructed from aluminum alloy, which is a high-strength material.

3.2 Design of a Robotic Elbow Joint

The shoulder joint adduction/abduction (q_3) is essential for the integration of the entire upper limb with the robot support section. The high loads and the long force arms result in considerable bending moments at this joint. To prevent excessive deformation of the motor shaft and ensure effective protection for the motor, the two parts are connected here by crossed roller bearings. Figure 8 illustrates the overall structure of the shoulder joint rehabilitation.

The elbow joint connects the large and small arms of the body's upper limbs. It plays a vital role in many of the movements of daily life, such as eating, drinking, and holding objects. The safe range of motion of the elbow joint varies from patient to patient due to differences in skeletal ligament limitations and different levels of disability. In this paper, an elbow joint limiting device that can flexibly change the limiting angle is designed in the elbow joint rehabilitation part. As illustrated in Fig. 9, the elbow joint limiting device is primarily comprised of a limiting block and a limiting disk. The internal and external rotation stops are fixed on the limit block, in conjunction with the internal and external rotation limit pins on the limit disk, which collectively serve to impose a hard limit on the elbow joint. The inner and outer mounting holes are evenly distributed on the limit disk, and the depth of the inner ring mounting holes is smaller than that of the outer ring. This configuration results in the internal rotation limit pins being mounted

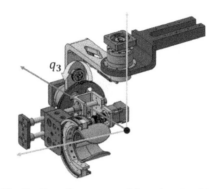

Fig. 8. Overall structure of the robot shoulder.

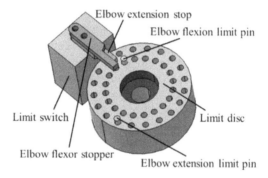

Fig. 9. Elbow joint limiting device structure diagram.

on the inner ring at a higher position than the external rotation limit pins mounted on the outer ring. The adjustment of the elbow flexion/extension limit angle is achieved by changing the mounting position of the limit pins.

The human upper limb is morphologically tapered from the trunk side to the palmar side. For the majority of people, the diameter of the large arm is larger than that of the small arm. Therefore, the large arm connectors are designed in a stepped shape to compensate for the difference in diameter between the large and small arms. At the same time, the elbow is also reserved for the installation of silicone pads. Silicone pads possess soft, skin-friendly properties that can markedly enhance the comfort of patients. Additionally, silicone is utilized for the inner lining of both the large and small arm wearers. To accommodate a range of patient sizes, the small arm wearer is attached to the small arm connector via the L bracket. This provides the small arm wearer with some flexibility in terms of length and height. Figure 10 depicts the overall structure of the shoulder and elbow joint.

3.3 Structural Design of Robot Wrist Joint

The structure of the wrist joint of the upper limb rehabilitation training robot comprises three parts, as illustrated in Fig. 11. The end fixation device is worn on the patient's

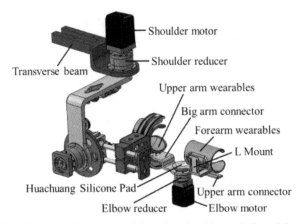

Fig. 10. Overall structure of the robot shoulder and elbow joints.

hand, and the level of disability and the degree of rehabilitation training required vary from one patient to another. In cases of mild disability, the patient is able to exert some control over the fingers to hook the grip. In more severe cases, however, the patient is unable to control the motor behavior of the upper limb and requires the use of medical tape to fix the hand with the grip. Consequently, the end fixation device is equipped with a quick grip adjustment function. The distance from the grip to the flexible parallel mechanism can be rapidly adjusted according to the patient's level of disability and the length of the lower arm. This design ensures the comfort and safety of the patient during rehabilitation training. As the end of the wrist rehabilitation mechanism and the whole robot, the end fixture is required to collect and record the position information in real time. Consequently, posture sensors have been installed in the end fixture with the objective of enabling precise control of the robot and the patient's post-rehabilitation evaluation. The small arm fixation device is connected to the shoulder and elbow rehabilitation part, and at the same time, it is necessary to design the fixation point of the wire pipe for driving the rope.

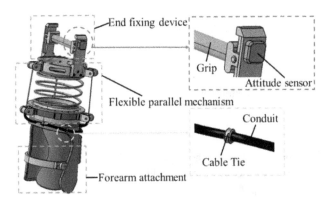

Fig. 11. Overall structure of the wrist joint part of the robot.

The end fixture is analogous to the human hand, while the small arm fixture is analogous to the human small arm. The flexible parallel mechanism connects the end and the small arm fixation device, which is analogous to the human wrist joint. Among these components, the movable platform simulates the end of the metacarpal bone, while the fixed platform simulates the end of the radius and ulna. The compression spring simulates the carpal bone and ligament complex, which provides support for the moving platform and decelerates it during motion. This design achieves a similar function to the radial carpal and intercarpal joints. Three cords simulate muscles to drive the parallel mechanism (Fig. 12).

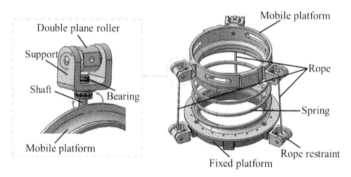

Fig. 12. Structural diagram of flexible parallel mechanism and rope restraining device.

In order to reduce the weight of the robot end, the servomotor driving the three ropes is mounted on the base part of the robot, as illustrated in Fig. 13. The winch is secured to one end of the connector by four evenly spaced light shafts and one threaded rod through the center. The threaded rod engages the threads in the center of the capstan, and the threaded rod is fitted with a bearing at the end of the connecting piece and a rigid connection at the end of the fixed base. This configuration allows the optical axis and the capstan to rotate together when the torque from the servomotor is transmitted to the connector. However, the threaded rod itself cannot rotate due to the constraints of the mounting and moves relative to the capstan. In this instance, the winch undergoes both a rotational movement and a translational movement in the direction of the optical axis. The rope is wound evenly and without overlap onto the drive capstan, and the length of the rope is calculated with precision based on the angle of rotation and the diameter of the capstan.

The measurement of rope tension is as important as that of rope length. In order to quickly and accurately obtain the rope pull force so as to control the flexible parallel mechanism and realize the fast response. In this paper, a rope tension measurement device consisting of three fixed pulleys and one pressure sensor is designed. Since the fixed pulleys alter the direction of the rope pull without affecting its magnitude, the rope pull is always half of the value measured by the sensor. Compared with installing a torque sensor at the output of the motor, the rope pulley force measurement device designed in this paper is easy to control at a later stage. Because it has lower cost and more concise calculation steps.

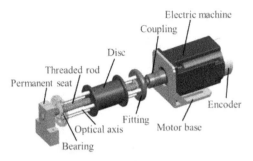

Fig. 13. Structure of Rope Drive Unit.

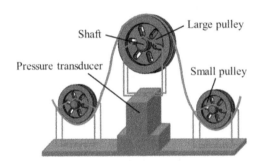

Fig. 14. Structure of rope tension measuring device.

3.4 Robot Overall Structure

This paper begins with an examination of the anatomy of the human upper limb, with a particular focus on the rehabilitation needs of stroke patients. A 6-degree-of-freedom rope-driven upper limb rehabilitation flexible parallel robot design is proposed. As illustrated in Fig. 14, the shoulder and elbow part of the robot employs a tandem mechanism with gravity compensation and offset compensation devices. Consequently, the torque requirement of the shoulder joint drive motor is reduced, and the motion of the shoulder and elbow joints with four degrees of freedom is achieved. The wrist part of the robot employs a rope-driven flexible parallel mechanism, which enables the motion of two degrees of freedom of the wrist joint. The flexible mechanism is designed to more effectively eliminate the unreasonable displacement between the system and the patient's joints, thereby enhancing the efficiency of the rehabilitation process. The robot is equipped with an adjustment mechanism to accommodate individual differences, thereby maximizing patient comfort (Fig. 15).

During the rehabilitation process, the patient's hand, small arm, and large arm were immobilized with the corresponding wearing devices in the robot. The robot's motion subs were utilized for joint synergistic training of multiple joints of the upper limbs. It is challenging to reach the upper limb's functional range of motion during the patient's rehabilitation process. Excessive range of motion may result in structural interference of the robot. Consequently, the joint range of motion of the robot is slightly smaller than the human body's limit range of motion.

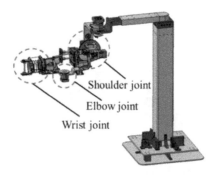

Fig. 15. Overall structure of the upper limb rehabilitation training robot.

4 Conclusion

The 6-degree-of-freedom rope-driven flexible parallel robot for upper limb rehabilitation proposed in this study is a well-designed and practical device. The range of motion of the upper limb was investigated by means of a detailed analysis of the human anatomy and the 3D motion capture system. Furthermore, the flexible structure of the shoulder, elbow, and wrist joints was designed to accommodate the necessary range of motion. The three joint mechanisms proposed in this paper represent a novel and practical approach to the design of rehabilitation robots. All of these devices can be utilized to meet the rehabilitation training needs of a diverse range of patients. In conclusion, this study is of great significance in addressing the inconsistency between traditional rehabilitation robots and the complex joint motion of the human body. Moreover, it offers a foundation for further research and applications in the field of upper limb rehabilitation.

Acknowledgements. This work was supported in part by the Jilin Province Science and Technology Department key research and development project, project number: 20220204102YY. And, the Jilin Provincial Department of Science and Technology has awarded the Excellence in Science and Technology Innovation and Entrepreneurship for Young and Middle-aged Talents (Team) Project with the code 20240601030RC.

Conflict of Interest. The authors declare no conflict of interest.

References

1. Tanaka, T., et al.: Pathophysiology, diagnosis, prognosis, and prevention of poststroke epilepsy: clinical and research implications. Neurology **102**(11), e209450–e209450 (2024)
2. Emel, D., et al.: Operational space analysis of human muscular effort in robot assisted reaching tasks. Robot. Auton. Syst. **125**, 103429 (2020)
3. Li, W., Liu, K., et al.: Development and evaluation of a wearable lower limb rehabilitation robot. J. Bionic Eng. **19**(3), 1–12 (2022)
4. Yuanyuan, C., Keping, L., Chunxu, L., et al.: A novel method based on long short-term memory network and discrete-time zeroing neural algorithm for upper-limb continuous estimation using sEMG signals. Biomed. Signal Process. Control **67** (2021)

5. Wanting, L., Keping, L., Zhongbo, S., et al.: A neural network-based model for lower limb continuous estimation against the disturbance of uncertainty. Biomed. Signal Process. Control **71**(PA) (2022)
6. Liu, K., Liu, Y., Zhang, Y., Wei, L., Sun, Z., Jin, L.: Five-step discrete-time noise-tolerant zeroing neural network model for time-varying matrix inversion with application to manipulator motion generation. Eng. Appl. Artif. Intell. **103** (2021)
7. Zhai, Y., Ma, X., Chen, D., Lei, J.: Joint motion control of flexible wearable upper limb rehabilitation robot. J. South China Univ. Technol. (Nat. Sci. Ed.) **49**(06), 19–27 (2021)
8. Sun, Z., Shi, T., Wei, L., et al.: Noise-suppressing zeroing neural network for online solving time-varying nonlinear optimization problem: a control-based approach. Neural Comput. Appl. **32**(15), 1–16 (2019)
9. Sun, Z., Tang, S., Jin, L., Zhang, J., Junzhi, Y.: Nonconvex activation noise-suppressing neural network for time-varying quadratic programming: application to omnidirectional mobile manipulator. IEEE Trans. Ind. Inf. **19**(11), 10786–10798 (2023)
10. Sun, Z., Tang, S., Zhang, J., et al.: Nonconvex noise-tolerant neural model for repetitive motion of omnidirectional mobile manipulators. IEEE/CAA J. Automatica Sinica **10**(08), 1766–1768 (2023)
11. Perry, J.C., Rosen, J., Burns, S.: Upper-limb powered exoskeleton design. IEEE/ASME Trans. Mechatron. **12**(4), 408–417 (2007)
12. Stienen, A.H.A., et al.: Dampace: design of an exoskeleton for force-coordination training in upper-extremity rehabilitation. J. Med. Dev. Trans. ASME **3**(3), 031003 (2009)
13. Mao, Y., Agrawal, S.K.: Design of a cable-driven arm exoskeleton (CAREX) for neural rehabilitation. IEEE Trans. Robot. **28**(4), 84–92 (2012)
14. Perry, J.C., Rosen, J.: Design of a 7 degree-of-freedom upper-limb powered exoskeleton. IEEE/ASME Trans. Mechatron. **12**(4), 408–417 (2007)

A Practical Method for Orchard Robots to Navigate Along Row Medians Using Tree Trunk Maps

Anmin Huang, Enbo Liu, Changguo Xu, Wei Tang(✉), Renyuan Zhang, and Xuebing Yuan

School of Automation, Northwestern Polytechnical University, Xi'an 710129, China
tangwei@nwpu.edu.cn

Abstract. Orchard tasks often require robots to navigate along the central axes of tree rows in the dynamic orchard environment, making traditional map-based path planning methods unsuitable for these environments. In this work, we propose a practical autonomous navigation solution tailored for orchard operations. We decompose the orchard navigation task into multiple straight-line segments, with the starting and ending points of each segment located on the central axis of the tree row. The waypoints are computed with a trunk map that contains only the trunk point clouds. In the actual navigation process, we sequentially connect all target points to form the robot's global path and utilize the Dynamic Window Approach (DWA) algorithm for path tracking and obstacle avoidance. Our experiments in real-world environments validate the feasibility of our autonomous navigation method. The proposed navigation approach does not require real-time detection of fruit trees and is capable of dynamic obstacle avoidance, thus offering broad application prospects.

Keywords: Dynamic environment · Orchard Robots · Autonomous navigation · path planning · Trunk Map

1 Introduction

Orchard robots can perform tasks such as harvesting, spraying, and fertilizing, contributing significantly to the advancement of agricultural intelligence [1]. A key technology enabling these robots to autonomously perform tasks is mobile robot autonomous navigation, which allows robots to autonomously plan paths and assign velocities to the actuation system. The qualities of paths directly impact the efficiency and safety of task execution. In orchard tasks, the robot needs to navigate past each tree sequentially while avoiding collisions, which increases the complexity of path planning. Therefore, developing a safe and efficient path planning strategy is crucial for achieving effective precision horticulture.

Orchards represent a semi-structured environment [2] where robots typically need to follow specific paths to perform tasks. Unlike urban settings, orchards usually lack predefined pathways to constrain the robot's trajectory. To prevent the robot from wandering aimlessly in the orchard, researchers commonly rely on visual sensors or LiDAR (Light Detection and Ranging) systems to extract the central axis of tree rows as the robot's path. Sharifi et al. [3] use the graph partitioning theory to categorize camera data into distinct classes, including terrain, trees, and sky. Subsequently, they applied the Hough transform to extract features from the classified orchard images, ultimately generating the desired central path for robot navigation. Chen et al. [4] focus on path planning at the end of rows in orchards. They employed a depth camera to detect the end of rows and then utilized a dynamic window path planner to generate collision-free paths for the robot. Opiyo et al. [5] extract the road medial axis in the orchard based on image processing and then use a two-input fuzzy logic controller to track the medial axis for robot navigation. Yang et al. [6] employ neural networks and pixel scanning to fit road edges in orchards, and calculate the centerline of the road using a weighted averaging method to generate paths for the robot. Despite the respective strengths of these methods, visual sensors are susceptible to environmental interference outdoors [7]. Therefore, vision-based navigation systems may not provide sufficient reliability for orchard robots.

LiDAR provides rich environmental feature information, including obstacle shapes and distances relative to the robot [8]. Consequently, many studies have developed LiDAR-based navigation systems for orchard robots. Researchers typically use diverse methods to filter out noise from the map and perform clustering on point clouds of fruit trees [9, 10]. Subsequently, they commonly utilize algorithms such as RANSAC [11–13] and LSM [14] to fit straight lines to the point clouds of tree trunks. The central axis of the tree rows is then extracted as the navigation path for the robot. In the navigation process, these algorithms use trajectory tracking methods or local path planning methods [15, 16] to ensure the robot follows the global path. These methods typically involve complex preprocessing of point cloud maps. Furthermore, they solely address the paths within tree rows, leading to insufficient stability when the robot turns at the ends of tree rows.

Considering the significance of tree trunks as fundamental static features in orchards, we propose a path planning and navigation method utilizing tree trunk point cloud maps. Our method divides the entire autonomous navigation task into multiple straight-line segments. For each segment, the method connects two points located on the central axis of tree rows to form the robot's global path. We also present a method for extracting the central axes of rows based on a trunk point cloud map [17], which includes only trunk point cloud data. To address obstacle avoidance in actual navigation tasks, our method integrates the Dynamic Window Approach (DWA) algorithm for path tracking and local obstacle avoidance. The primary contributions of this work are outlined as follows:

- We propose a practical scheme for orchard robots to navigate along the central axes of tree rows, addressing the specific requirements of orchard tasks. Our method divides the autonomous navigation task into multiple segments of linear navigation, ensuring smooth transitions between tree rows.
- We introduce a novel path planning method for orchard robots based on tree-trunk maps. Our method filters out features that could interfere with extracting the central axes of tree rows before map construction, which reduces the computational pressure

during navigation. Additionally, our method incorporates obstacle avoidance during the path-following process, enhancing the robot's safety.

Section 2 presents the overall framework of our method. Section 3 details the technical aspects of our approach. Section 4 demonstrates the navigation performance of our method in real-world environments. Section 5 summarizes the paper and discusses future research directions.

2 System Framework

During tasks like spraying, the robot needs to proceed along the central axis of tree rows to efficiently reach fruit trees on both sides. We translate this unique navigation requirement into a multi-segment navigation problem. As shown in Fig. 1, each navigation segment is a straight line, with both the starting and ending points located on the central axis of the tree row. Within this navigation framework, the orchard navigation problem can be divided into two sub-problems: central axis extraction and autonomous navigation based on the defined paths.

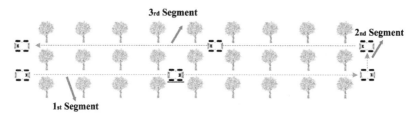

Fig. 1. Autonomous navigation in an orchard

Our navigation scheme mainly comprises three components: trunk map construction, path planning, and trajectory tracking. The overall framework of the scheme is illustrated in Fig. 2. The detection and extraction of trunk point cloud in the process of autonomous navigation will increase the computational pressure of the control system. Therefore, we designed a central axis extraction method using the trunk map, thereby eliminating the need for target detection during navigation.

The trunk map is obtained using SLAM algorithms, with trunk point clouds as the input. This process is detailed in our previous work [17]. The global path must ensure that the robot moves along the central axes of the rows and transitions smoothly between rows. We achieve this by selecting points at each end of the central axis and connecting them sequentially to form the global path. For actual autonomous navigation, the robot must avoid obstacles such as pedestrians. Hence, we use the DWA algorithm for velocity allocation and local path planning. This process is performed on a two-dimensional occupancy grid map, where obstacles are projected onto the map. Our navigation scheme is practical because it is tailored for orchard tasks, consider the computational simplicity and the robot safety simultaneously.

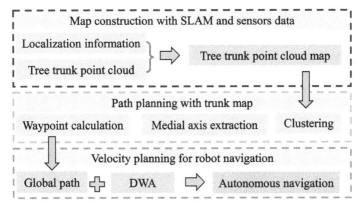

Fig. 2. Overall framework of the orchard navigation system

3 Method

In this section, we elaborate on each component of the proposed orchard robot navigation scheme. First, we explain the process of constructing the trunk map and provide a detailed description of how to calculate navigation points using this map. Building on this, we describe how to generate a two-dimensional grid map with obstacle information. Finally, we introduce the basic principles of the DWA algorithm.

3.1 Tree Trunk Map Construction

Our method depends on trunk maps to calculate navigation waypoints and plan paths. Therefore, the first step is to construct a trunk map, which contains only point clouds of tree trunks. The map construction process involves three steps: data collection, extraction of target point clouds, and map construction.

Data Collection. In this step, the robot collects data from the LiDAR, camera, and IMU. Before data collection, sensor calibration is required. Sensor synchronization is necessary to acquire data from all sensors simultaneously due to their different frequencies. Additionally, spatial registration is needed because the coordinates of the same object may differ across sensor coordinate systems, necessitating alignment based on the relative positions of the sensors.

Target Point Cloud Extraction. Compared to 3D point cloud data, 2D image data is less dense, making it easier to detect trunk features. Through experimental validation, we verify that the YOLOX algorithm has high detection accuracy for tree trunks and does not require a high-powered GPU for practical applications. Therefore, we first use the YOLOX [18] algorithm to detect the pixel coordinates of the trunks in the image, and then obtain the point cloud features of the trunks based on the relative transformation relationship between the camera and the LiDAR.

The YOLOX algorithm marks trunk positions with detection boxes. After projecting the point cloud data onto a 2D image, we cluster the point clouds within the detection boxes. The most abundant type of point cloud within each detection box is considered as trunk point cloud and retained, while other noise points within the detection boxes and point clouds outside the detection boxes are removed.

Map Construction. We utilize the LIO-SAM [19] algorithm to construct the trunk map. The LIO-SAM algorithm, as an advanced and popular mapping algorithm, not only offers high accuracy but also has low hardware requirements. It's worth noting that the input data for the mapping algorithm includes raw point cloud, trunk point cloud, and IMU data. During the mapping process, the raw point cloud data is used to build laser odometry, which determines the robot's pose. The algorithm stitches the trunk point cloud based on the robot's pose and optimizes the map in the backend using both LiDAR and IMU data.

3.2 Calculation of Navigation Waypoints

Navigation along the central axis of a row requires calculating the axis coordinates, which typically involves extracting fruit tree features. We propose directly extracting row lines using trunk maps, bypassing the need to extract tree features during navigation, thereby improving the efficiency of autonomous navigation. In this section, we detail how to calculate the coordinates of these navigation target points using the trunk point cloud map.

Determining the central axes in 3D space is overly intricate and dispensable, given that the trajectories of mobile robots are confined to two dimensions. Therefore, the purpose of this section is to calculate the x and y coordinates of the navigation points by extracting the central axes of the row. Traditionally, midline extraction is executed within the horizontal plane, often entailing intricate line fitting procedures. In this work, we introduce a more straightforward methodology. The systematic arrangement of tree trunks in orchards serves as a foundational aspect for our approach. We start by establishing a 3D coordinate system, with the horizontal plane serving as the XOY plane and aligning the x-axis parallel to the tree row, as depicted in Fig. 3(a). Subsequently, we project the map along the x-axis, setting all points' x coordinate to 0, as illustrated in Fig. 3(b).

(a) (b) (c) (d)

Fig. 3. The trunk map and clustering results

In the YOZ plane, the point clouds of trees within the same row exhibit substantial overlap, whereas significant gaps are observed between distinct rows of trees. Consequently, clustering trees in the plane and segmenting the orchard into distinct units is straightforward. In this study, we employ the Euclidean Cluster for this process. This method involves placing one of the tree points into a queue and subsequently computing the distance to other points within the vicinity of that point. This process can be formulated as

$$d = \sqrt{(x_1 - x_2)^2 + (y_1 - y_2)^2}, (x_1, y_1) \in L_1, (x_2, y_2) \in R \quad (1)$$

where (x_1, y_1) is one of the points in queue L_1, R is the domain of the point (x_1, y_1), (x_2, y_2) is the coordinate of the point in R, and d is the Euclidean distance between two points. If d is below the threshold, the algorithm will enqueue (x_2, y_2) into queue L_1. Conversely, if d exceeds the threshold, a new queue will be created to store (x_2, y_2). After traversing the point cloud map, the map is classified into different categories, as shown in Fig. 3 (c) and (d), where point clouds of the same color represent one category.

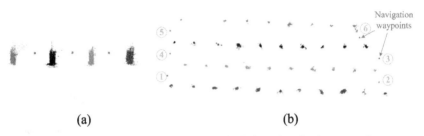

Fig. 4. Extraction of medial axes and calculation of navigation waypoints

Since the tree trunks are aligned parallel to the *x*-axis, the medial axis is projected as a single point in the YOZ plane. The *y* coordinates of these points can be easily obtained using the clustered point cloud map. As depicted in Fig. 4(a), the midpoints of the two types of tree rows can serve as the *y* coordinate to be solved. It is worth noting that the shape of the point cloud map may influence the calculation of midpoints for tree rows. The extraction process of the tree trunk point cloud may not completely filter out the canopy point cloud, resulting in a small number of other outliers in the point cloud map in addition to the tree trunk point cloud. If these point cloud data are involved in the calculation of navigation point coordinates, it will inevitably cause the robot's trajectory to deviate from the centerline of the rows. Additionally, it is impossible for trees in the same row to be perfectly aligned on a straight line, which can also introduce errors in the calculation of navigation point coordinates.

If there are very few residual point clouds from fruit tree branches or leaves, they are typically located at higher altitudes. Therefore, calculating the coordinates of the medial axes of the tree rows using points below this height can mitigate the influence of point cloud noise. Besides, to prevent calculation errors caused by individual trees deviating from the row, we use the median of the *y* coordinates of each tree row point cloud to represent that row of fruit trees. After obtaining the median for each tree row, the *y* coordinate can be calculated as

$$y_{k,k+1} = \frac{y^k_{z=z_0} + y^{k+1}_{z=z_0}}{2} \quad (2)$$

In Eq. (2), k and $k+1$ are the numbers of the rows, $y_{z=z_0}^{k}$ and $y_{z=z_0}^{k+1}$ are the median y coordinates of the point clouds. This calculation step is performed along the line where $z = z_0$. In practical applications, the value of z_0 is chosen based on the shape of the tree trunk map, avoiding potential residual outliers at the top and bottom that may not have been completely filtered out. $\{y = y_{k,k+1}, z = z_0\}$ is the wanted expression the central axis. And $y_{k,k+1}$ also serves the y coordinate of the navigation waypoint between the two tree rows.

In the XOY plane, it is straightforward to obtain the minimum and maximum values of the x-axis coordinates for each row of point clouds. During the transition from one row of trees to another, the robot needs to maneuver around the fruit trees to avoid collisions. Therefore, the x coordinate of the navigation points needs to be at a certain distance from the extreme values of the x coordinates of the adjacent point clouds. The calculation process for the x coordinate of the navigation points can be represented as

$$x_{k,k+1}^{1} = x_{k}^{min} - \delta \tag{3}$$

$$x_{k,k+1}^{2} = x_{k}^{max} + \delta \tag{4}$$

where $x_{k,k+1}^{1}$ and $x_{k,k+1}^{2}$ are the x coordinates of the two navigation points in this row. x_{k}^{min} and x_{k}^{max} represent the minimum and maximum values of the point cloud's X-coordinate, respectively, while δ denotes the spacing between the navigation point and the adjacent tree trunks in the x-axis direction. There are two navigation points between every two rows of trees $\left(x_{k,k+1}^{1}, y_{k,k+1}\right), \left(x_{k,k+1}^{2}, y_{k,k+1}\right)$. The positions of the navigation points are illustrated in Fig. 4(b).

3.3 Path Planning and Navigation

During the actual navigation process, the robot needs to a adjust its velocity based on the global path and respond to unforeseen dynamic obstacles. We employ the DWA algorithm to accomplish this. The core of the DWA algorithm involves sampling and optimizing the robot's velocity within the velocity space. The calculation of the velocity space takes into account the robot's performance, dynamic characteristics, and environmental obstacles:

$$V_r = V_s \cap V_a \cap V_d \tag{5}$$

In Eq. (5), V_r represents the range of feasible velocities, V_a represents the range of velocities that will not cause collisions or abrupt turns for the robot, V_s represents the range of velocities that the robot can achieve under the maximum motor speed limit, and V_d represents the range of velocities that the robot can attain at the next moment under the limitation of robot acceleration. The velocity range V_a and V_d can be calculated as

$$V_a = \{(v, w) | v \leq \sqrt{2 dist(v, w) \times a_v}, w \leq \sqrt{2 dist(v, w) \times a_w}\} \tag{6}$$

$$V_d = \{(v, w) | v \in [v_a - a_v \cdot t, v_a + a_v \cdot t], w \in [v_w - a_w \cdot t, v_w + a_w \cdot t]\} \tag{7}$$

In Eq. (6), v, w, a_v, a_w are the linear velocity, angular velocity, linear acceleration, and angular acceleration of the robot, respectively. $dist(v, w)$ is the closest distance between the trajectory of the robot and the obstacle. Under the restrictions of Eq. (6), the trajectory of the robot does not coincide with the obstacle.

In Eq. (7), v_a and v_w are the current linear and angular velocities of the robot. t is the time period of a local path planning process. Equation (7) represents the range of velocities that the robot can actually achieve under the limit of its own acceleration.

Optimizing the robot's speed within the velocity space can yield the most appropriate speed. The evaluation function for the optimization process is:

$$G(v, w) = \sigma(\alpha \cdot heading(v, w) + \beta \cdot dist(v, w) + \gamma \cdot velocity(v, w)) \quad (8)$$

In Eq. (8), $heading(v, w)$ is a progress towards the goal location. It is maximal if the robot moves directly towards the target. α, β, and γ are the weight coefficients of each part. The function σ smoothes the weighted sum of the three components and results in more side-clearance from obstacles. The goal of optimization is to maximize $G(v, w)$ such that the robot moves toward the goal point with the maximum safe speed achievable. If the robot maintains constant velocity and angular velocity for a period of time, it is possible to predict the robot's position at time $k \cdot \Delta t$ in the future.

$$\begin{aligned} x_k &= x + v\Delta t \sum_{i=1}^{k} \cos(\theta_{i-1}) \\ y_k &= y + v\Delta t \sum_{i=1}^{k} \sin(\theta_{i-1}) \\ \theta_k &= \theta + k\omega \Delta t \end{aligned} \quad (9)$$

In Eq. (9), (x, y, z) is the current state of the robot, (x_k, y_k, z_k) forms the local trajectory of the robot. The robot's speed and local trajectory output by the DWA algorithm take into account the robot's dynamic characteristics and the obstacles in the environment, ensuring the robot's safety. Therefore, using the DWA algorithm for local path planning further enhances the applicability of our navigation method.

4 Experimental Results

4.1 Dataset

Using our self-built robot platform, we conduct autonomous navigation experiments in a real environment. In this section, we provide the autonomously planned path and the actual navigation trajectory of the robot, demonstrating the practical effectiveness of our method in real-world environments. This robot is equipped with a 32-line LiDAR, cameras, IMU, and various other sensors, as shown in Fig. 5(a). The specific experimental scenario is set within a forest, as shown in Fig. 5(b). During the experiment, the robot not only navigated along the centerline to reach each target point but also autonomously avoided obstacles. These results prove the practicality of our autonomous navigation solution, enabling the robot to perform tasks in the orchard safely and efficiently.

(a) Experimental equipment   (b) experimental scene

Fig. 5. Experimental equipment and experimental scene.

4.2 Actual Experiment

Before autonomous navigation, we constructed a tree trunk point cloud map, which has been previously shown in Fig. 3. Using the tree trunk point cloud map, we calculated the multi-segment navigation target points with the proposed navigation point calculation method, as shown in Table 1.

Table 1. Coordinates of navigation waypoints.

Number	Coordinates of waypoints		
	x (m)	y (m)	yaw (deg)
1	4.916	0.278	0
2	53.910	0.278	0
3	53.910	5.266	−180
4	5.579	5.266	−180
5	5.579	10.879	0
6	49.290	10.879	0

By connecting the navigation points in sequence, the robot's global path can be obtained, as shown in Fig. 6. For further comparison, we also used the commonly applied A* algorithm to plan a path in this environment, as shown in Fig. 7.

In Fig. 6, the robot's global path is readily derived by sequentially connecting navigation points. A crucial factor is that our path predominantly aligns with the centerline of the tree rows. Admittedly, achieving perfect consistency in the distance from each tree to the global path is challenging due to the inherent curvature of tree rows. Nonetheless, this deviation is non-essential since our primary aim is to enable the robot to access fruit trees on both sides evenly during the spraying task, a criterion guaranteed by our path planning method.

A key difference between Fig. 6 and Fig. 7 is that the latter includes an additional layer of virtual obstacles. This layer is designed to prevent the robot from moving freely between the tree rows. Our path planning method is specifically designed for orchard

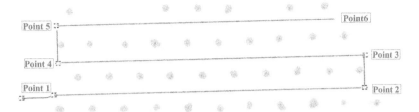

Fig. 6. The global path planned by our method.

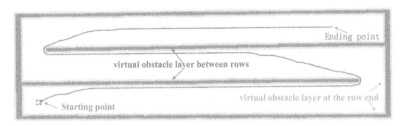

Fig. 7. The global path planned with A*.

tasks. Upon receiving the final target, it employs a unique approach to divide the entire navigation process into multiple straight-line segments. In contrast, the A* algorithm directly plans the shortest collision-free path from the robot's current position to the destination. Therefore, the virtual obstacle layer is essential to ensure that the path generated by the A* algorithm passes by each tree. However, even with the processed map, the A* algorithm cannot guarantee that the robot will move along the centerline. The comparison between Fig. 6 and Fig. 7 illustrates that conventional mobile robot path planning methods cannot be directly applied to orchard environments. In contrast, our method is specifically designed to adapt to the unique requirements of orchard robots.

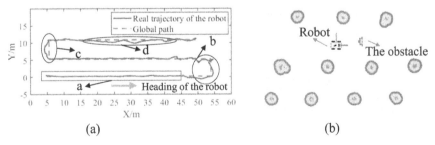

Fig. 8. The real trajectory during navigation.

To further validate the actual effectiveness of our navigation solution, we compare the robot's actual trajectory during autonomous navigation with the global path, with the result shown in Fig. 8. During autonomous navigation, the maximum speed of the robot is approximately 2 m/s. Figure 8(a) shows that the robot's actual trajectory closely aligns with the planned global path. However, in some specific areas, the trajectory deviates from the ideal path due to the complexity of the orchard environment. Uneven ground increases the difficulty of controlling the robot, particularly evident in areas b and c. Additionally, the robot deviates from the global path to avoid unexpected obstacles, as shown in area d. Figure 8(b) illustrates the visualized map when a pedestrian appears in front of the robot. Our navigation solution maps pedestrians onto the tree trunk map and uses the DWA algorithm for obstacle avoidance. This capability allows our solution to be truly applicable to real-world orchard tasks. Region a is a smooth section without obstacles. We evaluated the algorithm's performance in tracking the centerline in this area, with results shown in Fig. 9.

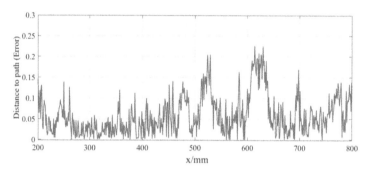

Fig. 9. Navigation error in area 'a.

The error curve indicates that when there are no obstacles blocking the global path, the robot can autonomously navigate along the centerline with minimal error. However, due to the abundance of weeds on the ground in our experimental environment (as shown in Fig. 5(b)), the robot's wheels frequently slipped, posing a challenge for control. Therefore, in certain areas, the navigation error reaches up to 0.15 m. Despite this, the error does not significantly impact the successful execution of the spraying task.

5 Conclusion

In this work, we propose a robot autonomous navigation method specifically designed for orchard tasks. To enable the robot to navigate along the central axis of tree rows, we introduce a path planning method based on trunk maps. We use trunk point clouds as input to construct a trunk map via a SLAM algorithm. From this map, we extract the central axis of the tree rows and plan the robot's global path accordingly. During navigation, we employ the DWA algorithm for path tracking and obstacle avoidance, ensuring the robot's safety. Our method allows the robot to autonomously navigate along the central axis of the rows without requiring feature detection, enhancing system stability and reducing computational load, making it highly practical. Test results in real-world environments demonstrate the effectiveness of our method. In the future, we aim to apply our method to larger and more complex environments.

Acknowledgments. This work is supported by A the Natural Science Basic Research Plan in Shaanxi Province of China (No. 2023-JC-YB-493), the China University Industry Research and Innovation Fund (No. 2021ZYA02014), the Innovation Chain of Key Industries in Industrial Field of Shanxi Province (2024GX-ZDCYL-02-06), and the Practice and Innovation Funds for Graduate Students of Northwestern Polytechnical University (No. PF2024011).

References

1. Bergerman, M., Maeta, S.M., Zhang, J., et al.: Robot farmers: autonomous orchard vehicles help tree fruit production. IEEE Robot. Autom. Mag. **22**(1), 54–63 (2015)
2. Dolgov, D., Thrun, S.: Autonomous driving in semi-structured environments: mapping and planning. In: International Conference on Robotics and Automation, Kobe, Japan, pp. 3407–3414. IEEE (2009)
3. Sharifi, M., Chen, X.: A novel vision based row guidance approach for navigation of agricultural mobile robots in orchards. In: International Conference on Automation, pp. 251–255. IEEE (2015)
4. Peng, C., Fei, Z., Vougioukas, S.G.: Depth camera based row-end detection and headland manuvering in orchard navigation without GNSS. In: 30th Mediterranean Conference on Control and Automation (MED), Athenian, Riviera, pp. 538–544. IEEE (2022)
5. Opiyo, S., Okinda, C., Zhou, J., et al.: Medial axis-based machine-vision system for orchard robot navigation. Comput. Electron. Agric. **185**, 106153 (2021)
6. Yang, Z., Ouyang, L., Zhang, Z., et al.: Visual navigation path extraction of orchard hard pavement based on scanning method and neural network. Comput. Electron. Agric. **197**, 106964 (2022)
7. Li, X., Qiu, Q.: Autonomous navigation for orchard mobile robots: a rough review. In: 36th Youth Academic Annual Conference of Chinese Association of Automation (YAC), Nanchang, Chinese, pp. 552–557. IEEE (2021)
8. Elhousni, M., Huang, X.: A survey on 3D LiDAR localization for autonomous vehicles. In: Intelligent Vehicles Symposium (IV), Las Vegas, NV, USA, pp. 1879–1884. IEEE (2020)
9. Li, Z., Liu, X., Wang, H., et al.: Research on robot path planning based on point cloud map in orchard environment. IEEE Access (2024)
10. Tao, X., Jingjing, F., Wenbo, C., et al.: Person recognition method in cross-country environment based on improved Euclidean clustering. Int. J. Pattern Recognit Artif Intell. **34**(14), 2056011 (2020)
11. Zhang, J., Chambers, A., Maeta, S., et al.: 3D perception for accurate row following: methodology and results. In: International Conference on Intelligent Robots and Systems, Tokyo, Japan, pp. 5306–5313. IEEE/RSJ (2013)
12. Fischler, M.A., Bolles, R.C.: Random sample consensus: a paradigm for model fitting with applications to image analysis and automated cartography. Commun. ACM **24**(6), 381–395 (1981)
13. Jacobs, L., Weiss, J., Dolan, D.: Object tracking in noisy radar data: comparison of Hough transform and RANSAC. In: International Conference on Electro-Information Technology, Rapid City, USA, pp. 1–6. IEEE (2013)
14. Jiang, A., Ahamed, T.: Navigation of an autonomous spraying robot for orchard operations using LiDAR for tree trunk detection. Sensors **23**(10), 4808 (2023)
15. Fox, D., Burgard, W., Thrun, S.: The dynamic window approach to collision avoidance. IEEE Robot. Autom. Mag. **4**(1), 23–33 (1997)

16. Rösmann, C., Feiten, W., Wösch, T., et al.: Trajectory modification considering dynamic constraints of autonomous robots. In: Robotics Proceedings of ROBOTIK 7th German Conference on VDE, pp. 1–6 (2012)
17. Liu, E., Lou, J., Tang, W., Wu, J., Liang, X.: A trunk map construction method for long-term localization and navigation for orchard robots. In: Yang, H., et al. (eds.) ICIRA 2023. LNCS, vol. 14267, pp. 442–455. Springer, Singapore (2023). https://doi.org/10.1007/978-981-99-6483-3_38
18. Ge, Z., Liu, S., Wang, F., et al.: YOLOX: exceeding yolo series in 2021. arXiv preprint arXiv:2107.08430 (2021)
19. Shan, T., Englot, B., Meyers, D., et al.: LIO-SAM: tightly-coupled Lidar inertial odometry via smoothing and mapping. In: International Conference on Intelligent Robots and Systems (IROS), Las Vegas, NV, USA, pp. 5135–5142, IEEE/RSJ (2020)

Recursive Neural Network: Small Target Detection in Remote Sensing Images

Changlin Yu[1], Juchao Zhang[1], Zhongyu Sun[2], Zaixiang Pang[1], Changxian Xu[1], and Zhongbo Sun[1(✉)]

[1] Department of Control Engineering, Changchun University of Technology, 130012 Changchun, China
zhongbosun2012@163.com

[2] Guangdong Open Laboratory of Geospatial Information Technology and Application, Guangzhou Institute of Geography, Academy of Sciences, Guangdong 510070, Guangzhou, China

Abstract. In this paper, a novel remote sensing image object detection algorithm is proposed by combining constraint energy minimization (CEM) and noise tolerance zeroing neural network (NTZNN). This algorithm combines traditional image processing methods with recursive neural network (RNN) and proposes a multi scene usable NTZNN-CEM object detection model for hyperspectral and RGB remote sensing images. Finally, through numerical simulation experiments and remote sensing image object detection experiments, it has been proven that the NTZNN-CEM algorithm has advantages such as fast detection speed and strong robustness, providing a new visual approach for improving the advanced perception of robots in complex environments.

Keywords: Recursive neural network · Remote sensing image · Object detection

1 Introduction

In the mid to late 20th century, with the development of information science, materials technology, spatial information development technology, and detector technology, remote sensing technology began to gradually develop [1]. Simply put, remote sensing is a long-distance non-contact detection technology. The development of remote sensing technology has gone through the stages of black and white images, color images, and multispectral images [2]. Hyperspectral imaging technology utilizes imaging spectrometers to achieve the joint acquisition of one-dimensional features that characterize spectral response and two-dimensional geometric information that reflects target distribution. This enables hyperspectral images to both depict targets in an image-based manner and detect spectra using fine electromagnetic waves, achieving the integration of image and spectral information. Hyperspectral remote sensing images have gradually been applied in fields such as disaster warning, species identification, agricultural planning, and sea ice detection due to their rich spectral band information. Remote sensing image object detection refers to the technique of identifying objects or targets of interest from remote sensing images and representing their contours in the form of rectangles or polygons. In the past few decades, many classic remote sensing image object detection algorithms have been proposed with the development of remote sensing images. Representative algorithms include spectral angle mapper (SAM), adaptive coherence estimator (ACE) and CEM algorithm [3], etc. Among them, The CEM algorithm has attracted the attention of researchers due to its advantage of only needing to know the spectral information of the target to be detected without obtaining background prior information. The main idea of the CEM algorithm is to design a pulse response filter to filter the image. Specifically, by passing the original signal through a filter and minimizing the total output energy while maintaining a constant energy of the target signal to be detected, the background is fully suppressed, achieving target detection. On the basis of the CEM algorithm, researchers have proposed the target trained interference optimized filter (TCIMF). The TCIMF algorithm can not only detect multiple targets simultaneously, but also remove interfering targets instead of suppressing them, greatly improving the detection effect and reducing the false alarm rate of target detection. In addition, the detection performance of traditional CEM algorithms is easily affected by the quality of the spectrum. To solve this problem, research [4] proposed a hierarchical CEM (hCEM) algorithm, which can suppress background information in layers while protecting target spectral information from damage, improving the accuracy of remote sensing image object detection. Although remote sensing images contain rich terrain information, processing and analyzing this information can solve many practical problems, remote sensing images have a large number of bands and a large amount of data. This makes the computational complexity of many analysis and processing designs based on remote sensing images very high. In addition, the difficulty in collecting label samples for remote sensing images and the high cost of manual annotation have hindered many deep learning methods that have used a large number of samples for model training. Therefore, how to combine traditional remote sensing image processing methods with neural network methods to design a remote sensing image object detection algorithm with fast detection speed, high detection accuracy, strong noise resistance, and multi scene availability is currently a key issue that needs further research.

In optimization theory, quadratic programming is an important type of optimization problem [5,6]. The objective function minimizes the energy output of the entire process while completing the main task. The constraints define the constraints and requirements of the problem, ensuring that the optimal solution satisfies all conditions. As an important branch of artificial intelligence, RNN models are considered powerful solvers for quadratic programming problems due to their parallel processing capabilities and hardware implementation feasibility [7,8]. The zeroing neural network (ZNN) model is a special type of RNN that can utilize derivative information to eliminate errors. Research [10] proposes a new finite time ZNN model with combined activation functions, which has faster finite time convergence speed and better robustness. Researchers have successfully applied these two ZNN models to image fusion denoising. Specifically, it is to vectorize each image row by row into a column of vector data, and then use the idea of data fusion for image fusion. The purpose of image fusion is to find the optimal fusion coefficient vector to fuse multiple images, minimizing the uncertainty of fusion information. By using the idea of data fusion, the image denoising problem is transformed into a quadratic programming problem with equality constraints. Then use these two improved ZNN models to solve the fusion coefficient vector. Finally, applying the fusion coefficient vector to a matrix composed of multiple noisy images in the same scene can remove additive Gaussian noise and improve image quality. Based on the widespread application of quadratic programming problems and the advantages of recurrent neural networks, this paper designs an NTZNN solver with noise suppression ability. By combining the CEM algorithm with the NTZNN network, a remote sensing image object detection algorithm suitable for multiple scenes is proposed. As shown in Fig. 1, this is the detection flowchart of the algorithm. The specific detection plan is as follows: Firstly, obtain spectral information of expected and unexpected targets, establish a CEM model, and obtain the quadratic programming model to be solved; Then, construct an NTZNN solver to solve the quadratic programming problem and obtain the optimal filtering coefficients that meet the accuracy requirements; Finally, the remote sensing images are filtered using the optimal filtering coefficients to achieve target detection.

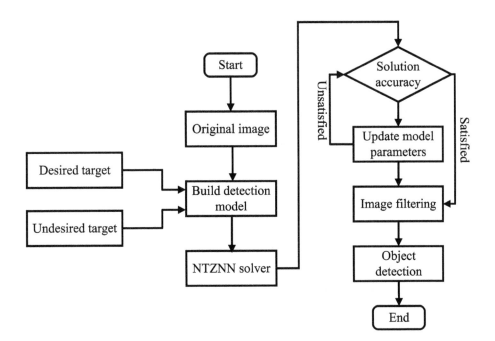

Fig. 1. Remote sensing image object detection algorithm flowchart

2 Technical Background

CEM is an important algorithm used for target detection in hyperspectral images. In the following, this paper will first introduce some of the necessary basic theories and mathematical derivations.

2.1 Hyperspectral Image Model

A hyperspectral image is a special three-dimensional image composed of multiple grayscale images. For example, if a hyperspectral image has L bands, it represents L-dimensional spectral domain information on each pixel. The grayscale values of pixels at the same position are plotted as curves to represent the spectral information of that pixel point. Assume that all the pixels of a hyperspectral image make up the matrix $S = [s_1, s_2, s_3, \cdots, s_N] \in \mathbb{R}^{L \times N}$, and the spectral vector of any one of the pixels is $s_i = [s_{i1}, s_{i2}, s_{i3}, \cdots, s_{iL}] \in \mathbb{R}^{L \times 1}$, where N is the total number of pixels in this hyperspectral image, and L is the number of bands. The designed linear filter coefficient vector is $\omega = [\omega_1, \omega_2, \omega_3, \cdots, \omega_L] \in \mathbb{R}^{L \times 1}$, keeps the output of the target spectrum constant, meanwhile, suppresses background output is minimal. According to the CEM algorithm, the following optimization problems can be obtained:

$$\begin{aligned} \min \quad & \omega^\top R \omega \\ \text{s.t.} \quad & d^\top \omega = I, \end{aligned} \tag{1}$$

where $d \in \mathbb{R}^{L \times 1}$ is the spectral vector of interest, $I \in \mathbb{R}^{1 \times 1}$ is the identity matrix, $R = (\sum_{i=1}^{N} s_i s_i^\top)/N$ is the autocorrelation matrix of the hyperspectral image. For this quadratic programming problem, the traditional approach is to use numerical methods to obtain the optimal filtering coefficient vector as follows:

$$\omega_{cem} = \frac{R^{-1} d}{d^\top R^{-1} d}, \tag{2}$$

then, filter the original image using the obtained optimal filtering coefficient vector ω_{cem}. In this way, a reconstructed image is obtained:

$$I_{cem} = \omega_{cem}^\top S. \tag{3}$$

where I_{cem} is the filtered output vector.

2.2 RGB Remote Sensing Image Model

The remote sensing images used in this paper were captured by the multispectral cameras of the GaoFen-1 and GaoFen-6 satellites [9]. The experimental images used in this article only use R, G and B bands. Assume that all the pixels of a hyperspectral image make up the matrix $P = [p_1, p_2, p_3, \cdots, p_N] \in \mathbb{R}^{3 \times N}$, and the spectral vector of any one of the pixels is $p_i = [p_{i1}, p_{i2}, p_{i3}] \in \mathbb{R}^{3 \times 1}$, where N is the total number of pixels in this hyperspectral image. The designed linear filter coefficient vector is $\boldsymbol{\omega} = [\omega_1, \omega_2, \omega_3] \in \mathbb{R}^{3\times 1}$. When any one pixel $\boldsymbol{p}_i$ passes through the filter, the output is:

$$y_i = p_{i1}\omega_1 + p_{i2}\omega_2 + p_{i3}\omega_3 = \boldsymbol{p}_i^\top \boldsymbol{\omega}, \tag{4}$$

therefore, the output energy of a single pixel after passing through a linear filter is y_i^2. Furthermore, the average output energy of N pixels in the whole RGB remote sensing image after passing through the linear filter is obtained :

$$\begin{aligned} E &= \frac{1}{N}\sum y_i^2 \\ &= \frac{1}{N}\sum (\boldsymbol{p}_i^\top \boldsymbol{\omega})^\top \boldsymbol{p}_i^\top \boldsymbol{\omega} \\ &= \boldsymbol{\omega}^\top (\frac{1}{N}\sum \boldsymbol{p}_i \boldsymbol{p}_i^\top)\boldsymbol{\omega} \\ &= \boldsymbol{\omega}^\top R \boldsymbol{\omega}. \end{aligned} \tag{5}$$

In the same way, the output of the target to be detected after passing through the linear filter is $\boldsymbol{d}^\top \boldsymbol{\omega}$. The output energy is $(\boldsymbol{d}^\top \boldsymbol{\omega})^2$. Furthermore, the following optimization problems can be obtained:

$$\begin{aligned} \min \quad & E \\ \text{s.t.} \quad & (\boldsymbol{d}^\top \boldsymbol{\omega})^2 = \boldsymbol{I}, \end{aligned} \tag{6}$$

equivalent to the following questions:

$$\begin{aligned} \min \quad & \boldsymbol{\omega}^\top R \boldsymbol{\omega} \\ \text{s.t.} \quad & \boldsymbol{d}^\top \boldsymbol{\omega} = \boldsymbol{I}. \end{aligned} \tag{7}$$

3 Theoretical Analysis

In this subsection, the integration process is introduced the traditional ZNN model and designed an NTZNN solver with faster convergence speed and stronger robustness. Then, through a specific numerical example, the traditional ZNN solver and the GNN solver was compared with the NTZNN solver. The solving advantages of the NTZNN solver were verified from a numerical simulation perspective.

3.1 Problem Statement

The CEM algorithm described in the previous section can be described as a quadratic programming problem with equality constraints in a more general form as follows:

$$\begin{aligned} \min \quad & \boldsymbol{x}^\top(t)\boldsymbol{H}(t)\boldsymbol{x}(t) + \boldsymbol{Z}^\top(t)\boldsymbol{x}(t) \\ \text{s.t.} \quad & \boldsymbol{P}^\top(t)\boldsymbol{x}(t) = \boldsymbol{q}(t), \end{aligned} \tag{8}$$

where $\boldsymbol{H}(t) \in \mathbb{R}^{n \times n}$ is a Hessian matrix, $\boldsymbol{Z}(t) \in \mathbb{R}^n$, $\boldsymbol{P}(t) \in \mathbb{R}^{n \times n}$ is a row-full-rank matrix, $\boldsymbol{q}(t) \in \mathbb{R}^n$ is a matrix of coefficients, $\boldsymbol{x}(t) \in \mathbb{R}^n$ is a vector of time states to be solved. In order to solve the equation-constrained time-varying quadratic programming problem (7), the following Lagrange function is established:

$$L(\boldsymbol{x}(t), \boldsymbol{\lambda}(t), t) = \frac{\boldsymbol{x}^\top(t)\boldsymbol{H}(t)\boldsymbol{x}(t)}{2} + \boldsymbol{Z}^\top(t)\boldsymbol{x}(t) \\ + \boldsymbol{\lambda}^\top(t)(\boldsymbol{P}(t)\boldsymbol{x}(t) - \boldsymbol{q}(t)), \quad (9)$$

where $\boldsymbol{\lambda}(t) \in \mathbb{R}^m$ is Lagrange multiplier vector, the derivatives $\boldsymbol{x}(t)$ and $\boldsymbol{\lambda}(t)$ are obtained by the Lagrangian multiplier method, the following equation can be obtained:

$$\begin{cases} \frac{\partial L(\boldsymbol{x}(t), \boldsymbol{\lambda}(t), t)}{\partial \boldsymbol{x}(t)} = \boldsymbol{H}(t)\boldsymbol{x}(t) + \boldsymbol{Z}(t) + \boldsymbol{A}^\top(t)\boldsymbol{\lambda}(t) = 0 \\ \frac{\partial L(\boldsymbol{x}(t), \boldsymbol{\lambda}(t), t)}{\partial \boldsymbol{\lambda}(t)} = \boldsymbol{P}(t)\boldsymbol{x}(t) - \boldsymbol{q}(t) = 0, \end{cases} \quad (10)$$

equation (10) is further transformed into the following system of linear equations:

$$\boldsymbol{W}(t)\boldsymbol{Y}(t) = \boldsymbol{V}(t), \quad (11)$$

where

$$\boldsymbol{W}(t) = \begin{bmatrix} \boldsymbol{H}(t) & \boldsymbol{P}^\top(t) \\ \boldsymbol{P}(t) & 0 \end{bmatrix},$$

$$\boldsymbol{Y}(t) = \begin{bmatrix} \boldsymbol{x}(t) \\ \boldsymbol{\lambda}(t) \end{bmatrix},$$

$$\boldsymbol{V}(t) = \begin{bmatrix} -\boldsymbol{Z}(t) \\ \boldsymbol{q}(t) \end{bmatrix}.$$

By literature the solution of the above system of linear equation (11) is the solution of quadratic programming problem (8).

3.2 Construction of Solver

The equation-constrained quadratic programming problem is transformed into a system of linear equations for solving, the approach of the original ZNN model is to construct an error function $e(t) = \boldsymbol{W}(t)\boldsymbol{Y}(t) - \boldsymbol{V}(t)$. The derivative of the error function is such that every element in $e(t)$ converges to zero. Theoretically eliminating the lag residuals of gradient neural network models in solving time-varying quadratic programming problems. It has been proven that the ZNN model has global exponential convergence for the theoretical solution of the time-varying convex quadratic programming problem under study. The ZNN model is obtained as follows:

$$\dot{\vartheta}(t) = -\gamma_1 \boldsymbol{W}^\top(t) e(t). \quad (12)$$

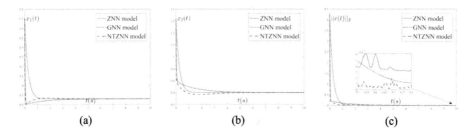

Fig. 2. Numerical simulation results in the absence of noise for the solver. (a) Profiles of neural states $x_1(t)$. (b) Profiles of neural states $x_2(t)$. (c) Profiles of residual errors $||e(t)||_2$

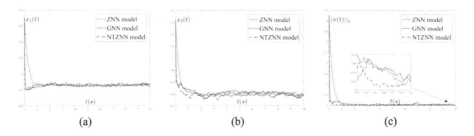

Fig. 3. Numerical simulation results in the random noise for the solver. (a) Profiles of neural states $x_1(t)$. (b) Profiles of neural states $x_2(t)$. (c) Profiles of residual errors $||e(t)||_2$

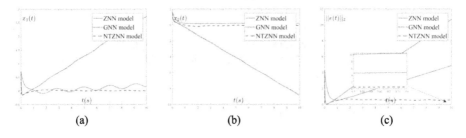

Fig. 4. Numerical simulation results in the hybrid noise for the solver. (a) Profiles of neural states $x_1(t)$. (b) Profiles of neural states $x_2(t)$. (c) Profiles of residual errors $||e(t)||_2$

where the parameter $\gamma_1 > 0$, is designed to improve the convergence speed. The solver used in this paper is to add an integral link on the basis of the ZNN model. The NTZNN model is obtained as follows:

$$\dot{\vartheta}(t) = -\gamma_1 \boldsymbol{W}^\top(t)\boldsymbol{e}(t) - \gamma_2 \boldsymbol{W}^\top(t) \int_0^t \boldsymbol{e}(\tau)\mathrm{d}\tau. \tag{13}$$

where the parameter $\gamma_2 > 0$, is designed to improve the convergence speed. What's more, in order to verify the noise suppression effect of the NTZNN model (13) in the actual acquisition and processing of images, the noise signal $\boldsymbol{\xi}(t)$ is introduced into the model, and the following result is obtained:

$$\dot{\vartheta}(t) = -\gamma_1 \boldsymbol{W}^\top(t)\boldsymbol{e}(t) - \gamma_2 \boldsymbol{W}^\top(t) \int_0^t \boldsymbol{e}(\tau)\mathrm{d}\tau + \boldsymbol{\xi}(t). \tag{14}$$

where $\boldsymbol{\xi}(t) \in \mathbb{R}^n$ represents noise signal.

3.3 Numerical Simulation

In this subsection, a numerical simulation experiment is designed to verify the convergence and robustness of the solver. The following is an example:

$$\begin{aligned} \min \quad & (sin(1)/4 + 1)\boldsymbol{x_1}^2(t) + (cos(1)/4 + 1)\boldsymbol{x_2}^2(t) \\ & + cos(1)\boldsymbol{x_1}(t)\boldsymbol{x_2}(t) + sin(3)\boldsymbol{x_1}(t) \\ & + cos(3)\boldsymbol{x_2}(t) \\ \text{s.t.} \quad & sin(3)\boldsymbol{x_1}(t) + cos(3)\boldsymbol{x_2}(t) = cos(2). \end{aligned} \tag{15}$$

Here, the relevant parameters of the numerical simulation will be explained: $\gamma_1 = 10$ and $\gamma_2 = 20$. The initial state is $x(0) = [1,1]^\top \in \mathbb{R}^2$. The random noise $\xi_1(0) \in [-20, 20]^{3\times 1}$. The hybrid noise $\xi_2(0) = [sin(3t), t, 1]^\top \in \mathbb{R}^2$. The simulation results are shown in Fig. 2 and Fig. 3. As is shown in Fig. 2(a) - Fig. 2(c): in the absence of noise, both solvers can quickly achieve stability with almost zero residual error. Among them, the NTZNN model has a faster convergence speed and better convergence performance than the ZNN model. As is shown in Fig. 3(a) - Fig. 3(c): in the case of constant noise, the NTZNN solver maintains a fast convergence speed while still having a low residual level. And Fig. 4(a) - Fig. 4(c) shows that in hybrid noise, the NTZNN solver still has strong robustness, this advantage has a excellent suppression effect on the unavoidable noise in the process of image acquisition and image processing, and improves the image quality.

4 Experimental Results

Remote sensing image object detection mainly utilizes the spectral difference between the target to be detected and the background to detect ground objects. In general, the spectral information of the target can be queried from the target database or spectral library, but there is no available spectral library to utilize. Therefore, this article takes the average spectral information of the region of interest in the remote sensing image as the target spectral information.

Fig. 5. Hyperspectral 3D image

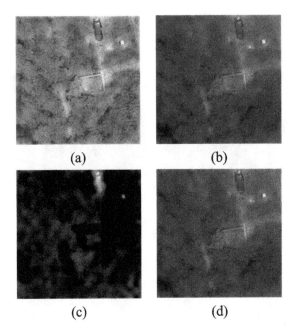

Fig. 6. Object detection results in hyperspectral image. (a) Pseudo color image. (b) Grayscale image of the 60th band. (c) Hyperspectral image after image processing. (d) Object detection of labeled ship

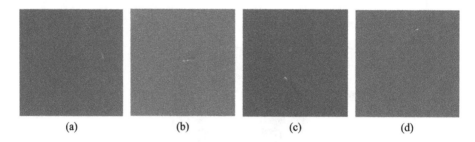

Fig. 7. The original ship images

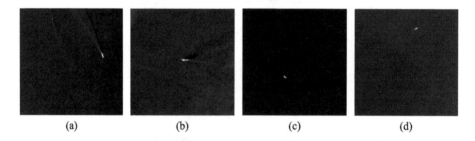

Fig. 8. Ship images after image processing

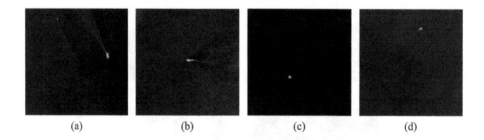

Fig. 9. Ship images after labeling

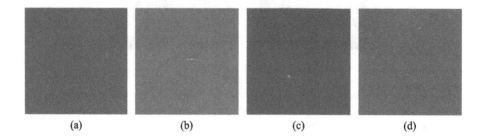

Fig. 10. Object detection of labeled ship

4.1 Hyperspectral Image Object Detection

As shown in Fig. 5, it is a 3D stereoscopic image display rendering of hyperspectral image data with 127 bands. This hyperspectral image was captured by an unmanned aerial vehicle high-speed imaging system, covering the visible to near-infrared spectral range. As shown in Fig. 6 (a) - Fig. 6 (b), the detection task of this section is to detect small car targets in this hyperspectral image, while courtyards and cabins are interference targets. Let the hyperspectral image pass through a filter designed by the NTZNN solver, while keeping the output energy of the car constant and minimizing the output energy to suppress interference targets and background. From the filtering effect shown in Fig. 6 (c), it can be seen that the detection algorithm effectively separates the target and background, thereby achieving small object detection in hyperspectral images. The detection results are shown in Fig. 6 (d).

4.2 RGB Remote Sensing Image Object Detection

As shown in Fig. 7, the remote sensing image dataset used in this experiment consists of only R, G and B consists of three bands. The detection task of this section is to detect small ship targets from the vast sea surface. From Fig. 8 - Fig. 10, it can be seen that compared to the vast sea level, although ship targets are very small, they can still be effectively detected through this detection algorithm. From hyperspectral images to RGB remote sensing images, this paper once again verifies the generalization ability and effectiveness of the object detection algorithm through detection tasks in different scenes.

5 Conclusions and Future Work

In this paper, a multi scene available object detection algorithm for hyperspectral and RGB remote sensing images is proposed by combining the CEM algorithm with an anti noise recursive neural network. Not only does it effectively utilize the rich spectral information in remote sensing images, but it also solves the problem of large data volume and complex operations in remote sensing images using the NTZNN solver. The numerical simulation results indicate that, the NTZNN solver has advantages such as fast convergence speed and strong noise resistance. Image experiments have shown that the detection algorithm can suppress interference with the minimum output energy of the target signal and background signal while keeping the output energy of the target signal unchanged, achieving the separation of the target and background, and effectively completing the task of remote sensing image object detection. Of course, there are still many areas for improvement in this research algorithm. Firstly, the construction of the detection model requires the spectral information of the target to be detected. However, within a certain band interval, different types of objects may exhibit the same spectral features, namely the phenomenon of same spectral foreign objects, which can reduce the effectiveness of target detection.

Therefore, in future research, sparse algorithms can be introduced to preprocess remote sensing images, increasing the spectral differences between targets and between targets and background, thereby achieving more accurate target detection. Secondly, in addition to introducing an integral loop in the traditional ZNN model to improve the noise resistance of the detection model, different drivers can also be introduced, such as finite time stable drivers, to enable the airborne camera to capture multiple consecutive frames of the same position. Through image fusion, the noise generated during the image acquisition process can be further removed, improving the accuracy of object detection.

Acknowledgments. The work is supported in part by the Key Science and Technology Projects of Jilin Province, China, under grant 20230201110GX and also in part by the Innovation and Entrepreneurship Talent funding Project of Jilin Province under grant 2022QN04 and also in part by the Changchun Science and Technology Project under grant 21ZY41.

References

1. Song, X., Zou, L., Wu, L.: Detection of subpixel targets on hyperspectral remote sensing imagery based on background endmember extraction. IEEE Trans. Geosci. Remote Sens. **59**(3), 2365–2377 (2021)
2. Zhang, S., Mu, X., Kou, G., Zhao, J.: Object detection based on efficient multiscale auto-inference in remote sensing images. IEEE Geosci. Remote Sens. Lett. **18**(9), 1650–1654 (2021)
3. Liufu, Y., Jin, L., Xu, J., Xiao, X., Fu, D.: Reformative noise-immune neural network for equality-constrained optimization applied to image target detection. IEEE Trans. Emerg. Top. Comput. **10**(2), 973–984 (2022)
4. Zou, Z., Shi, Z.: Hierarchical suppression method for hyperspectral target Detection. IEEE Trans. Geosci. Remote Sens. **54**(1), 330–342 (2016)
5. Zheng, X., Liu, M., Jin, L., Yang, C.: Distributed collaborative control of redundant robots under weight-unbalanced directed graphs. IEEE Trans. Ind. Inf. **20**(1), 681–690 (2024)
6. Sun, Z., Tang, S., Jin, L., Zhang, J., Yu, J.: Nonconvex activation noise-suppressing neural network for time-varying quadratic programming: application to omnidirectional mobile manipulator. IEEE Trans. Ind. Inf. **19**(11), 10786–10798 (2023)
7. Jin, L., Yan, J., Du, X., Xiao, X., Fu, D.: RNN for solving time-variant generalized Sylvester equation with applications to robots and acoustic source localization. IEEE Trans. Industr. Inf. **16**(10), 6359–6369 (2020)
8. Liu, M., Wu, H., Shi, Y., Jin, L.: High-order robust discrete-time neural dynamics for time-varying multilinear tensor equation with $\mathcal{M}$-tensor. IEEE Trans. Indr. Inf. **19**(9), 9457–9467 (2023)
9. Chen, J., Chen, K., Chen, H., Zhou, Z., Shi, Z.: A degraded reconstruction enhancement-based method for tiny ship detection in remote sensing images with a new large-scale dataset. IEEE Trans. Geosci. Remote Sens. **60**, 1–14 (2022)
10. Xiao, L., Liao, B.: A convergence-accelerated Zhang neural network and its solution application to Lyapunov equation. Neurocomputing **193**, 213–218 (2016)

Mobile Robot Path Planning Method Based on Weight Coefficient Improved A* Algorithm

Tao Qin[1,2,3], Hao Chu[1,2], Jia Wang[1,2], Peng Ren[1,2], Min Fu[1(✉)], and Xi Wu[2,3(✉)]

[1] School of Mechanical Engineering, Hubei University of Arts and Science, Xiangyang 441053, Hubei, China
[2] Xiangyang Key Laboratory of Rehabilitation Medicine and Rehabilitation Engineering Technology, Xiangyang 441053, Hubei, China
[3] Department of Rehabilitation Medicine, Xiangyang Central Hospital, Affiliated Hospital of Hubei University of Arts and Science, Xiangyang 441021, China

Abstract. Aiming at the shortcomings of traditional A* algorithm planning such as long path calculation time, multiple search nodes, and multiple turning points, an improved A* algorithm based on weight coefficient optimization is proposed. By comparing Euclidean distance, Chebyshev distance, and Manhattan distance, it is shown that Manhattan distance has shorter search time and fewer turning points, so Manhattan distance is selected as the estimated cost function; By improving the weight coefficients of the actual cost function and the estimated cost function, the disadvantages of traditional A* algorithm such as long calculation time and multiple search nodes are solved; The resulting path is smoothed through a Bezier curve, resulting in a smooth path. Experiments show that the improved A* algorithm has short computing time, fewer search nodes, fewer turning points, and smooth trajectory.

Keywords: Mobile robot · A∗ algorithm · Path planning

1 Introduction

Mobile robot path planning refers to planning a conflict-free trajectory from the starting point to the end point according to the information of the surrounding environment detected by each sensor on the robot, and according to the parameters set in the given algorithm. Currently, there are many path planning algorithms such as Rapidly-exploring Random Tree (RRT) algorithm, Ant Colony algorithm, A* algorithm and so on.

The RRT algorithm [1] is a sampling-based search algorithm that effectively solves the incompleteness restriction in multiple dimensions. The algorithm is very blind and purposeful, especially in high dimensionality or high dynamics, which can cause long search time, consume a lot of resources, and easily fall into the dead domain with local minima problem. Zong Changfu et al. [2] proposed a RRT method based on region sampling for the local path problem of unmanned vehicles under complex road conditions and improved it. Combining the Gaussian distribution sampling technique with the partial deviation sampling technique effectively improves the optimization speed of the samples;

Wang Jiankun et al. [3] use the obstacle boundary information to deal with the two problems of the RRT algorithm failing to find the optimal path and its long planning time, and the experiments show that their improved RRT algorithm can find a better path faster; Yang Ying et al. [4] addressed the issues of high randomness and non-asymptotic optimization in the RRT algorithm by proposing improvements in region sampling for target point selection and obstacle expansion, and optimized the algorithm by establishing the region sampling to select the target point and the obstacle expansion method, and the improved algorithm effectively reduces the occupied spatial memory, the running time, and the number of nodes.

The core idea of the ant colony algorithm is that during iterative searches, the algorithm is prone to interruptions, and the mobile robot is likely to fall into local optimal solutions [5]. To overcome these shortcomings, Chen Xiong et al. introduced pheromones into the ant colony algorithm, and based on this, an adaptive pheromone volatility factor was introduced to increase its search range and further improve its computational efficiency. Jiang Ming et al. [6] enhanced the search efficiency in the early stage of the algorithm by regulating the initial pheromone concentration. Additionally, an adaptive volatility factor was introduced to improve the global nature of the algorithm.

Mobile robot would not fall into the local optimum; Liu Chang'an et al. solved the problem of slow convergence of the ant colony algorithm based on the adaptive correction strategy of the target point; and drew on the principle of the wolf pack allocation to solve the problem that the problem that ant algorithm is easy to fall into local minima.

A* algorithm is the first one proposed by Prof. P.E. Hart [7, 8] in his paper. A* algorithm is based on Dijkstar's algorithm g(n), a cost function is added to evaluate the cost of the path needed to reach the target node from the start node, and the two are added to get the heuristic function, which judges the next path according to the value of the next step, thus obtaining an optimal path, and thus is more efficient than Dijkstar's algorithm. Than Dijkstar algorithm. However, because the evaluation function used in the A* algorithm is relatively simple, resulting in more folds at the corners, which is not conducive to the movement of the mobile robot, so, nowadays, scholars and experts in various countries, keep optimizing and improving the A* algorithm according to their practical needs. Du Wanru et al. proposed a synchronized bidirectional search method based on Hermite difference and optimized it, which effectively reduces the redundant nodes and improves the path planning accuracy and efficiency. Liu Y-T et al. [9] combined the A* algorithm with Floyda algorithm in order to solve the problems of many turning points, redundant points and large turning angles in the obstacle area, realized a reverse tracking by using Floyda algorithm, thus shortening the time of reverse tracking. Wang Hongbin et al. used adaptive arc optimization algorithm with weighted obstacle step adjustment algorithm to effectively shorten the path length, reduce the total degree of turning angle and improve the path planning efficiency. Lao Cailian et al. for the traditional A* algorithm to obtain the path of more inflection points, using the key point selection strategy to improve, the optimized algorithm path is smoother and more efficient.

2 Traditional A* Algorithm

2.1 Description of the Problem

Path planning for mobile robots indicates that given a start point and a target point with known information about the surroundings, a mobile robot can autonomously plan an optimal route avoiding all obstacles. The A* algorithm is one of the most efficient search methods for solving the shortest paths, but there are some drawbacks, such as: the A* algorithm gets line segments, and there are many turning points between the line segments, which means that the mobile robot will consume a lot of energy and time when turning, therefore, this paper proposes an improved A* algorithm based on this, to improve the search efficiency and at the same time smoothing the path to get a smoother path.

2.2 Principles of the Traditional A* Algorithm

The traditional A* algorithm is one of the most efficient direct search algorithms. The idea of heuristic search is used on the basis of guaranteeing the optimal path. The so-called heuristic search is to select the point with the lowest cost from the target point as the next search of the heuristic function when the next node selection is made for the currently searched node, and then jump to it. The computational function of the A* algorithm is shown in Eq. 1.

$$f(n) = g(n) + h(n) \qquad (1)$$

where $f(n)$ is the total cost function, $g(n)$ represents the actual cost from the start node to the current node, and $h(n)$ is the estimated cost from the current node to the target node. Refers to the actual cost function from the start node to the current node n, and refers to the estimated cost function from the current node n to the target node, where is the heuristic function of the A* algorithm, and H is the most important part of the cost function, and its selection relates to the accuracy and success of the A* algorithm. The traditional A* algorithm chooses the Euclidean distance, as shown in Eq. 2, but the Euclidean distance has more inflection points, which is not conducive to the mobile robot driving, and it will be optimized later.

$$h(n) = \sqrt{(x_n - x_g)^2 + (y_n - y_g)^2} \qquad (2)$$

Where (x_n, y_n) denotes the center coordinate of the raster where the current node n is located, and (x_n, y_n) denotes the center coordinate of the previous one where the target node g is located.

In the algorithm presented in this paper, point S is the starting point of the mobile robot, and point M is the optimal point obtained by the cost function $f(n)$.

Child node obtained by traversing the surrounding grid with the point M is N, and the final target point of the mobile robot is G. The algorithm flow is shown in Fig. 1.

The pseudo-code of the traditional A* algorithm is shown in Fig. 1.

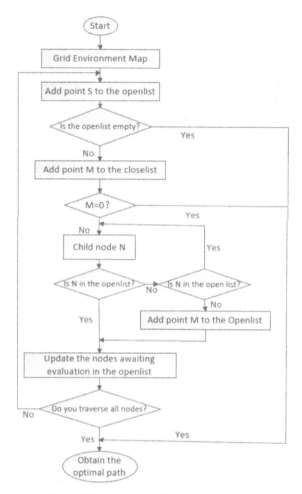

Fig. 1. Flowchart of traditional A* algorithm

As shown in Eq. 1, an appropriate estimated cost function $h(n)$ can improve the efficiency and accuracy of path search. The cost function $f(n)$ of the traditional A* algorithm is shown in Eq. 1, and the choice of different estimation cost function $h(n)$ corresponds to different efficiency and accuracy. When $h(n) = 0$, the A* algorithm is degraded to Dijkstra's algorithm, which can find the optimal path, but the nodes searched for are particularly large, which affects the search efficiency; when the estimated cost function $h(n)$ is relatively large, there is no guarantee that the algorithm can find the optimal path, which defeats the purpose of the A* algorithm. The choice of the appropriate estimated cost function $h(n)$ is to ensure that the final path is both the shortest path, but also to save the search nodes, improve the search efficiency of the premise. First, the more useful cost function consists of: Euclidean distance, Chebyshev distance, Manhattan distance, and the cost function of the final path is the shortest path.

(1) Euclidean distance

The traditional A* algorithm uses the Euclidean distance as shown in Eq. 2, Euclidean distance is a commonly used distance formula that refers to the actual distance between two points, or the natural length of a vector (i.e., the distance from a point to the origin), i.e., the sum of the squares of the differences between the two points and the root sign, the Euclidean distance has more inflection points, which is not conducive to the movement of mobile robot traveling.

(2) Chebyshev distance

The Chebyshev distance is a metric in vector space. It refers to the distance between two points defined as the maximum of the absolute value of the difference between the individual coordinate values of the two points. The Chebyshev distance $h(n)$ expression is shown in Eq. 3, where (x_1, y_2), (x_2, y_2) denote the coordinate values of the two points.

$$h(n) = \max(|x_1 - x_2|, |y_1 - y_2|) \tag{3}$$

(3) Manhattan Distance

The Manhattan distance was introduced by Hermann Minkowski in the 19th century. It refers to a geometric term used in geometric metric space to express the sum of the absolute axial distances between two points on a standard coordinate system. The expression for the Manhattan distance $h(n)$ is shown in Eq. 4, where (x_1, y_2), (x_2, y_2) denote the coordinate values of the two points.

$$h(n) = |x_1 - x_2| + |y_1 - y_2| \tag{4}$$

In order to verify which of the three distances has fewer search nodes, shorter search time, and shorter paths, the three distances are compared and experimented in two environments in a raster graph of size 35 × 35, Fig. 2 represents the Euclidean distance, Fig. 3 represents the Chebyshev distance, and Fig. 4 represents the Manhattan distance, and Table 1 represents the performance comparisons of the three distances.Performance comparison of three distances.

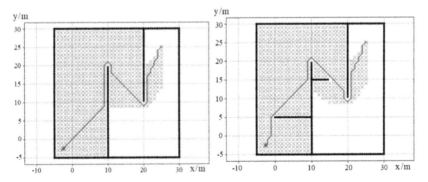

Fig. 2. A* algorithm based on Euclidean distance

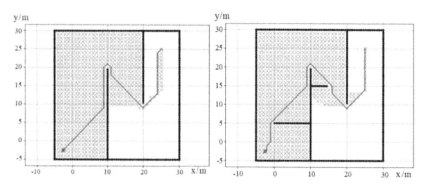

Fig. 3. A* algorithm based on Chebyshev distance

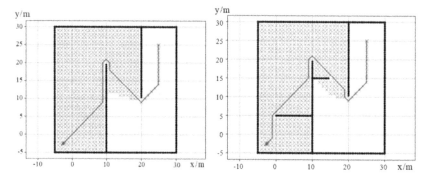

Fig. 4. A* algorithm based on Manhattan distance

Table 1. Comparison of the performance of the three distances

	$h(n)$ Selection	Number of search nodes	Running time/s
The first scenario	Euclidean distance	735	7.5036
	Chebyshev distance	695	7.0854
	Manhattan distance	673	6.8646
The second scenario	Euclidean distance	723	7.3023
	Chebyshev distance	679	6.8579
	Manhattan distance	659	6.6559

From Figs. 2, 3, and 4, it can be seen that the Manhattan distance plans out fewer path turning points than the other two distances, and therefore the mobile robot will consume less energy and time in operation.

As can be seen from Table 1, the path lengths obtained from the three distances for different scenarios are the same, but the Manhattan distance is the least number of nodes to be searched and the shortest time to be used by the three distances for different scenarios, so in this paper, we choose the Manhattan distance as the estimated cost function $h(n)$.

3 Improvement of the A* Algorithm

3.1 A* Algorithm Based on Improved Weight Coefficients

For the cost function $f(n)$ of the traditional A* algorithm, the weights of the actual cost function $g(n)$ and the estimated cost function $h(n)$ can be changed to reduce the useless search intervals, thus improving the search efficiency and reducing the search time.

In the cost function $f(n)$, if the weight of the actual cost function $g(n)$ is 1 and the weight of the estimated cost function $h(n)$ is 0, then the A* algorithm can be regarded as Dijkstra's algorithm, which is more inclined to the breadth-first search, i.e., do not take into account the efficiency of the algorithm, but only consider the accuracy of the results; if the weight of the actual cost function $g(n)$ is 0, and the weight of the estimated cost function $h(n)$ is 1, then the A* algorithm can be regarded as the best-first search. Best-first search, this algorithm has a stronger heuristic that is, the accuracy of the search results is not the focus of the object of consideration, but pay more attention to the efficiency of the algorithm, often planning the path is not the optimal solution, therefore, a reasonable allocation of the actual cost function $g(n)$ and the estimated cost function $h(n)$ weight ratio is conducive to reducing the useless search intervals, thereby improving the search efficiency, reducing the search time, the algorithm to produce a shorter path.

During the exploration of the A* algorithm above, it can be found that when the proportion of $h(n)$ is small, the heuristic information share of the cost function $f(n)$ is weak, and although a better path can be achieved, it will also directly lead to an increase in the workload of the search; when the proportion of $h(n)$ is large, the heuristic information share of the cost function $f(n)$ is strong, and although the workload of the search has been reduced, it cannot guarantee that the path searched for is the optimal solution. Therefore, this paper proposes the concept of optimizing the weight ratio of the actual cost function and the estimated cost function, so as to achieve the purpose of balancing the shortest path to reduce the search time. In this paper, the weight coefficients of the actual cost function $g(n)$ and the estimated cost function $h(n)$ are constructed as shown in Eq. 5.

$$\frac{1}{1+k} + \frac{k}{1+k} = 1 \qquad (5)$$

Where k is the independent variable, the value range is, and the sum of the two is 1. When the independent variable k changes from 0 to positive infinity, the first coefficient gradually decreases from 1 to 0, and the second coefficient gradually increases from 0 to 1, which are inversely proportional to each other, and the introduction of the two coefficients into the A* algorithm's cost function can freely regulate the ratio of the actual cost function $g(n)$ to the estimated cost function $h(n)$ to meet the demand. As shown in Eq. 6.

$$f(n) = \frac{1}{1+k}g(n) + \frac{k}{1+k}h(n) \quad k \in [0, \infty) \qquad (6)$$

When using the method of weighted scale factor, the speed of the search cannot be considered only and the planned path is ignored, so the dynamic weighting is introduced for planning, i.e., at the beginning of the search, it is more important to reach the range of the region where the destination is located quickly, so the second coefficient of Eq. 6 should be larger, and at the end of the search is almost over, it is more important to get the optimal path to reach the target point, at this time, the first coefficient of Eq. 6 should be be larger. In summary, the dynamic weighting method is as follows: when the search just started, the estimated cost function $h(n)$ is larger, and its weight coefficient is taken as small, at this time, the improved A* algorithm will prioritize to the target point area close to the target point, when close to the target point range, the estimated cost function $h(n)$ is smaller, and its weight coefficient should be taken as small, at this time, the improved A* algorithm will prioritize to search for the optimal path and reduce the search rate.

The simulation diagram of the A* algorithm with improved weight coefficients is shown in Fig. 5, and the performance comparison before and after the improvement is shown in Table 2. Comparison of the simulation results with the graphs shows that by rationally allocating the weight ratio between the actual cost function $g(n)$ and the estimated cost function $h(n)$ effectively reduces the useless search intervals, reduces the search nodes, and speeds up the search time.

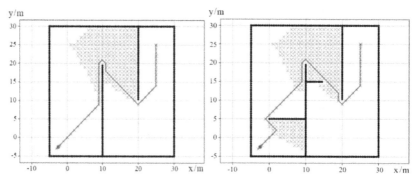

Fig. 5. A* algorithm based on improved weight coefficients

3.2 Optimized Path Planning Method

In practical path planning, the final planned path should be path-continuous and path curvature-continuous, and the path conforms to the dynamics of the mobile robot, which facilitates the movement of the mobile robot. However, the traditional A* algorithm is the path obtained in the raster environment, the path has more turns, and the corner of the turns is not smoothed (i.e., the path curvature is not continuous). And the smooth path is more favorable for mobile robot operation, in order to solve this problem, the obtained path needs to do puffing processing. In this section, Bessel curves are used to smooth the paths obtained by the above improved A* algorithm.

Table 2. Performance comparison of A* algorithm before and after improvement

	Arithmetic	Number of search nodes	Running time/s
The first scenario	A* algorithm	673	6.8646
	Improvement of the A* algorithm	286	2.9172
The second scenario	A* algorithm	659	7.0831
	Improvement of the A* algorithm	395	4.164

Bezier curves are parametric curves that are widely used in practical engineering. Bezier curves are mathematical curves applied to a two-dimensional plane, which can be plotted as a smooth curve based on the coordinates of two or more points. The mathematical principles and formulas of Bezier curves are described below.

As shown in Fig. 6, assuming the existence of A, B, C does not share the line of the three points, so that the line is connected with a line to get the line segment AB and the line segment BC. in the line segment AB to take a point D, in the line segment BC to take a point, so that the D, E point to meet $\frac{AD}{AB} = \frac{BE}{BC}$, and then connect the point D, E, in the new line segment DE to take a point F, so that the point F meets the $\frac{AD}{AB} = \frac{BE}{BC} = \frac{DF}{DE}$, then a point F on the bezier curve has been determined, next point D from the line segment AB point A towards point B at the same time, the point E from the line segment BC point B towards point C, then all the F points connected, then the bezier curve is obtained. AB of point A toward point B at the same time, point E from the line segment BC of point B toward point C to move, this time all the F points will be obtained to connect, you get the Bessel curve, as shown in Fig. 7.

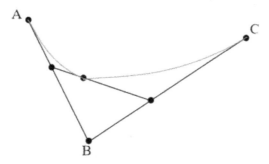

Fig. 6. Bessel curve diagram

The Bessel curve formula is shown, where P_i represents the control on the Bessel curve and t represents the independent parameters of the Bessel curve. When $n = 1$, it is a first-order Bessel curve with two points, representing a straight line. When $n = 2$, it is a second-order Bessel curve with three points, representing a parabola, and when $n \geq 3$, it is a higher-order Bessel curve with $n + 1$ points.

$$B(t) = \sum_{i=0}^{n} \binom{n}{i} P_i (1-t)^{n-i} t^i$$

$$= \binom{n}{1} P_0 (1-t)^n t^0 + \binom{n}{1} P_1 (1-t)^{n-1} t^1$$

$$+ \cdots + \binom{n}{n} P_n (1-t)^0 t^n, t \in [0, 1] \quad (7)$$

The Bessel curve is applied to the improved A* algorithm and smoothed at each turn, as shown in Fig. 7 for the simulation results after processing of the two scenarios, where the red path is obtained without the Bessel curve and the blue curve is the path fitted using the Bessel curve. The experiments show that the paths with continuous curvature are obtained after the Bessel curve smoothing process, and the obtained smooth paths can make the mobile robot spend less time and reduce the energy consumption when turning.

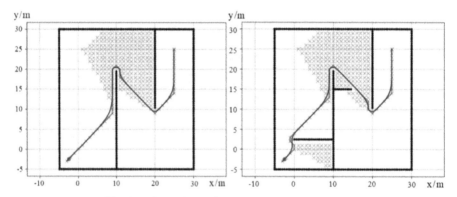

Fig. 7. A* algorithm after Bessel curve optimization

4 Conclusion

This paper focuses on the path planning problem of mobile robot, and proposes a mobile robot path planning method based on weight coefficients to improve the A* algorithm, by improving the weight coefficients to solve the shortcomings of the traditional A* algorithm with long computation time and many search nodes; in view of the problem that the path has many folds, Bessel curves are introduced to smooth the path, and a smooth path is finally obtained. Experiments show that the improved A* algorithm reduces the number of search nodes, reduces the search time and turning points, improves the execution efficiency of the algorithm, and smoothes the path, which effectively reduces the energy loss of the mobile robot in the process of operation.

Acknowledgments. This work was supported by Hubei Provincial Natural Sci-ence Foundation under Grant No. 2024AFC025, Science and Technology Innova-tion Team of Hubei University of Arts and Science under Grantr 2022pytd01, Graduate Innovation Program Project of Hubei University of Arts and Science under Grantr YCX202408.

References

1. Wang, W., Deng, H., Wu, X.: Path planning of loaded pin-jointed bar mechanisms using rapidly-exploring random tree method. Comput. Struct. **209**, 65–73 (2018)
2. Zong, C., Han, X., Zhang, D., et al.: Research on local path planning based on improved RRT algorithm. Proc. Inst. Mech. Eng. Part D J. Automob. Eng. **235**(8), 2086–2100 (2021)
3. Wang, J., Li, X., Meng, Q.H.: An improved RRT algorithm incorporating obstacle boundary information. In: IEEE International Conference on Robotics & Biomimetics (2016)
4. Ying, Y., Li, Z., Ruihong, G., et al.: Path planning of mobile robot based on improved RRT algorithm. In: 2019 Chinese Automation Congress (CAC), pp. 4741–4746 (2019)
5. Liu, J., Yang, J., Liu, H., et al.: An improved ant colony algorithm for robot path planning. Soft. Comput. **21**(19), 5829–5839 (2017)
6. Sahu, C., Parhi, D.R., Kumar, P.B.: An approach to optimize the path of humanoids using adaptive ant colony optimization. J. Bionic Eng. **15**(4), 623–635 (2018)
7. Li, Y.-Y., Liu, F.-G.: Path planning algorithm for mobile robot based on improved ant colony algorithm. J. Phys. Conf. Seri. **2083**(4) (2021)
8. Hart, P.E., Nilsson, N.J., Raphael, B.: A formal basis for the heuristic determination of minimum cost paths. IEEE Trans. Syst. Sci. Cybern. **4**(2), 100–107 (1968)
9. Liu, Y.-T., Sun, R.-Z., Zhang, T.-Y., et al.: Warehouse-oriented optimal path planning for autonomous mobile fire-fighting robots. Secur. Commun. Netw. **2020** (2020)

Wolf Pack Algorithm: An Overview

Wei Xu[1,2,3]([✉]), Yueming Wang[2,3], Peng Xu[1,2,3], Tianqi Qiu[1,2,3], Tong Yan[1,2,3], and Zhirui Wang[1,2,3]

[1] China North Vehicle Research Institute, Beijing 100072, China
[2] China North Artificial Intelligence and Innovation Research Institute, Beijing 100072, China
[3] Collective Intelligence and Collaboration Laboratory, Beijing 100072, China
xuwei1507@163.com

Abstract. Heuristic algorithms have evolved rapidly, leading to numerous theoretical breakthroughs and wide applications in various fields. Swarm intelligence algorithms, as an important branch of heuristic algorithms, have attracted significant attention from researchers. With the expansion of application scenarios and increasing problem complexity, swarm intelligence algorithms have faced considerable challenges in dealing with high-dimensional, multimodal complex function optimization. As a novel swarm intelligence algorithm, the Wolf Pack Algorithm (WPA) has emerged as an efficient tool for addressing such issues due to its unique swarm characteristics and the mechanism that simulates wolf pack hunting behavior. A systematic review and summary of WPA from the perspectives of biological characteristics and algorithm principles are of paramount significance. Subsequently, a comparison between WPA and commonly used swarm intelligence algorithms is conducted. Then, the research progress of WPA is discussed in terms of both theory and application. Finally, inadequacies of WPA are explored, and the future prospects are presented.

Keywords: Heuristics algorithm · Swarm intelligence algorithm · Wolf Pack Algorithm (WPA) · Application field

1 Introduction

With the increase in the scale and complexity of engineering systems, optimal problems have become more complicated. In recent years, swarm intelligence (SI) algorithms, as an effective tool for solving various optimization problems, have gained increasing attention from researchers. In fact, the concept of SI algorithms primarily originates from the observation and inspiration drawn from biological swarms in nature. These algorithms have naturally evolved to exhibit collaborative, stable, self-organizing behaviors, and adaptability to the environment at the macroscopic level through individual autonomous decision-making and simple information exchange mechanisms.

In 1975, John Holland laid the foundation for the development of swarm intelligence algorithms through his research on genetic algorithms [1]. Subsequently, Beni and Wang introduced the concept of swarm intelligence while studying cellular automata systems, demonstrating that systems composed of non-intelligent individuals can exhibit collective intelligent behavior [2,3]. These studies have driven the development of swarm intelligence theory and provided significant inspiration for subsequent swarm intelligence algorithms. Currently, commonly used swarm intelligence algorithms include the Ant Colony Optimization (ACO) algorithm, the Artificial Bee Colony (ABC) algorithm, and the Pigeon-Inspired Optimization (PIO) algorithm. These algorithms have been widely employed in traffic control [4,5], industrial manufacturing [6,7], national defense and military [8–10] and other fields. They generally offer advantages of high robustness, self-organization, intelligent emergence, flexibility and low resource consumption. The practical results in [11–15] have demonstrated the feasibility and efficiency of these algorithms in resolving large-scale complex computing tasks.

However, it is noteworthy that the Wolf Pack Algorithm (WPA), when compared to commonly used swarm intelligence algorithms, was proposed later and has had a shorter development period. Despite this, it exhibits great performance in tackling nonlinear optimization problems. It also possesses significant merits in terms of global convergence and computational robustness, particularly when solving complex functions with high-dimensional multi-modalities. As an efficient and challenging algorithm, WPA has attracted increasing research interest up to now.

In this article, an overview of the WPA is provided, commencing with a discussion of its biological principles and proceeding to an elaboration of the principles and steps of the algorithm. Subsequently, the fundamental characteristics of WPA are explored and a comparison is conducted with other commonly utilized swarm intelligence algorithms. Furthermore, a brief introduction to the research status of WPA is presented. Finally, conclusions and future prospects are drawn.

2 Basic Principle and Model of WPA

In this section, an overview of the research background of WPA is mainly presented. The biological principles of WPA are initially introduced. Next, by drawing inspiration from these principles and simulating the hunting behavior of wolves, the algorithmic fundamentals are subsequently summarized.

2.1 The Biology of WPA

As highly adaptable animals, wolves inhabit a diverse range of environments, including open woodlands, arid regions, and arctic tundra. To hunt prey in these environments, wolves rely on pack strength to increase hunting efficiency through a high level of organization and a clear division of labor. Among them, the lead scout, owing to its acute senses and enduring stamina, patrols at the forefront of the pack, searching for potential prey. Once a target is spotted, it rapidly communicates the information to its companions. After target confirmation, the chasers run after the prey from different directions, aiming to drive it into a preset surrounded area. Meanwhile, the surrounders move rapidly in an arc or semicircle formation, forming a tight hunting circle. To prevent the prey from escaping, the blockers are responsible for blocking its escape routes and ensuring it remains within the hunting range of the wolves. When the prey is cornered, the experienced alpha launches the final attack on the prey.

On the other hand, the highly collaborative nature that wolves show during the hunting process is largely determined by their diverse interaction styles. Members communicate through various vocalizations, such as howls, barks, and whimpers, to convey different types of information, like long-distance communication, signals for gathering together, or feedback on individual status. Wolves utilize barks or whimpers to indicate direction or express urgency in close contact. In addition, wolves employ numerous body movements to convey information, exhibiting intentions for attack, defense, or preparation for pursuit through body postures. Moreover, some actions like nodding, tail wagging, and eye contact are also used to communicate intentions or issue warnings. When necessary, wolves communicate with other members through touch or nibbling, particularly during critical moments such as maintaining formation or adjusting positions. While tracing and surrounding prey, the wolf pack will dynamically adjust its positions according to the environment and prey behavior, forming a tight encirclement through the coordination of visual communication and movement directions. Once the prey is captured, the alpha wolf will take the first bite, followed by the distribution of food according to the hierarchical structure of the pack. In summary, wolves exhibit an exceptional survival strategy in the natural world through their cohesive cooperation, keen perception, and intelligent decision-making. This biological principle not only lays a solid foundation for the design of Wolf Pack Algorithm, inspiring researchers to develop efficient optimization methods, but also profoundly reveals the sophistication of natural complex system operations.

2.2 Principle and Model of WPA

The WPA simulates the hunting strategies and prey distribution mechanisms of wolf packs in nature, abstracting three intelligent behaviors: searching, calling, and besieging. The leadership mechanism and pack renewal principle are introduced in WPA. This simulation not only enables the algorithm to achieve efficient and precise searching in specific environments, but it has also been successfully extended to solve various function optimization problems, demonstrating its wide applicability and efficiency. Moreover, the social structure of the wolf pack is explicitly captured in the WPA, which incorporates three primary roles: the alpha wolf (leader), scout wolves (contenders), and hunter wolves (followers), as depicted in Fig. 1. Each role serves a distinct purpose in WPA, with the alpha wolf guiding the overall direction of the pack, scout wolves conducting reconnaissance and confrontation, and hunter wolves executing and besieging prey. This well-defined collaborative model enables the WPA to achieve goals more efficiently and orderly when addressing practical problems.

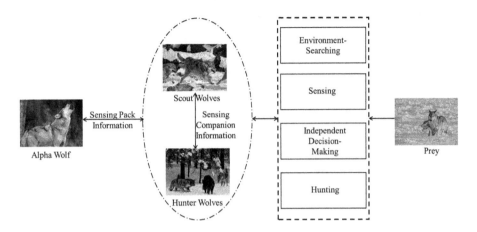

Fig. 1. Wolf pack social organizational structure.

Refer to the WPA proposed by Wu et al. [28] for a clearer introduction to the principle. The specific steps are as follows:

Set searching region as a $N \times D$ Euclidean space, where N denotes the sum of artificial wolves, D represents the number of variables to be optimized, the position vector of any artificial wolf i is $X_i = \chi_{i1}, \chi_{i2}, ..., \chi_{iD}$. In addition, $Y_i = f(X)$ and Y_{lead} signify the objective function value of the artificial wolf i and the lead wolf, respectively. Three behaviors and two mechanisms of WPA will be discussed in detail below.

Alpha Wolf Generation Mechanism. Utilize the following equation to initialize the positions of the wolf pack:

$$\chi_{id} = rand(\max_d - \min_d) + \min_d \tag{1}$$

where χ_{id} is the dth $(d = 1, 2, ..., D)$ variable value of the artificial wolf i, $\max_d$ and $\min_d$ denote the upper and lower bounds of χ_{id} in D-dimensional space, respectively. In addition, the artificial Wolf with the optimal objective function value is appoint as the lead wolf, it does not engage in subsequent search or hunting processes, but rather guides the pack towards the optimal position until it is superseded by wolves possessing more superior target values in the subsequent iteration processes.

Scouting Behavior. Based on the biological principles of a wolf pack, during the initial phase of hunting, scout wolves are sent out to search for prey. Correspondingly, in the WPA, S_{num} artificial wolves are designated as scout wolves, and their social status ranks second only to the lead wolf. First, calculate the objective function value Y_i of scout wolf i at the current position. If $Y_i > Y_{lead}$, it indicates that the scout wolf i is closer to the prey than the lead wolf. At this time, the scout wolf i is appointed as the lead wolf, and then, $Y_{lead} = Y_i$. If $Y_i < Y_{lead}$, the scout wolf i makes independent decisions, moving forward in R directions with step size $step_a$ (searching step size), records the objective function value Y_{ir} and then returns to the original position. Select the direction with the maximum Y_{ir} ($r = 1, 2, ..., R$) to move. At this moment, the position of scout wolf i in the D-dimensional space is:

$$\chi_{id}^r = \chi_{id} + \sin\left(2\pi \times \frac{r}{R}\right) \times step_a^d \quad (2)$$

Now, the objective function value of the scout wolf i satisfies $Y_{ir} > Y_{i0}$ (Y_{i0} is the objective function value at the current moment), and update the position X_i of the scout wolf i. Repeat the above process until $Y_i > Y_{lead}$ or the number of wolf searching (T) reaches the maximum number T_{max}.

Calling Behavior. The lead wolf summoned the M_num hunter wolves through howling, and they quickly gathered towards the lead wolf with step size $step_b$. The position vector of the hunter wolf at the $t+1$th iteration is:

$$x_{id}^{t+1} = x_{id}^t + step_b^d \frac{g_d^t - x_{id}^t}{|g_d^t - x_{id}^t|} \quad (3)$$

In the process of hunter wolves attacking, they still follow the lead wolf generation mechanism satisfying winner-take-all generation rule. If the optimal objective function value Y_i of hunter wolf i satisfies $Y_i < Y_{lead}$, hunter wolf i will continue to advance in the direction of the lead wolf until the distance satisfies $d_{is} < d_{near}$, then it will enter a besieging state. The decision distance d_{near} can be estimated by the following formula:

$$d_{near} = \frac{1}{Dw} \sum_{d-1}^{D} \left| \max_d - \min_d \right| \quad (4)$$

where w denotes distance decision factor.

Besieging Behavior. Owing to the fact that the lead wolf is closest to the prey, the position of the lead wolf is regarded as the current position of the prey. For the kth iteration wolf pack, the position of the prey in the d-dimensional space is G_d^t, and the besieging behavior of the wolf pack is as follows:

$$x_{id}^{t+1} = x_{id}^t + \lambda \times step_c^d \times |G_d^t - x_{id}^t| \quad (5)$$

where λ is a uniformly distributed random number in the range $[-1, 1]$, and $step_c$ is the attack step length. If the optimal objective function value of the hunter wolf after the besieging behavior is greater than the optimal objective function value of its original position state, the position of the hunter wolf will be updated; otherwise, the position does not change.

The relationship of each behavior step in the d-dimensional space is shown:

$$step_a^d = \frac{step_b^d}{2} = 2step_c^d = \frac{|max_d - min_d|}{S} \qquad (6)$$

where $step_a$, $step_b$, and $step_c$ are the step sizes of scouring behavior, calling behavior, and besieging behavior, respectively. S is the step size factor.

Renewing Rule of Wolf Pack. Consider the stronger-survive renewing rule of wolf pack, mapped to the WPA, it means that K artificial wolves with the worst fitness value are chosen to be removed, and then K artificial wolves are randomly generated. Where $K \in \left[\frac{n}{2\beta}, \frac{n}{\beta}\right]$ is a random integer and β represents population renewing proportional coefficient.

In summary, the pseudocode of WPA is illustrated in Algorithm 1.

Algorithm 1. the pseudocode of Wolf Pack Algorithm

Input the parameters of WPA including the maximum number of repetitions in scouting behavior T_{max}, distance decision factor w, step factor S, and population renewing proportional coefficient β
Output the optimal objective value
1: **Initialize** artificial wolf pack $X_i = \chi_{i1}, \chi_{i2}, ..., \chi_{iD}$
2: Select the artificial wolf with the optimal objective value as the initial lead wolf $Y_{lead} = \max Y_i$
3: Set iteration counter for initial population $g := 0$
4: **while** $g < G_{max}$ **do**
5:     Scouting behavior
6:     **if** $Y_i > Y_{lead}$ **then**
7:         renew the lead wolf
8:     **else if** $Y_i < Y_{lead}$ & scouting repetition number $T < T_{max}$ **then**
9:         for each of the R directions, take one step with step size $step_a$
10:     **else**
11:         update the position of scouting wolves as in Eq.(2)
12:     **end if**
13:     Calling behavior
14:     **if** $Y_i > Y_{lead}$ **then**
15:         renew the lead wolf and start the calling behavior
16:     **else if** $Y_i \leq Y_{lead}$ & $d_{ir} \leq d_{near}$ **then** ▷ d_{ir} is the distance between the lead wolf X_{lead} and scout wolf X_i
17:         hunter wolves advance to the lead wolf with the calling step size $step_b$
18:     **else**
19:         update the position as in Eq.(3)
20:     **end if**
21:     Besieging behavior

22:        **if** $Y_i > Y_{lead}$ **then**
23:            renew the lead wolf
24:        **else if** $Y_i < Y_{lead}$ **then**
25:            wolves move to the lead wolf with the besieging step size $step_c$
26:        **else**
27:            update the position as in Eq.(6)
28:        **end if**
29:        Population updating with stronger-survive renewing rule
30:        g++
31:        Restart the scouting behavior, calling behavior and besieging behavior
32: **end while**

3   Basic Characteristics of the Pack Algorithm

As an emerging swarm intelligence algorithm, WPA has garnered significant attention and undergone rapid development. Through a comprehensive review of relevant literature, the following salient features of WPA are distilled:

1. **Entirety:** In the social system of wolves, a distinct division of labor prevails. While individuals work independently, they also influence and communicate information among each other.
2. **Replaceability:** For the WPA, the position of the lead wolf represents the optimal objective value of the considered problem. During the iteration process, the replacement of the lead wolf follows a winner-take-all generation rule, and it will be updated according to change in the optimal objective value.
3. **Robustness:** Analogous to wolves in their natural environment, the survival of the wolf pack does not perish that a few wolves do not find high-quality resources. Similarly, WPA is resilient to suboptimal performance of local wolf, guaranteeing optimal solution exist.
4. **Feedback:** During the search phase, each artificial wolf has the ability to make its own decisions. After finding the optimal objective value, the lead wolf will howl, feeding the information back to the surrounding wolves, so that they gather around it. This positive and negative feedback process gives WPA a unique advantage in solving the optimization problem.

It is worth noting that different swarm intelligence algorithms exhibit varying performance for different application problems. To gain a deeper understanding of the characteristics of WPA, we compare the Wolf Pack Algorithm with other swarm intelligence algorithms, and the results are summarized in Table 1.

WPA owns advantages in terms of global search power, robustness, and parallelism, rendering it a highly efficient and reliable approach for solving multi-dimensional functions and complex optimization problems, particularly in scenarios demanding swift search speeds and global optimal solutions.

Table 1. Comparison of swarm intelligence algorithms

Algorithm name	Merit	Demerit	Application
Wolf Pack Algorithm (WPA)	1.Adaptability and flexibility 2.Efficient search capability 3.Robustness 4.Dynamic nature 5.Parallelism 6.Ease of implementation	1.Lack of information exchange 2.Long convergence time 3.Sensitivity to parameters 4.Susceptibility to local optimal	WPA eminently suites continuous optimization problems and excels in the realm of high-dimensional, multi-peak complex function solving [16,17].
Artificial Bee Colony algorithm (ABC)	1.Probabilistic search strategy 2.Division of labor 3.Self-organization and cooperation 4.Simple yet powerful	1.Sensitivity to parameters 2.Premature convergence 3.Computational complexity 4.Limited exploration capability 5.Difficulty in balancing exploration and exploitation 6.Dependence on randomness	ABC algorithm commonly utilizes to solve combinatorial optimization problems, large-scale search problems, and shop scheduling problems [18,19].
Ant Colony Optimization algorithm (ACO)	1.Parallelism and distributed nature 2.Positive feedback mechanism 3.Robustness and flexibility 4.Global search capability	1.Slow convergence 2.Sensitivity to parameters 3.Stagnation in local optima 4.Difficulty in handling discretization of continuous variables	ACO algorithm has been found to be effective in solving the Traveling Salesman Problem (TSP), backpacking problems, path planning problems, and resource allocation problems [20,21].
Pigeon-Inspired Optimization algorithm (PIO)	1.Efficient exploration and exploitation 2.Highly adaptive 3.Fast convergence speed 4.Scalability	1.Limited theoretical foundation 2.Sensitivity to parameters 3.Premature convergence 4.Difficulty in balancing exploration and exploitation 5.Limited applicability to large-scale problems	PIO algorithm exhibits significant potential in solving global optimization problems, both unconstrained and constrained optimization problems, and UAV obstacle avoidance problem [22,23].

4 Research Status and Application Scenarios at Home and Abroad

As a prominent swarm intelligence approach, the WPA exhibits ease of implementation and superior optimization capabilities, which have garnered significant attention from the scholarly community. This section delves into the progress of the WPA, encompassing both domestic and international research statuses, as well as its diverse applications.

4.1 Research Status at Home and Abroad

Since the 1980s, researchers have introduced numerous swarm intelligence algorithms that emulate the collective behavior of organisms. Over time, the theoretical framework of swarm intelligence algorithms has undergone continuous refinement, and their optimization capabilities have been progressively enhanced in numerous practical applications, offering a novel approach to tackle a broad spectrum of intricate problems. In this study, we introduce a novel group swarm intelligence algorithm, the Wolf Pack Algorithm. Initially, in 1971, wolf biologist Mech provided a comprehensive account of wolf ecology and pack behavior in [24]. Subsequently, Yang et al. introduced the Wolf Pack Search (WPS) algorithm in [25], only on fundamental hunting behaviors. In 2011, Liu et al. formally introduced the Wolf Colony Algorithm (WCA) in [26], which elaborately described searching and besieging behaviors. Notably, WCA shares fundamental similarities with intelligent swarm and particle swarm algorithms, both being statistical optimization techniques.

In contrast to other swarm intelligence algorithms, the WPA exhibits remarkable diversity in its expression forms. In 2013, Zhou et al. examined the hunting behavior of wolves within the context of the WCA and introduced the lead wolf in [27] to find the global optimal solution for optimization problems. Similarly, Wu et al., drawing inspiration from Mech and Yang et al., introduced three intelligent behaviors and two mechanisms in [28]. This was achieved by segmenting the prey capture and food distribution behaviors into scouting, calling, and besieging behaviors, and considering the winner-take-all generation rule of the lead wolf and the stronger-survive renewing rule of the wolf pack. The WPA has highlighted the distinct division of labor among wolves and emphasizes the pivotal role of the lead wolf. Subsequently, Wu et al. introduced random survival update rules in [29] to enhance the convergence speed and precision of the WPA.

Although the performance of the WPA is commendable, it also has limitations that attract scholars to study. For instance, Li et al. addressed the demerits of the WPA, including inadequate artificial wolf interaction, slow convergence, and susceptibility to local optima, by introducing an improved search strategy in [30]. Hui et al. introduced phase factors to change scout wolves' updating rules [31], developing the Grey Wolf Pack Algorithm (GWPA) to improve the flexibility of scout wolves during searching behavior. Wang et al. introduced a Differential Evolution-based Wolf Pack Algorithm (DWPA) in [32], incorporating differential evolution strategies, which avoid the vulnerabilities of local optima and high computational costs in the WPA. Escobedo et al. modeled wolves and prey as interacting particles in [33], revealing that cooperation enhances group lethality and impedes prey escape. However, their hunting environment was simplified, and individual perception ranges were idealized. Muro et al. found through multi-agent simulations in [34] that effective communication and hierarchical structure were not necessary for successful wolf hunting. Noting that the WPA is a relatively recent swarm intelligence algorithm, it has flourished and been extensively implemented in practical systems.

4.2 Research on the Application of the WPA

Nowadays, with the rapid development of theoretical research on WPA, it has received more and more attention, and has been implemented in practical problems such as image segmentation [35,36], optimal scheduling [37,38] and path planning [39,40]. Image segmentation, as a classic problem in the field of image processing, is of great significance for improving the efficiency of image processing and analysis, and promoting the development of computer vision applications. The WPA is introduced into image segmentation, which improves the accuracy and efficiency at the same time. For example, Wang simulated wolves' perception of prey odor concentration to realize information sharing among artificial wolves, and proposed an automatic image segmentation method in [41] to optimize the clustering center by WPA to improve image segmentation accuracy. Jiao et al. introduced a periodic random disturbance strategy in [42] to dynamically adjust algorithm weights in wolf pack scouting behavior, introduced chaotic global search into WPA hunting behavior, combined the improved WPA with new generalized entropy to achieve image segmentation, and made the results more accurate and clear. Menassel et al. introduced the WPA algorithm into fractal image research in [43], which reduced the coding time and obtained a better compression ratio, thus reducing the complexity of the research.

On the other hand, WPA also has practical significance in optimizing resource utilization, reducing costs and improving efficiency, etc. For example, Wu et al. proposed a binary WPA in [44] to solve the 0–1 backpack problem by defining motion operators and binary coding the position, step size and intelligent behavior of intelligent wolves. The author proposed an improved binary WPA in [45] to solve the multidimensional knapsack problem. The application of WPA can make the solution of knapsack problem more comprehensive and efficient, and can deal with different types of problems and constraints. In addition, in order to improve the operational efficiency of hydropower stations, Zhou et al. introduced the WPA in [46] to solve the optimal coincidence allocation problem of hydropower stations, and compared it with genetic algorithm and particle swarm optimization algorithm. It was proved that the algorithm had certain advantages in global convergence and local convergence. Li et al. proposed an adaptive WPA in [47], which was based on the characteristics of high dimension and multiple constraints for the load problem of operating units in a hydropower plant, combined with the differential evolution algorithm. Compared with the calculation results of genetic algorithm and WPA, the proposed adaptive WPA had good global searching ability. The hydropower station can deal with load distribution under different conditions more comprehensively and flexibly, and realize economic, environmental protection while ensuring stable operation.

In the realm of unmanned aerial vehicles (UAVs), reasonable trajectory planning and task allocation significantly enhance the efficacy of UAVs in executing diverse missions. For instance, Liu et al. employed an equivalent terrain simulation approach, equating enemy threats and terrain obstacles in combat zones to mountains, and implemented the WPA to effectively orchestrate the flight paths of UAVs in [48]. Zhang et al. introduced a UAV cluster and enclosure control strategy in [49], rooted in the interaction mechanisms of wolf hunting spaces, which imposed lower demands on on-board sensing capabilities and accounts for heterogeneous attributes, thereby rendering it more compatible with practical task environments. By refining the traditional WPA algorithm, simulation validation in [50] confirmed the superior stability and convergence speed of the proposed control framework, making it apt for multi-UAV path planning and minimizing the operational cost of UAV clusters. Chen et al. advanced a refined two-part WPS algorithm in [51] to address the collaborative task allocation challenge in multi-UAV systems. In [52], Zhao et al. integrated a clustering algorithm to prioritize task allocation in UAV clusters based on wolf pack behaviors, enhancing task allocation efficiency and reducing flight distances and times for UAV cluster mission execution. In [53], Wang et al. modeled the behavioral characteristics of a wolf pack in its natural environment and exploited it to solve a UAV swarm dynamic task allocation problem in complex scenes. In [54], Fan proposed a UAV path planning method based on improved WPA, simulations found that the presented algorithm could find the shortest path with shorter time.

5 Conclusions and Outlook

Drawing upon the fundamental principles of swarm intelligence, this paper offers a comprehensive exposition of the core idea and evolutionary trajectory of the WPA. It further undertakes a systematic comparison between the WPA and other commonly used swarm intelligence algorithms. It's worth noting that the WPA emerges as a novel and efficient swarm intelligence algorithm, exhibiting distinct advantages in terms of ease of implementation, swift convergence rates, and robust performance. However, given the relatively nascent stage of its development, the WPA faces numerous challenges. Specifically, in addressing complex, high-dimensional problems, the global search efficiency is limited, potentially resulting in incomplete exploration of the search space and the omission of potential optimal solutions. Furthermore, the random nature and cooperative behavior among wolves predisposes it to becoming trapped in local optima. Additionally, the WPA possesses numerous parameters, the selection of which significantly impacts algorithm performance. Improper parameter choice may lead to performance degradation or a slowdown in convergence speed.

On the other hand, wolves exhibit various ways of interaction when hunting. However, this intricate mechanism of interactions is streamlined in WPA, thereby restricting the diversity and adaptability of the algorithm to a certain degree. Furthermore, the WPA tends to overstate the predominance of the lead wolf, whereas in nature, the efficacy of the hunt relies predominantly on the intimate collaboration and diverse strategic interactions among the wolves within the pack.

In the future, we will delve deeper into the theoretical underpinnings of the WPA to enhance its performance and practical applicability. Initially, we aim to devise novel search strategies or algorithmic mechanisms that optimize the global search capabilities, particularly when tackling complex, high-dimensional problems. Concurrently, we will investigate the impact of parameters on the algorithm performance and leverage techniques such as adaptive parameter tuning and optimization to mitigate the effects of parameter choices on performance. Moreover, to accurately simulate the collaborative and interactive mechanisms of wolves in nature, we will intensify our research in fields such as wolf biology and sociology to gain a profound understanding of the interaction ways exhibited by wolves during hunting activities. This knowledge will aid us in designing more naturalistic and efficient WPA. On the application front, we will integrate the collaborative behavioral mechanisms of wolves, the ground mechanics theory of off-road legged robots, and the theory of swarm intelligence collaboration, conducting research on the application of a swarm of off-road legged robots pursuing a mobile target in an unknown environment, which aims to address the bottleneck problem of balancing high individual mobility with swarm collaboration in challenging environments.

Despite the numerous challenges, we must believe that no matter how the future unfolds, the WPA will always hold a significant position in swarm intelligence algorithms and will continue to attract numerous scholars to conduct research on it.

Acknowledgment. This research was supported by National Natural Science Foundation (9224830038).

References

1. Holland, J.H.: Adaptation in Natural and Artificial Systems: An Introductory Analysis with Applications to Biology, Control, and Artificial Intelligence. MIT press, America (1992)
2. Beni. G., Wang, J.: Swarm intelligence in cellular robotic systems. In: Robots and Biological Systems: Towards a New Bionics. Springer, Berlin, Heidelberg (1993)
3. Beni. G.: Swarm intelligence. In: Complex Social and Behavioral Systems: Game Theory and Agent-Based Models, pp. 791–818 (2020)
4. Shaikh, P.W., El-Abd, M., Khanafer, M., et al.: A review on swarm intelligence and evolutionary algorithms for solving the traffic signal control problem. IEEE Trans. Intell. Transp. Syst. **23**(1), 48–63 (2020)
5. SS. V. C.: A multi-agent ant colony optimization algorithm for effective vehicular traffic management. In: 2020 International Conference on Swarm Intelligence (ICSI), pp. 640–647. Springer (2020)
6. Pan, Q.K., Wang, L., Mao, K., et al.: An effective artificial bee colony algorithm for a real-world hybrid Flowshop problem in steelmaking process. IEEE Trans. Autom. Sci. Eng. **10**(2), 307–322 (2012)
7. Wu, X., Shen, X., Li, C.: The flexible job-shop scheduling problem considering deterioration effect and energy consumption simultaneously. Comput. Ind. Eng. **135**, 1004–1024 (2019)
8. Duan, H.B., Shao, S., Su, B.W., et al.: New development thoughts on the bio-inspired intelligence based control for unmanned combat aerial vehicle. Sci. Chin. Technol. Sci. **53**, 2025–2031 (2010)
9. Yu, Y.P., Liu, J.C., Wei, C.: Hawk and pigeon's intelligence for UAV swarm dynamic combat game via competitive learning pigeon-inspired optimization. Sci. Chin. Technol. Sci. **65**(5), 1072–1086 (2022)
10. Zhang, B., Duan, H.: Three-dimensional path planning for uninhabited combat aerial vehicle based on predator-prey pigeon-inspired optimization in dynamic environment. IEEE/ACM Trans. Comput. Biol. Bioinform. **14**(1), 97–107 (2015)

11. Sharma, S., Jain, R.: EACO: an enhanced ant colony optimization algorithm for task scheduling in cloud computing. Int. J. Secur. Appl. **13**(4), 91–100 (2019)
12. Xing, H., Zhu, J., Qu, R., et al.: An ACO for energy-efficient and traffic-aware virtual machine placement in cloud computing. Swarm Evol. Comput. **68**, 101012 (2022)
13. Babar, M., Khan, M.S., Din, A., et al.: Intelligent computation offloading for IoT applications in scalable edge computing using artificial bee colony optimization. Complexity **2021**(1), 5563531 (2021)
14. Li, J., Han, Y.: A hybrid multi-objective artificial bee colony algorithm for flexible task scheduling problems in cloud computing system. Cluster Comput. **23**, 2483–2499 (2020)
15. Wang, H., Zhao, J.: A novel high-level target navigation pigeon-inspired optimization for global optimization problems. Appl. Intell. **53**(12), 14918–14960 (2023)
16. Zhu, Q., Wu, H., Li, N., et al.: A chaotic disturbance wolf pack algorithm for solving ultrahigh-dimensional complex functions. Complexity **2021**(1), 6676934 (2021)
17. Peng, Q., Wu, H.S., Zhu, Q.: An interactive wandering Wolf Pack algorithm for solving high-dimensional complex functions. In: 11th International Conference on Information Science and Technology (ICIST), pp. 344–355. IEEE (2021)
18. Kaya, E., Gorkemli, B., Akay, B., et al.: A review on the studies employing artificial bee colony algorithm to solve combinatorial optimization problems. Eng. Appl. Artif. Intell. **115**, 105311 (2022)
19. Rahman, M.A., Sokkalingam, R., Othman, M., et al.: Nature-inspired metaheuristic techniques for combinatorial optimization problems: overview and recent advances. Mathematics **9**(20), 2633 (2021)
20. Wang, Y., Han, Z.: Ant colony optimization for traveling salesman problem based on parameters optimization. Appl. Soft Comput. **107**, 107439 (2021)
21. Zhang, D., You, X., Liu, S., et al.: Dynamic multi-role adaptive collaborative ant colony optimization for robot path planning. IEEE Access **8**, 129958–129974 (2020)
22. Cui, Z., Zhao, L., Zeng, Y., et al.: Novel PIO algorithm with multiple selection strategies for many-objective optimization problems. Complex Syst. Model. Simul. **1**(4), 291–307 (2021)
23. Qiu, H., Duan, H.: A multi-objective pigeon-inspired optimization approach to UAV distributed flocking among obstacles. Inf. Sci. **509**, 515–529 (2020)
24. Mech, L.D.: The wolf: the ecology and behavior of an endangered species. J. Wildl. Manag. **52**(3). https://doi.org/10.2307/3799810(1971)
25. Yang, C., Tu, X., Chen, J.: Algorithm of marriage in honey bees optimization based on the wolf pack search. In: 2007 International Conference on Intelligent Pervasive Computing (IPC), pp. 462–467. IEEE (2007)
26. Liu, C., Yan, X., Liu, C., Wu, H.: The wolf colony algorithm and its application. Chin. J. Electron. **20**(2), 212–216 (2011)
27. Zhou, Q., Zhou, Y.Q.: Wolf colony search algorithm based on leader strategy. Appl. Res. Comput. **30**(09), 2629–2632 (2013) (In Chinese)
28. Wu, H.S., Zhang, F.M., Wu, L.S.: New swarm intelligence algorithm-wolf pack algorithm. Syst. Eng. Electron. **35**(11), 2430–2438 (2013) (In Chinese)
29. Wu, H., Zhang, F.: A uncultivated wolf pack algorithm for high-dimensional functions and its application in parameters optimization of PID controller. In: 2014 IEEE Congress on Evolutionary Computation (CEC), pp. 1477–1482. IEEE (2014)
30. Li, G.L., Wei, Z.H., Xu, L.: Wolf pack algorithm based on modified search strategy. J. Comput. Appl. **35**(06), 1633–1636+1687 (2015)
31. Hui, X.B., Guo, Q., Wu, P.P.: An improved wolf pack algorithm. Control Decis. **32**(07), 1163–1172 (2017) (In Chinese)

32. Wang, Y.X., et al.: Research of improved wolf pack algorithm based on differential evolution. Appl. Res. Comput. **36**(08), 2305–2310 (2019) (In Chinese)
33. Escobedo, R., et al.: Group size, individual role differentiation and effectiveness of cooperation in a homogeneous group of hunters. J. R. Soc. Interface **11**(95), 20140204 (2014)
34. Muro, C., et al.: Wolf-pack (Canis lupus) hunting strategies emerge from simple rules in computational simulations. Behav. Proc. **88**(3), 192–197 (2011)
35. Chen, C., Xuan, S.B., Lei, H.X.: Image segmentation based on wolf pack algorithm and 2D maximum entropy. Comput. Eng. **44**(01), 233–237 (2018) (In Chinese)
36. Wachs-Lopes, G.A., Santos, R.M., Saito, N.T., et al.: Recent nature-inspired algorithms for medical image segmentation based on Tsallis statistics. Commun. Nonlinear Sci. Numerical Simul. **88**, 105256 (2020)
37. Wang, J.Q., Jia, Y.Y., Xiao, Q.Y.: Application of wolf pack search algorithm to optimal operation of hydropower station. Adv. Sci. Technol. Water Res. **35**(03), 1–4+65 (2015) (In Chinese)
38. Du, J., Zhang, Z., Li, M., et al.: Retracted Article: optimal scheduling of integrated energy system based on improved grey wolf optimization algorithm. Sci. Rep. **12**(1), 7095 (2022)
39. Ye, Y., Zhang, H.Z.: Wolf pack algorithm for multi-depot vehicle routing problem. Appl. Res. Comput. **34**(09), 2590–2593 (2017) (In Chinese)
40. Fang, Y.J., Tang, M.: Three-dimensional routing optimization for AVS/RS's composite operation. Comput. Integr. Manuf. Syst. **21**(03), 702–708 (2015) (In Chinese)
41. Wang, F.Z.: Automatic segmentation of FCM image based on the optimization algorithm of wolf swarm pack. Control Eng. Chin. **25**(09), 1727–1732 (2018) (In Chinese)
42. Jiao, R.F., Fan, J.L.: Novel generalized entropy image segmentation based on improved wolf pack algorithm. Appl. Res. Comput. **36**(10), 3142–3144+3167 (2019) (In Chinese)
43. Menassel, R., Nini, B., Mekhaznia, T.: An improved fractal image compression using wolf pack algorithm. J. Exp. Theor. Artif. Intell. **30**(3), 429–439 (2018)
44. Wu, H.S., et al.: A binary wolf pack algorithm for solving 0-1 knapsack problem. Syst. Eng. Electr. **36**(08), 1660–1667 (2014) (In Chinese)
45. Wu, H. S., et al.: Improved binary wolf pack algorithm for solving multidimensional knapsack problem. Syst. Eng. Electron. **37**(05), 1084–1091 (2015) (In Chinese)
46. Zhou, X.H., Yang, K., Wang, X.Y.: Application of wolf pack search algorithm in optimal load dispatching of hydropower station. Water Pow. **43**(02), 81–84 (2017) (In Chinese)
47. Li, L., Lai, X.D., Chen, X.M.: Research on inner-plant optimal operation of hydropower station based on improved wolf swarm algorithm. Water Res. Pow. **37**(06), 164–168 (2019) (In Chinese)
48. Liu, Y.L., et al.: Track planning for unmanned aerial vehicles based on wolf pack algorithm. J. Syst. Simul. **27**(08), 1838–1843 (2015) (In Chinese)
49. Zhang, D.F., Duan, H.B., Fan, Y.M.: UAV swarm containment control inspired by spatial interaction mechanism of wolf-pack foraging. Sci. Sin. (Technologica) **52**(10), 1555–1570. (In Chinese)
50. Jiang, C.S.: Research on multi UAV path planning system based on improved wolf swarm algorithm. Nanjing University Of Information Science And Technology. https://doi.org/10.27248/d.cnki.gnjqc.2022.000881 (2022) (In Chinese)

51. Chen, Y., Yang, D., Yu, J.: Multi-UAV task assignment with parameter and time-sensitive uncertainties using modified two-part wolf pack search algorithm. IEEE Trans. Aerosp. Electron. Syst. **54**(6), 2853–2872 (2018)
52. Zhao, Y.M., Zhang, J.L.: Clustering based task allocation algorithm for unmanned aerial vehicle wolf pack. AI-View **4**, 31–39+47 (2021) (In Chinese)
53. Wang, Z, Zhang, J.: A task allocation algorithm for a swarm of unmanned aerial vehicles based on bionic wolf pack method. Knowl.-Based Syst. **250**, 109072 (2022)
54. Fan, H.: UAV path planning method based on improved wolf pack algorithm. J. Electron. Inf. Sci. **8**(5), 31–37 (2023)

A Discrete Time-Varying Zeroing Neural Dynamics for Solving Equality Constrained Optimization

Jie Zhou[1], Qiaowen Shi[1], Ruicong Wang[1], Chao Mou[2], Dimitrios K. Gerontiti[3], and Yang Shi[1(✉)]

[1] School of Information Engineering, Yangzhou University, Yangzhou 225127, China
shiy@yzu.edu.cn
[2] School of Information Science and Technology, Beijing Forestry University, Beijing 100083, China
[3] Department of Information and Electronic Engineering, International Hellenic University, Thessaloniki, Greece

Abstract. In this paper, time-varying nonlinear optimization (TNO) problems are studied, and a new discrete time-varying zeroing neural dynamics (DZND) model is proposed to solve the discrete time-varying equality constrained optimization (DTECO) problems. Firstly, a continuous time-varying zeroing neural dynamics (CZND) model of equality constraints is established using the Lagrange method. Thereafter, the four-step Zhang discretization formula (FZDF) is employed to discretize the CZND model, resulting in the four-step DZND (FDZND) model. Notably, the truncation error of the FDZND model is raised to the fourth-order, thereby improving calculative accuracy. Theoretical analysis indicates that the FDZND model is convergent and stable. Besides, the FDZND model is compared with the Taylor-type DZND (TDZND) model and Euler-type DZND (EDZND) model to further verify its effectiveness and superiority. Among them, the residual errors of TDZND and EDZND are $\boldsymbol{O}(g^3)$ and $\boldsymbol{O}(g^2)$, respectively, where g denotes the sampling gap. During the experiment, the impact of different values of parameter on the residual errors and the effective interval of step size s is also assessed. The experimental results indicate that the truncation error of the FDZND model is smaller.

Keywords: Zeroing neural dynamics · Discrete time-varying equality constrained optimization · Four-step Zhang discretization formula

1 Introduction

The optimization problem with nonlinear equality constraints is a type of optimization method that is widely applied in theoretical research and engineering across various fields [1]. It has always been extensively studied by researchers due to its fundamental status. Many researches can be modeled as nonlinear optimization problems, especially neural network [2,3], mechanical control [4,5] and operations research [6]. For example, in [7], a flexible framework for general mixed-integer nonlinear programming (MINLP) was introduced, named Minotaur. This framework facilitated both algorithm exploration and structure exploitation, all while maintaining computational efficiency. In [8], an application-agnostic open-source library for differentiable nonlinear least squares (DNLS) optimization, built on PyTorch, offered a unified framework for end-to-end structured learning in robotics and vision. In [9], a new factor graph-based approach was proposed to address the discrete-time finite-horizon linear quadratic regulator problem with auxiliary linear equality constraints within and across time steps.

When addressing objective functions dependent on time, it becomes essential to consider the time-varying factors and devise more efficient algorithms to handle nonlinear optimization problems [10,11]. When employing traditional static methods to address time-varying problems, delay errors may arise. This is attributed to the dynamic nature of both the objective function and constraint condition evolving over time. Neural networks have gained significant attention in solving dynamic optimization problems. Their ability to model complex, nonlinear relationships and adapt to changing conditions makes them suitable for discrete time-varying optimization [12]. Drawing insights from historical data and making predictions or decisions based on the current state of the problem, neural networks can offer approximate solutions to dynamic optimization problems [13].

To effectively address time-varying nonlinear optimization (TNO) problems, the zeroing neural dynamics (ZND) or Zhang neural network (ZNN) has been established [14]. ZND represents a specialized form of recurrent neural network (RNN) designed for addressing real-time computing problems. The ZND method has found application in solving various time-varying problems [6], as evidenced by its successful application in scenarios such as quadratic programming [15] and matrix inversion [16].

Given the inherent advantages of ZND in solving many TNO problems, especially its significant role in circuits. We need to utilize ZND to develop continuous time-varying ZND models (CZND) [17]. The challenge lies in how to use dynamic discrete models to adapt to nonlinear equality constrained optimization (ECO). The problem of discrete time-varying ZND (DZND) arises when the objective function and constraints vary over discrete time [18].

The structure of this article is as follows. The second section introduces the backdrop of equality constraint issues and presents the CZND model using Lagrangian method. The third section is dedicated to the fourth-order discrete-time ZND (FDZND) model, which is obtained by applying four-step Zhang discretization formula (FZDF). In the fourth section, we choose the Taylor-type discrete formula and the traditional Euler formula to compare with the FDZND. The fifth section validates the efficacy of the FDZND model via numerical experiments, specifying the metrics used for validation. Furthermore, a set of control experiments explores the influence of parameter a on the precision of truncation error and the effective interval of step size s. Finally, the entire article is summarized in the sixth section. The primary contributions and content of the paper are outlined below:

- This paper focuses on the real-time calculation of the FDZND model, which sets it apart from the general investigation of TNO.
- The proposed model introduces the use of the general FZDF to transform the CZND model into the FDZND framework. This is an application of the FZDF to discretize the CZND model, presenting improved solutions to the discrete time-varying ECO (DTECO) problems.
- The fourth-order FDZND model offers higher computational accuracy with the optimal parameter. Subsequent numerical experiments have validated the effectiveness of this model.

2 Problem Formulation and CZND Model

2.1 Problem Formulation

To begin with, let us contemplate the following continuous time-varying ECO (CTECO) problem [19]:

$$\min_{x(t)\in\mathbb{R}^n} y(x(t), t) \in \mathbb{R}$$
$$\text{s.t. } D(t)x(t) = c(t), \tag{1}$$

where $y(x(t), t) \in \mathbb{R}$ indicates a time-varying nonlinear convex function that is second-order differentiable with time $t \in [t_0, t_j] \subseteq [0, +\infty)$. $x(t) \in \mathbb{R}^n$ is a vector that changes over time t, and that is what we need to solve for in real-time. $D(t) \in \mathbb{R}^{m\times n}$ is a matrix of rank m, and $c(t) \in \mathbb{R}^m$ is a vector in m row.

Note that the objective function $y(x(t), t)$ must satisfy the convexity inequality [20]:

$$y(lx_1(t_j) + (1-l)x_2(t_j), t_j) \leq lf(x_1(t_j), t_j) + (1-l)y(x_2(t_j), t_j),$$

where the domain of $x(t_j)$ must be a convex set for each t_j. This requirement holds true for every $x_1(t_j)$ and $x_2(t_j)$ within the prescribed limits, and $0 \leq l \leq 1$.

The above formula (1) about CTECO problem can be redescribed as DTECO problem as follows:

$$\min_{x_{i+1}\in\mathbb{R}^n} y(x_{i+1}, t_{i+1}) \in \mathbb{R}$$
$$\text{s.t. } D_{i+1}x_{i+1} = c_{i+1}, \tag{2}$$

in which $y(x_{i+1}, t_{i+1})$, D_{i+1} and c_{i+1} are generated from the above continuous information. x_{i+1} changing within time gap $[t_i, t_{i+1}) \subseteq [t_0, t_j] \subseteq [0, +\infty)$ need to be determined. The symbol t_{i+1} represents the sampling time and is stated as $t = (i+1)g$. Here, $g > 0$ signifies the sampling interval, and i takes values of $0, 1, 2, \cdots$ serving as the updating index.

Note that at the current moment t_{i+1}, we possess information such as x_{i-1}, $y(x_{i-1}, t_{i-1})$, D_{i-1}, x_i, $y(x_i, t_i)$, D_i and their derivatives. However, unknown information, including x_{i+1}, $y(x_{i+1}, t_{i+1})$, is not accessible. Thus, within the computational time interval $[t_i, t_{i+1})$, the aim of this paper is to ascertain the uncertain solution x_{i+1} corresponding to the nonlinear function $y(x_{i+1}, t_{i+1})$ with equality constraints using both current and former data.

2.2 CZND Model

To solve ECO problems, we use the Lagrange method to build the following function [21]:

$$A(x(t), a(t), t) = y(x(t), t) + a^T(t)(D(t)x(t) - c(t)), \quad (3)$$

in which $a(t) = [a_1(t), ..., a_m(t)]^T \in \mathbb{R}^m$ represents the Lagrange multiplier vector, and $a^T(t)$ represents a transpose matrix. According to the Lagrange method, the solution $x(t)$ to the formula (1) about CTECO problem is equivalent to that derived from the equations provided below:

$$\begin{cases} \frac{\partial A(x(t), a(t), t)}{\partial x(t)} = \frac{\partial y(x(t), t)}{\partial x(t)} + D^T(t)a(t) = 0 \\ \frac{\partial A(x(t), a(t), t)}{\partial a(t)} = D(t)x(t) - c(t) = 0. \end{cases} \quad (4)$$

To tackle the formula (4) mentioned above, we introduce the following definition:

$$f(t) = [x^T(t), a^T(t)]^T = [f_1(t), ..., f_n(t), f_{n+1}(t), ..., f_{n+m}(t)]^T \in \mathbb{R}^{n+m},$$

and set the first-order partial derivative of $A(x(t), a(t), t)$ in relation to $x(t)$ and $a(t)$, respectively:

$$z(f(t), t) = \begin{bmatrix} \frac{\partial y(x(t), t)}{\partial x(t)} + D^T(t)a(t) \\ D(t)x(t) - c(t) \end{bmatrix} = \begin{bmatrix} z_1(f(t), t) \\ \vdots \\ z_n(f(t), t) \\ z_{n+1}(f(t), t) \\ \vdots \\ z_{n+m}(f(t), t) \end{bmatrix} \in \mathbb{R}^{n+m}. \quad (5)$$

In order to achieve the theoretical solution $x^*(t)$ of formula (4), $z(f(t), t)$ should be $\mathbf{0}$. Then, continuing to take the derivative of time t, and the equation can be obtained:

$$\dot{z}(f(t), t) = \frac{\partial z(f(t), t)}{\partial f^T(t)} \dot{f}(t) + \frac{\partial z(f(t), t)}{\partial t} = \begin{bmatrix} \frac{\partial^2 y(x(t), t)}{\partial x \partial x^T} & D^T(t) \\ D(t) & 0 \end{bmatrix} \dot{f}(t) + \dot{z}_t(f(t), t). \quad (6)$$

To make formula (6) easier to understand, the Hessian matrix $H(\boldsymbol{f}(t),t)$ and the partial derivative $\dot{\boldsymbol{z}}_t(\boldsymbol{f}(t),t)$ with respect to time are defined as follows:

$$H(\boldsymbol{f}(t),t)) = \frac{\partial \boldsymbol{z}(\boldsymbol{f}(t),t)}{\partial \boldsymbol{f}^{\mathrm{T}}(t)} = \begin{bmatrix} \frac{\partial^2 y(\boldsymbol{x}(t),t)}{\partial \boldsymbol{x}\partial \boldsymbol{x}^{\mathrm{T}}} & D^{\mathrm{T}}(t) \\ D(t) & 0 \end{bmatrix} \quad (7)$$

and

$$\dot{\boldsymbol{z}}_t(\boldsymbol{f}(t),t) = \frac{\partial \boldsymbol{z}(\boldsymbol{f}(t),t)}{\partial t} = \begin{bmatrix} \frac{\partial z_1(\boldsymbol{f}(t),t)}{\partial t} \\ \vdots \\ \frac{\partial z_n(\boldsymbol{f}(t),t)}{\partial t} \\ \frac{\partial z_{n+1}(\boldsymbol{f}(t),t)}{\partial t} \\ \vdots \\ \frac{\partial z_{n+m}(\boldsymbol{f}(t),t)}{\partial t} \end{bmatrix}, \quad (8)$$

in which $\partial^2 y(\boldsymbol{x}(t),t)/\partial \boldsymbol{x}\partial \boldsymbol{x}^{\mathrm{T}}$ signifies the second-order partial derivative of $y(\boldsymbol{x}(t),t)$ regarding $\boldsymbol{x}(t)$. According to the formula of ZNN design method [14], the following formula can be obtained:

$$\dot{\boldsymbol{z}}(\boldsymbol{f}(t),t) = -\mu \boldsymbol{z}(\boldsymbol{f}(t),t), \quad (9)$$

where $\mu > 0$ serves as a parameter to adjust the convergence rate of the ZNN formula. Ultimately, we can integrate formulas (6), (7), (8) and (9) to derive the following CZND model:

$$\dot{\boldsymbol{f}}(t) = -H^{-1}(\boldsymbol{f}(t),t)(\mu \boldsymbol{z}(\boldsymbol{f}(t),t) + \dot{\boldsymbol{z}}_t(\boldsymbol{f}(t),t)), \quad (10)$$

in which $H(\boldsymbol{f}(t),t)$ is nonsingular and positive definite for all time t.

3 Four-Step Discretization Formula and FDZND Model

3.1 Four-Step Discretization Formula

In addressing the DTECO problem (2), it is essential to discretize formula (10) for improved computation. Founded on the four-step ZeaD formula previously investigated by Zhang et al. [22], which is a widely employed numerical method, the general FZDF is typically formulated in the following derivative form:

$$\dot{\varphi}_i = \frac{3a+1}{3g}\varphi_{i+1} - \frac{8a-1}{2g}\varphi_i + \frac{6a-1}{g}\varphi_{i-1} - \frac{24a-1}{6g}\varphi_{i-2} + \frac{a}{g}\varphi_{i-3} + \boldsymbol{O}(g^3). \quad (11)$$

In this expression, the symbol $\boldsymbol{O}(g^3)$ denotes the truncation error, and $g > 0$ represents the sampling interval. It is important to note that parameter a belongs to the interval $(1/12, 1/6)$. When φ_{i+1} is isolated, formula (11) can be reformulated as:

$$\varphi_{i+1} = \frac{3g}{3a+1}\dot{\varphi}_i + \frac{24a-3}{6a+2}\varphi_i - \frac{18a-3}{3a+1}\varphi_{i-1} + \frac{24a-1}{6a+2}\varphi_{i-2} - \frac{3a}{3a+1}\varphi_{i-3} + \boldsymbol{O}(g^4). \quad (12)$$

3.2 FDZND Model

In the aftermath, by utilizing the general FZDF (12), we discretize the CZND model (10) and establish the FDZND model in the following manner:

$$\begin{aligned}\boldsymbol{f}_{i+1} = & -\frac{3}{3a+1}H^{-1}(\boldsymbol{f}_i,t_i)(sz(\boldsymbol{f}_i,t_i)+g\dot{z}_t(\boldsymbol{f}_i,t_i)) + \frac{24a-3}{6a+2}\boldsymbol{f}_i \\ & -\frac{18a-3}{3a+1}\boldsymbol{f}_{i-1} + \frac{24a-1}{6a+2}\boldsymbol{f}_{i-2} - \frac{3a}{3a+1}\boldsymbol{f}_{i-3} + O(g^4),\end{aligned} \quad (13)$$

in which $\boldsymbol{f}_{i+1}$ is equivalent to $\boldsymbol{f}(t_{i+1})$. Besides, $s = g\mu > 0$ denotes the step size and $s \in (0, 1/3)$. The range of step size s is also related to parameter a, the specific relation in the Table 1. It is important to highlight that the truncation error exhibits fourth-order precision. Consequently, formula (13) is referred to as a fourth-order optimization formula, and it is a general formula with the parameter to solve DTECO problem (2).

Theorem 1. *Note that the FDZND model (13) exhibits zero-stability, consistency, and convergence when $a \in (1/12, 1/6)$.*

Proof. In accordance with the findings from the linear K-step method [24] presented in prior results, the characteristic polynomial for formula (11) can be expressed as follows:

$$p(\lambda) = \lambda^4 - \frac{24a-3}{6a+2}\lambda^3 + \frac{18a-3}{3a+1}\lambda^2 - \frac{24a-1}{6a+2}\lambda + \frac{3a}{3a+1}.$$

We can identify four roots that fulfill the condition when setting $p(\lambda) = 0$. To guarantee the zero-stability of the FDZND model (13), it is imperative that these roots satisfy $|\lambda| \leq 1$, with $|\lambda| = 1$ being simple. Thus, the range of values for parameter a can be determined as $a \in (1/12, 1/6)$. Besides, formula (13) is of fourth-order. With reference to the K-step method, the FDZND model (13) displays convergence, characterized by a truncation error of $O(g^4)$. Upon thorough analysis, the proof has been concluded.

Table 1. The relationship between step size s and parameter a of the FDZND model

a	Specific FDZND Model	Range of s
1/11	$\boldsymbol{f}_{i+1} = -\frac{33}{14}H^{-1}(\boldsymbol{f}_i,t_i)(sz(\boldsymbol{f}_i,t_i)+g\dot{z}_t(\boldsymbol{f}_i,t_i)) - \frac{9}{28}\boldsymbol{f}_i + \frac{15}{14}\boldsymbol{f}_{i-1} + \frac{13}{28}\boldsymbol{f}_{i-2} - \frac{3}{14}\boldsymbol{f}_{i-3} + O(g^4)$	$(0, 4/33)$
1/10	$\boldsymbol{f}_{i+1} = -\frac{30}{13}H^{-1}(\boldsymbol{f}_i,t_i)(sz(\boldsymbol{f}_i,t_i)+g\dot{z}_t(\boldsymbol{f}_i,t_i)) - \frac{3}{13}\boldsymbol{f}_i + \frac{12}{13}\boldsymbol{f}_{i-1} + \frac{7}{13}\boldsymbol{f}_{i-2} - \frac{3}{13}\boldsymbol{f}_{i-3} + O(g^4)$	$(0, 4/15)$
5/48	$\boldsymbol{f}_{i+1} = -\frac{16}{7}H^{-1}(\boldsymbol{f}_i,t_i)(sz(\boldsymbol{f}_i,t_i)+g\dot{z}_t(\boldsymbol{f}_i,t_i)) - \frac{4}{21}\boldsymbol{f}_i + \frac{6}{7}\boldsymbol{f}_{i-1} + \frac{4}{7}\boldsymbol{f}_{i-2} - \frac{5}{21}\boldsymbol{f}_{i-3} + O(g^4)$	$(0, 1/3)$
1/9	$\boldsymbol{f}_{i+1} = -\frac{9}{4}H^{-1}(\boldsymbol{f}_i,t_i)(sz(\boldsymbol{f}_i,t_i)+g\dot{z}_t(\boldsymbol{f}_i,t_i)) - \frac{1}{8}\boldsymbol{f}_i + \frac{3}{4}\boldsymbol{f}_{i-1} + \frac{5}{8}\boldsymbol{f}_{i-2} - \frac{1}{4}\boldsymbol{f}_{i-3} + O(g^4)$	$(0, 593/2112)$

4 Taylor-Type DZND and Euler-Type ZDND

4.1 Taylor-Type ZDND

Theorem 2. *Here is the Taylor differential formula [23]:*

$$\dot{\boldsymbol{f}}_i = \frac{2\boldsymbol{f}_{i+1} - 3\boldsymbol{f}_i + 2\boldsymbol{f}_{i-1} - \boldsymbol{f}_{i-2}}{2g} + \boldsymbol{O}(g^2). \tag{14}$$

Proof. Utilizing the Taylor expansion, the following is observed:

$$\boldsymbol{f}_{i+1} = \boldsymbol{f}_i + g\dot{\boldsymbol{f}}_i + \frac{g^2}{2!}\ddot{\boldsymbol{f}}_i + \boldsymbol{O}(g^3), \tag{15}$$

then, separate the derivative $\dot{\boldsymbol{f}}_i$ to obtain:

$$\dot{\boldsymbol{f}}_i = \frac{\boldsymbol{f}_{i+1} - \boldsymbol{f}_i}{g} - \frac{g}{2!}\ddot{\boldsymbol{f}}_i - \boldsymbol{O}(g^2). \tag{16}$$

Similarly, we can also derive the equations containing $\boldsymbol{f}_{i-1}$ and $\boldsymbol{f}_{i-2}$ to get the following formulas:

$$\dot{\boldsymbol{f}}_i = \frac{\boldsymbol{f}_i - \boldsymbol{f}_{i-1}}{g} + \frac{g}{2!}\ddot{\boldsymbol{f}}_i - \boldsymbol{O}(g^2), \tag{17}$$

and

$$\dot{\boldsymbol{f}}_i = \frac{\boldsymbol{f}_i - \boldsymbol{f}_{i-2}}{2g} + g\ddot{\boldsymbol{f}}_i - \boldsymbol{O}(g^2). \tag{18}$$

Combining formula (16) with (18) and subtracting (17), we derive the following Taylor discretization formula (14) and the proof has been concluded.

For comparison with FDZND (13), we use Taylor discretization formula (14) to discretize CZND model (10) and formulate the following Taylor-type DZND (TDZND) model:

$$\boldsymbol{f}_{i+1} = -H^{-1}(\boldsymbol{f}_i, t_i)(s\boldsymbol{z}(\boldsymbol{f}_i, t_i) + g\dot{\boldsymbol{z}}_t(\boldsymbol{f}_i, t_i)) + \frac{3}{2}\boldsymbol{f}_i - \boldsymbol{f}_{i-1} + \frac{1}{2}\boldsymbol{f}_{i-2} + \boldsymbol{O}(g^3), \tag{19}$$

in which $s = g\mu > 0$ denotes the step size, and the truncation error of TDZND model is $\boldsymbol{O}(g^3)$.

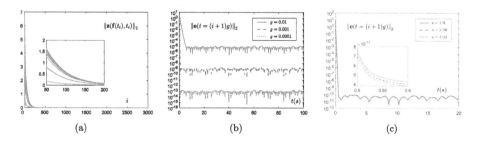

Fig. 1. The experimental results of the model (13) for solving DTECO problem (2). (a) The trajectory of solution residual errors $\|z(f(t_i), t_i)\|_2$. (b) Residual errors $\|e(t = (i+1)g)\|_2$ of the FDZND model (13) with $g = 0.01$, $g = 0.001$ and $g = 0.0001$. (c) Residual errors $\|e(t = (i+1)g)\|_2$ of the FDZND model (13) with $a = 1/9$, $a = 1/10$ and $a = 1/11$.

4.2 Euler-Type DZND

The conventional Euler forward finite difference formula is introduced as follows [21]:

$$\dot{f}_i = \frac{f_{i+1} - f_i}{g} + O(g). \tag{20}$$

Likewise, Euler-type DZND (EDZND) can be obtained by discretizing CZND model (10) by applying Euler-type discretization formula (20):

$$f_{i+1} = -H^{-1}(f_i, t_i)(sz(f_i, t_i) + g\dot{z}_t(f_i, t_i)) + f_i + O(g^2). \tag{21}$$

Here, where $s = g\mu > 0$ represents the step size, the truncation error of the EDZND model is $O(g^2)$.

5 Numerical Experiments

In this part, we carry out simulation experiments to verify the effectiveness of the FDZND model (13). In addition, we also select TDZND model (19) and EDZND model (21) for comparative experiments and show the influence of different values of parameter during the process. Let us start with a concrete example of DTECO problem (2) to calculate x_{i+1} at each calculative time gap $[t_i, t_{i+1}) \subseteq [t_0, t_j] \subseteq [0, +\infty)$,

$$\begin{aligned}
\min\ y(x_{i+1}, t_{i+1}) &= 0.4(\sin(0.1t_{i+1}) + 5)x_1^2(t_{i+1}) + 0.6(\cos(0.1t_{i+1}) + 7)x_2^2(t_{i+1}) \\
&+ 2\sin(t_{i+1})x_1(t_{i+1})x_2(t_{i+1}) + 0.1\cos(t_{i+1})x_1(t_{i+1}) + 0.3\sin(t_{i+1})x_2(t_{i+1}) \\
\text{s.t.}\ \sin(0.1t_{i+1})x_1 &+ \cos(0.1t_{i+1})x_2 = \sin(t_{i+1}),
\end{aligned} \tag{22}$$

where $D_{i+1} = [\sin(0.1t_{i+1}), \cos(0.1t_{i+1})]$, $c_{i+1} = \sin(t_{i+1})$ and $x_{i+1} = [x_1(t_{i+1}), x_2(t_{i+1})]^T$.

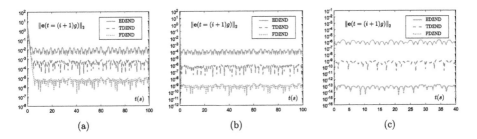

Fig. 2. The results of the comparison of different models with the same parameter $a = 1/11$ and the same step size $s = 0.05$. (a) Residual errors of model EDZND, TDZND and FDZND with $g = 0.01$. (b) Residual errors of model EDZND, TDZND and FDZND with $g = 0.001$. (c) Residual errors of model EDZND, TDZND and FDZND with $g = 0.0001$.

As depicted in Fig. 1a, there are ten curves with random initial values. The initial $\boldsymbol{f}_1$ is randomly generated vector of three rows and one column. Subsequent data iterate from $\boldsymbol{f}_2$ to $\boldsymbol{f}_{i+1}$ according to the FDZND model (13). The trajectory of solution residual errors $\|\boldsymbol{z}(\boldsymbol{f}(t_i), t_i)\|_2$ quickly trend towards zero. Meanwhile, if the initial value $\boldsymbol{f}_1$ is determined to be $[0, 0.5, 1]$, we can see the steady-state residual errors $\|\boldsymbol{e}(t = (i+1)g)\|_2$ of FDZND model (13) at different sampling gap. Specifically, when given initial conditions of step size $s = 0.05$ and parameter $a = 1/11$, the order of the residual errors generated by the new discrete model are 10^{-5}, 10^{-9} and 10^{-13} corresponding to $g = 0.01$, $g = 0.001$ and $g = 0.0001$, respectively. The numerical results, displayed in Fig. 1b and demonstrate the residual errors of FDZND model (13) are consistent with the variation of the fourth-order precision.

Unlike other models, the FDZND is a model with the parameter, and the variation of parameter a will also have effects on the results of errors. First we unify the initial variables with step size $s = 0.05$ and sampling gap $g = 0.001$. Then we continue the error experiment of FDZND model (13) by selecting different values of parameter. Specific results are shown in Fig. 1c, when parameter a is taken as $1/11$, $1/10$ and $1/9$ respectively, based on the effective value range of a, the residual errors $\|\boldsymbol{e}(t = (i+1)g)\|_2$ approach 10^{-10} at the same time. But in detail, there are slight differences that the residual error is relatively smaller when parameter $a = 1/11$. Therefore, according to the results, we can infer that in the range of values, the smaller a is, the better the actual accuracy of the model will be.

To substantiate the reliability and superiority of FDZND (13), we establish an additional controlled experiments, using TDZND model (19) and EDZND model (21). Specific experimental operations are as follows. Aiming at the same DTECO problem (2) presented, three models are used to solve the problem and related experiments are carried out. The most important variable is the sampling gap g, other parameters remain consistent. When the sampling gap $g = 0.01$, the truncation errors of the three models can be seen from Fig. 2a. Among them, the EDZND error is stable at 10^{-2}, the TDZND error is stable at 10^{-3}, and the

FDZND error is 10^{-5}. The residual errors $\|e(t=(i+1)g)\|_2$ of FDZND model (13) is significantly smaller. In addition, when $g = 0.001$ and $g = 0.0001$, the corresponding error plots are depicted in Fig. 2b and Fig. 2c. The residual errors of EDZND model (21) are 10^{-4} and 10^{-6}. The residual errors of TDZND model (19) are 10^{-6} and 10^{-9}. They all fit their own order of error, where EDZND model (21) is the second-order and TDZND model (19) is the third-order. From the Fig. 2b and Fig. 2c, it can be seen that the corresponding residual errors $\|e(t=(i+1)g)\|_2$ for FDZND are 10^{-9} and 10^{-13}. This indicates that FDZND model (13) is still changing according to the fourth-order, and compared with EDZND (19) and TDZND (21), the computational accuracy of FDZND (13) has been further improved.

6 Conclusion

In this article, our primary focus is to introduce FDZND model (13), which effectively tackles the challenges associated with the DTECO problem (2). Firstly, we establish the CZND model (10) about the CTECO problem (1) using the Lagrange method for convenient research. Subsequently, the dynamic equation of the CZND model (10) is discretized into the FDZND model (13) using the general FZDF (12). This FDZND model (13) not only effectively solves DTECO problem (2) but also enhances the accuracy of the truncation error. Further theoretical analysis indicates that the FDZND model (13) exhibits zero-stability, consistency, and convergence with a truncation error of $O(g^4)$. For comparison, we also choose TDZND model (19) and EDZND model (21) to conduct experiments together. In the end, we validate the feasibility of FDZND model (13) through simulation experiments. Additionally, we determine the optimal values of parameter a and the limiting range of the step size s. It is crucial to execute FDZNN model (13) without relying on unknown data, considering that the function $y(\bm{x}_{i+1}, t_{i+1})$ changes over time. In other words, we need to employ existing data to calculate the unknown optimal solution $\bm{x}_{i+1}$. Given the computational nature of DTECO problem (2), time consumption is inevitable. Therefore, it is vital to develop an efficient discrete-time model with enhanced accuracy, such as FDZND model (13), to meet the demand for rapid calculations. Building on the research above, we will continue to study the impact of multi-parameter discrete models on accuracy and the comparison of different models under inequality constraints. Concurrently, we will explore the model's applications in specific fields, such as robotic control and other engineering fields, with a focus on practical implementation in the future.

Acknowledgment. This work was supported by the National Natural Science Foundation of China (with number 61906164), by the Natural Science Foundation of Jiangsu Province of China (with number BK20190875), by the Yangzhou University Top-level Talents Support Program (2021), by Qinglan project of Yangzhou University (2021), by the Postgraduate Research & Practice Innovation Program of Jiangsu Province (with numbers KYCX21_3234, SJCX22_1709, KYCX24_3748 and KYCX24_3749), and in part by the Yangzhou University Training Program of Innovation and Entrepreneurship for Undergraduates.

References

1. Wei, L., Jin, L., Yang, C., Chen, K., Li, W.: New noise-tolerant neural algorithms for future dynamic nonlinear optimization with estimation on Hessian matrix inversion. IEEE Trans. Syst. Man Cybern. Syst. **51**(4), 2611–2623 (2021)
2. Tan, N., Yu, P., Zhong, Z., Zhang, Y.: Data-driven control for continuum robots based on discrete zeroing neural networks. IEEE Trans. Ind. Inf. **19**(5), 7088–7098 (2023)
3. Qi, Y., Jin, L., Luo, X., Shi, Y., Liu, M.: Robust k-WTA network generation, analysis, and applications to multiagent coordination. IEEE Trans. Cybern. **52**(8), 8515–8527 (2022)
4. Li, J., Mao, M., Uhlig, F., Zhang, Y.: Z-type neural-dynamics for time-varying nonlinear optimization under a linear equality constraint with robot application. J. Comput. Appl. Math. **327**(8), 155–166 (2018)
5. Jin, L., Zheng, X., Luo, X.: Neural dynamics for distributed collaborative control of manipulators with time delays. IEEE/CAA J. Autom. Sinica. **9**(5), 854–863 (2022)
6. Jin, L., Wei, L., Li, S.: Gradient-based differential neural-solution to time-dependent nonlinear optimization. IEEE Trans. Autom. Control **68**(1), 620–627 (2023)
7. Mahajan, A., Leyffer, S., Linderoth, J., et al.: Minotaur: a mixed-integer nonlinear optimization toolkit. Math. Prog. Comput. **13**, 301–338 (2021)
8. Pineda, L., Fan, T., Monge, M., et al.: Theseus: a library for differentiable nonlinear optimization. In: Advances in Neural Information Processing Systems (NeurIPS), vol. 25, pp. 3801–3818. Curran Associates, New Orleans (2022)
9. Yang, S., Chen, G., Zhang, Y., et al.: Equality constrained linear optimal control with factor graphs. In: IEEE International Conference on Robotics and Automation (ICRA), vol. 35, pp. 9717–9723. IEEE, Xi'an (2021)
10. Qi, Y., Jin, L., Li, H., Li, Y., Liu, M.: Discrete computational neural dynamics models for solving time-dependent Sylvester equation with applications to robotics and MIMO systems. IEEE Trans. Ind. Inf. **16**(10), 6231–6241 (2020)
11. Guo, D., Lin, X., Su, Z., Sun, S., Huang, Z.: Design and analysis of two discrete-time ZD algorithms for time-varying nonlinear minimization. Numer. Algor. **77**, 23–36 (2017)
12. Shi, Y., Zhang, Y.: New discrete-time models of zeroing neural network solving systems of time-variant linear and nonlinear inequalities. IEEE Trans. Syst. Man Cybern. Syst. **50**(2), 565–576 (2020)
13. Jin, L., Zhang, Y., Qiu, B.: Neural network-based discrete-time Z-type model of high accuracy in noisy environments for solving dynamic system of linear equations. IEEE Trans. Syst. Man Cybern. Syst. **29**(11), 1217–1232 (2018)
14. Jin, L., Zhang, Y.: Continuous and discrete Zhang dynamics for real-time varying nonlinear optimization. Numer. Algor. **73**, 115–140 (2016)
15. Zhang, X., Chen, L., Li, S., et al.: Design and analysis of recurrent neural network models with non-linear activation functions for solving time-varying quadratic programming problems. CAAI Trans. Intell. Technol. **6**(4), 394–404 (2021)

16. Zhang, Y., Li, S., Weng, J., Liao, B.: GNN model for time-varying matrix inversion with robust finite-time convergence. IEEE Trans. Neural Netw. Learn. Syst. **35**(1), 559–569 (2024)
17. Guo, D., Zhang, Y.: Zhang neural network for online solution of time-varying linear matrix inequality aided with an equality conversion. IEEE Trans. Neural Netw. Learn. Syst. **25**(2), 370–382 (2014)
18. Xie, Z., Jin, L., Du, X., Xiao, X., Li, H., Li, S.: On generalized RMP scheme for redundant robot manipulators aided with dynamic neural networks and nonconvex bound constraints. IEEE Trans. Ind. Inf. **15**(9), 5172–5181 (2019)
19. Liufu, Y., Jin, L., Xu, J., Xiao, X., Fu, D.: Reformative noise-immune neural network for equality-constrained optimization applied to image target detection. IEEE Trans. Emerg. Topics. Comput. **10**(2), 973–984 (2022)
20. Marcucci, T., Petersen, M., von Wrangel, D., Tedrake, R.: Motion planning around obstacles with convex optimization. Sci. Robot. **8**(84), 7843 (2023)
21. Cheng, Q., Liu, C., Shen, J.: A new Lagrange multiplier approach for gradient flows. Comput. Methods Appl. Mech. Eng. **367**, 113070 (2020)
22. Guo, J., Zhang, Y.: Stepsize interval confirmation of general four-step DTZN algorithm illustrated with future quadratic programming andtracking control of manipulators. IEEE Trans. Syst. Man Cybern. Syst. **51**(3), 1662–1670 (2021)
23. Zhang, Y., He, L., Hu, C., Guo, J., Li, J., Shi, Y.: General four-step discrete-time zeroing and derivative dynamics applied to time-varying nonlinear optimization. J. Comput. Appl. Math. **347**(3), 314–329 (2019)
24. Shi, Y., Zhao, W., Li, S., Li, B., Sun, X.: Direct derivation scheme of DT-RNN algorithm for discrete time-variant matrix pseudo-inversion with application to robotic manipulator. Appl. Soft Comput. **133**, 109861 (2023)

Workspace Analysis Based on a Serial-Parallel Hybrid Robot: Representing Robot Capabilities

Xinze Tian, Baoshi Cao^(✉), Le Qi, Xueai Li, Yang Liu, Kui Sun, Fenglei Ni, and Zongwu Xie

State Key Laboratory of Robotics and Systems, Harbin Institute of Technology, Harbin 150001, China
cbs@hit.edu.cn

Abstract. Calculating the dexterity value of a certain point is the foundation for demonstrating the dexterity of the robot. Furthermore, the criteria for calculating the dexterity value of the given point determines the authenticity of the capability map. Traditional methods that use Jacobian matrix to find inverse kinematic to determine whether a pose is reachable exhibit uncertainty around singularities. Thus, this article proposes an approach for calculating the dexterity of points based on a serial-parallel hybrid 7-degree-of-freedom robot. By improving the inverse kinematics solving process and selecting the optimal solutions, this method addresses the issues of low efficiency and inaccuracy in calculations near singular points. Additionally, this method does not require consideration of the configuration of the robot's end-effector axis, thus offering broader applicability. By analyzing the characteristics of the capability map and explaining the reasons behind their formation, verify the practicality and potential applications of this criteria.

Keywords: Redundant Robot · Hybrid Serial-Parallel Robot · Inverse Kinematics · Workspace Characteristics · Capability Map

1 Introduction

1.1 Related Work

Inverse kinematics is a prerequisite for determining the dexterity of a given point. With the advancement of robotic technology and the development of related theories, there is an increasing need for more dexterous robot in various scenarios. Generally, as the degrees of freedom increase, the dexterity of the robot also increases. Therefore, 7-degree-of-freedom (DOF) robot is becoming more popular. Determining the existence of inverse kinematic (IK) solution is the foundation of analyzing the characteristics of the capability map. Due to their redundant degrees of freedom, they pose challenges in solving kinematic inverse problems. To obtain their IK, the Monte Carlo method can be used to traverse the joint space to find feasible solutions, and there are also many improved methods based on the Monte Carlo approach [1]. This method has the advantage of avoiding complex analytical derivations but requires excessive computer memory and slow computation. Professor Simas proposed an extended Jacobian matrix that can better compute inverse kinematics [2]. The Jacobian matrix offers many advantages for the subsequent kinematic work of redundant robots. Utilizing various properties of the Jacobian matrix can conduct manipulability analysis [3], facilitate obstacle avoidance [4], and aid in object grasping planning [5]. A more common approach is to define the surplus degrees of freedom and fix the redundant degrees of freedom. Professor Sinha [6] defined two joint angle parameters to solve the inverse kinematics problem of robots with joint offsets in specific configurations. Wang S. proposed a new concept of the arm angle based on a specific robot configuration and derived a closed-form inverse solution by combining it with the Jacobian matrix [7]. Professor Tringali, by selecting appropriate initial joint trajectories and incorporating multiple cost functions, has found the optimal solution through global search [8]. Professor Masayuki Shimizu proposed an improved version of the "arm angle" parameter [9], which addresses the issue of the 0 plane being indeterminable in certain situations.

To obtain the robot's workspace, the traditional method is to traverse the joint space and plot the end points (Monte Carlo method). However, this method can only provide rough conclusions, indicating that the robot can reach a certain point in space, but the posture information at this point cannot be obtained. This poses difficulties for subsequent trajectory planning and obstacle avoidance tasks. Some professors have proposed the concept of a "service sphere", using the distance between the robot's end effector and the origin of the last joint coordinates as the radius of the "service sphere" to analyze the dexterous workspace of the robot [10]. They traverse the joint space to determine whether a particular pose has an inverse kinematic solution. Some professors have analyzed the DLR-Kuka Light-weight Robotarm, using inverse kinematics to determine whether a particular pose has a solution, thereby analyzing the robot's dexterous workspace [11]. Canran Li applied this process to a parallel robot and analyzed the dexterity of its workspace [12]. Based on Professor Zacharias's research findings, Professor Jingdong Zhao develop a new CCDJAP-IK method to solve the IK problem by combining the cyclic coordinate descent (CCD) and joint angle parameterization (JAP) methods, and analyzed the workspace of the SSRMS-type manipulator based on this method [13].

1.2 Contribution and Structure of This Article

Traversing the joint space to determine if a particular pose has an inverse kinematic solution is computationally slow and the results depend heavily on the number of joint angles chosen. The Jacobian matrix and its improvement methods are limited by the singularity characteristics of the Jacobian matrix, resulting in the inverse solution at singular points not always being accurate. Therefore, this article adopts an inverse kinematics solving approach. However, existing inverse kinematics solving strategies lack a detailed explanation and solutions for the multiple solutions problem. Given this deficiency, this research provides a detailed explanation of this issue. Next, a method to determine whether a given pose has an inverse kinematic solution is proposed, which has the advantage of avoiding singularities.

Currently, most analyses of the workspace dexterity for 7-DOF robots are based on the DLR-Kuka Light-Weight Robotarm, all its joints are rotary joints. Importantly, its final joint is a roll joint, allowing the end-effector's roll angle to be arbitrarily chosen without affecting dexterity. The previous methods for analyzing the dexterity of robots are only applicable to robots with a similar joint configuration and lacks general applicability. This paper based on an existing serial-parallel hybrid robot with a relatively general configuration (its last rotational axis is not a roll axis), to provide an analysis strategy when the roll joint affects its workspace dexterity.

In Sect. 2, this article introduces the robot's joint configuration, solves the inverse kinematics, and focus on methods to address various problems encountered during programming calculations. In Sect. 3, the research defines the capability map, proposes a method to determine whether a given pose has an inverse kinematic solution, and presents a method for discretizing the pose matrix to establish a dexterity metric suitable for the robot. By determining whether each pose has an inverse kinematic solution, the research calculates the dexterity values for various points in space. Finally, the characteristics of the resulting capability map are analyzed, and the reasons for its formation are explained.

2 Inverse Kinematic Solving and Refine

2.1 Inverse Kinematic of the Robot

The robot used in this paper is an anthropomorphic robot arm, which is a typical SRS configuration robot. SRS robot, also known as humanoid hands, are commonly used as arms for humanoid robots since they have a structure similar to the human arm. In fact, SRS robot consists of three parts: the shoulder (three revolute joints), the elbow (one revolute joint), and the wrist (three revolute joints). The three joints of the shoulder and wrist can be equivalent to a spherical joint. Additionally, the three joint axes of the shoulder and wrist intersect at one point, thus satisfying the Piper criterion. The improved DH parameter table for this robot is shown in Table 1. The configuration diagram of the robot is as shown in Fig. 1. At the wrist, the pitch and yaw joints are replaced by a 2-DOF parallel mechanism. The limitations of each joint angle are shown in Table 2. The kinematic forward solution can be easily obtained from the DH parameters, which will not be further elaborated here.

To address the redundant degrees of freedom, a parameter representing the redundant degree of freedom is needed. Lee and Bejczy proposed a joint parameterization method, in which one of the joints serves as the redundant degree of freedom, and its rotation angle is the redundant parameter. However, this method is only effective for certain robots and is not applicable to our SRS robot at least. Currently, a more effective method is to define the robot's self-motion parameter as the redundant parameter: for SRS-configured robots, when the base and end effector are stationary, the other joints of the robot can still move. This motion is represented by a parameter, namely the arm angle. This article adopts this method to describe the redundant degrees of freedom of our robot. As shown in Fig. 2. The research defines the arm angle as the angle between the plane determined by the shoulder, elbow, and wrist points and the 0 plane, as shown in Fig. 2. The initial plane is defined as the plane when θ_3 equals to 0. It can be verified that when this condition is satisfied, the joint angles can be uniquely determined, thus the initial plane can be determined [9].

Table 1. The improved DH parameter table of the robot

i	α_{i-1}	a_{i-1}	d_i	θ_i
1	−90°	0	114	−90° + θ_1
2	−90°	0	0	−90° + θ_2
3	−90°	0	−250	−90° + θ_3
4	−90°	0	0	θ_4
5	−90°	0	250	−90° + θ_5
6	−90°	0	0	90° + θ_6
7	90°	0	0	90° + θ_7

Table 2. The limitations of each joint angle

θ	Max	Min
θ_1	−5π/6	5π/6
θ_2	−π/6	11π/6
θ_3	−5π/6	5π/6
θ_4	−π/2	7π/9
θ_5	−5π/6	5π/6
θ_6	−π/9	π/9
θ_7	−7π/18	π/9

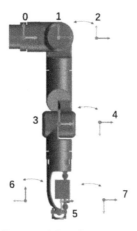

Fig. 1. The configuration diagram of the robot and it's Coordinate system settings

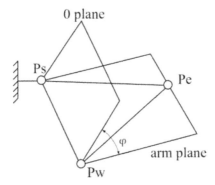

Fig. 2. Definition of arm angle φ

When the manipulator pose T is given, the vector $^0x_7$ from the base to the wrist of the virtual spherical joint can be determined. Since the end point, the base, and the vector from the base to the shoulder are all fixed and determined, the vector $^0x_{sw}$ from the shoulder to the wrist is also fixed and determined, which can be represented by Formula 1. The self-motion of our robot is a rotational motion around the vector $^0x_{sw}$. According to Rodrigues' formula, this article can obtain the rotation matrix $^0R_\varphi$ when the arm angle is φ. From Eq. 2, the research can derive the rotation matrix represented by the initial moment and the arm angle for any coordinate system. Where $^0u_{sw}$ is the unit vector of $^0x_{sw}$.

$$^0x_7 = {}^0x_{bs} + {}^0x_{se} + {}^0x_{ew} = {}^0x_{bs} + {}^0x_{sw} \tag{1}$$

$$^0R_\varphi = I_3 + \sin\varphi \left[{}^0u_{sw}\times\right] + (1-\cos\varphi)\left[{}^0u_{sw}\times\right]^2 \tag{2}$$

$$^0R_i = {}^0R_\varphi {}^0R_i^{ini} \tag{3}$$

In this robot, the position of the manipulator's hand is only related to $\theta_1, \theta_2, \theta_3$, and θ_4. Therefore, this article first calculates these four angles. Among them, θ_4 represents the angle between the upper arm and the forearm. According to the mechanical structure, θ_4 is only related to the position of the manipulator's hand and the lengths of the upper and forearm. It can be directly calculated, as shown in Eq. 4. This leaves us with considering only the first three angles. From Eq. 3, $^0R_3$ can be expressed in terms of its initial state and the arm angle. Here, $^0R_3^{ini}$ needs to compute the initial values of θ_1 and θ_2, namely the values of θ_1 and θ_2 when θ_3 equals 0. It is important to note that, due to our DH parameter definition, at this moment when "$\theta_3 = 0$", the corresponding θ_3 should be set to 90°. When the above conditions are met, the angle of the shoulder still needs to satisfy the requirements of the manipulator's hand position. Therefore, θ_1^{ini} and θ_2^{ini} can be solved. This will be discussed in detail in Sect. 2.2.

Substituting Eq. 2 into Eq. 3, and setting i to 3 in Eq. 3, Formula 5 can be derived.

$$\theta_4 = \pi - \arccos\frac{l_{se}^2 + l_{ew}^2 - l_{sw}^2}{2l_{se}l_{ew}} \tag{4}$$

$$^0R_3 = A_s sin\varphi + B_s cos\varphi + C_s \qquad (5)$$

A_s, B_s and C_s are constant matrices given by

$$A_s = \left[^0u_{sw}\times\right]{}^0R_3^{ini} \qquad (6)$$

$$B_s = -\left[^0u_{sw}\times\right]^2{}^0R_3^{ini} \qquad (7)$$

$$C_s = {}^0u_{sw}{}^0u_{sw}^T{}^0R_3^{ini} \qquad (8)$$

and the rotation matrix $^0R_3$ is given by

$$^0R_3 = \begin{pmatrix} \times & \times & sin\theta_1 cos\theta_2 \\ cos\theta_2 sin\theta_3 & cos\theta_2 cos\theta_3 & -sin\theta_2 \\ \times & \times & cos\theta_1 cos\theta_2 \end{pmatrix} \qquad (9)$$

Where × represents the values that are not required for subsequent calculations. By equating the corresponding elements on both sides of Eq. 5, the formula for calculating the shoulder joint angles can be derived:

$$tan\theta_1 = \frac{a_{s13}sin\varphi + b_{s13}cos\varphi + c_{s13}}{a_{s33}sin\varphi + b_{s33}cos\varphi + c_{s33}} \qquad (10)$$

$$sin\theta_2 = -a_{s23}sin\varphi - b_{s23}cos\varphi - c_{s23} \qquad (11)$$

$$tan\theta_3 = \frac{a_{s21}sin\varphi + b_{s21}cos\varphi + c_{s21}}{a_{s22}sin\varphi + b_{s22}cos\varphi + c_{s22}} \qquad (12)$$

where a_{sij}, a_{sij} and a_{sij} are the (i, j) element of the matrices A_s, B_s and C_s, respectively. When the arm angle is determined, the shoulder joint angles can be calculated using these equations.

Similarly, by substituting Eq. 2 into Eq. 13, and then moving the known matrices to one side, Eq. 14 can be obtained.

$$^0R_7 = {}^0R_\varphi {}^0R_3^{ini}{}^3R_4{}^4R_7 \qquad (13)$$

$$^4R_7 = A_w sin\varphi + B_w cos\varphi + C_w \qquad (14)$$

Where A_w, B_w and C_w are constant matrices given by

$$A_w = {}^3R_4^T A_s^T {}^0R_7^T \qquad (15)$$

$$B_w = {}^3R_4^T B_s^T {}^0R_7^T \qquad (16)$$

$$C_w = {}^3R_4^T C_s^T {}^0R_7^T \qquad (17)$$

and the rotation matrix $^4R_7$ is given by

$$^4R_7 = \begin{pmatrix} \times & \times & sin\theta_5 cos\theta_6 \\ cos\theta_6 sin\theta_7 & cos\theta_6 cos\theta_7 & -sin\theta_6 \\ \times & \times & cos\theta_5 cos\theta_6 \end{pmatrix} \quad (18)$$

Where $\times$ represents the values that are not required for subsequent calculations. By equating the corresponding elements on both sides of Eq. 14, the formula for calculating the shoulder joint angles can be derived:

$$tan\theta_5 = \frac{a_{w13} sin\varphi + b_{w13} cos\varphi + c_{w13}}{a_{w33} sin\varphi + b_{w33} cos\varphi + c_{w33}} \quad (19)$$

$$sin\theta_6 = -a_{w23} sin\varphi - b_{w23} cos\varphi - c_{w23} \quad (20)$$

$$tan\theta_7 = \frac{a_{w21} sin\varphi + b_{w21} cos\varphi + c_{w21}}{a_{w22} sin\varphi + b_{w22} cos\varphi + c_{w22}} \quad (21)$$

At this point, the formulas for the 7 angles of the manipulator arm have all obtained. In the next section, this article will discuss issues such as singular points and multiple solutions encountered when the value of φ continuously changes.

2.2 Multiple Solution Problem Encountered During the Calculation

When φ continuously changes from $-\pi$ to π, the research aims for the joint angles to also change continuously: 1. Without jump discontinuities, as sudden changes are unattainable in reality; 2. Their derivatives are also continuous, which helps reduce impacts during the motion.

According to the research by Professor Masayuki Shimizu and his team, singular points can be obtained from the angle calculation formulas for a given T matrix. By setting a singular tolerance, a range of singular angles centered around the singular points can be generated. Setting the φ value in an interval far from this range of singular angles can help avoiding the influence of singular angles. In the initial calculation, this article uses nearby singular φ angles as replacements for the calculation strategy. Further elaboration is unnecessary here.

First, let us consider θ_4. Its formula contains an arccos function, which outputs values within the range of $[0, \pi]$. When a value x is determined, arccosx mathematically has both positive and negative solutions. However, θ_4 represents the angle between the two arms, which is always positive, so the negative solution does not affect the calculation.

From the above calculation, it can be seen that θ_1^{ini} and θ_2^{ini} are the foundation of the entire calculation process, determining its correctness. According to the calculation method described in Sect. 2.1, three equations for calculating θ_1^{ini} and θ_2^{ini} can be obtained:

$$p_x = -250 c_2 s_1 - 250 s_1 s_2 sin\theta_4 - 250 c_2 s_1 cos\theta_4 \quad (22)$$

$$p_y = 250 s_2 - 250 c_2 sin\theta_4 + 250 s_2 cos\theta_4 + 114 \quad (23)$$

$$p_z = -250c_2c_1 - 250c_1s_2\sin\theta_4 - 250c_1c_2\cos\theta_4 \qquad (24)$$

Where $c_i = \cos\theta_i^{ini}$, $s_i = \sin\theta_i^{ini}$, $i = 1, 2$.

It can be observed that p_y is only related to θ_2^{ini}, thus a formula for calculating θ_2^{ini} can be derived:

$$\theta_2^{ini} = \arcsin\frac{p_y - 114}{250\sqrt{2\cos\theta_4 + 2}} + \arctan\frac{\sin\theta_4}{1 + \cos\theta_4} \qquad (25)$$

Then, θ_1^{ini} can be calculated using p_x and p_z:

$$\theta_1^{ini} = \arcsin\frac{p_x - p_z}{-250\sqrt{2}\left[\cos\theta_2^{ini}(1 + \cos\theta_4) + \sin\theta_2^{ini}\sin\theta_4\right]} + \frac{\pi}{4} \qquad (26)$$

It can be seen that there are two types of calculation formulas: the arcsin type and the arctan type. The arcsin type returns values within the range of $[-\pi/2, \pi/2]$, but mathematically, it has solutions that fall on $[-\pi, -\pi/2]$ and $[\pi/2, \pi]$. Therefore, the calculated angles need to be adjusted accordingly:

$$\alpha' = \begin{cases} \pi - \alpha, \alpha > 0 \\ -\pi - \alpha, \alpha < 0 \\ \pi, \alpha = 0 \end{cases} \qquad (27)$$

Where α represents the value returned by the arcsin function. When $\alpha = 0$, there should be two possible corrections of $\pm\pi$, however, $\pm\pi$ are equivalent, so selecting either one for calculation is sufficient.

Similarly, corrections need to be applied for the arctan type as well:

$$\beta' = \begin{cases} \beta - \pi, \beta > 0 \\ \beta + \pi, \beta < 0 \\ \pi, \beta = 0 \end{cases} \qquad (28)$$

Where β represents the value returned by the arctan function. When $\beta = 0$, there should be two possible corrections of $\pm\pi$, however, $\pm\pi$ are equivalent, so selecting either one for calculation is sufficient.

Since the calculation formula for θ_1^{ini} involves θ_2^{ini}, and θ_2^{ini}, due to the aforementioned correction process, has uncertainty, θ_1^{ini} cannot be directly calculated. Fortunately, the calculation formula for θ_2^{ini} does not include θ_1^{ini}, so it can be calculated first. The formula for θ_2^{ini} includes one arcsin type and one arctan type, each producing two candidate values, resulting in four different θ_2^{ini} calculation results. Substituting each θ_2^{ini} into the calculation formula for θ_1^{ini} will generate two different candidate values for θ_1^{ini}, resulting in eight different candidate values for θ_1^{ini}. Thus, there will be 32 different combinations of θ_1^{ini} and θ_2^{ini}, among which only one combination will correctly satisfy the definitions of these two angles. That is, the position vector of the T matrix obtained by calculating the forward kinematics from $[\theta_1^{ini}, \theta_2^{ini}, \pi/2, \theta_4, \times, \times, \times]$ is the same as the position vector of the predetermined T matrix. Where "×" represents variables that have no effect on this calculation process and can be arbitrarily set.

The final step is to correct all joint angles except for θ_4. As shown by the previous calculations, formulas 10, 11, 12, 19, 20 and 21 are also of arcsin and arctan types, which can be corrected using formulas 27 and 28. Unlike correcting θ_1^{ini} and θ_2^{ini}, there are unknown combinations (up to 64) that satisfy their definitions, meaning the T matrix obtained by calculating the forward kinematics from $[\theta_1, \theta_2, \theta_3, \theta_4, \theta_5, \theta_6, \theta_7]$ is exactly the same as the predetermined T matrix. At this point, filtering out each set of solutions is needed. Before doing so, the research defines two types of jumps: normal jumps occur when the φ value is near its singular point, causing the joint angles to jump, which is unavoidable; abnormal jumps occur when selecting a set of solutions, resulting in jumps in certain joint angles from the previous φ angle to the next φ angle due to the multiple solutions problem. In some cases, this can be avoided by selecting the appropriate set of solutions. Professor Masayuki Shimizu's research shows that "normal jumps" result in jumps of π, and from our calculation process, in "abnormal jumps", the magnitude of jumps for arctan type is also π, while for arcsin type, the magnitude is uncertain. For example, when the value of arcsin x is 0, the magnitude of the "abnormal jump" is π, while when the value of arcsinx is 1, the magnitude of the "abnormal jump" is 0. Therefore, it is not always possible to accurately distinguish between the types of jumps at this moment (arctan type jumps are consistent with singular point jumps, while arcsin type jumps, when the magnitude is small, cannot be distinguished from normal continuous functions). In this case, this research can only calculate the total jump between each set of solutions and the previous solution and select the solution with the smallest jump as the optimal solution strategy. In summary, the criteria for selecting a set of solutions are as follows: (1) The joint angles are within the limits specified in Table 2; (2) No "abnormal jumps" occur compared to the solution obtained from the previous φ angle, i.e., the smallest jump.

This selection method brings another question: how to choose the solution for the joint angle combination under the first φ angle? The strategy this article adopt is to select the solution that best fits the range of joint angles in Table 2. If there is a solution that falls entirely within its restricted range, this research choose that set of solutions. If not, this article selects the solution with the smallest deviation from the restricted range.

These are solutions to specific problems encountered during the inverse kinematics calculation. Herein, programming experiments are conducted on our strategy and the following chart are obtained, as shown in Fig. 7 and formula (29).

Its default setting is:

$$T = \begin{bmatrix} 1 & 0 & 0 & 250 \\ 0 & -1 & 0 & -136 \\ 0 & 0 & -1 & 0 \\ 0 & 0 & 0 & 1 \end{bmatrix} \qquad (29)$$

The theoretically calculated singular points are: $\theta_1, \theta_2, \theta_3$ are singular at $\varphi = 0$, while the remaining joint angles do not experience singularities. Figure 3 further confirms the correctness of the theoretical calculation: θ_1 and θ_3 are of the arctan type and experience a "normal jump" of magnitude π at $\varphi = 0$, while θ_2 is of the arcsin type and experiences a singularity with a discontinuous derivative at $\varphi = 0$. Note that θ_5 undergoes a jump of magnitude 2π at $\varphi = 0$, which is a normal transition from $-\pi$

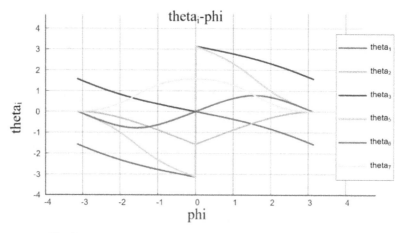

Fig. 3. The function plots of each joint angle θ_i with respect to φ

to π, not a singularity. Through this graph, this article can obtain all the IK solutions for a given pose. Furthermore, this article can select the optimal solution by applying various constraints, such as joint limits and avoiding singularities. If there exists a φ that satisfies the conditions under the constraints, the pose is achievable; otherwise, it is not. This will serve as the foundation for subsequent work.

Currently, the inverse kinematics solution for a given pose that satisfies the joint angle constraints is obtained. Next, this paper will put forward a method based on Fig. 3 to determine whether an inverse kinematics solution exists for a given pose. By applying the method to analyze various points in the space, the desired capability map will be acquired.

3 The Capability Map of the Robot

The robot's capability map is composed of the dexterity values of various points in space, representing the robot's dexterity within the workspace. To obtain the capability map, this article needs to uniformly discretizes the pose matrix first. Then, based on the discretization method, the research establishes a method for calculating the dexterity value of a point (3.1). Next, the criteria for determining whether there is an inverse kinematic solution for a certain pose are established (3.2). Finally, by calculating the dexterity value of various points in space using these criteria, the capability map is proposed (3.3).

3.1 Uniformly Discretize Poses and the Dexterity Calculation Criteria

Due to the uniformly discretized joint angles in joint space, the Cartesian space poses obtained from forward kinematics are not uniform. They are densely distributed at singular points and cannot be used as a method for distributing poses. Professor Gerhard Kurz [14] present a novel discretization method that is based on a quaternion representation in conjunction with a recursive subdivision scheme of the four-dimensional hypercube, also known as the tesseract. While this method allows for the direct discretization of SO(3), its underlying principles are complex, making it challenging to implement in programming. This article adopts the method of first uniformly discretizing one axis of the coordinate system and then rotating the coordinate system around this axis to distribute poses uniformly. For positions, the space is evenly divided into equally sized voxels, and the centers of the voxels are taken as the coordinates of the position points.

Using the method proposed by Professors E. Saff and A. Kuijlaars [15] for uniformly distributing points on a sphere, this article obtained the spherical coordinates of each point on the sphere. By rotating a coordinate system coinciding with the static coordinate system according to these spherical coordinate parameters, this article can obtain a coordinate system with the z-axis pointing to the uniformly distributed points on the sphere. Setting this coordinate system as the reference (0 position), rotating around the z-axis yields different poses. Assuming there are m points uniformly distributed on the sphere, and each coordinate system corresponding to a point rotates n times around the z-axis (a total rotation of 360°), then at the center of a voxel, this article can obtain mn uniformly distributed poses. Professor Zacharias F. [16] in his study of the DLR-LWR robotic arm, treated each point on the sphere as a basic unit. He examined the final step of rotating n coordinate systems around the z-axis. If at least one pose matrix could be achieved, he considered this basic unit achievable. The final dexterity index was then the ratio of achievable sphere points to the total. This was because the rotation axis of the last joint of the robot coincided with the z-axis (roll axis). Our robot's joint configuration differs from this, so this article treated each coordinate system rotated around the z-axis as a basic unit and assessed its achievability. This method has better general applicability because it can be used for the next steps regardless of whether the last axis is a roll axis (if the angle of the last axis does not affect the dexterity of the spherical point, then the dexterity of each point in space will increase by the same value). To simplify calculations, the dexterity index was based on the number of achievable poses, rather than their ratio to the total number of poses (FIg. 4).

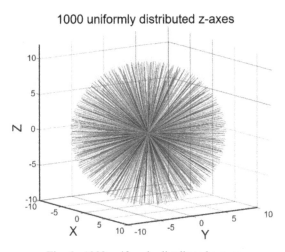

Fig. 4. 1000 uniformly distributed z-axes

When the joint angles are unrestricted and can rotate arbitrarily, the robot can achieve any pose within its workspace. However, when the joint angles are limited (as specified in Table 2), the achievable poses will be reduced. Given a pose, this article can use the method described in Sect. 2 to plot the angle curves that each joint angle needs to reach in order to achieve this pose. Based on the following two criteria, the research selects the arm angle value:

1. The joint angles must be within the limitation range at the given arm angle φ.
2. The arm angle φ must be away from singular points ($\varphi \notin$ [singularity-tolerance, singularity + tolerance], where tolerance = 0.1 rad).

Using these two criteria, this article can obtain φ that both meet the joint angle limits and avoid singular points (if such φ exist). After filtering, if there are still usable φ values, it means that the pose can be achieved. If not, it indicates that the pose cannot be achieved. To expedite the computation, assess the reachability of positions first. If reachable, then proceed with the aforementioned evaluations.

3.2 Analysis of the Capability Map

Analyzing the dexterity of each point in a plane allows for the generation of the capability map. By discretizing various points in the $z = 0$ plane, with $x \in [-500, 500]$ and $y \in [-386, 614]$ divided into 32 regions each, this article obtained 1024 positions for the robot. Thirty points were uniformly distributed on each sphere at every position, with each point corresponding to a coordinate system rotating 12 times around the z-axis, at intervals of 30°, resulting in 360 poses generated at each voxel center. The number of achievable poses by the robot serves as the dexterity value for each point. The dexterity of each point is depicted in the following graph (Fig. 5).

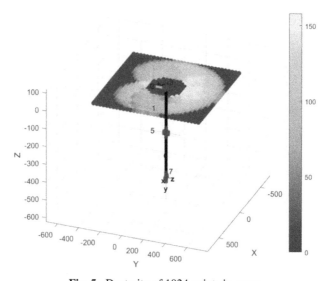

Fig. 5. Dexterity of 1024 points in space

The top-down view is shown in Fig. 6. This diagram exhibits characteristics similar to the conclusions of Professor Franziska[11]:

1. Overall, as the distance from the shoulder equivalent ball joint increases, the robot's dexterity decreases. When the distance exceeds 500mm, the dexterity of the robot becomes zero, as it surpasses the total length of the robot.
2. The diagram illustrates that in the z = 0 plane, the robot exhibits the highest dexterity in the region approximately between y = 250 and y = 450, which corresponds to the mid to far portion of the robot's "front end." Due to the wide range of θ_2 angle restrictions, there are also regions with relatively high dexterity in the area symmetrically positioned around y = 114. The dexterity in these regions reaches roughly half of all achievable poses, mainly due to the limited range of θ_6 and θ_7.
3. Within approximately a 170 mm radius centered at the shoulder ball joint, this is attributed to the angle restriction of θ_4. Specifically, as shown in Fig. 7, the smaller the minimum angle between the two arms, the smaller the zero-dexterity region near the shoulder. With θ_4 restricted to $[-\pi/2, 7\pi/9]$, for the "front" of the mechanical arm, where both arms are positioned in the region where z < 0; and for the "rear" of the mechanical arm, where θ_2's restriction range exceeds 180°, both arms can be positioned in the region where z > 0. Hence, the minimum angle between the two arms in the "rear" configuration is $(1-7/9)\pi = 40°$. Using cosine theorem, the radius of the unreachable region (indicated by the red lines) can be calculated to be 171mm. The blue lines in the figure represent the reachable region. The "rear" configuration distinguished by the """ in the upper right corner.
4. The dexterity diagram in front of the robot presents a complete semicircle, while the dexterity diagram behind is truncated, which is caused by the limitation of θ_1. The region within ±30° behind cannot be realized.

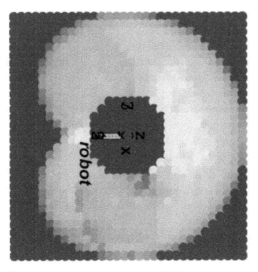

Fig. 6. Top view of Dexterity of 1024 points in space

5. The image is generally symmetrical, but in the front, the upper side consistently exhibits slightly better dexterity, while in the rear, the lower side shows slightly better dexterity. This is caused by the asymmetry in the limitation range of θ_4.

By removing the $z = 0$ constraint, this article will obtain the dexterity data for points in the space for this robot. Similar to Fig. 6, there will be regions with zero dexterity and regions with higher dexterity. This information can be utilized for optimizing robot path planning and task allocation to ensure that the robot efficiently accomplishes tasks within its workspace.

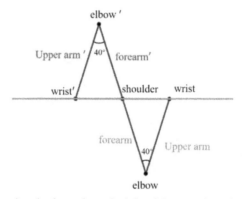

Fig. 7. Diagram illustrating the formation principle of the zero dexterity region centered at the shoulder.

4   Conclusion

This article first improves the process of solving inverse kinematics, focusing on addressing the issue of multiple solutions. Next, by establishing a criterion for determining whether a given pose has an inverse kinematics solution, the issue of avoiding singularities is resolved. Thirdly, by developing a more general method for calculating the dexterity value of a point, the research resolves the issue of computation strategies being non-universal for different rotational joint configurations. Lastly, based on the proposed approach, this paper creates a capability map of the robot, conducts qualitative and quantitative analyses of the robot, and explains the characteristics and formation reasons of this map. This diagram exhibits characteristics similar to the conclusions of Professor Zacharias, demonstrating its correctness. Through analysis, this map generally aligns with real-world expectations and provides valuable insights for subsequent tasks such as obstacle avoidance. Subsequently, we will apply this map in trajectory planning tasks to further verify its accuracy.

References

1. Stejskal, T., Svetlík, J., Ondočko, Š: Mapping robot singularities through the Monte Carlo method. Appl. Sci. **12**(16), 8330 (2022)
2. Simas, H., Di Gregorio, R.: A technique based on adaptive extended Jacobians for improving the robustness of the inverse numerical kinematics of redundant robots. J. Mech. Robot. **11**(2), 020913 (2019)
3. Miteva, L., Pavlova, G., Trifonov, R., Yovchev, K.: Manipulability analysis of redundant robotic manipulator. In: Proceedings of the 21st International Conference on Computer Systems and Technologies, pp. 135–140 (2020)
4. Li, W., Xiong, R.: Dynamical obstacle avoidance of task-constrained mobile manipulation using model predictive control. IEEE Access **7**, 88301–88311 (2019)
5. Taunyazov, T., Zhang, H., Eala, J.P., Zhao, N., Soh, H.: Refining 6-DoF grasps with context-specific classifiers. In: 2023 IEEE/RSJ International Conference on Intelligent Robots and Systems (IROS), pp. 6861–6867. IEEE (2023)
6. Sinha, A., Chakraborty, N.: Geometric search-based inverse kinematics of 7-dof redundant manipulator with multiple joint offsets. In: 2019 International Conference on Robotics and Automation (ICRA), pp. 5592–5598. IEEE (2019)
7. Wang, S., Liu, Z., Ma, Z., Chang, H., Huang, P., Lu, Z.: A closed-form solution for inverse kinematics of redundant space manipulator with multiple joint offsets. Adv. Space Res. **72**(5), 1844–1860 (2023)
8. Tringali, A., Cocuzza, S.: Globally optimal inverse kinematics method for a redundant robot manipulator with linear and nonlinear constraints. Robotics **9**(3), 61 (2020)
9. Shimizu, M., Kakuya, H., Yoon, W.-K., Kitagaki, K., Kosuge, K.: Analytical inverse kinematic computation for 7-DOF redundant manipulators with joint limits and its application to redundancy resolution. IEEE Trans. Robot. **24**(5), 1131–1142 (2008)
10. He, Z., Wang, J., Zhang, X., Huang, G., Song, M., Fu, J.: Dexterous workspace analysis of industrial robot for machining based on service sphere. In: 2021 IEEE International Conference on Robotics and Biomimetics (ROBIO), pp. 469–474 (2021)
11. Zacharias, F., Borst, C., Hirzinger, G.: Capturing robot workspace structure: representing robot capabilities. In: 2007 IEEE/RSJ International Conference on Intelligent Robots and Systems, vol. 16, no. 2, pp. 3229–3236 (2007)
12. Li, C., Wang, N., Chen, K., Zhang, X.: Prescribed flexible orientation workspace and performance comparison of non-redundant 3-DOF planar parallel mechanisms. Mech. Mach. Theory **168**, 104602 (2022)
13. Zhao, J., et al.: Inverse kinematics and workspace analysis of a novel SSRMS-type reconfigurable space manipulator with two lockable passive telescopic links. Mech. Mach. Theory **180**, 105152 (2023)
14. Kurz, G., Pfaff, F., Hanebeck, U.D.: Discretization of SO (3) using recursive tesseract subdivision. In: 2017 IEEE International Conference on Multisensor Fusion and Integration for Intelligent Systems (MFI), pp. 49–55. IEEE (2017)
15. Saff, E.B., Kuijlaars, A.B.J.: Distributing many points on a sphere. Math. Intell. **19**, 5–11 (1997)
16. Zacharias, F., Borst, C., Wolf, S., Hirzinger, G.: The capability map: a tool to analyze robot arm workspaces. Int. J. Humanoid Robot. **10**(04), 1350031 (2013)

Path Planning and Gait Switching for Quadruped Robots in Perceptually Complex Environments

Weijun Tian[1], Kuiyue Zhou[1], Jian Song[1], Xu Li[1], Zhu Chen[1], Ziteng Shen[1], Ruizhi Wang[2], Lei Jiang[2], and Qian Cong[1(✉)]

[1] Key Labotatory of Bionic Engineering of Ministry of Education, Jilin University, Changchun 130022, China
congqian@jlu.edu.cn
[2] North-Vehicle Research, Fengtai District, Beijing 100072, China

Abstract. There are still many challenges in achieving stable movement and adaptability to different terrains for quadruped robots in unstructured environments. This paper, based on the Gazebo simulation platform, utilizes LiDAR as the primary means of environmental perception, supplemented by a depth camera, to achieve efficient perception and recognition of complex environments. To address the task requirements of quadruped robots, a comprehensive environmental perception and navigation system was developed, including global map construction, local navigation map generation, precise balance control, and global positioning. Based on the generated global and local maps, path planning for the quadruped robot was achieved using a sliding window A* path planning algorithm. Finally, by perceiving obstacles and adjusting speed in real-time, speed commands are sent to the robot controller, enabling real-time gait switching and obstacle avoidance, thereby enhancing the quadruped robot's ability to cope with complex environments. A complete framework was developed for quadruped robots based on recognizing and perceiving complex environments, conducting path planning, and switching gaits in real-time.

Keywords: Complex environment perception · Route planning · Real-time gait switching

1 Introduction

In the field of footed robots, quadrupedal robots are one of the most popular research directions [1]. Quadrupedal robots can quickly adapt and cope with various challenges in complex environments, and are able to autonomously cross obstacles, climb stairs, and cope with complex terrains like living beings, which can be widely used in military, industrial, and social service fields [2–4]. However, there are still many challenges to their stable movement in unstructured environments and their ability to adapt to different terrains [5]. The first problem to be solved is to efficiently recognize complex environments for path planning, based on which different gaits are adopted for different environments to enhance motion stability and adaptability.

In recent years, the perception of complex terrain and robot localization have been deeply studied at home and abroad. Depth camera, as an important tool in the field of robotics and computer vision, provides us with the ability to acquire three-dimensional spatial information [6]. Saudabayev [7] et al. used a depth camera as an effective tool for terrain recognition, and achieved 96.71% accuracy in recognizing five types of terrains, namely, uneven, flat ground, staircase upward, staircase downward, and impenetrable, which helped the hybrid robots with multiple motion modes to choose their motion strategies. LIDAR, as an advanced active remote sensing technology, can detect, localize, and identify targets by emitting laser pulses and receiving their signals reflected back from the target [8, 9], which has the advantages of high density and high resolution, and can provide rich environmental information [10]. Steinvall [11] and others have shown that 3D LIDAR can be widely used in robotics, fast terrain visualization, augmented vision, reconnaissance and target recognition, weapon guidance (including aiming point selection), etc. It can rapidly generate 3D target information and efficiently recognize complex terrain. After solving the problem of perception and recognition of complex terrain, researchers have proposed a series of solutions for path planning of quadruped robots. Jin [12] et al. proposed a fusion algorithm to reach a specified target area quickly and safely in complex dynamic environments. By optimizing the parameters and improving the structure of the algorithm, the obstacle avoidance function of the algorithm in complex environments was improved. Angulo [13] et al. proposed a strategy optimization algorithm for learning adaptive motion primitives to find the next action strategy by using reinforcement learning method to address the problem of poor real-time path planning in dynamic and static environments. Tonola [14] et al. proposed a strategy optimization algorithm to address the problem of mobile robots being unable to cope with the possibility of moving and unforeseen obstacles in unstructured environments in time. Problem, proposed a strategy based on sampling path replanning, which can reduce the search complexity even in complex high-dimensional scenarios, and thus achieve the purpose of optimizing the path. On this basis, how to switch different gaits for different environments on a given path has become a new research hotspot. Lee [15] proposed a quasi-dynamic gait called hybrid walking gait and a new gait switching algorithm for quadrupedal walking robots, which generates the original end-of-foot trajectory by using some easy-to-define parameters. Liu [16] proposed a gait transition method for quadrupedal robots based on changing time series, swing phase and stance. Transition method, where the swing phase and stance phase are separated by a finite state machine (FSM), and the sequence of leg hopping events is changed so that the durations of the hopping and touchdown events are variable, and gait drive is realized through the combination of time and event drive. Chen [17] proposed a novel gait switching based on a flexible gait planner (FGP) and a gait feedback regulator (GFR) with behavioral rules. Hierarchical control framework. This gait planner selects the optimal foothold and changes the gait type based on safe footholds and leg stability margins and motion margins. Koo [18] et al. proposed a quasi-static gait transition control method for a quadrupedal walking robot, based on the observation of the locomotory behavior of quadrupedal animals exhibiting abrupt and discrete changes in velocity-dependent gait patterns, by predefining the gait transition patterns and based on the current and desired leg postures thus determining the gait sequence.

At this stage, the tasks of quadrupedal robots in environment perception mainly include the acquisition of information about the state of environmental structures, map construction and localization. The correlation between the perception tasks and the subsequent model control part is not strong, resulting in the advantages of environment perception not being fully utilized. Moreover, the traditional quadruped robot control method has great limitations in the application of dynamic unknown environment. Therefore, in this paper, through the perception and identification of complex environment, real-time map construction and localization, on the basis of path planning, the distance between the robot and obstacles is obtained through environment perception, the safe speed is calculated, and the speed command is transmitted to the controller to select the appropriate gait to realize gait switching, which gives full play to the advantages of environment perception. Switching, giving full play to the potential of environment perception to realize more intelligent and autonomous navigation, obstacle avoidance and target tracking functions.

2 Methods

2.1 Complex Environment Perception and Map Construction and Localization

Quadruped robots perceive complex environments, and the ways of acquiring environmental information are divided into two main categories: one is depth camera-based environmental sensing, and the other is LiDAR-based environmental sensing. In this paper, LIDAR-based environmental sensing is adopted, and depth camera is used as an auxiliary to make the quadruped robot localization and map building more accurate. Using multi-sensor fusion technology, the environmental information obtained by LiDAR, depth camera and IMU, as well as the robot's own motion state information are filtered or optimized to obtain a relatively accurate environmental information and the robot's state information, so as to build a map of the surrounding environment and localize the robot in the map.

The walking and obstacle avoidance functions of the quadruped robot require it to have high-precision environment sensing ability, so it obtains real-time information about the surrounding environment through sensors such as LiDAR, including the location, shape, size of obstacles and the height of the ground. This information will be used as the basic data for robot decision-making and planning. In order to realize global navigation, a global map needs to be constructed for the robot. The map should contain all the key information about the robot's working environment, such as the walkable area, obstacle locations, and target points. However, the global map cannot fully meet the real-time navigation needs of the robot. Because in the actual operation process, the robot may encounter some unknown obstacles or dangerous situations. At this point, it is necessary to use sensors such as LiDAR to generate local navigation maps in real time, so that the robot can adjust the trajectory and landing point in time.

In addition, quadrupedal robots also need to carry out accurate balance control during the movement process. This requires the ability to obtain the robot's state information in real time, such as attitude, velocity, acceleration, etc., and calculate the actual position of the robot based on this information. By matching with the global map, the exact position of the robot in the global coordinate system can be determined, thus realizing global localization. The simulation model of the quadruped robot is built in Gazebo as shown in Fig. 1.

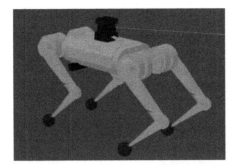

Fig. 1. Simulation model under Gazebo.

Aiming at the task requirements of quadruped robots, a set of complete environment sensing and navigation system including global map construction, local navigation map generation, precise balance control and global localization is constructed. This system can provide the robot with omni-directional and multi-level environment sensing capabilities, ensuring that it can stably and efficiently accomplish tasks in various complex environments.

2.2 A* Path Planning Algorithm Based on Sliding Window

After completing the perception of the complex environment and map construction and localization, the quadruped robot is subjected to path planning. Path planning is divided into global path planning and local path planning. Given a start point and a goal point, a smooth curve with the shortest distance is planned according to the environment map built in advance to guide the goal point to complete the global planning. Local path planning is to compensate for the shortcomings of global path planning, through the quadruped robot movement process of real-time sensors to build a local environment map for planning. As the global path planning is based on the established map for planning and does not take into account the map will temporarily add or reduce certain obstacles, resulting in the planned path is not optimal, and add local path planning can help the robot to understand the surrounding environment, so that it can be updated in a timely manner to the planned global path, to achieve the shortening of the distance to the goal or obstacle avoidance function.

The traditional A* pathfinding algorithm is suitable for static environment and can be used for global path planning, but for the obstacles that appear suddenly, there is the problem of not being able to adjust the path in time to achieve the avoidance effect. Therefore, the A* path planning algorithm with sliding window is used for local path planning. The essence of the sliding window is a dynamically updated local map, which moves with the robot and always contains the current position of the robot and a certain area around it. Within this local map, path planning using the A* algorithm ensures that the most up-to-date information about the environment is perceived at each planning time.

2.3 Gait Switching in Different Environments

The safety distance is determined by measuring the distance between the quadruped robot and the surrounding obstacles, calculating the feasible velocity range, obtaining a velocity value in the interval, and feeding the velocity command to the controller, which selects the optimal gait that matches the velocity to achieve the effect of autonomous gait switching.

3 Results and Analysis

3.1 Map Construction

The steps of global map building process usually include the following stages:

1. Environmental information acquisition: environmental information is acquired through sensors such as LiDAR and cameras. LIDAR can scan the surrounding environment and obtain distance and location information of obstacles, while cameras can obtain richer visual information. This information is the basis for constructing the global map.
2. Feature Extraction and Matching: Through feature extraction of the collected environmental information, key feature points in the environment, such as corner points and edges, are extracted. Meanwhile, feature matching is carried out to match the features collected by different sensors or at different times to establish a consistent representation of the environment.
3. Map construction and updating: on the basis of feature extraction and matching, the global map is constructed. Based on the extracted feature points and matching results, the positional relationship of the elements in the environment can be determined, and then the global map can be constructed. In addition, with the movement of the robot and the acquisition of new environment information, the global map needs to be updated and maintained to keep the accuracy and real-time performance of the map.
4. Map optimization and correction: In order to improve the accuracy and stability of the global map, the map is optimized and corrected. Methods such as loopback detection are utilized to detect and correct accumulated errors in the map, and multi-sensor fusion technology is utilized to improve the robustness and accuracy of the map.

In this paper, 3D LiDAR and Cartographer algorithm are used to build the map, which mainly relies on 2D planar information in the process of constructing the global map [19]. Therefore the point cloud data is projected onto the 2D plane. This conversion is achieved by using the pointcloud_to_laserscan method, which efficiently converts 3D line bundles to 2D line bundles.

The Cartographer algorithm is applicable to both 2D and 3D scenes [20]. It consists of two main components, Local SLAM and Global SLAM. Local SLAM is responsible for constructing a series of submaps by processing the scans data and incorporating new scans using scan matching technique. Global SLAM, on the other hand, adds submaps through closed-loop detection and builds a global map. The closed-loop detection adopts the efficient Branch-and-Bound Approach (BBA) to realize the scan matching, and the specific flow is shown in Fig. 2.

The IMU (Inertial Measurement Unit) projects the tilted data to the horizontal plane by attitude detection and gravity direction in the global map construction and provides the initial predicted values [21]. Ceres scan matcher utilizes the data integrated by the IMU to perform position optimization. Meanwhile, the method is also able to set the corresponding weight parameters according to the demand in order to realize more accurate matching effect.

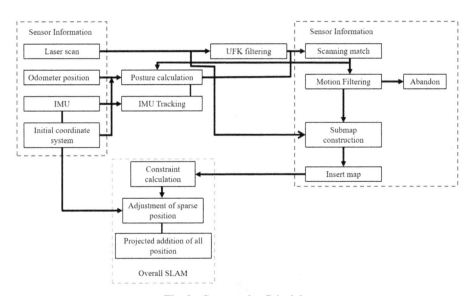

Fig. 2. Cartographer Principle.

The environment map built by the quadruped robot in Gazebo is shown in Fig. 3(a). The global map obtained by using Cartographer's algorithm is shown in Fig. 3(b). The global map is rasterized, which is based on the principle of dividing a continuous space into a series of discrete raster cells, each of which represents a specific region or state. This processing method can simplify the representation and computation of the map, making it easier for robots or other intelligences to understand and use the map information. In global map rasterization processing, the map is usually divided into uniformly sized rasters, and each raster is assigned a specific value or attribute, such as indicating whether the area is an obstacle, passable, etc. By rasterizing the global map it is also possible to easily implement operations such as storing, querying and updating the map [22]. In addition, the rasterized map can be combined with algorithms such as path planning, navigation, etc., to provide reliable environment sensing and decision support for robots or other intelligences. The obtained rasterized map is shown in Fig. 3(c).

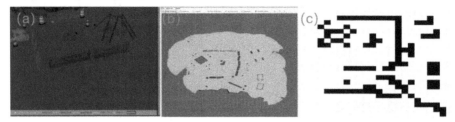

Fig. 3. Global map construction. (a) Simulation environment; (b) Global map; (c) Gridded map.

Local maps and global maps are basically the same in the way they are constructed, and their differences are, firstly, different scopes: local maps usually only cover the environment around the robot, while global maps cover the whole application scene or area; secondly, different real-time features: local maps are usually constructed in real time to reflect the current state of the environment, while global maps can be pre-constructed, or constructed step by step during operation; in addition, different accuracy requirements, since local maps only cover the surrounding environment, their accuracy and detail requirements are usually higher than global maps to ensure the safety and accurate navigation; finally, different update frequencies. In addition, the accuracy requirements are different: since local maps only cover the surrounding environment, their accuracy and detail requirements are usually higher than those of global maps to ensure the safety and accurate navigation of robots or vehicles; finally, the update frequency is different: local maps need to be updated in real time with the movement of robots to reflect the changes in the environment, while global maps are updated relatively infrequently. The local map construction is shown in Fig. 4.

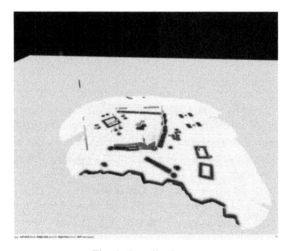

Fig. 4. Localized map.

3.2 Laser Positioning Algorithm

Initialization Positioning

Initialized positioning determines the starting position of the robot in global space. In Gazebo, a virtual simulation environment for quadruped robots, the initial position data is directly accessible. When the robot is stationary, the system can obtain this position information by subscribing to a specific topic (e.g., model_state).

Two important coordinate systems are included in the localization process: the Map coordinate system and the Odom coordinate system. The Map coordinate system is the coordinate system used by the robot when constructing the map, which is the reference frame for the map data. The Odom coordinate system, on the other hand, is the reference coordinate system when the robot moves, and it records the robot's trajectory. During the initialization and localization process, these two coordinate systems are overlapped to form a common reference system for subsequent navigation and motion control of the robot. As shown in Fig. 5.

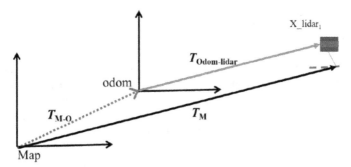

Fig. 5. Coordinate system related to laser positioning.

In Fig. 5, TM stands for the transformation of the Map coordinate system to the Lidar coordinate system, TM-O stands for the transformation of the Map coordinate system to the Odom coordinate system, and TOdom-Lidar stands for the transformation of the Odom coordinate system to the Lidar coordinate system.

Laser Point Cloud Processing

The point cloud filtering, which plays a central role in processing LiDAR data, is processed first. Although the raw point cloud data can show the details of the environment in detail, they usually contain a large number of discrete and isolated points, which may cause interference for subsequent analysis. Therefore, these raw data need to be filtered to distill purer and more useful information. To achieve this goal, a statistical filtering algorithm is used in this paper. The main purpose of this algorithm is to remove unnecessary data points. Assuming that there are n neighboring points near a point a in the point cloud, and the distance from a to them is d_j, the average distance d_{ave} from point a to them is calculated as:

$$d_{ave} = \frac{\sum_{j=1}^{n} d_j}{n} \tag{1}$$

Based on d_{ave} the mean μ and standard deviation σ are calculated, and σ describes the degree of dispersion of these distance values. Combining μ and σ, a reasonable distance threshold d_{thr} is set. If the mean distance d_{ave} of point r exceeds this threshold, then point a is considered to be a noisy point and it is removed from the point cloud data.

$$d_{thr} = \mu \pm \cdot \sigma \cdot \alpha \tag{2}$$

Second, ground point clouds are removed. Distinguishing ground point clouds from non-ground point clouds is critical for accurately identifying roadway obstacles when processing environmental sensing data. Obstacles are separated before clustering to eliminate ground point clouds from interfering with the clustering. Considering the mounting height of the LiDAR on the robot, this paper first excludes point cloud data that are obviously too high, as they are likely not ground point clouds. In order to separate the ground point cloud more precisely, this paper adopts the RANSAC (Randomized Sampling Consistent) algorithm.

The core idea of the RANSAC algorithm is to find an optimal mathematical model to describe the distribution of point cloud data by iterating. In each iteration, the algorithm randomly selects a small number of points from the original point cloud dataset and uses these points to fit a planar model. The algorithm evaluates how well the remaining points match that planar model, treating those points that fit the model as in-points (i.e., terrestrial point clouds) and those that do not as out-points (i.e., non-terrestrial or noisy point clouds). Through multiple iterations and comparing the effects of different models, the RANSAC algorithm is eventually able to determine a planar model that best fits the distribution of the point cloud data. Using this model, ground point clouds can be accurately distinguished from non-ground point clouds, thus avoiding misidentifying ground point clouds as obstacle point clouds. This processing method not only improves the accuracy of obstacle clustering, but also provides a reliable data base for subsequent navigation tasks.

Next, laser point cloud matching is performed. Normal Distribution Transformation (NDT) is a unique point cloud matching algorithm that utilizes the statistical properties of the 3D point cloud to construct a multi-dimensional normal distribution model of the reference points. When two frames of point cloud data are well matched, the probability density between them is relatively high, which reflects the similarity and consistency between the point cloud data. Compared with traditional point cloud matching methods, the NDT algorithm performs well in terms of localization accuracy and matching speed. It not only realizes high-precision localization, but also its matching speed is faster compared to the ICP (Iterative Nearest Point) algorithm, which gives the NDT algorithm an advantage in application scenarios with high real-time and accuracy requirements.

In the NDT algorithm, the point cloud data is mapped onto a smooth plane and a probability density function (PDF) is used to describe the shape of the surface. Through an optimization approach, the algorithm seeks the transformation matrix that maximizes the sum of the probability densities, which includes transformations such as translations and rotations. To solve this problem, the NDT algorithm employs Newton's method to optimize the maximized likelihood to obtain the corresponding point cloud transformation parameters. The mesh probability density function of the algorithm is a mathematical model used to describe the probability of the distribution of points in the point cloud data. With the function in Eq. 3, the NDT algorithm is able to capture the statistical properties of the point cloud data more accurately, and thus achieve more precise point cloud matching and localization.

$$p(x) = \frac{1}{\sigma\sqrt{2\pi}} \exp(-\frac{(x-\mu)^2}{2\sigma^2}) \qquad (3)$$

Based on the above elements a multi-sensor system is composed and the flow of multi-sensor fusion strategy used in this paper is shown in Fig. 6.

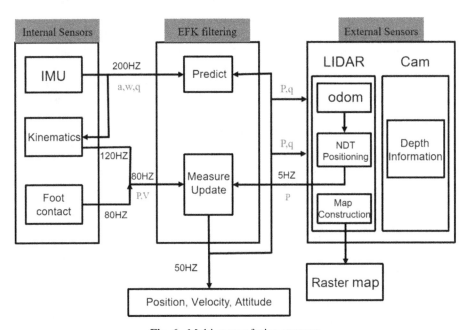

Fig. 6. Multi-sensor fusion strategy.

3.3 Path Planning Algorithm

The steps of the sliding window A* based path algorithm are:

1. map construction: a previously constructed gridded map is utilized, in which each grid represents a small area, which can be a passable open space, an obstacle or an unknown area. On this map, the current and calibrated positions of the robot are set as the starting and ending points for path planning.
2. Sliding Window Setting: On the grid map, a sliding window is created with the current position of the robot as the center. The size of this window needs to be adjusted according to the actual situation to ensure that it can cover all the areas that the robot may move to. At the same time, the size of the window will also affect the efficiency and response speed of the algorithm.

3. Path planning: Inside the sliding window, the A* algorithm is used for path planning. The current position of the robot is set as the start node and the target position is set as the end point, after which a heuristic function (the sum of the total cost g(n) from the start node to the target node and the estimated cost h(n) from the current node to the target node) is utilized to guide the search process. Since the value of g(n) is a fixed value computed from the identified path nodes, the key of the algorithm is to find the minimum value of h(n). To achieve the above, two lists are generally used: the OPEN list holds the traversable nodes and the CLOSE list holds the traversed nodes. Continuously iterating and updating the open list and the close list can find the optimal path from the start node to the end point. The schematic diagram of A* algorithm based on sliding window is shown in Fig. 7.
4. Dynamic update: As the robot moves and the environment changes, the sliding window needs to be constantly updated. After each update, the start node is put into the OPEN list and traverse the surrounding eight nodes with this node as the parent node and put them into the OPEN list. At the same time, the start node is put into the CLOSE list. Next, calculate the f(n) value of all the nodes in the open list and select the node with the smallest f(n) as the next parent. Keep looping the process until the target node is traversed. Eventually, a shortest path is connected by each grid node that has been traversed as a parent node. The simulation process is shown in Figs. 8.

3.4 Gait Switching

Obstacle Distance Calculation

The obstacle distance is first calculated for stationary obstacles or known obstacles, and the distance between the robot and the obstacle is obtained by using the previously created global map to get the position information of the obstacle and combining it with the robot's own position. Obstacles around the robot can also be detected using laser sensors or vision sensors. LIDAR gets the distance to the obstacle by measuring the time of flight of the laser and multiplying it by the speed of light to get the round trip distance. Vision sensors utilize a depth camera to get the depth information of the obstacles directly within the camera's view angle, thus getting the distance of the obstacles.

Determination of Safety Distances

Next determine the safe distance, the safe distance Ssafe is the minimum distance from an obstacle that the robot must maintain to ensure that a collision does not occur. That is, the distance required for the robot to come to a complete stop from its current speed at maximum deceleration. A safe distance threshold is determined based on the robot's dimensions, kinematic properties, and safety requirements.

By the basic physical equations of motion 4:

$$v^2 = u^2 + 2as \quad (4)$$

Therefore, the safe distance S_{safe} can be calculated by Eq. 5:

$$S_{safe} = \frac{V_{cur}^2}{2 \times a_{max}} \quad (5)$$

Fig. 7. Schematic diagram of sliding window A* algorithm.

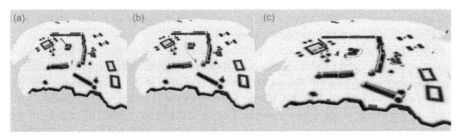

Fig. 8. Schematic diagram of simulation process. (a) Initial location map; (b) Global path planning map; (c) Localized path planning maps.

where a_{max} denotes the maximum deceleration of the robot, i.e., the maximum braking force that the robot can exert in an emergency situation. V_{cur} denotes the current speed of the robot.

As can be seen from Eq. 5, the a_{max} of the robot needs to be calculated before deriving the safe distance. When determining the a_{max}, a certain safety margin should be allowed to ensure that the braking performance of the robot will not be significantly degraded due to external factors (e.g., slippery surfaces, load variations, etc.) in real-world applications. This process may require several iterations and adjustments to obtain a_{max} values that are both safe and effective.

Newton's second law can be used to calculate deceleration. The braking force F is equal to the robot's mass m multiplied by the deceleration a. However, the braking force is also limited by the friction between the tires and the ground, which is equal to the robot's weight multiplied by the coefficient of friction µ. The coefficient of friction, µ, usually ranges from 0 to 1, depending on the material and condition of the ground. For example, dry concrete may have a high coefficient of friction (about 0.7 to 0.9), while wet or icy surfaces may have a low coefficient of friction (about 0.2 to 0.4). The coefficient of friction is thus set to 0.6 in the system.

Setting the braking force equal to the friction force gives Eq. 6, which solves for the deceleration a.

$$F = ma$$
$$F_{friction} = \mu \cdot m \cdot g \tag{6}$$

Further the value of maximum deceleration a_{max} can be deduced from Eq. 6.

$$a_{max} = F_{friction}/m = \mu \cdot g \tag{7}$$

Where g is the acceleration of gravity, which is about 9.81 m/s², the maximum deceleration $a_{max} = 0.6 \times 9.81 \approx 6.87$ m/s².

Calculation of the Feasible Speed Range

Finally, the feasible speed range is calculated. Based on the distance to the obstacle and the safe distance threshold, the maximum velocity at which the robot can safely pass is calculated. Also, a feasible velocity range is determined by considering the robot's kinematic constraints. This range should ensure that the robot will neither collide with an obstacle nor exceed its kinematic capabilities.

The safety margin S_{mar} is a very important parameter that ensures that the robot has enough space to stop in case of an emergency braking to avoid collision with an obstacle. The choice of safety margin should be based on the size of the robot and the specific application environment. It is a common and conservative practice to choose half the height of the robot as the safety margin. This is because the center of gravity of the robot may shift forward during an emergency stop, especially if the robot is fast or has a low coefficient of friction on the ground. Choosing half the height as a safety margin ensures that even in this case, the robot has enough room to come to a complete stop without making contact with an obstacle. In practice, the robot control system constantly measures the distance to the obstacle and dynamically adjusts the speed of the quadruped robot to maintain safety.

In order to calculate the safe speed, it is necessary to ensure that the quadrupedal robot can stop safely within the distance to the nearest obstacle, as shown in Eq. 8.

$$S_{safe} \leq d_{min} - S_{mar} \tag{8}$$

where d_{min} denotes the distance between the robot and the nearest obstacle; V_{safe} denotes the safe speed of the robot, i.e., the maximum speed at which the robot can travel without colliding with an obstacle; and S_{mar}, the margin of safety, denotes an additional distance that is used to ensure that the robot does not come into contact with an obstacle during an emergency braking.

Equation 5 is carried over to Eq. 8 to obtain Eq. 9:

$$\frac{V_{safe}^2}{2 \times a_{max}} \leq d_{min} - S_{mar} \qquad (9)$$

Solving the inequality gives a safe speed range, i.e.:

$$Vsafe \leq sqrt(2 \times a_{max} \times (d_{min} - S_{mas})) \qquad (10)$$

The quadruped robot through the above steps, as well as the information measured by the sensor in real time, if no obstacle is detected by default to take a diagonal trotting gait, the speed is selected as 1 m/s. Otherwise, the safe speed range can be calculated in real time through the formula 10 and select the appropriate value within the range, which is transmitted to the controller to select the optimal gait in particular, so as to realize the real-time gait switching.

Simulation Analysis

The gait switching simulation test of the quadruped robot is carried out in the quadruped robot simulation environment constructed above to obtain the supporting force on each leg and foot end of the quadruped robot, as well as the speed change of the quadruped robot, and the test results are shown in Fig. 9.

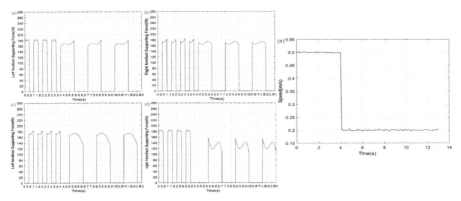

Fig. 9. Simulation results. (a) Force curves of left forefoot; (b) Force curves of right forefoot; (c) Force curves of left hindfoot; (d) Force curves of right hindfoot; (e) Velocity change curve.

The test results show that the distance between the robot and the obstacle measured by the sensor in 0–4 s is 4 m, and the speed is 0.5 m/s calculated by the formula, and according to the supporting force on the robot's foot end, it can be seen that the robot adopts a diagonal trotting gait at this time; the robot's distance between the sensor and the obstacle in 4–13 s is 2 m, and the speed is 0.2 m/s calculated by the formula, and according to the supporting force on the robot's foot end, it can be seen that the robot adopts a jogging gait at this time, so as to realize the optimal gait switching. According to the supporting force on the robot's foot end, it is known that the robot adopts a slow walking gait at this time, thus it can be seen that the robot calculates the safe speed range in real time through the real-time information measured by the sensors, and transmits it to the controller to select the optimal gait, so as to realize the gait switching.

4 Conclusion

This paper takes quadrupedal robot as the research object, and builds a simulation model of quadrupedal robot in gazebo, based on the environment sensing of LiDAR, using depth camera as an auxiliary to sense the complex environment, and combining with Cartographer algorithm to realize the localization of quadrupedal robot. After that, the global map, gridded map and local map are constructed by sensing the complex terrain, which provides the basis for the subsequent path planning part. A* algorithm based on sliding window is used for local path planning to realize real-time obstacle avoidance and navigation. Finally, we obtain the actual speed of the robot through the acquired global environment map and local environment map information, and feedback the speed command to the controller, so that the controller can select the optimal gait through the feedback speed information, thus realizing real-time and autonomous gait switching through environment perception. A complete framework for path planning and real-time gait switching based on recognizing and sensing complex environments is constructed for quadruped robots.

Acknowledgements. This research was funded by the Science and Technology Development Program of Jilin Province, China (Grant No. 20230101117JC), National Natural Science Foundation of China (Grant No. 51305157).

Declarations
Data Availability Statement. No data were used to support this study

Conflicts of Interest. The authors declare no conflict of interest.

References

1. Li, Y., et al.: Towards object tracking for quadruped robots. J. Vis. Commun. Image Represent. **97**, 103958 (2023)
2. Gao, X.H., Luo, Z., Li, C.S., Sun, Y.H., Qiu, Y.: A quadruped bionic robot and its control method. CN201910440141.8, 22 January 2024
3. Yang, Y.X., Han, B.L., Luo, X.: Simultaneous localization and construction of indoor navigation maps for mobile robots. Sci. Technol. Eng. **18** (2021)
4. Feng, J.H., Qu, X.: Analysis of typical leg structures of quadruped robots. China Sci. Technol. Inf. **19**, 86–87 (2022)
5. Jia, W.C., Huang, Z.S., Sun, Y., Pu, H.Y., Ma, S.G.: Toward a novel deformable robot mechanism to transition between spherical rolling and quadruped walking. In: 2017 IEEE International Conference on Robotics and Bionics (IEEE ROBIO 2017), pp. 1539–1544 (2017)

6. Xiang, X.Q., Pan, Z.G., Tong, J.: A study of depth camera applications to computer vision and graphics. Comput. Sci. Explor. **5**(6), 481–492 (2011)
7. Saudabayev, A., Kungozhin, F., Nurseitov, D., Varol, H.A.: Depth image based terrain recognition for supervisory control of a hybrid quadruped. In: 2014 IEEE 23rd International Symposium on Industrial Electronics (ISIE), pp. 1532–1537 (2014)
8. Wang, Y.F.: Perspective invariant gait recognition based on kinect skeletal joint information, Master's thesis, Shandong University (2017)
9. Yang, Y.R., Li, F.: Research on key technology of high-precision navigation map based on laser point cloud scanning. Mod. Comput. **9**, 23–26 (2018)
10. Zhou, Y.C.: A review of Lidar principles based on laser triangulation methods. Electron. Softw. Eng. **19**, 94–95 (2016)
11. Steinvall, O., Larsson, H., Gustafsson, F., Chevalier, T., Persson, Å., Klasén, L: Characterizing targets and backgrounds for 3 D laser radars. Mil. Remote Sens. **5613**, 51–66 (2004)
12. Jin, Q., Tang, C., Cai, W.: Research on dynamic path planning based on the fusion algorithm of improved ant colony optimization and rolling window method. IEEE Access **10**, 28322–28332 (2021)
13. Angulo, B., Panov, A., Yakovlev, K.: Policy optimization to learn adaptive motion primitives in path planning with dynamic obstacles. IEEE Robot. Autom. Lett. **8**(2), 824–831 (2023)
14. Tonola, C., Faroni, M., Beschi, M., et al.: Anytime informed multi-path replanning strategy for complex environments. IEEE Access **11**, 4105-4116 (2023)
15. Lee, Y.H., et al.: A gait transition algorithm based on hybrid walking gait for a quadruped walking robot. Intell. Serv. Robot. **8**(4), 185–200 (2015)
16. Liu, A., Zhang, X.Y., Zhang, K.G.: Gait transition of quadruped robot using time sequence control based on finite-state machine. Appl. Mech. Mater. **2746**, 423–426 (2013)
17. Chen, Z.H., Li, J.H., Wang, S.K., Wang, J.Z., Ma, L.L.: Flexible gait transition for six wheel-legged robot with unstructured terrains. Robot. Auton. Syst. **150**, 103989 (2022)
18. Koo, I.M., et al.: Biologically inspired gait transition control for a quadruped walking robot. Auton. Robots **39**(2), 169–182 (2015)
19. Zhao, Q., He, M.: Continuous laser SLAM conformal localization method based on known occupancy raster maps. CN110531766A, 03 January 2019
20. Luo, Q., Li, S.B., Ruan, W.J.: Cartographer SLAM construction method for ROS robots. Autom. Appl. **64**(1), 110–112 (2023)
21. Soken, H.E., Hajiyev, C.: UKF for the identification of the pico satellite attitude dynamics parameters and the external torques on IMU and magnetometer measurements. In: 2009 4th International Conference on Recent Advances in Space Technologies, pp. 547–552 (2009)
22. Yao, C.: Research on 3D state sensing and autonomous localization methods for quadruped robots in unstructured environments. Master's thesis, Harbin Institute of Technology (2020)

Real-Time Obstacle Avoidance and Pathfinding for Robot Manipulators Based on Deep Reinforcement Learning

Jun Hu[1], Jianliang Mao[2(✉)], Xin Zhou[2], and Chuanlin Zhang[1]

[1] College of Computer Science and Technology, Shanghai University of Electric Power, Shanghai 200240, China
[2] College of Automation Engineering, Shanghai University of Electric Power, Shanghai 200090, China
jl_mao@shiep.edu.cn

Abstract. In dynamic environments, safe motion planning for robots is one of the frequently encountered challenges in real applications. To address this issue, this paper proposes a real-time obstacle avoidance and pathfinding controller (ROAPC) for robot manipulators using a combination of deep reinforcement learning (DRL) and artificial potential field (APF) methods. Specifically, the soft actor-critic (SAC) algorithm coupled with the hindsight experience replay (HER) algorithm is developed to address sparse reward issues and enhance control performance, especially in tasks with multiple target points. In this approach, the reward function in DRL is computed based on the attraction and repulsion forces of the robot's current position calculated using the APF method, where attraction is considered as positive reward and repulsion as negative reward, with the sum of both forces representing the reward at the robot's current position. This method effectively guides the robot during exploration, significantly improving convergence speed. The effectiveness of the proposed method is verified by evaluating the real-time obstacle avoidance and path planning tasks of a six-degree-of-freedom robot manipulator in a simulation environment.

Keywords: reinforcement learning · obstacle avoidance · path planning · artificial potential field

1 Introduction

In recent years, the development of robotics technology has enabled robots to assist humans in service and production. Early robot manipulators could only perform repetitive tasks on industrial production lines. Today, with the development of artificial intelligence and the advancement of sensor technology, the development of robot manipulator is gradually moving towards intelligence and flexibility [1]. The application of technologies such as computer vision, force sensors, and machine learning enables robot manipulator to perceive and understand the surrounding environment and respond accordingly [2,3]. This intelligent robot manipulator can not only adapt to different working environments, but also perform more complex and diverse tasks [4,5].

Deep reinforcement learning (DRL) is a key field driving the development of artificial intelligence. Through trial and error and self-feedback, DRL enables autonomous systems to make real-time decisions in dynamic environments. It has achieved significant accomplishments in various areas such as autonomous driving, gaming, resource optimization, healthcare, and natural language processing [6]. Robots no longer rely on mathematical models for motion control to achieve tasks, but can achieve task goals through autonomous learning. For instance, Safaoui et al. [7] proposed an tractable motion planner, which leverages the advantages of DRL and constraint control-based trajectory planning. The proposed method can handle the agent's state and control constraints, and enforces collision avoidance with high probability between agents and with static obstacles in the workspace. Gu et al. [8] demonstrated that a state-of-the-art DRL algorithm based on off-policy training of deep Q functions can be extended to complex 3D manipulation tasks and can efficiently learn deep neural network policies for training on real physical robots. , further reducing training time by parallelizing the algorithm across multiple robots and pooling their policy updates asynchronously. Yang et al. [9] proposed a humanoid motion planning method for a robot arm based on human arm physics and DRL. By analyzing and learning the human arm motion data collected by the VICON optical motion capture system, humanoid motion rules are extracted. Reinforcement learning based on deep deterministic policy gradient (DDPG) and hindsight experience replay (HER) algorithms are used to train the robot arm in human-like movements. Mehta et al. [10] proposed a model-free DRL method based on waypoints. Instead of learning a low-level policy, the robot now learns a trajectory of waypoints and then interpolates between those waypoints using the existing controller. This proposed method learns new tasks faster than state-of-the-art baselines. Schoettler et al. [11] proposed a method that combines DRL with prior information to solve various difficult industrial tasks with visual input and different natural reward specifications. Haarnoja et al. [12] proposed an approach to learn expressive energy-based policies for continuous states and actions that improves exploration and compositionality, allowing skills to be transferred between tasks. Melika et al. [13] proposed an improved Q-learning by combining Dyna Q-learning with artificial potential field (APF) that can accelerate the learning process even with poor parameter selection. In conclusion, DRL has demonstrated its versatility and effectiveness in various applications, significantly enhancing the capabilities and performance of autonomous systems [14,15]. Given the feasibility of the above work, we also use the DRL method to achieve real-time dynamic obstacle avoidance and pathfinding tasks for the robot manipulator.

Motivated by the above analysis, this paper puts forward a real-time obstacle avoidance and pathfinding controller (ROAPC) for robot manipulators based on the DRL and APF. First, construct the attractive field and repulsive field in the APF algorithm as a reward field, which reduces the difficulty of reward function design. Then, the soft actor-critic (SAC) [16] algorithm combined with the hindsight experience replay (HER) algorithm, is introduced to train cooperatively, improving the convergence speed of training. Finally, the training results are verified in the environment.

The remainder of this paper is organized as follows. Section 2 covers the preliminaries of the algorithm background. The specific implementation process of the proposed ROAPC is detailed in Sect. 3. Section 4 presents the simulation results and analysis, while Sect. 5 provides the conclusions.

2 Preliminaries

In this section, two main algorithms including SAC and APF are presented.

2.1 Soft Actor-Critic

Soft actor-critic not only maximizes the cumulative reward, but also makes the strategy more random. Therefore, a regular term of entropy is added to the goal of reinforcement learning, defined as

$$\pi^* = \mathop{\mathrm{argmax}}_{\pi} \sum_{t=0}^{T} \gamma^t \mathbb{E}_{(s_t,a_t) \sim \rho_\pi}[r(s_t, a_t) + \alpha \mathcal{H}(\pi(\cdot|s_t))] \quad (1)$$

where $\mathcal{H}(\cdot)$ is the entropy term, α is the entropy temperature coefficient, which is used to control the effect of the entropy term on the target. a_t is the agent action, s_t is the environment state, $r(s_t, a_t)$ is the reward for the agent after performing the action.

In order to reduce the bias of Q value estimation, SAC adopts the following update rules:

$$y(r, s', d) = r + \gamma(1-d)[\min_{i=1,2} Q_{\theta_i}(s'_t, a'_t) - \alpha \log \pi_\phi(a'_t|s'_t)] \quad (2)$$

where $y(r, s', d)$ is the target Q value, γ is the discount factor, and d is the termination signal.

When learning a policy, SAC minimizes the objective function Q_w:

$$J_Q(w) = \mathbb{E}_{(s_t,a_t,s_{t+1}) \sim \mathcal{D}} \left[\frac{1}{2} \Big(Q_w(s_t, a_t) - (r(s_t, a_t) \right. \\ \left. + \gamma \left(Q_{\bar{\omega}}(s_{t+1}, a_{t+1}) - \alpha \log(\pi_\theta(a_{t+1}|s_{t+1})) \right) \Big)^2 \right] \quad (3)$$

where $Q_{\bar{\omega}}$ denotes a target soft Q-function.

α can be a fixed value or can be adjusted adaptively. The goal of adaptive adjustment is to make the entropy of the strategy close to the target value $\mathcal{H}$:

$$J(\alpha) = \mathbb{E}_{a_t \sim \pi_t}[-\alpha \log \pi_t(a_t|s_t) + \mathcal{H}] \quad (4)$$

2.2 Artificial Potential Field

The core of the APF is to construct a potential field function. The robot explores the potential field to achieve obstacle avoidance and pathfinding tasks. The force field $U(q)$ is divided into attractive field $U_{att}(q)$ and repulsive field $U_{rep}(q)$. The intuitive effect is shown in Fig. 1.

$U_{att}(q)$ is usually defined as a function of the distance between the robot and the target point. When the robot approaches the target, the attractive force decreases, defined as

$$U_{att} = \frac{1}{2}k_{att} \parallel q - q_{goal} \parallel^2 \tag{5}$$

where k_{att} is the coefficient of attraction, q_{goal} is the target position and q is the robot position, $\parallel \cdot \parallel$ denoting the Euclidean distance.

$U_{rep}(q)$ keeps the robot away from obstacles, usually increases as the distance between the robot and the obstacle decreases, defined as

$$U_{rep}(q) = \begin{cases} \frac{1}{2}k_{rep}(\frac{1}{\parallel q-q_{obs} \parallel} - \frac{1}{d_0})^2, & if \parallel q - q_{obs} \parallel \leq d_0 \\ 0, & if \parallel q - q_{obs} \parallel > d_0 \end{cases} \tag{6}$$

where k_{rep} is the repulsion coefficient, q_{obs} is the obstacle position and d_0 is the range of repulsion.

The total force field $U(q)$ is the synthesis of the attractive potential field and the repulsive potential field:

$$U(q) = U_{att}(q) + U_{rep}(q) \tag{7}$$

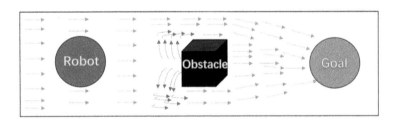

Fig. 1. APF power field.

3 Controller Design

In this section, in order to achieve obstacle avoidance and pathfinding for the robot manipulator, we combine APF with DRL and use HER to assist DRL training. An overview of the proposed control framework is depicted in Fig. 2. The detailed design process is as follows.

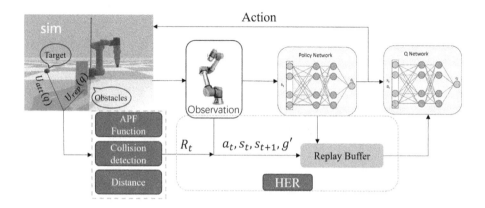

Fig. 2. The control framework of the proposed ROAPC.

3.1 APF-Based DRL Design

Environment Setting: In order to facilitate training, a simulation environment needs to be constructed. This paper construct a training environment through PyBullet simulation software. First, construct a simulation environment based on the real scene. Then, deploy the algorithm in the training environment. Finally, save the training results and play them back in the constructed scene.

Action Space: The action space a_t consists of joint velocities, which are the speeds of the six joints of the six-axis robot manipulator. The range of the action space is set within [-1 rad/s, 1 rad/s]. It is worth noting that controlling the robot manipulator through joint speed can avoid singularities.

State Space: The state space s_t is chosen as $[S_{bot}, S_{obs}, S_{goal}]$, where $S_{bot} = [J_s, J_v, J_p]$ is the robot state information in which J_s is the end position of the robot manipulator, J_v is the joint angle, J_p is the joint velocity. S_{obs} is the relative coordinates between the obstacle and the robot manipulator and S_{goal} is the distance between the end of the robot manipulator and the target.

3.2 Reward Potential Field Construction

Artificial Potential Field: The idea of the APF is applied to the design of the reward function. Attractive and repulsive fields are constructed, where the region of the attractive field provides positive rewards and the region of the repulsive field provides negative rewards. The composite field formed by the attractive and repulsive fields determines the reward at the robot's current position. The reward goal can be defined as

$$R_{U(q)} = R_{U_{att}(q)} - R_{U_{rep}(q)} \qquad (8)$$

Repulsive Field Construction: In actual application scenarios, it is difficult to accurately express the distance between the robot and obstacles, especially when encountering non-spherical obstacles. To solve this problem, this paper adopts a more conservative method. The formula is defined as

$$U_{rep} = \sum_{i=1}^{N} U_p(i) \tag{9}$$

where $U_p(i)$ is the repulsive field of the defined calculation points and N is the number of calculation points.

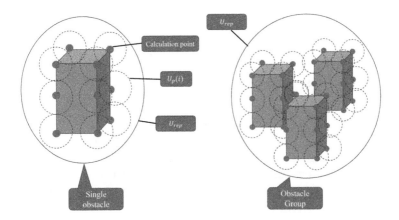

Fig. 3. Non-spherical obstacle repulsion field calculation example.

Figure 3 shows non-spherical obstacles. A series of calculation points are selected on the outer boundary of the obstacle. These points are used to calculate the distance between the robot and a certain area of the obstacle. From these points, the repulsive force $U_p(i)$ is constructed. The repulsive force $U_p(i)$ constitutes the repulsive force U_{rep} of the entire obstacle. It is worth noting that when constructing repulsion U_{rep}, the range of repulsion U_{rep} should be larger than the volume of the obstacle: $U_{rep} > V_{obs}$, where V_{obs} is the volume of the obstacle.

Reward Function Design: The reward function design uses the attraction and repulsion in the APF algorithm, and changes the force field in the APF algorithm into a reward field. Reward function is defined as

$$R = R_{att} + R_{collision} - R_{rep} - R_{dis} \tag{10}$$

The attraction design is defined as

$$R_{att} = \alpha \cdot d \tag{11}$$

where d is the distance between the end position of the robot and the target point, and α is the attract gain constant.

The repulsion design is defined as

$$R_{rep} = \begin{cases} \beta\left(\frac{1}{\partial} - \frac{1}{D(q)}\right)^2, & D(q) \leq \partial \\ 0, & D(q) > \partial \end{cases} \quad (12)$$

where $D(q)$ is the distance between the robot and the obstacle, β is the repulsion gain constant, and ∂ is the action threshold range of the obstacle.

The collision reward is defined as

$$R_{collision} = \begin{cases} -400, & collision \\ 0, & otherwise \end{cases} \quad (13)$$

When a collision occurs, a large negative reward is set as a penalty, otherwise, the collision reward is 0.

The distance reward is defined as

$$R_{dis} = \eta \cdot d \quad (14)$$

where d is the distance between the robot and the target point, and η is the gain constant. The distance reward is designed to speed up the efficiency of the robot's exploration towards the target point while balancing the attractive field reward to prevent the robot from obtaining larger rewards in invalid areas for an extended period.

Hindsight Experience Replay: In order to avoid the sparse reward function problem during the training process and improve the convergence speed of multiple target points, this paper introduces the HER algorithm to assist the SAC algorithm training.

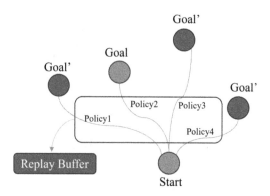

Fig. 4. HER algorithm diagram.

Algorithm 1 APF-based DRL Training

1: Initialize online Q network, target Q network, and policy network with weights ω, $\bar{\omega}$, θ;
2: Initialize replay buffer $\mathcal{R}$;
3: **for** each episode **do**
4:    Initialize environment;
5:    **for** each step **do**
6:       $a_t = \text{Policy}(s_t)$;
7:       $r_t = \text{APF}(s_t, a_t)$;
8:       $s_{t+1}, g' = \text{Env.step}(a_t, s_t)$;
9:       Add$(s_t, a_t, r_t, s_{t+1}, g')$ into $\mathcal{R}$;
10:      Check collision information in real-time;
11:    **end for**
12: **end for**
13: **for** each gradient step **do**
14:    Update online Q network weights:
      $\omega \leftarrow \omega - \lambda_Q \hat{\nabla}_\omega J_Q(w_i)$;
15:    Update policy weights: $\theta \leftarrow \theta - \lambda_\pi \hat{\nabla}_\theta J_\pi(\theta)$;
16:    Adjust temperature: $\alpha \leftarrow \alpha - \lambda \hat{\nabla}_\alpha J(\alpha)$;
17:    Update target Q network weights:
      $\bar{\omega} \leftarrow \tau \omega + (1-\tau)\bar{\omega}$;
18: **end for**

HER samples the trajectory τ from the environment: $\tau = (s_0, a_0, s_1, a_1, ..., s_t, a_t)$, where s_t represents the state and a_t represents the action. For each trajectory, a new target g' is generated, which is a certain state s_i in the trajectory, that is $g' = s_i$. Store the redefined target's trajectory $((s_t, a_t, s_{t+1}, r'(s_t, a_t, g'), g'))$ into the experience replay buffer, where s_{t+1} is the state after execute a_t. This process is shown in Fig. 4. Finally, the sample from the playback buffer and update the $Q\ network$ parameters: $Q(s, a, g') \leftarrow Q(s, a, g') + \alpha(r'(s_t, a_t, g') + \gamma \max_{a'} Q(s', a', g') - Q(s, a, g'))$.

3.3 Training Setting

Constructing a dynamic obstacle avoidance environment and deploying the algorithm in this environment for training. During the training process, the model is saved in real time. After the training is completed, the model is deployed to the environment for testing. The number of training episodes is 2000, and the maximum step size of each episode is 2000.

In order to obtain the best model during the training process, the average reward is calculated every 1000 training steps, and the model with the highest reward is saved in real time. Algorithm 1 summarizes the specific implementation of DRL. The parameter settings used in the training process are shown in the Table 1.

Table 1. Training Parameters.

Parameter	Definition	value
Θ	Policy Network Size	24 × 256 × 64 × 6
Ω	Q Network Size	30 × 256 × 64 × 1
γ	Discount Factor	0.95
M	Minibatch Size	256
λ	Learning Rate	$3e^{-4}$
α	Attract Gain Constant	0.2
β	Repulsive Gain Constant	30
∂	Action Threshold	0.3
η	Gain Threshold	0.1

4 Simulation Results and Analysis

In this section, a series of training and validation are carried out in a simulation environment to demonstrate the effectiveness of the method.

4.1 Training and Testing Results

In order to test the performance of the best model, we conduct a hundred rounds of tests on the model. When the target points randomly appeared in the work space and the obstacles had random velocities, the task success rate of the model reached more than 98%. From the success rate of the model every 1000 steps during the training process, it can be seen that the success rate of the model after convergence can be maintained above 90% in most cases.

Traning Results: During the test, the target point is randomly generated in the workspace $W = [[0.3, 0.4]_x, [-0.5, -0.6]_y, [0.2, 0.4]_z]$, and the obstacle speed is randomly generated within the range $V = [0.1 \text{ m/s}, 0.3 \text{ m/s}]$. The training result is shown in Fig. 5. The green line in figure represents the trajectory at the end of the robot manipulator. It can be seen that the robot manipulator lifts up in advance, bypasses the obstacle, and then moves towards the target point.

Expanding Test: The test environment shown in Fig. 5 is the same as the training environment, and it can be seen that the task can be successfully completed in this environment. In order to test the generalization of ROAPC, a new obstacle is added in the training environment, which has not appeared in the training environment. As shown in Fig. 6, the robot manipulator can still complete the task successfully. This demonstrates that the method has a certain level of generalization.

Figure 7(a) shows the change in each joint angle over time during the robot manipulator's task execution. Figure 7(b) displays the change over time of the

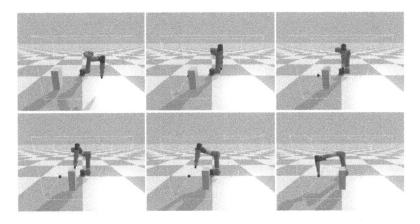

Fig. 5. Training environment test results.

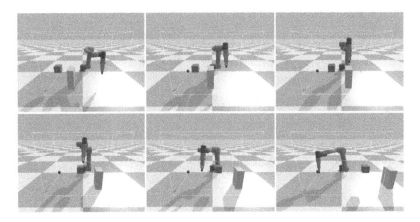

Fig. 6. Expanding test results.

distance between the end of the robot manipulator and the obstacle, where the action threshold is the range of repulsive force. It can be observed from Fig. 7(b) that the end of the robot manipulator is consistently outside the range of repulsive force.

4.2 Comparative Analysis

In order to verify the effectiveness of the method, two combinations of SAC with HER (SH) and SAC are used for comparison. In these two combinations, the reward function uses the commonly used reward calculation method: $R = R_{collision} - R_{dis}$.

Figure 8 shows the comparison of reward functions for three combination training. Due to the role of APF, the convergence level of ROAPC will be higher. It can also be clearly seen that ROAPC has the highest convergence level and

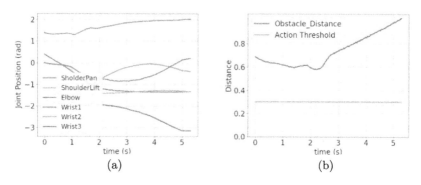

Fig. 7. Simulation results: (a) The real-time joint angle. (b) The real-time distance between the end of the robot manipulator and the obstacle centroid and the action threshold.

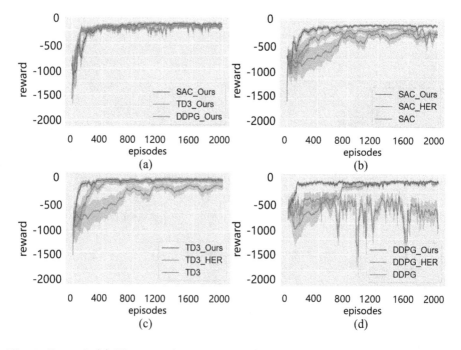

Fig. 8. Reward: (a) The reward convergence of the three algorithms SAC, TD3, and DDPG under the ROAPC framework. (b) The reward convergence of the three combinations of SAC training. (c) The reward convergence of TD3. (d) The reward convergence of DDPG.

fast convergence speed, and the combination of SH can also converge quickly, but it is difficult to converge when using the SAC algorithm alone. In addition, twin delayed deep deterministic policy gradient (TD3) and DDPG algorithms are also used for comparative verification, which can also show the superiority of the ROAPC framework.

5 Conclusion

In this paper, the APF algorithm has been combined with DRL to propose a real-time obstacle avoidance and pathfinding controller (ROAPC). Simultaneously, the SAC algorithm and the HER algorithm have been used to train in a dynamic obstacle avoidance environment. From the training process, it has been observed that this method has greatly improved the training efficiency and convergence speed of the algorithm. Judging from the experimental results, this method has effectively complete real-time obstacle avoidance and pathfinding tasks. In future work, this method can be applied in more complex scenarios to test the algorithm's performance when encountering an uncertain number and irregularly shaped obstacles.

Acknowledgement. This work was supported in part by the National Natural Science Foundation of China under Grants 62203292 and 62173221, in part by the Ministry of Education Chunhui Plan Cooperative Research Projects under Grant 202200890.

References

1. Wang, B., Dong, J.: A visual servo reinforcement learning control of uncalibrated manipulators with multi-channel gain decision. IEEE Trans. Inst. Meas. Control (2024). https://doi.org/10.1177/01423312241239716
2. Zhu, T., Mao, J., Han, L., Zhang, C., Yang, J.: Real-time dynamic obstacle avoidance for robot manipulators based on cascaded nonlinear MPC with artificial potential field. IEEE Trans. Ind. Electron. **71**, 7424–7434 (2024)
3. Han, L., Mao, J., Zhang, C., Kay, R.W., Richardson, R.C., Zhou, C.: A systematic trajectory tracking framework for robot manipulators: an observer-based nonsmooth control approach. IEEE Trans. Ind. Electron. **71**, 11104–11114 (2023)
4. Pan, Y., Xia, F., Mao, J.: A robot manipulator grasping method based on improved YOLOX. In: 2022 4th International Conference on Electrical Engineering and Control Technologies (CEECT), pp. 1279–1283. Shanghai, China (2022)
5. Dawson, C., Gao, S., Fan, C.: Safe control with learned certificates: a survey of neural lyapunov, barrier, and contraction methods for robotics and control. IEEE Trans. Robot. **39**, 1749–1767 (2023)
6. Zhao, W., Queralta, J.P., Westerlund, T.: Sim-to-real transfer in deep reinforcement learning for robotics: a survey. In: 2020 IEEE Symposium Series on Computational Intelligence (SSCI), pp. 737–744. IEEE (2020)
7. Safaoui, S., Vinod, A.P., Chakrabarty, A., Quirynen, R., Yoshikawa, N., Di Cairano, S.: Safe multi-agent motion planning under uncertainty for drones using filtered reinforcement learning. IEEE Trans. Robot. **40**, 2529–2542 (2024)
8. Gu, S., Holly, E., Lillicrap, T.P., Levine, S.: Deep reinforcement learning for robotic manipulation. arXiv preprint arXiv:1610.00633 **1**, 1 (2016)
9. Yang, A., Chen, Y., Naeem, W., Fei, M., Chen, L.: Humanoid motion planning of robotic arm based on human arm action feature and reinforcement learning. Mechatronics **78**, 102630 (2021)

10. Mehta, S.A., Habibian, S., Losey, D.P.: Waypoint-based reinforcement learning for robot manipulation tasks. arXiv preprint arXiv:2403.13281 (2024)
11. Schoettler, G., et al.: Deep reinforcement learning for industrial insertion tasks with visual inputs and natural rewards. In: RSJ International Conference on Intelligent Robots and Systems (IROS), pp. 5548–5555. Las Vegas, USA (2020)
12. Haarnoja, T., Tang, H., Abbeel, P., Levine, S.: Reinforcement learning with deep energy-based policies. In: International Conference on Machine Learning, pp. 1352–1361. Singapore, Singapore (2017)
13. Ataollahi, M., Farrokhi, M.: Online path planning of cooperative mobile robots in unknown environments using improved q-learning and adaptive artificial potential field. J. Eng. **2023**(2), e12231 (2023)
14. Li, J., Shi, H., Hwang, K.S.: Using goal-conditioned reinforcement learning with deep imitation to control robot arm in flexible flat cable assembly task. IEEE Trans. Autom. Sci. Eng. **21**, 1–12 (2023)
15. Hu, Z., Zheng, Y., Pan, J.: Grasping living objects with adversarial behaviors using inverse reinforcement learning. IEEE Trans. Rob. **39**(2), 1151–1163 (2023)
16. Haarnoja, T., et al.: Soft actor-critic algorithms and applications. arXiv preprint arXiv:1812.05905 (2018)

A Novel Building Construction Inspection Method Based on Naive Bayes Model by Fusing BIM and Lidar Point Cloud

Boyu Jiang[1,2], Liting Fan[1(✉)], Yang Zhang[2,3(✉)], Yu Han[1,2], and Zhongjiang Cheng[2]

[1] Mechanical Engineering School, Shenyang Jianzhu University, Shenyang 110168, China
fanliting@hotmail.com
[2] Sino-German College of Intelligent Manufacturing, Shenzhen Technology University, Shenzhen 518118, China
[3] Mechanical Industry Key Laboratory of Intelligent Robotics Technology for 3C, Shenzhen Technology University, Shenzhen 518118, China
zhangyang@sztu.edu.cn

Abstract. As the construction industry progresses and develops, construction inspection of the built environment plays a vital role in the success of a building project. This paper introduced a building construction quality monitoring method that combined building information modeling and LiDAR point cloud technology. The method first collected the point cloud data of the building environment, and preprocessed point cloud data including removing outliers and alignment; then, the point cloud generated by the BIM model was compared and analyzed with the actual point cloud to obtain the relative relationship between the two point clouds; finally, the results were determined by a Naive Bayes classification model to assess the construction quality. This method provided a complete set of solutions for construction quality verification, and promoted the construction industry to move towards intelligent and precise management.

Keywords: Construction monitoring · Point cloud comparison · BIM technology · Naive bayes classifier

1 Introduction

Construction has grown rapidly. It has become a key industry in the country's economy. Progress tracking and quality inspection have been problems for the building construction sector [1]. There are a number of drawbacks to the old manual monitoring technique. Firstly, it costs more in terms of labor and time because it requires a lot of human resources to monitor and report. Secondly, the outcomes of manual monitoring could contain some inaccuracies and be influenced by personal experience. Thirdly, due to time and space limits, manual monitoring is not able to keep an exhaustive eye on all work and details and may overlook some crucial information. As a result, it's critical to lower labor expenses, accelerate the detection process, and enhance the precision and efficiency of detection [2].

Numerous academics have studied quality and schedule inspection in the construction of buildings. To increase project transparency and efficiency, Lam K C and Ng S T investigated the possibilities of web-based technologies for gathering, organizing, evaluating, and sharing quality data. They also created a quality management system that makes quality data collection possible for all project participants [3]. Wang LC investigated the efficacy of RFID-based quality management applications to improve the testing and management of concrete samples, automated information collection, and informational management of laboratory quality inspections [4]. In order to improve the quality of construction, BoschéF created a model object that can automatically recognize computer designs based on big laser scanning methods and calculate construction dimensions to manage build dimensions and ensure build dimension accuracy [5]. Zoran Pučko et al. from the University of Maribor, Slovenia, used 3D scanning devices mounted on top of workers' heads to scan the construction environment in real time and record the location and timestamps of the captured point clouds, which were then matched to the 4D-BIM model when the corresponding point clouds were registered to enable progress monitoring [6]. Christopher Kroppa et al. from Ruhr-University Bochum, Germany, used the method of combining and comparing image information with BIM models to achieve progress monitoring of local target monitoring ranges [7]. Wang J et al. Dynamically combined BIM and LiDAR technologies to realize real-time data acquisition and construction quality control at building construction sites [8]. Qu T et al. fused low-altitude drone tilt-photography and BIM technology to dynamically monitor construction site progress through model comparison [9].

In recent years, with the progress and development of informatization in the construction industry, BIM (Building Information Modeling) technology has gradually become a popular object in the industry [10]. It can help to realize the integration of building information, from the design, construction, operation of the building until the end of the whole life cycle of the building, all kinds of information are always integrated with a three-dimensional model information database, which facilitates the collaborative work of all the participants based on BIM and the sharing of resources, which not only reduces the pressure of the designer, but also improves the efficiency of the whole construction work [11]. With the continuous development of robotics, the application of mobile robots in the field of building construction has become a popular research, and the study of monitoring robots in building construction is an important direction [12]. The integration of BIM and robotics is an innovative revolution in the field of construction. This combination not only greatly improves the accuracy and efficiency of construction, but also enhances safety. At the level of construction monitoring, the real-time monitoring and data analysis functions provided by the combination of the two ensure the fine management of the entire construction process, improve monitoring accuracy and efficiency, and strongly guarantee the quality of the project. At the same time, it also plays a key role in promoting intelligence and driving the digital transformation of the industry. Therefore, this study combines BIM technology and LiDAR technology to propose a method that can efficiently monitor the quality of building construction. This method detects the quality of building construction by scanning the building scene with LiDAR, collecting point cloud data, and comparing it with the point cloud data generated by the BIM model. This system can perform rapid operation and continuous repetitive operation, and after scanning a room or a floor, it can move to the next environment, and the point cloud data generated from different environments are independent data packages, which do not affect each other and greatly improve the work efficiency.

The rest of the paper is organized as follows: Section 2 describes the overall scheme design of the method. Section 3 describes preprocessing the point cloud data. including denoising, finding feature points, aligning with ICP and parameters for point cloud matching. Section 4 presents the experimental validation session of the method. Section 5 presents the conclusions and research directions.

2 Design of the Construction Inspection Program

In order to achieve an accurate assessment of the construction quality of a building project, this study proposes a systematic assessment scheme which centers on the use of advanced point cloud matching techniques to examine whether the construction activities meet the expected quality standards. This is a typical binary classification problem. In this context, this study adopts Naive Bayes model classifier as a solution [13]. It is deeply rooted in the Bayesian principle and skillfully assumes conditional independence among features to find clear classification boundaries in a complex data landscape. For a given training dataset, the joint probability distribution model of input and output variables is first learned based on the assumption of conditional independence of features. Subsequently, when faced with a new assessment case, Bayesian principle is utilized to find the output with the largest a posteriori probability, as a way to scientifically and efficiently determine the state of engineering quality. Given that the parameters involved are all continuous variables and each measurement represents a continuous scale value. It is challenging to calculate their exact probabilities directly. Thus, to address this characteristic, it is assumed that each feature of the sample set D obeys a normal distribution, the standard deviation and mean of each feature under the corresponding classification are calculated, and the probability density function of the normal distribution is utilized to estimate the corresponding probability value. The following formula is the probability density function formula:

$$P(x_i \mid D) = \frac{1}{\sqrt{2\pi}\sigma_i} \exp\left(-\frac{(x-\mu_i)^2}{2\sigma_i^2}\right) \quad (1)$$

where i denotes the i-th feature dimension, and σ_i and μ_i denote the corresponding standard deviation and expectation under the i-th feature, respectively. Integrating the probability density functions of all features, the final classification conditional probability can be written as:

$$P(x \mid D) = \prod_{i=1}^{n} p(x_i \mid D) \qquad (2)$$

This model is not only able to accurately quantify the likelihood of occurrence of each observation, but also able to effectively overcome the obstacle of probability calculation for continuous data, further enhancing its practicality and accuracy.

An outline of the flow of this program is shown in Fig. 1. The first step is the acquisition of the design point cloud model. By acquiring the design BIM model of the building to be evaluated and extracting the pure geometric form information from it, it's converted into a simplified triangular mesh model (Mesh model). Subsequently, a uniform point cloud sampling strategy is implemented on this Mesh model and appropriate parameter configurations are set to get the design point cloud model of this BIM model. Next is the acquisition of the actual point cloud model. The 3D Lidar technology is utilized to fully scan the physical building, collect the point cloud data in the actual environment, and perform the necessary preprocessing operations, covering the noise elimination and point cloud alignment steps. In this process, low-pass filtering is applied to reduce the number of point cloud points and exclude anomalies, while rough alignment by feature point matching and fine alignment by iterative closest point (ICP) algorithm are combined to integrate the point cloud data collected from multiple viewpoints, and ultimately form an accurate actual point cloud model. We compare the above designed point cloud model to the actual one and get relative distance metrics, like average distance and standard deviation, to assess the quality. They measure how well the model matches reality and help us see if the construction meets the standards.

In following the guiding principles of the structural engineering module of Evaluating Standard For Excellent Quality of Building Engineering on dimensional tolerances for concrete structures, we've specified the upper limit of dimensional deviation that constitutes a competent build. Using this benchmark, the dimensions of the original BIM model were tuned to generate a version of the critical BIM model reflecting the boundary of the dimensional deviation tolerance. By comparing this critical BIM model with the point cloud data generated from its original BIM model, we defined a distance threshold within the construction quality compliance. This threshold constitutes a quantitative criterion for evaluating construction accuracy, and the model is trained with it. The test data is brought into the model to verify that the construction results can be judged to be up to standard.

For further validation, this study constructed a simulated room as the inspection object in the experimental session, and executed point cloud comparison experiments from the new BIM model to the design BIM model for multiple dimensional deviation scenarios, from which multiple sets of relative distance data were obtained. After comprehensive analysis, the quantitative judging metrics established in this study are mean distance and standard deviation. The data obtained from the comparison experiments were used as the training set for the plain Bayesian algorithm, in which the standard deviation and the mean distance were two independent features, and their corresponding standard deviation and expectation were calculated. The result of comparing the designed point cloud with the actual point cloud is brought into the model as test data to calculate and discriminate whether the data meets the criteria or not. The experiment further reveals that there is an obvious linear correlation between relative distance and dimensional deviation, i.e., as dimensional deviation increases, relative distance also increases, confirming the close correlation between point cloud matching and dimensional error, thus verifying the practicality and effectiveness of the method of this study. This study not only provides a general construction quality assessment method, but also lays a theoretical and practical foundation for the implementation of refined construction management using BIM technology.

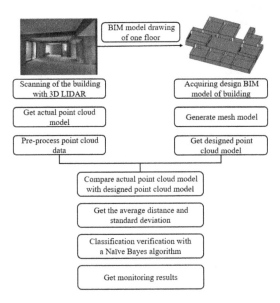

Fig. 1. The overall program flow

3 Pre-processing of LiDAR Point Cloud Data

During the acquisition of Lidar point cloud data, due to various factors such as system noise, object surface reflections, environmental interference and so on, the data may contain some outliers or noisy points. These outlier points, if not properly processed, will adversely affect the subsequent point cloud processing sessions (e.g.segmentation, feature extraction, alignment, etc.), leading to errors in the model results. Therefore, it is necessary to pre-process the point cloud data during the processing of point cloud data to ensure the accuracy and reliability of the point cloud data and improve the data quality.

3.1 Remove Outliers

Denoising of 3D construction completed building data is an important preprocessing step for effective application of building quality monitoring. The noisy points are set as redundant point cloud data points for the monitoring target, and are removed by means of noise filtering. The low-pass filtering function [14] usually involves smoothing, which improves data quality by reducing rapidly changing parts of the point cloud, such as measurement errors or cluttered points. The basic principle is to allow low-frequency signals (corresponding to slowly changing shape features) to pass through while suppressing or attenuating high-frequency signals (corresponding to sharp changes such as noise). The underlying surface is estimated by fitting a plane in a local range, setting an appropriate threshold radius, and removing points outside the range as outliers. The working principle is shown in Fig. 2. The blue points are the fitted plane point cloud points, and the green, orange and yellow points are the inspection points. Assuming that the set range radius is R and the number of neighboring points is 5, observe the number of points within the radius of the green, orange and yellow points. Greater than 5 means that the point meets the requirement; on the contrary, the point is eliminated. To preserve corner points or sharp edges, the algorithm is run repeatedly by choosing a smaller radius and a relatively high error threshold. Setting the range radius neighborhood point count to 10 or more, each point will be filtered based on the attributes of its 10 or more nearest neighbors around it. A suitable number of neighboring points can help to better preserve shape details while removing isolated noise points.

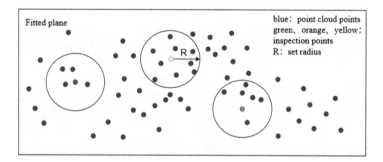

Fig. 2. The low-pass filtering principle

Due to the way the algorithm works, it is very powerful on planar surfaces, such as walls, etc. The target group to be monitored in this work is the building complex after the construction is completed, which consists of structures such as walls, columns, doors, etc., so this method is used in this paper for denoising.

3.2 Align Point Cloud Data

Point cloud alignment refers to the unification of point clouds under different coordinate systems into the same coordinate system. It finds a rigid-body transformation from system 1 to system 2. This transformation merges the clouds into the same system. The point cloud alignment process is shown in Fig. 3.

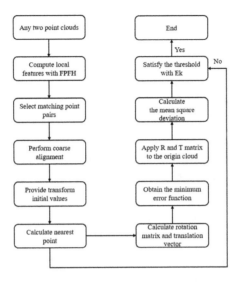

Fig. 3. The point cloud alignment process

The rigid body transformation process consists of rotational and translational transformations. Assuming the origin cloud Q=(X,Y,Z) then the rigid body transformation of Q is:

$$Q' = RQ + T \tag{3}$$

where Q' is the transformed point cloud, R is the rotation matrix and T is the translation matrix.

Rotational transformation means that the point cloud is rotated around the X, Y, and Z coordinate axes. Let the rotation matrix of the original point cloud Q rotated by an angle of α around the X-axis be denoted as $R_X(\alpha)$, the rotation matrix of the angle of β around the Y-axis be denoted as $R_Y(\beta)$, and the rotation matrix of the angle of rotation around the Z-axis of γ be denoted as $R_Z(\gamma)$, then the expressions for $R_X(\alpha)$, $R_Y(\beta)$, and $R_Z(\gamma)$ are, respectively, as follows:

$$R_X(\alpha) = \begin{bmatrix} 1 & 0 & 0 \\ 0 & \cos\alpha & -\sin\alpha \\ 0 & \sin\alpha & \cos\alpha \end{bmatrix} \tag{4}$$

$$R_Y(\beta) = \begin{bmatrix} 1 & 0 & 0 \\ 0 & \cos\alpha & -\sin\alpha \\ 0 & \sin\alpha & \cos\alpha \end{bmatrix} \tag{5}$$

$$R_Z(\gamma) = \begin{bmatrix} 1 & 0 & 0 \\ 0 & \cos\alpha & -\sin\alpha \\ 0 & \sin\alpha & \cos\alpha \end{bmatrix} \quad (6)$$

Then the rotation matrix R of the point cloud Q can be expressed as:

$$R = R_X(\alpha) \cdot R_Y(\beta) \cdot R_Z(\gamma) \quad (7)$$

Continuing the translation transformation for the rotationally transformed point cloud, the point cloud is moved along the X, Y, and Z axes by the translations t_X, t_Y, and t_Z, respectively, and the translation matrix T can be expressed as:

$$T = \begin{bmatrix} t_X & t_Y & t_Z \end{bmatrix}^T \quad (8)$$

Combining the rotation and translation matrices, the point cloud Q obtained by rigid body transformation can be expressed as Q':

$$\begin{bmatrix} X' \\ Y' \\ Z' \end{bmatrix} = R_X(\alpha) \cdot R_Y(\beta) \cdot R_Z(\gamma) \begin{bmatrix} X \\ Y \\ Z \end{bmatrix} + \begin{bmatrix} t_X \\ t_Y \\ t_Z \end{bmatrix} \quad (9)$$

The key to aligning point clouds is to find a good rigid-body transformation matrix. Then, use it to rotate and move the two sets of points. They have the same scale but different positions. This makes the data from the two viewpoints have the smallest error after the transformation. And they will overlap more.

Coarse alignment is an alignment method that is performed when the original point cloud and the target point cloud do not know any initial relative position at all. The main purpose of this method is to quickly estimate a rough point cloud alignment matrix when the initial conditions are unknown. For any initial state of the two point clouds, the two point clouds are made to be roughly aligned, giving initial values to the rotation matrix R and translation vector T. The FPFH [15] local feature based 3D point cloud coarse alignment method aligns two point clouds by calculating the local feature descriptors of each point in the point cloud data, and obtaining matching point pairs by comparing the descriptors for coarse alignment. The formula for FPFH is as follows:

$$FPFH(p_q) = SPFH(p_q) + \frac{1}{k} \sum_{i=1}^{k} \frac{1}{\omega_k} \cdot SPFH(p_k) \quad (10)$$

where the weight ω_k depends on the distance between the center point p_q and a certain nearest neighbor point p_k in a given metric space to measure the weight of the point pair (p_q, p_k).

In order to obtain a sufficient number and quality of correctly matched correspondences, the feature point description should be descriptive, robust and unique. More importantly, it should be robust to rigid transformations.

Fine alignment is the process of further optimizing to get more accurate transformations based on the initial values obtained from coarse alignment. The ICP algorithm [16] is a popular algorithm for fine alignment, which completes the rigid transformation of the point cloud by an iterative strategy. This algorithm has a core idea. First, based on the principle of nearest Euclidean distance from a point to a point, search for several corresponding pairs of points in the original point cloud and the target point cloud to form a set of corresponding pairs of points; Then, on the basis of this set of corresponding pairs of points, compute the matrix of rigid-body transformations by using quaternionic numbering method; Next, apply the computed transformation matrix to the original point cloud to update the point cloud; And then, compute the mean-square deviation to determine whether it meets the threshold value or not; If it doesn't meet, repeat the above process until the point cloud reaches a point of rigid-body transformation. The above process is repeated until the upper limit of iteration is reached, then the iteration is stopped and the point cloud alignment is realized with the transformation matrix corresponding to the last iteration.

The ICP algorithm's basic principle is to find the closest neighboring points (p_i, q_i) in the target point cloud P and the origin cloud Q. This is done according to certain constraints. Then, it computes the optimal matching parameters R and t to minimize the error function. The specific process of ICP algorithm is as follows. First, compute the nearest points of the origin cloud P and the target cloud Q according to them to get the matching point set. The nearest distance calculation formula is:

$$\|p_i - q_i\| \tag{11}$$

where i is any point in the point cloud data.

Based on the set of matched points, the rotation matrix R and translation matrix T are solved to minimize the error function E(R, t). The error function E(R, t) is:

$$E(R,t) = \frac{1}{n}\sum_{i=1}^{n}\|q_i - (Rp_i + t)\|^2 \tag{12}$$

where n is the number of nearest neighbor pairs, p_i is a point in the target point cloud P, q_i is the nearest point corresponding to p_i in the source point cloud Q, R is the rotation matrix, and t is the translation vector.

The rotation matrix R and translation matrix T are then applied to the original point cloud Q to calculate the mean square deviation E_k between the two point clouds after the transformation:

$$E_k = \frac{1}{n}\sum_{i=1}^{n}\|p_i - q_i\|^2 \tag{13}$$

Repeat the above steps until the error difference between two neighboring iterations is less than a threshold value or reaches a set number of iterations, then the algorithm is terminated and the point cloud fine alignment is completed.

3.3 Parameters for Point Cloud Matching

After 3D point cloud matching, approximate distances are obtained based on the relationship between the two point clouds, and a system of relative distance parameters constitutes the cornerstone for assessing the geometric similarity between two sets of point clouds and the quality of matching. This system covers the maximum distance, the minimum distance, the average distance, the standard deviation, and the maximum error, each of which depicts the fit of the corresponding pairs of points between the point clouds in different dimensions, and together contribute to the accuracy and robustness of the matching algorithm. These parameters and their computational formulas are discussed below.

The minimum distance represents the Euclidean distance between the two closest points in two sets of point clouds, and is a direct measure of the degree of localized closest match between point clouds. Its calculation formula is:

$$D_{\min} = \min_{i,j}(d_{ij}) \tag{14}$$

where d_{ij} denotes the distance between the point in the ith point cloud and the corresponding point in the jth point cloud, and the minimum value is obtained by comparing all possible pairs of points.

The maximum distance lies at the other extreme and identifies the furthest degree of separation between matched pairs of points, reflecting the largest inconsistency or potential mismatch region in the point cloud matching. The formula is calculated as:

$$D_{\max} = \max_{i,j}(d_{ij}) \tag{15}$$

where d_{ij} denotes the distance between the point in the i-th point cloud and the corresponding point in the j-th point cloud, and the maximum value is obtained by comparing all possible point pairs. The magnitude of this value directly affects the overall robustness assessment of the matching, and too large a value often indicates that the matching algorithm needs to be further optimized.

The average distance is the average of the distances of all matched pairs of points and is used to generalize the general tightness of matching between point clouds. Its formula is:

$$D_{\mathrm{mean}} = \frac{1}{N}\sum_{i=1}^{N} d_i \tag{16}$$

where N is the total number of matched point pairs and d_i is the distance between each pair of points. A lower average distance indicates a better overall match quality.

Compared to the mean distance, the standard deviation further reveals the dispersion of point-to-distance in point cloud matching, and is a key statistic for evaluating the accuracy and consistency of the matching, which is calculated as:

$$\sigma = \sqrt{\frac{1}{N}\sum_{i=1}^{N}(d_i - D_{\mathrm{mean}})^2} \tag{17}$$

where d_i is the alignment error of the i-th point, which may include deviations in position and direction.

The relative distance parameter not only grasps the overall effect of point cloud alignment globally, but also diagnoses the accuracy and stability of the matching precisely in local details. The mean distance and standard deviation, as the core parameters therein, play an irreplaceable role in ensuring the accuracy and reliability in the field of 3D reconstruction.

4 Comparative Validation of Point Cloud Models

To verify the feasibility of the proposed construction quality assessment method based on point cloud matching metrics, a comprehensive experiment was designed and implemented in this study. The experiment first constructed a simulated quadrilateral room using colored blocks as a simplified model of the state of completed building construction. Then, a BIM model of the room was drawn with Revit. It was ensured that the model followed the design of the axial network and elevation. The model had to meet the design for wall connections and component specifications. Based on this BIM model, a design point cloud model was generated. The experimentally constructed simulated room, BIM diagram and design point cloud model are shown in Fig. 4.

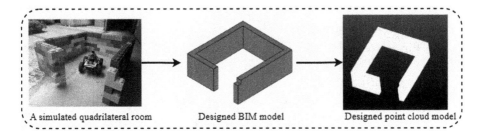

Fig. 4. Experimental room,BIM model and its point cloud model

Then, a mobile robot platform with integrated LiDAR technology was used to scan the simulated room in all directions to obtain the point cloud data of the room. A preprocessing process was carried out on the obtained data, including noise reduction, alignment fusion of point cloud data from different viewpoints, etc., to obtain more accurate 3D point cloud data, and the preprocessing results are shown in Fig. 5.

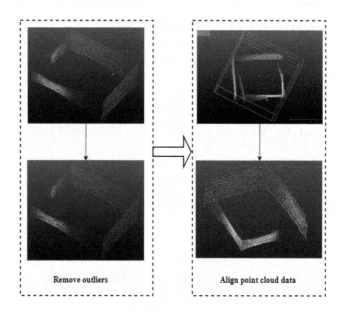

Fig. 5. The pre-processing results of point cloud

Table 1 shows the transformation matrix for point cloud alignment, from which the rotation matrix and translation matrix of the rigid body transformation can be known.

Table 1. Tranformation matrix

R	0.160	−0.979	0.086
	0.982	0.156	−0.049
	0.035	0.092	0.991
T	0.0512	−0.734	0.026

The actual point cloud data is compared and analyzed with the design point cloud data generated based on the BIM model. The comparison visualization is shown in Fig. 6.

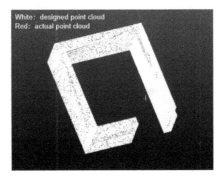

Fig. 6. The visualization of comparison results

The comparison of the two point clouds produced the relative distance information. Table 2 shows the specific values of them.

Table 2. Approximate distances

Parameter	Data
Min dist.	0
Max dist.	0.116849
Avg dist.	0.0125987
Sigma	0.0157707
Max error	0.01417

The histogram is shown in Fig. 7, from which it can be seen that 99 percent of the point clouds are within the relative distance threshold of 0.05, which reflects the overall closeness of the point cloud matching and the good quality of the point cloud comparison. Min distance refers to the minimum value of the distance from each point selected from one point cloud to the nearest point in the other model, and max distance indicates the maximum value. They can reflect the closest proximity between two sets of point clouds. Avg distance is the average of the distances of all points to their nearest neighbors. This value can be used as an overall indicator to assess the degree of average deviation of the two data. When comparing a physically scanned point cloud with a design model point cloud, a smaller average distance usually means a better agreement between the physical and the design. The Sigma value reflects the distribution of distances between point clouds. A small standard deviation means that most point-to-point distances are close to the average distance, i.e., the deviation between point clouds is relatively uniform.

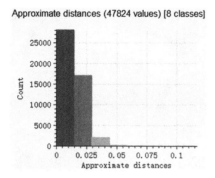

Fig. 7. Histogram of approximate distances

In order to further corroborate the feasibility of the method, this validation will also perform comparison experiments. By purposefully adjusting the data of the original BIM model, we've created a new design point cloud model and compare it with the actual scanned point cloud above. We observe how the relative distance between the two point clouds changes if the actual point cloud doesn't match the one from the new BIM model. Figure 8 presents a direct comparison view of the two sets of design point clouds, where the green point cloud maps the geometry of the original BIM model, while the red point cloud highlights the state of the adjusted new BIM model, visualizing the inconsistency between the two.

Fig. 8. Comparison of the two design point clouds

Figure 9 shows the visualization of the design point cloud derived from the new BIM model against the actual point cloud, where the specially marked red circle area highlights the significant gap between the two, implying the direct correspondence between the model size change and the actual build deviation.

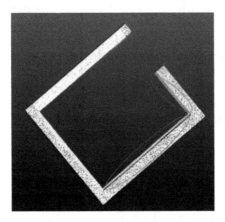

Fig. 9. Point cloud comparison based on new BIM models

According to Evaluating Standard For Excellent Quality of Building Engineering, the permissible error of surface flatness of fair-faced wall is 5 mm, and the permissible error of flatness of plastered is 8 mm. The permissible deviation of verticality of each layer is 5 mm; The permissible deviation of verticality of the whole height is ≤ 10 m is 10 mm; The permissible deviation of verticality of the whole height is > 10 m is 20 mm. Table 3 shows the range of dimensional deviations (mm) for structural engineering.

Table 3. The structural engineering dimensional deviation

Concrete structure	Reinforcing steel bar	Thickness of cover to reinforcement	Column,Beam	±5
			Slab,Wall,Shell	±3
	Concrete	Axis	Foundation	10
			Wall,Column,Beam	8
		Elevation	Story height	±10
			Whole height	±30

This comparative experiment is designed to perform the comparison test with the qualified and unqualified differentiation criteria with a limit of 8 mm deviation of the wall-column-beam at the axial position. A qualified range does 8 times of comparison test, each deviation increasing 1 mm. An unqualified range does also do 8 times of comparison experiment, each deviation increasing 2 mm. Since the maximum distance, minimum distance and maximum error have no obvious difference in this group of comparison experiments, the two parameters of the average distance and the standard deviation are chosen as the quantitative criterion.

After 16 comparison tests, the specific values of the two indicators constitute the model training dataset for this experiment. Figure 10 visualizes the dynamic curves of these two key parameters with experimental conditions. Subsequently, the collected training set was analyzed and modeled using Naive Bayes model algorithm to construct a Naive Bayes prediction model. Based on the deviation values mentioned above, a further force of 16 additional matching experiments were performed with the aim of obtaining a completely new dataset of mean distances and standard deviations. This dataset is a test set for the Naive Bayes model and is used to verify the prediction accuracy of it. The parameters of the new dataset were sequentially brought into the trained model for validation. Results show that a total of 13 sets of data were predicted to be in line with the actual situation, while 3 sets of data were not in line with the actual situation, and the resulting accuracy of the model was calculated to be 81.3 percent, which can be seen that the results are relatively accurate.

Applying the parameters in Table 2 as test data in the Bayesian model, it is verified that the comparison result is qualified and meets the construction quality standard. Meanwhile, the line graph of the experimental data can show the linear relationship between the point cloud matching degree and the dimensional deviation, and the larger the deviation value is, the larger the average distance and standard deviation value is. The experiment confirms the effectiveness and practicality of this method, which provides a reliable new way for construction quality judgment.

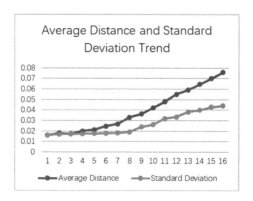

Fig. 10. Indicator change curves

5 Conclusion

This paper proposes a building construction quality and progress detection method, that is, based on the mobile robot carrier, integrating BIM technology, using 3D LIDAR to obtain the point cloud data of the building and the point cloud data of the BIM model to compare and detect whether the building construction meets the standards. The method comprehensively scans the building to obtain 3D point cloud data through 3D LIDAR technology, and then carries out the pre-processing process for the point cloud data, including de-noising, alignment and other steps, to optimize the data set and ensure the accuracy and completeness of the data set. Then the design point cloud model is generated based on the BIM model of the building, and finally, by comparing the actual point cloud with the design point cloud data, a simple Bayesian classifier is used to determine whether the construction quality meets the standard. The experimental results show that this method can accurately capture the building point cloud data, process and analyze the data, and obtain quantitative criterion to judge the quality and progress of building construction. The application of this paper will help to improve the quality and progress monitoring of building construction and provide strong support for the development of the construction industry. Future research will focus on optimizing and upgrading the method, improving its accuracy and stability, and broadening the application scenarios to adapt to a wider and more complex construction environment and higher requirements for monitoring needs, bringing more intelligent and refined management tools to the construction field.

Acknowledgments. This work was supported in part by the Natural Science Foundation of Top Talent of SZTU [Grant: GDRC202328] and the Educational reform project of Shenzhen Technology University [Grant No. 20231002]

References

1. Kim, S., Peavy, M., Huang, P.C., Kim, K.: Development of BIM-integrated construction robot task planning and simulation system. Autom. Constr. (2021). https://api.semanticscholar.org/CorpusID:234830216
2. Brosque, C., Fischer, M.: Safety, quality, schedule, and cost impacts of ten construction robots. Constr. Robot. **6**(2), 163–186 (2022). https://eurekamag.com/research/080/535/080535223.php
3. Lam, K.C., Ng, S.T.: A cooperative internet-facilitated quality management environment for construction. Autom. Constr. **15**(1), 1–11 (2006). https://doi.org/10.1016/j.autcon.2005.01.009, https://www.sciencedirect.com/science/article/pii/S092658050500049X
4. Wang, L.C.: Enhancing construction quality inspection and management using RFID technology. Autom. Constr. **17**(4), 467–479 (2008). https://doi.org/10.1016/j.autcon.2007.08.005, https://www.sciencedirect.com/science/article/pii/S0926580507001057
5. Bosché, F.: Automated recognition of 3D cad model objects in laser scans and calculation of as-built dimensions for dimensional compliance control in construction. Adv. Eng. Inform. **24**(1), 107–118 (2010). https://doi.org/10.1016/j.aei.2009.08.006, https://www.sciencedirect.com/science/article/pii/S1474034609000482, informatics for cognitive robots

6. Kropp, C., Koch, C., König, M.: Interior construction state recognition with 4D BIM registered image sequences. Autom. Constr. **86**, 11–32 (2018). https://doi.org/10.1016/j.autcon.2017.10.027, https://www.sciencedirect.com/science/article/pii/S0926580517304405
7. Pučko, Z., Šuman, N., Rebolj, D.: Automated continuous construction progress monitoring using multiple workplace real time 3D scans. Adv. Eng. Inform. **38**, 27–40 (2018). https://doi.org/10.1016/j.aei.2018.06.001, https://www.sciencedirect.com/science/article/pii/S1474034617305086
8. Wang, J., et al.: Integrating BIM and LiDAR for Real-Time Construction Quality Control. J. Intell. Robot. Syst. **79**(3), 417–432 (2014). https://doi.org/10.1007/s10846-014-0116-8
9. Qu, T., et al.: Construction site monitoring using UAV oblique photogrammetry and bim technologies. In: Proceedings of the 22nd Conference on Computer Aided Architectural Design Research in Asia (CAADRIA) (2017). https://api.semanticscholar.org/CorpusID:174790593
10. Annenkov, A.: Monitoring the deformation process of engineering structures using BIM technologies. Int. Arch. Photogram. Remote Sens. Spat. Inf. Sci. XLVI-5/W1-2022, 15–20 (2022). https://doi.org/10.5194/isprs-archives-XLVI-5-W1-2022-15-2022, https://isprs-archives.copernicus.org/articles/XLVI-5-W1-2022/15/2022/
11. Azhar, S., Nadeem, A., Mok, j., Leung, B.: Building information modeling (BIM): a new paradigm for visual interactive modeling and simulation for construction projects (2008)
12. Bryde, D., Broquetas, M., Volm, J.M.: The project benefits of building information modelling (BIM). Int. J. Project Manage. **31**(7), 971–980 (2013). https://doi.org/10.1016/j.ijproman.2012.12.001, https://www.sciencedirect.com/science/article/pii/S0263786312001779
13. Balaji, V., Suganthi, S., Rajadevi, R., Krishna Kumar, V., Saravana Balaji, B., Pandiyan, S.: Skin disease detection and segmentation using dynamic graph cut algorithm and classification through naive bayes classifier. Measurement **163**, 107922 (2020). https://doi.org/10.1016/j.measurement.2020.107922, https://www.sciencedirect.com/science/article/pii/S0263224120304607
14. Tsirikolias, K.: Low level image processing and analysis using radius filters. Digit. Signal Process. **50**, 72–83 (2016). https://doi.org/10.1016/j.dsp.2015.12.001, https://www.sciencedirect.com/science/article/pii/S1051200415003565
15. Rusu, R.B., Blodow, N., Beetz, M.: Fast point feature histograms (FPFH) for 3D registration. In: 2009 IEEE International Conference on Robotics and Automation, pp. 3212–3217 (2009). https://doi.org/10.1109/ROBOT.2009.5152473
16. Chan, T.O., Lichti, D.D., Belton, D., Nguyen, H.L.: Automatic point cloud registration using a single octagonal lamp pole. Photogram. Eng. Remote Sens. **82**(4), 257–269 (2016). https://doi.org/10.14358/PERS.82.4.257, https://www.sciencedirect.com/science/article/pii/S0099111216300817

Development and Implementation of a Six-Legged Skiing Robot for Cross-Country Skiing Techniques

Liangyu Wang, Yunpeng Yin, Limin Yang, Feng Gao[✉], and Xianbao Chen

State Key Laboratory of Mechanical System and Vibration, School of Mechanical Engineering, Shanghai Jiao Tong University, Shanghai 200240, China
gaofengsjtu@gmail.com

Abstract. This paper develops a novel six-legged skiing robot capable of cross-country skiing on complex snowy terrains that are not downhill. The robot emulates human cross-country skiing techniques, featuring a parallel ski board connection configuration with high mechanical performance and stability, and a ski pole mechanism that transitions between support and swing states. By estimating the snow conditions, the skiing robot selects the most optimal cross-country skiing technique for the current environment and utilizes gait planning to achieve various skiing techniques such as double-pole and diagonal stride. An improved centroid balance controller (CBC) is utilized during cross-country skiing, coordinating the force distribution between the ski poles and skis. Finally, field experiments conducted in natural snowy environments validate the terrain adaptability, stable mobility, and steering capabilities of the skiing robot on complex snowy terrains.

Keywords: Six-legged Skiing Robot · Cross-Country Skiing · Terrain Adaptability

1 Introduction

Adapting to complex terrains has always been a research focus for legged robots. Significant progress has been made in the stability and agility of legged robots on conventional terrains [1–3], but achieving stable movement in snowy environments, characterized by wet, soft, and low-temperature conditions, remains a challenge. While some researchers have developed skiing robots, research on skiing robots is still in its infancy, primarily focusing on humanoid robots and downhill skiing.

Yoneyama et al. [4] developed a bipedal skiing robot using an open-loop control method to glide on artificial grass slopes, focusing on the relationships between joint movements, reaction forces, and turning trajectories. Lahajnar et al. [5] developed a bipedal skiing robot capable of parallel skiing and introduced ZMP control into bipedal robot skiing. However, this robot could not display speed control during skiing. Han et al. [6] showcased a bipedal skiing robot at the 2018 PyeongChang Winter Olympics, with a research focus on recognizing markers on ski slopes and planning skiing paths using deep learning algorithms. Wu et al. [7] developed a servo-driven bipedal skiing robot and trained its turning model using a deep reinforcement learning control method. The first hexapod skiing robot et al. [8] debuted at the 2022 Beijing Winter Olympics, achieving high-speed skiing and obstacle avoidance on intermediate slopes. Subsequently, et al. [9] utilized ducted fans to enable the hexapod skiing robot to ski without relying on gravity.

In addition to alpine skiing, cross-country skiing holds a significant position in the realm of skiing sports [10]. Unlike alpine skiing, which converts gravitational potential energy into kinetic energy, cross-country skiing achieves movement on non-downhill snowy terrain through the coordinated use of ski poles and skis, giving rise to various skiing techniques. This paper aims to develop skiing robots capable of stable cross-country skiing on non-downhill snow surfaces, enhancing the adaptability of skiing robots to complex snowy environments.

The remainder of this paper is organized as follows. Section 2 introduces the mechanical design and analyzes the motion models of skis and ski poles. Section 3 proposes a decision model that selects the optimal cross-country skiing technique by estimating terrain conditions, and implements each skiing technique through gait planning and center of mass balance control. Section 4 experimentally validates the control strategies for cross-country skiing. Section 5 concludes the paper and discusses future work.

2 System Design

2.1 Mechanism Design

As shown in Fig. 1, the hexapod skiing robot has overall dimensions of approximately 1.5 m × 0.8 m × 1.0 m (length × width × height) and a total mass of about 50 kg. The robot consists of a body and six legs, designated as the left front leg (LF), left middle leg (LM), left hind leg (LH), right front leg (RF), right middle leg (RM), and right hind leg (RH). Each front and hind leg is connected to the skis via ball joints and Hooke hinges, while the middle legs on each side function as ski poles in alpine skiing. Each leg has the same configuration, featuring a three-degree-of-freedom design formed by the hip abduction/adduction (HAA) joint, the hip flexion/extension (HFE) joint, and the knee flexion/extension (KFE) joint in series. Each joint is driven by composite drive units, with the three composite drive units of each leg centrally mounted at the hip joint to improve the response characteristics of the leg mechanism. The composite drive units consist of actuators, torque sensors, encoders, harmonic reducers with a reduction ratio of 50, and brushless motors. The high reduction ratio allows each joint to output a torque of up to 140Nm, enabling the execution of complex skiing maneuvers and supporting a total payload of up to 40kg. Additionally, the robot's body is equipped with an Inertial Measurement Unit (IMU) to sense the body's posture, angular velocity, and acceleration. The external body is fitted with GPS and radar for navigation and obstacle avoidance functions.

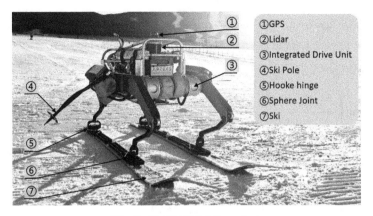

Fig. 1. Six-legged skiing robot.

2.2 Kinematics

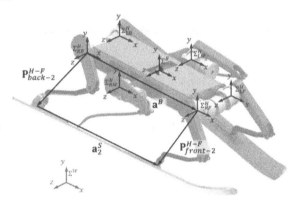

Fig. 2. Coordinate systems of six-legged skiing robot

As shown in Fig. 2, a body coordinate system Σ^B is established with the robot's body center of mass as the origin. A single leg coordinate system Σ^H is established with the origin at the intersection of the HAA joint axis and the HFE joint axis of each leg. The world coordinate system Σ^W is established with the origin at the projection of the robot's initial position center of mass on the ground. According to the Denavit-Hartenberg (D-H) method, the transformation matrix of the foot tip coordinates in the robot body coordinate system can be obtained as follows:

$$^BT_3 = {^BT_0}\,{^0T_1}\,{^1T_2}\,{^2T_3} \tag{1}$$

where $^{i-1}T_i$ is the transformation matrix from the $(i-1)^{th}$ coordinate system to the ith coordinate system.

Therefore, when the foot tip coordinates $\mathbf{p}_i^F = \begin{bmatrix} p_{ix}^F & p_{iy}^F & p_{iz}^F \end{bmatrix}^T$ are known, the coordinates of each joint in the corresponding leg can be obtained.

$$\mathbf{q}_i = \begin{bmatrix} q_i^{HAA} & q_i^{HFE} & q_i^{KFE} \end{bmatrix}^T$$

$$= \begin{bmatrix} \arctan\left(\dfrac{-\sqrt{p_{iy}^{F2} + p_{iz}^{F2} - L_1^2}}{sign(right)L_1}\right) - \arctan\left(\dfrac{p_{iy}^F}{p_{iz}^F}\right) \\ \arctan\left(\dfrac{p_{ix}^F}{\sqrt{p_{iy}^{F2} + p_{iz}^{F2} - L_1^2}}\right) - \arccos\left(\dfrac{p_{ix}^{F2} + p_{iy}^{F2} + p_{iz}^{F2} - L_1^2 + L_2^2 - L_3^2}{2L_2\sqrt{p_{ix}^{F2} + p_{iy}^{F2} + p_{iz}^{F2} - L_1^2}}\right) \\ \arccos\left(\dfrac{p_{ix}^{F2} + p_{iy}^{F2} + p_{iz}^{F2} - L_1^2 - L_2^2 - L_3^2}{2L_3 L_2}\right) \end{bmatrix}$$

(2)

where L_i represents the lengths of the segments in the single leg mechanism, and $sign(right)$ is an identification function for whether the leg is on the right side. For a right-side leg, the function returns 1, and for a left-side leg, the function returns -1.

During the skiing motion, robot's movement effect is primarily determined by the motion state of the skis. Therefore, it is necessary to establish a constraint relationship between the coordinates of the front and hind feet based on the motion state of the skis.

$$\mathbf{p}_{front-i}^F = \mathbf{p}_{back-i}^F + \mathbf{a}_i^S - \mathbf{a}^B \quad (i = 1, 2) \qquad (3)$$

where $\mathbf{a}^B$ is the robot body vector or the initial ski vector, with its direction along the positive x-axis and its length equal to the distance between the centers of the two ski hinges. $\mathbf{a}_i^S$ is the ski vector, where the right ski is numbered 1 and the left ski is numbered 2. This vector can be calculated based on the Euler angles of the skis:

$$\mathbf{a}_i^S = Rot(\alpha_i^S, \beta_i^S, \gamma_i^S)\mathbf{a}^B \quad (i = 1, 2) \qquad (4)$$

Due to the coupling between the tilting angle of the tiger hinge and its two-dimensional motion coordinates in the tangential plane, the ski has five degrees of freedom in motion. Therefore, the Euler angles in the equation above can be omitted, resulting in a simplified ski vector:

$$\mathbf{a}_i^S = Rot(\beta_i^S, \gamma_i^S)\mathbf{a}^B \quad (i = 1, 2) \qquad (5)$$

where β_i^S, γ_i^S represent the pitch angle and the yaw angle of the skis, respectively.

3 Control Strategy

Unlike the acquisition of kinetic energy in downhill skiing, which primarily comes from the conversion of gravitational potential energy, in cross-country skiing, we need to achieve the conversion of thrust work into kinetic energy in the forward direction through the coordinated use of ski poles and skis. In cross-country skiing, athletes evaluate the terrain features to adopt appropriate technical movements for the most efficient movement on snow. Common cross-country skiing techniques include double poling and diagonal stride.

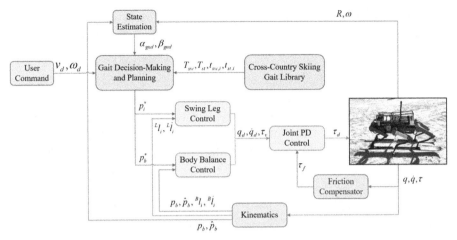

Fig. 3. Control framework of the skiing robot for cross-country skiing.

The overall control framework for the ski robot's cross-country skiing is shown in Fig. 3. After receiving the commands for speed and angular velocity $v_d, \omega_d \in \mathbb{R}^3$, the ski robot estimates the terrain condition based on body posture information detected by the IMU and joint kinematic parameters measured by encoders. Based on the terrain condition, it selects an appropriate gait from the cross-country skiing gait library and plans the trajectory according to the selected gait.

Gait control includes swing leg control and body balance control, using an improved centroid balance controller method to optimize the solution for tip forces. Due to the large joint friction resistance caused by high reduction ratio reducers in the robot's joint drive units, joint friction is compensated based on data from joint torque sensors. The final calculated actual joint output torque is sent to the driver for control in the form of current.

3.1 State Estimation

In cross-country skiing, athletes often decide which skiing technique to use based on factors such as terrain slope, snow conditions, and energy consumption status. This paper primarily analyzes how the ski robot estimates terrain slope and selects and implements various skiing techniques to adapt to different snow surface terrains, thereby achieving efficient and stable cross-country skiing.

Due to the significant zero drift error in the yaw angle of the IMU data, we establish an advance coordinate system Σ^A with the robot's body center as the origin, the y-axis always pointing upwards along the direction of gravity, and the plane P_{x-y} always coinciding with the plane of the robot body coordinate system P^B_{x-y}. Thus, the coordinates of the foot end in the advance coordinate system are:

$$\mathbf{p}_i^{A-F} = Rot\left(\alpha^{IMU}, \beta^{IMU}\right)\left(\mathbf{p}_i^{H-F} + \mathbf{p}_i^{B-H}\right) \tag{6}$$

According to geometric relationships, the unit normal vector of the slope $\mathbf{n}_G \in \mathbb{R}^3$ on which the robot is situated satisfies the following equation, where S_g represents the set of all feet in contact with the ground.

$$\left(\mathbf{p}_i^{A-F} - \mathbf{p}_j^{A-F}\right)^T \mathbf{n}_G = 0, \forall i, j \in S_g \tag{7}$$

Since the four legs connected to the skis remain in contact with the ground for an extended period, the above equation is over-constrained. There exists a least-squares solution, which can be obtained through QP (Quadratic Programming) decomposition. This allows us to determine the terrain slope $\mathbf{g}_{gnd} \in \mathbb{R}^2$.

$$\mathbf{g}_{gnd} = \begin{bmatrix} \alpha_{gnd} \\ \beta_{gnd} \end{bmatrix} = \begin{bmatrix} -\arcsin(\mathbf{n}_{Gy}) \\ \arcsin(\mathbf{n}_{Gx}/\cos(\alpha_{gnd})) \end{bmatrix} \tag{8}$$

where α_{gnd} and β_{gnd} represent the lateral slope and forward slope of the terrain relative to the robot's direction of movement, respectively.

Since the forward mobility of the ski robot is greater than its lateral mobility, the impact of the components of $\mathbf{g}_{gnd}$ on the cross-country skiing gait varies. By assigning different weights $\mathbf{W}_{gnd} \in \mathbb{R}^{2\times 2}$, the composite terrain slope can be determined.

$$g_{gnd} = \mathbf{g}_{gnd}^T \mathbf{W}_{gnd} \mathbf{g}_{gnd} \tag{9}$$

3.2 Gait Decision-Making and Planning

In cross-country skiing techniques, based on the slope, skiing gaits can be divided into double pole, diagonal stride, and herringbone climb. Double pole is suitable for flat or slightly downhill terrain, diagonal stride is suitable for flat or slightly undulating terrain, and herringbone climb is suitable for steeper uphill terrain. The scheduling of each skiing technique gait is shown in the Fig. 4. Since the gait distribution of diagonal stride and herringbone climb is the same, we treat them as a single gait in the planning of cross-country skiing for ski robots.

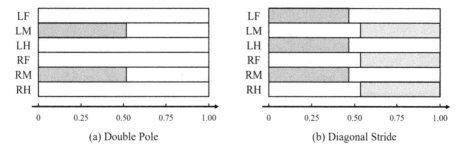

Fig. 4. Gait scheduler of double pole and diagonal stride

Based on the coefficient of friction between the skis and the snow surface, the non-slip slope constraint can be calculated. When $-g_\mu \leq g_{gnd} < g_\mu$, the double pole gait is used. By controlling the direction and trajectory of the pole movements on both sides, the robot can achieve forward movement, turning, or stationary turning on gentle slopes. When $g_{gnd} \geq g_\mu$, the robot uses the diagonal stride gait. By alternately stepping with the skis in a "V" shape and using diagonal pole support, it can move on steeper slopes. g_μ can be calculated based on the friction coefficient μ of the snow.

$$g_\mu = \arctan \mu \tag{10}$$

3.3 Swing Leg Control

In our previous research [11], by using a cycloid-based spatial compliance trajectory, we designed a gait trajectory for the swing leg that smoothly connects the swing trajectory and the support trajectory. The expression for this trajectory is as follows:

$$\mathbf{p}_{\xi_i}(t_{sw,i}) = \begin{bmatrix} p_{x,\xi_i} \\ p_{y,\xi_i} \\ p_{z,\xi_i} \end{bmatrix} = \frac{\mathbf{p}_i^* - \mathbf{p}_{\xi_i=0}}{2\pi}(\xi_i - \sin(\xi_i)) + \begin{bmatrix} 0 \\ 0 \\ \frac{h_z}{2} \end{bmatrix}(1 - \cos(\xi_i)) \tag{11}$$

where $\mathbf{p}_{\xi_i} \in \mathbb{R}^3$ denotes the function of the swing time $t_{sw,i}$ for the ith leg, $\xi_i = 2\pi \frac{t_{sw,i}}{T_{sw}} \in [0, 2\pi]$ represents the swing phase, $\mathbf{p}_i^*$ indicates the target foothold position to be calculated later, $\mathbf{p}_{\xi_i=0}$ is the position of the tip before lifting (at $t_{sw,i} = 0$), and h_z is the step height that needs to be raised during the swing. This trajectory is continuously differentiable, as illustrated in Fig. 5.

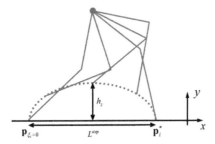

Fig. 5. Swing trajectory based on cycloid spatial composite trajectory

When the ski robot uses the double poling gait, it can achieve translation and turning by altering the support trajectory. Turning includes gliding turns and stationary turns. This is achieved by controlling the input v_b and the duration of the support phase to determine the poling step length L^{step} and the direction change angle γ^{step}.

$$\begin{bmatrix} L^{step} \\ \gamma^{step} \end{bmatrix} = \begin{bmatrix} v_{b,x} \\ v_{b,\omega} \end{bmatrix} T_{st} \tag{12}$$

From this, the contact trajectory length and curvature radius on the left and right sides of the ski robot during movement can be calculated.

$$C_p(\mathbf{v}_b) = \begin{bmatrix} L_{outside}^{step} \\ R_{outside}^{step} \\ L_{inside}^{step} \\ R_{inside}^{step} \end{bmatrix} = \begin{bmatrix} L^{step} \\ \dfrac{L_{outside}^{step}}{2\sin\left(\dfrac{\gamma^{step}}{2}\right)} \\ L_{outside}^{step} \dfrac{R_{outside}^{step}\cos\left(\dfrac{\gamma^{step}}{2}\right) - W^{mid}}{R_{outside}^{step}\cos\left(\dfrac{\gamma^{step}}{2}\right)} \\ \dfrac{L_{inside}^{step}}{2\sin\left(\dfrac{\gamma^{step}}{2}\right)} \end{bmatrix} \quad (13)$$

where $L_{outside}^{step}$ and $R_{outside}^{step}$ represent the chord length and curvature radius of the outer trajectory along the turning path, respectively. W^{mid} is the distance between the coordinate systems of the LM and RM legs. Based on the initial position of the contact trajectory, the swing down and swing up trajectories of the ski poles are generated. As shown in the Fig. 6, the contact trajectory of the ski poles is represented by the purple solid line in Σ^B, and the center of mass movement trajectory of the robot is represented by the red solid line in Σ^W. Finally, the double poling gait for forward or turning motion is completed through gait timing control.

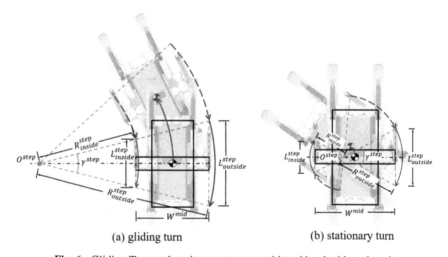

(a) gliding turn   (b) stationary turn

Fig. 6. Gliding Turn and stationary turn are achieved by double pole gait

When the ski robot uses the diagonal stride gait, according to the Spring-Loaded Inverted Pendulum (SLIP) model, the pre-selected value for the target touchdown point of the ith leg can be obtained as:

$$\mathbf{p}_{pre,i} = \mathbf{p}_B + \mathbf{R} \cdot {}^B\mathbf{p}_{HAA,i} + \frac{T_{st}}{2}\left(\mathbf{v} + \boldsymbol{\omega} \times {}^B\mathbf{p}_{HAA,i}\right)$$
$$+ (T_{sw} - t_{sw,i})\left(\mathbf{v}_d + \boldsymbol{\omega}_d \times {}^B\mathbf{p}_{HAA,i}\right) \quad (14)$$

where $\mathbf{p}_B$ represents the current position of the body, $\mathbf{R} \in SO(3)$ represents the current orientation, calculated from the Euler angles measured by the current Inertial Measurement Unit (IMU), and ${}^B\mathbf{p}_{HAA,i}$ is the position of the HAA joint of the ith leg in the body coordinate system. $\mathbf{v}$ and $\boldsymbol{\omega}$ are the current velocity and angular velocity of the body, respectively. $\mathbf{v}_d$ and $\boldsymbol{\omega}_d$ are the desired velocity and angular velocity. T_{sw} is the time duration of the stance phase, T_{sw} is the total duration of the swing phase, and $t_{sw,i}$ is the time the current leg has been in the swing phase.

When the terrain slope is steep, to prevent the skis from slipping on the snow, the angle between the two skis is increased, making the skis form a V-shape distribution. This increases the edge angle of the skis, enabling a herringbone climbing gait. At this time, the robot's forefeet will have a displacement $\Delta \mathbf{p}_i$ from the originally pre-selected touchdown points. According to Eqs. (4) and (6), the actual touchdown points of the forefeet can be calculated as:

$$\mathbf{p}_{front-i} = \mathbf{p}_{back-i} + Rot(\beta_i^S, \frac{T_{st}}{2}\omega_y + (T_{sw} - t_{sw,i})\omega_{d,y} + (-1)^i \delta g_{gnd})\mathbf{a}^B \quad (i = 1, 2) \quad (15)$$

where ω_y denotes the yaw component of the robot's angular velocity, $\omega_{d,y}$ denotes the yaw component of the planned angular velocity, and δ represents the conversion ratio between the slope angle and the angle between the two skis.

3.4 Body Banlance Control

In our previous research [11], we implemented complex terrain balance control using the centroid balance control (CBC). In cross-country skiing, we improved the CBC by differentially adjusting the tip forces on the supporting legs of the ski poles and skis. This enabled us to achieve body balance control that is adapted to the special gaits in cross-country skiing.

Assuming the mass of the legs is negligible compared to the body mass, and the body mass is concentrated at the Center of Mass (CoM), with the effects of Coriolis and centrifugal forces ignored, the simplified dynamics of the robot satisfy:

$$\begin{cases} m(\ddot{\mathbf{p}}_B + \mathbf{g}) = \sum_{i=1}^{\mu} \mathbf{f}_i \\ \hat{\mathbf{R}} \cdot {}^B\mathbf{I} \cdot \hat{\mathbf{R}}^T \dot{\omega}_B^* = \sum_{i=1}^{\mu} \hat{\mathbf{R}} \cdot {}^B\mathbf{l}_i \times \mathbf{f}_i \end{cases} \quad (16)$$

In the equation, m is the mass of the robot, $\mathbf{g}$ is the gravitational acceleration, ${}^B\mathbf{I}$ is the inertia matrix of the body in the frame $\sum^B$. μ represents the number of supporting legs, ${}^B\mathbf{l}_i$ is the position of the tip in the frame $\sum^B$, and $\mathbf{f}_i$ is the Ground Reaction Force (GRF) of the ith leg.

By solving for the virtual forces generated by CBC, feedback control of the body balance state can be achieved. The control equation is:

$$\begin{cases} \ddot{\mathbf{p}}_B^* = \mathbf{K}_{Pp}(\mathbf{p}_B^* - \hat{\mathbf{p}}_B) + \mathbf{K}_{Dp}(\dot{\mathbf{p}}_B^* - \hat{\dot{\mathbf{p}}}_B) \\ \dot{\boldsymbol{\omega}}_B^* = \mathbf{K}_{P\omega}(\log(\mathbf{R}^*\hat{\mathbf{R}}^T)) + \mathbf{K}_{P\omega}(\boldsymbol{\omega}_B^* - \hat{\boldsymbol{\omega}}_B) \end{cases} \quad (17)$$

where $\hat{\mathbf{p}}_B, \hat{\dot{\mathbf{p}}}_B$, and $\hat{\boldsymbol{\omega}}_B$ are the actual position, velocity, and angular velocity of the robot, and $\mathbf{p}_B^*, \dot{\mathbf{p}}_B^*$, and $\boldsymbol{\omega}_B^*$ are the desired position, velocity, and angular velocity of the robot. $\mathbf{K}_{Pp}, \mathbf{K}_{Dp}, \mathbf{K}_{P\omega}$ and $\mathbf{K}_{P\omega}$ are the diagonal matrices of proportional and derivative gains corresponding to position and attitude, respectively. Log(*) is the mapping from the rotation matrix to the rotation vector. Through the above PD control adjustments, the control values of the CoM acceleration and angular acceleration are obtained.

Rewriting Eq. (17) in matrix form gives:

$$\underbrace{\begin{bmatrix} \mathbf{I}_{3\times3} & \cdots & \mathbf{I}_{3\times3} \\ [\hat{\mathbf{R}} \cdot {}^B\mathbf{l}_1]\times & \cdots & [\hat{\mathbf{R}} \cdot {}^B\mathbf{l}_6]\times \end{bmatrix}}_{\mathbf{A}} \underbrace{\begin{bmatrix} f_1 \\ \vdots \\ f_6 \end{bmatrix}}_{\mathbf{f}} = \underbrace{\begin{bmatrix} m(\ddot{\mathbf{p}}_B + \mathbf{g}) \\ \hat{\mathbf{R}} \cdot {}^B\mathbf{I} \cdot \hat{\mathbf{R}}^T \dot{\boldsymbol{\omega}}^* \end{bmatrix}}_{\mathbf{b}} \quad (18)$$

where $\mathbf{I}_{3\times3}$ is the identity matrix. $[*]\times$ represents the antisymmetric matrix.

By formulating a QP problem, the above over-constrained system can be solved.

$$\mathbf{f}^* = \arg\min_{\mathbf{f}\in\mathbb{R}^{18}} \left((\mathbf{Af} - \mathbf{b})^T \mathbf{S}((\mathbf{Af} - \mathbf{b})) + \delta \mathbf{f}^2\right), \quad (19)$$
$$s.t.\ \mathbf{Cf} < \mathbf{D}$$

Among them, the diagonal matrix $\mathbf{S} \in \mathbb{R}^{18\times18}$ is the selection matrix used to identify whether the corresponding leg is in the support phase. The elements are zero when the corresponding leg is in the swing phase. When the leg is in the support phase, different weight values are assigned to the corresponding elements in $\mathbf{S}$ based on the bearing characteristics of the ski pole and ski-connected legs, so that more load is distributed to the ski-supporting legs. δ is the weight factor of the CBC, and matrices $\mathbf{C}$ and $\mathbf{D}$ represent the friction cone constraints. The virtual forces on the supporting legs $\mathbf{f}^*$ can be optimized using the above balance optimizer model.

4 Experiments

We conducted cross-country skiing experiments with the skiing robot at the Chifeng Ski Resort in Inner Mongolia, where the local temperature was -10 °C. The operator remotely sent movement commands to the skiing robot via a remote control handle and a communication system based on ZeroMQ.

4.1 Cross-Country Skiing Using Double Pole Technique

When the skiing robot is on flat snow terrain, it uses the double pole technique. It moves forward and turns by pushing off the ground with ski poles. The experimental results are shown in Figs. 7 and 8. Figure 7 shows that the robot advances 0.5 m with each push of the ski poles, with a maximum stride length of ± 0.5 m in the double pole gait. Figure 8 shows the robot making an in-place turn of 50° in a clockwise direction, with a maximum achievable in-place turning angle of ± 55°.

Fig. 7. Six-legged skiing robot moves forward using the double pole technique.

Fig. 8. Six-legged skiing robot rotates using the stationary turn technique.

Due to the high symmetry of the ground reaction forces on the left and right feet in the double pole technique of the skiing robot, we analyzed the forces on the tips of the three legs on the right side. As can be seen from the Fig. 9, when the ski poles touch the ground, the forces on the supporting legs connected to the skis change in the direction opposite to the forces on the ski poles.

4.2 Cross-Country Skiing Using Diagonal Stride Technique

The skiing robot conducted diagonal stride experiments at the bottom of a beginner slope. Using the planning and control methods described in the article, the skiing robot

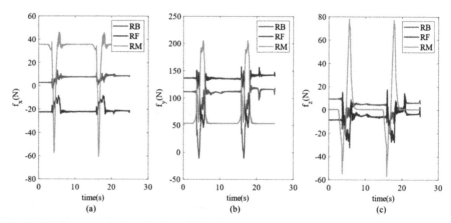

Fig. 9. The force received on the tips of the three legs on the right side along (a) the x-axis, (b) the y-axis, (c) the z-axis, when using double pole technique.

was able to stably achieve forward, backward, sideways movement, and turning on a slope with a certain gradient, as shown in Fig. 10. Analyzing the forces on the tips of the three legs on the right side as an example, the force distribution in each direction is shown in Fig. 11.

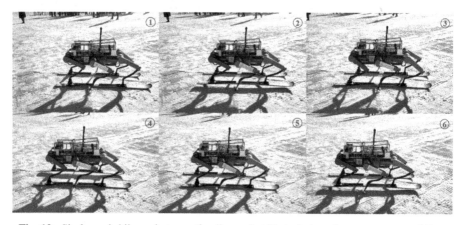

Fig. 10. Six-legged skiing robot uses the diagonal stride technique for cross-country skiing.

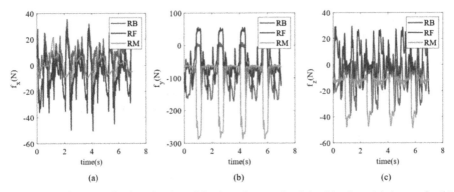

Fig. 11. The force received on the tips of the three legs on the right side along (a) the x-axis, (b) the y-axis, (c) the z-axis, when using diagonal stride technique.

5 Conclusion

This paper presents the development of the hardware system and the construction of the control system for a hexapod skiing robot used in cross-country skiing. By estimating the terrain conditions, the hexapod skiing robot can select the most suitable skiing technique from its cross-country skiing gait library, and achieve swing leg and body balance control through gait optimization and an improved centroid balance controller (CBC). Ultimately, it achieves movement and turning on non-downhill and even uphill terrain, demonstrating stronger adaptability to complex snowy terrains compared to existing skiing robots.

In future work, we will continue to optimize the cross-country skiing gaits to improve their dynamic performance. This research will provide important references for the movement of legged robots on soft geological surfaces.

References

1. Paul, V., Maxim, L., Subhrajit, B., et al.: Search-based planning for a legged robot over rough terrain. In: 2009 IEEE International Conference on Robotics and Automation, Kobe, Japan (2009), pp. 2380–2387 (2009)
2. Semini, C., Tsagarakis, N.G., Guglielmino, E., Focchi, M., et al.: Design of HyQ – a hydraulically and electrically actuated quadruped robot. Proc. Inst. Mech. Eng. Part I: J. Syst. Control Eng. **225**(6), 831–849 (2011)
3. Winkler, A.W., Bellicoso, C.D., Hutter, M., Buchli, J.: Gait and trajectory optimization for legged systems through phase-based end-effector parameterization. IEEE Robot. Autom. Lett. **3**(3), 1560–1567 (2018)
4. Yoneyama, T., Kagawa, H., Unemoto, M., Iizuka, T., Scott, N.W.: A ski robotsystem for qualitative modelling of the carved turn. Sports Eng. **11**(3), 131–141 (2009)
5. Lahajnar, L., Kos, A., Nemec, B.: Skiing robot - design, control, and navigation in unstructured environment. Robotica. **27**(4):567–577 (2009)
6. Han, Y.H., Jeon, H.J., Cho, B.K.: Development of a humanoid robot for the 2018 ski robot challenge. Int. J. Precis. Eng. Manuf. **21**(7), 1309–1320 (2020)

7. Wu, Z.G., Ye, J.T., Wang, X.R., Li, F.S.: Control of ski robot based on deep reinforcement learning. In: International Conference on Security, Pattern Analysis, and Cybernetics (SPAC), pp. 211–215 (2021)
8. Gao, F., Li, S., Gao, Y., Qi, C.K., Tian, Q.Y., Yang, G.Z.: Robots at the Beijing 2022 Winter Olympics. Sci. Robot. **7**(65), eabq0785 (2022)
9. Yang, L., et al.: Design and control of a novel six-legged robot for flat, downhill, and uphill skiing. In: International Conference on Intelligent Robotics and Applications, pp. 469–480 (2023)
10. Lind, D.A., Sanders, S.P.: The Physics of Skiing: Skiing at the Triple Point. Springer Science & Business Media (2013)
11. Yin, Y.P., Zhao, Y., Xiao, Y.G., Gao, F.: Footholds optimization for legged robot walking on complex terrain. Front. Mech. Eng. **18**(2), 26 (2023)

Soft Actuators and Sensors

Design of the Pole-Climbing Robot Based on Yoshimura Origami Actuator

Shilong Liu, Gangqiang Tang, Kangning Tan, Xiaofeng Yu, Dong Mei, Shunan An, and Yanjie Wang(✉)

Jiangsu Provincial Key Laboratory of Special Robot Technology, Hohai University, Changzhou Campus, Changzhou 213200, China
yj.wang1985@gmail.com

Abstract. Origami structure has good flexibility and folding ability. Based on the excellent axial deformation ability of Yoshimura origami structure, a pole-climbing robot driven by Yoshimura-ori actuators is designed. Firstly, a Yoshimura-ori actuator composed of Yoshimura-ori structure, thermoplastic urethane (TPU) sheet and polyethylene (PE) film is proposed and the actuator model is designed and fabricated. The relationship between the length of Yoshimura-ori actuator and the change of pressure is investigated. Then, a pneumatic adapter that can integrate and combine Yoshimura-ori actuators is proposed, and its design basis is analyzed. The working diameter range of the ring-shaped Yoshimura-ori actuator combination is measured, and the prototype of the pole-climbing robot is built. Finally, the control strategy of the pole-climbing robot is formulated, and its climbing performance is tested. The experimental results show that the pole-climbing robot has good climbing ability, and its ring structure can adapt well to the diameter size of the pole to realize the climbing function.

Keywords: Yoshimura-ori structure · Yoshimura-ori actuator · pneumatic adapter · pole-climbing robot

1 Introduction

Pole-climbing robot is a kind of robot designed to crawl and move on the surface of vertical pole or pipe, which has been widely concerned and studied for its advantages of strong flexibility and no need for human intervention [1]. It is often used to perform hazardous tasks that require operation on high or vertical surfaces, such as maintenance and overhaul of pipes [2, 3] or other structures [4, 5]. Traditional pole-climbing robots are composed of rigid joints and connecting rods. Most of them are driven by electromagnetic motors [6] and hydraulic drives [7], which can stably and powerfully complete climbing actions. However, they always have large volume and weight, poor environmental adaptability and slow climbing speed.

With the development of advanced soft materials, soft actuators such as pneumatic artificial muscle [8] and origami actuators [9] have received more and more attention because of their advantages of simple structure, lightweight material and good biological adaptability. They can meet the needs of pole-climbing robots for lightweight and flexibility, and there have been relevant studies in the field of pole-climbing robots [10]. Pneumatic artificial muscle has relatively good flexibility and environmental adaptability, but it is driven by positive pressure and its deformation rate is relatively small [11]. Origami actuator is made of origami structure as the skeleton, which has the advantages of large folding ratio and fast transformation [12]. Among them, Yoshimura-ori structure has good axial deformation ability and has typical application in engineering [13]. Based on this, it is of great potential to develop and design a pole-climbing robot based on Yoshimura-ori actuator, which has good climbing performance and fast climbing speed.

In this paper, we made a Yoshimura-ori actuator based on the Yoshimura-ori structure. Then a special pneumatic adapter for the interconnection between the Yoshimura-ori actuators is designed. The prototype of the pole-climbing robot is built based on the two key components of the Yoshimura-ori actuator and pneumatic adapter. Finally, the climbing function of the pole-climbing robot is verified through the built experimental platform.

2 Design and Test of the Yoshimura-ori Actuator

2.1 Design of the Yoshimura-ori Actuator

Yoshimura-ori structure has good axial deformation ability, and it can produce extreme shrinkage deformation under negative pressure. In this paper, the Yoshimura-ori structure is designed based on Ref. [14], as shown in Fig. 1(a) and 1(b) and the fabrication material is polyethylene terephthalate (PETE) film with a thickness of 0.15 mm. As shown in Fig. 1(c), the initial length of the folded origami skeleton is approximately 125 mm and the weight is 3.5 g.

The production process of the Yoshimura-ori actuator is shown in Fig. 2. Firstly, a Yoshimura-ori skeleton is fabricated using laser-cut PETE film. Secondly, the connection parts on the skeleton are bonded with UV glue, and then the skeleton is folded into Yoshimura-ori structure. Thirdly, due to the cavity characteristics of Yoshimura-ori structure, and in order to maintain the length of the skeleton after each contraction and deformation, 3D printed TPU sheets (thickness of 0.15 mm) are used to bond the two ends of the origami structure. At the same time, the installation tubes at both ends are heat treated, and the end faces of the air tubes are formed with convex rings and bonded to the TPU sheets. Then, the structure is encapsulated by hot-pressed PE film. Finally, the two ends of the origami structure are locked tightly with plastic rolling band locks.

As shown in Fig. 2, in order to facilitate the installation of the air tubes, the center of the TPU sheet designed in this paper has a circular hole with a diameter of 4 mm, whose size can be adjusted according to the size of the outer diameter of the connected air tube. The connected air tubes are polyurethane (PU) rigid tubes, which can provide a certain axial support force when the actuator is integrated.

2.2 Test of the Yoshimura-ori Actuator

The physical picture of the Yoshimura-ori actuator is shown in Fig. 3(a), its initial length is about 125 mm, the weight is 5.5 g. It is a compact and lightweight device. As shown

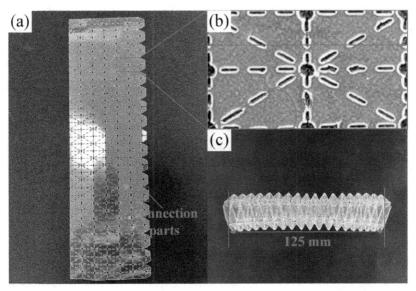

Fig. 1. Design of the Yoshimura-ori structure. (a) The laser-machined 2D sheet of a 3 × 18 Yoshimura-ori made of PETE film. (b) The constituent unit of Yoshimura-ori. (c) The obtained eighteen-layer Yoshimura-ori structure.

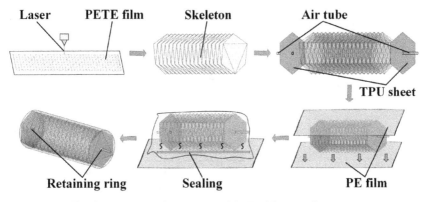

Fig. 2. The production process of the Yoshimura-ori actuator.

in Fig. 3(b), when the given air pressure is -45 kPa, the Yoshimura-ori actuator produces a considerable shrinkage deformation in the axial direction, shrinking to 21.6 mm within 1.2 s, and the shrinkage amount reaches 82.72%. It can be seen that the designed Yoshimura-ori actuator has a very large folding ratio and a very fast response speed, with excellent driving performance and good sealing.

In order to investigate the relationship between the length of Yoshimura-ori actuator and the pressure, we tested a single actuator with the pressure increment of -5 kPa. The experimental results are shown in Fig. 4. It can be seen that in the negative pressure range of 0 kPa - 15 kPa, the Yoshimura-ori actuator produces an obvious contraction

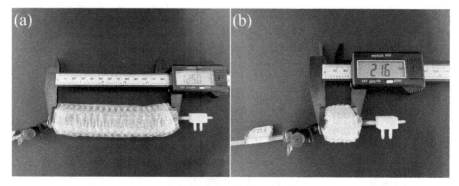

Fig. 3. The state diagram of the actuator based on Yoshimura-ori structure. (a) The state of being stretched. (b) The state of being compressed.

in the length direction, while in the negative pressure range of 15 kPa - 45 kPa, the deformation of Yoshimura-ori actuator in the length direction tends to be gentle. In general, as the negative pressure increases, the length of the Yoshimura-ori actuator continues to decrease.

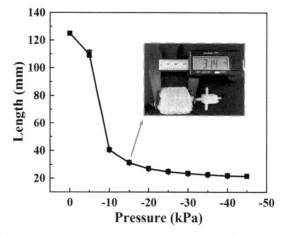

Fig. 4. The relationship between the length of the Yoshimura-ori actuator and the pressure.

3 Design of the Pneumatic Adapter and the Pole-Climbing Robot

3.1 Design of the Pneumatic Adapter

In order to integrate the designed Yoshimura-ori actuator to realize more complex motions, a special pneumatic adapter is designed to realize the connection between Yoshimura-ori actuator and its connection with the external air path. As shown in Fig. 5(a), the pneumatic adapter is designed with 6 round platforms, the size of which can be adjusted according to the size of the inner diameter of the connecting air tube to realize the connecting function. Among them, the round platform a and b, the round platform c and d are hollow round platforms, and the two are connected, so that the Yoshimura-ori actuator has the function of communicating with the external air path. The ventilation direction is shown in Fig. 5(a), the red dotted line is the airflow direction of the Yoshimura-ori actuator under negative pressure, and the blue solid line is the internal airflow direction of the Yoshimura-ori actuator when the contraction state changes to the relaxation state. The round platform e and f are solid round platforms, which are only used for connections between Yoshimura-ori actuators. In this paper, 3D printing technology is used to manufacture the pneumatic adapter. The manufacturing material is future resin 8000 and the weight is 2 g. The physical figure of the pneumatic adapter is shown in Fig. 5(b).

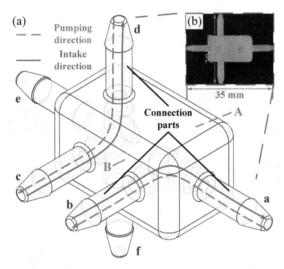

Fig. 5. Pneumatic adapter. (a) Three-dimensional model. (b) Concrete figure.

3.2 Design of the Pole-Climbing Robot

To achieve climbing on the pole surface, the robot actuator should have the axial deformation ability. Therefore, inspired by the arm and leg movements of a monkey climbing a tree, the pole-climbing robot is built based on the Yoshimura-ori actuator and the pneumatic adapter designed, as shown in Fig. 6. The pole-climbing robot consists of three parts: Group 1, Group 2 and Group 3. Groups 1 and 3 are connected in a ring by three Yoshimura-ori actuators and three pneumatic adapters respectively, which are used to complete the holding action of the pole surface during the climbing process of the pole-climbing robot. The three Yoshimura-ori actuators of Group 2 are successively connected to the corresponding pneumatic adapters of Group 1 and Group 3, which are used to complete the overall lifting action during the climbing process of the pole-climbing robot. As shown in Fig. 6, the overall height of the pole-climbing robot is about 220 mm and the weight is about 61.5 g, which has the advantages of lightweight and low cost compared with the traditional pole-climbing robot.

In addition, the pole-climbing robot has a total of 9 external air tubes (4 × 2.5 mm) connected to pneumatic adapters. Each Yoshimura-ori actuator corresponds to an external air tube to provide a channel for internal airflow. The external air tubes corresponding to the three parts of the Yoshimura-ori actuators in Group 1, Group 2 and Group 3 are respectively integrated in a four-way pneumatic quick joint, which is communicated with the external air source. Therefore, the pole-climbing robot has 3 air channels communicated with the outside. In this paper, PU tube is used as the external air tube of the pole-climbing robot, which can reduce its interference to the actuator during the climbing process of the pole-climbing robot.

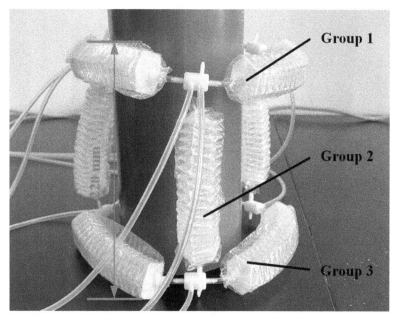

Fig. 6. Pole-climbing robot.

The action of pole-climbing robot to hold the pole surface during the climbing process is realized by the simultaneous contraction of the ring-shaped Yoshimura-ori actuator groups. At the same time, the Yoshimura-ori actuator is a flexible actuator. Therefore, the size of the pneumatic adapter is directly related to the degree of fit of the pole-climbing robot with the pole surface during the climbing process. The larger the size of the pneumatic adapter, the lower the fit degree between the pole-climbing robot and the pole surface. Therefore, without affecting the function of the pneumatic adapter, the robot with smaller pneumatic adapters, will have the better performance. The size of the designed pneumatic adapter is shown in Fig. 5(b). At the same time, the position distribution of the round platform connected by the pneumatic adapter is related to the distribution of the external air tubes, which will significantly affect the climbing height and the continuity of climbing actions of the pole-climbing robot, and then affect the performance of the pole-climbing robot. Based on this, the round platform distribution of the pneumatic adapter designed is shown in Fig. 5(a). Among them, the round platform b and c that need to be connected to the external air tubes are located on the B plane. The A plane is in the state of bonding with the pole surface during the climbing process, so the round platform connection position is not set on this plane.

3.3 Test of the Ring-Shaped Yoshimura-Ori Actuator Combination

The diameters of the climbing poles of the pole-climbing robot are different in different working environments. Therefore, we measured the maximum and minimum diameters of the tangent circles formed by the ring-shaped Yoshimura-ori actuator combination. As shown in Fig. 7(a), select the appropriate round cardboard as a reference. In the relaxed state, the maximum diameter of the tangent circle is about 130 mm. As shown in Fig. 7(b), in the contracted state, the minimum diameter of the tangent circle is about 56 mm. Therefore, the pole-climbing robot can realize the climbing task of the diameter of the pole in the range of 56 mm - 130 mm.

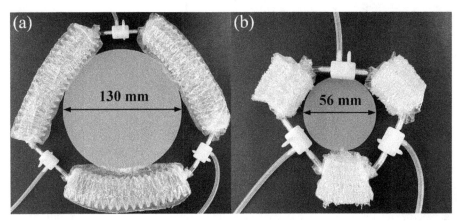

Fig. 7. The working diameter of the pole-climbing robot. (a) Maximum working diameter. (b) Minimum working diameter.

4 Climbing Testing

According to the pole-climbing robot designed, we built its control platform. The air compressor provides a stable air source, and the vacuum generator uses the positive air source to generate negative pressure. The airflow of the three air channels of the pole-climbing robot is controlled by a proportional pressure valve respectively. The PC sends instructions to the STM32 through the serial port to control the proportional pressure valve group. Therefore, the internal air pressure control of Yoshimura-ori actuator is realized. The precise attitude adjustment of the pole-climbing robot will be coordinate after the addition of position sensors in the future.

We developed the control strategy of the pole-climbing robot, as shown in Fig. 8. It should be noted that before the execution of the climbing action, each air channel of the pole-climbing robot is in a state of negative pressure tightening. At this time, the overall height of the pole-climbing robot is about 110 mm. When the system is stable, the pole-climbing robot begins to perform the set actions according to the control strategy.

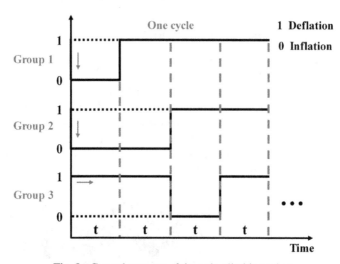

Fig. 8. Control strategy of the pole-climbing robot.

Here we used a water pole with an outer diameter of 114 mm as the climbing object of the pole-climbing robot to test its actual climbing ability, as shown in Fig. 9. It should be pointed out that the working pressure of each part of the pole-climbing robot set here is -45 kPa, and the working time interval $t = 7$ s. After a control cycle, the pole-climbing robot climbs about 90 mm, and the time spent is 28 s. The climbing performance of the pole-climbing robot is greatly affected by the connection position, length and weight of the external air tubes, which may cause the pole-climbing robot to slip and fall during the climbing process after a certain height. Meanwhile, since the Yoshimura-ori actuator designed is a flexible actuator, the three Yoshimura origami actuators in group 2 have low stiffness in the climbing direction and slightly bend in the relaxed state. These are the directions that we will further improve the pole-climbing robot in the future.

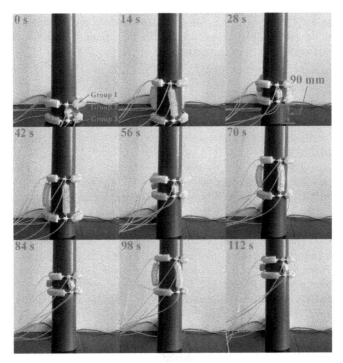

Fig. 9. Climbing test of the pole-climbing robot.

5 Conclusion

In this paper, the design process and performance test of a pole-climbing robot are introduced. The Yoshimura-ori actuator, which forms the backbone of the robot, has a shrinkage rate of 82.72% within 1.2 s under −45 kPa air pressure, indicating excellent deformation performance and fast response speed. The length of the actuator decreases with the increase of negative pressure. In addition, a pneumatic adapter is proposed to realize the integrated connection between the Yoshimura-ori actuators. Through the pneumatic adapter, the Yoshimura-ori actuator can be connected to the external air path to realize the telescoping function. The pole-climbing robot is integrated by the Yoshimura-ori actuators and pneumatic adapters, which is fast and easy to assemble and has lightweight. The working diameter range of the pole-climbing robot is determined through the test of the ring-shaped Yoshimura-ori actuator combination. Finally, the pole-climbing robot is built, which consists of two ring-shaped Yoshimura-ori actuator combinations for holding the pole surface and one Yoshimura-ori actuator combination for lifting the robot. The control strategy of the pole-climbing robot is formulated and the experiment platform is built. The pole-climbing robot is driven in combination by the experiment platform. When the working interval is set to 7 s, the pole-climbing robot climbs 90 mm in one control cycle (28 s), indicating that it has good climbing ability.

Acknowledgement. This research was supported by the Ministry of Education Joint Fund (8091B032250), the Fundamental Research Funds for the Central Universities (B240205045). The authors gratefully acknowledge the supports.

References

1. Tang, D., Yu, W., Lv, X., et al.: Research progress on pole-climbing robots: a review. Recent Pat. Eng. **18** (2023)
2. Zhang, Y., Guan, E., Li, P., et al.: A novel magnetic circuit design method for a permanent magnetic chuck of a wall-climbing robot. Energies **15**(18), 6653 (2022)
3. Lu, Z.J., Wu, S.L., Feng, Y., et al.: Climbing robot based on triangle wheels obstacle crossing design: modeling simulation and motion analysis. J. Braz. Soc. Mech. Sci. Eng. **45**(10), 539 (2023)
4. Liu, Z., Lu, J., Du, H., et al.: Research on climbing robot for transmission tower based on foot-end force balancing algorithm. Actuators **12**(12), 441 (2023)
5. Lin, T.H., Putranto, A., Chen, P.H., et al.: High-mobility inchworm climbing robot for steel bridge inspection. Autom. Constr. **152**, 104905 (2023)
6. Qiaoling, D., Yan, L., Sinan, L.: Design of a micro pole-climbing robot. Int. J. Adv. Rob. Syst. **16**(3), 1729881419852813 (2019)
7. Ban, Y., Lyu, K., Ba, S., et al.: Monkeybot: a climbing and pruning robot for standing trees in fast-growing forests. Actuators **11**(10), 287 (2022)
8. Zhong, S., Gai, Z., Yang, Y., et al.: A contraction length feedback method for the McKibben pneumatic artificial muscle. Sens. Actuators, A **334**, 113321 (2022)
9. Junfeng, H.E., Guilin, W.E.N., Jie, L.I.U., et al.: A modular continuous robot constructed by Miura-derived origami tubes. Int. J. Mech. Sci. **261**, 108690 (2024)
10. Guan, Q., Liu, L., Sun, J., et al.: Multifunctional soft stackable robots by netting–rolling–splicing pneumatic artificial muscles. Soft Rob. **10**(5), 1001–1014 (2023)
11. Kalita, B., Leonessa, A., Dwivedy, S.K.: A review on the development of pneumatic artificial muscle actuators: force model and application. Actuators **11**(10), 288 (2022)
12. Kim, W., Byun, J., Kim, J.K., et al.: Bioinspired dual-morphing stretchable origami. Sci. Robot. **4**(36), eaay3493 (2019)
13. Li, S., Stampfli, J.J., Xu, H.J., et al.: A vacuum-driven origami "magic-ball" soft gripper. In: 2019 International Conference on Robotics and Automation (ICRA), pp. 7401–7408. IEEE, Montreal, QC, Canada (2019)
14. Zhang, Q., Fang, H., Xu, J.: Yoshimura-origami based earthworm-like robot with 3-dimensional locomotion capability. Frontiers Robot. AI **8**, 738214 (2021)

A Soft Pneumatic Gripper Integrated Strain and Piezoresistive Sensors for Grasping Detection

Xin Zhao, Jianfeng Wang, Gangqiang Tang, Dong Mei, Chun Zhao, and Yanjie Wang[✉]

Jiangsu Provincial Key Laboratory of Special Robot Technology, Hohai University, Changzhou Campus, Changzhou 213200, China
yj.wang1985@gmail.com

Abstract. The matching mechanical impedance between the flexible sensors and the soft gripper will endow the soft pneumatic gripper with excellent actuating performance and sensing ability. In this paper, a conductive elastomer based on Polydimethylsiloxane (PDMS) doping carbon conductive filler is proposed, which has similar mechanical properties with the body material of the gripper. The resistive strain senso was fabricated based on a conductive elastomer, and the piezoresistive sensor was assembled by two conductive elastomers with microstructures, which were used to monitor bending deformation and pressure changes, respectively. Two essential factors of the conductive filler type and the MWCNTs mixing ratio have been investigated to improve the sensitivity and mechanical properties of proposed sensors. MWCNTs with large aspect ratio has been selected as the conductive filler. The resistance strain sensor, filled with 8 wt%, displays good angular discrimination ability with a sensitivity of 0.107 kΩ/°. The piezoresistive sensor exhibits good force sensitivity within 0 ~ 350 kPa range. The sensors have been integrated into the designated area of a soft pneumatic gripper and well reflect the diameter and weight of the grasped object.

Keywords: Conductive Elastomer · Strain sensor · Piezoresistive sensor · Soft pneumatic gripper · Grasping detection

1 Introduction

Compared with rigid continuum robots, soft robots with the inherent material properties make the interaction between environment and robots safer and more efficient [1]. With its high flexibility, safety and adaptability, soft pneumatic gripper has been widely used in medical industry [2], industrial manufacture [3], human-computer interaction [4] and other fields. Soft grippers have been developed with a variety of types to realize the different grasping functions [5–8]. Among them, the pneumatic soft finger has the characteristics similar to human hands [9]. The deformation of the finger can enlarge the grasping range, and finally realize the dexterous grasping. To further improve the autonomy and adaptability of the soft pneumatic gripper in unstructured environments, it is necessary to develop the ability to sense both its internal state and the external surroundings in real-time. The feedback information generated can improve the handling effect of objects and enhance the interactive ability with the environment. However, many grippers are designed without feedback function, and the contact state between the gripper and the gripped object is unclear. As a result, it is hard to perceive the object information and automatically adjust the grasping strategy to meet various work needs. A variety of flexible sensors have been developed to improve the interaction level between the gripper and the environment. These flexible sensors are commonly utilized to convert force and deformation into resistance [10], capacitance [11], voltage [12] and other information. Besides, magnetic sensors [13] and optical fiber sensors [14] have also been developed and implemented in soft grippers. Although there are many approaches for soft grippers sensing, there are still many limitations and challenges [15] to properly integrating stretchable or flexible sensors with a soft pneumatic gripper. In particular, the mechanical impedance mismatch between the sensor and the soft gripper will not only reduce the sensitivity and stability of the flexible sensor due to the low mechanical coupling, but also limit the ability of the soft gripper to undergo large deformations due to the increased stiffness.

To solve the problems of complex process and poor compatibility of the existing flexible sensors, a conductive elastomer based on Polydimethylsiloxane (PDMS) doping carbon conductive filler was fabricated for strain sensing, and the piezoresistive sensor was assembled and manufactured by transferring microstructures on the conductive elastomer. The appropriate contents of multi-walled carbon nanotubes (MWCNTs), carbon black (CB) and carbon fiber (CF) in the PDMS matrix have been investigated to enhance the sensitivity and durability of the flexible sensor. The optimized preparation process endows the conductive elastomer with great mechanical and electrical properties. The electrical experiments have been carried out to demonstrate the deformation and pressure response characteristics of the proposed sensors, respectively. The soft pneumatic gripper was manufactured using mold casting method. The similar mechanical characteristics of flexible sensors and the gripper body material make them well integrated into a whole structure, which can realize the both autologous and extraneous sensing ability without sacrificing the actuating performance of the soft gripper. The effectiveness of the proposed sensors in the grasping detection of the soft pneumatic gripper has been proved by grasping objects with different diameters and weights.

2 Materials and Methods

2.1 Materials and Experimental Configuration

Polydimethylsiloxane (PDMS, Sylgard 184) was purchased from Dow Corning Chemical Company (Midland, MI, USA). Multi-walled carbon nanotubes (MWCNTs, with diameters of 8–15 nm and lengths of ~ 50 μm) and carbon black (CB, 30–40 nm in particle sizes and 125 m2/g in specific surface area) were purchased from XFNANO Tech Co., Ltd (Nanjing, China). Carbon fiber (CF, with diameters of 7 μm and lengths of 1/3 mm) was purchased from Toray Industries, Inc. (Shanghai, China). The isopropyl alcohol solution (purity ≥ 99.7%) was purchased from Aladdin (Shanghai, China). The two-component silica gel material (E630) was purchased from Hongyejie Tech Co.,

Ltd. (Shenzhen, China). The experimental platform for performance evaluation of the resistive sensors mainly consists of a push-pull dynamometer, a digital multimeter, and an upper computer. The resistance sensors were stretched and loaded using a push-pull dynamometer, then the resistance changes were recorded by a digital multimeter synchronously. During the dynamic response test of the resistive sensors, the stepper motor actuated the linear slide table to drive the resistive strain sensor to get stretched and released, and the loading and unloading on the piezoresistive sensor were applied by the pressing element driven by the vibration exciter. The control system for operating and sensing feedback of soft pneumatic grippers is shown in the Fig. 1.

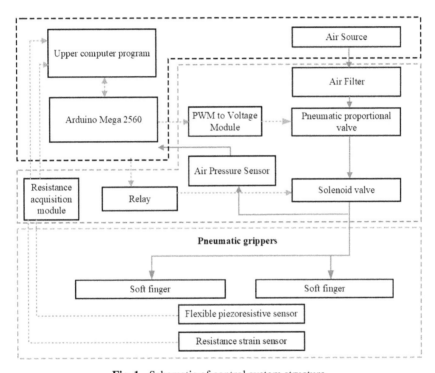

Fig. 1. Schematic of control system structure.

2.2 Optimization Process of the Fabrication of the Conductive Elastomer

The conductive elastomer is the main sensing element of the resistance sensor, which mechanical and electrical properties are closely related to the sensing characteristics of the sensors. Resistive sensors inevitably require sufficient strength and ductility of the substrate, PDMS (polydimethylsiloxane) is chosen as the substrate material of flexible sensors in this work. The conductivity and mechanical performances of the conductive elastomer are largely determined by the type and content of the conductive filler, thus affecting the sensitivity and tensile properties of the sensor. In order to enhance the sensing performance and compliance of the sensors, the effect of conductive fillers on the conductive elastomer will be further investigated. To select the appropriate conductive fillers, multi-walled carbon nanotubes (MWCNTs), carbon black (CB) and carbon fiber (CF) were mixed with PDMS respectively. Then the resistivity, Shore hardness and elastic modulus of the obtained conductive elastomer samples (size of 30 mm × 10 mm × 1 mm) were tested and compared (the average value was taken after three tests). To obtain improved stretch ratio and enhanced sensitivity, the factors of conductive filler content have also been investigated. Under the same preparation conditions, the tensile properties of the conductive elastomers with four filler contents of 6 wt%, 8 wt%, 10 wt% and 12 wt% were compared by concentration gradient experiments. The sensitivity of resistance sensor can be calculated by $GF = (\Delta R/R)/(\Delta L/L)$. R and L represent the initial resistance and the initial length of the samples, respectively, while ΔR denotes the resistance change and ΔL is the length change of the samples.

2.3 Fabrication of Resistive Strain Sensor and Piezoresistive Sensor

Since PDMS is a cross-linked polymer, the conductive filler is improved dispersed in the matrix after being pre-mixed with PDMS prepolymer and then for cross-linking curing. The specific preparation process is shown in Fig. 2. Firstly, the conductive filler with the corresponding mass fraction was added into the isopropyl alcohol solution (the mass ratio of conductive filler to isopropanol was 1:100), and the conductive filler dispersion was obtained after stirring for 30 min with a magnetic stirrer. Then the PDMS prepolymer was added to the prepared dispersion, and the dispersion was magnetically stirred for 30 min to obtain the conductive filler/PDMS prepolymer dispersion, which was placed in a vacuum drying oven for 12 h to volatilize the solvent. At this time, in order to avoid hardening and cracking of the conductive mixture caused by too high temperature, the temperature of the vacuum oven is 50 °C. After Solvent volatilization, the cross-linking agent with the mass of 1/10 of the PDMS was added into the obtained conductive filler /PDMS prepolymer mixture. Next, the conductive mixture was uniformly mixed by an electric blender for 5 min, and the mixture was injected into prepared molds after air bubbles are eliminated by vacuum. The uncured conductive mixture was filled in the mold with a smooth surface by coating and scraping, and the cured conductive elastomers were obtained after heat curing at 60 °C for 8 h. Finally, the conductive silver adhesive was used for fixing the conductive tapes at two sides of the cut conductive elastomer to obtain the resistive strain sensor. During the fabrication of the piezoresistive sensor, the microstructure on the surface of the sand paper was transferred to one side of the conductive elastomer to enhance the sensitivity. Two conductive elastomers with the microstructure were vertically stacked face-to-face, then the piezoresistive sensor was obtained after packing by the pure PDMS layer.

2.4 Fabrication of the Soft Finger and Assembly with the Sensors

The soft pneumatic gripper is obtained by casting the two-component silica gel material into 3D printed molds for curing and molding, the resistive strain sensor is installed on the upper silica gel layer of the limiting layer to prevent a large bending measurement error caused by touching objects, and the piezoresistive sensor is installed on the lower silica gel layer of the limiting layer which can be directly contacted with the object

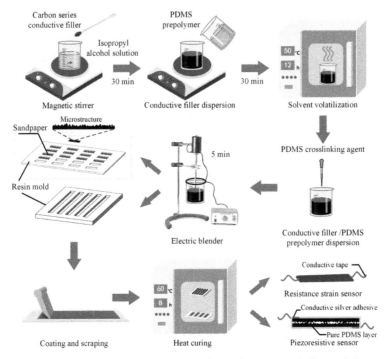

Fig. 2. The manufacturing process of the resistive strain sensor and piezoresistive sensor.

to measure the contact force. The specific manufacturing process is shown in Fig. 3. Firstly, the main body mold and the bottom limiting layer mold of the soft pneumatic gripper were fabricated by 3D printing. Then the silica gel A and B components were mixed uniformly in a mass ratio of 1:1, and the defoamed silica gel solution was slowly poured into the assembled mold until the silica gel was adequately filled in the whole mold. The mold was placed in a constant-temperature drying oven at 60 °C for 5 h and then take out to obtain the main body of the soft pneumatic gripper and the upper and lower silica gel layers of the bottom limiting layer. The resistive strain sensor and the piezoresistive sensor were embedded into reserved grooves of the silica gel layers respectively, and then assembling and compacting to form a limiting layer according to the sequence of the silica gel layer-paper-silica gel layer, wherein silica gel solution was used as an adhesive between the layers. After heating and curing, a bottom limiting layer integrated with a resistive strain sensor and a piezoresistive sensor was obtained. Finally, the bottom limiting layer was attached to the main body of the soft pneumatic gripper through a silica gel adhesive, and the soft pneumatic gripper with sensing capability was obtained after curing. In order to verify the feasibility of the sensors and the soft pneumatic gripper, a two-finger gripper was assembled for grasping tests.

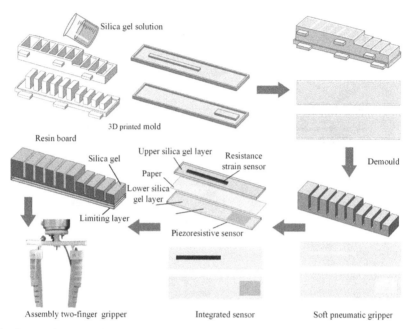

Fig. 3. A soft pneumatic gripper integrated with the strain sensor and piezoresistive sensor.

3 Results and Discussion

3.1 Performances of the Conductive Elastomer

The conductivity of the conductive elastomer depends on the concentration of the conductive filler in the substrate material. In the case of well dispersion of conductive fillers, the resistivity and concentration will show an obvious percolation effect. To investigate the percolation concentration interval of three conductive fillers, the resistivity of the samples doped with different conductive fillers are shown in Fig. 4 (a). It can be seen that the percolation concentration of the three conductive fillers from low to high is MWCNTs, CB and CF, because the diameter of MWCNTs and the particle size of CB are nano-scale, which is better dispersed than the micro-scale of CF. As a typical one-dimensional nanomaterial, MWCNTs has a large aspect ratio, which is easier to form conductive network than CB particles with 0-dimensional structure. Therefore, the MWCNTs can produce good conductivity at a lower doping concentration. As the concentration of conductive fillers increases, the charge transfer resistance and resistivity of each sample cohort gradually decrease, suggesting formation of a more complete conductive network within the elastomers. PDMS elastomer (prepolymer: crosslinking agent = 10:1) has good elastic deformation ability and low elasticity modulus, with Shore hardness of 43 HA. The doping of conductive fillers will inevitably affect the mechanical properties of PDMS elastomer. As shown in Fig. 4 (b), CF/PDMS composite elastomers have the highest hardness, which is due to the fact that carbon fiber has the highest percolation threshold and requires a larger mass fraction (34 wt%–42 wt%) to be conductive, thus sacrificing the flexibility. The hardness of MWCNTs/PDMS and

CB/PDMS composites elastomers increased slowly with the increase of conductive filler concentration. Further, the stress-strain curves of the samples were obtained using a universal tensile testing machine, and the elastic modulus calculated are shown in Fig. 4 (c). The elastic modulus of CF/PDMS elastomers varies in a wide range, and the elongation at break is less than 50%. The elastic modulus of MWCNTs/PDMS and CB/PDMS composite elastomers were similar. In conclusion, the conductive elastomer fabricated using 8wt% MWCNT has both good conductivity and flexibility. In order to enhance the sensing performance of the flexible sensor, the influence of the MWCNTs concentration on the sensitive characteristics of the conductive elastomer was investigated. The relative change of the resistance values of MWCNTs/PDMS elastomers with different MWCNT contents in the stretched state is shown in Fig. 4 (d). With the increase of tensile strain, the $\Delta R/R$ of MWCNTs/PDMS elastomers increases gradually, which is due to the internal conductive network structure of the elastomer change from dense to sparse. Under the same $\Delta L/L$, the MWCNTs/PDMS conductive elastomer with 8% MWCNTs has the optimal tensile sensitivity. With the further increase of MWCNTs content, the internal conductive network tends to be saturated, and the hardness will become larger, which weakens the deformation ability and leads to the lower sensitivity.

3.2 Sensing Performances of the Sensors

To measure the bending sensing performance of the resistive strain sensor, an empty slot with an arc length of 70 mm and a bending angle ranging from 0° to 180° in increments of 30° was created via 3D printing. The sensor was then affixed to the inner surface of one side of the slot to measure the corresponding resistance value. Figure 5 (a) displays the change in resistance of the resistive strain sensor at different bending angles. As the bending angle increases from 0° to 180°, the resistance of the resistive strain sensor increases linearly, resulting in a sensitivity of 0.107 kΩ/°. This effect is attributed to the change in the internal conductive network caused by the bending strain. Figure 5 (b) depicts the dynamic response signals of the resistive strain sensor at various bending angles. The resistive strain sensor exhibits dynamic response characteristics within two bending ranges of 30°−60° and 60°−90°. Specifically, the signal amplitude remains consistent with the peak shape, indicating excellent signal repeatability. The sensing signal's wave trough within the 60°−90° bending range nearly aligns with the wave crest of the sensing signal in the 30°−60° bending range, demonstrating the excellent angle recognition ability of the resistive strain sensor. Within the 120°−180° range, the resistive strain sensor shows a more prominent dynamic response signal as the bending angle increases, demonstrating that the sensor still has exceptional bending angle recognition ability even with large deformations. To evaluate the pressure response characteristics of the piezoresistive sensor, static loads ranging from 0–350 kPa were applied, as illustrated in Fig. 5 (c). The relative resistance change of the piezoresistive sensor displays two reliable linear response regions as the load increases. The sensitivity is 0.008 kPa^{-1} in the range of 0–20 kPa and 1.141×10^{-4} kPa^{-1} in the range of 20–350 kPa. This is due to the existence of microstructure makes the internal structure of the piezoresistive sensor larger, and the larger Poisson's ratio leads to greater deformation of the piezoresistive sensor at a very low pressure. As the pressure increases, the contact between the microstructures tends to become saturated and the Poisson's ratio of the

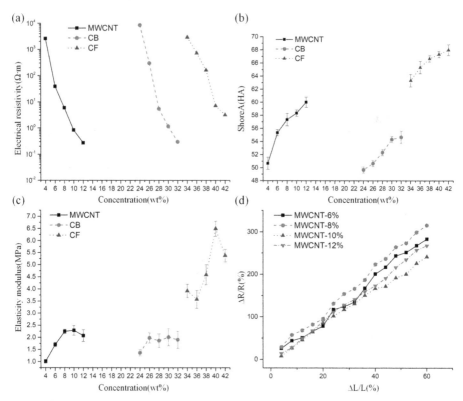

Fig. 4. Optimization of electromechanical properties of conductive elastomers (a) Effect of different types of conductive fillers on the conductivity of conductive elastomers (b) Effect of different types and concentrations of conductive fillers on the hardness of conductive elastomers (c) Effect of different types and concentrations of conductive fillers on the modulus of elasticity of conductive elastomers (d) Static tensile properties of MWCNT/PDMS conductive elastomers at different concentrations.

piezoresistive sensor decreases, resulting in a decrease in the deformation capability and sensitivity. To test the dynamic response characteristics of the piezoresistive sensor, dynamic loads of 5kPa, 10kPa and 15kPa were applied to the same sensor sample, respectively, and the dynamic response signals obtained are shown in Fig. 5(d). As the dynamic load decreases, the amplitude of ΔR decreases accordingly, indicating that the piezoresistive sensor has a good ability to detect the pressure. The sensing signal shows consistent peaks and troughs when subjected to the same pressure load, indicating the flexible piezoresistive sensor has a high degree of repeatability accuracy.

3.3 Grasping Detection of the Soft Gripper

To demonstrate the potential applications in grasping detection, the soft pneumatic gripper with sensing capabilities was fixed at the end of the six-axis mechanical arm. A two-finger gripper was implemented for grasping tests., and the switching between the

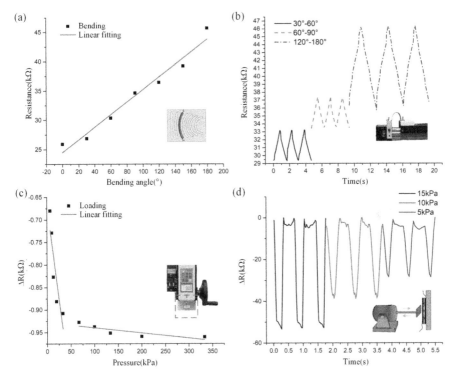

Fig. 5. Sensing performances of the sensors (a) Static bending response of the resistive strain sensor (b) Dynamic response of the resistive strain sensor (c) Relative resistance change of the piezoresistive sensor during loading (d) Dynamic response of the piezoresistive sensor

free state and the bending state of the soft pneumatic gripper was regulated by a pneumatic experimental platform. When the soft pneumatic gripper bent to fit the target object, the corresponding resistance change values of the resistive strain sensor and piezoresistive sensor were recorded. To demonstrate the feasibility of the soft pneumatic gripper integrated flexible strain sensor, a two-finger gripper grasps plastic tubes with outer diameters of 10.5 mm, 32 mm, 50 mm and 60 mm respectively, and the resistance change of the strain sensor is shown in Fig. 6(a–d). The loading-unloading grasping experiments have been conducted and the peak values in the sensing signals are utilized to represent the different diameters of grasping objects. The resistance value of the strain sensor in its free state is 27.6 kΩ. By gripping a circular plastic tube with an outer diameter of 10.5 mm, the response resistance of the strain sensor increases to 34.17 kΩ, an increase of 23.80%. As the diameter of the plastic tube increases, the bending degree of the soft gripper decreases during grasping, thus the increase in strain sensor response resistance decreases (13.19%, 9.71%, 7.79% at 32 mm, 50 mm and 60 mm diameters respectively). These results prove that the proposed strain sensor can detect the diameter size of the objects grasped by the soft pneumatic gripper, and the sensing accuracy is higher for small-sized objects.

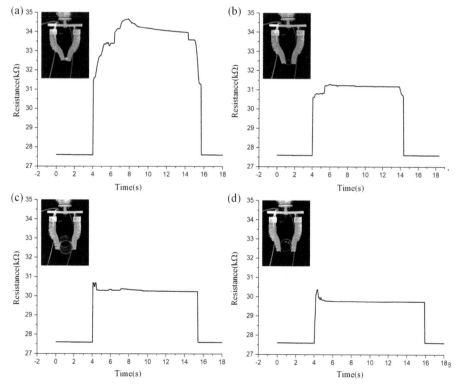

Fig. 6. Grasping objects with different diameters (a) Outer diameters of 10.5 mm (b) Outer diameters of 32 mm (c) Outer diameters of 50 mm (d) Outer diameters of 60 mm

The grasping experiments on four objects with different weights of a table tennis ball, a hollow plastic ball, an apple and a weight were performed to prove the effectiveness and feasibility of the soft pneumatic gripper integrated piezoresistive sensor. The resistance change of the piezoresistive sensor is shown in Fig. 7. When a table tennis ball weighing 2.7 g was grasped, the resistance value of the piezoresistive sensor was reduced from 159 kΩ to 110 kΩ, and the grasping force was close to be 0.4 N (the relative resistance change rate is 30.82%), as shown in Fig. 7 (a). In contrast, when a hollow plastic ball weighing 64 g was grasped, the soft pneumatic gripper requires more air pressure to provide a larger force to grasp the plastic ball, and the corresponding grasping force was increased to 0.75 N (the relative resistance change rate is 42.94%), as shown in Fig. 7 (b). As the weight of the target object increases, the output force of the soft gripper increases, thus the resistance change rate of the piezoresistive sensor increases. However, due to the low sensitivity limit of the piezoresistive sensor at larger pressures, the resistance change rate tends to grow slowly, being 61.84% and 66.18% at 125 g and 500 g weight, respectively, as shown in Fig. 7 (c) and Fig. 7 (d). The experimental results demonstrate that the proposed piezoresistive sensor can detect the grasping force between the objects and the soft pneumatic gripper, and the sensing accuracy is higher for small-mass objects.

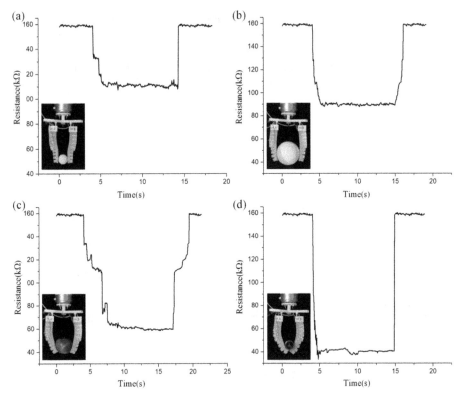

Fig. 7. Grasping objects with different weights (a) a table tennis ball weighing 2.7 g (b) a hollow plastic ball weighing 64 g (c) an apple weighing 125 g (d) a weight weighing 500 g

4 Conclusion

In this work, a resistive strain sensor and a piezoresistive sensor assembled by conductive elastomers has been proposed to detect deformation and force respectively. The essential factors of the type of conductive filler and the mixing ratio of MWCNTs, together with the optimization of preparation process, have been investigated to improve the sensor performances in terms of sensitivity, compliance, and stretch ratio. The loading experiments have been performed to investigate the sensing characteristics of sensors. The sensitivity of the resistive strain sensor is 0.107 kΩ/°, exhibiting a good angular discrimination ability. And the piezoresistive sensor shows two reliable linear response regions in the range of 0–350 kPa. The resistive strain sensor and piezoresistive sensor have been integrated into the soft pneumatic gripper to test the grasping perception, and the distinct response signals have validated its effectiveness. The two-finger gripper with integrated sensors can obtain the information (diameter and weight) of the target object by identifying the curvature and output force of the soft pneumatic gripper. Compared with the traditional sensor integration on the inner surface, the developed sensors are constructed from the similar material as the gripper, thus show a similar mechanical impedance and do not impede the gripping strength or adaptability. The arrangement of two sensors enables the soft pneumatic gripper to simultaneously detect both size and weight information of the target object. In addition to obtaining the target object information, it is expected to synchronously extract the curvature or state information of the pneumatic gripper by integrating flexible sensors to accurately control the soft gripper and safely interact with the environment in future work.

Acknowledgment. This work was supported in part by the the Ministry of Education. Joint Fund (8091B032250) and the Fundamental Research Funds for the Central Universities (B240205045).

References

1. Rus, D., Tolley, M.T.: Design, fabrication and control of soft robots. Nature **521**(7553), 467–475 (2015)
2. Roh, Y., Kim, M., Won, S.M., et al.: Vital signal sensing and manipulation of a microscale organ with a multifunctional soft gripper. Sci. Robot. **6**(59) (2021)
3. Wang, Z.K., Or, K., Hirai, S.: A dual-mode soft gripper for food packaging. Robot. Auton. Syst. **125**, 103427 (2020)
4. Huang, H.M., Tang, S.J., Chai, W.Q., et al.: MCSG: a morphology configurable soft gripper with self-adaption modular composite finger. IEEE Trans. Industr. Electron. **71**(1), 708–717 (2024)
5. Li, H.L., Yao, J.T., Wei, C.J., et al.: An untethered soft robotic gripper with high payload-to-weight ratio. Mech. Mach. Theory **158**, 104226 (2021)
6. Wu, M.X., Zheng, X.W., Liu, R.S., et al.: Glowing sucker octopus (Stauroteuthis syrtensis)-inspired soft robotic gripper for underwater self-adaptive grasping and sensing. Adv. Sci. **9**(17) (2022)
7. Wang, Y.J., Yang, Z.W., Zhou, H., et al.: Inflatable particle-jammed robotic gripper based on integration of positive pressure and partial filling. Soft Rob. **9**(2), 309–323 (2022)
8. Li, S.G., Stampfli, J.J., Xu, H.J., et al.: A vacuum-driven origami " magic - ball " soft gripper. In: International Conference on Robotics and Automation, pp. 7401–7408. IEEE, Montreal, CANADA (2019)
9. Mosadegh, B., Polygerinos, P., Keplinger, C., et al.: Pneumatic networks for soft robotics that actuate rapidly. Adv. Func. Mater. **24**(15), 2163–2170 (2014)
10. Gao, Q.W., Li, H., Zhang, J.J., et al.: Microchannel structural design for a room-temperature liquid metal based super-stretchable sensor. Sci. Rep. **9**(1), 5908 (2019)
11. Pyo, S., Lee, J., Bae, K., et al.: Recent progress in flexible tactile sensors for human-interactive systems: from sensors to advanced applications. Adv. Mater. **33**(47) (2021)
12. Zhao, X., Tang, G.Q., Zhao, C., et al.: Bio-inspired artificial receptor with integrated tactile sensing and pain warning perceptual abilities. Mach. **10**(11), 968 (2022)
13. Hellebrekers, T., Kroemer, O., Majidi, C.: Soft magnetic skin for continuous deformation sensing. Adv. Intell. Syst. **1**(4) (2019)
14. Sareh, S., Jiang, A., Faragasso, A., et al.: Bio-inspired tactile sensor sleeve for surgical soft manipulators. In: International Conference on Robotics and Automation, pp. 1454–1459. IEEE, Montreal, Hong Kong (2014)
15. Dou, W.Q., Zhong, G.L., Cao, J.L., et al.: Soft robotic manipulators: designs, actuation, stiffness tuning, and sensing. Adv. Mater. Technol. **6**(9), 2100018 (2021)

Drift-Free Ionotronic Sensing

Canhui Yang(✉)

Southern University of Science and Technology, Shenzhen 518055, China
yangch@sustech.edu.cn

Abstract. Skin-like soft pressure sensors enable artificial haptic technologies for myriad applications in robotics, healthcare and beyond. A soft sensor must detect pressure with both high sensitivity and high accuracy. However, for existing soft pressure sensors, viscoelastic creep of the soft materials causes signal drift, which can result in unreliable measurements that might lead to an incorrect trigger or safety concerns. Among the many types of soft pressure sensor, ionotronic sensors exhibit superior sensing properties owing to the nanoscale charge separation at the electric double layer. However, signal drift is particularly prevalent in ionotronic sensors owing to leakage of the ionic solvent, in addition to the viscoelastic creep. This talk will introduce our recent advances in realizing drift-free ionotronic sensing. We do so by designing and copolymerizing a leakage-free and creep-free polyelectrolyte elastomer containing two types of segments: charged segments having fixed cations to prevent ion leakage and neutral slippery segments with a high crosslink density for low creep. We show that an ionotronic sensor using the polyelectrolyte elastomer barely drifts under an ultrahigh static pressure of 500 kPa (close to its Young's modulus), exhibits a drift rate two to three orders of magnitude lower than that of the sensors adopting conventional ionic conductors and enables steady and accurate control for robotic manipulation. Such drift-free ionotronic sensing potentializes highly accurate sensing in robotics and beyond.

Keywords: Ionotronic Sending · Signal Drift · Drift-Free Sensing

1 Introduction

Biological systems have evolved tightly integrated pressure sensing, controlling, and actuation for environmental adaptation and survival. Such closed-loop integration is also pervasive and plays a pivotal role in artificial engineering systems [1–3], such as automatic pilot and drive, industrial robots, virtual reality, electro-tactile devices, and exoskeleton manipulators. Of primary significance for artificial closed-loop integration is the acquisition of sensing signals accurately and stably, which demands highly sensitive and reliable pressure sensors. The widely used capacitive pressure sensors feature structural simplicity, high tolerance of noise, and low power consumption [4], but they suffer from low signal-to-noise ratio due to the dielectric layer between the two electrodes, which possesses a limited capacitance per unit area on the order of 10^{-7} F/m^2. The emerging ionotronic (or iontronic) sensors [5], typically consist of a layer of ionic conductor sandwiched between two layers of electronic conductor, resolve the issue by eliminating the dielectric layer [6]. In an ionotronic sensor, the ionic conductor and the electronic conductor are in contact with each other. An electric double layer (EDL) forms at the ionic conductor/electronic conductor interface. The EDL separates charges of opposite polarities at nanometer scale such that, the capacitance per unit area reaches ~ 10^{-2} F/m^2, yielding an ultra-high signal-to-noise ratio [7, 8]. However, existing ionotronic sensors are susceptible to signal drift and do not sense stimuli reliably. The poor sensing stability significantly impedes the practical deployments of ionotronic sensors.

The signal drift of ionotronic sensors is related to the stability of the employed ionic conductors in two aspects: the leakage of ingredients and the creep of polymer network. For the sensors using gels, either ionogels or ionic hydrogels, the signal drift primarily originates from the leakage of solvent molecules, a process inherent to gel materials. Subject to compression, the strain energy of the polymer network increases. Thermodynamics dictates that the gel expels solvent molecules to reduce the free energy of mixing [9]. Meanwhile, due to its poroelastic nature, the gel gradually thins down as the solvent molecules diffuse out of the gel [10]. In addition, osmocapillary phase separation, caused by the Laplace pressure, tends to pull the solvent molecules out of the gel [11, 12], especially when the feature size of the surface asperities is much smaller than the osmocapillary length in a soft gel. These processes lead to the leakage of solvent molecules, expanding the effective area of the EDL to up-drift the signal of the sensor. The recently developed ionically conductive elastomers are immune to solvent leakage [13], yet they are still vulnerable to ion leakage when both the cations and anions are mobile. Leakage-free ionic conductors have been synthesized by engrafting at least one type of ionic moieties to the polymer backbone [14, 15]. Nevertheless, in stark contrast to the leakage of ingredients, the influences of the creep of polymer network on the sensing stabilities of ionotronic sensors remain unexplored, leaving signal drift a grand challenge for ionotronic sensing.

We note that accurate and reliable ionotronic sensing requires drift-free ionotronic sensor, which in turn requires ionic conductors that are free of leakage and creep at the same time. Herein, to realize drift-free ionotronic sensing, we first rationally design and synthesize a leakage-free and creep-free polyelectrolyte elastomer by elaborating the chemistries and the recipe of the ingredients. The obtained polyelectrolyte elastomer can sustain a step stress of 200 kPa for 12 h and a cyclic load of peak stress of 400 kPa for 100,000 cycles without creep. In addition, a low hysteresis of 2.26% at 15% tensile strain and a low tackiness of 20.78 J m^{-2} to gold electrode have been achieved. The resulting ionotronic sensor can maintain stable signal under 500 kPa for 48 h. Remarkably, we show that the sensor responds to a cyclic compression with square waves at 400 kPa without any noticeable signal drift, which has been reported for ionotronic sensing for the first time. We further show that the sensor also accurately senses the superposition of static and dynamic loads with an average stress of 375 kPa. The accurate and stable sensing capability makes ionotronic sensing practically useful for applications across fields.

2 Results and Discussion

Drift-free ionotronic sensors are promising as artificial skins, e.g. for human-machine interactions (Fig. 1a). On the device level, the sensors must give accurate and stable feedback upon stimulation for safe interactions and are desired to operate over a broad range of pressure and working frequency with high response speed and high sensitivity. When a step constant compression is applied, a drift-free ionotronic sensor step-responses and maintains the signal stably over time. When the compression is removed, the sensor instantaneously and completely recovers to the original state without residual signals. In this work, we fabricate the ionotronic sensor by sandwiching a layer of micro-structured ionic conductor between two layers of electronic conductors.

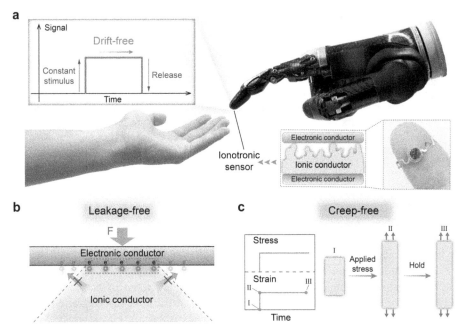

Fig. 1. (a) Illustration of a drift-free ionotronic sensor as an artificial skin for human-machine interactions. Subject to a step stimulus, the sensor step-responses and maintains the signal stably. When the stimulus is removed, the sensor recovers instantaneously and completely. The ionotronic sensor used in this work consists of a layer of micro-structured ionic conductor sandwiched between two layers of electronic conductors. The bottom-right image shows the appearance of the sensor, which employs a polyelectrolyte elastomer for the ionic conductor and gold for the electronic conductor. (b) Schematic of being leakage-free. Subject to compression, the ingredients of the ionic conductor do not leak. (c) Schematic of being creep-free. Subject to a step stress, the ionic conductor step-responses and holds the deformation.

On the material level, the employed ionic conductor must be leakage-free (Fig. 1b). When the electronic conductor contacts the ionic conductor, the charges in the electronic conductor (e.g. electrons) and the charges in the ionic conductor (e.g. cations) accumulate at the interface to form an EDL. The capacitance of the sensor is proportional to the area of EDL. Subject to a compressive force, the ingredients of the ionic conductor should not leak to avoid enlarging the effective area of EDL. The employed ionic conductor must further be creep-free (Fig. 1c). The viscoelastic creep of an ionic conductor is the macroscopic consequence of microscopic molecular rearrangements, which also causes the increment of the area of EDL. Subject to a step constant stress, the ionic conductor should step-response and maintain the strain stably over time.

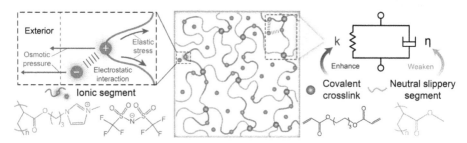

Fig. 2. Designing principles of a leakage-free and creep-free polyelectrolyte elastomer. For leakage-free, the polymer network contains no solvent and has cations engrafted to the polymer chains. For creep-free, the ionic segments are copolymerized with neutral slippery segments and the polymer network has a high covalent crosslink density. The chemical structures of the ionic segment, AMT, the covalent crosslinker, HDDA, and the neutral slippery segment, MA, are illustrated.

Following the above principles, on the molecular level, we have designed and synthesized a leakage-free and creep-free polyelectrolyte elastomer (Fig. 2). For leakage-free, the polymer network contains no solvent and has cations engrafted to the polymer chains and mobile anions. When in contact with other materials, an osmotic pressure Π builds up between the interior and the exterior of the polymer network due to the difference in ion concentration, $\Pi \sim cRT$, where c is the ion concentration, R is the ideal gas constant, and T is the absolute temperature. As a result, both the cations and anions tend to diffuse outwards inherently. However, long-range directional diffusion of the engrafted cations will stretch the interconnected polymer chains, inducing entropic elastic stress to counteract the osmotic pressure to prevent the leakage of cations. Meanwhile, the anions are also confined within the polymer network due to the electrostatic interactions with the cations.

For creep-free, the polymer network contains neutral slippery segments and has a high crosslink density. Since the ionic segments simultaneously contribute to the ionic conductivity and the interactions between polymer chains, the polymer network of a polyelectrolyte elastomer is intrinsically viscoelastic. Assume that the polyelectrolyte elastomer obeys the Kelvin-Voigt model, consisting of an elastic spring of stiffness k in parallel with a dashpot of viscosity η. On one hand, copolymerizing the ionic segments with neutral slippery segments lessens the contribution of viscosity by weakening the interchain interactions. On the other hand, increasing the covalent crosslink density enhances the contribution of entropic elasticity by suppressing the fluctuations of polymer chains. Therefore, the applied constant stress is mostly carried by the elastic spring whereas the dashpot carries negligible stress, so that the polyelectrolyte elastomer is creep-free.

The design strategy can be illustrated by various chemistries. Here we use 1-(3-(acryloyloxy)propyl)-3-methylimidazolium bis(trifluoromethane)sulfonimide (AMT) for the ionic segment, methyl acrylate (MA) for the neutral slippery segment, and 1,6-hexanediol diacrylate (HDDA) as the covalent crosslinker to synthesize a network of poly(1-(3-(acryloyloxy)propyl)-3-methylimidazolium bis(trifluoromethane)sulfonimide-co-methyl acrylate) (P(AMT-co-MA)). Since ionic species are generally hygroscopic, we elaborately synthesize AMT with hydrophobic moieties to minimize the potential complications caused by humidity. The cation of AMT contains a vinyl group for free radical photo-polymerization. The monomer of MA contains short and low-polarity side chain. Diluting AMT with MA effectively reduces the friction between polymer chains.

In addition to being leakage-free and creep-free, other aspects of the polyelectrolyte elastomer also need to be rationally tailored for high-performance ionotronic sensors. We systematically investigate the effects of crosslink density and the molar ratio of AMT:MA on the mechanical and electrical properties of the randomly copolymerized network of P(AMT-co-MA). In addition, we further toughen the P(AMT-co-MA) network with physically interpenetrated PMA long chains and probe the effects of PMA content. The resulting polyelectrolyte elastomer, termed P(AMT-co-MA)-PMA, is highly creep-resistant that the optimized sample maintains mechanical performances, e.g. strain, and electrical performances, e.g. impedance, stably over 40,000 s when subjected to a constant stress of 200 kPa (Fig. 3a). The marked creep resistance of P(AMT-co-MA)-PMA is also manifested under dynamic loads. Under a cyclic triangular wave load with a peak stress of 400 kPa and a frequency of 1 Hz, the peak strain of the sample barely changes over 100,000 cycles (Fig. 3b).

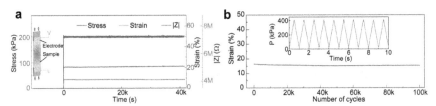

Fig. 3. (a) The variations of strain and impedance of P(AMT-co-MA)-PMA with time under constant tensile stress of 200 kPa. (b) The variation of peak strain of P(AMT-co-MA)-PMA with time under cyclic tension with a maximum stress of 400 kPa. The inset shows the loading profile.

For comprehensive optimizations, we first tune the crosslink density of poly(1-(3-(acryloyloxy)propyl)-3-methylimidazolium bis(trifluoromethane)sulfonimide (PAMT). The addition of crosslinks shortens the polymer chain length and embrittles the polymer network. Consequently, the stretchability and the work of fracture, defined as the area underneath the stress-strain curve, decreases while the Young's modulus increases when the crosslink density increases. Subject to a constant stress of 50 kPa, the PAMT samples with 1 mol% crosslinker creep to rupture and the PAMT samples with 3 mol% crosslinker creep by 18.6% after 2 h. We set the crosslinker content to be 3 mol% and then tune the molar ratio of AMT:MA of P(AMT-co-MA). The mechanical properties escalate but the electrical performance, characterized by the capacitance per unit area between P(AMT-co-MA) and gold electrode, gets worse as the amount of the neutral monomer MA increases. Besides, the low strength and toughness are unsatisfactory for robust ionotronic sensors, whereas the P(AMT-co-MA) with a molar ratio of AMT:MA of 1:2 barely creeps under a constant stress of 50 kPa.

Setting the molar ratio of AMT:MA to be 1:2, we next turn to the toughener PMA. As expected, P(AMT-co-MA)-PMA becomes more stretchable and tougher with the addition of PMA, although the Young's modulus mostly keeps constant. Moreover, because the operation of the ionotronic sensor involves the contact and separation between the ionic conductor and the electronic conductor, the adhesion at the EDL interface is detrimental for separation and retards the recovery of sensors, which is often the culprit of baseline drift [16]. As such, a low interfacial adhesion is desired for rapid and complete detachment. Recall that we have used gold for the electrode. We perform tack tests to access the adhesion between P(AMT-co-MA)-PMA and gold. The adhesion energy increases while the capacitance per unit area decreases with the content of PMA. Finally, we set the content of PMA to be 10 wt% to accommodate mechanical properties, interfacial adhesion, and electrical properties.

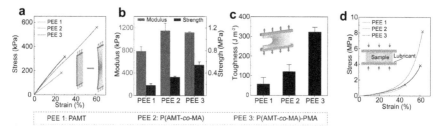

Fig. 4. (a) Uniaxial tensile stress-strain curves, (b) modulus and strength, (c) toughness, (d) uniaxial compressive stress-strain curves of PAMT, P(AMT-co-MA), and P(AMT-co-MA)-PMA.

The uniaxial tensile curves of the optimized PAMT, P(AMT-co-MA), and P(AMT-co-MA)-PMA, represented by PEE1, PEE2, and PEE3, respectively, are compared in Fig. 4a. The toughened PEE3 possesses the largest fracture strain, 61.3%, and the highest tensile strength, 560 kPa (Fig. 4b), whereas its Young's modulus is comparable to that of PEE2. Also, PEE3 has the highest fracture energy, 323.5 J/m^2, measured by the pure shear test (Fig. 4c), and the largest fracture strain and the highest compressive strength, 8.2 MPa, measured by uniaxial compression (Fig. 4d). Hereafter, we will refer to the optimized P(AMT-co-MA)-PMA as PEE for concision unless otherwise specified.

A tack test shows that the surface of PEE is non-tacky and exhibits a low adhesion energy of 20.78 J/m^2 with gold. Under dynamic compression, the delayed recovery of the deformation of ionic conductor will cause overmeasurement of stress. To examine the recovery of PEE, characterized by hysteresis, we perform cyclic tests by stretching a PEE sample to 15% strain and unloading to zero force. Hysteresis is defined as the energy dissipated during one loading cycle divided by the work done by external work during that loading cycle. The stress-strain curves of loading and unloading almost coincide with each other, giving an average hysteresis of 2.26% over ten cycles.

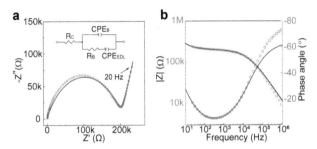

Fig. 5. (a) Nyquist plot, and (b) bode phase plot of P(AMT-*co*-MA)-PMA. The gray lines are theoretical fittings using the equivalent circuit model in the inset of (a).

Ionic conductivity and charge density of ionic conductors are essential for the functions of ionotronic sensors. We conduct ac-impedance measurements using gold electrodes and obtain the Nyquist plot (Fig. 5a) and the Bode phase plot (Fig. 5b) for PEE, and PAMT and P(AMT-*co*-MA). By fitting the impedance data to the equivalent circuit model in Fig. 5a, the capacitance per unit area between PEE and gold is 2.18×10^{-3} F/m^2 and the conductivity of PEE is 2.47×10^{-5} S/m. The decent ionic conductivity and charge density are ascribed to the low glass transition of PEE, -6.9 °C, which facilitates selective ion transport through localized segmental chain motion and ion hopping. The notable comprehensive properties of PEE lay a solid foundation for the marvelous performances of ionotronic sensors.

We fabricate an ionotronic sensor by sandwiching a layer of the optimized PEE between two layers of Au deposited on polyimide (PI) (Fig. 6). For the sake of broad-range high sensitivity, we construct graded intrafillable architectures on the surfaces of PEE and one PI-Au electrode. A flat PET-Au is used as another electrode, a 50 μm thick polydimethylsiloxane (PDMS) ring is used as the spacer, and two 100 μm thick PDMS films are used as the seals for the assembly of the whole sensor. Subject to a pulse loading of ~ 2.5 kPa, the sensor exhibits a response time of ~ 3.8 ms and a recovery time of ~ 5.8 ms, respectively. The rapid responses and complete recovery are attributed to the low hysteresis of PEE and the low adhesion between PEE and Au. The initial capacitance of the sensor, with a layer of air between PEE and Au, is on the order of 1 pF. When a load is applied to bring Au into contact with PEE, the capacitance rises sharply to the order of 1000 pF, giving an extremely high signal-to-noise ratio. Subject to a monotonic compression, the sensor achieves sensitivities of 3.3 kPa^{-1} within 200 kPa, 2.6 kPa^{-1} within 200 ~ 500 kPa, and 1.1 kPa^{-1} within 500 ~ 1000 kPa. The maintenance of high sensitivity over a broad range of pressure is attributed to the graded intrafillable microstructures on the surfaces of PEE and PI-Au and the robust mechanical properties of PEE.

Reliable sensing is vital for practical applications, such as the precise feedback for closed-loop systems and machine learning-based intelligent sensing systems and has been a formidable challenge for laboratory level ionotronic sensors. Our sensor exhibits

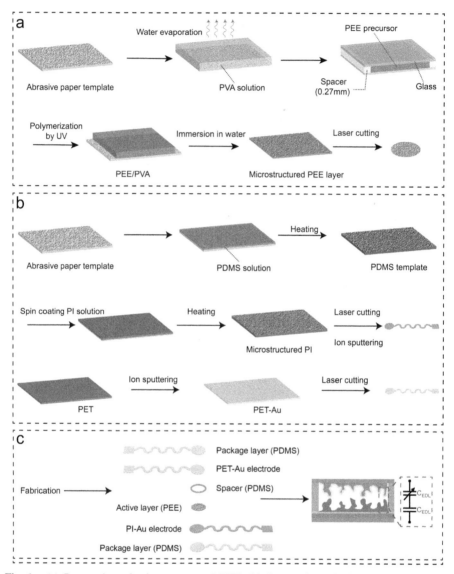

Fig. 6. (a) Preparation of micro-structured PEE. (b) Preparation of micro-structured PI-Au electrode and PET-Au electrode. (c) Fabrication of ionotronic sensor.

negligible signal drift under either long-term high static pressure or cyclic loads with square waves. We apply a static pressure of ~ 500 kPa to the sensor, and its capacitance is maintained at ~ 1.410 nF over 48 h, and rapidly recovers to the original value (~ 1 pF) upon release (Fig. 7a). Microscopic inspection shows that the surface of PET-Au electrode is clean, indicating no leakage (inset of Fig. 7a). Next, we apply a cyclic load of 400 kPa using square-waves with each wave enduring for 20 s. The sensor outputs square-wave signals accordingly for each cycle over a total of 1000 cycles (Fig. 7b).

The drift-free response is also verified in a more complicated situation—a superposition of static pressure of 375 kPa and dynamic compression with a periodic fluctuation of 50 kPa and a frequency of 2 Hz, and the response of the sensor is in phase with the stimuli (Fig. 7c).

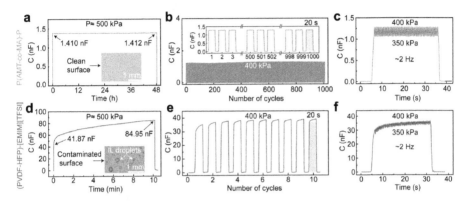

Fig. 7. (a) Capacitance of the PEE-based sensor varies with time under static compression of 500 kPa for 48 h. The inset shows the clean surface of the Au electrode after the test. (b) Cyclic compression of the PEE-based sensor under square waves, each endures for 20 s, over 1000 cycles at 400 kPa. The inset zooms in on the signals at the initial, middle, and final three cycles. (c) Response of the PEE-based sensor subject to the superposition of static and dynamic loads. The average stress is 375 kPa and the amplitude and frequency of the fluctuation are 50 kPa and 2 Hz, respectively. (d) Capacitance of an ionogel-based sensor varies with time under static compression of 500 kPa for 10 min. The inset shows the contaminated surface of the Au electrode after the test. (e) Cyclic compression of the ionogel-based sensor under square waves, each endures for 20 s, over 10 cycles at 400 kPa. (f) Response of the ionogel-based sensor subject to the same superposition of static and dynamic loads as before.

A control sensor using ionogel exhibits substantial signal drift. We use microstructured 1-ethyl-3-methylimidazolium bis(trifluoromethylsulfonyl)imide infused poly(vinylidene fluoride-co-hexafluoropropylene) ((PVDF-HFP)-[EMIM][TFSI]) ionogel, a widely used ionic conductor in ionotronic sensors, for comparison. Under a static compression of 500 kPa, the capacitance drifts by ~ 102.9% within 10 min, and the surface of the PET-Au electrode is contaminated by leaked ionic liquid (Fig. 7d). Accordingly, the strain creeps from 44% to 54%. The signal also drifts in load-unload cycles (Fig. 7e), or in the case of superposed static and dynamic compression (Fig. 7f). The high stability of the signal is further verified when subject to 10,000 cycles of load-unload with a peak pressure of 400 kPa, whereas the control sensors using (PVDF-HFP)-[EMIM][TFSI] ionogel or phosphoric acid doped poly(vinyl alcohol) (PVA-H_3PO_4) hydrogel generate drifting signals (Fig. 8).

Previous efforts on flexible pressure sensors have mostly focused on improving sensing properties (e.g., sensitivity, response time, working range, signal linearity, and operation bandwidth), whereas the accuracy of transduction has been largely overlooked. For polymer-based sensors, signal drift is a common issue causing inaccurate measurement,

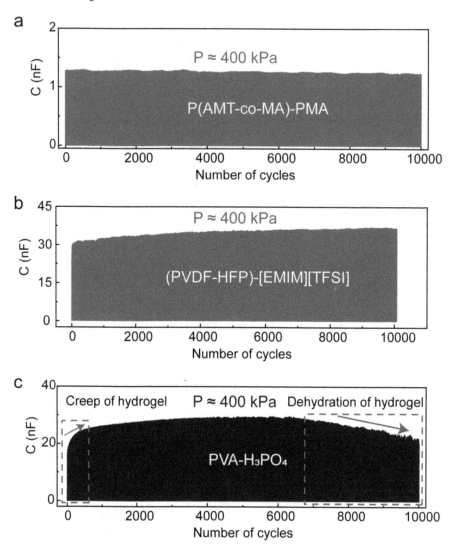

Fig. 8. Cyclic compressive test of (a) PEE-based sensor, (b) ionogel-based sensor, and (c) hydrogel-based sensor over 10,000 cycles at 400 kPa at a frequency of 0.2 Hz.

specifically for applications with prolonged high pressures. Our work shows that a rationally designed leakage-free and creep-free polyelectrolyte elastomer enables drift-free ionotronic sensing.

The softness and the creep-free characters of PEE are balanced—short chains are often used in polymers to reduce creep, but this increases the stiffness of the material. Our polyelectrolyte elastomer exhibits high softness (E ~ 1.12 MPa) and high toughness (~300 J/m^2) comparable to that of the commonly used PDMS elastomers.

The polyelectrolyte elastomer may find applications in reliable electrophysiological signal collection and strain sensing. The material is expected to be nontoxic because ions are trapped in the polymer network; by contrast, traditional ionogels can hardly be used to interface biological tissues and electrodes because of the leakage of ionic liquid. The low-creep and low-hysteresis of PEE are also highly desired for strain sensing in both robotics and human body because of the low residual deformation or delay in response.

3 Conclusion

In summary, we report the first achievement of drift-free ionotronic sensing. We note the two prerequisites: leakage-free and creep-free. The former excludes gel materials, and the latter imposes new challenges for the rational design and synthesis of ionically conductive polymer networks. In principle, polyelectrolyte elastomers are the materials of choice for EDL-based ionotronic sensors when sustained mechanical loads are indispensable. We successfully fabricate a drift-free micro-structured ionotronic sensor by elaborating a double network polyelectrolyte elastomer with optimized mechanical and electrical properties and demonstrate its extremely stable sensing performances via the deliberate manipulation of a fragile cherry tomato. Ionotronic sensors, inborn with high sensitivity and high signal-to-noise ratio, will find numerous applications without the disease of signal drift.

References

1. Yao, K., et al.: Encoding of tactile information in hand via skin-integrated wireless haptic interface. Nat. Mach. Intell. **4**, 893–903 (2022)
2. Zhu, M.L., et al.: Haptic-feedback smart glove as a creative human-machine interface (HMI) for virtual/augmented reality applications. Sci. Adv. **6**(19), eaaz8693 (2020)
3. Zhu, M., Sun, Z., Chen, T., Lee, C.: Low cost exoskeleton manipulator using bidirectional triboelectric sensors enhanced multiple degree of freedom sensory system. Nat. Commun. **12**, 2692 (2021)
4. Wan, Y.B., Wang, Y., Guo, C.F.: Recent progresses on flexible tactile sensors. Mater. Today Phys. **1**, 61–73 (2017)
5. Chang, Y., et al.: First decade of interfacial iontronic sensing: from droplet sensors to artificial skins. Adv. Mater. **33**, 2003464 (2021)
6. Yang, C., Suo, Z.: Hydrogel ionotronics. Nat. Rev. Mater. **3**, 125–142 (2018)
7. Bai, N., et al.: Graded intrafillable architecture-based iontronic pressure sensor with ultra-broad-range high sensitivity. Nat. Commun. **11**, 209 (2020)
8. Liu, Q., et al.: High-porosity foam-based iontronic pressure sensor with superhigh sensitivity of 9280 kPa(-1). Nano-micro-Lett **14**, 21 (2021)
9. Rubinstein, M., Colby, R.H.: Polymer Physics, vol. 23. Oxford University Press, New York (2003)
10. Biot, M.A.: General theory of three-dimensional consolidation. J. Appl. Phys. **12**, 155–164 (1941)
11. Zhu, J., Liu, Q.: The osmocapillary effect on a rough gel surface. J. Mech. Phys. Solids **170**, 105124 (2023)
12. Zhu, J., Yang, C., Liu, Q.: Experimental characterization of elastocapillary and osmocapillary effects on multi-scale gel surface topography. Soft Matter **19**, 8698–8705 (2023)
13. Shi, L., et al.: Highly stretchable and transparent ionic conducting elastomers. Nat. Commun. **9**, 1–7 (2018)

14. Yuan, J., Mecerreyes, D., Antonietti, M.: Poly (ionic liquid)s: an update. Prog. Polym. Sci. **38**, 1009–1036 (2013)
15. Kim, H.J., Chen, B., Suo, Z., Hayward, R.C.: Ionoelastomer junctions between polymer networks of fixed anions and cations. Science **367**, 773–776 (2020)
16. Zhang, P., et al.: Stretchable heterogeneous polymer networks of high adhesion and low hysteresis. ACS Appl. Mater. Interfaces **14**, 49264–49273 (2022)

Design and Analysis of an Exoskeleton Robotic Actuator for Lumbar Spine Assisted Rehabilitation

Lisheng Wang[1], Linsen Xu[1,2,3]([✉]), Zhihuan Wang[1], Liangzhi Ye[1], and Huan Mei[1]

[1] College of Mechanical and Electrical Engineering, Hohai University,
Changzhou 213000, China
lsxu@hhu.edu.cn
[2] Changzhou Key Laboratory of Intelligent Manufacturing Technology and Equipment,
Changzhou 213000, China
[3] Suzhou Research Institute, Hohai University, Suzhou 215004, China

Abstract. Based on the biological structure of the Elephant Trumpet class, a soft body actuator that can satisfy the above requirements is designed by combining the extension PAM and contraction PAM. This will allow the lumbar spine assisted rehabilitation exoskeleton robot to provide support function to reduce the compression force of the lumbar spine joints and to meet the required output force requirement. The actuator is a variable stiffness pneumatic artificial muscle (VSPAM) with both extension and contraction functions. A new mathematical model of the VSPAM's output force is developed using the energy conservation principle after the kinematic analysis of the device is completed. A strong correlation is found in quasi-static studies examining the relationship between the output force experimental data of VSPAM and the new mathematical model. Stiffness experiment results confirm the VSPAM's ability to have variable stiffness at a range of particular lengths, showing that the stiffness of the VSPAM can be changed without reference to a particular length. Ultimately, an exoskeleton robot prototype for lumbar spine assisted rehabilitation is built for lumbar rehabilitation training. The experimental results show that the VSPAM has several advantages over traditional soft actuators, such as the capacity to change the stiffness at particular lengths and the ability to contract and extend relative to the VSPAM's initial length to generate contraction and extension forces.

Keywords: Soft Body Actuator · Variable Stiffness · Kinematic

1 Introduction

China's aging population has grown significantly in recent years, and as a result, many elderly people suffer from various chronic pains from chronic diseases [1], while lumbar skeletal and muscular disorders are starting to rise to the top of the list of diseases in many industrialized nations (such as China, India, and the US) as a result of fast-paced lifestyles and inadequate exercise [2]. Exoskeleton robots are a type of assistive-replacement rehabilitation robots, meaning they may help with mobility as well as rehabilitation. In order to lessen muscular fatigue, avoid underlying musculoskeletal problems, and restore limb movement functions like HAL, BLEEX, and EXO, exoskeleton robotics has been employed [3], However, the most of these robots disregard lumbar support and fail to take into account the physiological makeup of the human lumbar vertebrae and how important they are to daily functioning. This has an impact on how comfortable and useful the aid is to wear and limits its potential for advancement [4, 5].

Since rigid institutions find it difficult to meet the demand for natural movement assistance, research on lumbar assisted rehabilitation technology has increased recently. Flexible lumbar assisted rehabilitation robots fall into two categories: passive assisted and active assisted. This is because the human lumbar spine has a high redundancy joint structure. In order to reduce the wearer's need to lift heavy objects when the back of the waist requires torque, wearers of passive assistance devices such as PLAD, Smart Suit Lite, and Passive Spine Exoskeleton, primarily use springs, elastic bands, and other elastic elements to connect the waist with the shoulders, thighs, and other parts of the human body through the elastic elements of the "energy storage - release" mechanism [6–8]. While researchers like Xiangpan Li, Yali Han, and others created a lumbar assisted exoskeleton robot with elastic components and saw some success, the robot's primary structure is made of flexible material, so it is unable to offer support functions that would lessen the compression force on lumbar spine joints [9, 10]. Smart Suit, LAD [11, 12], and other assisted robots use a combination of elastic elements and flexible cords for active drive to reduce the lumbar and back muscle mobility during human movement; in terms of active assistance, researchers primarily use flexible drive methods to provide assistance for the lumbar spine; In order to present the lumbar-assisted exoskeleton H-WEXv2, Hyun et al. [13] built up a stiff support back plate at the back using a mixed drive of elastic parts and flexible wires. These robots can only help with tensile forces in the sagittal plane; they are unable to aid with compression forces on lumbar spine joints, and they will also create joint parasitic force, which will have an impact on how comfortable it is to wear.

To solve the drawbacks of the preceding two approaches, scientists have created soft robots by studying flexible features such as octopus tentacles, snakes, and elephant trunks [14–16], as well as bionics [17, 18]. The benefit of soft robots is that the variable stiffness flexible structure may modify the stiffness to an appropriate value within the range of maintaining safety to fulfill the demand of assisting and supporting, providing a new option for assisted rehabilitation exoskeleton robots. However, conventional soft robots are unable to produce a significant output force to meet the aiding need due to material limitations [19].

Thus, this work suggests an exoskeleton robot for lumbar spine supported rehabilitation that can do both extension and contraction assisted motions with a high output force, in order to overcome the aforementioned issues. Figure 1 depicts the general layout of the exoskeleton robot for lumbar spine supported rehabilitation. It is primarily made up of the following components: VSPAM, Lumbar Actuator Base, Lumbar Aluminum Plate, Sliding Rail and Connecting Fasteners. This research primarily investigates the output force and variable stiffness of the actuator since the magnitude of force that the actuator can output determines how much force the robot can output.

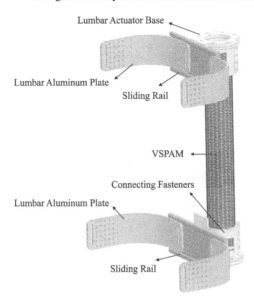

Fig. 1. Lumbar spine assisted rehabilitation exoskeleton robot

2 Design and Manufacture of VSPAM

The actuator is a variable stiffness pneumatic artificial muscle (VSPAM) with both extension and contraction functions, and the VSPAM consists of a combination of contraction PAM and extension PAM. The design of the two end caps is the first step in the production of VSPAM. The process of manufacturing VSPAM begins with the design of two end caps, as seen in Fig. 2(a). The middle of the two end caps has three square-shaped connecting ports that are used to connect the contraction PAM's hoses; the holes inside the three connecting ports are used to fill the contraction PAM with high-pressure gases; There are openings in the middle of the end caps that are utilized to feed high-pressure gasses to the extension PAM through the gas tubes once the high-pressure gas has been sent there via the pneumatic tubes. After that, the hose is wrapped in PET braid, which is slightly longer than the hose overall but still ensures that the braid angle is less than 54.7°. The braid is then securely fastened with nylon ties, and the contraction PAM that has been created is displayed in Fig. 2(b).

As shown in Fig. 2(c), a 48 mm inner diameter hose is used to wrap the contraction PAM, and the hose is then wrapped in PET braid. Since the PET braid is far longer than the hose, it is firmly packed together, restricting the radial expansion of the hose to solely axial elongation. After locking the nylon tie securely to prevent it from leaking, the VSPAM is physically shown in Fig. 2(d).

In order to study the relationship between the length of VSPAM and the supply air pressure design the experimental setup shown in Fig. 3. The experiments to investigate the relationship between supply pressure and VSPAM length consisted of gradually and independently inflating each PAM (contraction PAM and extension PAM) from 0 to 0.5 MPa in steps of 50 kPa. Contraction PAM is able to shrink by 26%, meaning that the

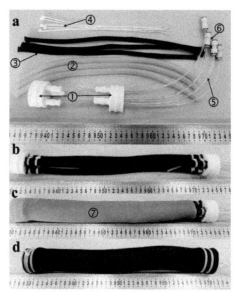

Fig. 2. Design and construction of VSPAM (a) Materials: ① end caps, ② hoses, ③ PET braid, ④ nylon ties, ⑤ gas tubes, ⑥ gas tube adapters (b) Contraction PAM (c) Extension PAM (d) VSPAM

minimum length of contraction PAM would be shorter than the unfilled (unpressurized) length of extension PAM with high pressure gas, which resulted in contraction PAM being compressed. Filling the contraction PAM with 0.5 MPa high-pressure gas while the extension PAM is not filled with high-pressure gas resulted in the VSPAM contracting from its rest length of 40.5 cm to 36 cm, which is 13% of the effective contracted length of the hose involved in the contraction, as shown in Fig. 3(d). Thus, the entire VSPAM is able to elongate and contract 13% from its resting length.

In its unpressurized state, the extension PAM measures 40.5 cm in length without the high-pressure gas charge. The contraction PAM will, however, be compressed to a length of 40.5 cm within the extension PAM's hose because it is 13% longer than this. The contraction PAM will be stretched until it reaches its maximum length when the extension PAM is supplied with high pressure gas to extend. The extension PAM will now be prevented from elongating any further by the contraction PAM. As illustrated in Fig. 3(d), the VSPAM extends 13% to 45 cm, or 13% of the effective length of 36 cm of the highly elastic latex hose involved in the elongation, from the contraction PAM's resting length of 40.5 cm to the point at which it is unable to extend any further.

3 Kinematic Analysis of VSPAM

Al-Fahaam H [20] described the general geometry of the pneumatic artificial muscle, as shown in Fig. 4, assuming that the middle portion of the pneumatic artificial muscle is a complete cylinder, and that the length of the pneumatic artificial muscle is L, and the diameter is D and β represent the braiding angles between a single braided wire and the central axis of the pneumatic artificial muscle. The length of the single braid is b, and

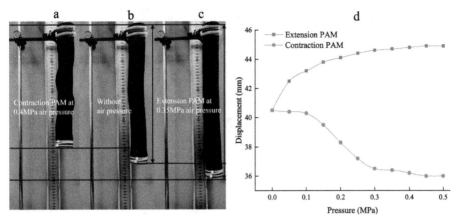

Fig. 3. Experiments to calculate the relationship between the length of VSPAM and the supply air pressure: (a) Contraction PAM at 0.4 MPa air pressure (b) Without air pressure (c) Extension at 0.35 MPa air pressure (d) Experimental results of the relationship between the length of VSPAM and the independent increase of the supply air pressure of the internal contraction PAM and the extension PAM

the length of the PET braid is n turns around the hose inside the pneumatic muscle. The length of the PET braid is longer than the length of the hose, i.e., the PET braid has to be compressed by an angle of β in order to be as long as the length of the hose.

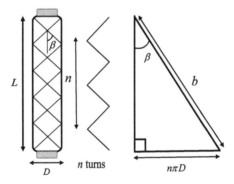

Fig. 4. General geometry model of a pneumatic artificial muscle

The kinematic study of the VSPAM is predicated on the supposition that there is no friction between the hose, the extension PAM and the contraction PAM, or the nylon threads of the PET braid. The geometric kinematic analysis of the VSPAM is shown in Fig. 5. The hose inner diameter for the extension PAM is four times larger than the hose inner diameter for the contraction PAM. As seen in Fig. 5(c), the contraction PAM is 13% longer than the extension PAM. Consequently, as seen in Fig. 5(d), at the rest length of the VSPAM, the contraction PAM will bend or compress inside the extension

PAM to match the extension PAM's length.

$$L_C = 1.13 L_E \tag{1}$$

$$L_E = \frac{1}{1.13} L_C \tag{2}$$

where L_C is the length of the contraction PAM and L_E is the length of the extension PAM.

The hose's inner diameter for the contraction PAM is four times larger than the hose's inner diameter for the extension PAM. Consequently, the static diameter of both hoses:

$$n_C = 1.13 n_E \tag{3}$$

$$4 b_C = 1.13 b_E \tag{4}$$

where n_C is the number of loops of contraction PAM PET braid, n_E is the number of loops of extension PAM PET braid, b_C is the length of the single braid of contraction PAM, and b_E is the length of the single braid of extension PAM.

According to Fig. 5(a) and (b), the geometrical parameters of contraction PAM and extension PAM are:

$$L_C = b_C \cos \beta_c \tag{5}$$

$$L_E = b_E \cos \beta_E \tag{6}$$

$$D_C = \frac{b_C \sin \beta_C}{n_C \pi} \tag{7}$$

$$D_E = \frac{b_E \sin \beta_E}{n_E \pi} \tag{8}$$

$$V_C = \frac{\pi D_C^2 L_C}{4} \tag{9}$$

$$V_E = \frac{\pi D_E^2 L_E}{4} \tag{10}$$

Where β_C is the angle between the braid and the axis of the contraction PAM hose, β_E is the angle between the braid and the axis of the extension PAM hose, D_C is the diameter of the contraction PAM, D_E is the diameter of the extension PAM, V_C is the volume of the contraction PAM, and V_E is the volume of the extension PAM.

Based on the PAM's cylindrical form, Chou and Hannaford [21] developed the following mathematical model of the PAM output force to replicate the output force of the VSPAM:

$$F = -P^1 \frac{dV}{dL} \tag{11}$$

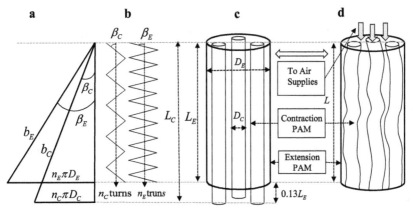

Fig. 5. Kinematics of VSPAM: (a) General geometry of PAM (contraction PAM and extension PAM) (b) Angles and number of turns of the braid of contraction PAM and extension PAM (c) Length relationship between contraction PAM and extension PAM (d) VSPAM design

where p' is the difference in air pressure inside and outside the PAM.

$$p' = (P_C - P_E) \qquad (12)$$

where P_C is the air pressure of the contraction PAM and P_E is the air pressure of the extension PAM.

Equation (11) may be solved for the contraction force produced by the contraction PAM by substituting Eqs. (5), (9), and (12).

$$F_C = -(P_C - P_E)\frac{dV_C/d\beta}{dL_C/d\beta} = \frac{b_C^2(P_C - P_E)}{4\pi n_C^2}(3\cos^2\beta_C - 1) \qquad (13)$$

The extension PAM is affected by the volume of the contraction PAM; in fact, the hollow cylindrical section of the extension PAM's core is occupied by the contraction PAM. Accordingly, the force produced by the extension PAM will be as follows as the part of the contraction PAM mitigates the real volume of the extension PAM.

$$F_S = P_E\frac{dV_S}{dL_E} = P_E\frac{dV_E - 3dV_C}{dL_E} \qquad (14)$$

where V_S is the actual volume of the cylinder representing the extension PAM.
Substituting (3) and (4) into Eq. (14) and simplifying gives:

$$F_S = \frac{b_C^2 P_E}{4\pi n_C^2}\left[1.13\left(3\cos^2\theta_C - 1\right) - 16\left(3\cos^2\theta_E - 1\right)\right] \qquad (15)$$

In VSPAM, the contraction PAM generates a force F_C and the extension PAM generates a force F_S, which are combined to obtain a combined force:

$$F = F_C - F_S = \frac{b_C^2}{4\pi n_C^2} \begin{bmatrix} P_C\left(3\cos^2\theta_C - 1\right) - \\ 10.08 P_E\left(3\cos^2\theta_C - 1\right) + \\ 16 P_E\left(3\cos^2\theta_E - 1\right) \end{bmatrix} \quad (16)$$

The contraction force F is generated by VSPAM when the value is greater than zero, and the extension force F is generated by VSPAM when the value is less than zero.

4 Experimental Validation

In order to verify the correctness of the VSPM kinematic model, the following is an experimental verification of the VSPM output force model to verify the VSPM variable stiffness. Using the mechanical properties of the driver VSPM, a prototype of lumbar spine assisted rehabilitation exoskeleton robot was designed, and rehabilitation training was carried out.

4.1 Experimental Validation of the VSPAM Output Force Model

The experimental setup depicted in Fig. 6 is utilized to verify the VSPAM output force model through experimentation. The unpressurized VSPAM had a resting length of 40 cm and is vertically hung within the fixture. The digital dynamometer is fixed to the test bench using a fixture as shown in Fig. 6(b) and (c), and the gas line supplying the high-pressure gas is connected to the gas line interface of the upper end cap. The lower end cap of the VSPAM is connected to the digital dynamometer, which is secured with a nylon rolled tape to limit the deformation of the VSPAM during the test period. The experiment started by raising the air pressure within the stretching PAM to 50 kPa (P_E) and recording the tensile force detected by the force transducer.

Figure 6(a) shows how to utilize the equipment to determine the contraction force. The contraction force is then measured and the air pressure (P_C) within the contraction PAM is progressively raised from 0 to 400 kPa in increments of 50 kPa. The experiment is then performed five times to get the average value. Next, the extension PAM is subjected to pressures of 75 kPa, 100 kPa, 125 kPa, and 150 kPa during the experiment.

Although the simplicity of the Chou-Hannaford model lends itself well to analysis, it has been reported in a number of studies that the average error between the mathematical model and the experimental results is expected because force losses are ignored; for example, these force losses between the braid and the hose, and between the nylon threads of the braid result in errors between the experimentally measured experimental values and the new model results of approximately a fixed percentage of the total force (20%) and increases with increasing force. To help compare the performance of VSPAM with theory, Choi I [22] uses a modified version of the Chou-Hannaford model [21]. Thus, in (16), it is now:

$$F = k_F(\pi r_0^2) P[a(1 - k_\varepsilon \varepsilon)^2 - b] \quad (17)$$

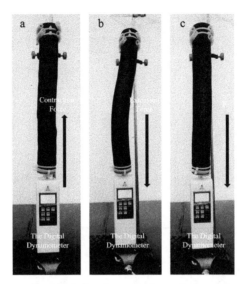

Fig. 6. Experimental setup for calculating the extension and contraction forces of VSPAM: (a) Calculation of the contraction force of VSPAM (b) Bending or lateral deformation of VSPAM in tension (c) Calculation of the extension force of VSPAM

where $a = 3/\tan^2(\alpha_0)$, $b = 1/\sin^2(\alpha_0)$, α_0 is the initial braid angle of the woven mesh. Furthermore, k_F is the force tuning parameter defined as:

$$k_F(p) = \frac{F_{meas,\max}(p)}{(\pi r_0^2)P(a-b)} \tag{18}$$

and, k_ε is the strain tuning parameter defined as:

$$k_\varepsilon(p) = \frac{1}{\varepsilon_{meas,\max}(P)}(1 - \frac{1}{\sqrt{3}\cos(\alpha_0)}) \tag{19}$$

This research uses the calibrated Chou-Hannaford model as a VSPAM output force model for comparison in order to prevent variations arising from material and structural factors. On a separate VSPAM, we ran quasi-static cyclic loading experiments in order to determine the tuning parameters of Eq. (18). We used a low-order polynomial fit to obtain the tuning parameters, adhering to the process described by Meller [23].

As demonstrated in Fig. 7, which displays the experimental results of the VSPAM output forces and its mathematical model (the top part of the figure shows the contraction force of the ECPAM and the bottom part shows the extension force of the ECPAM), the difference between the predicted and actual VSPAM output forces can be better determined by doing this. The combined force of the VSPAM for the cases of Behaves like a contraction force in the 400 kPa and 50 kPa cases, with a maximum force of about 60 N. The discrepancy between the actual and theoretical values is within 10%.

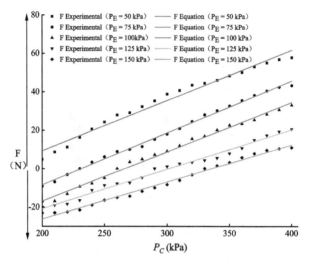

Fig. 7. Experimental results of VSPAM output force and its mathematical modeling

4.2 Experimental Verification of VSPAM Variable Stiffness

To confirm that the VSPAM's stiffness can be changed without affecting its length, a stiffness experiment is carried out using the experimental setup seen in Fig. 3. The VSPAM is once more suspended vertically, but this time its distal end is free. With the contraction PAM pressured to 0.14 MPa, the VSPAM, which is initially at its unpressurized length of 40.5 cm, is shortened by 5 mm relative to its initial unpressurized length. The axial displacement of the VSPAM under various loads is then measured, and the experiment is repeated five times to determine the average value. After that, the pressure in the extension PAM is increased until the length of the VSPAM is restored to 40.5 cm. The pressure in the extension PAM is recorded as 0.04 MPa.

The experiment is run five times in order to average the axial displacement of the VSPM under various loads. The ECPAM, which has a length of 40.5 cm, exhibits variation in length with varying additional loads, as illustrated in Fig. 8. The stiffness of the VSPAM can be ascertained by analyzing the gradient of the resulting force and displacement curve. In this case, the stiffness is 1925 N/m when the contraction PAM and extension PAM have combined loads of 0.14 MPa and 0.04 MPa, respectively.

Increasing the contraction PAM pressure to 0.20MPa again caused the ECPAM to become shorter than the initial length, therefore the extension PAM pressure is again increased until the initial VSPAM length of 40.5 cm is reached, the extension PAM pressure required to reach this point is 0.095 MPa and using the same method the stiffness of the ECPAM was calculated to be 2,449 N/m. The ECPAM becomes shorter than the initial length when the contraction PAM pressure is increased to 0.20 MPa. Consequently, the extension PAM pressure is increased once more until the initial VSPAM length of 40.5 cm is reached. The extension PAM pressure needs to reach this point is 0.095 MPa, and the stiffness of the ECPAM is determined to be 2,449 N/m using the same method. The VSPAM's stiffness, at 0.26 MPa for contraction and 0.12 MPa for extension, is 3474 N/m. This further confirms that the stiffness may be adjusted at the starting length of

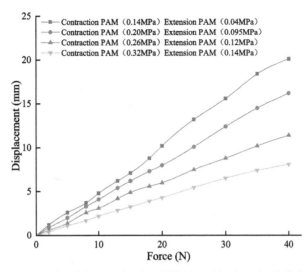

Fig. 8. Experimental results of the length of an ECPAM with a length of 40.5 cm varying with different additional loads at a specific inlet air pressure

40.5 cm. Additionally, the VSPM's rigidity is 4790 N/m at contraction PAM pressure of 0.32 MPa and an extension PAM pressure of 0.14 MPa. Table 1 displays the experimental outcomes for each of the four studies. It is evident that varying stiffness may be attained with an identical VSPAM length.

Table 1. Experimental results on the stiffness of ECPAM with a length of 40.5 cm.

Length of VSPAM (cm)	Air pressure of Contraction PAM (MPa)	Air pressure of Extension PAM (MPa)	Stiffness of VSPAM (N/m)
40.5	0.14	0.04	1925
40.5	0.20	0.095	2449
40.5	0.26	0.12	3474
40.5	0.32	0.14	4790

4.3 Experiment Using Lumbar Spine Assisted Exoskeleton Rehabilitation Robot for Lumbar Assistance

Using the mechanical characteristics of the driver VSPAM, we create a prototype exoskeleton robot for lumbar spine assisted rehabilitation in this chapter. Figure 9(a) displays the waist's natural bending state diagram along the sagittal plane, and Fig. 9(b) illustrates how the contraction PAM, which is introduced in earlier chapters, can produce a contraction force of roughly 60N, which can help the human body perform rehabilitation exercises. The VSPM's contraction PAM produces contraction force in the sagittal plane to support the human body's back state diagram. The human waist is forced to an upright position by the contraction PAM when it produces the greatest contraction force, as seen in Fig. 9(c); Then, the extension PAM of VSPAM is filled with high-pressure gas, and the contraction PAM is reduced by the pressure of high-pressure gas, and the VSPM will generate an extension force to assist the human body to bend the waist as shown in Fig. 9(d) and (e);

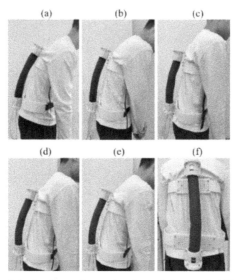

Fig. 9. The prototype of the lumbar spine assisted exoskeleton rehabilitation robot is used for lumbar assist training

The human lumbar spine is bent after the lumbar spine assists the rehabilitation exoskeleton robot as shown in Fig. 9(f). To sum up, the application of VSPAM to the lumbar spine assisted rehabilitation exoskeleton robot not only meets the requirements of contraction force and extension force, but also solves the problem that the weight of the rigid robot is too heavy.

5 Conclusion

In order to help the elderly carry out lumbar rehabilitation training, this paper designs a lumbar spine assisted rehabilitation exoskeleton robot driver with both contraction and extension functions, and introduces the design, manufacture and application of VSPM. Combining contraction and extension PAM allow them to elongate and contract and generate forces in both directions. A mathematical model is established to describe the output force of ECPAM and the mathematical model is experimentally verified, but the loss of force is ignored, for example, the friction between the braided and the hose and between the nylon threads of the braid is assumed, resulting in an error of 10% between the experimental results and the theoretical value. VSPAM can demonstrate the ability to change the stiffness of VSPAM independently of its position by adjusting the internal air pressure values of the contraction and extension PAM to change the stiffness, and perform stiffness experiments.

In the future, we will try to come up with more interesting applications of curved and spiral PAM to explore more possibilities for them.

Acknowledgement. This work was supported in part by Changzhou Social Development Science and Technology Support Program, No. CE20225037; Jiangsu special project for frontier leading base technology, No. BK20192004; Changzhou Science and Technology Program Project (Key Laboratory), No. CM20223014; Suzhou key industry technology innovation - prospective application research project, No. SYG202143.

References

1. Chen, Y.M., Liu, Z.F., et al.: The aging trend of Chinese population and the prediction of aging population in 2015–2025. Chinese J. Soc. Med. **35**(5), 408–483 (2018)
2. Li, C.Y., Shi, Y.: Analysis of risk factors of cervical spondylosis. Chinese J. Acupuncture Moxibustion. **9**(3), 128–130 (2020)
3. Adam, B.Z., Homayoon, K., Andrew, C.: Biomechanical design of the Berkeley lower extremity exoskeleton (BLEEX). IEEE/ASME Trans. Mechatronics. **11**(2), 128–138 (2006)
4. Konrad, S., Wilfried, J.E., Hans, W.R.: Exoskeleton toenhance industrial production. Mob. Serv. Robot. **12**, 53–60 (2014)
5. Chen, S., Wu, H.F., Liu, S., et al.: Development of waist assist mechanism for wearable handling assist robot. Mech. Eng. Technol. **10**(2), 248–256 (2021)
6. David, M.F., Mohammad, A., Joan, M.S.: PLAD stiffness affects the lumbar flexion/extension moment and the posterior chain EMG during symmetrical lifting tasks. J. Electromyogr. Kinesiol. **19**(6), 403–412 (2009)
7. Yumeko, I., Takayuki, T., Yoshihito, S., et al.: Motion-based-design of elastic material for passive assistive device using musculoskeletal model. J. Robot. Mechatronics. **23**(6), 978–990 (2011)
8. Zhang, H.H., Abhijit, K., Frank, C.S.: Design and preliminary evaluation of a passive spine exoskeleton. J. Med. Devices **10**(1), 011002 (2016)
9. Li, X.P., Han, J.H., Guo, B.J., et al.: Research on wearable waist-assisted robot based on flexible pneumatic actuator. J. Autom. **42**(12), 1849–1858 (2016)
10. Wu, J.X., Han, Y.L., Ke, Z.Y., et al.: Research on flexible exoskeleton robot technology. Electromech. Eng. Technol. **50**(02), 127–129 (2021)
11. Takayuki, T., Yuta, S., et al.: Smart suit: soft power suit with semi-active assist mechanism - prototype for supporting waist and knee joint. In: International Conference on Control, Automation and Systems. Seoul, Korea, Oct. 14–17, 2008, pp. 2002–2005 (2008)
12. Lee, J.-W., Kim, G.: Design and control of a lifting assist device for preventing lower back injuries in industrial athletes. Int. J. Precis. Eng. Manuf. **20**(10), 1825–1838 (2019). https://doi.org/10.1007/s12541-019-00183-0
13. Dong, J.H., Lim, H.S., Park, S.I., et al.: Singular wire-driven series elastic actuation with force control for a waist assistive exoskeleton, H-WEX v2. IEEE/ASME Trans. Mechantronics. **25**(2), 1026–1035 (2020)

14. Kohei, N., Helmut, H., Kang, R., et al.: A soft body as a reservoir case studies in a dynamic model of octopus inspired soft robotic arm. Front. Comput. Neurosci. **7**, 1–19 (2013)
15. Tang, Z.L., Wang, H.Y., Zhang, H.K., et al.: Experimental investigation on the forward speed of passive wheeled serpentine robot. Mod. Manuf. Technol. Equipment. **283**(6), 86–89 (2020)
16. Tian, J.W., Wang, T.M., Shi, Z.Y., et al.: Kinematic analysis and experiment of elephant-like trunk robotic arm. Robotics **39**(5), 585–594 (2017)
17. Gao, W.X., Wang, H.L.: Research process and development prospect study of bionic robot. Heilongjiang Sci. **9**(1), 26–27 (2018)
18. Li, Z.Y.: Development application and prospect of soft robot. Sci. Technol. Commun. **10**(23), 109–110 (2018)
19. Li, H.L., Yao, J.T., Zhou, P., et al.: Untethered high-load soft gripping robots: a review. J. Mech. Eng. **56**(1), 1–15 (2020)
20. Al-Fahaam, H., Nefti-Meziani, S., Theodoridis, T., et al.: The design and mathematical model of a novel variable stiffness extensor-contractor pneumatic artificial muscle. Soft Rob. **5**(5), 576–591 (2018)
21. Chou, C.P., Hannaford, B.: Measurement and modeling of McKibben pneumatic artificial muscles. IEEE Trans. Robot. Autom. **12**(1), 90–102 (1996)
22. Do, B.H., Choi, I., Follmer, S.: An all-soft variable impedance actuator enabled by embedded layer jamming. IEEE/ASME Trans. Mechatron. **27**(6), 5529–5540 (2022)
23. Meller, M.A., Bryant, M., Garcia, E.: Reconsidering the McKibben muscle: Energetics, operating fluid, and bladder material. J. Intell. Mater. Syst. Struct. **25**(18), 2276–2293 (2014)

Variable Stiffness Performance Analysis of Layer Jamming Actuator Based on Bionic Adhesive Flaps

Liangzhi Ye[1], Linsen Xu[1,2,3](✉), Zhihuan Wang[1], Lisheng Wang[1], and Huan Mei[1]

[1] College of Mechanical and Electrical Engineering, Hohai University, Changzhou 213022, China
lsxu@hhu.edu.cn
[2] Changzhou Key Laboratory of Intelligent Manufacturing Technology and Equipment, Changzhou, China
[3] Suzhou Research Institute, Hohai University, Suzhou, China

Abstract. The layer jamming mechanism is widely applied to soft actuators but is limited by the non-fluid layer material with a narrow range of stiffness variation. Inspired by the excellent adhesive ability of geckos, the bionic adhesive flaps with tilted semicircular micropillars are designed for the layer jamming mechanism. A prototype of the layer jamming actuator based on the bionic adhesive flaps is fabricated. A variable stiffness theoretical model of the layer jamming structure is established, and the shear adhesive force of the bionic adhesive flap during detachment is calculated based on the Kendall viscoelastic band model. The measurement results of shear adhesive forces show that the critical shear adhesive forces of the bionic adhesive flaps are increased by a factor of 3.2 compared to the PET flaps. The variable stiffness performance of the layer jamming actuator based on bionic adhesive flaps is evaluated by two stiffness test methods, and the maximum stiffness reaches 8.027 N/mm, which is 1.5 times higher than that of the layer jamming actuator based on PET flaps, verifying the feasibility and superiority of the application of the bionic adhesive flaps to the layer jamming mechanism to improve stiffness.

Keywords: Variable Stiffness · Layer Jamming Mechanism · Bionic Adhesive Flaps · Soft Actuator

1 Introduction

Rigid robots can perform tasks accurately and efficiently, but they cannot passively adapt to complex unstructured environments [1]. Although the lack of flexibility and adaptability can be made up by increasing the number of joints for high degrees of freedom, it also increases the control complexity, weight, and cost of the overall system [2]. Instead, many researchers have been attracted to soft robots due to their inherent flexibility, adaptability, safety [3]. However, soft robots normally generate limited output forces, and low stiffness cannot resist the large external forces. Therefore, variable stiffness technology has become an internationally popular topic for researching soft robots [4].

In recent studies, the main technologies for achieving variable stiffness include phase-change materials [5], antagonism principle [6] and jamming mechanisms [7]. Usually, a high temperature, high voltage/current, and strong magnetic field are required for phase-change materials and the antagonism principle, and the response time for rigid-flexible state switching is too long [5]. Therefore, jamming mechanisms stand out from a crowd of variable stiffness technologies. Compared to other jamming mechanisms, the layer jamming is still the most suitable choice in application scenarios with volume and weight constraints, even though restrictions on non-fluid planar sheets under stress easily lead to damage to the jamming structure, making it impossible to detach partially [8]. In response to the drawback that layer jamming mechanism provides stiffness dependent on layer orientation, which usually limits the application scenario to a single planar structure making it unsuitable for robots with bending motions, a novel pneumatic layer jamming structure that only requires complex fabrication techniques is proposed to allow for out-of-plane bending [9, 10]. However, the stiffness of the layer jamming mechanism obtained by the negative pressure-activated is still not significant enough, and higher stiffness can be obtained by changing the flaps materials and designing structured surfaces.

Geckos are able to crawl easily on vertical walls and even ceilings. This ability benefits from their toes with a multi-scale hierarchical structure consisting of tiny setae 5-10 μm in diameter and 30-130 μm in length, each of which splits into more than 100–1000 nm-sized spatulas at its end [11–13]. Autumn et al. verified for the first time that geckos are in close contact with surfaces through the multiscale hierarchical structure, mainly using weak and small-scale van der Waals forces for adhesion, in addition to other types of non-covalent forces acting, such as capillary forces [14, 15]. Inspired by the adhesion ability of geckos, researchers have biomimetically designed multiscale hierarchical structures to fabricate adhesive materials that resemble the ideal anisotropic behaviors of geckos with strong adhesion in the griping direction and almost zero adhesion in the releasing direction [16–19].

In this paper, inspired by the adhesive ability of geckos, the bionic adhesive flaps with tilted semicircular micropillars are designed for the layer jamming mechanism and a layer jamming actuator is fabricated based on the bionic adhesive flaps. The fabrication process of the bionic adhesive flaps and the layer jamming actuator are described in detail in the following section. Then a variable stiffness theoretical model about the layer jamming structure is established and the shear adhesive force of the bionic adhesive flaps is calculated based on the Kendall viscoelastic band model. In the final section, the feasibility and superiority of applying the bionic adhesive flaps to the layer jamming mechanism are verified by experiments, and the variable stiffness performance of the layer jamming actuator based on the bionic adhesive flaps is evaluated.

2 Design and Fabrication

The layer jamming actuator based on the bionic adhesive flaps consists of two modules: the soft actuator and the layer jamming structure, as shown in Fig. 1. By comparing and analyzing the simulation results [20], it is found that the bending motion ability of the soft actuator is best when the air chamber cross-section is fan-ring shaped. The three air chambers soft actuator, which is made of silicone casting, placed on the inside, and the pressure in the three air chambers can be independently controlled to achieve the bending movements in different directions and angles. In order to avoid excessive radial expansion of the soft actuator during loading, restraining rings are assembled in the surface to act as constraints. The layer jamming structure that achieves variable stiffness is surrounded on the outside of the soft actuator. Laser-cut polyethylene terephthalate (PET) sheets are commonly used as flaps materials. To improve stiffness performance, the bionic adhesive flaps are made of the PET sheets bonded to the bionic adhesive material, which is made of polyurethane (PU). The flaps are wrapped around the surface of the soft actuator using a nylon thread, and a latex membrane is wrapped around the flaps to form a confined space.

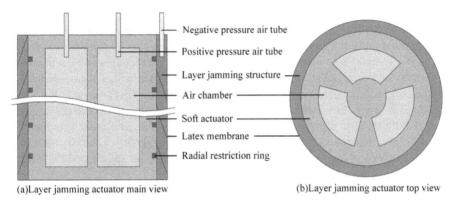

Fig. 1. Layer jamming actuator structure schematic

After controlling the pressure in the air chambers to move the soft actuator to a specified position, a negative pressure is applied to the latex membrane to activate the layer jamming mechanism. When jamming occurs, the flaps are squeezed against each other, and the sharp rise in interlayer friction increases the difficulty of relative movement of the flaps and improves the resistance to deformation of the layer jamming actuator. Adjusting the negative pressure inside the latex membrane will control the change of the stiffness of the layer jamming actuator.

2.1 Bionic Adhesive Flaps Fabrication

Bionic adhesive flaps are made of bionic adhesive materials bonded to the PET sheets. Inspired by the surface structure of the gecko's toe, as shown in Fig. 2, the micropillars of the adhesive material are designed in the form of inclined semi-cylinders as shown in Fig. 3(d). Under negative pressure, the flaps slide in the + Y direction, and when the negative pressure is released, the flaps slide in the -Y direction, and the negative pressure is loaded in the -Z direction. The micropillars contact the substrate with the flat surface when sliding occurs in the + Y direction, and with the curved surface when sliding occurs in the -Y direction. Adhesive materials have anisotropic shear adhesive capabilities, which manifested in larger range of variable stiffness and shorter response times for rigid-flexible state switching in layer jamming structure.

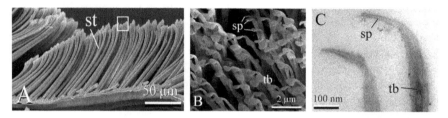

Fig. 2. Surface structure of gecko's toe [13]

The mold turning process is selected to obtain a large area of adhesive material. The concave mold that could replicate micropillars is fabricated by 3D printing. Reoflex 30 polyurethane A and B components are mixed 1:1, placed in vacuum chamber to remove air bubbles and then poured onto the concave mold treated with release agents. The polyurethane is homogenised on a homogenising machine at 500 rpm/min for 2 min, placed again in vacuum chamber to remove air bubbles and to allow the polyurethane to enter fully into the negative cavity of the molds (Fig. 3a). The mold is removed to obtain the polyurethane adhesive materials after curing (Fig. 3b). The bionic adhesive flaps are made by gluing the adhesive materials to the laser cut and shaped PET sheets, as shown in Fig. 3(c).

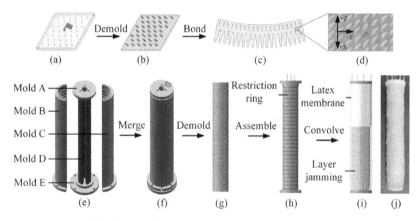

Fig. 3. Layer jamming actuator fabrication process

2.2 Soft Actuator Fabrication

The separated molds required for casting are fabricated by 3D printing, as shown in Fig. 3(e). The three air chamber molds D are mounted on the base mold E. The left and right molds B and C are merged and locked with a hoop, and bolted and fastened to the mold E to avoid infiltration of silicone from the bottom gap during pouring. Next, the two components of E620 silica gel A and B 1:1 are mixed, placed in vacuum chamber to remove air bubbles and inject into the molds treated with release agents, placed them again in vacuum chamber to remove air bubbles and make full contact. The end-cap mold A is installed to fix the air chamber molds B (Fig. 3f). All molds are removed to obtain the soft actuator after the silicone solidifies (Fig. 3g), and the restriction rings are assembled in the groove on the side of the soft actuator. The air chambers and the air pump are connected with the air tube, and sealed at both ends with silicone. The base and end caps are mounted on both ends of the soft actuator respectively and bonded and sealed with special glue to ensure air tightness (Fig. 3h). The bionic adhesive flaps are wrapped around the surface of the soft actuator by nylon thread passing through the holes and slots. A latex membrane is wrapped around the outside and sealed with glue to form a confined space (Fig. 3i), and accessing the air pipe to connect with the vacuum pump to complete the fabrication of the layer jamming actuator based on the bionic adhesive flaps, as shown in Fig. 3(j).

3 Theoretical Modeling

3.1 Variable Stiffness Theoretical Model

When the negative pressure activates the layer jamming mechanism, jamming occurs and the movement of the flaps are restricted, increasing the resistance to deformation of the overall structure. After removing the negative pressure, the flaps return to the free state. The stiffness of the flaps in the free state due to external forces is usually not considered separately in theoretical modelling or is taken into account within the inherent stiffness of the soft actuator. However, when wrapping the flaps around the surface of the soft actuator, not only does the nylon thread exert a certain amount of pressure, but also the soft actuator squeezes the curved side flaps during movement, causing a slight interaction force between the flaps. The stiffness provided by this is limited, so this part of the stiffness is not considered. The maximum friction force before the flaps sliding in the jamming state is defined as [21]

$$F = \mu n W L P \tag{1}$$

where μ is the coefficient of friction, n is the number of contact surfaces between the flaps, P is the applied negative pressure, W is the width of the flap, and L is the length of the contact surface. Assuming that the number of contact surfaces, width and length of the flaps are kept constant, the friction can be improved by increasing the negative pressure and friction coefficient. Designing bionic adhesive flaps will effectively improve the surface roughness and friction coefficient.

To further analyze the specific effect of the multilayer jamming structure on the stiffness, the Euler-Bernoulli assumption is usually used to define the bending stiffness and quantify the stiffness performance, and the soft actuator is simplified into a cantilever beam structure, from which the bending stiffness model is developed. In order to simulate the loading of the air chambers that makes the soft actuator bend, a bending force F_b is applied at the end of the actuator, which produces a maximum displacement of δ. The bending stiffness of the beam will be defined as:

$$K = \frac{F_b}{\delta} = \frac{3EI}{l^3} \quad (2)$$

where E is the modulus of elasticity of the beam, I is the area moment of inertia and l is the length. In multi-layer structures, considering that each layer is independent, the stiffness depends on the sliding phenomena between the layers and the area moments of inertia. In fact, when the layers are not coupled, as shown in Fig. 4(b), the moment of inertia of a single layer flap of rectangular cross-section $b \times h$ is:

$$I_Z = \int_{-h/2}^{h/2} y^2 dA = \int_{-h/2}^{h/2} y^2 b dy = \frac{bh^3}{12} \quad (3)$$

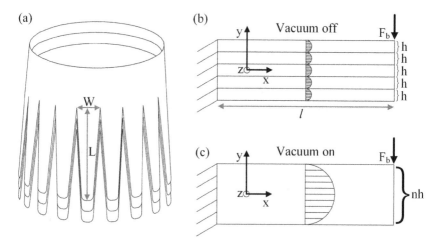

Fig. 4. Variable stiffness analysis

When no negative pressure is applied within the latex membrane, the flaps remain free and slide against each other. The overall inertia of the multilayer flaps is:

$$I_Z = \sum_{i=1}^{n} \frac{bh_i^3}{12} = \frac{nbh^3}{12} \quad (4)$$

However, when negative pressure is applied within the latex membrane, the flaps are squeezed and the resulting friction prevents the flaps from sliding to creating jamming, as shown in Fig. 4(c), so the multi-layer flaps can be considered as a whole beam with a moment of inertia is:

$$I_Z = \int_{-nh/2}^{nh/2} y^2 b dy = \frac{b(nh)^3}{12} \quad (5)$$

After removing the negative pressure, the flaps will return to the free state again. Ideally, without taking into account the bending stiffness effect of the soft actuator itself, the bending stiffness of the multi-layer flaps in the jamming state is n^2 times higher than in the free state.

3.2 Shear Adhesive Forces Calculation

Since the JKR theory does not consider the role of tangential forces, the Kendall viscoelastic band model is used in this paper, and the micropillar at the time of adhesion is regarded as a viscoelastic band, as shown in Fig. 5. When the surface is peeled off at an angle of θ with the substrate surface, the peeling length is Δc, and the energy required to generate a new surface is $-\omega b \Delta c$, and ω is the equivalent surface adhesion energy per unit area. The work done by the external force F is $F(1-\cos\theta)\Delta c$, and the elastic deformation energy in the peeling area is $F^2 \Delta c/bdE$. The strain energy stored for restoring the original state is $-F^2 \Delta c/2bdE$.

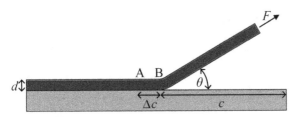

Fig. 5. Kendall viscoelastic band model

When proposing the viscoelastic band model, Kendall considered that the bending stiffness of the band depends on the third power of the thickness d, and the contribution of bending to the change of elastic performance during the peeling process can be neglected. He assumes that the equivalent adhesion energy per unit area is fixed to a constant and avoids the problem of the distribution of adhesive forces along the length, with an undivided area of action. Assuming that energy can be conserved, all the above energies are summed. The required peeling force is

$$F = bdE(\cos\theta - 1 + \sqrt{(\cos\theta - 1)^2 + \frac{2\omega}{dE}}) \qquad (6)$$

When negative pressure is applied, the micropillars make contact with the substrate in flat surface, and when negative pressure is removed, contact with the substrate in curved surface. Due to the low Young's modulus of the polyurethane material, the curved surface in contact with the substrate elastically deforms to form a limited contact width c_{eq}:

$$c_{eq} = 8\left[\frac{W(1-v^2)R^2}{\pi E}\right]^{1/3} \qquad (7)$$

Since the classical Kendall model applies to films of rectangular cross-section and does not apply to micropillars of semicircular cross-section with radius R, the peel force equation needs to be rederived and multiple by the maximum number of micropillars, N, in contact with the substrate, and the modified peeling force equation in the shear direction is

$$F_\tau = N\left[\cos\theta \times \frac{\pi R^2 E}{2}(\cos\theta - 1 + \sqrt{(\cos\theta - 1)^2 + \frac{4\omega b}{\pi R^2 E}})\right] \quad (8)$$

4 Performance Evaluation

The layer jamming actuator based on the bionic adhesive flaps is fabricated with a length of 200 mm, a diameter of 30 mm, and three air chambers. In order to evaluate the feasibility of bionic adhesive flaps for layer jamming mechanism to improve stiffness and the variable stiffness performance of layer jamming actuator, multiple sets of experiments are carried out.

4.1 Shear Adhesive Forces Measurement

A test apparatus for measuring the critical shear adhesive forces of the polyurethane bionic adhesive flaps under a specific preload is shown in Fig. 6(a). Under the action of certain mass of weights (50 g and 100 g), the PET sheets are contacted with the bionic adhesive flaps fixed on an elevating pad, and the right side is connected to a dynamometer through a pulley. The peak value of the dynamometer during the process of the flaps from static to sliding are recorded, which are the critical shear adhesive forces.

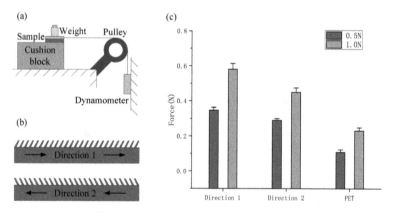

Fig. 6. Shear adhesive forces measurement

In addition, to assess the anisotropy of the shear adhesive forces of the polyurethane bionic adhesive flaps, the peaks during the process are recorded respectively in the adhesion direction (Direction 1) and the releasing direction (Direction 2), as shown in Fig. 6(b). The measurement results are shown in Fig. 6(c), where the ratio of the critical shear adhesive forces of the bionic adhesive flaps in the adhesion direction and the releasing direction is about 1.2 under the pre-pressure of 0.5 N, while the critical shear adhesive forces in the adhesion direction is 3.2 times higher than that of the conventional PET flaps. The bionic adhesive flaps also show a consistent trend under the preload of 1.0 N. The measurement results verify the feasibility and superiority of the bionic adhesive flaps for layer jamming mechanism to improve stiffness.

4.2 Variable Stiffness Performance Testing

In most cases, soft actuators are not sufficient to handle tasks that require forces output, so variable stiffness structures are required to hold the shape and resist external forces for operation, making stiffness an important indicator for evaluating the performance of soft actuators. The feasibility and superiority of bionic adhesive flaps for layer jamming actuators are verified by testing the stiffness of soft actuators respectively with 0° bending, and 90° axial compression under different negative pressure-activated jamming states, and setting up a control group of layer jamming actuator based on PET flaps. The test platform is shown in Fig. 7, which contains a gripper, a digital dynamometer, and a vertical and horizontal test bench. The arrows in the figure show the direction of displacement.

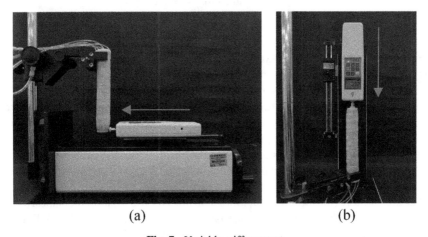

(a) (b)

Fig. 7. Variable stiffness test

During the tests, the dynamometer is in contact with the end of the layer jamming actuator. The dynamometer moves from 0-10 mm, 2 mm at a time, and the number shown is the force at the end of the actuator. The vacuum pressures are set to 0 kPa, 10 kPa, 20 kPa and 30 kPa, to test the relationship between the displacement and the end forces of the actuators under different vacuum pressures.

The experimental results of the actuators 0° bending and 90° axial compression state are respectively shown in Fig. 8. Each group is repeated five times. And the data are the average of the five experimental results, which can be analyzed and obtained: The higher the vacuum pressure inside the latex membrane, the higher the actuator end forces at the same displacement. Under the same vacuum pressure and the same displacement, the end force of the layer jamming actuator based on bionic adhesive flaps(BAF) is higher than that of the layer jamming actuators based on PET flaps in general. The stiffness test results strongly demonstrate the feasibility and superiority of bionic adhesive flaps for layer jamming actuator.

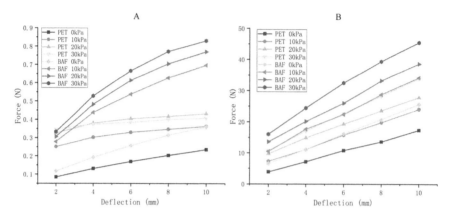

Fig. 8. Variable stiffness test results

According to Eq. 2, the max stiffness of the layer jamming actuator based on the bionic adhesive flaps reaches 8.027 N/mm, which is 1.5 times higher compared to 5.344 N/mm for the layer jamming actuator based on the PET flaps at 90° compression. The max stiffness of the layer jamming actuator based on the bionic adhesive flaps are increased by 2.84 times at 0° bending and 2.45 times at 90° compression respectively.

Unexpected phenomenon occurs during testing. The differences in the end force of the layer jamming actuator based on the bionic adhesive flaps and the PET flaps at 0 kPa are hypothesized to be caused by manufacturing errors and measurement errors. At 0° bending, the slip generated by the micropillar relying only on the bionic adhesive flaps at small displacements is not sufficient to generate high shear adhesive forces, so that the end force of the layer jamming actuator based on the bionic adhesive flaps occurs to be lower than that of the layer jamming actuator based on the PET flaps at 2 mm displacement. As the displacement increases, the end force of the layer jamming actuator based on the bionic adhesive flaps gradually increases and leads. Due to the smooth surface of the PET flaps, it is prone to slip when an external force is applied. It is hypothesized that the end force at 30 kPa is higher than 20 kPa for the layer jamming actuator based on PET flaps before 4 mm displacement, however, the end force at 30 kPa is lower than 20 kPa is caused by slippage after 4 mm at 0° bending.

5 Conclusion

In this paper, the bionic adhesive flaps with tilted semicircular micropillars are designed inspired by the adhesive ability of geckos and a prototype of the layer jamming actuator based on bionic adhesive flaps is fabricated. The Euler-Bernoulli assumption is used to establish a variable stiffness theoretical model, and shear adhesive force of the bionic adhesive flaps is calculated by the Kendall viscoelastic band model. The measurement results show that the critical shear adhesive force of the bionic adhesive flaps in the adhesion direction is 1.2 times higher than that in the releasing direction and 3.2 times higher compared to the PET flaps. Variable stiffness performance of the layer jamming actuator based on the bionic adhesive flaps are evaluated under different negative pressures at 0° bending and 90° compression. The maximum stiffness of the layer jamming actuator based on the bionic adhesive flaps reaches 8.027 N/mm at 30 kPa, which is 1.5 times higher than 5.344 N/mm for the layer jamming actuator based on the PET flaps at 90° compression. The max stiffness of the layer jamming actuator based on the bionic adhesive flaps are increased by 2.84 times at 0° bending and 2.45 times at 90° compression respectively. Testing results demonstrate effectively the feasibility and superiority of the bionic adhesive flaps for layer jamming mechanism to enhance the stiffness. This research can be applied to soft grippers and reconfigurable robotic arms with large stiffness requirements for improving the gripper's load capacity and resistance to interference from external forces. Future work may focus on the specific effects of micropillars dimension and geometry on stiffness and practical applications.

Acknowledgment. This research was funded by Jiangsu Special Project for Frontier Leading Base Technology, grant number BK20192004; Fundamental Research Funds for Central Universities, grant number B240201190; Changzhou Social Development Science and Technology Support Plan, grant number CE20225037; Changzhou Science and Technology Plan, grant number CM20223014; Suzhou Key Industrial Technology Innovation Forward-Looking Application Research Project, grant number SYG202143.

References

1. Ibrahimi, M., Paternò, L., Ricotti, L., et al.: A layer jamming actuator for tunable stiffness and shape-changing devices. Soft Rob. **8**(1), 85–96 (2021)
2. Clark, A.B., Rojas, N.: Design and workspace characterisation of malleable robots. In: 2020 IEEE International Conference on Robotics and Automation (ICRA), pp. 9021–9027. IEEE (2020)
3. Marchese, A.D., Katzschmann, R.K., Rus, D.: A recipe for soft fluidic elastomer robots. Soft Rob. **2**(1), 7–25 (2015)
4. Wang, T., Hao, Y., Yang, X., et al.: Soft robotics: structure, actuation, sensing and control. J. Mech. Eng. **53**(13), 1–13 (2017)
5. Shang, Z., Ma, J., Wang, S.: Review of variable stiffness mechanisms in minimally invasive surgical manipulators. J. Mech. Eng. **58**(21), 1–15 (2022)
6. Giannaccini, M.E., Xiang, C., Atyabi, A., et al.: Novel design of a soft lightweight pneumatic continuum robot arm with decoupled variable stiffness and positioning. Soft Rob. **5**(1), 54–70 (2018)
7. Gerez, L., Gao, G., Liarokapis, M.: Laminar jamming flexure joints for the development of variable stiffness robot grippers and hands. In: 2020 IEEE/RSJ International Conference on Intelligent Robots and Systems (IROS), pp. 8709–8715. IEEE (2020)
8. Fitzgerald, S.G., Delaney, G.W., Howard, D.: A review of jamming actuation in soft robotics. In: Actuators, vol. 9, pp. 104. MDPI (2020)

9. Kim, Y.J., Cheng, S., Kim, S., et al.: A novel layer jamming mechanism with tunable stiffness capability for minimally invasive surgery. IEEE Trans. Rob. **29**(4), 1031–1042 (2013)
10. Kim, Y.J., Cheng, S., Kim, S., et al.: Design of a tubular snake-like manipulator with stiffening capability by layer jamming. In: 2012 IEEE/RSJ International Conference on Intelligent Robots and Systems, pp. 4251–4256. IEEE (2012)
11. Murphy, M.P., Kim, S., Sitti, M.: Enhanced adhesion by gecko-inspired hierarchical fibrillar adhesives. ACS Appl. Mater. Interfaces **1**(4), 849–855 (2009)
12. Tian, Y., Pesika, N., Zeng, H., et al.: Adhesion and friction in gecko toe attachment and detachment. Proc. Natl. Acad. Sci. **103**(51), 19320–19325 (2006)
13. Persson, B.N.J., Gorb, S.: The effect of surface roughness on the adhesion of elastic plates with application to biological systems. J. Chem. Phys. **119**(21), 11437–11444 (2003)
14. Autumn, K., Sitti, M., Liang, Y.A., et al.: Evidence for van der Waals adhesion in gecko setae. Proc. Natl. Acad. Sci. **99**(19), 12252–12256 (2002)
15. Autumn, K., Liang, Y.A., Hsieh, S.T., et al.: Adhesive force of a single gecko foot-hair. Nature **405**(6787), 681–685 (2000)
16. Shi, W., Cheng, X., Cheng, K.: Gecko-inspired adhesives with asymmetrically tilting-oriented micropillars. Langmuir **38**(29), 8890–8898 (2022)
17. Zhang, Y., Ma, S., Li, B., et al.: Gecko's feet-inspired self-peeling switchable dry/wet adhesive. Chem. Mater. **33**(8), 2785–2795 (2021)
18. Dong, X., Zhang, R., Tian, Y., et al.: Functionally graded gecko setae and the biomimics with robust adhesion and durability. ACS Appl. Polymer Mater. **2**(7), 2658–2666 (2020)
19. Shi, Z., Tan, D., Wang, Z., et al.: Switchable adhesion on curved surfaces mimicking the coordination of radial-oriented spatular tips and motion of gecko toes. ACS Appl. Mater. Interfaces **14**(27), 31448–31454 (2022)
20. Li, T., Cui, B., Liu, H., et al.: Design and experiment of a soft pneumatic actuator with variable stiffness by magnetic-induced. J. Mech. Eng. **59**(3), 1–12 (2023)
21. Liu, Z., Xu, L., Liang, X., et al.: Stiffness-tuneable segment for continuum soft robots with vertebrae. Machines **10**(7), 581 (2022)

Research on End-Effector Decoupling Control Strategy Based on Dual Force Sensors

Ying Zhong[1,2], Han Chen[2], Chin-Yin Chen[2(✉)], Junjie Dai[2], Yuncai Zhao[1], and Chi Zhang[2]

[1] School of Mechanical and Electrical Engineering, Jiangxi University of Science and Technology, Ganzhou 341000, Jiangxi, China
[2] Zhejiang Key Laboratory of Robotics and Intelligent Manufacturing Equipment Technology, Ningbo Institute of Materials Technology and Engineering, Chinese Academy of Sciences, Ningbo 315201, China
yeyuze@nuaa.edu.cn

Abstract. This paper proposes a decoupling control algorithm based on dual force sensors to address the coupling between force and motion of end-effector, industrial robots, and end-effector series connection, friction, and coupling forces caused by nonlinear factors. Install a force sensor for decoupling between the end-effector and the industrial robotic arm and another between the end-effector and the polishing head to obtain the interaction force in contact with the workpiece and feedback to the control circuit. In order to verify the effectiveness of decoupling, the decoupling control algorithm was integrated into impedance and admittance control. The goal of eliminating coupling forces was achieved by separating the effects of various inherent dynamics in the system (such as inertial effects and friction) from the required control inputs. Decoupling frees the control system from these dynamic entanglements, enabling it to respond more accurately and adaptively to external forces and environmental disturbances. Experimental results have shown that the bandwidth of the system is increased after decoupling, which can improve the system's anti-interference ability and tracking performance.

Keywords: End-effector · Impedance control · Admittance control · Decoupling

1 Introduction

In the manufacturing and surface processing fields, the grinding and polishing tasks performed by end-effector [1] are paramount, as their precision and stability directly influence the quality of workpiece surfaces and processing efficiency [2]. Traditional grinding and polishing processes often rely on experience and manual adjustments, which pose limitations when dealing with workpieces of complex shapes and materials.

Impedance control [3] and admittance control [4], as emerging control strategies, have gradually garnered attention in the manufacturing and automation fields. However, relying solely on impedance/admittance for grinding and polishing methods has limitations. Firstly, impedance or admittance control methods may fail to provide precise control over the machining process. Due to the involvement of complex mechanics and dynamic variations during grinding and polishing, more than relying on impedance or admittance control may achieve the desired machining quality and surface finish. Secondly, handling nonlinear characteristics poses a challenge. Nonlinear factors [5] such as friction, frictional forces, and nonlinear characteristics of nitrogen gas springs during grinding and polishing may lead to inaccuracies in the established models, resulting in errors in force control methods designed based on these models, thus undermining stability and predictability in the machining process. Therefore, it is necessary to eliminate coupling disturbances among end-effector. Several scholars have proposed methods for end-effector decoupling [6]. Shin [7] decoupled three drive joints to enhance the stiffness matrix under decoupling conditions, thereby improving the accuracy and response characteristics of parallel end-effector, albeit with limitations in practical usage, particularly applicable to redundant parallel machine tools with multiple passive joints. Baron [8] proposed the utilization of joint force sensors to decouple the translational and rotational degrees of freedom of the end-effector, thereby enhancing the precision of robotic arm movements. However, compared to a single end-effector, a joint data decoupled parallel end-effector poses a higher risk of failure due to the increased number of components involved, wherein the failure of any component may lead to the entire system's malfunction. Iskandar [9] introduced an extended Cartesian impedance control force tracking algorithm, achieving complete dynamic decoupling in contact direction and motion space; nonetheless, this decoupling method overlooks the influence of disturbances, resulting in residual errors in force control. Sandy [10] proposed an end-effector decoupling method based on visual-inertial sensors, enabling the robotic arm to perform tracking tasks under unknown base motion. However, this control method necessitates complex algorithms and computational processes for handling image data, thereby augmenting the system's computational burden and latency and imposing certain requirements regarding the shape and position of objects in the environment. Oh [11], based on the robust motion tracking method studied, devised an inertia decoupling dynamic method for expanding the task space of robotic arms, incorporating a disturbance observer designed to mitigate disturbances. The design of this method necessitates estimation and constraint of uncertainties and disturbances, potentially amplifying the complexity of the design process. Furthermore, the performance of the disturbance observer is subject to estimation errors, thus necessitating appropriate treatment and compensation for estimation errors. Chen [12] used decoupling algorithm to render stiffness, which was done without environment contact. Chen [13] combined the proposed method with traditional force control to improve response speed. The method that distinguishes this paper from the above authors is to use force sensors to decouple the end-effector, and to verify the important effect of decoupling through stiffness rendering (in contact with the environment) and experimental verification of impedance and admittance control design.

The structure of this article is as follows. The second part describes the structural characteristics of the end-effector and establishes its dynamic model. The third part provides an overview of the design of traditional force controllers and impedance/admittance controllers, along with corresponding control diagrams. The fourth part provides a detailed introduction to the experimental setup and validation process, clarifying the impact of coupling on system performance. Finally, the fifth section provides a comprehensive summary and synthesis of the entire manuscript, emphasizing the significance and potential application value of the proposed methodology.

2 System Dynamic Modeling

2.1 Mechanical Structure of the End-Effector

This study focuses on integrating a mechanical system and an end-effector, as illustrated in Fig. 1. Industrial robots, characterized by their expensive workspace, facilitate precise position control during polishing operations, while end-effectors are known for their low inertia and high responsiveness, enabling effective force adjustment.

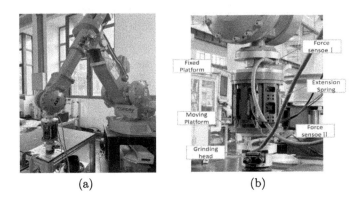

Fig. 1. (a) Mechanical system; (b) End-effector.

The section delineates the design and configuration of the grinding and polishing robotic force control system constructed herein. The system comprises an industrial robot paired with a force-regulated end-effector, which regulates the latter's position and orientation. Leveraging its high responsiveness and low inertia attributes, the force-regulated end-effector is employed to effectuate constant force for active force control. Its schematic representation is illustrated in Fig. 1.

Comprised of a voice coil motor, tension spring, nitrogen spring, and force sensor, among others, the end-effector embodies a comprehensive design. Additional components include the mobile platform, fixed platform, fixed casing, mobile inner casing, guide rails, positional encoders, force sensors, and pneumatic polishing apparatus. The voice coil motor serves as a direct drive motor, enabling linear motion without the need for transmission mechanisms. Tension springs aim to augment system stiffness, improving response time and control bandwidth. The mass of the end-effector is 5.5 Kg, with a damping of 400 Ns/m and a stiffness of 3354 N/m. The industrial robot furnishes precise posture control during polishing, while positional sensors provide feedback on the end-effector's displacement. Concurrently, the force-regulated end-effector makes minute adjustments upon contact with the workpiece and engages in active force control, preventing the industrial robot's need for precise positional control.

2.2 Establish Dynamic Model

The end-effector under investigation in this study exhibits a compact structure, where frictional forces present equate to damping terms. Assuming that the end-effector's motion direction remains perpendicular to the workpiece surface through trajectory planning methods applied to the industrial robot, it is postulated that the force-regulated end-effector under scrutiny operates as a single-degree-of-freedom system, moving solely along the Z-axis. When the end-effector operates without contact with the workpiece, it is modeled as a second-order system, with the fixed and mobile platforms representing a mass block. When in contact with the workpiece, it can also be regarded as a three spring mass system, as shown in Fig. 2.

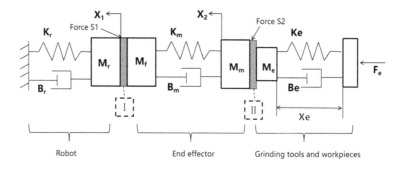

Fig. 2. Model of simplified of the End-effector system

The simplified dynamic model pertaining to the vertical force direction exerted on the workpiece is depicted in Fig. 2, where M_r, B_r, and K_r denote the mass, damping, and stiffness of the industrial robot's end-effector, respectively. X_1, X_2, and X_e represent the positions of the industrial robot's end-effector (the fixed platform's position of the end-effector), the displacement of the mobile platform, and the position of the workpiece, respectively. M_m, M_f, B_m, K_m, and F signify the mass of the mobile platform, mass of the fixed platform, mechanical damping, mechanical stiffness, and the output force of the voice coil motor respectively. K_e and B_e denote the total stiffness and damping coefficient of the grinding tool and workpiece environment (after this called environmental stiffness/damping). M_e and M_w respectively represent the grinding tool's mass and the workpiece's inertia. F_e denotes the force exerted on the workpiece. $\dot{X}_2$, $\dot{X}_1$ and $\dot{X}_e$ denote the velocities of the mobile platform and the fixed platform of the end-effector, and the velocity of the workpiece respectively, wherein $(X_2 - X_1)$ can be measured through the position grating encoder installed on the end-effector.

Consequently, the dynamic equations governing the fixed platform of the end-effector are derived as follows:

$$F - K_r X_1 - B_r \dot{X}_1 + K_m (X_2 - X_1) + B_m \left(\dot{X}_2 - \dot{X}_1\right) = (M_r + M_f) \ddot{X}_1 \quad (1)$$

The dynamic equations governing the mobile platform of the end-effector are as follows:

$$F + K_m(X_2 - X_1) + B_m(\dot{X}_2 - \dot{X}_1) - K_e(X_e - X_2) - B_e\left(\dot{X}_e - \dot{X}_2\right) = (-M_m - M_e)\ddot{X}_2 \quad (2)$$

The contact force formula is:

$$F_e = M_w \ddot{X}_e + K_e(X_e - X_2) - B_e(\dot{X}_e - \dot{X}_2) \quad (3)$$

The desired contact force is expressed as:

$$F_d = M_d \ddot{X}_d + B_d \dot{X}_d + K_d X_d \quad (4)$$

Contact force not only arises due to the series connection between the robotic arm, end-effector, and workpiece but also experiences interference from nonlinear factors such as friction in the end-effector, thereby compromising the precision of force control. A key focus lies placing force sensors within the end-effector, as illustrated in Fig. 2, where two force sensors are installed at respective positions. The force sensors are installed in the end-effector acquire forces as follows:

$$F_{s1} = F - M_f \ddot{X}_1 + K_m(X_2 - X_1) + B_m(\dot{X}_2 - \dot{X}_1) \quad (5)$$

$$F_{s2} = -M_e \ddot{X}_2 + K_e(X_e - X_2) + B_e(\dot{X}_e - \dot{X}_2) \quad (6)$$

Force Sensor F_{s1}, F_{s2}, as Eqs. (5) and (6), can measure the mechanical impedance of the end-effector, the inertia of the end-effector's fixed platform, and the output force of the voice coil motor. The opposing forces on its measuring surface include the impedance and end inertia of the industrial robot. In this study, the forces collected by Force sensor S1 are utilized for the decoupling control algorithm of the end-effector.

$$F_{s1n} = M_r \ddot{X}_1 + K_r X_1 + B_r \dot{X}_1 \quad (7)$$

$$F_{s2n} = F + M_m\ddot{X}_2 + K_m(X_2 - X_1) + B_m(\dot{X}_2 - \dot{X}_1) \tag{8}$$

Force Sensor F_{s2} measures the impedance and inertia of the polishing tool and workpiece. The forces on its measuring surface also include the mechanical impedance of the end-effector, the inertia of the end-effector of movable platform, and the output force of the voice coil motor. Positioning the force sensor at this location can achieve direct feedback on contact force. The measurable Reaction force by F_{s1n} and F_{s2n} at positions, respectively, are as (7) and (8).

3 Principle of End-Effector Control

Traditional force control inputs the expected force and feedback contact force as errors into the force controller $H(s)$, but the nonlinear factors inherent in the end-effector can result in poor controller performance. Based on this, this article adds a decoupling control algorithm on this basis. The main control framework of this paper is illustrated in Fig. 3. The green dashed box represents the force controller, in the fourth section, which undergoes traditional force control experiments with and without decoupling to validate the proposed methodology's feasibility. Building upon the designed force loop, an impedance loop, depicted by the red dashed box in the Fig. 3, is introduced and experimentally validated. Additionally, the blue dashed box represents the admittance loop. By equivalently treating the impedance loop as a position, force-tracking experiments are conducted in Sect. 4 to assess the efficacy of decoupling.

In contrast to conventional position or velocity control methodologies, impedance control finds enhanced applicability in scenarios necessitating interaction with uncertain, dynamic, or variable environments. Building upon the foundation of impedance control, this paper leverages decoupling control to mitigate the impact of coupled forces mentioned earlier. The schematic representation of decoupling-based impedance control is illustrated below, as depicted in the accompanying Fig. 3. The impedance control algorithm formula is;

$$F_d = M_d(\ddot{X} - \ddot{X}_d) + B_d(\dot{X} - \dot{X}_d) + K_d(X - X_d) \tag{9}$$

Assuming that the expected position does not change with time, $\ddot{X}_d = \dot{X}_d = 0$, it can be simplified as;

$$F_d = M_d\ddot{X} + B_d\dot{X} + K_d(X - X_d) \tag{10}$$

Decoupling is mainly achieved by eliminating the force measured by F_{s1}, but during the elimination process, it also compensates for the output force F of the motor. Therefore, it is necessary to provide an F_{st} that meets the input force requirements of the motor while decoupling. The force F' relationship between a motor and the end-effector can be obtained as,

$$F' = F + F_{st} - F_{s1} \tag{11}$$

Therefore, the decoupled contact force is

$$F_{s2} = F_d + M_m\ddot{X}_2 \tag{12}$$

This means that only the inertia of the end-effector impacts the contact. As shown in the experimental results, there has been a significant improvement.

In Fig. 3, $P(s)/Z(s)$ represents the position controller/impedance controller while. Although impedance control leverages adjustments in the relationship between position and force to achieve desired impedance characteristics through parameter tuning, it fails to eliminate control output, inevitably resulting in residual errors. These errors are transmitted to the voice coil motor through the force controller, preventing the desired output force from being obtained.

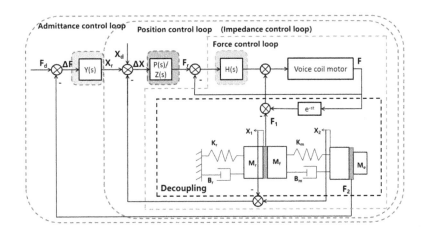

Fig. 3. Decoupling based admittance control block diagram.

In Fig. 3, $Y(s)$ represents the admittance controller, $P(s)$ denotes the position controller. The difference between the desired force F_d and the feedback force $S2$ from the end-effector is inputted to the admittance controller, which adjusts its parameters to drive the output reference position X_r. The realization of admittance control typically necessitates the utilization of force sensors to monitor the interaction forces between the robot's end-effector and the surface of the workpiece, thereby facilitating real-time adjustments of the robot's motion through control algorithms. This paper adopts a PID control-based approach for admittance control. The design of the admittance controller entails integrating an impedance loop as the positional loop foundation, supplemented by an additional admittance loop in the outer loop, thereby completing the design of the admittance controller. The decoupled control diagram for admittance control is illustrated in the accompanying Fig. 4. If a reference contact force F_r is given to the admittance controller, the control algorithm equation of the admittance controller can be simplified as

$$F_0 = M_d \ddot{X} + B_d \dot{X} + K_d(X_r - X) \tag{13}$$

$$Y(s) = \frac{1}{M_d s^2 + B_d s + K_d} \tag{14}$$

By connecting the formula (3), it can be obtained that

$$\Delta F = F_d - M_m s^2 \qquad (15)$$

The admittance compliance control effect can be achieved as long as the admittance controller's parameter meets the output reference position of 0 and the position controller is adjusted.

4 Experiments

4.1 Comparison Experiment of Traditional Force Control Tracking

Figure 4(a) shows the force tracking experimental platform. Figure 5 experimentally verifies the constant force tracking ability of the proposed method under traditional force control for the end effector. Although traditional PID controllers are used, the force tracking performance in Fig. 5(a) is better than the effect after decoupling without decoupling. The force tracking experiment starts at approximately 0.08 s and maintains a constant force of 10 N in contact with the workpiece, stopping at around 7 s. Figure 5(a) does not settle at 10 N when stopped, indicating that traditional force control alone is less stable than the proposed method. In addition, the evaluation indicators corresponding to the experimental results are shown in Table 1. Fmax and Fmin contact forces are indicators for adjusting the response speed of the control system under environmental disturbances, while the VAR and mean absolute error MAE of contact force changes reflect the force tracking accuracy of the control system.

Fig. 4. (a) Force tracking experimental system; (b) PD controller stiffness rendering experimental platform.

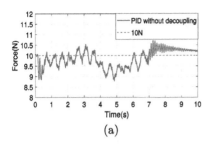 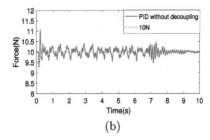

Fig. 5. Experiment on PID control of end-effector force tracking 10N: (a) Without decoupling; (b) Decoupling.

Table 1. PID control of force tracking analysis.

Control methods	Fmax	Fmin	VAR	MAE
PID	10.6N	8.4N	0.17N	0.35N
The proposed method	11.1N	9.3N	0.03N	0.13N

4.2 Impedance Controller Stiffness Rendering

To evaluate the effectiveness of the proposed method in presenting the stiffness of the end-effector, the usual approach is to use an impedance controller (PD controller) to drive the end-effector while applying a sinusoidal expected force to obtain the output position of the end-effector. As shown in Fig. 5(b), it is the stiffness rendering experimental platform of the impedance controller (PD controller). When conducting stiffness rendering experiments, K_P is used to replace the stiffness value of the given PD controller, with K_P values of 10 N/mm, 15 N/mm, and 20 N/mm, respectively. Figure 6(a) shows the stiffness rendering of the end-effector when it is not in contact with the environment. It can be clearly seen that the stiffness rendering experiment of the impedance controller without decoupling will have viscous characteristics, and the stiffness displayed at this time will be affected by the mechanical stiffness. Chen [12] has also studied stiffness rendering experiments, but has not verified the influence of environmental stiffness. In order to evaluate the stiffness rendering effect after contact with the environment, Fig. 6(b) shows the measurement results of environmental stiffness simulated using springs. After fitting the curve, the stiffness of the spring (considered as environmental stiffness) $K_e = 26$ N/mm is obtained.

Figure 7 shows the experimental results of the proposed method without contact or contact with the environment. The blue dashed line, red dashed line, and yellow dashed line represent the stiffness rendering of the decoupled PD controller without contact with the environment. At this point, the displayed stiffness is exactly equal to the stiffness value of the PD controller. This indicates that decoupling weakens the hysteresis loop and minimizes the influence of mechanical stiffness on the end-effector. In Fig. 7, the solid purple lines, solid green lines, and solid blue lines represent the stiffness rendering experiments of

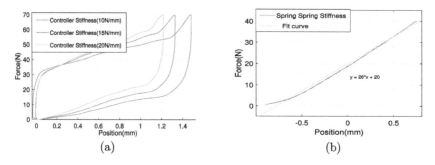

Fig. 6. Experimental verification of setting control stiffness $K_p = 10, 15, 20$ N/mm; (a) The relationship between the position and force of PD and mechanical stiffness without decoupling; (b) The measured spring stiffness is $K_e = 26$ N/mm.

the decoupled PD controller after contact with the environment. However, in contact with the environment, the stiffness exhibited at this time is the sum of the values of K_P and K_e. It can be concluded that in a decoupled state (without contact with the environment), the stiffness of the system is mainly determined by the stiffness of the controller. The controller controls the motion of the end-effector through sensors and actuators, and the stiffness exhibited by the system is relatively ideal. When the end-effector comes into contact with the environment, the stiffness and characteristics of the environment will affect the dynamic response of the overall system. At this point, the overall stiffness of the system is determined by the stiffness of the controller and the stiffness of the environment, and the stiffness relationship between the two is in series. In this case, the stiffness not only depends on the performance of the controller design, but also on the influence of environmental factors.

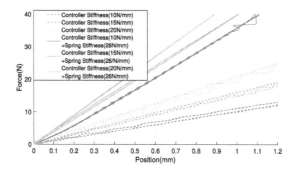

Fig. 7. Decoupling stiffness rendering of end-effector and environment contact and non-contact.

4.3 Impedance/Admittance Control Contact Force Comparison Experiment

The contact force experiment involves transitioning from a non-contact phase to a contact phase, where the grinding head's contact force gradually increases from 0 to 10N. Desired contact force remains constant at 10N throughout, as illustrated in Fig. 8.

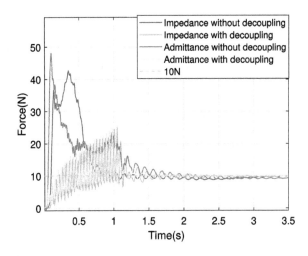

Fig. 8. Experiment on impedance/admittance control with and without decoupling on a contact force of 10 N.

From the Fig. 8, it is evident that without decoupling, the impedance exhibits a significant contact force overshoot, reaching an amplitude of approximately 42.7 N. In contrast, the decoupled impedance demonstrates a reduced overshoot with a contact force amplitude of 25.2 N. Although decoupled impedance and admittance control exhibit a suppressive effect on overshoot in contact force regulation, the presence of damping terms within the impedance/admittance controller may lead to force divergence during contact instants. Consequently, it is imperative to adjust the controller parameters appropriately to ensure that the stability and efficacy of the control system are effectively maintained. The Table 2 provides a comparison of settling time and contact force overshoot for impedance control and impedance control with decoupling, as well as for admittance control and admittance control with decoupling. Similarly, when using admittance control, there is a significant impact force with an amplitude of 48.1 N. In contrast, the decoupled admittance control results in a reduced impact force amplitude of only 25.0 N. In conclusion, under the influence of decoupling, both impedance and admittance control exhibit shortened times to reach steady-state contact force and reduced maximum overshoot in contact force, with reductions of approximately half in both time and overshoot.

Table 2. Contact force analysis results for impedance and admittance.

Control methods	Overshoot(Fmax)
Impedance without decoupling	367%(46.7 N)
Impedance with decoupling	152%(25.2 N)
Admittance without decoupling	381%(48.1) N
Admittance with decoupling	150%(25.0 N)

4.4 Step Response Experiment of Admittance Control

In order to verify the speed of decoupling admittance response and ensure that the control system exhibits good responsiveness and accuracy in practical applications, the experimental results are shown in Fig. 9. On the basis of traditional force control methods, this article further designs an admittance controller and conducts step response experiments to compare it with other proposed control methods. Chen [13] used the proposed method to obtain the step response of traditional control, as shown in Fig. 9(a), where the solid blue line represents the result of the proposed method. The blue solid line in Fig. 9(b) has a shorter settling time.

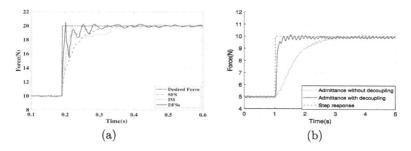

Fig. 9. Step response experiment (a) Response experimental diagram of [9] (b) Admittance control step response.

The red dashed line in Fig. 9(b) represents the contact force response 5 to 10 N. In contrast, the green solid line represents the admittance response of the contact force between 5 N and 10 N, and the blue solid line represents the admittance step response based on the decoupling method. It is evident that compared to traditional admittance control, the decoupled admittance response exhibits a significantly shortened response time. The red dashed line reaching 10 N takes about 2.1 s, the blue solid line settles at around 2.5 s, and the green solid line reaches and settles at 10 N after about 4.8 s. Compared with admittance control, the response time calculation for decoupling admittance step response is reduced by about 6.75 times. The proposed method significantly shortens the rise time and settling time of the step response, indicating that Decoupling can optimize a system's dynamic response characteristics, improve its dynamic response speed and stability, and thus achieve faster and more accurate force control and tracking.

5 Conclusions and Future Work

This paper investigates the dynamic characteristics of force-controlled end-effector based on theoretical and experimental approaches, focusing on dynamic decoupling of kinematics. The findings indicate that decoupling using force sensors enhances control performance and reduces settling time in force impedance and force-admittance control of the end-effector. In the experiments conducted, the comparison between the implementation before and after decoupling indicates that the impedance and admittance control performance after decoupling is superior. In the future, further research plans will be proposed to reduce the vibration introduced by decoupling control and optimize the decoupling effect.

Acknowledgement. This work was supported by the National Key Research and Development Program of China (2022YFB4702500), the National Natural Science Foundation of China (U23A20616), and the Key Research and Development Program of Zhejiang Province (2022C01096).

References

1. Mohammad, A.E.K., Hong, J., Wang, D.: Design of a force-controlled end-effector with low-inertia effect for robotic polishing using macro-mini robot approach. Robot. Comput. Integr. Manuf. **49**, 54–65 (2018)
2. Ma, Z., Poo, A.N., Ang, M.H., Jr., Hong, G.S., See, H.H.: Design and control of an end-effector for industrial finishing applications. Robot. Comput. Integr. Manuf. **53**, 240–253 (2018)
3. Martín-Martín, R., Lee, M.A., Gardner, R., Savarese, S., Bohg, J., Garg, A.:Variable impedance control in end-effector space: an action space for reinforcement learning in contact-rich tasks. In 2019 IEEE/RSJ International Conference on Intelligent Robots and Systems (IROS), pp. 1010–1017. IEEE (2019)
4. Fujiki, T., Tahara, K.:Series admittance-impedance controller for more robust and stable extension of force control. ROBOMECH J. **9**(1), 23 (2022)
5. Liu, X., Zhao, F., Ge, S.S., Wu, Y., Mei, X.: End-effector force estimation for flexible-joint robots with global friction approximation using neural networks. IEEE Trans. Industr. Inf. **15**(3), 1730–1741 (2018)
6. Li, R., Vuong, N.D., Chew, C.M., Lim, C.W.: Improving force control using zero coupling impedance criterion in series manipulator systems. IFAC Proc. Volumes **46**(5), 549–554 (2013)
7. Shin, H.P., Lee, D.: A new decoupling method for explicit stiffness analysis of kinematically redundant planar parallel kinematic mechanism. Math. Problems Eng. **2015**(1), 957269 (2015)
8. Baron, L., Angles, J.: The kinematic decoupling of parallel manipulators using joint-sensor data. IEEE Trans. Robot. Autom. **16**(6), 644–651 (2000)

9. Iskandar, M., Ott, C., Albu-Schäffer, A., Siciliano, B., Dietrich, A.: Hybrid force-impedance control for fast end-effector motions. IEEE Robot. Autom. Lett. **8**(7), 3931–3938 (2023)
10. Sandy, T., Buchli, J.: Dynamically decoupling base and end-effector motion for mobile manipulation using visual-inertial sensing. In :2017 IEEE/RSJ International Conference on Intelligent Robots and Systems (IROS), pp. 6299–6306. IEEE (2017)
11. Oh, Y., Chung, W.K.: Disturbance-observer-based motion control of redundant manipulators using inertially decoupled dynamics. IEEE/ASME Trans. Mechatron. **4**(2), 133–146 (1999)
12. Chen, H., Dai, J., Chen, C.Y., An, Y.,Huang, B.: Force sensor-based linear actuator stiffness rendering control. In: International Conference on Intelligent Robotics and Applications, pp. 162–173 (2023)
13. Chen, C.Y., Dai, J., Yang, G., Wang, C., Li, Y., Chen, L.: Sensor-based force decouple controller design of macro-mini manipulator. Robot. Comput. Integr. Manuf. **79**, 102415 (2023)

MLP-Depth: An Improved Visuo-Tactile 3D Reconstruction Method Applied to TIRgel Sensor

Shixin Zhang[1,2], Yuhao Sun[2], Funchun Sun[3], Huaping Liu[3], Yiyong Yang[1], and Bin Fang[2(✉)]

[1] School of Engineering and Technology, China University of Geosciences (Beijing), Beijing 100083, China
zhangshixin@email.cugb.edu.cn, yangyy@cugb.edu.cn
[2] School of Artificial Intelligence, Beijing University of Posts and Telecommunications, Beijing 100876, China
fangbin1120@bupt.edu.cn
[3] State Key Laboratory of Intelligent Technology and Systems, Beijing National Research Center for Information Science and Technology, Department of Computer Science and Technology, Institute for Artificial Intelligence, Tsinghua University, Beijing 100084, China
{fcsun,hpliu}@tsinghua.edu.cn

Abstract. TIRgel sensor has pioneered a new visuo-tactile sensing mechanism that integrates visual and tactile modalities through the remote/near vision conversion of the focus-adjustable camera. To further expand its tactile function, this paper proposes a 3D reconstruction method, MLP-Depth, based on the photometric stereo. First, we press the sensor with a calibration ball with a known size. Then, the corresponding depth value of each pixel is obtained by calibrating the contact area and resolving the sphere geometry. Finally, a direct mapping between RGB and depth is constructed based on MLP. Experiments show that the MLP-Depth has high reconstruction precision, especially for unknown objects, with high reconstruction robustness.

Keywords: TIRgel · Visuo-tactile sensing · 3D reconstruction

1 Introduction

Since Gelsight and Tactip, vision-based tactile sensors (VTS) have gradually developed in the field of robotic sensing [1]. Compared with electronic tactile sensors, the VTSs have the advantages of high-density tactile information and homogeneity of tactile data [2]. With the acceleration of the development process of visual-tactile fusion, the advantage of data isomorphism has been further highlighted [3]. In addition, the simple structure of the VTSs is favored by researchers. As an important structural part, the VTSs are integrated into the manipulator, robotic palm, and robotic arm [4,5].

The most conventional VTSs consist of coatings, elastomers, acrylics, LEDs, and cameras [6]. The coating is attached to the surface of the elastomer to block the external ambient light and enhance the intensity of the internal light signal. When an object is in contact with an elastomer, its surface geometry leads to irregular deformation of the elastomer, and light is scattered through the coating into the camera lens, reflecting the edge features of the contact area in the image due to the intensity difference. The researchers also attach a marker layer under the coating for the quantitative characterization of contact deformation [7]. The deformation state is derived by tracing the displacement of the markers. The coating and marker layer serve as the core functional layer of the VTSs, and together with the elastomer they are regarded as the contact module [8]. They are the transfer medium of tactile features to provide tactile information with different properties.

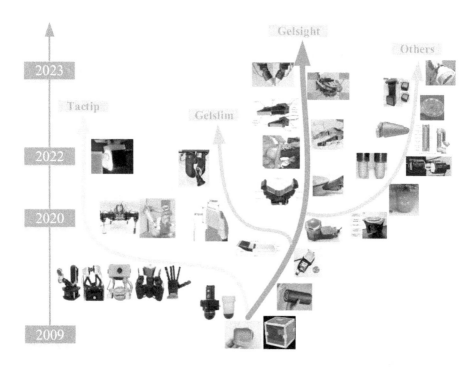

Fig. 1. Development process of the VTSs over the past 15 years.

Photometric stereo is the basis of 3D reconstruction based on visuo-tactile sensing [9]. Irradiating the elastic inner surface from multiple directions, the irregular scattering of light by the coating creates a hierarchical gradient distribution for the contact area. The light in each direction can provide a gradient measurement. To simplify the illumination system, the Gelsight uses multi-directional lighting with different light colors (red, green, and blue lights) [10].

Each illumination represents a gradient measurement on the image channel (RGB). The mapping between RGB values and deformation gradients G_x and G_y is solved, and then the deformation depth is calculated with the Fast Poisson solver [11]. To solve the problem of Gelsight's multi-light and color integration, Lin et al. [12] proposed a novel visuo-tactile sensing mechanism (Dtact), which utilized the light absorption characteristics of black silicone to realize the tactile presentation contrary to the Gelsight. Under a black background, the Dtact reduces background noise and indirectly creates a near-linear RGB-gradient mapping. In the previous work, we proposed the TIRgel sensor [13], a VTS that integrated internal and external vision. Under tactile mode, the TIRgel reduced light contrast and created a dark image background. The luminosity information in the contact region had a significant gradient change, which provided a possibility for 3D reconstruction.

This paper proposes a 3D reconstruction method applied to the TIRgel sensor. Due to a stable tactile imaging environment, we directly construct the mapping between RGB and deformation depth. First, we press the elastomer with a calibration ball with a known size. The contact area is obtained by Hough circle transformation and manual adjustment. Then, the deformation depth is calculated based on the sphere geometry. Finally, the MLP model is trained with pixel coordinates and RGB as input and depth value as output. The experimental results show that the 3D reconstruction precision of MLP-Depth is higher than MLP-Gradient's. The main contribution of this work is to expand 3D reconstruction for the TIRgel sensor, further applying it to robot operation.

2 Related Work

2.1 VTS Development

The research of visuo-tactile sensing originated in the 1960s [14]. Limited to the immaturity of imaging and image recognition technology, the VTSs have not aroused widespread interest. Since the 21st century, visuo-tactile sensing has developed rapidly. This section divides the development process into three stages (in Fig. 1):

1) Before 2010; In 2009, MIT researchers proposed the modern visuo-tactile sensing system, namely Gelsight [6]. Later, a marker layer was introduced to complement the force measurement function of the Gelsight. This configuration was widely recognized. Another sensing mechanism, Tactip [15,16], developed by the University of Bristol, used embedded bionic pins to simulate human receptors to obtain contact information.

2) 2010-2020; This decade has been an important development period for the VTSs. Researchers have promoted the iteration and development of the VTSs in terms of sensor structure, sensing function, and robot application expansion, such as TH-Tactile [17] and Gelslim [18].

3) 2020 to present; With the increasing demand for robot-embodied intelligence, higher requirements are put forward for the VTS integration. In recent years, micro VTSs have gradually replaced the original sensing components of

robots, providing robots with local to global tactile perception, such as fingertip [19], finger [20], and palm [5].

Considering the convenience of visual-tactile fusion and information alignment, researchers have gradually explored the integration scheme of internal and external vision, such as STS [21] and SpecTac [22]. The TIRgel sensor is our first attempt in this field [13], and its visual/tactile expression has high versatility. This paper aims to expand its tactile sensing.

2.2 3D Reconstruction Based on Visuo-Tactile Sensing

According to the technical approach, 3D reconstruction based on visuo-tactile sensing can be divided into five categories: 1) photoscopic stereo, 2) binocular depth calibration, 3) optical flow, 4) deep learning, and 5) depth camera. Method 1 is suitable for coated-type VTSs [23]. On the premise of multi-color light/multi-directional illumination, the contact depth is solved by constructing the association between RGB and gradient. Method 2 is suitable for marker-type VTSs [24]. The binocular camera tracks the same marker and obtains local depth information according to parallax. In theory, the smaller (denser) the markers, the better the continuity of the depth distribution. Method 3 is also suitable for marker-type VTSs, but only for dense randomly marker layers and monocular cameras [25]. The deformation depth is derived from Gaussian density distribution. Method 4 is suitable for any VTS [26], and the output contains parameters related to depth information, such as gradient angle and disparity. The difficulty of this method lies in large-scale data sets, which restricts its wide application. Method 5 applies only to VTSs using depth cameras [27]. Limited by sensor size, the popularity of this method is low. The TIRgel sensor gives up the coating, but the sensing mechanism is similar to that of the Gelsight sensor. Therefore, the 3D reconstruction approach is more inclined to photometric stereo.

3 Sensor Design and 3D Reconstruction Method

3.1 Sensor Design and Principle

The TIRgel sensor consists of a lenticular elastomer, an LED, an acrylic lens, and an adjustable focus camera (in Fig. 2(a)). We perform total internal reflection inside the elastomer, leveraging the luminosity information to represent the tactile features. When contact causes deformation, the law of light propagation inside the elastomer is broken, and part of the light refracts through the elastomer surface to the object. The geometry of the object's surface causes this light to scatter irregularly, which is received by the camera. These luminosity differences present multiple layers of depth features in the image, representing geometric features of the contact area. Visual and tactile modality conversion is controlled by the camera's remote/near imaging adjustment. In remote imaging, the camera can observe the external environment; In near imaging, the camera can capture the contact details of the elastic surface. When imaging contrast is reduced, the hierarchy of tactile imaging is further amplified, which is more conducive to tactile representation.

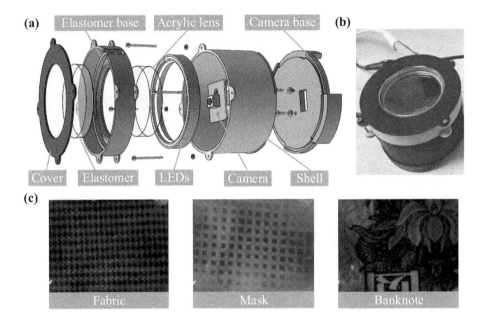

Fig. 2. (a) Structure of the TIRgel sensor. (b) TIRgel sensor prototype. (c) Tactile imaging of the TIRgel sensor.

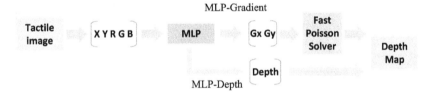

Fig. 3. 3D reconstruction flow of MLP-Gradient and MLP-Depth.

3.2 3D Reconstruction Method

As shown in Fig. 3, the 3D reconstruction process based on the photometric stereo contains: 1) the gradients G_x and G_y of the contact region are obtained; 2) the depth is calculated via the Fast Poisson solver. If the first step obtains the depth value directly, we can skip the second step. Among them, the gradient/depth is obtained by analyzing the sphere geometry. First, we press the elastomer with a vernier card and label the pixel length of the contact area in the tactile image. The pixel-millimeter conversion ratio is calculated based on the actual length provided by the vernier caliper and pixel length. The elastomer is then pressed with a pre-printed calibration ball (hemisphere) with a known size (in Fig. 4(a)), and the contact area boundary is calibrated by Hough circle transformation (in Fig. 4(b)). We also develop an assistance calibration system to improve the calibration precision. Based on Hough circle detection, the center of

Fig. 4. Tactile image calibration. (a) Original tactile image. (b) Hough circle transformation. (c) Manual adjustment.

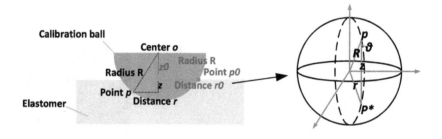

Fig. 5. Geometric analysis of sphere to obtain gradient G_x and G_y and depth values.

the contact region, the pixel values, and their image coordinates are determined by manual fine-tuning (in Fig. 4(c)).

The radius R of the sphere is known. The distance r between pixels and the region center is converted to actual length by the pixel-millimeter conversion ratio. From the geometric relationship, gradients $G_x = \frac{\partial z}{\partial x}$ and $G_y = \frac{\partial z}{\partial y}$ are obtained as follows:

$$x^2 + y^2 + z^2 = R^2 \tag{1}$$

$$\begin{cases} \frac{\partial z}{\partial x} = -\frac{x}{r} * \frac{r}{z} \\ \frac{\partial z}{\partial y} = -\frac{y}{r} * \frac{r}{z} \end{cases} \tag{2}$$

$$\frac{r}{z} = \tan(\arcsin(\frac{r}{R})) \tag{3}$$

$$\begin{cases} \frac{\partial z}{\partial x} = -\frac{x}{r} * \tan(\arcsin(\frac{r}{R})) \\ \frac{\partial z}{\partial y} = -\frac{y}{r} * \tan(\arcsin(\frac{r}{R})) \end{cases} \tag{4}$$

The circular outline in the tactile image represents the outermost area where the sphere comes into contact with the elastomer (in Fig. 5). Point p_0 is one of the points on the outline, as shown in Fig. 4(b). The distance z_0 from the sphere center is calculated by the equation (5).

$$z_0 = \sqrt{R^2 - r_0^2} \tag{5}$$

$$\Delta z = z - z_0 \tag{6}$$

where the vertical distance between p and p_0 is the press depth Δz.

In calibration, we collect 100 tactile images and record the coordinates, RGB, gradient values, and corresponding depth values of each pixel. Among them, pixel coordinates and RGB are the inputs, and gradient/depth are the labels. We then use the above data set to train an MLP. Referring to the literature [28], we construct an MLP consisting of 3 hidden layers (5-32-32-2/1). Although it is a small neural network, it produces continuous results involving the RGB changes across the image. The purpose of introducing pixel coordinates in the input is to take into account the nonlinear relationship of gradients in different contact regions. This is because the light intensity decreases with distance. The illumination system of the TIRgel sensor cannot guarantee uniform illumination over the whole area. The output type depends on the output forms. '2' represents the output gradient G_x and G_y, and '1' represents the output depth value. We name the two methods as MLP-Gradient and MLP-Depth. The significant difference between them is that the gradient requires the depth to be solved using a discrete sine transform (Poisson solver).

When calibrating the contour of the contact region, we find that the calibration precision of p_0 will affect the accuracy of the depth label. Both Hough circle transformation and manual adjustment make it difficult to achieve precision positioning. Hence, we require evaluating label precision. On the one hand, the gradient value obtained by point p calibration is used to calculate depth D. On the other hand, the depth D_1 is calculated according to the point p_0 geometry relationship. The results show that their difference is less than 5 parts per thousand. Consequently, the calibration precision of p_0 is within the error range.

4 Experiment

This section performs three experiments. Firstly, the tactile visualization of the TIRgel sensor is verified. Secondly, the 3D reconstruction precision of MLP-Gradient and MLP-Depth is tested. Finally, the reconstruction robustness of MLP-Depth on other contact objects is tested.

In tactile modality, we use OpenCV to obtain internal camera parameters to adjust the image contrast. Then, we press the elastomer with the fabric, mask, and banknotes. Tactile imaging is shown in Fig. 2(c). The contact area is highly visible due to huge luminosity differences. The uncontacted area is dark, in sharp contrast to the contact areas. The experimental results show that the luminosity information effectively visualizes tactile features.

MLP-Gradient and MLP-Depth are implemented by PyTorch 1.8 and Python 3.9. The hardware includes an Intel Core i7-8750H processor, two 8 GB memory chips (DDR4), and a GPU (GeForce RTX 2060 6G). The data set is divided into training sets, verification sets, and test sets by 80%, 10%, and 10%. The depth map reconstructed by the two methods is shown in Fig. 6. The color of the depth map indicates the change trend. We find that the color intensity decreases from the center of the contact area in all directions. This situation is consistent with the depth changes of the sphere. In addition, the depth trend is symmetrical. We think it is related to the introduction of pixel coordinates. Coordinate

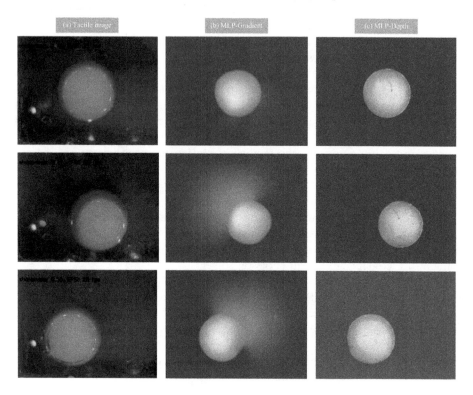

Fig. 6. (a) Tactile images. (b) Depth map predicted by the MLP-Gradient. (c) Depth map predicted by the MLP-Depth.

information allows the model to learn the dynamic fluctuations in light intensity caused by changes in location. It makes up the problem of gradient dispersion caused by uneven illumination in space. This section adopts MSE to evaluate the reconstruction precision of the two methods. We aim to quantitatively compare the applicability of the two methods to TIRgel sensors. Their errors are 0.0364 and 0.028.

To further evaluate the robustness of both methods, we use test objects that the model has not learned, not limited to spheres, such as a cylinder, a cube, an irregular body, and a tube (in Fig. 7). The results show that the MLP-Depth still has high applicability to new test objects. The depth boundary is sharp, and the plane tends to be flat. In contrast, the MLP-Gradient fails to predict a smooth depth trend. The depth of the region edge diverges seriously, and the depth of the plane region fluctuates greatly. In general, the MLP-Gradient produces smoother results during 3D reconstruction. However, this method is not necessarily suitable for the TIRgel sensors. This is because TIRgel's sensing mechanism reduces the effect of noise (stable dark background) and provides complete gradient data. In addition, directly constructing a mapping between RGB and depth weakens the nonlinear error of the gradient. In a word, it indi-

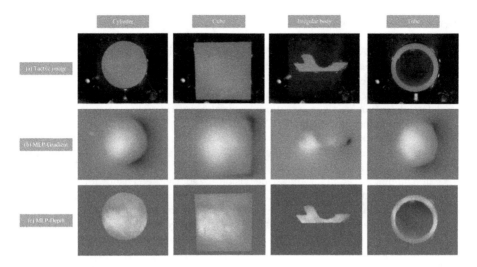

Fig. 7. 3D reconstruction of unknown objects. (**a**) Tactile images. (**b**) Depth map predicted by the MLP-Gradient. (**c**) Depth map predicted by the MLP-Depth.

rectly forms an implicit expression of them. The MLP-Depth skips the inverse solution of the gradient to depth. It can be regarded as an end-to-end reconstruction method, thus effectively simplifying the process of 3D reconstruction. In summary, the MLP-Depth is more suitable for the 3D reconstruction function development in the TIRgel sensor.

5 Conclusion

This paper proposes a 3D reconstruction method based on photometric stereo, MLP-Depth, which expands the 3D reconstruction function of the TIRgel sensor. Due to the high stability of tactile imaging, the TIRgel has advantages in reducing noise and retaining complete gradient information, which provides the basis for simplifying the 3D reconstruction process. To construct the mapping between RGB and depth, we use the hemispherical calibration ball to calibrate the pixel coordinates, RGB, and depth values, and achieve nonlinear expression through MLP. The experimental results verify that the MLP-Depth has higher reconstruction precision than the MLP-Gradient, especially for unknown objects. In future work, we will further optimize the sensing mechanism to adapt to the tactile imaging of complex objects. In addition, we need to consider the effect of object color on the robustness of 3D reconstruction.

Acknowledgments. This work was supported by the National Natural Science Foundation of China under Grant (62173197) and the National Natural Science Fund for Key International Collaboration (62120106005). The corresponding author was Bin Fang.

References

1. Tippur, M.H., Adelson, E.H.: GelSight360: an omnidirectional camera-based tactile sensor for dexterous robotic manipulation. In: 2023 IEEE International Conference on Soft Robotics (RoboSoft), pp. 1–8. IEEE (2023)
2. Fang, B., Long, X., Sun, F., Liu, H., Zhang, S., Fang, C.: Tactile-based fabric defect detection using convolutional neural network with attention mechanism. IEEE Trans. Instrum. Meas. **71**, 1–9 (2022)
3. Gao, Y., Matsuoka, S., Wan, W., Kiyokawa, T., Koyama, K., Harada, K.: In-hand pose estimation using hand-mounted RGB cameras and visuotactile sensors. IEEE Access **11**, 17218–17232 (2023)
4. Van Duong, L., et al.: Large-scale vision-based tactile sensing for robot links: design, modeling, and evaluation. IEEE Trans. Rob. **37**(2), 390–403 (2020)
5. Zhang, S., Yang, Y., Shan, J., Sun, F., Xue, H., Fang, B.: PaLmTac: a vision-based tactile sensor leveraging distributed-modality design and modal-matching recognition for soft hand perception. IEEE J. Sel. Top. Sign. Process. **18**(3) (2024)
6. Yuan, W., Dong, S., Adelson, E.H.: GelSight: high-resolution robot tactile sensors for estimating geometry and force. Sensors **17**(12), 2762 (2017)
7. Yuan, W., Li, R., Srinivasan, M.A., Adelson, E.H.: Measurement of shear and slip with a GelSight tactile sensor. In: 2015 IEEE International Conference on Robotics and Automation (ICRA), pp. 304–311. IEEE (2015)
8. Zhang, S., et al.: Hardware technology of vision-based tactile sensor: a review. IEEE Sens. J. **22**(22), 21410–21427 (2022)
9. Johnson, M.K., Adelson, E.H.: Retrographic sensing for the measurement of surface texture and shape. In: 2009 IEEE Conference on Computer Vision and Pattern Recognition, pp. 1070–1077. IEEE (2009)
10. Dong, S., Yuan, W., Adelson, E.H.: Improved GelSight tactile sensor for measuring geometry and slip. In: 2017 IEEE/RSJ International Conference on Intelligent Robots and Systems (IROS), pp. 137–144. IEEE (2017)
11. Athar, S., Patel, G., Xu, Z., Qiu, Q., She, Y.: VisTac towards a unified multi-modal sensing finger for robotic manipulation. IEEE Sen. J. **23**(20) (2023)
12. Lin, C., Lin, Z., Wang, S., Xu, H.: DTact: a vision-based tactile sensor that measures high-resolution 3D geometry directly from darkness. In: 2023 IEEE International Conference on Robotics and Automation (ICRA), pp. 10359–10366. IEEE (2023)
13. Zhang, S., .: TIRgel: a visuo-tactile sensor with total internal reflection mechanism for external observation and contact detection. IEEE Rob. Autom. Lett. **8**(10), 6307–6314 (2023)
14. Abad, A.C., Ranasinghe, A.: Visuotactile sensors with emphasis on GelSight sensor: a review. IEEE Sens. J. **20**(14), 7628–7638 (2020)
15. Ward-Cherrier, B., et al.: The TacTip family: soft optical tactile sensors with 3D-printed biomimetic morphologies. Soft Rob. **5**(2), 216–227 (2018)
16. Lepora, N.F.: Soft biomimetic optical tactile sensing with the tactip: a review. IEEE Sens. J. **21**(19), 21131–21143 (2021)
17. Fang, B., et al.: A dual-modal vision-based tactile sensor for robotic hand grasping. In: 2018 IEEE International Conference on Robotics and Automation (ICRA), pp. 4740–4745. IEEE (2018)
18. Donlon, E., Dong, S., Liu, M., Li, J., Adelson, E., Rodriguez, A.: GelSlim: a high-resolution, compact, robust, and calibrated tactile-sensing finger. In: 2018 IEEE/RSJ International Conference on Intelligent Robots and Systems (IROS), pp. 1927–1934. IEEE (2018)

19. Lambeta, M., et al.: Digit: a novel design for a low-cost compact high-resolution tactile sensor with application to in-hand manipulation. IEEE Rob. Autom. Lett. **5**(3), 3838–3845 (2020)
20. Gomes, D.F., Lin, Z., Luo, S.: GelTip: a finger-shaped optical tactile sensor for robotic manipulation. In: 2020 IEEE/RSJ International Conference on Intelligent Robots and Systems (IROS), pp. 9903–9909. IEEE (2020)
21. Hogan, F.R., Jenkin, M., Rezaei-Shoshtari, S., Girdhar, Y., Meger, D., Dudek, G.: Seeing through your skin: recognizing objects with a novel visuotactile sensor. In: Proceedings of the IEEE/CVF Winter Conference on Applications of Computer Vision, pp. 1218–1227 (2021)
22. Wang, Q., Du, Y., Wang, M.Y.: Spectac: a visual-tactile dual-modality sensor using UV illumination. In: 2022 International Conference on Robotics and Automation (ICRA), pp. 10844–10850. IEEE (2022)
23. Roberge, E., Fornes, G., Roberge, J.P.: StereoTac: a novel visuotactile sensor that combines tactile sensing with 3D vision. IEEE Robo. Autom. Lett. **8**(10), 6291–6298 (2023)
24. Zhang, C., et al.: GelStereo 2.0: an improved GelStereo sensor with multimedium refractive stereo calibration. IEEE Trans. Industr. Electron. **71**(7), 7452–7462 (2023)
25. Du, Y., Zhang, G., Wang, M.Y.: 3D contact point cloud reconstruction from vision-based tactile flow. IEEE Rob. Autom. Lett. **7**(4), 12177–12184 (2022)
26. Do, W.K., Jurewicz, B., Kennedy, M.: DenSetact 2.0: optical tactile sensor for shape and force reconstruction. In: 2023 IEEE International Conference on Robotics and Automation (ICRA), pp. 12549–12555. IEEE (2023)
27. Huang, I., Liu, J., Bajcsy, R.: A depth camera-based soft fingertip device for contact region estimation and perception-action coupling. In: 2019 International Conference on Robotics and Automation (ICRA), pp. 8443–8449. IEEE (2019)
28. Wang, S., She, Y., Romero, B., Adelson, E.: GelSight wedge: measuring high-resolution 3D contact geometry with a compact robot finger. In: 2021 IEEE International Conference on Robotics and Automation (ICRA), pp. 6468–6475. IEEE (2021)

Design and Performance Testing of Electro-fluidic Soft Actuator

Yuze Ye[1], Qingsong He[1,2(✉)], Lin Xie[1], Changli Yang[1], and Shouyi Ni[1]

[1] Jiangsu Provincial Key Laboratory of Bionic Functional Materials, College of Mechanical and Electrical Engineering, Nanjing University of Aeronautics and Astronautics, Nanjing 210016, China
heqingsong@nuaa.edu.cn

[2] State Key Laboratory of Mechanics and Control of Aerospace Structures, Nanjing University of Aeronautics and Astronautics, Nanjing 210016, China

Abstract. Electro-fluidic actuators have become an investigated hotspot for their inherent adaptability and security of human-machine interaction. This paper points to combining the characteristics of dielectric elastomers and fluid actuators and developing electro-fluidic soft actuators by modifying Al_2O_3 on the surface of nano $BaTiO_3$ to move forward the dielectric constant and breakdown field strength and by utilizing the silicone rubber material as a substrate. Tests on the actuation strain and current performance of the electro-fluidic soft actuator under diverse loads were carried out, which appeared that the maximum actuation strain of the electro-fluidic soft actuator was 17.20% under 100 g load, the critical breakdown current of the actuator was 115 μA~130 μA, and the maximum electro-mechanical conversion efficiency of the actuator was 67.93% under different loads. Experimental results show that an appropriate load is beneficial to improving the energy utilization of the actuator. Finally, the development of electro-fluidic soft actuators has opened new avenues for materials development and application, contributing to the development of soft robots.

Keywords: Electro-fluidic Soft Actuator · Actuation Strain · Breakdown Current · Articulated Actuate Mechanism

1 Introduction

For a long time, robots have been progressively undertaking different errands in mechanical generation and everyday life. Conventional rigid robots are composed of parts and structures with certain hardness and firmness [1]. In spite of the fact that they have an expansive load-bearing capacity and exact movement capabilities, their tall, unbending nature makes it troublesome for them to perform assignments in unstructured situations [2]. Soft robots, characterized by their adaptable materials and structures, have noteworthy focal points in adaptability, compliance, and versatility [3]. They are broadly utilized in areas such as getting a handle on unpredictable objects [4], therapeutic surgeries [5], mechanical generation [6], and agrarian gathering [7].

Soft actuators made of flexible substances are fundamental elements of soft robots, such as dielectric elastomer actuators [8] (DEAs), fluid actuators [9], shape memory alloys [10]/polymers [11] (SMAs/SMPs), ion polymer-metal composites [12], liquid crystal elastomers [13], and hydrogels [14]. These soft actuators can attain bending [15], elongation/contraction [16], torsion [17], and spiraling [18] movement via several stimuli consisting of fluids [19], heat [20], electricity [21], magnetism [22], light [23], humidity [24], and chemical substances [25]. Compared to different actuators, gadgets made of DEAs are preferred by researchers for their fast response, excessive flexibility, lightweight, low cost, and excessive output energy [26–28].

DEAs consist of an elastic membrane sandwiched between two flexible electrodes. When voltage is applied, electrostatic stress compresses the membrane, and due to the fact that the quantity of the elastomer stays regular throughout deformation, the membrane elongates perpendicular to the utilized electric-powered field. Upon elimination of the electric field, the membrane relaxes and returns to its initial state [29–31]. Silicone rubber [32], polyurethane [33, 34], and acrylic resin [35] are the three most broadly used dielectric elastomer materials. However, due to the low dielectric consistency of these materials, excessive actuating voltages are required to result in mechanical work, hindering similar functions of DEAs [36].

Currently, there are two important strategies to decorate the performance of DEAs. The first entails enhancing the polymer chains inside the polymer [37], including excessive dielectric constant fillers [38] or conductive fillers [39] to expand their dielectric constant. The second approach is to enhance the actuating performance of the actuator by means of the use of the fluidity and anti-breakdown ability of dielectric fluids [40–42]. In the first method, Racles *et al.* [43] used vinyl cyanide to hydrosilylation poly(dimethyl-co-methyl hydrogen siloxane), synthesizing an elastomer with hydrogen propyl facet groups dispensed on the PDMS main chain, increasing the dielectric constant from 2.4 to 6.5, reaching 10% strain under an actuating electric field of 40 V/μm. Galantini *et al.* [44] functionalized the surface of MWCNTs by grafting acrylonitrile or amino acid monomer onto them, then dispersed them into a polyurethane matrix. The effects confirmed that the addition of 0.5 wt % MWCNTs to the PU matrix doubled the strain under the same electric field (5.5 V/μm) compared to pure PU. Huang *et al.* [45] prepared ethylene-vinyl acetate (EVM) composite materials with BaTiO$_3$ fillers with the use of a melt mixing method. The results confirmed that the introduction of nano-BaTiO$_3$ particles into the nano-BaTiO$_3$/EVM composite fabric expanded its dielectric constant, thermal conductivity, and mechanical strength. However, the addition of excessive dielectric constant fillers or conductive fillers to polymers commonly increases their dielectric constant; however, it normally leads to an extensive reduction in breakdown field strength, thereby limiting the actuating voltage of polymer materials. Therefore, Huang *et al.* [46] employed a surface modification method by coating nanostructured BaTiO$_3$ with Al$_2$O$_3$. This method decreased electric field distortion at the interface between high-dielectric-constant ceramics and low-dielectric-constant polymers, minimized viable contact and structural defects between adjacent nanoparticles, and improved the breakdown strength of the polymer materials. The second method for developing an electro-fluidic soft actuator includes a polymer film with chambers filled with dielectric fluid. When voltage is applied, the film compresses, inflicting the fluid within its chambers to flow under pressure, further compressing the film, thus improving the actuating performance and operational effectivity of DEAs. Acome [41] *et al.* first proposed combining the multifunctionality of fluid-driven actuators with the muscle-like performance of DE actuators to boost a hydraulically amplified self-healing electrostatic (HASEL) actuator composed of silicone rubber, successful in self-repairing after dielectric breakdown for over 50 cycles. Wang [47] *et al.* investigated the linear contraction performance of the high-strain hydraulically amplified self-healing electrostatic (HS-Peano-HASEL) actuator and designed a tubular pump based totally on the artificial circular muscle (ACM) of HS-Peano-HASEL. Tang [48] *et al.* developed a self-sustaining soft electric fluid actuator (SEFA) and utilized it to create an underwater robotic accomplishing a swimming speed of ~0.13 body lengths per second.

This study combines the method of increasing the dielectric constant of materials with the structural advantages of electro-fluidic soft actuators. It uses nanostructured $BaTiO_3$ as a high dielectric constant filler, conducts interface modification experiments by surface modification of Al_2O_3 through nanostructured $BaTiO_3$ [46, 49], and develops an electro-fluidic soft actuator based on silicone rubber. The performance of the electro-fluidic soft actuator was tested, and the actuator was used to construct a joint drive device, verifying the feasibility of its application.

2 Structural Design and Preparation Method

2.1 Design and Principle of Electro-fluidic Soft Actuator

Based on the principle of electrostatic adsorption, this study designed an electro-fluidic soft actuator, as shown in Fig. 1a. The actuator consists of a silicone rubber membrane, dielectric fluid, conductive carbon paste, bracket, and wires. The silicone rubber membrane is composed of silicone rubber material and nanoparticle materials resistant to breakdown, with a length of 90 mm, a height of 75 mm, and a thickness of 0.6 mm. The dielectric fluid, resistant to breakdown, fills the inside cavity of the silicone rubber membrane, with dimensions of 70 mm 35 mm, as shown in Fig. 1b. As the conductive carbon paste is excessive flexibility and adhesion, it is utilized to both sides of the electro-fluidic soft actuator membrane the usage of a mold as actuating electrodes. The dimensions of the conductive carbon paste are smaller than the inner cavity of the silicone rubber membrane to decorate the breakdown resistance of the actuator, measuring 60 mm 30 mm. The bracket is used to pre-stretch the silicone rubber membrane to prevent instability breakdown under high voltage. With a pre-stretching ratio coefficient of 2.5, the size after pre-stretching is 17.5 mm. Additionally, the wires are fixed on the bracket and linked to the conductive carbon paste to provide energy to the actuator. When a high voltage is utilized by means of the wires to the carbon paste on both sides of the actuator, a high-voltage electric field exists between the carbon pastes, producing Maxwell stress, which compresses the silicone rubber membrane in the thickness direction. Since silicone rubber is incompressible, the silicone rubber elastomer generates actuating displacement in the vertical direction. Furthermore, when the silicone rubber membrane is compressed in the thickness direction, the liquid inner the silicone rubber membrane is additionally compressed. Due to the incompressibility and proper flowability of the liquid, it expands in the plane perpendicular to the thickness direction of the silicone rubber membrane, in addition to advertising the growing actuation displacement of the actuator [41], as shown in Fig. 1a.

In order to discover the effect of several influencing factors on the deformation of electro-fluidic soft actuators, an experimental platform proven in Fig. 1c was set up. The actuator used to be suspended without load, and a laser displacement sensor was once used to measure the deformation displacement of the actuator's backside earlier than and after deformation, from which the most driving strain of the actuator underneath no load was calculated.

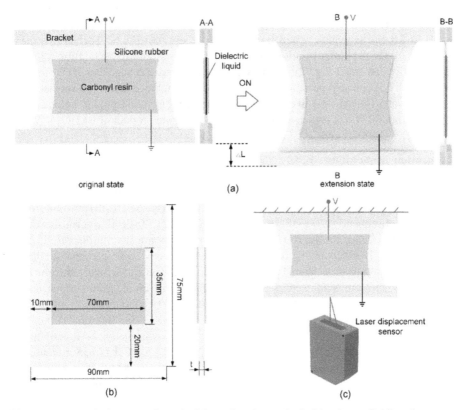

Fig. 1. Structure design, actuating principle, and testing method of the electro-fluidic soft actuator. a) Structure composition and actuating principle of the electro-fluidic soft actuator; b) Dimension of the electro-fluidic soft actuator; c) Testing method for the actuation strain of the electro-fluidic soft actuator.

2.2 Preparation of Electro-fluidic Soft Actuator

Materials. Ammonium formate, formic acid, nano barium titanate powder ($BaTiO_3$) with an average diameter of 100 nm bought from McKlin Company, aluminum sulfate octa decahydrate ($Al_2(SO_4)_3 \cdot 18H_2O$) bought from China National Pharmaceutical

Group Corporation, Ecoflex 00–30 supplied by means of Smooth-On Company, tetrahydrofuran (chromatographic grade, ≥99.9%, barring stabilizer) bought from Sigma Company. High-pressure insulating oil was purchased from Aukelei Lubricant Company, conductive lubricating grease was bought from SZ Junyi Lubrication Technology Company, and BOOP film was bought from Yilihua Film Packaging Materials Company. All chemicals were used as acquired except in addition purification. All experimental water used to be deionized water.

Preparation of $BaTiO_3$-modified Materials. According to reference [49], initially, 12.612 g of ammonium formate was dissolved in 1000 mL of deionized water and vigorously stirred for 5 min, observed by using the addition of formic acid to modify the pH to 4.6. Subsequently, 2 g of $BaTiO_3$ powder and $Al_2(SO_4)_3 \cdot 18H_2O$ (6.4 mM) were delivered to the buffer solution and vigorously stirred. The above mixture was then ultrasonically dispersed for 10 min and vigorously stirred and heated at 70 °C for two hours. Finally, suspended particles were filtered out from the solution and washed with deionized water (DI) at least five times. After the reaction, solid samples were accrued and heated at 300 °C for two hours to achieve the ultimate product of $BaTiO_3$@Al_2O_3 nanoparticles ($BaTiO_3$ core, Al_2O_3 shell).

Preparation of Actuator. Firstly, the 1.028 g (2.57% silicone rubber mass) of the synthesized $BaTiO_3$@Al_2O_3 nanoparticles is weighed and positioned into a beaker. Then, 6 g of tetrahydrofuran (THF) is added, and the beaker is sealed with plastic wrap to avoid THF evaporation. The mixture is ultrasonically dispersed for 10 min and stirred uniformly. Subsequently, 20 g of component A of Ecoflex 00–30 is vigorously stirred into the beaker. After the $BaTiO_3$@Al_2O_3 nanoparticles are wholly dispersed, 20 g of component B is added and vigorously mixed. Once utterly combined, the mixture is poured onto a glass surface cleaned with alcohol and placed on a horizontal platform. Due to gravity, the mixture is allowed to flow and spread evenly on the glass surface earlier than being placed in a vacuum drying oven at 70 °C for 30 min to treatment into a film, referred to as $BaTiO_3$@Al_2O_3/Ecoflex. The $BaTiO_3$@Al_2O_3/Ecoflex film is then cut into two rectangles as per the pre-designed dimensions. Additionally, the BOOP film is cut into a barely smaller rectangle than the $BaTiO_3$@Al_2O_3/Ecoflex film. Subsequently, the $BaTiO_3$@Al_2O_3/Ecoflex and BOOP films are alternately layered to form a sandwich structure. Next, components A and B of Ecoflex 00–30 are uniformly mixed and applied to three sides of the sandwich structure, which is then placed in a vacuum drying oven for 30 min to cure, making sure the edges of the $BaTiO_3$@Al_2O_3/Ecoflex rectangular film are bonded on three sides. The BOOP film in the middle of the sandwich structure is removed, and a small amount of stress insulation oil is injected with the use of a syringe. Component A and B of Ecoflex 00–30 are again mixed and applied to the fourth side of the sandwich structure for sealing, which is then placed in a vacuum-drying oven for 30 min to cure. Finally, carbon grease is utilized, wires are linked on each side of the actuator, and the actuator film is pre-stretched with the use of a 3D-printed frame, as depicted in Fig. 2.

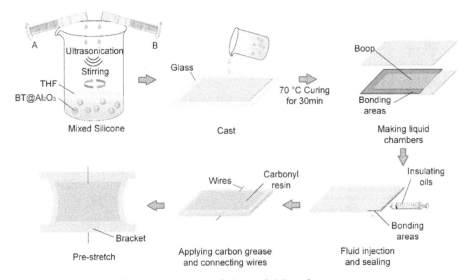

Fig. 2. Preparation of electro-fluidic soft actuator

3 Characteristics of the Actuator

3.1 Design of Test Circuit

In arrange to test the actuating performance and electromechanical efficiency of the optimized actuator, it is essential to control high-voltage and low-voltage transfers in entirely different arrangements, conduct performance tests of the actuator, and design the estimation framework principle as appeared in Fig. 3(a). The actuator is associated with high-voltage relay 1 (CRSTHV 24 V, Ningbo Yinzhou Group Ji Electronic Co., Ltd.) and resistor R (10 kΩ) through wires, in arrangement with the high-voltage control supply (RK2674A, Shenzhen Merik Electronic Innovation Co., Ltd.). The PC controls the opening and closing of low-voltage relay 1 to control the on-off state of high-voltage relay 1, subsequently actuating the actuator through a data acquisition card (Model USB-6001, DAQ). Resistor R realizes real-time monitoring and collection of the actuator's supply current. Due to the high-capacitance impact of the actuator, when the driving voltage is detached, the actuator gradually contracts and returns to its original length as the charge dissipates. In order to quicken this process, this paper simultaneously interfaces the anode and cathode of the actuator to the ground through high-voltage relay 2 to quickly eliminate the stored charge inside the actuator. The PC controls the on-off state of high-voltage relay 2 through a data acquisition card by controlling the opening and closing of low-voltage relay 2.

The measurement system control flow chart appears in Fig. 3b. When the test starts, firstly, the number of test cycles for the actuator is to begin with set on the PC side; furthermore, the laser displacement sensor is enacted to get real-time displacement information through the data acquisition card.; at that point, the PC sends commands through the data acquisition card to control the closure of low-voltage relay 1 to cause the closure of high-voltage relay 1, realizing the actuator's high-voltage drive. Hence, after the actuator works steadily for a period, the PC sends instructions through the data acquisition card once more to open low-voltage relay 1, causing high-voltage relay 1 to open, provoking the actuator to return to its original state. The actuator's capacitance under high voltage shows a capacitive energy storage impact. At that point, the PC sends instructions through the data acquisition card to shut down low-voltage relay 2, causing high-voltage relay 2 to shut, holding up for 0.1s to discharge the charge from the actuator to the ground totally. At last, it is decided whether the number of test cycles for the actuator surpasses the set value. In case it does, the test ends; otherwise, low-voltage relay 1 is revived, and the process rehashes until completion.

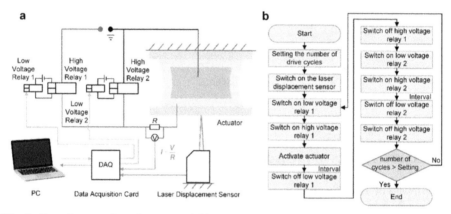

Fig. 3. Test of actuator's performance. a) Measurement system schematic diagram; b) Measurement system control flow chart.

3.2 Results and Analysis of the Test

Calculate the actuation strain according to Eq. (2) (i.e., the strain generated by applying high voltage rather than external load), where is the original length of the actuator under load, is the deformation length of the driver after applying voltage U under load, and is the original length of the actuator.

$$\varepsilon(U, Load) = \frac{L(U, Load) - L(0, Load)}{L(0, 0)} \times 100\% \tag{1}$$

The actuation strain increments and, after that, diminishes with the increment of connected voltage, as appeared in Fig. 4a. The maximum actuation strain comes to within the load range of 100 g–150 g, where an actuation strain of ~ 17.20% can be accomplished at 16 kV. When the load is less than 100 g–150 g, the increment can continuously eliminate the unsteady wrinkles caused by the pre-stretching of the actuator's film so that the displacement created by the actuator contributes altogether within the vertical direction. So, the actuator's actuation strain increments with the increment of the applied voltage. When the load exceeds 100 g–150 g, with the increment of the load, the stress-strain curve of the film of the actuator shifts towards the origin [50], coming about in a sharp increment in modulus of the film of the actuator under slight strain, hence lessening the actuation strain of the actuator. From Fig. 4b, it can be observed that with the increment of actuation voltage and load, the actuation current too increments. At the same time, when the current surpasses 115 µA–130 µA, the actuator, by and large, encounters breakdown phenomena. Hence, the actuation current can be utilized as one of the critical criteria for judging the occurrence of breakdown damage within the actuator, giving a security limit for subsequent tests.

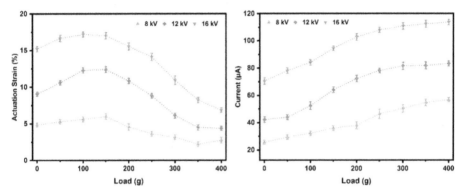

Fig. 4. Actuation strain and actuation current. a) The effect of different test voltages and actuation loads on the actuation strain; b) The effects of different test voltages and actuation loads on the actuation current.

The electromechanical efficiency of a drive is calculated based on the mechanical (output) energy and electrical (input) energy expended throughout the drive cycle. To decide the electromechanical effectiveness of the drive, we performed the cycle that appeared in Fig. 5a. Sometime after the cycle is executed, we will hang 50 g, 100 g, 150 g, 200 g, 250 g, 300 g, 350 g, 400 g weights to test the actuating performance of the actuator. The test voltage is set to 12 kV to diminish the actuator's risk of breaking down during the actuating process. The test voltage and load change curve with time under 100 g load appear in Fig. 5a and b. At that point, the current and displacement curves were obtained through the test individually. The test current and displacement curves under 100 g load appear in Fig. 5c and d. When voltage is given to the actuator at the 5th second, the voltage and current of the actuator will surge due to the inertia of the actuator and after that stabilize after a wavering of approximately 1 s. After stabilization, the actuator undergoes creep deformation under Maxwell stress, so the displacement increments gradually. When the control is turned off at 15 s, the actuator displacement quickly weakens by 90% within 3 s, and the final 10% of the displacement takes 6–7 s to eliminate due to the viscoelasticity of the material gradually. In addition, this paper employs the numerical integration method to get the electrical and mechanical energy, respectively, according to Eqs. (3) and (4).

$$W_{el} = \int UI dt \qquad (2)$$

$$W_{mech} = FS \qquad (3)$$

$$\eta = \frac{W_{mech}}{W_{el}} \tag{4}$$

where W_{el} is the input electric energy, W_{mech} is the work done by the driver, U, I, t are the input voltage, current and power-on time respectively, and are the load force and actuation displacement, and are the electromechanical conversion efficiency.

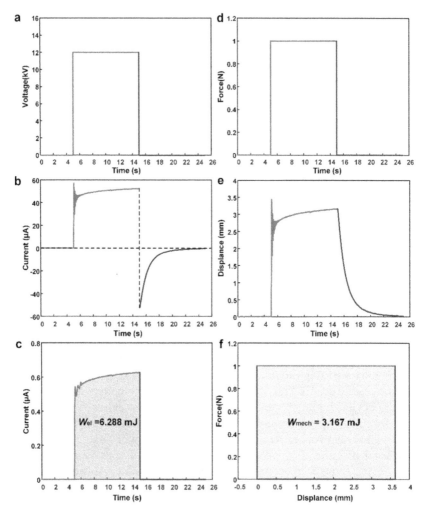

Fig. 5. Test and analysis of electromechanical efficiency. a–b) Test voltage and load change curve with time under 100g load; c–d) Test current curve and displacement curve under 100 g load; e–f) Electrical energy and mechanical energy under 100 g load.

Hence, the electrical and mechanical energy at a 100 g load appears in Fig. 5e and f, with electromechanical conversion effectiveness calculated to be 50.89%. So also, the efficiencies for loads of 50 g, 150 g, 200 g, 250 g, 300 g, 350 g, and 400 g were calculated as 24.82%, 65.09%, 67.93%, 64.44%, 52.32%, 44.87%, and 48.60%, individually. As the actuating load increments, the electromechanical conversion efficiency begins with increments. Then, it diminishes, showing that suitable loads are advantageous to progressing the energy utilization of the actuator.

4 Conclusion and Future Work

In this paper, by modifying Al_2O_3 on the surface of nano-$BaTiO_3$ to progress the dielectric constant and breakdown field strength, a kind of electro-fluidic soft actuator with dielectric elastomer and fluidic actuator drive characteristics is designed based on silicone rubber material. The electro-fluidic soft actuator's structure, actuating principle, and arrangement handle are described, and execution tests and preparatory application experiments of the electro-fluidic soft actuator are carried out. The results appear that the electro-fluidic soft actuator can achieve a driving strain of ~17.20% at a load range of 100 g-150 g and a voltage of 16 kV. The maximum electro-mechanical conversion efficiency of the actuator is 67.93% under 100 g load and different driving voltages, and the critical breakdown current is 115 μA~130 μA. Compared with traditional DEAs, the work in this paper has higher actuation strain, provides a new path for the development of DEAs, and can provide a useful reference for researchers studying dielectric elastomers and soft fluid actuators. At last, the design of electro-fluidic soft actuators progresses the state of the craftsmanship of soft actuators, thus providing new solutions in regions such as agribusiness, manufacturing, and disaster response opening new avenues for material development and robotic system design investigation.

In the future, we will conduct simulations based on FEA to analyze the deformation mechanism of the electro-fluidic soft actuator. In addition, we plan to develop an expression robot with facial muscle movement using the electro-fluidic soft actuator. Finally, we also hope to study new dielectric materials to reduce the driving voltage of the electric soft actuator and design soft robots in combination with bistable structures to expand the application environment of the electro-fluidic soft actuator.

Acknowledgements. The authors are deeply grateful for financial support from the National Natural Science Foundation of China (No. 52375293), the Open Fund of Laboratory of Aerospace Servo Actuation and Transmission (No. LASAT-2021-05), the Open Fund of Key Laboratory of Advanced Technology for Small and Medium-sized UAVs (No. XCA22054-06).

References

1. Shintake, J., Cacucciolo, V., Floreano, D., et al.: Soft robotic grippers. Adv. Mater. **30**(29), 1707035 (2018)
2. Goh, G.D., Goh, G.L., Lyu, Z., et al.: 3D printing of robotic soft grippers: toward smart actuation and sensing. Adv. Mater. Technol. **7**(11), 2101672 (2022)

3. Qu, J., Mao, B., Li, Z., et al.: Recent progress in advanced tactile sensing technologies for soft grippers. Adv. Func. Mater. **33**(41), 2306249 (2023)
4. Dou, W., Zhong, G., Cao, J., et al.: Soft robotic manipulators: designs, actuation, stiffness tuning, and sensing. Adv. Mater. Technol. **6**(9), 2100018 (2021)
5. Fang, G., Chow, M.C., Ho, J.D., et al.: Soft robotic manipulator for intraoperative MRI-guided transoral laser microsurgery. Sci. Robot. **6**(57), eabg5575 (2021)
6. Lee, J.-Y., Seo, Y.-S., Park, C., et al.: Shape-adaptive universal soft parallel gripper for delicate grasping using a stiffness-variable composite structure. IEEE Trans. Industr. Electron. **68**(12), 12441–12451 (2020)
7. Hong, Y., Zhao, Y., Berman, J., et al.: Angle-programmed tendril-like trajectories enable a multifunctional gripper with ultradelicacy, ultrastrength, and ultraprecision. Nat. Commun. **14**(1), 4625 (2023)
8. Banet, P., Zeggai, N., Chavanne, J., et al.: Evaluation of dielectric elastomers to develop materials suitable for actuation. Soft Matter **17**(48), 10786–10805 (2021)
9. Chen, F., Song, Z., Chen, S., et al.: Morphological design for pneumatic soft actuators and robots with desired deformation behavior. IEEE Trans. Robot. (2023)
10. Liang, X., Yuan, C., Wan, C., et al.: Soft self-healing robot driven by new micro two-way shape memory alloy spring. Adv. Sci., 2305163 (2023)
11. Li, Y., Zhang, F., Liu, Y., et al.: A tailorable series of elastomeric-to-rigid, selfhealable, shape memory bismaleimide. Small, 2307244 (2023)
12. He, Q., Yin, G., Vokoun, D., et al.: Review on improvement, modeling, and application of ionic polymer metal composite artificial muscle. J. Bionic Eng. **19**(2), 279–298 (2022)
13. Maurin V, Chang Y, Ze Q, et al. Liquid Crystal Elastomer–Liquid Metal Composite: Ultrafast, Untethered, and Programmable Actuation by Induction Heating. Advanced Materials, 2302765 (2023)
14. Jiao, D., Zhu, Q.L., Li, C.Y., et al.: Programmable morphing hydrogels for soft actuators and robots: from structure designs to active functions. Acc. Chem. Res. **55**(11), 1533–1545 (2022)
15. Liu, S., Wang, F., Liu, Z., et al.: A two-finger soft-robotic gripper with enveloping and pinching grasping modes. IEEE/ASME Trans. Mechatron. **26**(1), 146–155 (2020)
16. Wei, Y., Li, S., Zhang, X., et al.: Smart devices based on the soft actuator with nafion-polypropylene-PDMS/graphite multilayer structure. Appl. Sci. **10**(5), 1829 (2020)
17. Wang, Z., Wang, Y., Wang, Z., et al.: 3D printing of electrically responsive PVC gel actuators. ACS Appl. Mater. Interfaces **13**(20), 24164–24172 (2021)
18. Ze, Q., Wu, S., Nishikawa, J., et al.: Soft robotic origami crawler. Sci. Adv. **8**(13), eabm7834 (2022)
19. Wu, F., Lin, X., Xu, Y., et al.: Light-driven locomotive soft actuator and multi-functional sensors based on asymmetric PVA/carbon/PE bilayer film. Sci. China Mater., 1–12 (2023)
20. Li, J., Wang, M., Cui, Z., et al.: Dual-responsive jumping actuators by light and humidity. J. Mater. Chem. A **10**(47), 25337–25346 (2022)
21. Xu, H., Bai, S., Gu, G., et al.: Bioinspired self-resettable hydrogel actuators powered by a chemical fuel. ACS Appl. Mater. Interfaces **14**(38), 43825–43832 (2022)
22. Mosadegh, B., Polygerinos, P., Keplinger, C., et al.: Pneumatic networks for soft robotics that actuate rapidly. Adv. Func. Mater. **24**(15), 2163–2170 (2014)
23. Guan, Q., Sun, J., Liu, Y., et al.: Novel bending and helical extensile/contractile pneumatic artificial muscles inspired by elephant trunk. Soft Rob. **7**(5), 597–614 (2020)
24. Yan, J., Zhang, X., Xu, B., et al.: A new spiral-type inflatable pure torsional soft actuator. Soft Rob. **5**(5), 527–540 (2018)
25. Nie, S., Huo, L., Ji, H., et al.: Deformation characteristics of three-dimensional spiral soft actuator driven by water hydraulics for underwater manipulator. Soft Rob. (2023)
26. Gratz-Kelly, S., Rizzello, G., Fontana, M., et al.: A multi-mode, multi-frequency dielectric elastomer actuator. Adv. Func. Mater. **32**(34), 2201889 (2022)

27. Zhang, Y., Ellingford, C., Zhang, R., et al.: Electrical and mechanical self-healing in high-performance dielectric elastomer actuator materials. Adv. Func. Mater. **29**(15), 1808431 (2019)
28. Bernat, J., Kolota, J., Rosset, S.: Identification of a nonlinear dielectric elastomer actuator based on the harmonic balance method. IEEE/ASME Trans. Mechatron. **26**(5), 2664–2675 (2020)
29. Panahi-Sarmad, M., Zahiri, B., Noroozi, M.: Graphene-based composite for dielectric elastomer actuator: a comprehensive review. Sens. Actuators A Phys. **293** (2019)
30. Sholl, N., Moss, A., Kier, W.M., et al.: A soft end effector inspired by cephalopod suckers and augmented by a dielectric elastomer actuator. Soft Rob. **6**(3), 356–367 (2019)
31. Li, Z., Gao, C., Fan, S., et al.: Cell nanomechanics based on dielectric elastomer actuator device. Nano-Micro Lett. **11**(1–19) (2019)
32. Xu, S., Nunez, C.M., Souri, M., et al.: A compact DEA-based soft peristaltic pump for power and control of fluidic robots. Sci. Rob. **8**(79), eadd4649 (2023)
33. Dong, J., Yan, H., Lv, X., et al.: Reprocessable polyurethane elastomers based on reversible ketal exchange: dielectric properties and water resistance. J. Mater. Chem. C **11**(4), 1369–1380 (2023)
34. Tan, T., Siew, W.H., Han, L., et al.: Self-healing of electrical damage in microphase-separated polyurethane elastomers with robust dielectric strength utilizing dynamic hydrogen bonding networks. ACS Appl. Polym. Mater. **5**(9), 7132–7143 (2023)
35. Yin, L.-J., Zhao, Y., Zhu, J., et al.: Soft, tough, and fast polyacrylate dielectric elastomer for non-magnetic motor. Nat. Commun. **12**(1), 4517 (2021)
36. Molberg, M., Crespy, D., Rupper, P., et al.: High breakdown field dielectric elastomer actuators using encapsulated polyaniline as high dielectric constant filler. Adv. Func. Mater. **20**(19), 3280–3291 (2010)
37. Madsen, F.B., Dimitrov, I., Daugaard, A.E., et al.: Novel cross-linkers for PDMS networks for controlled and well distributed grafting of functionalities by click chemistry. Polym. Chem. **4**(5), 1700–1707 (2013)
38. Zhang, C., Zhang, Q.: Deep eutectic solvent inclusions for high-k composite dielectric elastomers. Front. Chem. Sci. Eng. **16**(6), 996–1002 (2022)
39. Quinsaat, J.E.Q., Alexandru, M., Nüesch, F.A., et al.: Highly stretchable dielectric elastomer composites containing high volume fractions of silver nanoparticles. J. Mater. Chem. A **3**(28), 14675–14685 (2015)
40. Kellaris, N., Gopaluni Venkata, V., Smith, G.M., et al.: Peano-HASEL actuators: Muscle-mimetic, electrohydraulic transducers that linearly contract on activation. Sci. Robot. **3**(14), eaar3276 (2018)
41. Acome, E., Mitchell, S.K., Morrissey, T., et al.: Hydraulically amplified self-healing electrostatic actuators with muscle-like performance. Science **359**(6371), 61–65 (2018)
42. Tang, W., Zhong, Y., Xu, H., et al.: Self-protection soft fluidic robots with rapid large-area self-healing capabilities. Nat. Commun. **14**(1), 6430 (2023)
43. Racles, C., Alexandru, M., Bele, A., et al.: Chemical modification of polysiloxanes with polar pendant groups by co-hydrosilylation. RSC Adv. **4**(71), 37620–37628 (2014)
44. Galantini, F., Bianchi, S., Castelvetro, V., et al.: Functionalized carbon nanotubes as a filler for dielectric elastomer composites with improved actuation performance. Smart Mater. Struct. **22**(5), 055025 (2013)
45. Huang, X., Xie, L., Hu, Z., et al.: Influence of $BaTiO_3$ nanoparticles on dielectric, thermophysical and mechanical properties of ethylene-vinyl acetate elastomer/$BaTiO_3$ microcomposites. IEEE Trans. Dielectr. Electr. Insul. **18**(2), 375–383 (2011)
46. Huang, X., Jiang, P.: Core–shell structured high-k polymer nanocomposites for energy storage and dielectric applications. Adv. Mater. **27**(3), 546–554 (2015)

47. Wang, X., Mitchell, S.K., Rumley, E.H., et al.: High-strain peano-HASEL actuators. Adv. Func. Mater. **30**(7), 1908821 (2020)
48. Tang, W., Lin, Y., Zhang, C., et al.: Self-contained soft electrofluidic actuators. Sci. Adv. **7**(34), eabf8080 (2021)
49. He, D., Wang, Y., Chen, X., et al.: Core–shell structured $BaTiO_3@Al_2O_3$ nanoparticles in polymer composites for dielectric loss suppression and breakdown strength enhancement. Compos. Part A Appl. Sci. Manuf. **93**, 137–143 (2017)
50. Qiu, Y., Zhang, E., Plamthottam, R., et al.: Dielectric elastomer artificial muscle: materials innovations and device explorations. Acc. Chem. Res. **52**(2), 316–325 (2019)

A Flexible Sensor Based on PVC Gel for Detections of Robotic Grasping

Qiyun Zhong[1,2], Qingsong He[1,2,3(✉)], Lin Xie[1,2], and Ziyan Shi[1]

[1] Jiangsu Provincial Key Laboratory of Bionic Functional Materials, College of Mechanical and Electrical Engineering, Nanjing University of Aeronautics and Astronautics, Nanjing 210016, China
heqingsong@nuaa.edu.cn
[2] Key Laboratory of Advanced Technology for Small and Medium-Sized UAV, Ministry of Industry and Information Technology, Unmanned Aerial Vehicles Research Institute, Nanjing University of Aeronautics and Astronautics, Nanjing 210016, China
[3] State Key Laboratory of Mechanics and Control of Aerospace Structures, Nanjing University of Aeronautics and Astronautics, Nanjing 210016, China

Abstract. The rapid evolution of the smart industry has propelled significant advancements in both the realms of flexible electronics and robotics. The fusion of flexible sensing with intelligent robots bestows upon them the capability of tactile sensing, a critical enhancement that elevates their intelligence, digitalization, and practical applicability. We have triumphantly developed an innovative poly(vinyl chloride)/multi-walled carbon nanotubes polymer gel (PVC/MWCNTs polymer gel, PMPG), renowned for its exceptional elasticity and sensitivity. This high-performing sensing gel was crafted through a physical cross-linking method, utilizing poly(vinyl chloride) as the base matrix and multi-walled carbon nanotubes as the reinforcing fillers. Optimally, at a PVC:DBA = 1:5 (1 wt% of MWCNTs), PMPG demonstrates a remarkable response time of merely 172 ms, coupled with the capacity for sustained, continuous measurements. The material's stability is commendable, enduring up to 2,500 successive measurements without degradation. By integrating PMPG with machine learning algorithms, the soft gripper is endowed with enhanced tactile sensing and responsive feedback capabilities, heralding a new era for soft robotics across diverse settings.

Keywords: Flexible Sensor · PMPG · Tactile Sensing

1 Introduction

As a pivotal segment within the intelligent industry, flexible sensors have experienced swift development, leveraging their inherent strengths of adaptability and flexibility. These attributes have facilitated their integration into a myriad of applications, encompassing health and sports monitoring [1–4], human-computer interaction [5, 6] and medical fields [7, 8]. The current landscape sees a diverse array of flexible sensors, crafted from conductive polymers [9, 10], hydrogels [11–13], and other elastic composites [14–16]. Conductive gels [17, 18], integral to flexible sensing, typically consist of an elastic matrix paired with a dielectric material. This composition predominantly features conductive ions, polymers, and particles. In the case of conductive gels that rely on ions for conductivity, achieving high conductivity necessitates a dense concentration of these ions. However, this approach can result in ion precipitation, adversely affecting the tensile properties of the composite material. When it comes to gels predicated on conductive polymers [19, 20], the direct cross-linking of monomers often yields a brittle end product, prone to fracture, with room for enhancement in biocompatibility. In contrast, carbon-based materials have emerged as promising contenders for flexible strain sensors [21–23], owing to their commendable electrical conductivity, flexibility, and stability. The ever-evolving practical application environments and advancements in science and technology have set the stage for new expectations from sensors. The next generation of flexible strain sensors is anticipated to exhibit enhanced ductility, accelerated response times, and superior repeatability, thereby meeting the escalating demands of modern applications.

The above mentioned better mechanical properties, physicochemical properties and biocompatibility are some of the goals we urgently need to achieve. Therefore, here we designed a polyvinyl chloride/multi-wall carbon nanotube polymer gel (PVC/MWCNTs polymer gel, PMPG) with high elasticity, linearity and sensitivity. PMPG was prepared by physical crosslinking method using polyvinyl chloride gel as elastomer matrix and MWCNTs as medium. The plasticizer dibutyl adipate and the polarity of the carbon tube enhance the sensing performance. The mechanical and electrical properties of PMPG can be adjusted by adjusting the component content. The prepared PMPG has excellent thermal stability, linearity, response speed and durability. In order to verify the feasibility of PMPG and the validity of the detection method, it is integrated into the robot's gripper by interacting with different objects. Using machine learning algorithm to learn feedback information and achieve classification prediction. Giving the feedback ability to the gripper can improve its intelligence and broaden the application of the robot in unstructured environment.

2 Results and Discussion

2.1 Preparation and Characterization Analysis

Figure 1 illustrates the process of preparing PMPG and the demonstration of its sensor capabilities. The plasticizer dibutyl adipate (DBA), the solvent tetrahydrofuran (THF), PVC, and MWCNTs were combined in a precise ratio and subjected to vigorous stirring followed by ultrasonic curing to yield the PMPG, as depicted in Fig. 1a. For an exhaustive walkthrough of the preparation methods, one should refer to the experimental section of the documentation. The PMPG sensor is constructed with a sandwich-like configuration, as outlined in Fig. 1b. It features electrodes positioned on either side of the PMPG, with an additional PVC film layer serving as an insulating barrier on the exterior of the electrodes. This design endows the PMPG pressure sensor with exceptional flexibility, allowing it to be flexed to a radius as small as 1 mm without compromising its structural integrity, as showcased in Fig. 1c. This level of pliability underscores the sensor's potential for diverse applications where adaptability is paramount.

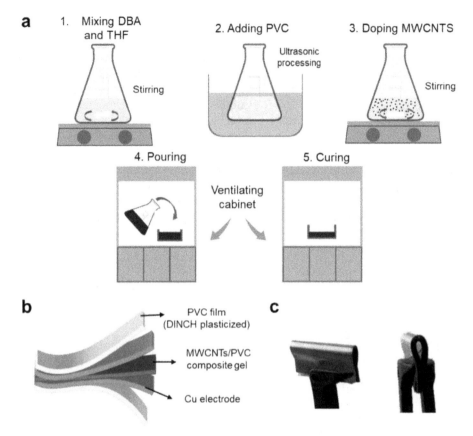

Fig. 1. Preparation of PMPG and sensor demonstration. (a) Preparation process of PMPG. (b) Schematic of sensor constructional decomposition and layering and demonstration of bending performance. (c) Bending of PMPG flexible pressure sensors.

Figure 2a shows the FT-IR test results of PMPG and its components. Curve a) shows the Fourier transform infrared spectra of MWCNTs, curve b) shows the FT-IR spectra of PVC, and curve C) shows the FT-IR spectra of DBA. Through comparison, it is found that the FT-IR results of gel are basically consistent with DBA, because the content of DBA in gel is the highest, and the proportion of PVC and MWCNTs is far lower than DBA. The experimental results show that there is a large amount of DBA in the gel, and the absorption band of DBA in the gel almost retains all the characteristics of pure DBA. Through a comprehensive comparison of the FTIR absorption spectra, it is not difficult to find that the gel band contains almost all the characteristic or superimposed peaks related to PVC and DBA, and no new absorption peaks have been found. When the content of PVC and DBA increased, the wave number and peak value of PVC and DBA groups in gel did not change significantly. Therefore, the PVC polymer chains in PMPG are filled and surrounded by DBA and MWCNTs, and there are no substantial chemical bonds between PVC, DBA, and MWNTs, which is a physical mixing state.

The thermal analysis of PVC and PMPG is elegantly captured in Fig. 2b and c, respectively. The thermogravimetric (TG) analysis reveals that the predominant weight loss occurs between 161 °C and 383 °C, with a substantial mass loss rate of 89.77%. This suggests a significant thermal degradation within this temperature range. Upon examining the differential scanning calorimetry (DSC) curve, a pronounced endothermic peak emerges at approximately 261 °C. This peak signals the melting temperature of the gel elastomer network, suggesting a phase transition for PMPG from a state of high elasticity to a state of viscous flow, occurring between 161 °C and 261 °C. Subsequently, the process identified is one of melting decomposition, predominantly characterized by the dehydrochlorination of PVC. The combined thermogravimetric-differential scanning calorimetry (TG-DSC) profile of PMPG indicates the absence of any phase transition within the range of 30 °C to 161 °C. This absence underscores the material's excellent thermal stability, thereby substantiating its reliability as a flexible sensing material. The consistent performance across a wide temperature span assures its potential for applications requiring robust thermal endurance.

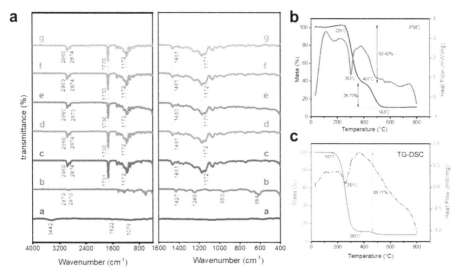

Fig. 2. Preparation and characterization of PMPG and sensor demonstration. (a) Fourier infrared spectra of PMPG and each component (a) MWCNTs; b) PVC; c) DBA; d) 1: 5 0 wt%; e) 1: 5 1 wt%; f) 1: 9 1 wt%; g) 1: 5 2 wt%). (b) Simultaneous thermal analysis curves of PVC and (c) PMPG.

2.2 Electrical and Electrochemical Characterization

Compared with traditional rigid sensors, flexible sensing gels usually have some nonlinearity, so it is necessary to study the linearity of the gels for the subsequent application compensation. Linearity describes the degree to which the output-input characteristic curve deviates from the fitted line under the condition of stable input [24], and the nonlinear error is quantified here. Figure 3a shows the linearity of PMPG. When the content of

PVC and DBA is unchanged (PVC: DBA = 1:5), the nonlinear error decreases with the increase of carbon tube content, and the linearity is better. When the carbon tube content is 2 wt%, the gel has a small nonlinear error, showing a good linearity, the corresponding nonlinear error is only 1.76%.

As can be seen from Fig. 3b, the sensitivity of PVC/MWCNTs sensing gel showed a certain drift phenomenon with the increase of strain. When PVC: DBA = 1:5, the sensitivity of PMPG is stable with the increase of strain. With the increase of carbon tube content, the sensitivity of the gel increases significantly. When the carbon tube content is 1 wt%, the sensitivity of the gel is more than double that of the gel when the carbon tube content is 0.5 wt%. The above results may be due to the interaction between the PVC polymer network and the carbon tube, and the change of DBA content leads to the more obvious dielectric properties of the gel, which has a certain impact on the voltage change. Under 5 cycles of pressurization and unloading, there is a certain mismatch between the output voltage and strain curve (Fig. 3c), which indicates that PMPG has hysteresis effect. This is because polyvinyl chloride gel is an elastic body, and its inherent mechanical properties cause deviations in the electrical response, but the hysteresis effect of PMPG will not have a great impact on the sensing performance. Figure 3d shows the influence of different strains on the output characteristics of the flexible sensing gel. With the increase of strain, the output voltage signal fluctuates slightly, which is due to the retarding effect of defects and polymer network on charge migration. Relatively, the gel has good stability. Figure 3e shows that the response time of the gel is only 189 ms. As can be seen from Fig. 3f, the sensing material with PVC: DBA = 1:5 (1 wt% of MWCNTs) shows good stability and reliability under long-term operation. In the first 100 times, there is a certain drift phenomenon, which is caused by the mechanical hysteresis of PMPG.

In order to analyze the electrochemical stability of the gel, the electrochemical impedance of PMPG was further measured. The electrochemical test platform was firstly built, as shown in Fig. 4a. The electrodes on both sides of the PMPG were connected to the electrodes of the electrochemical analyzer, which were analyzed and collected by the electrochemical analyzer and displayed on the host computer. The capacitive impedance arcs of the PMPG electrode system in the Nyquist diagram (Fig. 4b) for the first quadrant are less than semicircular circular arcs, which is in accordance with the impedance frequency response curves of the composite element (RQ). The constant phase angle element is characterized by the fact that as the value of the index n increases, the capacitive characteristics of the element become more pronounced. The change in the index n of the constant phase angle element Q is positively correlated with the carbon tube content, indicating that there is charge migration between the two electrodes of the gel, and that the higher the carbon tube content, the greater the amount of charge gathered on the electrodes on both sides, making the capacitive characteristics of the element Q more pronounced. From the Bode plot (Fig. 4c), it can be seen that when the frequency is lower than 104 Hz, the phase of the electrode system tends to decrease, while the impedance decreases accordingly, and the capacitance of the electrode system decreases; when the perturbation frequency is in the range of 104 Hz~106 Hz, the phase of the electrode system gradually increases close to 90°, and the impedance mode is close to 0, which indicates that the resistance of the electrode system is constantly decreasing in

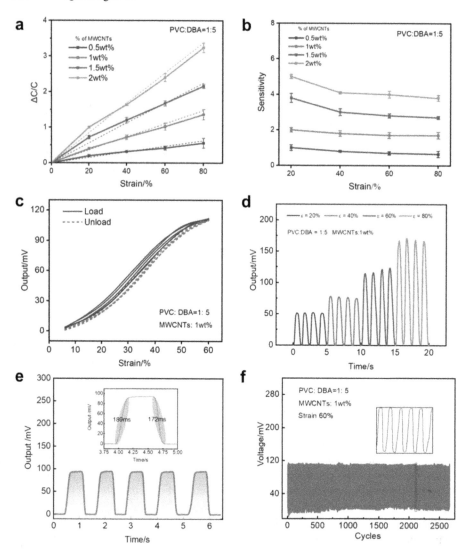

Fig. 3. Electrical characterization of PMPG. (a) Linearity of PMPG with different MWCNTs contents. (b) Sensitivity of PMPG with different MWCNTs contents. (c) Hysteresis properties of PMPG. (d) Compressive properties of PMPG with different strains. (e) Response time of PMPG. (f) Stability of 2500 cycles of stretching.

the process. The impedance is mainly composed of the capacitive resistance, and in this case, the polarization resistance Rp is equal to the reaction resistance Rt. By comparing the electrochemical impedance characteristics of the electrode system of PVC sensing gels with different DBA contents, it can be found that, with the increase in the content of MWCNTs, the reaction resistance Rt of the gels decreases, which suggests that the multi-walled carbon nanotubes can improve the electrical conductivity of the gels. The conductivity results of PMPG are shown in Fig. 4d. Carbon tube doping can improve the conductivity of the gel. When the carbon tube content is 2 wt%, the conductivity of the gel is between 10.6 μS/cm~25.4 μS/cm, which is more than 30 times higher than that of PVC gel without carbon tube (0.31~0.36 μS/cm). In addition, cyclic voltammetry tests were performed on gel, and the results are shown in Fig. 4e. At different scanning rates, there is no obvious oxidation and reduction peak in a charge-discharge cycle range of −0.5 V~0.5 V, which indicates that IL has good stability and only migrates under voltage without chemical reaction.

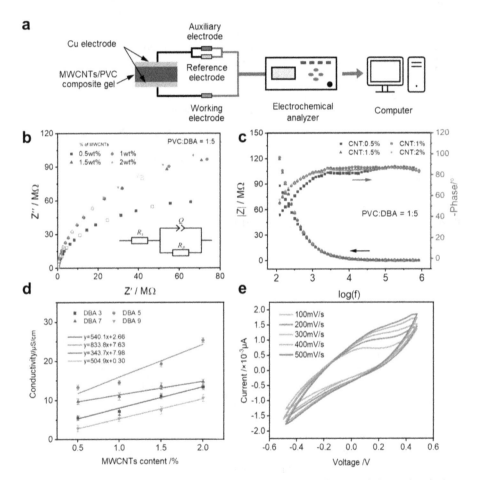

Fig. 4. Electrochemical characterization of PMPG. (a) Schematic diagram of electrochemical test platform. (b) Electrochemical resistance Nyquist plot, (c) bode plot, (d) electrical conductivity and (e) cyclic voltammetry of PMPG.

2.3 Mechanical Characterization

PMPG has good flexibility and adjustable mechanical properties. The excellent flexibility of PMPG is demonstrated through macroscopic deformation, as shown in Fig. 5a, PMPG has good resistance to puncture and shear, which can resist the damage of sharp objects. Figure 5b shows that PMPG still has good resilience under different degrees of pressing. The stress-strain curves of PMPGs do not have an obvious yield phase, unlike metallic materials, which exhibit an increase in stress with strain (Fig. 5c). When PVC: DBA = 1:3 and the content of MWCNTs is 2 wt%, PMPG exhibited the best toughness with a maximum stress of 224 kPa. In addition, the maximum stress of PMPG increased with the increase in the mass fraction of MWCNTs when the DBA content was certain. Carbon nanotubes become an ideal reinforcement for polymer matrix composites because of their excellent mechanical properties, and the present experiments also demonstrated that the doping of MWCNTs improved the mechanical properties of the gels. Meanwhile, the maximum stress of PMPG decreased with the increase of DBA content at the constant mass fraction of MWCNTs, indicating that DBA decreased the mechanical properties of the gel matrix. This is because PMPG is a physically crosslinked polymer network, and too much plasticizer occupies the solid space inside the gel, resulting in the polymer network becoming sparse, which leads to a decrease in the mechanical properties. The Young's modulus of PMPG is also correlated with the contents of MWCNTs and DBA (Fig. 5d). The Young's modulus of PMPG increased with the increase of MWCNTs content, while the increase of DBA content resulted in the decrease of Young's modulus. When PVC: DBA = 1:3 and the content of MWCNTs is 2 wt%, the Young's modulus of PMPG reaches up to 71.3 kPa. It is not difficult to understand that the increase of DBA content improves the softness of PMPG, while MWCNTs decreases the softness of PMPG.

2.4 Detections of Robotic Grasping Using PMPG Sensors

To substantiate the capabilities of the PMPG sensor and the efficacy of the detection methodology, this research endeavored to integrate the sensor into a robotic gripper system. Employing a two-fingered flexible robot, harnessing the PMPG to gather data that was pivotal for analyzing the state of the grip and the nature of the objects being gripped. The schematic of the sensor acquisition system is delineated in Fig. 6a. The PMPG sensors are seamlessly integrated into the gripper, with the resultant signals during the gripping process being captured by a National Instruments (NI) data acquisition module. These signals undergo filtration through a microcontroller before being relayed to a computer, where an algorithm performs learned predictions based on the data. The assembled signal reception system is adept at displaying the output signals from the tactile sensing elements in real time, as depicted in the physical setup of Fig. 6b. The system comprises an acquisition unit coupled with a computer. The acquisition unit is tasked with signal acquisition and filtering, while the computer is responsible for the real-time analysis and visualization of the sensing data. Upon contact with an object, there is a marked escalation in the output voltage, as indicated in Fig. 6c. This surge in voltage can be logically correlated with an increase in the gripper's exerted force, resulting in a more intimate coupling between the sensor and the object. Throughout the

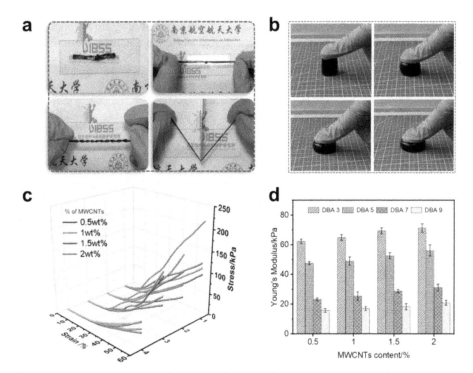

Fig. 5. Mechanical characterization of PMPG. (a) Knotting, torsion, puncture and shear resistance tests, (b) compression performance, (c) stress-strain graph and (d) Young's modulus of PMPG.

gripping phase, the output voltage maintains a steady state. Upon releasing the object, the sensing output reverts to its original condition. The successful execution of this demonstration not only validates the viability of the sensor system but also highlights its suitability for sensing applications in environments that are either unoccupied or require specific sensing conditions, showcasing the system's adaptability and robustness.

Flexible sensing elements are integrated into the soft gripper, which can sense and feedback the pressure when grasping an object. However, due to the existence of certain nonlinearities in the sensing element, here machine learning algorithms are combined to learn and classify the feedback data of different target objects for prediction, and accurately recognize the grasped objects. In this paper, K-Nearest Neighbor (KNN) algorithm is used, in which the K value is very important for the measure of the weights of neighboring samples and the guarantee of the accuracy of category prediction. Therefore, the optimal K value is determined by the method of cross-validation, and the cross-validation results are shown in Fig. 6d, which shows that a K value of 3 corresponds to the highest prediction accuracy of 98.6%. A model is built based on this value to predict the classification results of the samples to be tested, and the prediction accuracy of the model is evaluated. Crawling training and testing were completed on the above experimental platform to verify the feasibility of the crawling strategy based on the KNN algorithm. The target objects selected for this experiment are mainly disposable water cups, foam balls and headphone boxes. After the algorithm analysis, the accuracy of model evaluation is 100%, and the results predicted by the cut program are completely consistent with the actual results. This provides ideas for the combination of machine learning and flexible sensors.

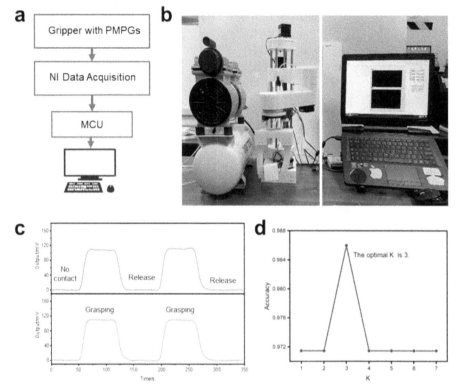

Fig. 6. Structure and application of PMPG-based tactile sensing array system integrated on soft gripper. (a) Schematic diagram of sensor acquisition system. (b) Physical image of the tactile gripper and the signal monitoring system diagram. (c) Real-time voltage signal response of the sensor to monitor the grasping motion of the gripper. (d) The accuracy corresponding to different K values.

3 Conclusion

We have crafted a highly elastic and sensitive flexible sensing material, PMPG, through a straightforward casting process. An in-depth examination was conducted to assess the various properties of PMPG, including its sensing capabilities, electrochemical behavior, and mechanical integrity, across a range of multi-walled carbon nanotubes (MWCNTs) concentrations. It was observed that as the MWCNTs content increased, the sensitivity, conductivity, maximum stress, and Young's modulus of PMPG also escalated, while the nonlinear error was notably reduced. The formulation of PMPG with PVC:DBA = 1:5

(1 wt% of MWCNTs) emerged as the optimal choice, showcasing the most impressive performance metrics. It boasts a rapid response time of merely 172 ms and maintains stable operation over 2,500 cycles, with an exceptionally low nonlinear error of just 1.76%. Moreover, PMPG has demonstrated remarkable stability, retaining its shape and dimensions even after 90 days of exposure to ambient air. The integration of PMPG into a haptic gripper for pressure detection and feedback represents a significant advancement. Utilizing the K-Nearest Neighbors (KNN) algorithm to process and analyze the feedback data, the system achieves precise haptic perception. Impressively, the system attains a perfect classification accuracy of 100% for three distinct objects. This accomplishment not only validates the viability of PMPG for haptic grippers but also paves the way for innovative integrations of machine learning with flexible sensors, sparking new avenues for technological synergy.

4 Experimental Section

4.1 Preparation of PMPG

The plasticizer dibutyl adipate and the solvent tetrahydrofuran were mixed in specific proportions and stirred at a speed of 400 r/min for 10 min. Polyvinyl chloride particles were slowly added to the above solution by ultrasonication for 10 min followed by stirring at 1500 r/min until the particles were completely dissolved. The speed was adjusted to 400 r/min and multi-walled carbon nanotubes were added to the precursor solution. The rotational speed was then adjusted back to 1500 r/min and after 48 h of stirring, the obtained mixed solution was cured by casting in a fume hood for 36 h to obtain PMPG.

Acknowledgements. This research was supported by grants from the Natural Science Foundation (Grant No. 52375293).

Conflict of Interest. The authors declare no conflict of interest.

References

1. Yang, T., et al.: Hierarchically microstructure-bioinspired flexible piezoresistive bioelectronics. ACS Nano **15**(7), 11555–11563 (2021)
2. Wang, Y., et al.: Stretchable temperature-responsive multimodal neuromorphic electronic skin with spontaneous synaptic plasticity recovery. ACS Nano **16**(5), 8283–8293 (2022)
3. Gao, W., et al.: Fully integrated wearable sensor arrays for multiplexed in situ perspiration analysis. Nature **529**(7587), 509–514 (2016)
4. Fan, W., et al.: Machine-knitted washable sensor array textile for precise epidermal physiological signal monitoring. Sci. Adv. **6**(11), eaay2840 (2020)
5. Niu, H., et al.: Perception-to-cognition tactile sensing based on artificial-intelligence-motivated human full-skin bionic electronic skin. Adv. Mater. **34**(31), 2202622 (2022)
6. Tao, K., et al.: Ultra-sensitive, deformable, and transparent triboelectric tactile sensor based on micro-pyramid patterned ionic hydrogel for interactive human–machine interfaces. Adv. Sci. **9**(10), 2104168 (2022)

7. Yang, F., et al.: Wafer-scale heterostructured piezoelectric bio-organic thin films. Science **373**(6552), 337–342 (2021)
8. Abramson, A., et al.: A flexible electronic strain sensor for the real-time monitoring of tumor regression. Sci. Adv. **8**(37), eabn6550 (2022)
9. Wang, D., et al.: Freestanding silver/polypyrrole composite film for multifunctional sensor with biomimetic micropattern for physiological signals monitoring. Chem. Eng. J. **404**, 126940 (2021)
10. Gao, L., et al.: Flexible pressure sensor with wide linear sensing range for human–machine interaction. IEEE Trans. Electron Devices **69**(7), 3901–3907 (2022)
11. Shen, Z., et al.: High-stretchability, ultralow-hysteresis conducting polymer hydrogel strain sensors for soft machines. Adv. Mater. **34**(32), 2203650 (2022)
12. Zhou, Y., et al.: Highly stretchable, elastic, and ionic conductive hydrogel for artificial soft electronics. Adv. Funct. Mater. **29**(1), 1806220 (2019)
13. Kong, W., et al.: Muscle-inspired highly anisotropic, strong, ion-conductive hydrogels. Adv. Mater. **30**(39), 1801934 (2018)
14. Wang, X., et al.: PDMS-based conductive elastomeric composite with 3D reduced graphene oxide conductive network for flexible strain sensor. Compos. A Appl. Sci. Manuf. **161**, 107113 (2022)
15. Ma, C., et al.: Robust flexible pressure sensors made from conductive micropyramids for manipulation tasks. ACS Nano **14**(10), 12866–12876 (2020)
16. Distler, T., Boccaccini, A.R.: 3D printing of electrically conductive hydrogels for tissue engineering and biosensors–a review. Acta Biomater. **101**, 1–13 (2020)
17. Ding, Y., Zhang, J., Chang, L., Zhang, X., Liu, H., Jiang, L.: Preparation of high-performance ionogels with excellent transparency, good mechanical strength, and high conductivity. Adv. Mater. **29**(47), 1704253 (2017)
18. Cao, Z., Liu, H., Jiang, L.: Transparent, mechanically robust, and ultrastable ionogels enabled by hydrogen bonding between elastomers and ionic liquids. Mater. Horiz. **7**(3), 912–918 (2020)
19. Wang, Z., et al.: Extremely stretchable and electrically conductive hydrogels with dually synergistic networks for wearable strain sensors. J. Mater. Chem. C **6**(34), 9200–9207 (2018)
20. Lee, Y.Y., et al.: A strain-insensitive stretchable electronic conductor: PEDOT: PSS/Acrylamide organogels. Adv. Mater. (Deerfield Beach Fla.) **28**(8), 1636–1643 (2015)
21. Han, J., et al.: A self-healable and highly flexible supercapacitor integrated by dynamically cross-linked electro-conductive hydrogels based on nanocellulose-templated carbon nanotubes embedded in a viscoelastic polymer network. Carbon **149**, 1–18 (2019)
22. Tang, W., Yan, T., Wu, J., Ying, Y.: Rapid fabrication of flexible and stretchable strain sensor by chitosan-based water ink for plants growth monitoring. Adv. Mater. Technol. **2**(7), 1700021 (2017)
23. Ha, K.H., et al.: Highly sensitive capacitive pressure sensors over a wide pressure range enabled by the hybrid responses of a highly porous nanocomposite. Adv. Mater. **33**(48), 2103320 (2021)
24. Huang, J., Tang, X., Wang, F., Wang, Z., Niu, Y., Wang, H.: Multi-hierarchical microstructures boosted linearity of flexible capacitive pressure sensor. Adv. Eng. Mater. **24**(9), 2101767 (2022)

A Soft Amphibious Robot with Buoyancy Control and Underwater Manipulation Capabilities

Yang Yang[1,2(✉)], Haozhe Zheng[1], Yuan Xie[1], Pei Jiang[3], and Yingtian Li[4]

[1] School of Automation, Nanjing University of Information Science and Technology (NUIST), Nanjing 210044, China
meyang@nuist.edu.cn
[2] Jiangsu Province Engineering Research Center of Intelligent Meteorological Exploration Robot, NUIST, Nanjing 210044, China
[3] State Key Laboratory of Mechanical Transmission for Advanced Equipment, Chongqing University, Chongqing, China
[4] Shenzhen Institutes of Advanced Technology, Chinese Academy of Sciences, Shenzhen, China

Abstract. Underwater equipment is critical for environmental applications. Conventional rigid underwater manipulators require considerable size and weight, hindering the application of underwater operations. Origami actuators have proven to be an effective technique and have been used in many applications. In this work, I propose a bionic soft amphibious robot based on a Z-shaped actuator and a twisted tower actuator. The soft robot can be fabricated by 3D printing technology and has a simple structure for easy operation. Two different types of programmable origami actuators are designed and fabricated, i.e., Z-shaped actuator and torsion tower actuator. Z-shaped actuator is used for the rear leg which enables the movement of the frog. Meanwhile, the torsion tower shaped actuator is used for the front legs to rotate the joints and movement on land. We designed a novel hybrid structure (rigid frame + soft actuator) gripper using the Z-shaped actuator to improve the gripping performance. And we use bellows to make the buoyancy unit of the soft robot. The origami actuators and were tested through a series of experiments, which showed that the robot was able to efficiently move and perform grasping maneuvers in water and on land. Our results demonstrate the effectiveness of these actuators in generating the desired motions and provide insight into the potential of applying 3D printed origami actuators to develop soft robots with bionic capabilities.

Keywords: Soft Body Robots · Origami Actuators · Underwater Manipulation · Bionic Robots · Amphibious Locomotion

1 Introduction

The ocean is rich in resources and a large variety of marine organisms, and has gradually become an important field for human exploration. Due to the special environment of high pressure, low temperature and no oxygen in the ocean, underwater robots have become an important equipment for human beings in underwater operations such as marine resource exploration, underwater biological sampling and transportation of marine waste. The rigidity of traditional rigid-body manipulators makes it very difficult to handle soft and fragile aquatic specimens [1]. In addition, the most commonly used drive methods are either motor-based drive mechanisms [2] or hydraulic pumps [3], both of which generate noise and vibration. Although they have high stability and controllability, the grasping coupling is less safe and adaptable, which cannot meet the needs of nondestructive grasping operations in complex marine environments, and brings great challenges to underwater operations such as biological sampling.

In recent years, soft actuators have been rapidly developed by virtue of better contact adaptability, which provides a new option to improve the adaptability of underwater robots. Soft robots made of flexible materials can realize continuous and frequent local deformation and have good adaptability to unknown environments [4]. Pneumatic soft actuators are widely used due to their safety, light weight and ability to provide continuous, natural motion [5]. Due to the soft-textured material and structural properties, pneumatic soft actuators typically exhibit lower forces and higher deformations. Compared to conventional rigid-body robots, soft-body robots offer a new approach to underwater manipulation. In particular, the inherent adaptability and waterproofness of soft-bodied actuators are well suited for grasping delicate and flexible objects underwater.

In this paper, a new soft amphibious robot based on Miura origami actuator and Kresling origami driver is proposed, see Fig. 1. The bionic soft robot parts are all fabricated by 3D printing technology, which is characterized by simple structure and light weight. The frog's movement mechanism of swimming, crawling, diving and surfacing, and grasping was observed and analyzed [6]. Through clever design, the motion trajectories of Miura origami and Z-shaped origami can fit the limbs, joints and organs of the animals. In particular, the Miura was employed as a gripper actuator to both counteract environmental pressure and increase the flow rate of the drive level [7]. In order to achieve compactness, lightweight and fast response simultaneously, innovations in the drive and control systems were needed in the development phase. The actuators were all 3D printed directly from thermoplastic elastomers (TPEs) through fused deposition modeling and heat-treated to withstand high fluid pressures. Meanwhile, the unique bistable properties of Miura Origami facilitate the responsiveness of the bionic amphibious soft robot. The pneumatic hardware control system we designed can well characterize the motion properties of the bionic soft-bodied robot. We use the bellows structure as the buoyancy unit of the robot, which can make the robot float and dive underwater [8, 9]. The robot is driven by four pneumatic circuits, which can realize swimming (straight/left/right), land crawling, grasping, and upward and downward dive in the water [10].

The main contributions of this paper include the following three points:

(1) The application of Miura origami and Z-shaped origami as actuators for bionic robots and the demonstration of the feasibility of this approach;
(2) Programmable motion control of bionic soft robots;
(3) The realization of an origami actuator-based animal bionic soft robot for aquatic and underwater locomotion for grasping and land locomotion.

The rest of the paper is organized as follows: Sect. 2 describes the design and working principle of the soft amphibious robot. Section 3 describes the fabrication and control of

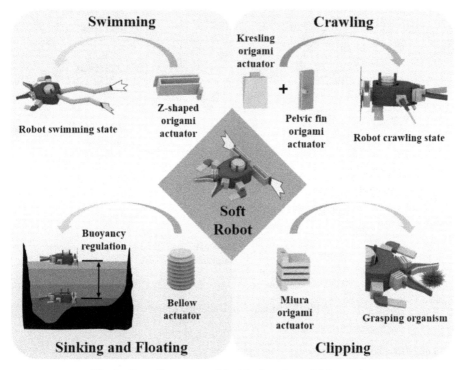

Fig. 1. Overall structure of the bionic soft amphibious robot

the soft amphibious robot [11]. In Sect. 4, the main focus is on testing the Miura origami actuator, experimenting with the soft robot's ability to swim, and analyzing the ability to manipulate the gripper [12, 13]. Finally, in Sect. 5, we summarize the article and present future work.

2 Design and Fabrication

2.1 Soft Actuator Design

Figure 2 shows a 3D model of a soft amphibious robot, modeled after a frog, divided into 4 main parts: legs, forelimbs, grippers and buoyant actuators. All designed actuators are integrated in a single robot body, the robot is modular and all parts are 3D printed, the green part is made of PLA material and the white part is made of TPE material, see Fig. 2. The robot is the middle part of the robot where the buoyant device is placed, and the top surface can be opened. There are two 7×30 mm rectangular holes at the back of the body, and the leg actuators extend through the rectangular holes to the inside of the soft robot. And four 4 mm round holes are placed at the rear of the robot, and the rubber hose extends through the holes to the inside of the quadruped soft robot. The surface of the gripper is smooth and has very little friction with the grasped object, so we pasted a rough material as a rough surface on the surface of the gripper for increasing the friction between the legs and the ground.

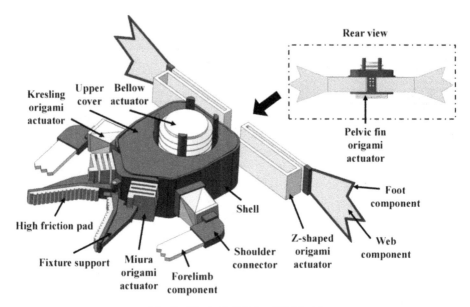

Fig. 2. Bionic Soft Robot 3D Model

The Miura soft actuator used in this paper is vacuum-driven, and the Miura origami method helps to quickly fold paper into multiple origami units, as shown in Fig. 3(a). Inspired by Miura Origami, we varied the length of the initial origami units to mimic the movement of a frog's legs in water and arranged them into a Z-shaped structure similar to a tubular structure. The Z-shaped origami actuator (ZSOA) was fabricated using 3D printing. Figure 3(b) shows the design of the Kresling-shaped origami actuator. In response to the needs of underwater sampling operations and the problems of the existing rigid hand structure, we designed a hybrid structure (rigid frame + soft actuator) gripper suitable for underwater operations by combining the functional characteristics of the Miura Origami structure. We then obtained relatively neutral buoyancy by placing the buoyancy unit at the center of the robot.

The gripper origami actuator can be used to complete the grasping function in water, and the gripper is pressurized by the internal fluid to produce a bending action to realize the contact with the object, which shows better performance in underwater operation applications, see Fig. 3(c). A bellows configuration soft body actuator is designed to be used in the buoyancy of bionic amphibious soft body robots, see Fig. 3(d) The pressure in the bellows can be adjusted to control the robots to work in the water.

2.2 Manufacturing Process

The origami actuator of the soft amphibian robot was printed in TPE by a 3D printer (KP3S, KINGROON, China), and the body and leg joints of the soft robot were printed in PLA. The soft actuator was printed as a single unit with no internal support. In this case, in order to guarantee the print quality of the top layer, it is necessary to reduce the print speed and provide sufficient cooling during the printing process. Strong and thin

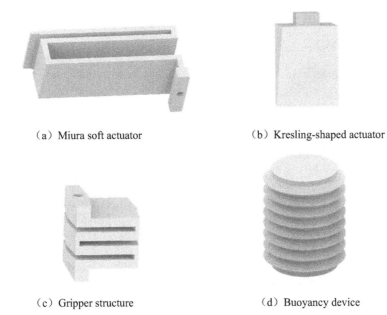

(a) Miura soft actuator (b) Kresling-shaped actuator

(c) Gripper structure (d) Buoyancy device

Fig. 3. Leg and forelimb actuator structures

walls are beneficial to promote twisting and contraction of the soft actuator. Considering that the nozzle diameter of the printer is 4 mm, we set the wall thickness to 1.2 mm. at the same time, we set the extrusion volume of the nozzle to 115% and the filling density to 100% to enhance the airtightness of the soft actuator, as shown in Table 1 for specific information.

Table 1. Partial setting parameters of the printer.

Setting	PLA	TPE
Layer height (mm)	**0.2**	0.1
Wall thickness (mm)	**1.2**	1.2
Filling density (%)	**25**	100
Printing speed (mm/s)	**50**	30
Nozzle temperature (°C)	210	220
Extrusion volume (%)	100	130
Fan cooling	ON	ON

3 Principle of Operation and Control

3.1 Principle of Operation of Soft Actuators

In complex underwater environments, soft-bodied robots have the advantage of inherent compliance over conventional rigid-bodied robots. On the other hand, by applying rigid parts in the design, better accuracy and larger payloads can be realized. A soft-bodied gripper consists of two parts: a Z-shaped origami actuator and a rigid part. Our gripper has two fingers, both of which are covered with a soft texture to increase friction. When not actuated, the origami actuator is in its initial state. When it is actuated by a vacuum, the origami actuator fills with gas and expands, which drives the rigid fingers into a bending motion.

Figure 4(a, b) shows the working process of the Kresling-shaped origami actuator. Kresling origami is a type of paper folding in which twisting motion occurs through predefined diagonal creases. The forelimbs of the soft amphibious robot have Kresling origami actuators with two oppositely oriented creases, and when it is actuated by a vacuum, the soft actuator achieves a compound motion of twisting and contracting, and the direction of twisting is related to the direction of the side creases, which is determined during the modeling of the actuator.

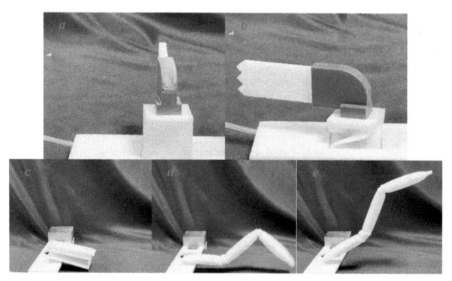

Fig. 4. Principle of operation of Z-folding actuators and Kresling-folding actuators

Figure 4(c, d, e) shows the Z-shaped origami actuator and the working process. We determined their unique swimming patterns by observing the frogs: expansion, propulsion, and recovery. During the expansion phase, the knee joints between the frog's thighs and calves were preferentially activated to adjust the position of the limbs for maximum range of webbing jumps on the water surface. During the propulsion phase, rapid movement of the ankle and hip joints generates a paddling force at the surface of the water to promote the frog's swimming motion, utilizing the inertia of this force to perform a gliding motion at the surface of the water. Finally, during the recovery phase, all three joints of the frog's legs are activated to return to the initial swimming position.

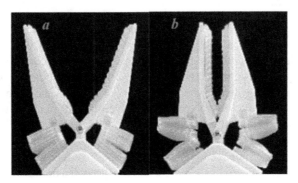

Fig. 5. Real prototype of the gripper

Figure 5(a, b) shows the motion of the gripper actuator. The gripper actuator is designed by using a hybrid structure of Z-shaped actuator and rigid fingers (rigid frame + soft actuator) so that the performance of the fetch can be better improved. When the Z-shaped origami actuator is activated, the origami structure will drive the rigid gripper to contract, thus realizing the fetch task.

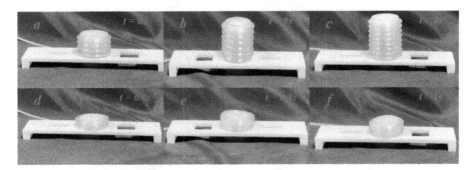

Fig. 6. Bellows buoyancy device movement process

Figure 6 shows the motion process of the bellows buoyancy actuator. The bellows actuator acts as a buoyancy unit in the robot, which can realize the two states of sinking and uplifting of the robot. In the sinking stage, the negative pressure pump is used to pump out the gas in the bellows, which reduces the buoyancy of the overall structure of the robot and realizes the sinking motion, and in the uplifting stage, the negative pressure pump stops pumping out the gas, and the gas line is disconnected with a solenoid valve, which restores the buoyancy unit to its original state and realizes the uplifting motion. We tested the contraction process of three different types of bellows, with the negative pressure set to 93 kPa, to test the time required for the three bellows to contract from the initial state to the final state.

3.2 Control Method

The control system of the soft amphibious robot is shown in Fig. 7. The control system consists of a vacuum pump, a positive pressure pump, an STM32F103 microcontroller, a 6-way relay module and six normally closed 2-position, 3-way solenoid valves. All these electronic components can be purchased online. The vacuum pump is used to provide negative pressure to drive the forelimb soft actuator to reverse and the buoyancy device to release pressure to sink the robot. The positive pressure pump is used to provide positive pressure to drive the hind limb leg actuators to expand and to drive the gripper to perform the grasping operation. STM32F103 is used to control the on-off of the relay. The solenoid valves are powered by an external power supply with a voltage of 12 V. The inlet holes of the solenoid valves are extended through a hose to the vacuum pump and positive pressure pump outlet ports, and the outlet holes are connected to each soft actuator separately through another hose. Pressure regulating valves are used to regulate the amount of pressure with a range of −93 kPa to 93 kPa.

Fig. 7. The control system

4 Experiments and Results

4.1 Robotic Swimming and Crawling Experiments

Figure 8(a) shows the swimming forward speed test. We inflate both leg actuators simultaneously and the actuators expand allowing the soft robot to swim forward. The duration of one complete cycle from the start of the robot's motion to its return to the initial state is denoted as T (i.e., cycle T = 1/f), while the internal positive pressure inside the actuators is denoted by P. We have tested that the maximum swimming distance of the robot is 100 mm and the swimming speed reaches 20 mm/ s under the inflation pressure P = 93 kPa and the test time t = 5 s. The robot can swim up to 20 mm/ s with the inflation pressure P = 93 kPa.

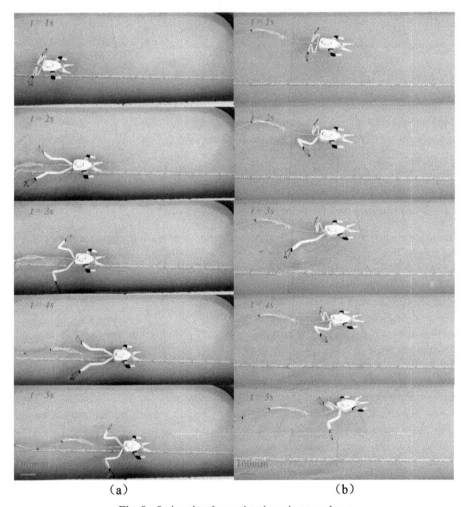

(a)   (b)

Fig. 8. Swimming forward and turning speed test

Figure 8(b) shows the swimming rotation speed test. The water maneuverability of the robot was evaluated to demonstrate its ability to swim flexibly in water. We tested the robot's ability to turn under 93 kPa pressure conditions. The results show that the robot's maneuverability can be well represented in water, and the maximum turning angle can reach 53.7° in time t = 5 s. The results show that the robot's maneuverability can be well represented in water.

Fig. 9. Crawling ability test

Figure 9 shows the crawling forward speed test. In order to evaluate the ground crawling speed of the robot, we controlled the length of a single cycle of the Kresling soft actuator by the relay opening and closing intervals. We set the crawling speed of the soft robot to 20 mm/s for a negative pressure P = 93 kPa and a motion cycle of 1.5 s. The soft robot was able to crawl at a speed of 20 mm/s.

4.2 Robot Sinking and Grasping Experiments

Figure 10(a) and (b) show the initial and final gripping states of the gripper, respectively. We placed the Miura origami gripper on a workbench and bent the soft actuator at different angles by means of the positive pressure of the regulator. We chose ten pressure values from 0 kPa to 50 kPa and measured the relationship between the gripper angle and positive pressure, and Fig. 10(c) shows the nonlinear relationship between the change of gripper angle and positive pressure.

Figure 11(a, b) shows the test of the maximum gripping force of the gripper under different air pressures. We fixed the gripper above the table and tested the maximum pulling force of the machine gripper under different pressure cases. Sixteen sets of pressure variations were selected at pressure 0kPa-150kPa to measure the relationship between the gripper pulling force magnitude and the positive pressure, and Fig. 11(c) shows the nonlinear relationship between the gripper's maximum clamping force and the positive pressure.

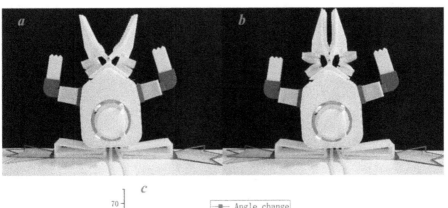
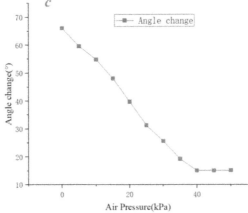

Fig. 10. Nonlinear relationship between gripper angle and positive pressure

Figure 12 shows the evaluation of the combined ability of the soft-bodied robot to swim and drop items at a fixed location. In order to verify the feasibility of the bionic soft robot, the robot demonstrated its good swimming ability and underwater spotting and dropping ability from its initial position Fig. 12(a), swimming in the water surface to the dropping location Fig. 12(b, c), using buoyancy device for diving and dropping the items Fig. 12(d, e), and finally surfacing in the swimming movement Fig. 12(f).

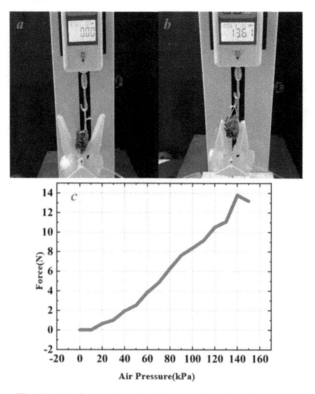

Fig. 11. Maximum clamping force as a function of pressure

5 Conclusion and Future Work

This work demonstrates the design and fabrication of 3D printed origami actuators for a bionic soft robot with amphibious locomotion and underwater manipulation capabilities. By applying Miura origami actuators and bellows actuators to a bionic soft robot, a pneumatically programmable bionic soft robot with swimming and turning capabilities, surfacing and diving, and grasping manipulation capabilities was developed. The soft robot was driven to swim and turn in water by driving the expansion of the leg structure. We fabricated the soft robot prototype and designed nine robot gaits, and tested them through a series of experiments to demonstrate its powerful and integrated amphibious capabilities and diving and grasping functions. The grasping function is promising for applications such as environmental detection, search and rescue operations in water. In future research, autonomous control of robotic motion and amphibious transitions will be investigated based on sensory feedback. In addition, the gripper of the amphibious robot needs to be upgraded in the grasping stability. And the integrated pH, turbidity and other water quality detection sensors and temperature and humidity sensors will be integrated into the soft robot so that it can perform some monitoring feedback information tasks. The bionic soft robot based on Miura origami actuator proposed in this paper can be improved in the following ways: (1) The bending angle of the gripper actuator restricts

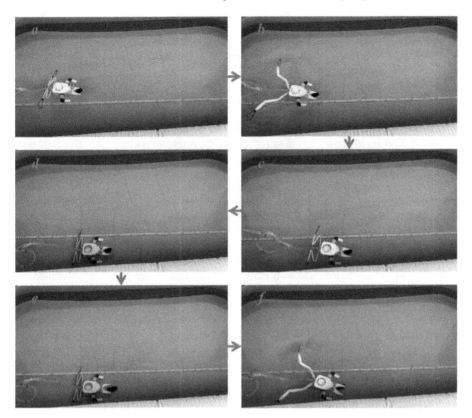

Fig. 12. The soft robot swim, dive and grasp object underwater.

the grasping function of large-size items, and the gripper's gripping force and accuracy test still need to be improved. (2) The bionic soft robot's body posture will be deviated to some extent when it dives and surfaces. We need to optimize the structure of the bionic soft robot so as to improve the stability of the soft robot.

Acknowledgement. This research was supported in part by the Research Project of State Key Laboratory of Mechanical System and Vibration (MSV202319) and the State Key Laboratory of Mechanical Transmission for Advanced Equipment (SKLMT-MSKFKT-202327).

References

1. Yang, Y., et al.: 3D printed origami actuators for a multi-animal inspired soft robot with amphibious locomotion and tongue hunting. Soft Robot. (2024). Ahead of print. https://doi.org/10.1089/soro.2023.0079
2. Wu, M., et al.: Glowing sucker octopus (stauroteuthis syrtensis)-inspired soft robotic gripper for underwater self-adaptive grasping and sensing. Adv. Sci. **9**(17) (2022)
3. Zhang, J., Liu, Q., Zhou, J., Song, A.: Crab-inspired compliant leg design method for adaptive locomotion of a multi-legged robot. Bioinspir. Biomim. **17**(2), 025001 (2022)

4. Hwang, J., Wang, W.D.: Shape memory alloy-based soft amphibious robot capable of seal-inspired locomotion. Adv. Mater. Technol. **7**(6), 2101153 (2022)
5. Lin, P.W., Liu, C.H.: Bio-inspired soft proboscis actuator driven by dielectric elastomer fluid transducers. Polymers (Basel) **11**(1), 142 (2019)
6. Stuart, H.S., Wang, S., Cutkosky, M.R.: Tunable contact conditions and grasp hydrodynamics using gentle fingertip suction. IEEE Trans. Rob. **35**(2), 295–306 (2019)
7. Stuart, H., Wang, S., Khatib, O., Cutkosky, M.R.: The ocean one hands: an adaptive design for robust marine manipulation. Int. J. Robot. Res. **36**(2), 150–166 (2017)
8. Huang, J., et al.: Modular origami soft robot with the perception of interaction force and body configuration. Adv. Intell. Syst. **4**(9), 2200081 (2022)
9. Kang, B., Lee, Y., Piao, T., Ding, Z., Wang, W.D.: Robotic soft swim bladder using liquid-vapor phase transition. Mater. Horiz. **8**(3), 939–947 (2021)
10. Simetti, E., et al.: Autonomous underwater intervention: experimental results of the MARIS project. IEEE J. Oceanic Eng. **43**(3), 620–639 (2018)
11. Casalino, G., et al.: Underwater intervention robotics: an outline of the italian national project MARIS. Mar. Technol. Soc. J. **50**(4), 98–107 (2016)
12. Stuart, H.S., Wang, S., Gardineer, B., Christensen, D.L., Aukes, D.M., Cutkosky, M.: A compliant underactuated hand with suction flow for underwater mobile manipulation. In: Proceedings of the 2014 IEEE International Conference on Robotics and Automation (ICRA), pp. 6691–6697. IEEE (2014)
13. Marani, G., Choi, S.K., Yuh, J.: Underwater autonomous manipulation for intervention missions AUVs. Ocean Eng. **36**(1), 15–23 (2009)

Deep Learning Network Based Time Series Prediction Model for Cyanobacterial Concentration Using a Many-Objective Algorithm

Bao Liu[✉] and Jiaxin Li

College of Control Science and Engineering, China University of Petroleum, Qingdao 266580, China
lb314423@163.com

Abstract. Blue-green algae are ancient organisms capable of photosynthesis with strong vitality. However, the toxins they produce pose a threat to human health and water safety. Global warming and water pollution have led to frequent outbreaks of algal blooms worldwide. Therefore, accurate prediction of blue-green algae concentration and early warning is crucial for effective algae management. However, current prediction models often lack accuracy and robustness, limiting their effectiveness in real-world applications.

To enhance cyanobacterial bloom prediction accuracy, this paper proposes a time series prediction model for cyanobacterial concentration. The main structure includes wavelet decomposition, a many-objective optimization algorithm, and Gated Recurrent Unit neural network. The main process involves three steps: initially, the cyanobacteria concentration data and environmental variables undergo discrete wavelet decomposition to extract low-frequency trends and high-frequency features. Then, the decomposed data are fed into a two-layer GRU network, fine-tuned by the many-objective optimization algorithm for prediction. Lastly, the predicted outputs are combined to derive the final concentration prediction.

To validate the model, we selected three metrics: RMSE (root mean square error), NSE (Nash-Sutcliffe efficiency coefficient), and CORR (correlation coefficient), to evaluate the prediction results. Meanwhile, we conducted tests in three regions: Morgan, Murray Bridge, and Tailem Bend, with RMSE values of 2721, 672, and 470 respectively; NSE values of 0.962, 0.979, and 0.969 respectively; and CORR values of 0.984, 0.990, and 0.986 respectively. The results demonstrate the generalizability of the model.

Keywords: Discrete Wavelet Transform · Gated Recurrent Unit · Many-objective Algorithm

1 Introduction

Cyanobacteria is one of the ancient photoautotrophic organisms with strong vitality [1]. It can increase rapidly, forming harmful algal blooms. [2] Therefore, accurately predicting the concentration of blue-green algae to achieve early warning is key to the prevention and control of blue-green algal blooms.

The current common modeling methods include mechanistic and data-driven methods. Mechanistic methods entail developing dynamic models to understand cyanobacteria growth. These models are intricate and demand the expertise of skilled modelers. Although data-driven methods are widely used nowadays, they still encounter challenges. It relies on data quality and struggles to predict complex models directly. Secondly, the model heavily depends on parameters, making it challenging to balance multiple objectives during tuning. Therefore, selecting suitable parameters has become a crucial aspect of modeling. Researchers have developed the GWO-SVM model to predict Chl-a concentration, showing promising accuracy. However, the model has limitations, such as GWO considering only a single criterion during parameter tuning and the model's low generalizability. [3].

To tackle these issues, we propose a time series prediction model for cyanobacterial concentration. Initially, wavelet decomposition is employed for complex data to improve input data quality. Secondly, enhanced many-objective optimization algorithm is used to fine-tune the deep learning architecture, aiming to address multiple objectives simultaneously and ensure comprehensive prediction result quality.

The main contributions of this paper are summarized as follows: 1) Decomposing complex concentration data and environmental variables using wavelet decomposition, and then inputting the same-level decomposition products into a time-series prediction network for forecasting. 2) Introducing a Manyobj-GRU time-series prediction network, aiming to adjust the hyperparameters of the dual-layer GRU through the proposed many-objective optimization algorithm. 3) Through comparison with other prediction models, we find that our proposed model demonstrates advantages in the domain of complex time-series prediction.

2 Methodology

To enhance the accuracy of cyanobacterial bloom prediction, this paper introduces a time series prediction model for cyanobacterial concentration utilizing a many-objective algorithm based on a deep learning network. The main components include: wavelet decomposition, a many-objective optimization algorithm, and a GRU neural network. The general frame diagram of the proposed model is shown in Fig. 1. Among them, the meanings of the input and output variables are shown in the table below. Below is a detailed description of each component (Table 1).

Table 1. Variables Declaration

Meaning	Definition	Variable
Flow rate (ML/day)	The amount of fluid passing through a surface per unit of time	Q
Flow velocity (m/s)	The speed at which a fluid flows through a given point	V
Water temperature (°C)	A measure of how hot or cold the water is	T
Salinity (muS/cm)	A measure of the concentration of dissolved salts in water	S
Concentration (number of cells/ml)	The amount or density of cyanobacteria present in a body of water	C

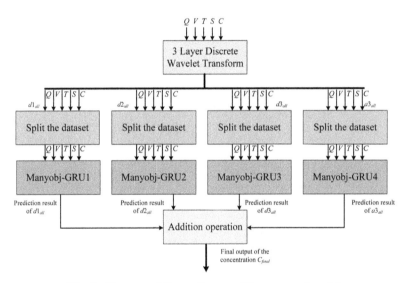

Fig. 1. The general frame diagram of the proposed model

2.1 Wavelet Decomposition

Wavelet transform is widely used in complex data processing, divided into continuous and discrete wavelet transforms [4]. Since the data used in this experiment is recorded weekly, DWT (discrete wavelet transform) is adopted, with the formula as follows:

$$DWT(a, b) = \frac{1}{\sqrt{|a|}} \int_{-\infty}^{+\infty} f(t) \cdot \psi(\frac{t-b}{a}) dt \qquad (1)$$

where, $DWT(a, b)$ is the wavelet coefficient, which represent the wavelet transform results of the signal at scale a and translation b; $f(t)$ donates the original signal; $\psi(\cdot)$ is wavelet function, which is a waveform function with a zero mean.

2.2 ARSBX-ILD-NSGA-III Many-Objective Optimization Algorithm

ARSBX-ILD-NSGA-III is the many-objective optimization algorithm proposed in this paper. It builds on the NSGA-III algorithm by incorporating the adaptive simulated binary crossover (ARSBX) strategy for population generation and the incremental lattice design (ILD) strategy for reference point generation. This approach improves population diversity and effectively addresses the rotational Pareto problem and its overall flowchart is shown in Fig. 2. Below is a detailed explanation of each component.

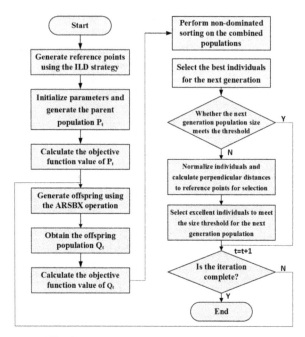

Fig. 2. Flowchart of ARSBX-ILD-NSGA-III

NSGA-III

NSGA-III is a commonly used many-objective optimization algorithm that employs a reference point-based niching strategy [5]. It aims to find the Pareto front through continuous iterations, making it similar to the true front. Although NSGA-III is popular and reliable, it has limitations in its reference point generation strategy and struggles with rotation problems.

ILD Reference Point Generation Strategy

In the original NSGA-III method, reference points are generated using Das and Dennis' strategy. However, if the decomposition parameter H is less than the number of objective functions M, the reference points are only generated on the boundary of the hyperplane.

Therefore, we introduce the ILD (incremental lattice design of weight vector set) reference vector generation strategy. Proposed by Takagi et al. in 2020 [6], this method addresses the limitations of Das and Dennis' reference point generation strategy. It expands the number of weight vectors using a decomposition parameter, ensuring the inclusion of intermediate weight vectors pointing toward the center of the Pareto front. Moreover, it maintains the uniform distribution of reference points formed by spatial weight vectors. The core formulas, denoted as (2), (3), and (4), represent the generation methods for boundary and interior reference points. Formula (4) represents the union of newly generated boundary and interior reference points.

$$L_{edge} = \lambda_{edge} + M \cdot e_j, j \in \{1, 2, ..., M\} \tag{2}$$

$$L_{inside} = \lambda_{inside} + 1 \tag{3}$$

$$L_{edge} = L_{edge} \cup L_{inside} \tag{4}$$

In Formula (2), L_{edge} represents the newly generated boundary reference points, where λ_{edge} denotes a portion of the edge reference points from the previous weight vector set, e_j represents standard basis vectors, and M is the number of objective functions. In Formula (3), L_{inside} represents the newly generated interior reference points, where λ_{inside} denotes a portion of the interior reference points from the previous weight vector set, and the vector $\mathbf{1} = (1, 1, ..., 1)$.

The initial coordinates are $(0, 0, ..., 0)$, and the loop of Formulas (2)–(4) is repeated H times. Finally, the obtained vector L is uniformly divided by $M \times H$, resulting in normalized reference vectors.

ARSBX Population Generation Strategy

For solving rotating Pareto set problems, the NSGA-III method is insufficient. Therefore, we introduce the ARSBX (adaptive simulated binary crossover for rotated many-objective optimization) strategy to address rotating Pareto sets in population generation. Proposed by Pan et al. in 2021 [7], this method incorporates rotation characteristics into SBX (simulated binary crossover) and introduces an adaptive selection strategy that uses both SBX and RSBX (simulated binary crossover for rotated many-objective optimization).

1) The core idea of the RSBX is to decouple the variables. The process is shown in Eq. (1):

$$\begin{cases} m = \frac{1}{N} \sum_{i=1}^{N} x_i \\ C_{i,j} = \frac{\sum_{k=1}^{D} (x_{i,k} - m_k)(x_{j,k} - m_k)}{N-1} \end{cases} \tag{5}$$

where, m is the mean vector; x_i is the decision vector of the ith individual; $x_{i,k}$ and m_k are the kth element of x_i and m, respectively; C is the covariance.

Moreover, according to the eigen-decomposition $Cv_i = \lambda_i v_i$, eigenvectors $v_1, ..., v_D$ of C can be get. Ultimately, using vector $V = [v_1, ..., v_D] (V \in R^{D \times D})$ and m, the generated offspring can be transformed back to the original position and orientation of the parent. Specifically represented by $O = V^{-1} O + m$, where O is decision vectors of offspring solutions and V^{-1} is the inverse matrix of V.

2) The introduction of adaptive operations aims to balance SBX and RSBX. While SBX performs adequately for rotation problems, it excels in many many-objective problems. However, RSBX may lead to slower convergence rates for these problems. Hence, to balance the convergence rates between rotation and non-rotation problems, adaptive operations are introduced.

Let the probabilities of generating populations with SBX and RSBX correspond to p_s and $1 - p_s$, respectively, with initial values set to 0.5 and updated every generation. The calculation formula for PS is given by Eq. (2):

$$\begin{cases} p_s = \frac{1}{1+\exp(-kq)} \\ q = (\frac{N_o^{(g)}+1}{N_r^{(g)}+N_o^{(g)}+2} - 0.5) * \frac{g}{g_{max}} \end{cases} \quad (6)$$

where, $k = M\sqrt{D}$; $N_o^{(g)}$ and $N_r^{(g)}$ are the number of offspring solutions generated by SBX and RSBX respectively, that survive from generation g; g_{max} is the maximum iterations.

2.3 GRU

Gate Recurrent Unit (GRU) [8] is a type of Recurrent Neural Network(RNN) that is widely used in the field of time series prediction. It incorporates update gate z and reset gate r to control information flow, with the calculation formulas shown in Eq. (7).

$$\begin{cases} z_t = \sigma(W_z x_t + U_z h_{t-1} + b_z) \\ r_t = \sigma(W_r x_t + U_r h_{t-1} + b_r) \\ h_t = z_t \odot h_{t-1} + (1 - z_t) \odot \hat{h}_t \\ \hat{h}_t = \tanh(W_h x_t + U_h(r_t \odot h_{t-1}) + b_h) \end{cases} \quad (7)$$

where, $\odot$ is vector element multiplication, h_t and $\hat{h}_t$ are the output and candidate status in t^{th} moment; z_t and r_t are status of update gate and reset gate in the tth moment; W_* and U_* are adjustable parameters and b_* is the bias.

2.4 Objective Function

In this paper, we selected four functions as our objective functions: CC (the computational complexity), RMSE (Root Mean Square Error) [9], NSE (Nash-Sutcliffe Efficiency) [10], and CORR (Correlation coefficient) [11]. Their calculations are shown in Eqs. (8) to (11).

$$CC = D_{input} + D_{input} \times Neu_1 + Neu_1 \times Neu_2 + Neu_2 \times D_{output} \quad (8)$$

$$RMSE = \sqrt{\frac{\sum_{t=1}^{N}(P_t - A_t)^2}{N}} \quad (9)$$

$$NSE = 1 - \frac{\sum_{t=1}^{N}(A_t - P_t)^2}{\sum_{t=1}^{N}(A_t - \overline{A})^2} \qquad (10)$$

$$CORR = \frac{\sum_{i=1}^{N}(A_t - \overline{A})(P_t - \overline{P})}{\sqrt{\sum_{i=1}^{N}(A_t - \overline{A})^2(P_t - \overline{P})^2}} \qquad (11)$$

In Eq. (8), D_{input} is the dimensionality of input, Neu_1 is the neuro number in the first layer, Neu_2 is the neuro number in the second layer, D_{output} is the dimensionality of output. In Eqs. (9) to (11), A_t means observed value, P_t is the predicted value, N is the number of samples, $\overline{A}$ is the average value of observed values.

2.5 Manyobj-GRU

This paper introduces the Manyobj-GRU temporal network model, depicted in Fig. 2. The process is as follows: Firstly, build a double-layer GRU neural network and identify adjustable hyperparameters. Secondly, create the ARSBX-ILD-NSGA-III many-objective optimization algorithm and initialize it. Next, we determine the CC, RMSE, NSE, and CORR as the objective functions to tune the two-layer GRU model. Lastly, choose suitable parameters (Fig. 3).

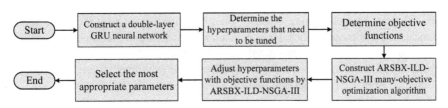

Fig. 3. Flowchart of ARSBX-ILD-NSGA-III

3 Experimental Details

3.1 Application Background

The Murray River is the longest river in Australia [12], stretching 2,575 km, but its ecological environment is concerning, with frequent blue-green algae blooms. To address this, we selected three sites along the Murray River from 1994 to 2017 to perform weekly sampling of four environmental variables (water flow, water velocity, water temperature, and salinity) and blue-green algae concentration. The data dimension for each site is [1248, 5].

3.2 Manyobj-GRU Model for Cyanobacterial Concentration Prediction

This paper proposes a time series prediction model for cyanobacterial concentration using a many-objective algorithm based on a deep learning network. This model aims to accurately predict the concentration of cyanobacteria for the next time step using historical data. Here is the process: Firstly, five variables are individually input into a three-layer wavelet transform, and their decomposed results are integrated into four components: $d1_{all}$, $d2_{all}$, $d3_{all}$, and $a1_{all}$. Then, the decomposed results are split into training and testing sets. We use data from the first 24 years as the training set and the last 3 years as the testing set. Next, the training set is fed into Manyobj-GRU for training and hyperparameter optimization, followed by testing the model with the testing set. The test results are saved, and subjected to non-dominated sorting, and the corresponding superior hyperparameters are stored. Finally, a set of parameters is selected from the saved hyperparameters population for the final presentation of GRU results.

In this paper, we developed our predictive model using a 64-bit Windows 10 operating system, 8 GB of RAM, and MATLAB 2018B as the programming environment. In manyobj-GRU, we optimized neuron counts and the learning rate of the two-layer GRU model using a population size of 10 over 15 iterations. The optimized model was then used for time series prediction.

4 Results and Discussions

4.1 Comparative Experiment Results in Three Sites

We compared it with baseline models like GRU and Wavelet-GRU (GRU sequentially predicts the data obtained from wavelet decomposition), all being two-layer networks with 100 neurons each. Figure 4 shows the prediction results of three sites, Table 2 summarizes the average metrics. It is worth noting that although four objective functions were used for parameter optimization, we only selected RMSE, NSE, and CORR as evaluation indexes when comparing the quality of the experimental models, similar to the standard time series model comparison experiments.

4.2 Comparative Experiment Results in Three Sites

From Table 2, we can see that the Manyobj-GRU model achieves the best prediction results in all three regions, demonstrating its general applicability. Additionally, compared to the GRU and Wavelet-GRU models, the average performance improvements across the three regions are: 79.9% and 39.5% in RMSE, 296.7% and 5.54% in NSE, and 84.6% and 2.6% in CORR, proving the superiority of our model.

From Fig. 4, we can also observe that decomposing complex data using wavelet transform and then making targeted predictions on the decomposed data yields significantly better results than directly predicting the original data. Furthermore, as shown in Table 2, we can see that using optimization algorithms for targeted parameter adjustment results in better outcomes compared to using preset parameters.

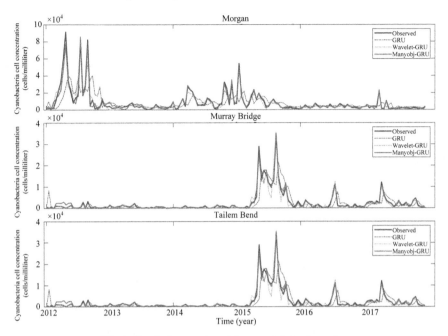

Fig.4. Prediction results of four models in three sites

Table 2. Summary of Metrics for the Three Models

Site / Models	GRU	Wavelet-GRU	Manyobj-GRU
In Morgan			
RMSE	12518	4277	2721
NSE	0.2126	0.9081	0.9628
CORR	0.4691	0.9582	0.9835
In Murray Bridge			
RMSE	3563	4277	672
NSE	0.2126	0.4182	0.9693
CORR	0.4691	0.6740	0.9897
In Tailem Bend			
RMSE	2400	695	470
NSE	0.1926	0.9322	0.9690
CORR	0.4999	0.9677	0.9859

4.3 Limitations and Further Research

Due to constraints on computational resources, our study utilized a relatively small population size and a limited number of iterations to derive the model parameters. While this approach allowed us to conduct the analysis within the available resources, it is important to acknowledge that the outcomes might be further refined and potentially improved with the application of a larger population size and an increased number of iterations. Future research could explore this by expanding these parameters to assess the impact on the model's accuracy and robustness, which could provide deeper insights and more reliable results.

5 Conclusions

This paper proposes a time series prediction model for cyanobacterial concentration using a many-objective algorithm based on a deep learning network. First, the complex cyanobacteria concentration time series data is decomposed, and each decomposed result is fed into a two-layer GRU, whose parameters have been tuned by a many-objective optimization algorithm, for prediction. The final time series prediction result is obtained by summing all the predicted results.

We tested the proposed model in three regions and found that it performed well, demonstrating its general applicability and versatility. Additionally, we compared the proposed model with two other models and found that our model performed the best. The average performance improvements across the three regions compared to the GRU and Wavelet-GRU models were: 79.9% and 39.5% in RMSE, 296.7% and 5.54% in NSE, and 84.6% and 2.6% in CORR, respectively, proving the superiority of our model.

However, due to computational resource constraints, there is still room for improvement in our model.

References

1. Paerl, H.W., Otten, T.G.: Harmful cyanobacterial blooms: causes, consequences, and controls. Microb. Ecol. **65**, 995–1010 (2013)
2. Batool, U., Tromas, N., Simon, D.F., Sauvé, S., Shapiro, B.J., Ahmed, M.: Snapshot of cyanobacterial toxins in Pakistani freshwater bodies. Environ. Sci. Pollut. Res. (2024)
3. Xia, J.J., Zeng, J.: Early warning of algal blooms based on the optimization support vector machine regression in a typical tributary bay of the Three Gorges Reservoir, China. Environ. Geochem. Health **44**, 4719–4733 (2022)
4. Majidi, N., Heidari, A., Fatehi, A., Heidarzadeh, H.: Estimation of earthquake frequency content and its effect on dynamic analysis using continuous and discrete wavelet transform. Scientia Iranica **29**, 2773–2788 (2022)
5. Deb, K., Jain, H.: An evolutionary many-objective optimization algorithm using reference-point-based nondominated sorting approach, Part I: solving problems with box constraints. IEEE Trans. Evol. Comput. **18**, 577–601 (2014)
6. Takagi, T., Takadama, K., Sato, H.: Incremental lattice design of weight vector set. In: Proceedings of the 2020 Genetic and Evolutionary Computation Conference Companion, pp. 1486–1494 (2020)

7. Pan, L.Q., Xu, W.T., Li, L.H., He, C., Cheng, R.: Adaptive simulated binary crossover for rotated multi-objective optimization. Swarm Evol. Comput. **60** (2024)
8. Fantini, D.G., Silva, R.N., Siqueira, M.B.B., Pinto, M.S.S., Guimaraes, M., Brasil, Jr., A.C.P.: Wind speed short-term prediction using recurrent neural network GRU model and stationary wavelet transform GRU hybrid model. Energ. Convers. Manage. **308** (2024)
9. Zhou, H.B., et al.: Low-complexity double-vector model predictive control with minimum root mean square error for three-phase three-level inverters. IEEE J. Emerg. Sel. Top. Power Electron. **11**, 5809–5819 (2023)
10. Mathevet, T., Le Moine, N., Andréassian, V., Gupta, H., Oudin, L.: Multi-objective assessment of hydrological model performances using Nash-Sutcliffe and Kling-Gupta efficiencies on a worldwide large sample of watersheds. C.R. Geosci. **355**, 117–141 (2023)
11. Chicco, D., Warrens, M.J., Jurman, G.: The coefficient of determination R-squared is more informative than SMAPE, MAE, MAPE, MSE and RMSE in regression analysis evaluation. Peer J. Comput. Sci., 24 (2021)
12. Bargrizan, S., Biswas, T.K., Joehnk, K.D., Mosley, L.M.: Sustained high CO2 concentrations and fluxes from Australia's largest river system. Mar. Freshw. Res. **73**, 540–551 (2022)

Research and Application of Key Technology of "One-Click Opening and Closing" of Hydropower Station Gate Based on Intelligent Portal Crane

Hailong Zhang[✉], Jin Yang, Hui Zeng, Xiaoxiang Wei, Wu Zhou, Wen Liu, Haiwei Lei, and Jun Chen

China Yangtze Power Co., Ltd. (CYPC), Yichang 443002, China
zhang_hailong@ctg.com

Abstract. Under the background of carbon peaking and carbon neutrality, the application of intelligent technology in the field of hydropower station operation and maintenance has received wide attention from the industry. In order to meet this challenge, this work proposed a key technology based on intelligent portal crane of hydropower station gates "one key opening and closing". In this work, we took the traditional gantry crane as the research object, and implemented the intelligent crane generalised system and personalised system modification to achieve the purpose of one-click opening and closing of the gates, reduction of personnel operation and hot standby control system for 7×24 h. This innovation not only improves the safety and operational efficiency of the gate opening and closing,operations of the hydropower plant, but also provides a new solution to the problem of preventing the escape of hydroelectric power plant turbine units, and significantly improves the intrinsic safety level of the hydroelectric power plant to prevent flooding of the plant.

Keywords: Intellectualise · Crane · one-click opening and closing

1 Introduction

Currently, most of the portal cranes in hydropower stations are still controlled manually by the traditional driver, which is complicated to operate and has poor safety performance, which affects the operation efficiency to a certain extent and may cause safety accidents. With the expansion of the scale of hydropower plants and the improvement of operation standards, the traditional portal crane has been difficult to meet the pursuit of high efficiency, safety and environmental protection in modern hydropower plants. Therefore, the research and development of an intelligent portal crane with intelligent, efficient and safe performance, and based on the intelligent portal crane to achieve the hydroelectric power station gate "one key opening and closing" has become an urgent need for the transformation of hydroelectric power station equipment.

Riverbed hydropower stations are mostly constructed in the middle and lower reaches of rivers with a wider river surface and smaller specific drop. Because of the low head and relatively large flow rate of this kind of hydropower station, only maintenance gates and accident gates are usually set up, and when there are reliable anti-runaway devices, it is not necessary to set up fast gates. The rapid development of artificial intelligence technology provides higher requirements and more possibilities for the design and construction of hydropower plants, promotes the safety, environmental protection, intelligence and adaptability of hydropower plants, and pushes the hydropower industry to develop in a more sustainable and efficient direction.

Relying on a hydropower station gantry crane intelligent transformation project, the project team carries out the research and application of the key technology of "one-click opening and closing" intelligent gantry cranes, aiming to improve the operational efficiency and safety of hydropower stations, reducing energy consumption and maintenance costs, promoting the intelligent upgrading of hydropower station equipment, and improving the technical level of hydropower stations.

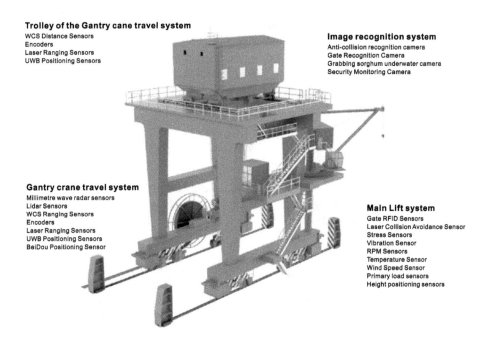

Fig. 1. Intelligent Portal Crane Sensing System

2 Current Status of Research

2.1 Anti-Fig:Vector-Imagerunaway Technology for Hydraulic Turbine Units

Runaway refers to the unit load dumping (or tripping) due to some kind of accident, and at this time, the speed control system refuses to operate, the water guide mechanism can not cut off the water flow, resulting in the unit from the rated speed up to the runaway speed operation. Prolonged runaway may cause damage to the unit resulting in a runaway accident.

According to the current standard, when the unit has effective anti-flight measures, the design of the accident door of the water inlet can be relatively simplified. Many low-head, high-flow, rotating-propeller units, such as the Fuchun River Power Station in Zhejiang and the Xijin Power Station in Guangxi, are mainly equipped with maintenance gates and accident gates. For these hydropower stations, the hydroelectric generating units are undoubtedly their core equipment, so the importance of runaway protection is self-evident.

At present, there is no uniform standard for the design of hydroelectric power plants to prevent flooding plant and gate flooding prevention technology, and there is a relative lack of relevant research. In this work, in order to cope with the challenges of the "post-hydropower era", the intelligent transformation of hydroelectric power station inlet gate opening and closing equipment is particularly critical. This transformation can not only improve the flood prevention capacity of the power station, reduce the loss of flooded plant, but also provide a strong guarantee for the safe and stable operation of the hydropower station [1].

2.2 Intelligent Sensing Technology

The monitoring of the crane's own state, working conditions and the surrounding environment is not only the basis for the realisation of intelligent and safe operation of cranes, but also the key to the application of a variety of advanced information technologies such as IoT, AI, digital twins and so on in the crane operating site [2].

As can be seen from the literature, many scholars are committed to how to integrate single-point or multi-source data to achieve the overall structural safety of cranes, dynamic operation safety and other high-level needs of intelligent perception. As far as the overall structural safety of cranes is concerned, Yan Yuchen established a tower cap tilt model, and achieved classification and identification of working conditions through monitoring data and the use of support vector machines [3]. These studies provide important technical support for crane structural safety.

In terms of dynamic operation safety, researchers have also proposed several innovative solutions. For example, the tower crane group operation monitoring system, through the sensor monitoring and Zigbee network to achieve the movement trajectory mapping of the tower group, to reduce the probability of collision to provide an effective means; ultrasonic technology-based collision monitoring methods and other methods to further enhance the safety of the tower crane in the dynamic operation.

In addition, for the problems such as crane driver operation errors, researchers have proposed a series of solutions, such as the full-situational safety risk perception system and visual camera tower crane operation activity monitoring method, which provides important support for improving the safety awareness of the operating driver and operational efficiency.

In summary, the application of intelligent perception in the field of cranes has great prospects. By integrating a variety of advanced technologies and research results, we can better realise the intelligent operation and safety management of cranes, and inject new vitality and power into the development of the engineering construction field. It is hoped that more research will continue to focus on and deepen this field in the future, and will make greater contributions to improving the safety and efficiency of crane operations.

2.3 Intelligent Planning Technology

Crane intelligent planning technology is one of the key core technologies to realise the intelligent operation of gantry machines, which involves the intelligent planning of gantry machine task sequences and operation paths, and is of great significance for cranes to complete operation tasks in complex and dynamic environments. In the literature and related materials, researchers have explored and improved crane intelligent planning technology in various [4–7].

In terms of task planning, the research focuses on the goal of crane automation and intelligent operation, and emphasises the importance of crane loading and unloading sequence optimisation and automatic generation. Different scholars such as Zhang Wenxia and Li Guojie proposed a research method based on a genetic algorithm to optimise the container loading and unloading sequence and limit the handling distance to improve the operation efficiency. Their research provides an effective method for the generation and optimisation of crane loading and unloading operation sequence.

In terms of path planning, researchers have explored various methods such as ant colony algorithm, neural network combined with sliding mode control, and genetic algorithm for crane handling path planning. Different scholars have designed various algorithms and strategies including simplified configuration space, bidirectional fast random search tree, improved RRT* strategy, etc. to improve the quality and success rate of the planned paths. Their work are dedicated to achieving real-time motion replanning and collision avoidance for crane paths in dynamic environments.

In addition, some researchers performed collision detection through multilayer depth images and proposed a planning method based on a master-slave parallel genetic algorithm to improve the path quality. There are also scholars who have studied the efficiency of lifting planning for mobile cranes, redefined the path planning problem and proposed intelligent planning methods. In addition, some research focuses on intelligent crane path planning and automatic generation methods based on experience learning, so that cranes can carry out independent analysis and judgement and autonomous decision-making by digitising and stereotyping the operating processes and rules of skilled drivers.

In summary,intelligent planning technology for cranes plays an important role in the intelligent operation of gantry machines, and related research covers task planning and path planning, etc., and continuously explores new methods and strategies, with the aim of improving the efficiency and safety of crane operation and promoting the development of intelligence for crane machines.

2.4 Intelligent Control Technology

Crane intelligent control technology has become one of the important technologies to achieve intelligent crane operation. This work reviews the application and research progress of control strategies based on particle swarm optimisation algorithm, fuzzy algorithm and neural network in the field of crane control.

The particle swarm optimisation algorithm and the fuzzy algorithm, as classical artificial intelligence algorithms, show excellent performance in crane control. Scholars use these algorithms to search for the optimal control parameters and achieve the rapid sway elimination control of cranes. For example, PID controllers, LQR controllers, and input shapers based on particle swarm algorithm tuning parameter, as well as self-resilient controllers and PID controllers based on Takagi-Sugeno fuzzy algorithm. These methods provide important ideas for improving crane control performance.

In recent years, artificial intelligence technology based on neural networks has been widely used. Many scholars use the learning and prediction ability of neural networks to adjust the classical controller parameters to achieve precise positioning of the crane weight and residual swing angle suppression. By approximating the unknown dynamics or parameters of the system through neural networks and designing the weight update method based on the Lyapunov method, the control effect of online real-time adjustment of weight parameters and ensuring system stability can be achieved. For example, sliding mode controller based on RBF neural network, adaptive controller based on neural network and other methods have been successfully applied on container mobile port and mast crane.

Methods combining the sliding mode controller and the neural network also show good control effect, which can achieve the compensation of unknown disturbances and the assurance of system stability. These researchers verified the method of using neural networks to estimate the unknown friction force online and designing online neural network weight update law through model experiments, which showed better control effects and improved the control performance of cranes.

Overall, the research on the application of particle swarm optimisation algorithms, fuzzy algorithms and neural networks in the intelligent control of cranes demonstrates the potential in improving crane control performance, achieving precise positioning and suppressing pendulum angle, and provides useful references and insights for future research in the field of intelligent control of cranes.

3 Intelligent Crane Generalised System Design

Intelligent cranes, as a core component of "Made in China 2025" and other national development strategies, are devices that integrate sensors, intelligent decision-making software and cranes. This kind of crane has a number of capabilities such as intelligent perception, data analysis, optimised decision-making, adaptive control, self-assessment and self-diagnosis, information sharing and universal network interconnection, and is a representative of high-performance lifting machinery. Intelligent cranes are developed on the basis of traditional cranes and automated cranes, and their universal systems include, but are not limited to, the following points [8–10].

3.1 Space Positioning System

At present, there are two types of commonly used positioning methods: one is relative addressing, such as rotary encoders, laser or radar ranging, visual recognition, etc. the other type is absolute addressing, such as limit switches, coding cable (Graeme line), linear encoder, BPS barcode, sprocket chain, and real-time absolute addressing of the radio, infrared, radio frequency, GPS and other parties. Due to the crane's large operating range, a single positioning method is difficult to achieve the required positioning accuracy, so the precise positioning of large areas, complex environments often use "relative convergence addressing , absolute positioning and addressing" of the integrated positioning technology.

3.2 Crane Anti-sway System

Crane anti-swing control refers to the crane lifting objects, through the control of the crane's action, to avoid the hook and the lifting object to produce swing, so as to improve the safety and efficiency of lifting. The control method usually includes two kinds of open-loop control and closed-loop control. Open-loop control can control the crane's action through the pre-calculated trajectory and speed of the hook to reduce or avoid swing. Commonly, there are predictive control based on mathematical models, time sequence control, control based on tables or charts, based on experimental results or experience and manual control. The advantage of open-loop control is that it is simple to implement and less expensive, but it is less robust to changes in system parameters and external disturbances, making it difficult to cope with complex changes in working conditions. Closed-loop control can monitor the motion status of the hook and the portal crane in real time by installing devices such as acceleration sensors or tilt sensors, and then adjust the crane in real time through the control algorithm to suppress the swing. Commonly, there are proportional-integral-derivative (PID) control, fuzzy logic control, adaptive control and predictive control. The advantage of closed-loop control is that it can more accurately respond to changes in system parameters and external interference, and improve control accuracy and stability, but the system is complex and costly.

3.3 Route Planning System

Path planning for intelligent cranes refers to planning a safe and collision-free path from the starting point to the end point based on evaluation criteria according to the environmental information obtained by the vision system or sensors, which requires comprehensive consideration of multiple factors such as the environment, safety, and efficiency. In recent years, the application of artificial intelligence technologies such as deep learning and machine learning has greatly improved the path planning technology. Such as genetic algorithms, simulated annealing algorithms, ant colony algorithms, etc., can improve the efficiency and accuracy of path planning. However, there are still some challenges and problems, for example how to deal with complex operating environments, how to improve the real-time and robustness of path planning, and how to reduce the error and improve the accuracy etc. In the future, with the continuous progress of technology and the continuous expansion of application scenarios, the path planning technology of intelligent cranes will be continuously optimised and improved to provide strong support for achieving more efficient and safer lifting operations!

3.4 Crane Identification and Gripping System

Lift identification and gripping technology is one of the very important technologies in intelligent cranes, and it is also one of the key technologies to achieve automation and intelligent lifting. This technology mainly involves the following aspects. Lift identification, take pictures or scan the lifting objects, and then use image processing and recognition algorithms to extract and classify the features of the lifting objects, in order to determine the type, size, weight and other information of the lifting objects; lifting object positioning, using GPS, LIDAR, ultrasonic and other technologies, to achieve accurate positioning and tracking of the lifting objects; grasping strategy, according to the type, size, weight and other information of the lifting objects, to formulate the corresponding grasping strategies and operation procedures according to the type, size, weight and other information of the lifting objects, to ensure the safety and stability of the lifting objects.

3.5 Security Monitoring and Remote Service System

Safety monitoring and remote service technology is an important part of intelligent cranes, mainly used to improve the safety, reliability and maintenance of equipment. Safety monitoring technology is used to monitor the operating status of the crane in real time, as well as to identify and warn of potential safety hazards. Remote service technology allows remote experts to provide fault diagnosis and maintenance guidance for lifting machinery. Through the Internet or wireless networks, operators can send the operating data and fault information of a crane to a remote service centre. Experts at the remote service centre can then analyse the data received and provide appropriate troubleshooting and maintenance advice. This helps to reduce downtime and improve equipment utilisation and maintenance efficiency.

4 Design of "One-Click Opening and Closing" Intelligent Portal Crane System

Universal system is the basic conditions that intelligent cranes should have, personalised systems and capabilities often determine the competitiveness and creativity of intelligent products. In the hydropower station gate opening and closing operations, the gantry crane (hereinafter referred to as "portal crane"), generally responsible for the opening and closing of multiple gates, also known as mobile opener. A hydroelectric power station intelligent portal crane should be in the strong wind, water flow, foreign body intrusion, dynamic obstacles and other external factors interference, autonomous planning, autonomous implementation and adaptive adjustment of gate opening and closing operations, to ensure high reliability.

Remote Intelligent Control Layer	Task management ——Inforation visualisation ——Multimodal interaction——Awareness recognition ——Assisted operations					
Integrated Processing Layer	**Basic systems:** automated control systems, remote monitoring systems, data acquisition and processing systems, fault warning and maintenance systems, database and management systems					
	Dedicated systems: walking intelligent positioning system, intelligent identification and collision avoidance system, automatic locking system for gates, anti-shaking and automatic pinning system for gripping sorghum, early warning system for crossing the line, comprehensive determination system for gates in place, and safety protection system.					
Intelligen Perception Layer	Millimetre wave radar sensors Lidar Sensors WCS Ranging Sensors Encoders Laser Ranging Sensors UWB Positioning Sensors BeiDou Positioning Sensor	WCS Distance Sensors Encoders Laser Ranging Sensors UWB Positioning Sensors	Gate RFID Sensors Laser Collision Avoidance Sensor Stress Sensors Vibration Sensor RPM Sensors Temperature Sensor Wind Speed Sensor Primary load sensors Height positioning sensors	Anti-collision recognition camera Gate Recognition Camera Grabbing sorghum underwater camera Security Monitoring Camera		
Local Control Layer	Main Operating Console, Local master control display, In-place control mainframe, PLC Mastere					
	PLC Substation for Gantry crane Data Switch Inverter Relays Contactor	Trolley PLC Substation Data Switch Trolley Inverter Relays Contactor	Main Lift PLC Substation Data switch Main hoist inverter	Rotary PLC Substation Data switches Rotary hoist inverters	Reel PLC Substation Data switch	
Action mechanism layer	gantry crane Motor Brake for gantry crane Windproof iron wedge for gantry crane Windproof ground anchor for gantry crane gantry crane warning light Mechanical Limit Position Switch	Trolley Motors Trolley Brake Trolley Limit Position Switch	Main Lifting Motor Main Lift Brake Underwater camera Underwater switches Grab beam positioning pins Gripper pump station Automatic locking Lifting Mechanism Limit Position Switch	Lifting motors Lifting brakes Slewing motors Slewing brake Lift height limit Slewing echanical Limit Position Switch	Intelligent Cable Reels	
	Gantry crane travel, WindproofSystem,	Trolley of the Gantry cane travel	Main Lift, Grab Sorghum, Lockingr	Rotation of Portal Cranee	Cable reel.	

Fig. 2. Key technology architecture of 'one-click opening and closing' intelligent ortal crane

4.1 Technology Architecture

Combined with the general technology of intelligent cranes and the actual business needs, the implementation of the hydropower station gate one-click opening and closing' intelligent portal cranes should at least include the following key technologies: walking intelligent positioning system, intelligent identification and collision avoidance system, automatic locking system for gates, anti-shaking and automatic pinning system for gripping sorghum and so on. The automation system upgrade of No.1 portal crane at the dam top of a hydropower station, on the basis of retaining the metal structure and mechanical drive mechanism of the original equipment, based on the gate lifting and lowering process for the design, transformation into a friendly human-machine interface, with perception, planning, execution, collaboration, learning, data and information management functions such as intelligent portal crane. Key technology architecture of one-click opening and closing' intelligent ortal crane , as show in Fig. 2.

4.2 Basic Systems

Automation Control System: automation control and operation of the portal crane is realised through the automation control system, including controllers, actuators and sensor components: opening/closing, speed adjustment and position control of the portal crane are realised.

Remote Monitoring System: remote monitoring and operation of the portal crane is realised through remote monitoring system and internet communication, including remote monitoring software and network communication equipment, so that the operation and maintenance personnel can monitor the running status, parameters and alarm information of the portal crane at any time and any place through mobile phones and computer terminal equipment.

Data Acquisition and Processing System: Real-time acquisition of status information of the portal crane through sensors and monitoring equipment, including opening degree, water level and flow data; the data acquisition and processing system is responsible for processing, storing and analysing the acquired data, providing real-time data and historical data analysis for the operation and maintenance personnel.

Failure Warning and Maintenance System: Failure warning and maintenance management is achieved through sensors and data analysis. Through this system, the operating status of the portal crane is monitored in real time, and once an abnormality or failure is found, an alarm will be sent to the operation and maintenance personnel, and corresponding maintenance guidance and fault diagnosis will be provided.

Database and Management System: the system need to establish a portal crane library to store and manage the relevant information of the portal cranes, including the model, parameters and operation records of the portal cranes; the database and management system is responsible for the establishment, maintenance and query of the portal crane library, so as to enable the operation and maintenance personnel to carry out the management of the portal cranes and data analysis.

4.3 Dedicated Systems

Intelligent Positioning System for Portal Crane Travelling: Setting up a set of "coarse positioning + precise positioning + feedback positioning + redundant positioning" flexible portal crane travelling automatic positioning system, which is a flexible portal crane travelling automatic positioning system consisting of coarse positioning system, precise positioning system, feedback positioning system and redundant positioning system, and can be applied to the on-site working environment, It can meet the requirements of positioning accuracy.

Intelligent Identification and Collision Avoidance System of the Portal Crane: including image recognition system, laser scanning system and radar system, the system can independently find and identify the obstacles, misplaced vehicles or people that may affect the normal operation of the portal crane, and according to the emergency situation to make acoustic and visual warnings, deceleration, or even stop the operation of the measures to ensure the safety of the portal crane and the surroundings; Image Recognition System: through the installation of cameras or laser scanners and other visual sensors, to detect the portal crane surroundings. Image recognition system: By installing cameras or laser scanners and other visual sensors, it carries out real-time monitoring and image recognition of the environment around the portal crane. Using image processing and machine learning algorithms, it can identify and classify obstacles, vehicles, people, etc., and judge their distance and relative position to the portal crane.

Gate Automatic Locking System: automatic locking of the rise and fall should be efficiently linked with the gate rise and fall operation, without the need for personnel assistance, the control equipment through the rapid interface docking to complete the automatic control process. Automatic locking mechanical emergency action mechanism, in the linkage system fails to manually complete the operation.

Grab Beam Anti-Shaking and Automatic Pin-Through System: the use of frequency converter control to complete the anti-shaking control, in the big car, trolley frequency converter to open the crane anti-shaking control program and on-site optimisation and debugging of the mathematical model parameters, to reduce the load occurs unnecessarily swinging.

Image Recognition System is able to realise the over-the-line early warning system: combined with the current operational tasks, manually or autonomously delineate the virtual safe operation area, and automatically warn when there are personnel, vehicles, etc. mistakenly enter the operation site.

Comprehensive Judgement System for Gate Positioning: after each lifting/falling operation, the system should integrate the three-dimensional coordinate position of the hook (gripping beam) and the real-time image of the gate and the gate groove to comprehensively judge whether "the gate has been opened" or "the gate has been closed", and save the real-time photos and relevant parameters of the beginning and the end of the operation. Comparison photos and related parameters are saved.

The Portal Crane Safety Protection System can realize vibration monitoring of the transmission motor and reducer, give the monitoring points of the key parts of the transmission according to the modelling analysis of the equipment manufacturing structure, and carry out on-line monitoring and analysis of the key points, and through the statistics of the vibration signals of the various phases, it can initially and quickly determine the health status of the monitoring object, and realize simple, fast and accurate diagnosis. When the equipment is in an abnormal state, the system automatically analyses and judges the monitoring point failure type in time, and provides predictive maintenance alarm prompts.

5 Key Process Control of "One-Click Opening and Closing" of Hydroelectric Power Station Gates

5.1 Flexible Travelling Automatic Positioning System

A hydropower station portal crane is usually responsible for the opening and closing operations of multiple gates, and the weight of a single gate may be in dozens of tonnes, while the gap between the gate and the gate slot is only about 2 cm. When the intelligent portal crane operates autonomously, the repetitive positioning accuracy has to reach the millimetre level, and once the positioning error exceeds the permissible range, it may cause collision accidents or even affect the operation safety of the hydropower unit. Procedure for automatic gate closure as show in Fig. 3.

To solve this problem, a set of flexible portal crane travelling automatic positioning system is designed. The system combines the combined use of coarse positioning, precise positioning, feedback positioning and redundant positioning to achieve accurate positioning of the portal crane. The coarse positioning mainly relies on the encoder and inertial navigation system for preliminary estimation; the precise positioning relies on the visual positioning system, which obtains the precise position and attitude information of the gantry relative to the reference point through the perception and identification of the environment

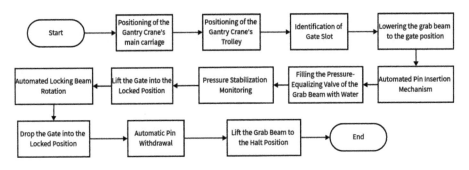

Fig. 3. Procedure for Automatic Gate Closure

around the gantry; the feedback positioning monitors and feeds back the travelling distance, speed and direction of the gantry in real time; and the redundant positioning introduces a variety of positioning technologies, such as satellite positioning, wireless signal positioning and redundant positioning introduces various positioning technologies, such as satellite positioning, wireless signal positioning and ultrasonic positioning, etc., and improves the reliability and accuracy of positioning through fusion processing.

In addition, a set of precise positioning control method for large-inertia gantry is designed. The method adopts a velocity closed-loop control strategy with progressive fast operation in the acceleration phase and slow operation based on an S-shaped curve in the deceleration phase. The speed planning strategy is matched with the position target. When approaching the target position, the system quickly adjusts and realises full closed-loop motion control of the motor in the current, position and speed loops. This facilitates precise control of the end actuator of the portal crane and improves operational stability even under heavy loads.

5.2 Autonomous Identification System for Gate Position Variations

The traditional manual recording of gate positional variations may result in incomplete records, which is not conducive to the full life cycle management and maintenance of the gate. In order to realise the "one-click opening and closing" of the gate, it is necessary to solve the problem of autonomous identification and recording of the opening and closing status of the gate.

To this end, a YOLO-based automatic identification method for hydroelectric power station gates is developed [11]. As shown in Fig. 4, which operates sequentially through the steps of locating the gate, locating the gate number plate and identifying the gate number. Firstly, a deep learning-based target detection model YOLO is used to locate the gate target in the real-time video and crop out the gate image. The, YOLO is used to locate and crop the number plate image in the intercepted gate image, and finally, the number plate image is input into a convolutional neural network-based character recognition model to obtain the actual content represented by the number plate and record

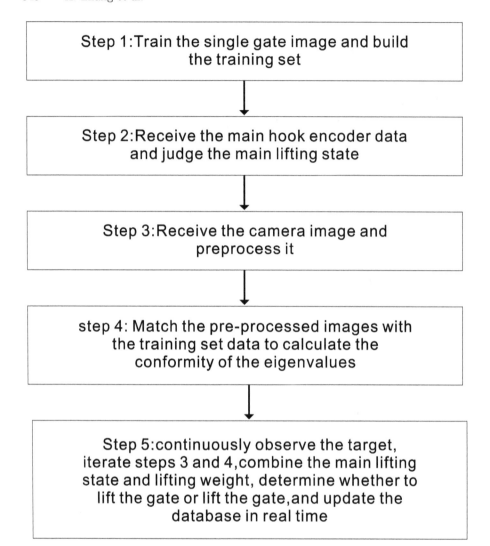

Fig. 4. Gate identification flow chart

it. This method makes comprehensive use of image processing technology and deep learning technology to achieve real-time dynamic and accurate identification of hydropower station gates, which lays a technical foundation for the digital management of hydropower station metal equipment.

5.3 Real-Time Sensing System for Gate Opening and Closing Status

The operation state perception of the gate after entering the water is the most critical link to realise the "one-click opening and closing" of the gate of the hydropower station. At present, the means of judgement of gate status in the industry mainly include marking on the cable of the gripping beam, installing a camera under high and clear water on the gripping beam of the opener and installing an encoder on the opener, etc. However, these methods have certain limitations, such as being greatly affected by light and clarity, and being unable to accurately reflect the true position of the gate.

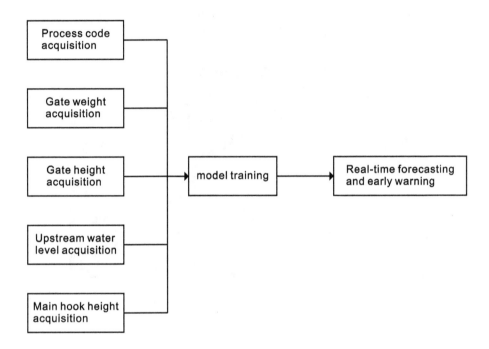

Fig. 5. Flow chart of gate opening and closing state prediction

In order to solve these problems, a real-time early warning method and device for gate opening and closing status based on TCN neural network was developed [12], which is shown in Fig. 5. The method realises real-time judgement of the gate status and early warning of abnormal situations by constructing a model, collecting relevant parameters and predicting the change of the main hook weight when the opener carries out gate opening and closing operations. Firstly, the whole process parameters affecting the state of the opening and closing gates in the normal operation process are acquired, and the input sequence is composed of the process code, gate weight, gate height, upstream water level and main hook height value, and the output sequence is composed of the main hook weight value. Then, the input and output sequences are used to train the prediction model of the main hook weight value based on the TCN neural network. Finally, the real-time comparison of the predicted value of the main hook weight with the difference between the measured value is carried out to realise the purpose of real-time warning of gate opening and closing status.

5.4 "One-Click Opening and Closing" Test

On 23 April 2024, the test of one-key open/close' of the inlet gate based on intelligent portal crane was successfully completed on the upstream dam surface of Unit 4 of a power station. After the operator gave the gate open/close command from the control platform, the intelligent portal crane completed 12 scheduled work processes by itself, such as travelling and positioning of the portal crane main carriage, and the total time consumed is more than 20 per cent less than manual operation.Screenshot of the test process as show in Fig. 6.

Fig. 6. Screenshot of the test process

6 Conclusions

A hydropower station faces the problem of tedious manual gate opening and closing work and potential safety hazards, and to solve this problem, an intelligent modification scheme is proposed and successfully applied. The intelligent portal crane integrates key technologies such as intelligent perception of human-machine environment, intelligent planning of portal crane "task-path-trajectory", intelligent anti-collision and anti-shaking control of portal crane, fault diagnosis of portal crane and safety situational awareness, and intelligent portal crane system control platform. By applying the intelligent portal crane to the inlet gate of hydropower station, it realises the function of "one-click opening and closing", and at the same time automatically updates the gate database. This not only makes up for the lack of fast gates in riverbed hydropower stations, but also improves the safety level of hydropower stations in preventing flooding of plants, and effectively improves the safety and maintenance management level of hydropower stations.

The promotion and application of intelligent portal crane in hydropower stations will help to promote the intelligent upgrading of metal structure equipment in hydropower stations, form a large unified "digital metal structure" system, and comprehensively improve the management level of metal structure equipment in hydropower stations.

References

1. Quanwei, W.: Research on the theory and application of health monitoring system of lifting machinery. Taiyuan University of Science and Technology [2024-05-21]
2. Li, P.: Introduction to Intelligent Manufacturing. Tsinghua University Press, Beijing (2021)
3. Yuqin, Y.A.N.: Tower crane steel structure health monitoring technology and experimental research. Shandong University (2011). https://doi.org/10.7666/d.y2045567
4. Huali, W., Jinhua, W., Xiuli. W.: PID controller parameter tuning based on improved particle swarm algorithm. In: Aeronautical Society of China. Aviation Society of China (2012)
5. Yao, W., Anhu, R., Yangyang. R.: Improved ant colony algorithm for UAV trajectory planning. Electro-Optics Control **04**, 43–48 (2024)
6. Qianwang, D., Likun, G., Zhengping, L., et al.: Crane lifting path planning based on multi-objective genetic algorithm. J. Hunan Univ. (Natural Science Edition), 2014(1). https://doi.org/10.3969/j.issn.1674-2974.2014.01.011.
7. Xuezhu, S., Xueliang, Z., Jinggang, Z., Zhimei .C.: Intelligent crane path planning and positioning anti-swing control strategy. Lifting Transp. Mach. **11**, 65–70 (2017)
8. Liu, W.S., Yue, W.S., Li, L.: Introduction to key technologies of intelligent cranes. Crane Transp. Mach. **09**, 57–59 (2017)
9. Guojie, L.: Key features of intelligent cranes and overall architecture of control system. J. Mech. Eng. **24**, 254–268 (2020)
10. Haogang, W.U., Yanhong, P.A.N., Chao, B.U.: Control system and key technology of intelligent crane. Lifting Transp. Mach. **05**, 69–72 (2018)
11. Hailong, Z., Yunhua, D., Gang, C., Hui, Z., Jian, L.: Automatic identification method of hydropower station gate based on YOLO. Hubei Province: CN115862021A [2023-03-28]
12. Zhang, H., et al.: Real-time early warning method and device for gate opening and closing status based on TCN neural network. Hubei Province: CN116579230A [2023-08-11]

Superior Performances of a Novel Soft Electroactive Actuator Based on High-Purity Single-Walled Carbon Nanotubes

Guangyao Hu[1,2], Weixing Feng[1,2], Nan Zhang[1,2], Longlong Wang[1,2], Dewen Niu[1,2], and Jie Ru[1,2(✉)]

[1] Key Laboratory of Green and Precise Synthetic Chemistry and Applications, Ministry of Education, Huaibei Normal University, Huaibei 235000, Anhui, China
rujie@chnu.edu.cn
[2] School of Chemistry and Materials Science, Huaibei Normal University, Huaibei 235000, Anhui, China

Abstract. Ionic electroactive polymer (iEAP) actuators have emerged as promising candidates for the advancement of artificial muscles, exhibiting great potential in applications within bionic robotics, space exploration, and the biomedical field. In this study, a novel iEAP actuator was developed utilizing high-purity single-walled carbon nanotube (SWCNT) electrodes and a Nafion/EMIBF$_4$ ion-exchange membrane through a simple and effective spray printing technique. The SWCNT actuator demonstrates significantly enhanced electrical conductivity (1.63 S/cm), attributed to the high electrical conductivity of SWCNT. These enhancements surpass those observed in activated carbon aerogel bucky gel electrode-based actuators. Through the evaluation of the electroactive behaviors of the SWCNT actuator under varying alternating square wave voltages (1–3 V) and frequencies (0.01–100 Hz), impressive results were obtained, including a substantial bending displacement of 10.28 mm and long-term operational stability up to 12,000 cycles (at 2 V, 1 Hz). This research introduces a simple and effective spray printing technique for the successful fabrication of iEAP actuators with superior electromechanical properties, holding promise for use as artificial muscles in the realm of bionic robotics.

Keywords: Ionic electroactive polymer · actuators · spray printing technique · electromechanical properties

1 Introduction

Electroactive polymer (EAP) actuators are attracting increasing research interest and attention in various fields of modern science and technology due to their remarkable ability to undergo significant deformation in response to external electrical stimuli [1, 2]. Consequently, EAP actuators are widely recognized as promising candidates for the development of 'artificial muscles,' with significant potential for applications in bionic robotics, space exploration, and the biomedical field [3, 4].

Ionic polymer metal composites (IPMCs), a common type of ionic electroactive polymer (iEAP) materials, typically consist of an inner ion-exchange polymer layer (such as Nafion) and metal electrodes (like Pd and Pt) on both sides, typically achieved through electroless plating processes [5, 6]. These actuators exhibit substantial deformation towards the anode side at relatively low voltages due to the swelling of the cathode side, driven by the flow of hydrated ions in the inner polymer layer towards the cathode side through ion nanochannels. However, the metal electrodes of IPMCs, fabricated through multiple electroless plating processes, often have rough surfaces and poor adhesion to the Nafion layer, negatively impacting the deformation of IPMCs. Moreover, these electrodes are prone to damage and cracking after numerous cyclic deformations, resulting in issues such as easy peeling, reduced repeatability, and rapid relaxation. The deformation behavior of IPMCs, including back relaxation in hydrated conditions and attenuation of deformation in air, is too unstable to be effectively controlled [6]. This instability significantly limits their potential applications.

In engineering disciplines, there is a pressing need for iEAP actuators that can operate durably and stably in air. In 2005, Asaka's group [7] introduced a pioneering category of iEAP actuators specifically engineered for long-lasting stable operation in air. These innovative actuators are constructed by hot-pressing a polymeric membrane with ionic liquid between two bucky-gel electrodes [8–10]. The electrodes are typically fabricated by casting a blended dispersion consisting of supporting polymers, nanoconductive materials, and ionic liquid. However, the presence of a substantial amount of non-conductive polymers in the electrodes often results in inferior conductivity compared to pure nanocarbon materials [10, 11]. Moreover, their volumetric capacitance tends to fall short of that exhibited by supercapacitor electrodes [12, 13]. These characteristics lead to delays in the electrochemical kinetic processes within the resultant actuators, necessitating compromises in their actuation performances.

To further enhance actuation capabilities, a range of exceptional nanocarbon materials, such as hierarchical carbon nanotubes and graphene mesh, have been developed for iEAP actuators [14, 15]. Leveraging the unique structure and electrochemical properties of these electrodes, the respective actuators have demonstrated significant orders of magnitude increases in power density compared to traditional bucky-gel actuators. Despite the advancements in actuation performance, the exploration of these exceptional nanomaterials remains largely confined to laboratory settings. The limited production and high cost of these materials significantly impede their practical applications in engineering.

In this study, we have employed a spray printing technique for the efficient and rapid fabrication of iEPA actuators utilizing single-walled carbon nanotube electrodes. The spray printing technique is highly effective, and we anticipate that actuators developed using this method will find widespread use in the field of soft robotics.

2 Experimental Section

2.1 Experimental Materials

Nafion solution (DE-520, 20 wt%) was purchased from DuPont Company (Shanghai, China). The high purity SWCNT were purchased from Chengdu Organic Chemical Co. Ltd (Chengdu, China). Table 1 shows the physical properties of the SWCNT. 1-Ethyl-3-methylimidazolium tetrafluoroborate (EMImBF$_4$, 99.9 wt%), N,N-dimethylacetamide (DMAc, 99 wt%) and anhydrous ethanol (EtOH, 99.5 wt%) were purchased from Aladdin (Shanghai, China). All the reagents were used as received.

Table 1. Physical properties of the SWCNT.

Outer Diameter	Purity	Length	Surface Area	Electric Conductivity	Ig/Id
<2 nm	>95 wt%	5–30 μm	>490 m2/g	>100 S/cm	>20

2.2 Preparation of Nafion/EMImBF$_4$ Membrane

1.25 g of Nafion solution (20 wt%), 0.25 g EMImBF$_4$, 9.25 g DMAc and 3.75 g H$_2$O were put into a glass sample bottle and continuously stirred for 4 h to prepare Nafion/EMImBF$_4$ casting solution. 11.12 g of the casting solution was poured in a glass container (50 mm × 50 mm × 30 mm) and evaporated thoroughly at 70 °C in open air to prepare Nafion/EMImBF$_4$ membrane. Then, the membrane was put into an oven to dry at 80 °C and 120 °C for 2 h, respectively, and finally treated at 150 °C for 30 min. The sizes of the prepared Nafion/EMImBF$_4$ membrane were 50 mm × 50 mm × (70 ± 5) μm (length × width × thickness).

2.3 Fabrication of Actuators

(a) Preparation of spraying solutions: 0.08 g of SWCNT were dispersed into 16 mL of EtOH by sonicating in ice-water bath for 45 min to prepare SWCNT/EtOH dispersion.
(b) Preparation of actuators: First, a 2 cm × 1.5 cm sized Nafion/EMImBF$_4$ membrane was fixed on a heating platform. Second, 0.1 mL of the casting solution was sprayed onto the membrane surface by using a spray gun. The platform was heated to 120 °C to completely remove DMAc and other solvents. After that, set amount of the SWCNT/EtOH solution was put into the spray gun and sprayed onto the membrane surface. The membrane was then heated to 80 °C to remove EtOH and to form a conductive surface, which will work as an electrode while the actuator working. After that, the above steps were repeated to prepare electrode on the other side of the Nafion/EMImBF$_4$ membrane. Finally, actuators with SWCNT electrode on both sides of the Nafion/EMImBF$_4$ membrane were successfully obtained, which was named SWCNT actuator. The actuators were cut into 20 mm × 2 mm × (95 ± 5) μm (length × width × thickness) sized specimens for characterization.

2.4 Characterizations

Morphological Observation: The micro morphologies of the actuators were examined using a field emission scanning electron microscope (FE-SEM, S-8200, Hitachi, Japan) to investigate the cross-sectional and interfacial structures of the actuators, as well as the microstructures of the electrodes.

Surface Resistance Measurement: The surface resistances of the electrodes were assessed with a four-probe resistance tester.

Electromechanical Testing: The electromechanical properties of the actuators were evaluated by measuring the deformation with the test apparatus depicted in Fig. 1e. The actuators were subjected to various voltages supplied by a power source (HM8143) controlled by Labview. A laser displacement tester (Keyence, LK-G80) was utilized to capture the bending displacement at a distance of 10 mm. Three samples of each type of actuator were tested concurrently, ensuring that the standard deviations of the recorded displacements did not exceed 20%.

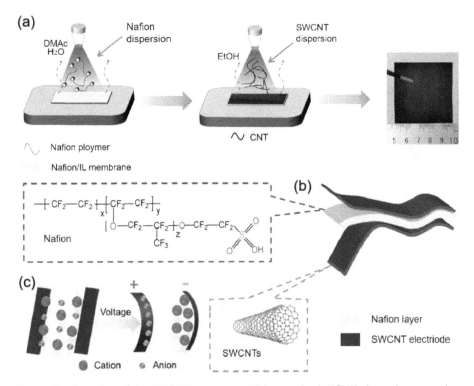

Fig. 1. Configuration of the SWCNT actuator: (a) Diagram for SWCNT electrode preparation. (b) Image of a SWCNT actuator. (c) Illustration for actuation mechanism.

3 Results and Discussion

3.1 Morphological Observation

Observation of the electrode surface microstructures and actuator cross-sections was carried out using a FE-SEM. The surface of the core layer was uniformly coated with SWCNT via spray printing to create an electrode film, displaying a relatively rough mesoporous structure. The rough microfibrous surfaces of the SWCNT electrode serve to increase its contact area with the inner Nafion membrane, while the porous structure facilitates the rapid injection of charge and migration of ions within the actuators. These characteristics play a crucial role in enabling the actuators to achieve substantial deformation.

As illustrated in Fig. 2e, the SWCNT actuator exhibits a typical sandwiched structure. Furthermore, as shown more distinctly in Fig. 2c, the SWCNT electrode adheres effectively to the Nafion membrane without delamination. This strong adhesion promotes accelerated ion migration both within and between layers of the actuators, thereby enhancing their electromechanical actuation properties.

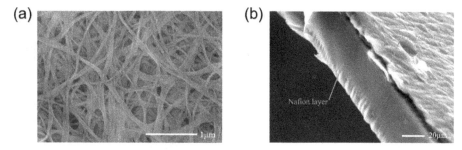

Fig. 2. SEM images of SWCNT electrode surface and SWCNT actuator's cross-section.

3.2 Electromechanical Properties

When applied to an electric field, charge and discharge processes will occur separately inside the actuator. Subsequently, cations migrate to and accumulate at the cathode side, while anions migrate to and accumulate at the opposite side. Due to the geometric effect of $EMIm^+$ and BF_4^-, the cathode expandes much larger than the anode does. Consequently, the actuator will bend toward the anode side (Fig. 1d). To investigate the electromechanical behaviors, we recorded the displacement of the actuators under applied square wave voltages (Fig. 3a).

The deformation curves shown in Fig. 3b clearly demonstrate that, as the actuator submits to a periodic voltage, the strain increases and decreases in accordance with the voltage variation, leading to a periodic deformation. All deformation curves keep the shapes in time, showing great stability and controllability for the actuators. Figure 3c illustrates that bending displacement significantly increases with higher applied voltage. According to the deformation mechanism of the capacitor-type actuator (Fig. 1d), higher

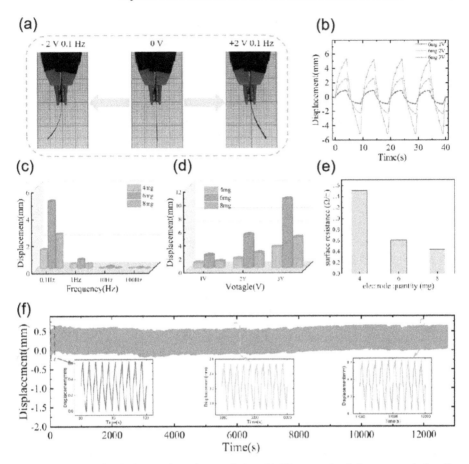

Fig. 3. Electromechanical actuation characteristics. (a) Photograph of the actuator's bending deformation under 2 V, 0.1 Hz square wave voltage. (b) Bending curves of the actuators under 2 V, 0.1 Hz square wave voltage. (c) Displacement under different applied amplitude. (d) Displacement under different applied frequencies. (e) Surface Resistance for Different Electrode Amounts. (f) Actuation durability of the SWCNT actuator under 2 V, 1 Hz square wave voltage.

voltage results in greater charge accumulation on the electrodes, leading to increased migration of working ions in the Nafion membrane towards the electrodes, thus causing more swelling and larger bending displacement. Additionally, Fig. 3d demonstrates that bending displacement of the actuator decreases markedly with the frequency increasing, as lower applied frequencies allow more time for bending to occur.

In addition, the surface resistance of the electrode layer was negatively correlated with the SECNT content, and the more SWCNT content, the lower the surface resistance, when the electrode content was 6 mg, the surface resistance was 0.613 Ω/□, which was a significant decrease in the resistance compared to the corresponding 1.507 Ω/□ when the electrode amount was 4 mg, but the effect was insignificant compared to that of the 8 mg electrode corresponding to a resistance of 0.438 Ω/□, so for the 6 mg electrode Driving performance analysis corresponding to SWCNT actuator. Actuator with electrode content of 6mg exhibited bending displacements of 1.94, 4.99, and 10.28 under 0.1 Hz square wave voltages with amplitude of 1 V, 2 V and 3 V, respectively.

The SWCNT actuator has also demonstrated relative durability in air. Figure 3f presents the actuator's cycling bending curves under ±2 V, 1 Hz square wave voltage in the air. The actuator continuously operated up to 12,000 cycles with only 15% initial drop. This is mainly caused by annealing of the actuator components. Nevertheless, the cycling operation of the SWCNT/PP actuator keeps significantly stable with comparison to those of actuators based on Pt or rGO electrodes [16, 17].

4 Conclusions

In summary, to optimize the preparation process and electromechanical properties of iEAP actuators and thereby advance their applications in engineering fields, we developed an efficient and straightforward spray printing technique for fabricating iEAP actuators employing high-purity SWCNT electrodes and ion-exchange membrane. Benefiting from the high electrical conductivity of SWCNT, the electric conductivity (1.63 S/cm) of the SWCNT actuator was significant. Based on high electrical conductivity and mechanical strength of SWCNT, the SWCNT actuator exhibited a substantial bending displacement of 10.28 mm (at 3 V, 0.1 Hz) with a long-life cycling stability more than 12,000 cycles (at 2 V, 1 Hz), surpassing the performances of the PP actuator in this study and most previously reported iEAP actuators. Benefiting from the significant achievements, we hope that the newly developed actuators would serve as alternative candidates with great promise for artificial muscles. What's more, the simple and efficient spray printing technique could be extended to an economical way for mass production for iEAP actuators.

References

1. Zhang, H., Lin, Z., Hu, Y., Ma, S., Liang, Y., Ren, L.: Low-voltage driven ionic polymer-metal composite actuators: structures, materials, and applications. Adv. Sci. **10**(10), 2206135 (2023)
2. Wei, S., Ghosh, T.K.: Bioinspired structures for soft actuators. Adv. Mater. Technol. **7**, 2101521 (2022)
3. Zhao, C., et al.: Ionic flexible sensors: mechanisms, materials, structures, and applications. Adv. Fun. Mater. **32**(17), 2110417 (2022)
4. Shi, M., Yeatman, E.M.: A comparative review of artificial muscles for microsystem applications. Microsys. Nanoeng. **7**(1), 95 (2021)
5. Ru, J., Zhao, D., Zhu, Z., Wang, Y.: Fabrication and characterization of a novel smart-polymer actuator with nanodispersed CNT/Pd composite interfacial electrodes. Polymers **14**(17), 3494 (2022)
6. Ru, J., et al.: A moisture and electric coupling stimulated ionic polymer-metal composite actuator with controllable deformation behaviour. Smart Mater. Struct. **27**, 02LT01 (2018)
7. Mukai, K., et al.: High performance fully plastic actuator based on ionic-liquid-based bucky gel. Electroch. Acta **53**, 5555–5562 (2008)

8. Kong, L., Chen, W.: Carbon nanotube and graphene-based bioinspired electrochemical actuators. Adv. Mater. **26**(7), 1025–1043 (2014)
9. Tang, X., et al.: A review of soft actuator motion: actuation, design, manufacturing and applications. Actuators **11**(11), 331 (2022)
10. Wang, F., Huang, D., Li, Q., Wu, Y., Yan, B., Wu, Z.: Sukho Park, Highly electroresponsive ionic soft actuator based on graphene nanoplatelets-mediated functional carboxylated cellulose nanofibers. Compos. Sci. Technol. **231**, 109845 (2023)
11. Mukai, K., Asaka, K., Sugino, T., Kiyohara, K., et al.: Highly conductive sheets from millimeter-long single-walled carbon nanotubes and ionic liquids: application to fast-moving, low-voltage electromechanical actuators operable in air. Adv. Mater. **21**, 1582–1585 (2009)
12. Palmre, V., Lust, E., Jänes, A., Koel, M., et al.: Electroactive polymer actuators with carbon aerogel electrodes. J. Mater. Chem. **21**, 2577–2583 (2011)
13. Izadi, N., Yasuda, S., Kobashi, K., Yamada, T., et al.: Extracting the full potential of single walled carbon nanotubes as durable supercapacitor electrodes operable at 4 V with high power and energy density. Adv. Mater. **22**, E235–E241 (2010)
14. Li, J., et al.: Superfast-response and ultrahigh-power-density electromechanical actuators based on hierarchal carbon nanotube electrodes and chitosan. Nano Lett. **11**(11), 4636–4641 (2011)
15. Ru, J., et al.: Controllable and durable Ionic electroactive polymer actuator based on nanoporous carbon nanotube film electrode. Smart Mater. Struct. **28**(8) (2019)
16. Tabassian, R., Kim, J., Nguyen, V., Kotal, M., Oh, I.: Functionally antagonistic hybrid electrode with hollow tubular graphene mesh and nitrogen-doped crumpled graphene for high-performance ionic soft actuators. Adv. Funct. Mater. **28**, 1705714 (2018)
17. Wang, F., et al.: Highly electro-responsive ionic soft actuator based on graphene nanoplatelets-mediated functional carboxylated cellulose nanofibers. Compos. Sci. Technol. **231**, 109845 (2023)

A Sound Absorber Based on IPMC Electro-Mechanical Conversion Mechanism

Tao Wang[1], Yachao Zhang[1], Bo Li[2], Ying Hu[1], Alvo Aabloo[3], and Longfei Chang[1,3(✉)]

[1] Anhui Province Key Lab of Aerospace Structural Parts Forming Technology and Equipment, Hefei University of Technology, Hefei 230009, People's Republic of China
feny.clf@hfut.edu.cn

[2] School of Mechanical Engineering, Xi'an Jiaotong University, Xi'an 710049, People's Republic of China

[3] Intelligent Materials and Systems Laboratory, Institute of Technology, University of Tartu, Nooruse 1, 50411 Tartu, Estonia

Abstract. Ionic polymer metal composite (IPMC) typically consists of a polyelectrolyte membrane sandwiched between two electrode layers of metals or nanocarbon materials. Due to its exceptional advantages, including high sensing performance, low driving voltage, rapid response speed, flexibility, large deformation, IPMC has been extensively explored in various field, such as electronic devices, bionic robots, biomedicine. However, the application of IPMC in the field of acoustic absorption has hardly been reported. In this paper, we investigated the sound absorption mechanism of IPMC and the acoustic properties of so-based acoustic structure through both experiment and simulation. The results showed that the IPMC membrane displayed an enhanced acoustic absorption ability at low frequencies.

Keywords: Flexible intelligent material · Ionic electro-active polymer · Ionic polymer metal composite · acoustic metamaterials

1 Introduction

Noise problems have become increasingly serious with global industrialization in recent years. These noises, especially below 1000 Hz, not only threaten the accuracy and stability of precision instruments but also have a detrimental impact on the physical and mental health of living beings [1, 2]. However, due to the unique physi-cal properties of low-frequency sound waves, it is challenging for traditional acous-tic materials to effectively absorb them in a limited space. Although acoustic met-amaterials with subwavelength dimensions have demonstrated effective sound ab-sorption in the low-frequency domain, most of these metamaterials have a fixed structure, and their acoustic properties are determined after fabrication[3, 4]. Consequent-ly, they are limited to functioning in a pre-determined frequency domain[5–7].

The application of flexible intelligent materials in acoustic systems brings highly innovative ideas to the field of low-frequency sound absorption [8, 9]. These flexible smart materials can respond to a wide range of external stimuli such as light [10, 11], electricity [12, 13] and magnetism [14, 15]. In recent years, flexible electro-active or magneto-active intelligent materials such as dielectric elastomers (DE) [16–18], poly vinylidene difluoride (PVDF) [19–21], magnetically active materials [22, 23], and carbon nanomaterials [24, 25] have been successfully applied to low-frequency acoustic structures. Modulation of the perforation conditions of acoustic surfaces, as well as physical properties such as surface tension or stiffness, can be achieved by modulating external stimuli, providing excellent design paths for structures with tunable low-frequency acoustic absorption or isolation [6, 26]. Moreover, the piezoelectric effect of PVDF converts and dissipates the mechanical energy in sound waves, thereby introducing an additional energy dissipation mechanism for low-frequency acoustic structures [19, 20].

Ionic electro-active polymers (EAPs), renowned for their bidirectional energy conversion, have been extensively explored across aerospace engineering, biomedicine, and soft robotics for their actuation and sensing capabilities [27–30]. Nevertheless, the dependence of electro-mechanical and mech-electrical conversion processes on mass transportation within nanochannels has led to sluggish reactions and heightened energy consumption, resulting in a narrow operational range and low efficiency [30]. Intriguingly, we have discovered a novel approach to leverage these limitations, effectively accelerating the attenuation of low-frequency sound energy.

This paper presents a thin-membrane acoustic metamaterial constructed from a representative ionic electroactive polymer material (IEAP), IPMC. The existence of three energy dissipation mechanisms in the IPMC acoustic structure in the presence of acoustic waves is hypothesized and subsequently verified through experiments and finite element method (FEM) simulation. It is anticipated that these findings will stimulate the development of diverse acoustic structures for the mitigation of low-frequency noise, consequently advancing the utilization of soft smart materials and acoustic metamaterials in practical settings.

2 Design and Experimental Methods

2.1 Design Description

IPMCs are typically composed of a polyelectrolyte membrane sandwiched between two electrode layers of metals or nanocarbon materials [29, 30]. In this paper, we use Nafion (DuPont)-based IPMC, with substrate membrane containing fluorocarbon backbones and numerous immobilized sulfonated side chains that facilitate extensive nano-mass transport channels [31, 32]. As illustrated in Fig. 1a, the application of external mechanical stress prompts the movement of cations in conjunction with water molecules within the matrix membrane. This movement leads to an uneven distribution of charges, which subsequently establishes a potential gradient between the two electrodes.

Figure 1b is a schematic of the acoustic metamaterial we designed, referred as IPMC-MA, which consists of an IPMC membrane and a 20 mm deep back cavity. As depicted in Fig. 1c, it is postulated that the IPMC-MA structure exhibits three distinct energy dissipation mechanisms when subjected to acoustic stress. Initially, incident sound waves cause stress on the membrane surface, which triggers an induced potential between the conducting electrodes. This conversion of the resultant electrical energy into thermal energy dissipates partial sound energy. Additionally, due to the hysteresis oscillations of the internal ions, the acoustic energy was converted into kinetic energy, resulting in additional acoustic energy dissipation. Moreover, the integration of the IPMC membrane and the rear cavity forms a mass-spring system, which culminates in damping dissipation. In order to verify the electromechanical conversion under acoustic pressure, we conducted a measurement and simulation of the sensing potential of the IPMC-MA samples.

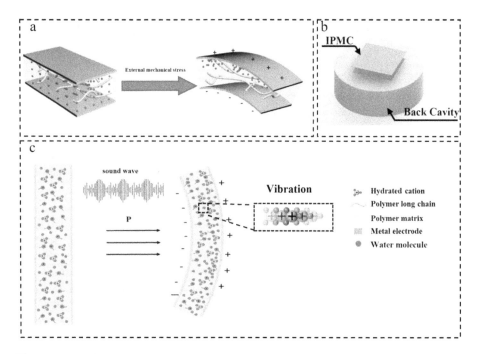

Fig. 1. Schematic diagram of (a) the sensing mechanism of IPMC under external mechanical stress. (b) the IPMC-MA structure. (c) the acoustic energy dissipation mechanisms in IPMC-MA structure.

2.2 Experiment

Based on our previously established fabrication process [31], as shown in Fig. 2, Pd-Au electroplated IPMC with Nafion-117 as the substrate membrane was fabricated as the primary acoustic absorbing material.

Sound Absorption Performance Test

The acoustic absorption test setup is depicted in Fig. 3. During the testing process, a computer is utilized to control the data acquisition card (NI USB-4431), which in turn regulates the output of sound waves from a power amplifier (Yamaha PG2500S).

Subsequently, the feedback data, which is based on the sound pressures measured by two microphones (B&K TYPE4958A) strategically positioned within the impedance tube (BSWA SW422), enables the calculation of the transfer function and the vertical incidence coefficient. Consequently, the absorption coefficient of the test specimen can be determined [23, 24].

Sensing Performance Test

To assess the sensing capability, the IPMC membrane was placed on an acoustic test rig and the two wires connecting the electrodes on the surface of the IPMC membrane were extended and connected to a data acquisition card (NI USB-6003). Measurements were conducted using a digital source meter (Keithley 6514) at various frequencies of sound pressure. Data were collected via the data acquisition card, and the corresponding induced potentials of the IPMC samples were recorded using the LabVIEW program (NI). During the experiment, three measurements were taken for each set of experiments, and the resulting data were averaged to reduce the impact of random errors.

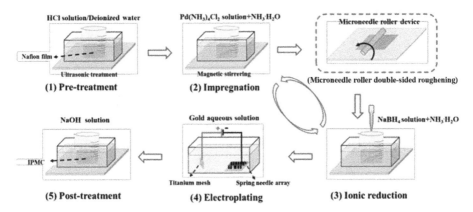

Fig. 2. Fabrication processes of IPMC membrane.

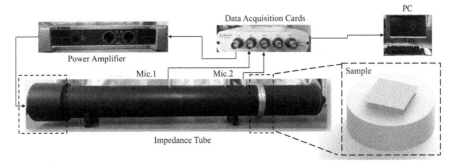

Fig. 3. The sound absorption test platform.

2.3 FEM Simulation

To verify the sound absorption mechanism, the commercial software COMSOL Multiphysics was employed to establish the sensing model of the IPMC acoustic absorber, as illustrated in Fig. 4. The anechoic boundary is defined as a perfectly matched layer, and the incident planar acoustic wave is defined in the background acoustic field with an acoustic pressure amplitude of 1 Pa, a sound velocity of 343 m/s, and the incident acoustic wave oriented along the normal direction to the surface of the IPMC membrane. Furthermore, the pressure acoustic domains are represented by an air medium for the air layer and the back cavity portion. The Dirichlet boundary conditions is set on the side surfaces of the IPMC membranes. The parameters utilized in this study are presented in Table 1.

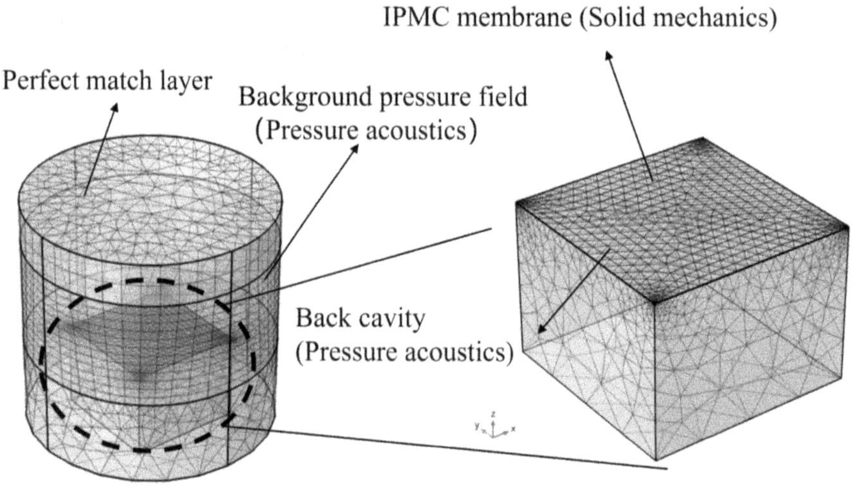

Fig. 4. The IPMC sensing FEM model.

Based on the sensing mechanism of IPMC [33, 34], three different physical fields are involved in the IPMC membrane (solid mechanics domain). The monitoring equations for the mechanical field are as follows:

$$\sigma_{eA} - \sigma_{eB} = \frac{E_{dry}}{3}\left(\left(\frac{1+W_0}{1+W_{V0}}\right)^{-\frac{4}{3}} - \left(\frac{W_0}{W_{V0}}\right)^{-\frac{4}{3}}\right) \qquad (1)$$

$$\begin{cases} W_0 = \frac{C_w}{\frac{\rho_w}{M_w} - C_w} \\ P^* = -\sigma_{eB} + \frac{E_{dry}}{3}\left(\left(\frac{1+W_0}{1+W_{V0}}\right)^{-\frac{4}{3}} - \left(\frac{W_0}{W_{V0}}\right)^{-\frac{4}{3}}\right) + \sigma^* \end{cases} \qquad (2)$$

Where σ_{eA} is the stress on the outer surface, and when coupled with acoustic field, σ_{eA} is regarded as the stress on the outer surface resulting from the incoming acoustic wave, σ_{eB} is the elastic stress in the inner surface, W_0 is the local volume fraction of water and σ^* is the characteristic stress resulting from the redistribution of cations and water, W_{V0} is the initial volume fraction of water. ρ_w is the density of water, M_w is the molar weight of water, C_w is the water concentration. P^* is the total pressure, E_{dry} is the elastic modulus of dry Nafion 117.

The inner transport process included the convective flux under the total pressure gradient, the electromigration of the built-in electric field, and the mutual coupling effect of cations and water. Accordingly, the dynamic transmission can be described by deriving the water flux, J_I, and the cation flux, J_W, as shown in Eq. (3), along with the mass continuity equation in Eq. (4). Due to the redistribution of cations, an intrinsic electric field is generated within the polymer, resulting in a voltage disparity between the two electrodes. The electric potential $\varnothing$ must adhere to the requirements stipulated by the equation Poisson (5).

$$\begin{cases} J_I = -d_{ll}\left(\nabla C_a + \frac{z_I C_a F}{RT}\nabla\varnothing\right) - N_{dI}d_{ww}\nabla C_w - C_a K \nabla P \\ J_W = -N_{dW}d_{ll}\left(\nabla C_a + \frac{z_I C_a F}{RT}\nabla\varnothing\right) - d_{ww}\nabla C_w - C_W K \nabla P \end{cases}, \quad (3)$$

$$\frac{\partial C_i}{\partial t} + \nabla J_i = 0 (i = a, W) \quad (4)$$

$$\nabla^2 \varnothing = -\frac{Z_I F(C_a - C_f)}{\varepsilon} \quad (5)$$

where R is the gas constant, T is the temperature and $\varnothing$ is the the induced voltage potential and C_a is the cation concentration. z_I is the valence of the cation, F is the faraday constant. d_{ww} is the diffusion coefficient of water and d_{ll} is the diffusion coefficient of the cations, N_{dW} is the water number of pump effect, and N_{dI} is the electroosmosis drag coefficient of cation, C_f is the concentration of the fixed ion. ε is the effective permittivity of the IPMC.

3 Results and Discussion

3.1 The Acoustic Absorption of IPMC-MA Structure

The measured acoustic absorption properties of double-sided roughened IPMC sample with IPMC-MA structure are presented in Fig. 5. The peak absorption coefficient of the double-sided roughened IPMC sample was 0.758, with a peak absorption frequency of 748 Hz. Moreover, the absorption curve exhibited multiple absorption peaks. To assess the mechanical-electrical conversion capability of IPMC during the noise absorption process. Four absorption peak frequencies of 230 Hz, 504 Hz, 748 Hz, and 1002 Hz were selected for testing and simulation purposes.

Table 1. Parameters used in FEM simulation (Saturated Nafion-117(Na^+)).

Parameters (Unit)	Value	Physical meaning
$\rho_w (kg/m^3)$	1000	Water density
$M_w (kg/mol)$	0.018	Molar weight of water
W_{V0}	0.5368	Initial volume fraction of water
$E_{dry}(Pa)$	1×10^9	Elastic modulus of dry Nafion 117
$C_W (mol/m^3)$	19405	Initial Water concentration
$F (C/mol)$	96485	Faraday constant
$T(K)$	300	Temperature
$d_{ll}(m^2/s)$	2×10^{-11}	Diffusion coefficient of Na
$d_{ww}(m^2/s)$	8×10^{-11}	Diffusion coefficient of water
N_{dI}	0.022875	Electroosmosis drag coefficient of cation
N_{dW}	1	Water number of pump effect
$K(m^2/(pa \cdot s))$	2×10^{-17}	Hydraulic permeability coefficient
z_I	1	Valence of Na Cation
$C_f (mol/m^3)$	1393.1	concentration of the fixed ion
ε	4.427×10^{-4}	Effective permittivity of the IPMC

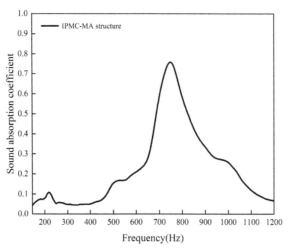

Fig. 5. The sound absorption coefficients of the IPMC-MA structure.

3.2 The Mech-Electrical Conversion Capability of the IPMC Samples Under Acoustic Pressure

The voltage measurements of the double-sided roughened IPMC samples under the peak absorption frequency acoustic field was plotted as depicted in Fig. 6a, and Fig. 6b to e illustrate the voltage signals generated by the samples and the simulation results at different sound field frequencies. The voltage value was calculated as the mean amplitude of the sensing curve. The voltage plots of the simulation and experimental results exhibited a high degree of correlation, both demonstrating that the voltage frequency increased in proportion to the frequency of the incident acoustic pressure. IPMC membranes with double-sided roughening displayed superior sensing capabilities. They produced an average voltage amplitude of approximately 3.3 mV at 504 Hz, while voltage signals of 1.9 mV, 1.3 mV, and 0.3 mV were generated at 230 Hz, 748 Hz, and 1002 Hz, respectively. These findings demonstrate that acoustic waves impinging on the surface of IPMC membranes can generate millivolt-level voltages whose frequency is corresponded to the acoustic wave frequency.

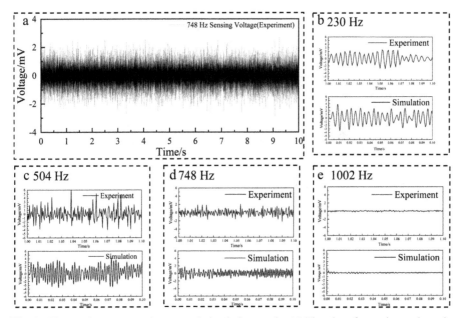

Fig. 6. The sensing test experiments and simulation results (a) The plot of experimental results at 748 Hz of double-sided roughness; The sensing potential of IPMC samples with double-sided roughening under acoustic pressure at frequencies of (b) 230 Hz; (c) 504 Hz; (d) 748 Hz; (e) 1002 Hz respectively.

Moreover, the sensed voltage was not linearly related to the magnitude of the acoustic wave frequency. It is particularly noteworthy that the sensed voltage is higher at 504 Hz acoustic field compared to other frequencies, which was most likely related to the resonance state of the membrane at different frequencies. Accordingly, the simulation of the sensing model enables the analysis of each vibration pattern and the sensed displacement at four frequencies. As illustrated in Fig. 7, the simulation results of the resonant displacement and voltage generation of the double-sided roughened IPMC membrane are juxtaposed with the experimental results. The membrane vibration modes at different frequency sound fields demonstrate localized non-homogeneous deformation. In addition, the mean values of resonant displacement at 230 Hz, 504 Hz, 748 Hz and 1002 Hz are 0.75 μm, 1.20 μm, 0.65 μm and 0.45 μm, respectively. These values were found to be positively correlated with the average voltage generated. From the results, it can be postulated that the vibration of the IPMC membrane induces uneven displacements on each side, leading to an inhomogeneous vibration of the hydrated ions and consequently establishing a potential gradient across the electrodes. The presence of conductive electrodes facilitates the rapid dissipation of the generated electrical energy. Additionally, in accordance with the principles of energy conservation, the kinetic energy of the internal hydrated ions is likely to contribute to the dissipation of acoustic energy.

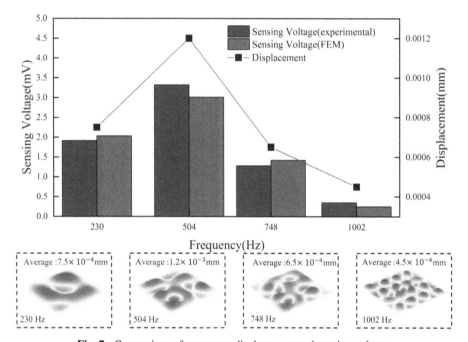

Fig. 7. Comparison of resonance displacement and sensing voltage.

4 Conclusion

This paper presents the development of a low-frequency acoustic metamaterial, the IPMC-MA absorber, based on the flexible intelligent IEAP material, IPMC. Under the acoustic field, three distinct energy dissipation mechanisms can be identified. Firstly, as in the case of resonant acoustic metamaterials, the fusion of the IPMC membrane with the back cavity establishes a mass-spring system, which results in damped dissipation. Furthermore, the application of acoustic stress generates an induced potential between the conducting electrodes, which subsequently converts the generated electrical energy into thermal energy. This process results in the dissipation of energy. In addition, hysteretic oscillations of internal ions absorb acoustic energy and convert it into kinetic energy, thus acting as a complementary dissipation mechanism.

Moreover, to verify the electromechanical conversion under acoustic pressure, a series of measurements and simulations were conducted on IPMC samples. These results demonstrated that IPMC can generate sensing voltages at acoustic pressures up to several hundred Hz, and that the voltage amplitude is positively correlated with the vibrational displacement of the membrane.

References

1. Holzman, D.C.: Fighting noise pollution: a public health strategy. Environ. Health Perspect. **122**(2), A58 (2014)
2. Yang, P., Xie, H., Li. Y. Jin., K.: The effect of noise exposure on high-frequency hearing loss among chinese workers: a meta-analysis. Healthcare (Basel, Switzerland) **11**(8), 1079 (2023)
3. Liao, G., Luan, C., Wang, Z., Liu, J., Yao, X., Fu, J.: Acoustic metamaterials: a review of theories, structures, fabrication approaches, and applications. Adv. Mater. Technol. **6**(5), 2000787 (2021)
4. Dong, E., Cao, P., Zhang, J., Zhang S., Fang, X., Zhang, Yu.: Underwater acoustic metamaterials. Natl. Sci. Rev. **10**(6), nwac246 (2023)
5. Kim, S., Kim, Y.H., Jang, J.H.: A theoretical model to predict the low-frequency sound absorption of a Helmholtz resonator array. J. Acoust. Soc. Am. **119**(4), 1933–1936 (2006)
6. Mei, J., Ma, G., Yang, M., Yang, Z., Wen, W., Sheng, P.: Dark acoustic metamaterials as super absorbers for low-frequency sound. Nat. Commun. **3**(3), 756 (2012)
7. R, Zhu., X, Liu., G, Hu., F, Yuan., G. L, Huang.: Microstructural designs of plate-type elastic metamaterial and their potential applications: a review. Int. J. Smart Nano Mater. **6**(1), 14–40 (2015)
8. Chang, L., et al.: Progress of low-frequency sound absorption research utilizing intelligent materials and acoustic metamaterials. RSC Adv. **11**(60), 37784–37800 (2021)
9. Wang, Y., Wang, Y., Wu, B., Chen, W., Wang, Y.: Tunable and active phononic crystals and metamaterials. Appl. Mech. Rev. **72**(4), 040801 (2020)
10. Xiao, J., et al.: Optical fibre taper-enabled waveguide photoactuators. Nat. Commun. **13**(1), 363 (2022)
11. Li, J., Zhou, X., Liu, Z.: Recent advances in photoactuators and their applications in intelligent bionic movements. Adv. Opt.Mater. **8**(18), n/a–n/a (2020)
12. Pelrine, R., Kornbluh, R., Pei, Q., Joseph, J.: High-speed electrically actuated elastomers with strain greater than 100%. Science **287**(5454), 836–839 (2000)
13. Koerner, H., Price, G., Pearce, N., Alexander, M., Vaia, R.: Remotely actuated polymer nanocomposites—stress-recovery of carbon-nanotube-filled thermoplastic elastomers. Nat. Mater. **3**, 115–120 (2004)
14. Kuang, X., et al.: Magnetic dynamic polymers for modular assembling and reconfigurable morphing architectures. Adv. Mater. **33**(30), 2102113 (2021)
15. Ze, Q., et al.: Magnetic shape memory polymers with integrated multifunctional shape manipulation. Adv. Mater. **32**(4), 1906657 (2020)
16. Lu, Z., Shrestha, M., Lau, G.: Electrically tunable and broader-band sound absorption by using micro-perforated dielectric elastomer actuator. Appl. Phys. Lett. **110**(18), 182901 (2017)
17. Lu, Z., Godaba, H., Cui, Y., Foo, C., Debiasi, M., Zhu, J.: An electronically tunable duct silencer using dielectric elastomer actuators. J. Acoust. Soc. Am. **138**(3), 236–241 (2015)

18. Zhang, Y., Li, B., Chang, L., Ma, F., Zhou, X., Chen, G.: Bistable sound insulator with an abrupt stiffness shift using magnetic-coupled dielectric elastomer actuator. Smart Mater. Struct. **31**(6), 065012 (2022)
19. Mohamed, M.A., Yao, K., Yousry, M.Y., Chen, S., Wang, J.: Open-cell poly (vinylidene fluoride) foams with polar phase for enhanced airborne sound absorption. Appl. Phys. Let. **113**(9), 092903 (2018)
20. Stathara, E.C., Yao, K., Zhang, L., Salloum, R., Mohamed, A.M., Tay, F.: Theoretical analysis on hybrid local piezoelectric and conductive effect on sound absorption performance of porous poly (vinylidene fluoride). Mater. Res. Express. **6**(8), 086204 (2019)
21. Xu, H., Kong, D.: Dynamic sound absorption characteristics of a series piezoelectric acoustic absorber regulated by voltage. J. Acoust. Soc. Am. **151**(6), 3807–3807 (2022)
22. Yu, K., Fang, N., Huang, G., Wang, Q.: Magnetoactive acoustic metamaterials. Adv. Mater. **30**(21), 1706348 (2018)
23. Cao, X., et al.: Magnetic-tunable sound absorber based on micro-perforated magnetorheological elastomer. Smart Mater. Struct. **29**(1), 015024 (2019)
24. Rahimabady, M., Statharas, E., Yao, K., Mirshekarloo, M., Chen, S., Tay, F.: Hybrid local piezoelectric and conductive functions for high performance airborne sound absorption. Appl. Phys. Lett. **111**(24), 241601 (2017)
25. Hosseinpour, A., Katbab, A., Ohadi, A.: Improving the sound absorption of a highly deformable nanocomposite foam based on ethylene-propylene-diene-monomer (EPDM) infused with multi-walled carbon nanotubes (MWCNTs) to absorb low-frequency waves. Eur. Polym. **178**, 111522 (2022)
26. Xing, T., et al.: Low frequency sound absorption of adjustable membrane-type acoustic metamaterials. Appl. Acoust. **188**, 108586 (2022)
27. Ma, S., Zhang, Y., Liang, Y., Ren, L., Tian, W., Ren, L.: High-performance ionic-polymer–metal composite: toward large-deformation fast-response artificial muscles. Adv. Funct. Mater. **30**(7), 08508 (2020)
28. Zhang, H., Lin, Z., Ma, Y.S., Liang, Y., Ren, L., Ren, L.: Low-voltage driven ionic polymer-metal composite actuators: structures, materials, and applications. Adv. Funct. Mater. **10**(10), 06135 (2023)
29. Zhao, C., et al.: Ionic flexible sensors: mechanisms, materials, structures, and applications. Adv. Funct. Mater. **32**(17), 10407 (2022)
30. Kim, J., Park, M., Kim, S., Jeon, M.: Effect of ionic polymer membrane with multiwalled carbon nanotubes on the mechanical performance of ionic electroactive polymer actuators. Polymers **12**(2), 396 (2022)
31. Rao, M., Tang, F., Li, Y., Chang, L., Zhu, Z., Aabloo, A.: Multi-physical modeling and fabrication of high-performance IPMC actuators with serrated interface. Smart Mater. Struct. **31**(9), 095023 (2022)
32. Schmidt-Rohr, K., Chen, Q.: Parallel cylindrical water nanochannels in Nafion fuel-cell membranes. Nat. Mater. **7**(1), 75–83 (2008)
33. Zhu, Z., Chang, L., Horiuchi, T., Takagi, K., Aabloo, A., Asaka, K.: Multi-physical model of cation and water transport in ionic polymer-metal composite sensors. J. Appl. Phys. **119**(12), 124901 (2016)
34. Zhu, Z., Asaka, K., Chang, L., Takagi, K., Chen, H.: Multiphysics of ionic polymer–metal composite actuator. J. Appl. Phys. **114**(8), 084902 (2013)

Advanced Intelligent and Flexible Sensor Technologies for Robotics

Design of a Wearable EEG Signal Acquisition System for Brain-Computer Interaction

Fei Fei[✉], Yiqi Wu, Ruonan Yang, Lizhi Mao, and Qianru Zhang

College of Automation Engineering, Nanjing University of Aeronautics and Astronautics,
Nanjing 211100, China
fei.fei@nuaa.edu.cn

Abstract. Electroencephalography (EEG) signals provide us with direct insights into brain function and play a vital role in fields such as neuroscience and medicine. The integration with wearable EEG devices has enabled long-term monitoring of specific EEG indicators, offering new methods for human-computer interaction. This not only holds significant potential for improving the quality of human life but also promotes the advancement of scientific research and has the potential to transform the landscape of medical and health services. This paper proposes and develops a wearable EEG signal acquisition system for brain-computer interfaces, with the following specific details: The system uses a main controller STM32F411CEU6, an EEG chip KS1092, a power supply chip IP5306, and protective circuits to build the peripheral circuits. The device dimensions are 7.5 × 5.0 × 3.5 mm, and the total weight is 132.2 g. The embedded software can collect EEG signals in real-time at a high sampling rate of 1 kHz and achieve information transmission through Bluetooth. In practical applications such as physiological response testing and focused task assessment, the system can accurately determine the state of the test subjects, demonstrating its potential for application in areas such as educational assessment, medical health, human-computer interaction, and cognitive research.

Keywords: Brain-Computer Interaction · EEG signals · Wearable devices · Focus task assessment

1 Introduction

Electroencephalogram (EEG) signals, generated by neuronal activity in the brain, are irregularly fluctuating signals with frequencies ranging from 0.5 to 100 Hz. Electrodes record these minute voltage changes on the scalp over time, capturing the dynamic images of bioelectric phenomena produced by neuron activation. EEG aggregates the activity of a vast number of neurons, encompassing ionic exchange and metabolic processes, providing a macroscopic representation of brain states.

Compared to common bioelectric signals in the human body such as electrocardiogram (ECG) and electromyogram (EMG), brainwave signals exhibit a high degree of randomness and diversity, significantly influenced by emotional and cognitive states.

This leads to a rich variability and extreme sensitivity to real-time changes. Prone to interference from external sources like muscle activity, eye movements, and cardiac electrical activity, brainwave signals often incorporate non-brain-originated artifacts, which augment the complexity of analysis. Consequently, the interpretation and analysis of brainwave signals necessitate specialized expertise and techniques [1–3]. While differing in frequency, amplitude, and morphology, all these bioelectric signals reflect the electrophysiological processes of physiological activities in the human body and are interconnected to some extent. For example, through their analysis, one can gain insights into the health status, diagnose illnesses, and even control bioelectrical driven prosthetics [4–6].

EEG signals can be divided into frequency bands: δ band (0.5–4 Hz), θ band (4–8 Hz), α band (8–12 Hz), β band (12–30 Hz), and γ band (>30 Hz). These frequency bands are associated with different brain states. For example, δ waves dominate during deep sleep and are related to bodily restoration and memory consolidation; their presence during wakefulness may indicate brain injury or drug effects. θ waves are common during light sleep, relaxation, meditation, and brain development in children and adolescents; in awake adults, increased θ activity may be associated with distraction, daydreaming, or light drowsiness. α waves are prominent in relaxed, eyes-closed, resting but alert states, especially in the occipital and posterior regions; suppression of α waves is related to a shift in brain activity toward external attention. β waves are associated with alertness, thinking, problem-solving, focused attention, and active consciousness, particularly in the frontal regions. γ waves are linked to high-level cognitive functions, consciousness, attention, and processes involving learning and memory. Therefore, EEG has widespread applications in clinical medicine, neuroscience research, and human-computer interaction [7, 8]. Compared to medical-grade electroencephalography (EEG) sensors, consumer-grade EEG devices offer a significantly lower price point, making them more accessible for routine medical monitoring and diagnostics. These devices are designed to be user-friendly and are often marketed for home use, allowing individuals to monitor various aspects of their brain activity with relative ease [9–13].

The work in this paper primarily involves designing an EEG signal acquisition system for brain-computer interfaces, achieving the collection of δ, θ, α, and β waves, and completing system verification and experimentation. On the hardware level, the focus is on PCB and related appearance design, which ensures functionality while enhancing portability. On the software side, embedded software was developed to control hardware operations, including signal collection and transmission. User-friendly PC software was also designed for displaying, analyzing, and managing collected EEG data. System verification was conducted through meticulous hardware and software testing, including electrical tests and communication protocol validation. Noise analysis was also performed to explore internal and external noise sources and measures were taken to reduce their impact, ensuring the stability and reliability of the system's hardware and software. Experimental application validation was also carried out using wavelet transform analysis, open-close eye tests, and concentration tests, demonstrating the system's practicality and potential application value in EEG research.

2 Hardware Circuit Design

The schematic includes the power supply circuit, acquisition circuit, and the minimum system board of the microcontroller unit (MCU). The power supply circuit serves two functions: charging the lithium battery and providing operating voltage for subsequent circuits. The acquisition circuit reads EEG signals at a fixed sampling rate, amplifying them simultaneously. The MCU is responsible for analog-to-digital conversion (ADC) of the amplified EEG signals, configuring the acquisition chip, and transmitting Bluetooth information. Given the design requirement for a wearable hardware system, this paper prioritizes minimizing signal interference and overall volume in both schematic and PCB design (Fig. 1).

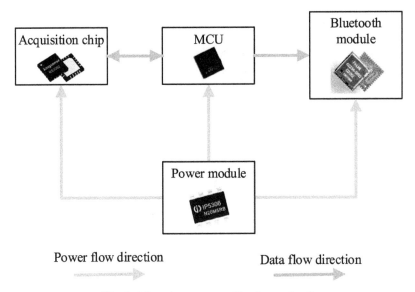

Fig. 1. The primary parts of hardware circuit.

This paper employs three primary integrated circuits: a power management chip, an acquisition chip, and an MCU chip. For the power management chip, the IP5306 is selected. As a highly integrated power management system-on-chip, the IP5306 encompasses functions such as a boost converter, lithium battery charge and discharge management, and signal light indication. Its high level of integration and built-in features allow for minimal peripheral components, effectively reducing the overall PCB size. However, given that this chip only boosts the Li-ion battery voltage of 3.7 V to 5 V, exceeding the subsequent circuit's operating voltage of 3.3 V, a low dropout linear regulator (LDO), the TPS7A2033, is added after the boost input of the IP5306. The TPS7A2033 boasts ultra-low noise performance and comprehensive protection against short circuits, over-temperature, and current limits, safeguarding both the regulator and the load under abnormal conditions.

Regarding the acquisition chip, suitable for processing microvolt-level voltage signals due to the nature of EEG signals, the article considers two main options in the market:

ADS1299 and KS1092. Here, the domestically produced KS1092 is adopted for EEG signal acquisition. It integrates a low-noise amplifier, filters, internal references, LDO, and reference bias circuits within a compact 20-pin QFN package measuring merely 3 mm * 3 mm, significantly contributing to PCB space-saving and the miniaturization of the overall device. It also supports configuration via SPI interface.

As for the MCU chip, the STMF411CEU6 is chosen. Based on the ARM Cortex-M4 architecture, it operates at a frequency of 100 MHz, facilitating rapid mathematical computations including floating-point operations. Its ADC module supports high-speed conversion with multiple sampling rate settings, peaking at 1 Msps (million samples per second), aligning well with the article's sampling rate requirements. Moreover, its ultra-thin package design facilitates the integration into the system (Fig. 2).

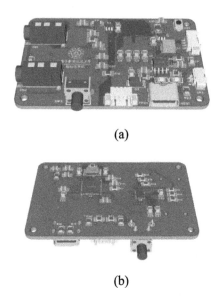

(a)

(b)

Fig. 2. 3D simulation view of PCB board. (a) front view. (b) back view.

After the key components were selected, this paper proceeded to determine the interfaces, which are categorized into two primary types: signal interfaces and power interfaces. In this work, the signal interfaces mainly include the signal acquisition interface, Bluetooth transmission interface, program download interface, and interaction interface; while the power interfaces consist of the lithium battery interface and charging input interface. Signal Interfaces: The signal acquisition interface employs a 4-pole audio jack, with two such jacks provided – one for connecting signal lines and the other for connecting the reference ground and the Right Leg Driver (RLD). Both the Bluetooth interface and the program download interface utilize 4-pin connections, unified by adopting the 1.25-4PWB terminal as the standard interface. The interaction interface, designed to initiate the boost output of the IP5306, features a tact switch with an extended button, selected based on ergonomic considerations to facilitate activation from outside the enclosure. Power Interfaces: The charging input interface was chosen with universality in mind, opting for the widely adopted Type-C interface to simplify the charging process for users. For the lithium battery interface, a 1.25-2PWB terminal was selected to ensure secure connection. Overall, these interface selections balance functionality, compatibility, and user convenience, reflecting a thoughtful integration of hardware design with practical application needs.

3 System Exterior Design

The overall exterior design of the system follows three design principles:

1. Miniaturization: The exterior design aims to be as compact and lightweight as possible, minimizing any burden on users.
2. Ergonomics and Comfort: Prioritizing user comfort, the design ensures that users do not experience discomfort during prolonged wear.
3. Adaptability: Overcoming individual differences in head shapes, the design is adjustable to accommodate various user preferences.

Based on these three principles, this paper designs the wearable EEG acquisition device as a head-mounted system. The entire wearable hardware circuit system is enclosed within a shell, which is then fixed onto a headband. Signal interfaces and power interfaces are routed out through spaces reserved in the shell. The reduction in PCB volume achieves miniaturization, while the headband, made of soft material, ensures comfort during wear. Additionally, the stretchable nature of the headband helps accommodate individual differences in head shapes (Fig. 3).

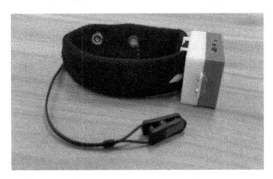

Fig. 3. Wearable EEG acquisition device as a head-mounted system.

As for the design of the top plate, it is initially determined based on the overall dimensions of the bottom plate and the positions of the through-holes (which connect the top and bottom plates). After assembly, perspective views are utilized to finalize the positioning of holes, providing space for charging, program downloading, and signal line connections. Additionally, due to the presence of indicator lights for the IP5306 and MCU on the PCB, small holes are left for these indicator lights to facilitate observation of the system status.

For the overall enclosure, there are mainly two connection points: one is between the bottom plate and the top plate, and the other is between the bottom plate and the headband. The force exerted between the plates is minimal due to the small size and lightweight nature of the entire system. Therefore, the impact of force at this connection point can be neglected compared to the connection with screws and nuts. However, for the connection between the bottom plate and the headband, as it may be subjected to external tensile forces, it is essential to analyze the structural strength of the bottom plate connection using Fusion360 and perform finite element analysis to obtain more accurate results. This analysis will help ensure the connection can withstand external forces effectively (Fig. 4).

Fig. 4. Finite element analysis of baseplate.

Since this paper only has two channels to select appropriate EEG positions, according to the 10–20 international standard electrode placement system, the frontal polar areas on both sides (FP1 and FP2 in Fig. 5) are chosen as the two signal inputs. The selection of FP1 and FP2 is primarily based on two reasons: Firstly, compared to other electrode positions, the two potentials in the frontal polar areas are not obscured by hair, requiring minimal preparation for daily device use (usually just a simple wipe to remove oils). Secondly, the frontal lobes, which are adjacent to the frontal polar areas, are associated with higher cognitive functions such as learning, language, decision-making, and emotion, which facilitates the subsequent experimental tasks.

As for the choice of electrode materials, the mainstream options include dry electrodes and wet electrodes. Although dry electrodes are widely used due to their convenience and are commonly found in portable devices and non-invasive monitoring systems, making them more compatible with the system described in this paper, wet electrodes, which can yield higher-quality EEG signals, were chosen for the preliminary validation environment. These electrodes consist of a silver chloride dry electrode internally and conductive gel externally, maintaining consistency with the electrode materials of the double-sided electrode clips and reducing artifacts caused by differences in electrode polarization levels.

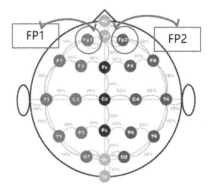

Fig. 5. 10–20 International standard lead system.

4 Experimental Results Processing and Analysis

Following the successful development and initial testing of the EEG signal acquisition system, this paper incorporates wavelet transform as an effective method for signal processing. Leveraging its unique advantages in time-frequency analysis, the wavelet transform conducts multi-scale analyses of the collected EEG signals, effectively removing noise while preserving transient features in the signal. To comprehensively validate the accuracy and practicality of the system, two pivotal experiments are meticulously designed: the eyes-open/eyes-closed experiment and the attention experiment. The eyes-open/eyes-closed experiment is straightforward and intuitive, observing the suppression and recovery of α waves. Conversely, the attention experiment involves subjects performing cognitive tasks to observe relevant evaluation metrics, thereby assessing levels of concentration.

4.1 Wavelet Analysis and Filtering Processing

In the analysis of EEG signals, both the time domain and frequency domain fail to adequately reveal the core characteristics of the EEG, as they extract features with limited dimensions, often resulting in suboptimal analytical outcomes. Wavelet transform, as an innovative signal processing technique, stands out for its ability to more finely adapt to the demands of our experiments, particularly in dissecting non-stationary signals like EEG, where it demonstrates unique advantages. In summary, wavelet transform captures transient features in EEG signals more comprehensively and flexibly, compensating for the inadequacies of conventional methods.

Given the system's need to efficiently handle large volumes of data, Discrete Wavelet Transform (DWT) is employed due to its discretization of time and scale, which reduces computational load, making it suitable for big data analysis. Hence, this paper adopts DWT, and below is the formula for its first level decomposition:

$$A_1(n) = \sum_k f(k) * h(k-n) \qquad (1)$$

$$D_1(n) = \sum_k f(k) * g(k-n) \tag{2}$$

In Eqs. 1 and 2, $f(k)$ represents the time series of the input signal. $h(n)$ serves as a low-pass filter, designed to generate approximation coefficients $A_1(n)$, which contain the low-frequency information of the signal. Conversely, $g(n)$ acts as a high-pass filter, aimed at producing detail coefficients $D_1(n)$ that encompass the high-frequency details of the signal. In both equations, the symbol $*$ denotes convolution operation.

The entire process entails recursively applying the first-level decomposition formula to attain deeper levels of approximation and detail coefficients, thereby constructing a multi-resolution analysis structure. At each decomposition level, the signal is separated into an approximation component and a detail component. The approximation part is further decomposed in the next layer, with this recursive process continuing until a predetermined number of decomposition levels is achieved.

Utilizing MATLAB in conjunction with the Signal Multiresolution Analyzer (SMA) toolbox, the procedure commences with importing a.csv file, which contains recorded signals from the host machine, into the MATLAB workspace and subsequently directing it into the SMA toolbox. The sampling frequency is configured to 1000 Hz, and the Daubechies wavelet basis, specifically Db8, is elected for the wavelet transform. The decomposition level is set to ten, marking the beginning of the analytical process.

Post-wavelet transformation, a bias attributed to hardware circuit DRL, contributing to 93.89% of the energy, is eliminated. Although an in-built calibration function in the host machine adjusts by subtracting the average value of the signal when shorted to a reference, this method fails to parallel the precision achieved through post-wavelet filtering. Concurrently, high-frequency components exceeding 30 Hz are discarded, given that the primary frequency bands of EEG signals—δ, θ, α, and β—are all beneath this threshold. The filtered data is then exported and saved. Reintroducing this cleansed dataset back into the toolbox, the subsequent steps isolate the EEG signals corresponding to these neural frequency bands. By selectively choosing detail levels within the SMA toolbox that match the desired frequency ranges, the signals are combined and exported. Leveraging MATLAB's plotting capabilities, Fig. 6 illustrates the resultant data, sequentially presenting δ, θ, α, and β bands from top to bottom. Notably, these amplitude representations have been magnified 360 times; dividing them by 360 restores their authentic amplitudes, which are consistent with EEG signal norms.

However, considering the inherent variability in EEG signals, supplementary validation is imperative to attest to the system's practical efficacy, despite the demonstrated visual representation.

4.2 Open and Close Eyes Experiments

In EEG experiments, the eyes-open/eyes-closed test serves as a common method for assessing variations in brain activity. This test compares EEG changes between the states of eyes open and eyes closed in participants, thereby analyzing the activity patterns of specific brain regions. With eyes open, external visual stimuli dominate the frequency components, leading to a reduction in α band activity (approximately 8–12 Hz)

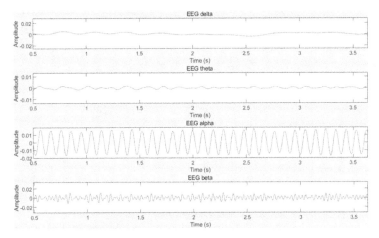

Fig. 6. EEG signals in different frequency band.

as visual stimulation and other attention-demanding tasks suppress α band. Conversely, during eyes-closed relaxation, endogenous brain oscillations take precedence, resulting in heightened α band activity, indicative of a relatively relaxed mental state [14].

This study employs the eyes-open/eyes-closed paradigm to observe EEG spectral changes, particularly focusing on α band responses, to validate the system's capability in measuring EEG accurately. Participants, comprising both males and females, were instructed to maintain an eyes-open state for ten seconds, followed by ten seconds of eyes-closed, totaling twenty seconds per trial, with multiple trials conducted. Data was acquired using the upper-level machine, saved, and subsequently imported into MATLAB, where it underwent wavelet transformation for noise and drift removal. Utilizing a signal analyzer toolbox, the waveforms corresponding to eyes-open and eyes-closed phases were segmented according to time. Frequency spectra and time-frequency energy spectra were then plotted for both conditions, laying the groundwork for subsequent analyses.

Figure 7 illustrates the temporal and spectral comparison of an experimental subject's eyes-open versus eyes-closed signals. From top to bottom, the figures depict the time-domain signal, frequency-domain spectrum, and time-frequency energy spectrogram. In both the frequency-domain spectrum and the time-frequency energy spectrogram, data cursors have been employed to highlight the α band. Analyzing the frequency-domain spectrum reveals a notably stronger response of α band during eye closure, with the amplitude approximately 4 dB higher compared to the eyes-open state (eyes closed: −53.93 dB; eyes open: −57.35 dB). Similarly, the time-frequency energy spectrogram echoes this finding, demonstrating an augmented energy level of α band during the relaxed, eyes-closed condition (brighter colors correspond to higher energy levels), further substantiating the enhanced α band response during eye closure. This evidence confirms that the system effectively captured the EEG signals differentiating between eyes-open and eyes-closed states, thereby validating its capability to record brain electrical activity.

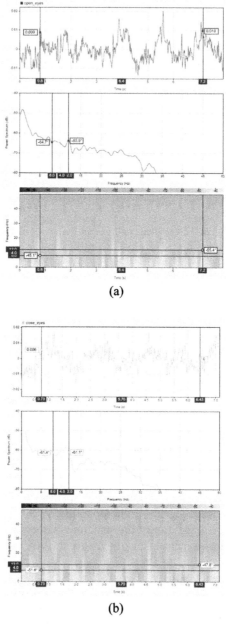

Fig. 7. Comparison of eye opening and closing signals in time domain and frequency domain. (a) with eyes open. (b) with eyes close.

4.3 Concentration Experiment

In conducting a concentration test, the analysis of EEG signals is employed to assess an individual's level of attention focus. Among the various EEG frequency bands, beta band (12–30 Hz) are associated with alertness and concentrated attention. An increase in beta wave activity is observed when individuals are actively engaged in cognitive tasks or maintaining high levels of attention. Theta band (4–8 Hz), on the other hand, become more prominent during mild to moderate lapses in attention, particularly indicating a decrease in attentiveness or fatigue in adults. Alpha band (8–12 Hz) relate to a state of relative relaxation while remaining awake and daydreaming; their suppression, or a decrease in alpha power in certain brain areas, is linked to focused attention. When focusing on a specific task or external stimulus, alpha activity in relevant brain regions decreases. Delta band (0.5–4 Hz) are typically associated with deep sleep and do not have a direct positive correlation with daily attention states.

To evaluate the experimental results and reinforce the practicality and reliability of the system, this study employs three distinct concentration assessment indices that complement each other:

The first index is the energy proportion of beta waves. Given the dominant role of beta wave patterns in attention analysis, this metric focuses on the frequencies within the beta1 and beta2 range, specifically 15–28 Hz, which are indicative of attention-related rhythms. After energy normalization, the value represents the percentage of beta band (15–28 Hz) in the EEG signal; a higher value signifies a greater proportion of beta band and thus, heightened concentration.

The second index adopted is the Theta/Beta ratio (TBR), which has proven particularly efficacious in the frontal region, making it a fitting criterion for the system's concentration test. A higher TBR is suggestive of reduced attention as it reflects a relative increase in theta activity compared to beta, indicative of a less focused mental state.

$$TBR = \frac{\theta_{power}}{\beta_{power}} \qquad (3)$$

The Theta/Beta Ratio (TBR) can be calculated from the Power Spectral Density (PSD). A higher TBR, indicating a relatively higher power in theta waves compared to beta waves, is commonly associated with Attention Deficit Hyperactivity Disorder (ADHD) or states of distraction. Conversely, a lower TBR signifies relatively enhanced beta activity, which is typically aligned with focused states.

The third index, one of the most widely applied methods for evaluating concentration, employs a formula introduced by Pope in 1995. This approach calculates cognitive engagement based on the energies in the alpha, beta, and theta frequency bands. Specifically, it is the ratio of beta wave energy to the sum of alpha and theta wave energies. Pope posited that during periods of intense focus, EEG signals are primarily characterized by beta waves, whereas during rest, they exhibit alpha or theta waves, or even lower frequency bands. Therefore, this ratio serves as an indicator of attentional focus, or cognitive engagement (CE), expressed as:

$$E_c = \frac{\beta_{power}}{\theta_{power} + \alpha_{power}} \qquad (4)$$

Here θ_{power}, α_{power} and β_{power} can all be derived from the PSD. A higher value of CE suggests a higher level of concentration.

While all three indices serve as reference points for assessing attention states, none should be used in isolation to determine concentration levels. Any assessment of attention must also account for individual differences, testing environments, task specificity, and standardized data processing methods to ensure the reliability and validity of the results.

In designing the concentration experiment, two groups were established: a focused group and a distracted group. The focused group was tasked with completing a 6x6 grid version of the popular and concise Schulte Grid attention test as quickly as possible without external disturbance, a globally recognized method for concentration training. Conversely, the distracted group was required to complete multiple unrelated tasks simultaneously while attempting to divert their attention (such as browsing the web while engaging in conversation or performing other specified tasks) (Fig. 8).

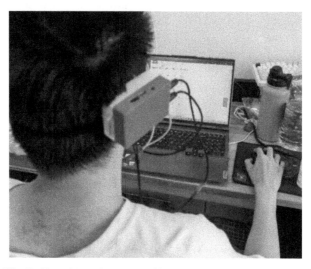

Fig. 8. Experimental process with wearable EEG sensor system.

In this study, two experimental groups were established with a time interval of less than 5 min between sessions to ensure environmental consistency, thereby ensuring that any differences observed were solely due to variations in concentration levels. The system designed in this study was utilized for data acquisition and recording. Data was processed using wavelet transform to eliminate drift and noise, and PSD was employed to calculate the energy in each frequency band, subsequently determining the three indices. Variations in these indices were then used to gauge the level of attention. By analyzing power changes in these specific frequency bands, the focused state of the participants could be assessed, providing empirical evidence for cognitive load assessment, studying learning efficiency, and neuro feedback training.

As illustrated in Table 1, it is evident that for all participants, the energy proportion of β waves and the level of cognitive engagement measured during the focused group were higher compared to those measured during the distracted group. Furthermore,

Table 1. Experimenters in different experimental groups of indicators.

No	Experimental group	Proportion of β band/%	TBR	Cognitive engagement E_c
1	Focus group	0.157173	0.966105	0.645158
	Distracted group	0.000072	5.842262	0.121999
2	Focus group	0.091067	0.995411	0.570800
	Distracted group	0.047940	1.409640	0.538961
3	Focus group	0.037790	2.791088	0.207820
	Distracted group	0.012654	3.801794	0.196494
4	Focus group	0.020705	3.976933	0.115967
	Distracted group	0.009485	11.289153	0.075426

the Theta-to-Beta Ratio (TBR) observed in the focused group was consistently lower than that recorded in the distracted group for each participant, indicating a reduced TBR, heightened cognitive involvement, and a greater proportion of β wave energy during focused states (with each participant serving as their own control) [15]. Analyzing these findings against theoretical frameworks, it can be concluded that the experimental outcomes align with expectations, affirming that variations in attentional focus—whether concentrated or dispersed—correspond to established theories. This, in turn, indirectly validates the successful acquisition of EEG signals by our system and the efficacy of signal processing methodologies employed.

An important note to add is that different participants exhibited varying values for the same metric, a phenomenon attributable to individual differences, environmental factors, and a multitude of other influences. When assessing levels of concentration using such metrics, efforts should be made to minimize extraneous variables, and comparisons are most meaningful when conducted within the same individual over different conditions. This underscores the necessity of controlling for external factors and maintaining consistency in experimental protocols to ensure the interpretability and reliability of the cognitive engagement indicators.

5 Conclusions

This paper presents the design and implementation of a wearable electroencephalogram (EEG) signal acquisition system, which comprehensively considers the synergistic operation of hardware and software. The system aims to provide a portable solution for EEG data collection in the fields of neuroscience, biomedical engineering, and human-computer interaction. The system design is divided into two main parts: hardware and software. In the hardware design aspect, the paper systematically introduces the component selection for EEG signal acquisition modules, circuit design, and PCB layout and routing, ensuring the quality and stability of signal acquisition. Moreover, focusing on the stability of electrode contact and user comfort, the exterior design has been optimized. Finite element analysis was employed to validate the mechanical strength of the structure. Regarding software design, the initialization setup and development of the embedded software were completed, along with the design of an upper computer software based on the Qt framework. This enabled real-time display and preliminary processing of the data, thereby enhancing the system's interactivity and practicality. System debugging and verification were also conducted through a series of rigorous tests, including electrical performance testing, communication protocol validation, and noise analysis, assuring the reliable operation of the entire acquisition system. Finally, relevant experiments were designed and executed, involving wavelet transform analysis, open and closed eye experiments, as well as concentration tests. These validations confirmed the effectiveness and accuracy of the system, laying the groundwork for subsequent analyses and applications of EEG data.

Acknowledgements. This research was funded by the Natural Science Foundation of the Jiangsu Higher Education Institutions of China under Grant No. 21KJB510049, the Graduate Research and Practical Innovation Program at Nanjing University of Aeronautics and Astronautics under Grant No. xcxjh20230329, and the Experimental Technology Research and Development Project at Nanjing University of Aeronautics and Astronautics under Grant No. SYJS202304Z.

References

1. Vidal, J.J.: Toward direct brain-computer communication. Annu. Rev. Biophys. Bioeng. **2**(1), 157–180 (1973)
2. Riedl, R., Minas, R.K., Dennis, A.R., et al.: Consumer-grade EEG instruments: insights on the measurement quality based on a literature review and implications for NeuroIS research. Inform. Syst. Neurosci. NeuroIS Retreat **2020**, 350–361 (2020)
3. Sabio, J., Williams, N.S., McArthur, G.M., et al.: A scoping review on the use of consumer-grade EEG devices for research. PLoS ONE **19**(3), e0291186 (2024)
4. Sawangjai, P., Hompoonsup, S., Leelaarporn, P., et al.: Consumer grade EEG measuring sensors as research tools: a review. IEEE Sens. J. **20**(8), 3996–4024 (2020)
5. Müller-Putz, G., Crell, M., Egger, J., et al.: Towards implantable brain-computer interface for communication in locked-in syndrome patients. Curr. Direct. Biomed. Eng. **9**(2), 1–4 (2023)
6. Kaveh, R., Doong, J., Zhou, A., et al.: Wireless user-generic ear EEG. IEEE Trans. Biomed. Circuits Syst. **4**, 727–737 (2020)
7. Schwendeman, C., Kaveh, R., Muller, R., et al.: Drowsiness detection with wireless, user-generic, dry electrode ear EEG. In: Annual International Conference of the IEEE Engineering in Medicine and Biology Society. IEEE Engineering in Medicine and Biology Society. Annual International Conference, pp. 19–12 (2022)
8. Shah, J., Chougule, A., Chamola, V., et al.: Novel welch-transform based enhanced spectro-temporal analysis for cognitive microsleep detection using a single electrode EEG. Neurocomputing **549** (2023)
9. LaRocco, J., Le, M.D., Paeng, D.G.: A systemic review of available low-cost EEG headsets used for drowsiness detection. Front. Neuroinform. **14**, 553352 (2020)
10. Jeon, J., Cai, H.: Multi-class classification of construction hazards via cognitive states assessment using wearable EEG. Adv. Eng. Inform. **53**, 101646 (2022)
11. Apicella, A., et al.: Enhancement of SSVEPs classification in BCI-based wearable instrumentation through machine learning techniques. IEEE Sens. J. **22**(9), 9087–9094 (2022)
12. Feng, L., Yang, L., Liu, S., Han, C., Zhang, Y., Zhu, Z.: An efficient EEGNet processor design for portable EEG-Based BCIs. Microelectron. J. **120**, 105356 (2022)

13. Arias-Cabarcos, P., Fallahi, M., Habrich, T., Schulze, K., Becker, C., Strufe, T.: Performance and usability evaluation of brainwave authentication techniques with consumer devices. ACM Trans. Privacy Secur. **26**(3), 1–36 (2023)
14. Yu, Z., Guo, S.: A low-cost, wireless, 4-channel EEG measurement system used in virtual reality environments. HardwareX **17**, e00507 (2024)
15. Kerson, C., deBeus, R., Lightstone, H., et al.: EEG theta/beta ratio calculations differ between various EEG neurofeedback and assessment software packages: clinical interpretation. Clin. EEG Neurosci. **51**(2), 114–120 (2020)

Enhancing Robotic Hand Control with Electronic Slime-Based Flexible Finger Joint Motion Sensor

Yu Feng[1], Hui Sun[1], Meng Chen[1,2], Xiaodong Yu[1], Cong Wu[1], Guanglie Zhang[1,2(✉)], and Wen Jung Li[1,2(✉)]

[1] Department of Mechanical Engineering, City University of Hong Kong, Hong Kong SAR 999017, China
{gl.zhang,wenjli}@cityu.edu.hk
[2] CAS-CityU Joint Laboratory for Robotic Research, City University of Hong Kong Shenzhen Research Institute, Shenzhen 518057, China

Abstract. The emergence of flexible wearable devices represents a significant leap forward in human-robot interaction (HRI), meeting the growing demand for both comfortable and versatile interfaces. Finger joint movements, the most intricate among human joint motions, require precise detection while comfortable deployment for seamless collaboration with robotic hands, which is hard for traditional rigid sensors. This study presents electronic slime crafted from a biocompatible polyvinyl alcohol (PVA) matrix combined with cost-efficient and highly effective carbon-based nanoparticles (graphite and carbon black) using a simple fabrication process. The electronic slime benefits from a unique island-bridge structure and tunneling effect between graphite flakes and carbon black granules, resulting in a high gauge factor of 2.95, a broad sensing range of up to 400%, and a low detection threshold of 1% strain. Easily applicable to fingers, this electronic slime is capable of detecting minute motion signals, such as subtle joint extensions and flexions. Additionally, it accurately captures finger motion signals to facilitate interaction with robotic fingers, underscoring its potential as a human-machine interface. This research paves the way for the development of ultra-flexible, readily deployable electronic skin suitable for wearable HRI applications.

Keywords: Flexible electronics · Epidermal sensor · Wearable sensor · Humanrobot interaction

1 Introduction

The rise of flexible wearable devices marks a significant advancement in human-robot interaction (HRI), catering to the growing demand for convenience and comfortability [1–6]. Traditional rigid electronic devices hinder seamless interfacing with human skin, affecting comfort and limiting interaction methods. Flexible sensors provide a versatile platform for various HRI applications, including small joint and large body motions

[7–10]. Flexible sensors can adhere to dynamic skin surfaces, enabling continuous real-time monitoring of physiological, which is essential for accurate and responsive HRI. Flexible sensors capture real-time physical, electrophysiological, and environmental signals, with wireless communication and signal processing bridging the input and output stages with the machine [11–17]. These systems ultimately enhance the interaction experience by leveraging mechanical actuators, robots, and various interactive interfaces. The integration of flexible epidermal electronics is crucial for advancing HRI technology, ensuring more natural and effective interactions. Among the various joint movements in the human body, finger joint movements are the most intricate and refined [18, 19]. Accurate detection and processing of these movement signals are crucial for achieving smooth interactions with robotic hands. Traditional rigid sensors are unable to conform to the flexible nature of fingers, thereby hindering effective HRI with robotic hands.

Epidermal electronics, a category of flexible electronic systems, can be applied to the body surface to monitor physiological signals, enable human-robot interactions, and provide therapeutic assistance. These systems come in various forms, including electronic patches [20–22], electronic tattoos [23–25], and electronic ink [26, 27], each distinguished by their physical properties. Although recent progress has been made in developing thin and well-integrated electronic patches, they still struggle with customization issues related to shape and size for specific applications. In contrast, electronic tattoos address this limitation by being pre-fabricated and tailored to the desired morphology before application to the skin. However, their fabrication complexity and the need for transfer printing during deployment challenge their skin conformity. Electronic ink offers on-demand customization by allowing direct application to the epidermal area, yet it generally suffers from a limited shelf life, and exposure to sweat can lead to performance degradation, detachment, or even failure.

Different from the above-mentioned types of epidermal electronics, "Silly Putty-like" materials, as flexible and deformable materials, have demonstrated their potential in flexible electronics due to self-healing ability, malleability, and viscoelasticity [28–30]. In this work, utilizing biocompatible polyvinyl alcohol (PVA) as a matrix while accompanied by low-cost and highly effective carbon-based nanoparticles (graphite and carbon black), electronic slime is proposed through a simple fabrication method. Owing to the island-bridge structure and tunneling effect between graphite flake and carbon black granular, electronic slime exhibits a high gauge factor (2.95), wide sensing range (up to 400%), and low detection limit (1% strain). Electronic slime can be conveniently deployed on-the-fly at fingers to measure small motion signals (small joint extension and flexion). Moreover, electronic slime is able to interact with robotic fingers by obtaining finger motion signals accurately, demonstrating the feasibility of a human-machine interface. This study paves the way for the development of ultra-flexible and easy-deployment electronic skin for wearable human-machine interfaces.

2 Principles of Electronic Slime for Hand Motion Tracking

2.1 Sensing Mechanism of Electronic Slime

Figure 1 illustrates the conductive sensing mechanism of electronic slime. Carbon black particles act as fillers in this mechanism to create an island-bridge structure through interconnected conductive pathways. These pathways significantly enhance the overall conductivity of the composite by bridging the gaps between graphite layers and linking different graphite particles. When the electronic slime deforms, its internal structure, composed of these carbon-based composites, changes accordingly. This deformation impacts the conductive pathways, either enhancing or diminishing them due to the shifting positions of the composite materials. Consequently, the electrical resistance of the electronic slime is altered.

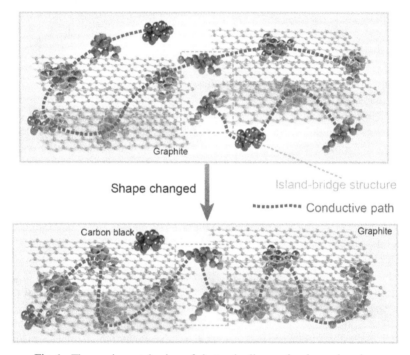

Fig. 1. The sensing mechanism of electronic slime under shape-changing.

The conductive sensing mechanism is fundamentally dependent on the intricate distribution of carbon black and graphite within the electronic slime matrix. Carbon black particles are crucial for maintaining electrical connectivity throughout the composite material despite their small size. When the electronic slime is subjected to mechanical forces such as compression, stretching, or bending, the spatial arrangement of these carbon particles changes; this alteration in the conductive network can lead to an increase in the number of contact points between conductive particles, thereby reducing resistance or a decrease in contact points, resulting in higher resistance.

2.2 Motion Model of the Finger

Finger joint movements primarily involve the metacarpophalangeal (MCP), proximal interphalangeal (PIP), and distal interphalangeal (DIP) joints, essential for tasks like grasping, typing, and manipulating objects. Figure 2a shows a static model of the hand, highlighting the thumb with two phalanges and the other fingers with three phalanges. The thumb has five degrees of freedom, critical for opposable functions, while the other fingers have four degrees each, resulting in 21 degrees of freedom for the entire hand. This complex articulation enables precise and coordinated fine motor skills. Both the thumb and other fingers share two degrees of freedom at the MCP joints: flexion-extension and abduction-adduction. These movements are facilitated by a combination of muscles and tendons. Figure 2b offers a detailed view of a single finger's anatomy and joint articulations.

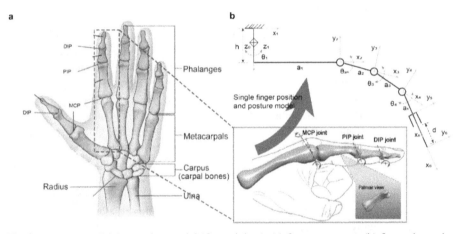

Fig. 2. Human small joint motion model (finger joints). (a) finger structure; (b) finger dynamics model.

The kinematic model of a single finger is analyzed using the Denavit-Hartenberg parameter model as follows:

$$^0_5I = {}^0_1I {}^1_2I {}^2_3I {}^3_4I {}^4_5I \tag{1}$$

Among it:

$$_1^0I = \begin{bmatrix} c\theta_1 & 0 & -s\theta_1 & a_1 c\theta_1 \\ s\theta_1 & 0 & c\theta_1 & a_1 s\theta_1 \\ 0 & -1 & 0 & h \\ 0 & 0 & 0 & 1 \end{bmatrix}, {}_2^1I = \begin{bmatrix} c\theta_2 & -s\theta_2 & 0 & a_2 c\theta_2 \\ s\theta_2 & c\theta_2 & 0 & a_2 s\theta_2 \\ 0 & 0 & 1 & 0 \\ 0 & 0 & 0 & 1 \end{bmatrix}, {}_3^2I =$$

$$\begin{bmatrix} c\theta_3 & -s\theta_3 & 0 & a_3 c\theta_3 \\ s\theta_3 & c\theta_3 & 0 & a_3 s\theta_3 \\ 0 & 0 & 1 & 0 \\ 0 & 0 & 0 & 1 \end{bmatrix}, {}_4^3I = \begin{bmatrix} c\theta_4 & -s\theta_4 & 0 & a_4 c\theta_4 \\ s\theta_4 & c\theta_4 & 0 & a_4 s\theta_4 \\ 0 & 0 & 1 & 0 \\ 0 & 0 & 0 & 1 \end{bmatrix}, {}_5^4I = \begin{bmatrix} 1 & 0 & 0 & d \\ 0 & 1 & 0 & 0 \\ 0 & 0 & 1 & 0 \\ 0 & 0 & 0 & 1 \end{bmatrix}.$$

The inverse solution obtained through algebraic methods is:

$$\theta = \theta_1 + \theta_2 + \theta_3 = A \tan 2(s_{123}, c_{123}) \tag{2}$$

Here are the Denavit-Hartenberg equation parameters. By solving for these parameters, the joint angles of the finger's movement can be estimated.

Although the detection of human joint movements demands high response speed, stability, and reliability from sensors, as analyzed previously, small joint movements are typically subtle and precise. Therefore, for the detection of small joint movements, the primary requirements for sensors are sensitivity and resolution.

3 Experimental Setup and Procedure

3.1 Fabrication of Electronic Slime

PVA, known for its widespread use as a synthetic polymer with biocompatibility, has been utilized to create various types of hydrogels serving different functions in biomedical applications and human-machine interfaces. This study employs PVA as the matrix material for preparing electronic slime, leveraging easy-to-obtain, low-cost, and environmentally friendly raw components. The preparation process, illustrated in Fig. 3, involves three steps. A mixed solution of PVA, glycerol, and TA is initially prepared at the desired concentration and stirred in an 80 °C water bath for 2 h. Once all chemicals are dissolved, graphite and carbon black powder are added to the mixture in a 60 °C water bath. Although graphite and carbon black are not water-soluble, the TA monomer can undergo oxidative polymerization, depositing on the surface of graphite. Meanwhile, carbon black is dispersed within the interlayer spaces due to the high reduction capacity of TA-modified graphite, ensuring uniform mixing. Subsequently, a borax pentahydrate solution is gradually introduced into the conductive mixture with continuous stirring to form electronic slime.

3.2 Sensing Performance Tests

For the electrical performance tests, electronic slime was molded into a cubic shape with dimensions of 20 mm in length, 10 mm in width, and 2 mm in thickness. Using a digital multimeter, the electrical signals of the electronic slime were measured. The conductivity (σ) of the electronic slime sample was calculated using the formula $\sigma = L/(R \times A)$, where L is the length of the sample, R is the resistance of the sample, and A denotes the cross-sectional area of the sample. The relative resistance variation was determined by the equation:

$$\Delta R/R_0 = (R - R_0)/R_0 \tag{3}$$

Where R_0 and R represent the resistance without and with applied strain, respectively.

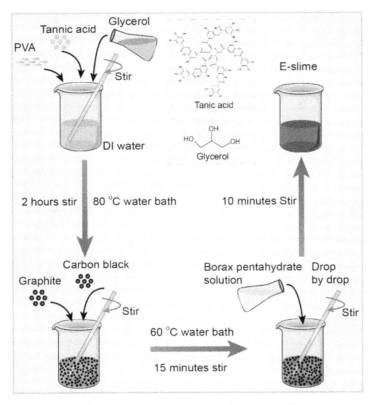

Fig. 3. The schematic preparation of electronic slime.

3.3 Experiments for Hand Motion Sensor

The electronic slime was applied to various targeted locations on the human body in different shapes and sizes. Wires were securely attached to the electronic slime using pressure-sensitive tape. A digital multimeter was used to detect electrical signals in real-time.

4 Demonstrations of Electronic Slime on Human-Robot Interaction

4.1 Sensing Performance of Electronic Slime

As shown in Fig. 4a, the relative resistance variation changes positively with the increase of applied strain due to the effect of the elongated internal electron transfer channels. Electronic slime exhibits a sensitivity of 2.95, which can be attributed to the island-bridge structure formed by carbon black and graphite and the tunneling effect. This unique combination makes electronic slime an excellent flexible strain sensor, particularly suitable for detecting small joint movements in fingers. The high sensitivity of electronic slime is a result of the effective conductive pathways established by the carbon black and graphite particles. The island-bridge structure ensures robust electrical connectivity even under deformation, while the tunneling effect further enhances the material's responsiveness to strain. These properties enable electronic slime to accurately detect and respond to minute movements, such as those of small finger joints.

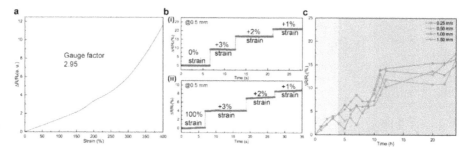

Fig. 4. The sensing performance of electronic slime. (a) The relative resistance variation curves of electronic slime as a function of strain; (b) The strain resolution of electronic slime under 0 and 100% strain load; (c) The relative resistance variation of electronic slime over time (room temperature) with different thicknesses.

Figure 4b demonstrates the strain resolution of electronic slime under varying strain loads (0% and 100% strain). This figure illustrates that each increment in strain results in a noticeable change in resistance, even when different reference strains are applied. Electrical stability is a crucial parameter for sensors made from hydrogel, and this was assessed by examining the resistance changes over time at room temperature, as shown in Fig. 4c. All test samples, which included four different thicknesses, exhibited a resistance variation of less than 5% within the first 4 h, gradually increasing to around 10% by the 10th hour. This result indicates that the sensor possesses essential electrical performance stability, making it suitable for relatively long-term storage and use.

These findings underscore that electronic slime maintains stable electrical conductivity, even when subjected to irregular and wrinkled skin surfaces and various types of deformation. The ability to detect strain increments reliably, coupled with its minimal resistance variation over time, suggests that electronic slime is well-suited for applications requiring consistent and durable performance. This stability ensures that electronic slime can be effectively used in wearable sensors, flexible electronics, and other applications where long-term reliability and precise strain detection are critical. Moreover, the stable electrical performance of electronic slime under different conditions highlights its potential for use in real-world scenarios, where sensors may be exposed to dynamic and unpredictable environments. The robust nature of electronic slime, as evidenced by its consistent resistance changes and electrical stability, positions it as a promising material for advanced technological applications, particularly in the fields of biomedical engineering and human-machine interfaces.

4.2 Finger Motion Detection of Electronic Slime

As shown in Fig. 5a, when the stretching angle of the finger increased from 60° to 120°, the relative resistance variation signal exhibited a correspondingly near-linear decrease ($R^2 = 0.98$), with a sensitivity of approximately 0.17% per degree. This sensitivity is due to the change in electronic slime strain, which indicates that electronic slime possesses high sensitivity to angular changes. Figure 5b illustrates the electrical signal response of electronic slime upon repeated measurements of finger bending motion at different angles (30°, 60°, and 120°). The results demonstrate that electronic slime has a rapid response rate to finger bending motion, approximately 2 s, and effectively detects repeated motions. Additionally, the results from cyclic detection (Fig. 5c), involving 1000 cycles over approximately 1500 s, further verify the durability and reliability of electronic slime for sustained use.

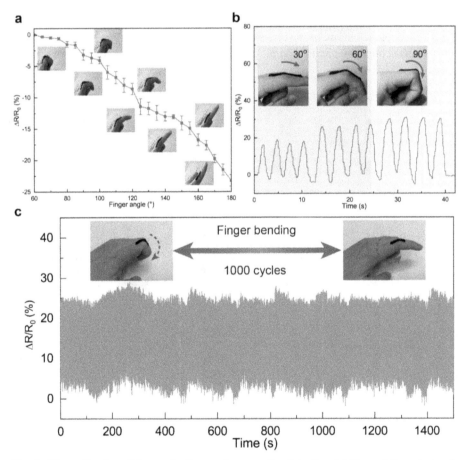

Fig. 5. The application of electronic slime on finger motion detection. (a) The real-time electronic slime's relative resistance variation as a function of finger position angle; (b) The real-time relative resistance variation under different finger bending angles (30°, 60°, and 90°); (c) The cyclic motion signal detection of human finger bending.

These findings highlight electronic slime's potential as an effective strain sensor for monitoring finger movements. Its high sensitivity and near-linear response to angular changes make it suitable for precise motion detection applications. The rapid response rate ensures that electronic slime can provide real-time monitoring, which is crucial for applications in wearable technology and human-machine interfaces. Furthermore, the durability demonstrated through extensive cyclic testing underscores the robustness of electronic slime in long-term applications. This durability, combined with its sensitivity and quick response, positions electronic slime as a promising material for developing advanced sensors in biomedical engineering, robotics, and other fields where accurate and reliable motion detection is essential.

4.3 Interaction Between Human Finger and Robotic Finger upon Electronic Slime

To manifest the human-robot interaction of electronic slime, two pieces of electronic slime were deployed in situ on the fingers (index finger and middle finger). In this system, a two-signal acquisition circuit is employed to convert the resistance variations of the film

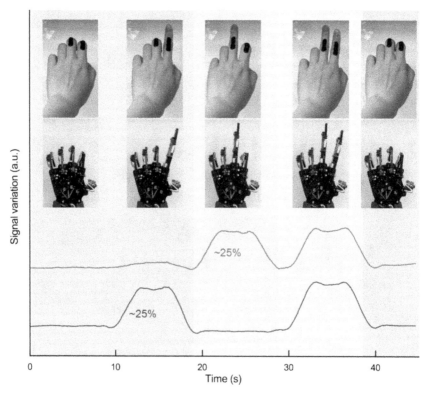

Fig. 6. The application of electronic slime on Human-robot interaction. The instant control of the robotic hand is demonstrated by the different gestures and the corresponding signal responses from two fingers (index finger and middle finger).

into an analog voltage signal. A low-pass filter is then used to eliminate high-frequency noise from the amplified voltage signal. Subsequently, an analog-to-digital converter (ADC) collects and digitizes the signal. Ultimately, an Esp32 processor governs the operation of the steering engines, thereby inducing the bending of the robotic fingers.

Figure 6b illustrates the instantaneous control of a robotic hand using the electronic slime by demonstrating the transition of four gestures. The figure also presents the corresponding signals generated by the two pieces of electronic slime mounted on the robotic fingers. This demonstration highlights the system's capability to accurately and rapidly interpret and replicate human hand motions. The real-time responsiveness and precision of the robotic hand underscore the effectiveness of electronic slime in providing reliable sensory feedback, thereby enabling the robotic system to mimic complex human gestures with high fidelity. The aforementioned experiment demonstrates that electronic slime possesses significant application value in the domain of wearable electronic devices and human-machine interfaces. This finding underscores the potential of electronic slime to enhance the performance and functionality of next-generation wearable technologies and interactive systems.

5 Conclusion

The rise of flexible wearable devices marks a significant advancement in human-robot interaction (HRI), addressing the need for more comfortable and versatile interfaces. Among the various joint movements in the human body, finger joint movements are the most intricate, and accurate detection of these movements is crucial for achieving seamless interactions with robotic hands, a task that traditional rigid sensors cannot accomplish effectively. In this study, we introduce electronic slime composed of a biocompatible polyvinyl alcohol (PVA) matrix integrated with cost-effective and efficient carbon-based nanoparticles (graphite and carbon black) fabricated through a straightforward method. The unique island-bridge structure and tunneling effect between graphite flakes and carbon black granules endow the electronic slime with a high gauge factor of 2.95, a wide sensing range of up to 400%, and a low detection limit of 1% strain. This electronic slime can be easily applied to fingers to detect subtle motion signals, such as small joint extensions and flexions. Furthermore, it effectively captures finger motion signals to interact with robotic fingers, showcasing its potential as a human-machine interface. This work significantly advances the development of ultra-flexible, easily deployable electronic skin for wearable human-machine interfaces.

Acknowledgments. This work was supported by the Hong Kong Research Grants Council (Project Number: 11216120), the University Grants Committee (Project Number: T42-717/20-R), the CRF-Collaborative Research Fund (Project Number: 8739045), and the InnoHK Project at the Hong Kong Centre for Cerebro-cardiovascular Health Engineering (COCHE).

References

1. Sanchez, V., Walsh, C.J., Wood, R.J.: Textile technology for soft robotic and autonomous garments. Adv. Funct. Mater. **31**, 2008278 (2021)
2. Liu, S., Rao, Y., Jang, H., Tan, P., Lu, N.: Strategies for body-conformable electronics. Matter. **5**, 1104–1136 (2022).
3. Xu, C., Solomon, S.A., Gao, W.: Artificial intelligence-powered electronic skin. Nat. Mach. Intell. **5**, 1344–1355 (2023)
4. Qu, J., et al.: Advanced flexible sensing technologies for soft robots. Adv. Funct. Mater. 2401311 (2024)
5. Lee, S., Liang, X., Kim, J.S., Yokota, T., Fukuda, K., Someya, T.: Permeable bioelectronics toward biointegrated systems. Chem. Rev. (2024)
6. Vicente, B.A., Sebastião, R., Sencadas, V.: Wearable devices for respiratory monitoring. Adv. Funct. Mater. 2404348 (2024)
7. Kim, D., Lee, J., Park, M.K., Ko, S.H.: Recent developments in wearable breath sensors for healthcare monitoring. Commun Mater. **5**, 1–14 (2024)
8. Hou, C., et al.: Boosting flexible electronics with integration of two-dimensional materials. InfoMat. e12555 (2024)
9. Suo, J., et al.: AI-enabled soft sensing array for simultaneous detection of muscle deformation and mechanomyography for metaverse somatosensory interaction. Adv. Sci. **11**, 2305025 (2024)
10. Suo, J., et al.: Wide-bandwidth nanocomposite-sensor integrated smart mask for tracking multiphase respiratory activities. Adv. Sci. **9**, 2203565 (2022)
11. Xing, X., et al.: Ultra-stretchable and high performance fibrous TENG with helically structured dual-channel Liquid Metal electrode. Chem. Eng. J. **493**, 152392 (2024)
12. Wang, Z., et al.: Directional moisture-wicking triboelectric materials enabled by laplace pressure differences. Nano Lett. (2024)
13. Wang, Y., et al.: Dual-adaptive heterojunction synaptic transistors for efficient machine vision in harsh lighting conditions. Adv. Mater. n/a, 2404160 (2024)
14. Wang, R., et al.: Fiber-based miniature strain sensor with fast response and low hysteresis. Adv. Funct. Mater. 2403918 (2024)
15. Wang, L., et al.: Moisture-enabled self-charging and voltage stabilizing supercapacitor. Nat. Commun. **15**, 4929 (2024)
16. Wang, J., Du, P., Hsu, Y.-I., Uyama, H.: Smart versatile hydrogels tailored by metal-phenolic coordinating carbon and polypyrrole for soft actuation, strain sensing and writing recognition. Chem. Eng. J. **493**, 152671 (2024)
17. Vo, T.H., Lam, P.K., Chuang, R., Shieh, F.-K., Sheng, Y.-J., Tsao, H.-K.: One-step, additive-free fabrication of highly stretchable and ultra-tough physical polyvinyl alcohol-based eutectogels for strain sensors. Chem. Eng. J. **493**, 152877 (2024)
18. Bae, S., Armstrong, T.J.: A finger motion model for reach and grasp. Int. J. Ind. Ergon. **41**, 79–89 (2011)
19. Xu, Y., et al.: A soft magnetoelectric finger for robots' multidirectional tactile perception in non-visual recognition environments. NPJ Flex Electron. **8**, 2 (2024)
20. Luo, J., et al.: A highly stretchable, real-time self-healable hydrogel adhesive matrix for tissue patches and flexible electronics. Adv. Healthcare Mater. **9**, 1901423 (2020)
21. Han, W.B., Lee, J.H., Shin, J., Hwang, S.: Advanced materials and systems for biodegradable, transient electronics. Adv. Mater. **32**, 2002211 (2020)
22. La, T., et al.: Two-layered and stretchable e-textile patches for wearable healthcare electronics. Adv. Healthcare Mater. **7**, 1801033 (2018)

23. Tang, L., Shang, J., Jiang, X.: Multilayered electronic transfer tattoo that can enable the crease amplification effect. Sci. Adv. **7**, eabe3778 (2021)
24. Kireev, D., et al.: Fabrication, characterization and applications of graphene electronic tattoos. Nat. Protoc. **16**, 2395–2417 (2021)
25. Gogurla, N., Kim, Y., Cho, S., Kim, J., Kim, S.: Multifunctional and ultrathin electronic tattoo for on-skin diagnostic and therapeutic applications. Adv. Mater. **33**, 2008308 (2021)
26. Huang, H., Feng, Y., Yang, X., Shen, Y.: Natural gum-based electronic ink with waterproofing self-healing and easy-cleaning properties for directly on-skin electronics. Biosens. Bioelectron. **214**, 114547 (2022)
27. Lee, G.-H., et al.: A personalized electronic tattoo for healthcare realized by on-the-spot assembly of an intrinsically conductive and durable liquid-metal composite. Adv. Mater. **34**, 2204159 (2022)
28. Li, Z., et al.: 3D-printable and multifunctional conductive nanocomposite with tunable mechanics inspired by sesame candy. Nano Energy **108**, 108166 (2023)
29. Chen, M., Murphy, B.B., Wang, Y., Vitale, F., Yang, S.: SMART silly putty: stretchable, malleable, adherable, reusable, and tear-resistible hydrogels. Small **19**, 2205854 (2023)
30. Feng, Y., et al.: Amoeba-inspired self-healing electronic slime for adaptable, durable epidermal wearable electronics. Adv. Funct. Mater. 2402393 (2024)

A Biocompatible Strain Sensor Based on Ni-GaIn and SA-Doped PAAM for Implantable Bioelectronics

Mingxi Tu[1,2], Jiawen Liang[1,3], Hongji Guo[1], Tianming Zhao[1(✉)], and Haibo Yu[1]

[1] State Key Laboratory of Robotics, Shenyang Institute of Automation, Chinese Academy of Sciences, Shenyang 110016, China
zhaotianming@sia.cn
[2] University of Chinese Academy of Sciences, Beijing 100049, China
[3] School of Mechanical Engineering and Automation, Northeastern University, Shenyang 110819, China

Abstract. With the rapid evolution of sensor technology, biomaterials, and micro/nano manufacturing techniques, the performance requirements for flexible electronic devices have been increasingly elevated. These devices not only need to exhibit exceptional flexibility and stability but also require a high level of biocompatibility to adapt to a variety of application scenarios ranging from attachment to the skin surface to implantation inside the body, ultimately facilitating the monitoring and feedback of internal human body information. In this study, by doping Ni particles in Liquid metal (Ni-GaIn) to regulate the surface tension and fabricating them with a biocompatible hydrogel (SA-doped PAAM), an implantable strain sensor was successfully developed. This method not only significantly improves the processability and moldability of liquid metal by reducing its surface tension but also endows the device with excellent stretchability through the construction of a stable hydrogel-liquid metal interface. The device possesses high stretchability and can serve as an implantable stress sensor, stably sensing motion information such as bending angles within biological tissues. This research provides new insights for the design and fabrication of implantable bioelectronics and holds promising application prospects in the field of biomedical engineering.

Keywords: Hydrogel · Liquid Metal · Biocompatibility · Implantable · Bioelectronics

1 Introduction

In recent years, flexible electronics have garnered significant attention in the biomedical field due to their unique advantages [1–4]. These electronic devices not only enable real-time monitoring of physiological parameters such as heart rate and deformation [5, 6] but also possess the capability to modulate tissues or nerves [7–9], leading to revolutionary changes in bioengineering detection [10–12]. In the manufacturing process of these flexible electronic devices, a common strategy is to fabricate serpentine electrodes on flexible substrates (such as PDMS and PI films) based on MEMS technology [13, 14]. These electrodes are used to capture electromyography signals or sense deformation to reflect heart rate. These devices exhibit excellent electrical performance while maintaining good flexibility, making them easy to attach to the skin surface. However, the uneven stress distribution caused by the large modulus difference between the electrodes and the substrate materials and the inflammatory response caused by the corrosion of the electrode material limit the development of bioelectronics.

The PAAM hydrogel doped with sodium alginate (SA-doped PAAM) [15], a highly biocompatible and stretchable biomaterial, exhibits excellent compatibility when in contact with biological tissues, avoiding the risks of allergies, toxicity, and mechanical damage [16–21]. However, its conductivity is poor, and the combination of other conductive materials is required to prepare bioelectronic devices. Liquid metal, as a conductive material with fluidity at room temperature, can match the high stretchability of SA-doped PAAM well [22–24]. Nevertheless, the high surface tension of liquid metal makes it difficult to process directly on the hydrogel surface.

In this paper, by doping Ni powder into the liquid metal, its processability was improved by regulating the surface tension. Subsequently, the liquid metal was encapsulated using SA-doped PAAM hydrogel to prepare a highly biocompatible and stretchable strain sensor. Through appropriate surface tension design, the sensor ensures that the liquid metal does not penetrate the network structure of the SA-doped PAAM, and its good fluidity matches the high stretchability of SA-doped PAAM. Due to its ability to detect changes in liquid metal shape caused by stretching, bending, and other deformations, this device can be implanted into the body as a strain sensor.

2 Materials and Methods

2.1 Materials

The chemicals N,N,N′,N′-tetramethylethylenediamine (TEMED, purity $\geq$ 99.5%), Ammonium persulfate (APS, purity $\geq$ 98%), and Acrylamide (AAm, purity $\geq$ 99.0%) were procured from Aladdin. Additionally, Sodium alginate (SA, CAS No. 9005-38-3) and N,N'-methylenebisacrylamide (MBA, purity $\geq$ 99%) were obtained from Sigma-Aldrich (Shanghai). The liquid metal (LM) utilized in this study was gallium-indium eutectic alloy (EGaIn) consisting of 75.5 wt% gallium and 24.5 wt% indium (supplied by Jiachun Metal, purity $\geq$ 99.99%), with a melting point of 15 °C. Furthermore, nickel powder (999 purity, 50 nm) was purchased from Jiachun Metal in China. All reagents were utilized in their as-received state without undergoing additional purification processes.

2.2 Preparation of SA-Doped PAAM Hydrogels:

A total of 5.5 mL of AAm solution (18.7 wt%) was dissolved in water and subsequently mixed with 4 mL of a sodium alginate (SA) solution (4 wt%). The resulting mixture was stirred for 15 min at room temperature. Subsequently, 375 μL of the cross-linking agent MBA (0.2 g/100 mL) and 102 μL of the initiator APS (0.2 mol/L) were added to the solution. The solution was then sealed and stirred for an additional 10 min. Next, 5 μL of the accelerator TEMED was introduced, and after thorough mixing and stirring for 5 min, the mixed solution was poured into the mold. Finally, the solution was cured under UV light at 180 W for 15 min, resulting in the formation of the SA-doped PAAM hydrogel.

2.3 Fabrication of the Strain Sensor:

Nickel powder was poured into the liquid metal and agitated on a shaking bed for 2 h to achieve a homogeneous mixture, resulting in the preparation of Ni-GaIn with mass fractions of 1 wt%, 2 wt%, and 3 wt%. Then, patterned Ni-GaIn was printed onto the SA-doped PAAM hydrogel using a screen printing process. Finally, the device was encapsulated using the SA-doped PAAM hydrogel.

2.4 Characterization

The conductivity of the strain sensor was assessed utilizing a digital multimeter (Keithley 2400, USA). Tensile, flexural, and cyclic tests were conducted on a material testing machine system (1ST; Tinius Olsen; USA). During the tensile and tensile cyclic tests, a maximum tensile extension of 20 mm was attained at a tensile velocity of 4 mm/min. Similarly, for the bending and flexural cyclic experiments, a maximum downward deflection of 10 mm was achieved at a tensile speed of 5 mm/min. The performance of the TMHA-based sensors was evaluated by employing a tensile testing machine alongside an LCR meter (Keysight E4980AL, USA). To verify the potential application capabilities of the sensors, a robot arm (Jaco2, Kinova, Canada) and a dexterous hand (RH56DFX, Inspired-robots, China) were utilized. A scanning electron microscope (Quattro S, Thermo Fisher Scientific, USA) with an accelerating voltage of 10–20 kV was used to observe the microstructural details of the devices under high vacuum. The hydrogels were freeze-dried for 48 h and finally sputtered with a 60 nm thick nanometric layer of gold.

3 Results and Discussion

3.1 Design and Fabrication of the Strain Sensor

Figure 1A shows the design and fabrication process of the device. The fabrication process is primarily divided into four steps: pouring, solidification, printing, and packaging. A detailed description of the fabrication process can be found in the Materials and Fabrication Methods section. Figure 1B-E shows scanning electron microscopy (SEM) images of the device. Figure 1B shows the top-view SEM image of the freeze-dried hydrogel material, revealing its complex network structure after freeze-drying. Figure 1C shows the Ni-GaIn coating on the SA-doped PAAM. Figure 1D is a cross-sectional SEM image of the device, and Fig. 1E is a magnified view of Fig. 1D, which reveals that Ni-GaIn is packaged by the SA-doped PAAM hydrogel without any diffusion. This is attributed to the stable interface formed between the oxide layer on the liquid metal surface and the abundant -OH bonds in the hydrogel [25]. In addition, this interface can effectively prevent the leakage of Ni-GaIn.

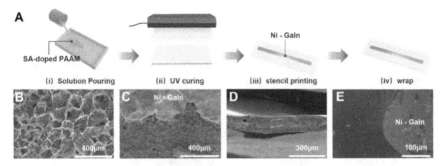

Fig. 1. (A) The design and fabrication of the strain sensor. (B-E) SEM images of the devices.

3.2 Surface Tension Regulation

EGaIn displays significant surface tension, making it challenging to directly print microcircuits on the surface of hydrogels. Consequently, reducing the surface tension of this liquid metal is crucial for enhancing its processability. Previous studies have shown that incorporating nickel powder into EGaIn can effectively lower its surface tension. Therefore, we prepared Ni-GaIn alloys with varying nickel mass fractions. As depicted in Fig. 2A, when the Ni content is 0 wt%, fabricating electrodes on the SA-doped PAAM surface using liquid metal is challenging, even for electrodes with a width of 5 mm. Numerous breakpoints are observed, and the electrode thickness is uneven. However, as the mass fraction of the nickel particles increased (Fig. 2B–D), the processability of Ni-GaIn gradually improved. Notably, when the nickel particle mass fraction reaches 3 wt%, it becomes feasible to fabricate 1 mm wide circuits on the SA-doped PAAM surface, which meets the processing requirements for small flexible electronics. Unless otherwise specified, the subsequent sections will utilize 3 wt% Ni-GaIn for experimental and analytical purposes.

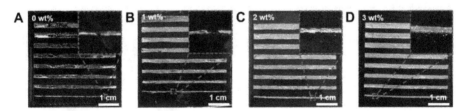

Fig. 2. The processability of Ni-GaIn at different concentrations: (A) 0 wt%, (B) 1 wt%, (C) 2 wt%, and (D) 3 wt%.

3.3 Biocompatibility

SA-doped PAAM is recognized as a biocompatible material. To further assess the biocompatibility of our strain sensor, we devised three experimental groups: (1) an SA-doped PAAM hydrogel (Fig. 3A); (2) an SA-doped PAAM hydrogel with a printed layer of Ni-GaIn on its upper surface (Fig. 3B); and (3) the device with complete package. After 72 h of cultivation, a fluorescence live/dead cell staining assay was performed. The results indicated that the cells in all the experimental groups A, B, and C exhibited robust survival and proliferation capabilities (Fig. 3D). These findings suggest that encapsulated Ni-GaIn PAAm/SA hydrogels hold significant potential in the field of implantable bioelectronics.

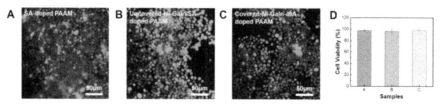

Fig. 3. Fluorescence live/dead cell staining assays with (A) SA-doped PAAM, (B) SA-doped PAAM with a printed layer of Ni-GaIn, and (C) the device with the complete package. (D) The cell viability of the three experimental groups.

3.4 Properties of the Strain Sensor

The device exhibited excellent electrical properties, as shown in Fig. 4. As shown in Fig. 4A and 4B, when the device is connected to an LED, the LED is successfully illuminated, indicating that the device possesses a certain level of electrical conductivity. Further observation in Fig. 4C and 4D reveals that after placing the device in a solution containing a pigment for six hours, the LED remains illuminated, which sufficiently proves that the device can operate stably in both air and water environments. Additionally, Fig. 4E shows the fluidic properties of the liquid metal, which can seamlessly integrate with the elasticity of SA-doped PAAM. Even under a stretch of more than 200%, the LED remains illuminated.

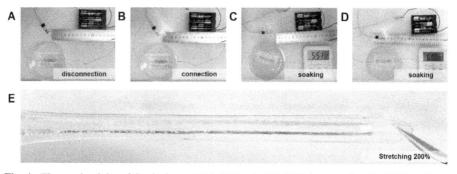

Fig. 4. The conductivity of the devices. (A) & (B) In air. (C)&(D) In water for 6 h. (E) Stretching.

Due to the fluidity of Ni-GaIn, the resistance of this device changes when it deforms, and this device can be considered a resistive strain sensor. As shown in Fig. 5A, the strain (S) can be determined using the following equation:

$$S(\%) = (L - L_0)/L_0 \times 100\% \tag{1}$$

where L_0 and L represent the lengths of the devices before and after stretching, respectively. With increasing strain, the relative resistance also increases. When the stretching strains are 10%, 20%, 30%, 40% and 50%, the relative resistance change rates are 5.78%, 15.62%, 27.14%, 39.91%, and 53.43%, respectively. The red line in Fig. 5A is the fitted result, and the fitting formula is as follows:

$$y = 1.1062x - 4.88 \tag{2}$$

Therefore, the sensitivity of this strain sensor to stretching can reach 1.1062. Figure 5B shows the repeatability of the device.

As shown in Fig. 5C, the relative resistance decreases with increasing bending angle. When the bending strains are 5%, 10%, 15%, 20% and 25%, the relative resistance change rates are −0.867%, −1.654%, −2.483%, −3.708%, and −4.531%, respectively.

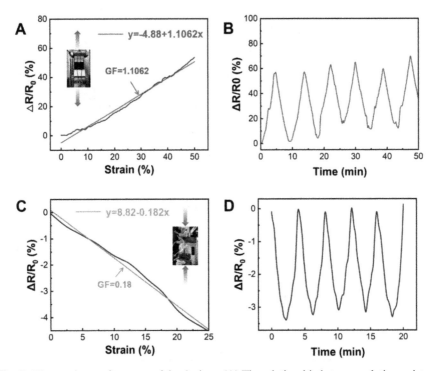

Fig. 5. The sensing performance of the devices. (A) The relationship between relative resistance and strain. (B) The repeatability of the strain. (C) Relationship between the relative resistance and bending angle. (D) The repeatability of bending.

The green line in Fig. 5C is the fitted result, and the fitting formula is as follows:

$$y = -0.182x + 8.82 \tag{3}$$

Therefore, the sensitivity of this strain sensor to the bending angle can reach 0.182. Figure 5D shows the repeatability of the device.

We integrated this flexible strain sensor into the joint of the robotic hand and detected the motion state of the joint in an underwater environment, as shown in Fig. 6. Figure 6A shows the testing system, with the flexible strain sensor attached to the knuckle of the robotic finger and placed in a water tank, where the resistance was detected using an LRC meter. As shown in Fig. 6C, our designed flexible strain sensor can stably sense joint motion in an underwater environment.

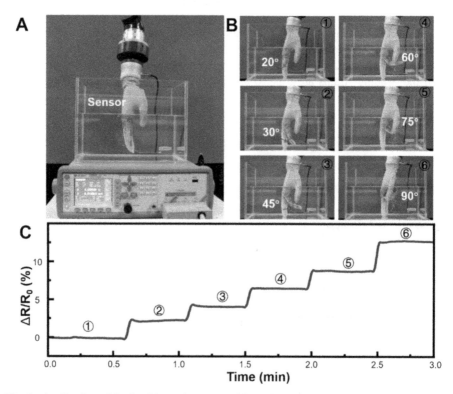

Fig. 6. Application of the flexible strain sensor with a robot hand for detecting motion in water. (A) Photograph of the experimental system. (B)&(C) Sensing performance of the device.

Due to the excellent biocompatibility of SA-doped PAAM, we placed this flexible strain sensor in commercially available pork, as shown in Fig. 7A. When the biological tissue deforms, the flexible strain sensor moves along with it and accurately reflects the degree of tissue deformation (Fig. 7B). This demonstration suggests that our flexible strain sensor can be implanted into organisms to detect limb movements. This work provides new ideas for the preparation of implantable bioelectronics.

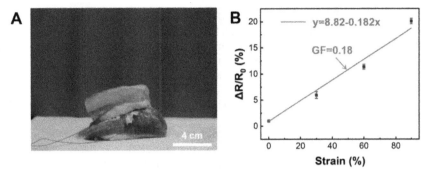

Fig. 7. Application of the flexible strain sensor in biological tissues.

4 Conclusion

In summary, a method for fabricating high-biocompatible, self-healing strain sensors based on SA-doped PAAM and Ni-GaIn was developed. The 3 wt% Ni-GaIn provides excellent processability, and the stable interface between the oxide layer of Ni-GaIn and the -OH groups on the SA-doped PAAM surface, as well as the good fluidity of the liquid metal, endows this device with high sensing performance. It also exhibits self-healing properties. We ultimately demonstrated the performance of this device within biological tissues. This work provides new insights for implantable bioelectronics and stretchable strain sensors.

Acknowledgements. The authors acknowledge the funding provided by the National Key R&D Program of China (Project No. 2022YFB4700100); the National Natural Science Foundation of China (Grant Nos. 62203154, 61973298); the Innovation Promotion Research Association of the Chinese Academy of Sciences (NO. 2022199); the Applied Basic Research Program of Liaoning Province, China (No. 2023JH2/101600037); and the China Postdoctoral Science Foundation (Grant No. 2022M723313).

References

1. Zhang, T., et al.: Flexible electronics for cardiovascular healthcare monitoring. Innov. **4**(5), 100485 (2023)
2. Li, N., et al.: Bioadhesive polymer semiconductors and transistors for intimate biointerfaces. Science **381**(6658), 686–693 (2023)
3. Hong, Y.J., et al.: Wearable and implantable devices for cardiovascular healthcare: from monitoring to therapy based on flexible and stretchable electronics. Adv. Funct. Mater. **29**(19), 1808247 (2019)
4. DY. Xu, et al.: Ultrasound-responsive aligned piezoelectric nanofibers derived hydrogel conduits for peripheral nerve regeneration. Adv. Mater. (2024)
5. Boutry, C.M., et al.: Biodegradable and flexible arterial-pulse sensor for the wireless monitoring of blood flow. Nat. Biomed. Eng. **3**(1), 47–57 (2019)
6. Ouyang, H., et al.: Symbiotic cardiac pacemaker. Nat. Commun. **10**(1), 1821 (2019)

7. Zhou, T., et al.: 3D printable high-performance conducting polymer hydrogel for all-hydrogel bioelectronic interfaces. Nat. Mater. **22**(7), 895–902 (2023)
8. Park, S., et al.: Adaptive and multifunctional hydrogel hybrid probes for long-term sensing and modulation of neural activity. Nat. Commun. **12**, 1 (2021)
9. Yin, Y., et al.: Hydrogel-coated microelectrode resists protein passivation of in vivo amperometric sensors. Anal. Chem. **95**(6), 3390–3397 (2023)
10. Liu, Y.X., et al.: Morphing electronics enable neuromodulation in growing tissue. Nat. Biotechnol. **38**(9), 1031–1036 (2020)
11. Han, W., et al.: Accelerated intestinal wound healing via dual electrostimulation from a soft and biodegradable electronic bandage. Nat. Electron. **7**(4), 299–312 (2024)
12. Liang, Q., et al.: Highly stretchable hydrogels as wearable and implantable sensors for recording physiological and brain neural signals. Adv. Sci. **9**(16), 2201059 (2022)
13. Sunwoo, S.H., Han, S.I., Park, C.S., et al.: Soft bioelectronics for the management of cardiovascular diseases. Nat. Rev. Bioeng. **2**, 8–24 (2024)
14. Park, S., et al.: Fully screen-printed PI/PEG blends enabled patternable electrodes for scalable manufacturing of skin-conformal, stretchable, wearable electronics. ACS Appl. Mater. Interfaces **15**(1), 2092–2103 (2024)
15. Yan, H., et al.: Hydrogen bond-mediated strong plasticization for high-performance alginate plastics. Adv. Mater. (2024)
16. Yang, P.-O., et al.: A flexible, stretchable and shape-adaptive approach for versatile energy conversion and self-powered biomedical monitoring. **27**(25), 3817–3824 (2015)
17. Sun, J.-S., et al.: Highly stretchable and tough hydrogels. **489**(7414), 133–136 (2012)
18. Hang, C.-Z., et al.: Highly stretchable and self-healing strain sensors for motion detection in wireless human-machine interface. Nano Energy **76**, 105064 (2020)
19. Trappmann, B., et al.: Extracellular-matrix tethering regulates stem-cell fate. Nat. Mater. **11**, 642–649 (2012)
20. Huang, T., et al.: Recent advances and progress on the design, fabrication and biomedical applications of Gallium liquid metals-based functional materials. Colloids Surf. B **238**, 113888 (2024)
21. Chongzhi, X., et al.: Selected phase separation renders high strength and toughness to polyacrylamide/alginate hydrogels with large-scale cross-linking zones. ACS Appl. Mater. Interfaces **13**(21), 25383–25391 (2021)
22. Lin, S., et al.: Stretchable hydrogel electronics and devices. Adv. Mater. **28**(22), 4497–4505 (2016)
23. Yan, J., et al.: Advances in liquid metals for biomedical applications. Chem. Soc. Rev. **47**(8), 2518–2533 (2018)
24. Dickey, M.D., et al.: Stretchable and soft electronics using liquid metals. Adv. Mater. **29**(27), 1606425 (2017)
25. Park, J.-E., et al.: Autonomous surface reconciliation of a liquid-metal conductor micropatterned on a deformable hydrogel. Adv. Mater. **32**(37), 2002178 (2020)

Advancing Human-Machine Interaction Using Intelligent Wearable Acoustic Sensors in Noisy Environments

Hui Sun[1], Xiaomeng Yang[1], Cong Wu[1], Yu Feng[1], Meng Chen[1,2], Guanglie Zhang[1,2(✉)], and Wen Jung Li[1,2(✉)]

[1] Department of Mechanical Engineering, City University of Hong Kong, Hong Kong SAR 999017, China
{gl.zhang,wenjli}@cityu.edu.hk

[2] CAS-CityU Joint Laboratory for Robotic Research, City University of Hong Kong Shenzhen Research Institute, Shenzhen 518057, China

Abstract. Noisy environments in various domains pose substantial communication barriers that can negatively impact work efficiency and increase safety risks. With the advancement in robotics technology, there's an increasing need for reliable and efficient voice recognition systems to ensure accuracy and safety during complex operations. This paper introduces a groundbreaking voice recognition method utilizing our innovative smart wearable acoustic sensor based on the ConformerLSTM architecture. The sensing device employs a deep learning model that integrates multiple acoustic features, specifically tailored for processing speech signals captured by acoustic sensors. Our approach involves training the model in both quiet and noisy environmental conditions to enable it to adapt to different environments and achieve approximately 80% recognition accuracy in high-noise settings, significantly outperforming traditional models and enhancing robustness. This study not only advances technology for processing acoustic sensor speech signals but also offers an efficient and reliable solution for speech recognition and synthesis across related fields.

Keywords: Wearable Acoustic Sensor · Speech Recognition · Multi-Feature Fusion

1 Introduction

With the rapid advancement of artificial intelligence technologies, speech recognition has been widely applied across various fields such as smart assistants, automatic translation, and assisted communication. In these applications, the collection of speech signals typically relies on devices such as microphones. However, traditional microphones often struggle with the interference of ambient noise in noisy environments, which can impact the accuracy and reliability of speech recognition. In contrast, acoustic sensors offer unique advantages and characteristics. Mounted directly on the user's throat, these sensors capture the activity of the throat muscles during speech through vibration sensing technology, effectively avoiding external noise interference. This makes them particularly suitable for use in noisy environments or situations where privacy is a major concern.

Due to the unique method of acquisition, the speech signals captured by acoustic sensors differ significantly in texture and characteristics from those collected by traditional microphones. These signals often contain more physiological information about the speech production mechanism, which is extremely valuable for certain specific medical and security applications. Examples include voice-assisted re-authentication systems, patient voice reconstruction, and highly confidential communication. However, due to the unique nature of throat speech signals, traditional speech recognition systems often struggle to adapt directly. Existing speech recognition methods, such as those based on deep learning for Automatic Speech Recognition (ASR) [1], are primarily designed for standard speech signals captured through microphones. Although these methods perform well in typical environments, they tend to be less effective when dealing with speech signals captured via acoustic sensors. This is mainly because of the significant acoustic characteristic differences in these signals, which make it difficult for models to capture the relevant speech features effectively.

Current speech recognition and classification approaches are largely based on deep learning technologies, such as Recurrent Neural Networks (RNN) [2], Long Short-Term Memory networks (LSTM) [3], Convolutional Neural Networks (CNN) [4], and the more recently popular Transformer models. These models demonstrate superior performance across various scenarios but each has its focus and limitations. RNNs and LSTMs are powerful tools for processing sequential data, capable of capturing long-term dependencies, which makes them particularly suitable for the temporally rich data of speech signals. However, RNNs are prone to issues like vanishing or exploding gradients, while LSTMs, though mitigating this issue to some extent, are computationally intensive and require longer training times. CNNs have achieved tremendous success in the field of image processing and have recently been applied to speech signal processing. With a natural advantage in extracting local features, CNNs are suitable for capturing short-term frequency features but are less effective at processing the temporal information in speech signals compared to RNNs and LSTMs. The Transformer model, based on a self-attention mechanism, can handle long-distance dependencies efficiently and is highly parallelizable, making it a mainstream model in the NLP field. However, Transformers require extensive data for training and demand considerable computational resources.

Due to the uniqueness of throat speech signals, traditional models often fail to directly apply. The acoustic characteristics of throat speech signals significantly differ from those captured by microphones, making many pretrained models unsuitable for direct transfer, requiring retraining and adjustment to specific acoustic features. Therefore, this study proposes a ConformerLSTM model that combines the spatial feature extraction capabilities of Conformer with the temporal information processing advantages of LSTM. By integrating multiple features, this model significantly improves the recognition accuracy of throat speech signals in complex environments, effectively overcoming the limitations of single models.

The process of converting recognized throat speech signals into normal speech using ChatTTS [5] voice generation technology not only enhances the naturalness and intelligibility of the voice but can also be applied to various important fields. For instance, in the medical field, this technology can help patients who have lost their ability to speak due to illness or surgery regain their communication capabilities. In the field of high-security communications, encrypted throat speech signals can be converted into normal speech, enabling secure communication. Moreover, this technology, which combines high-accuracy recognition and high-quality voice generation, is of significant importance for the development of more humanized human-computer interaction systems. It not only improves the naturalness of interaction and user experience but also provides more accurate and effective voice interaction services in noisy environments. Overall, the throat speech signal recognition and classification method combining Conformer and LSTM, along with the voice generation process using ChatTTS proposed in this paper, not only enhances the technical level of the system but also expands the scope and depth of applications of speech recognition technology, offering broad practical utility and profound societal impact (Fig. 1).

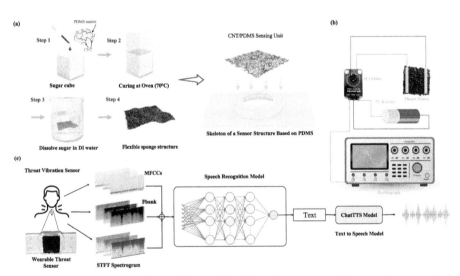

Fig. 1. Flowchart of Speech Recognition. (a) The fabrication process of the acoustic sensor detection unit; (b) Schematic of signal acquisition for the throat vibration sensor; (c) Deep learning-based throat speech recognition and speech synthesis using multi-features fusion.

2 Method

2.1 Fabrication and Signal Acquisition of CNT/PDMS Acoustic Sensor

In this study, CNT/PDMS nanocomposites are a crucial component for the fabrication of throat vibration sensors. In our previous works [6–8], we developed a highly sensitive and stable acoustic sensor using CNT/PDMS nanocomposites materials. The preparation process of this composite material initially involves mixing multi-walled carbon nanotubes (MWCNTs), polydimethylsiloxane (PDMS), and isopropyl alcohol (IPA). IPA not only acts as a solvent partially dissolving the CNTs and PDMS but also facilitates subsequent processing steps. Specifically, 0.2 g of MWCNTs with diameters of 10–20 nm and lengths of 10–30 μm are uniformly dispersed in IPA, followed by 20 min of ultrasonication to ensure complete dispersion. Subsequently, 10 g of PDMS base elastomer is added to the dispersion and subjected to another 20 min of ultrasonication to enhance the mixing effect.

The mixture is then heated on a hotplate at 55 °C to evaporate the IPA, after which 1 g of PDMS curing agent is added in a 10:1 weight ratio and the mixture is mechanically stirred for uniform blending. Finally, the CNT/PDMS mixture undergoes vacuum treatment to remove any air bubbles. To create a porous structure suitable for vibration signal capture, the CNT/PDMS solution is applied to the surface of a sugar cube, and another sugar cube is placed on top before curing in an oven at 70 °C for about 2 h. After curing, the sugar matrix is dissolved in deionized water, yielding a CNT/PDMS sponge sheet approximately 400 μm thick. This technique not only allows for the production of sponge samples with varying CNT concentrations (3wt%) but also enables precise control over the thickness of the samples by adjusting the amount of solution used, thus meeting specific application needs.

The main body of the acoustic sensor is made from polydimethylsiloxane (PDMS), which forms the basic structure of the sensor. The sensor features a circular cavity that is open at both the top and bottom, resembling a partially opened bottle cap. To create this structure, we first used Solidworks software to design the assembly drawings, followed by the use of the WENEXT 8200Pro for 3D printing the molds. This printer employs a precision and durable class-ABS stereolithography resin produced by WENEXT. During the assembly process, a CNT/PDMS sponge structure flexible sensor was installed at the top opening of the PDMS acoustic resonance cavity. The electrical connections of the sensor utilized two strips of copper tape as electrodes, connected to the flexible sensor with conductive silver paste. This assembly was then solidified using a hot air gun at 120 °C for approximately 2 min to ensure a secure bond. Finally, the throat vibration signals were amplified using a GY-MAX4466 audio signal amplifier and collected and analyzed by an oscilloscope. This design not only enhances the practicality of the sensor but also improves the efficiency and accuracy of signal collection.

2.2 Experimental Setup

Data Description. In this experiment, we collected throat vibration signals using acoustic sensors to construct a specific dataset aimed at exploring and analyzing speech recognition technology. This dataset includes data from two experimental participants (one male and one female), who were asked to read 15 different English words. To assess the robustness of the speech recognition system under varying environ-mental conditions, data collection was conducted in two settings: a normal environment and one with ambient noise. Each word was repeated 32 times. Of these repetitions, 20 were designated as the training set to train the speech recognition model, while the remaining 12 served as the test set to evaluate the model's performance on unseen data. Through this approach, our objective is to comprehensively analyze these data and assess the effectiveness and accuracy of the model in processing real-world speech signals, especially in less-than-ideal environments.

Training Procedure. This study employs a highly efficient speech recognition system constructed using a Conformer model combined with a Bidirectional Long Short-Term Memory network (BiLSTM) [9, 10]. Initially, audio files in WAV format are loaded from a local dataset, from which three acoustic features are extracted: Mel-Frequency Cepstral Coefficients (MFCC), Mel Spectrogram (Fbank), and Short-Time Fourier Transform spectrogram (STFT). Sequence padding techniques are used to ensure temporal consistency across all input data, and the extracted features are concatenated along the feature dimension. The model's input layer receives the processed feature data, enhanced by positional encoding to bolster the temporal information within the sequence. Subsequently, the data passes through several Conformer modules, each comprising a feed-forward network, depthwise separable convolution, and multi-head attention mechanism, effectively capturing both local and global dependencies of the speech signals. The BiLSTM layer further extracts sequence features, enhancing the model's capability to process time-series data. Finally, the results of speech recognition are output through a fully connected layer. During the model training process, the Adam optimizer and categorical cross-entropy loss function are employed, with the training spanning 300 epochs.

2.3 Model Architecture Design

The speech classification model (as shown in Fig. 2) employs a Conformer architecture that adeptly combines convolutional, feed-forward, and multi-head self-attention layers to address complex classification tasks. Initially, the model accepts an input of a specific shape, to which positional encoding is applied using sinusoidal functions, infusing temporal context into the data. The architecture's main body consists of multiple Conformer blocks, each structured to enhance feature representation through a sequence of operations: a feed-forward layer with normalization and ReLU activation, a convolution module incorporating pointwise and depthwise convolutions with additional normalization and dropout for regularization, followed by a multi-head attention mechanism that refines the focus on various sequence segments for superior contextual interpretation, culminating in a second feed-forward sequence that stabilizes and enriches the processed features. Subsequent to the Conformer blocks, a bidirectional LSTM layer captures temporal dependencies from both directions of the input sequence, which is then flattened and passed through a final dense layer with 128 units and ReLU activation. The architecture concludes with a dropout layer for regularization and a softmax-activated output layer that categorizes the inputs into distinct classes, encapsulating a robust method for speech classification (Fig. 2).

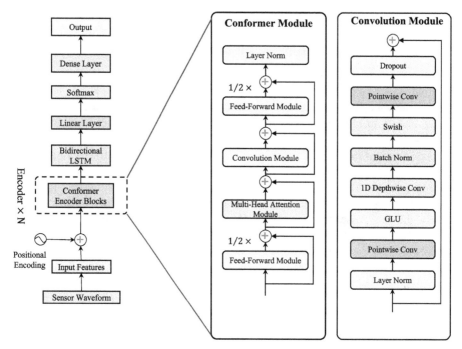

Fig. 2. ConformerLSTM-based Speech Recognition Neural Network Architecture.

3 Experimental Results and Analysis

3.1 Performance of ConformerLSTM Model

In this study, we compared the effectiveness of SVM [11], DeepSpeech [12], Transformer [13], and ConformerLSTM in classifying throat speech signals. By analyzing the confusion matrices from the test results of each method, we gained a deeper understanding of how different models perform with this type of unique speech data.

Firstly, SVM, as a traditional machine learning algorithm, has certain advantages in handling nonlinear problems but shows limitations in processing high-dimensional data. Therefore, it exhibits moderate performance in the complex task of throat speech signal recognition, achieving a maximum accuracy of 71%. DeepSpeech and Transformer, as deep learning-based models, are better equipped to handle and learn from the complex features within large datasets, thus enhancing recognition accuracy. However, as end-to-end speech-to-text models, DeepSpeech and Transformer have limitations in processing the specific acoustic characteristics of throat speech, achieving a classification accuracy of 69.44%. The ConformerLSTM model stood out in this study, combining the spatial feature extraction capabilities of Conformer with the temporal information processing strengths of LSTM. Furthermore, we also explored the changes in the training loss function of ConformerLSTM under different configurations, as illustrated in Fig. 3. It is evident that as the number of Conformer Blocks increases and the input features are optimized, the training loss progressively decreases, further validating the importance of model configuration optimization in enhancing recognition performance. Particularly during multi-feature fusion, ConformerLSTM demonstrated superior processing ability and accuracy. Experiments conducted on the ConformerLSTM model with different input features and numbers of Conformer Blocks yielded results as shown in Fig. 4. These results clearly indicate significant improvements in classification performance with increases in Conformer Blocks and adjustments to the input feature combinations.

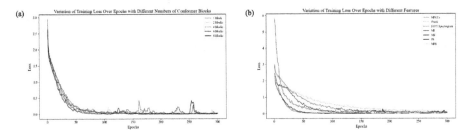

Fig. 3. Changes in the Training Loss Function of the ConformerLSTM Speech Classification Model Under Different Input Features and Network Configurations.

3.2 Comparison of Different Speech Recognition Methods

As illustrated in Table 1 and Fig. 5a–c, significant differences in Precision, Recall, and F1 Score are observed among four distinct speech recognition technologies: SVM, Deep-Speech, Transformer, and ConformerLSTM. ConformerLSTM consistently demonstrates higher Precision, Recall, and F1 Score in most instances, indicating its effectiveness in accurately identifying positive classes. This variation may stem from the differences in the internal mechanisms that these speech classification models employ to process sequential data. The Transformer relies on a global attention mechanism, while ConformerLSTM combines long short-term memory with its unique attention mechanism, allowing for more refined information processing.

Table 1. Comparison of Throat Speech Recognition Rates by Different Methods

No	Methods	Accurarcy
1	SVM	71%
2	Transformer	69.44%
3	DeepSpeech	69.44%
4	ConformerLSTM	80.00%

3.3 Effects of Different ConformerLSTM Configurations

Table 2 and Fig. 5d–f delve into the specific impacts of employing varying numbers of Conformer Blocks (1, 2, 4, 6, 8) within the ConformerLSTM model. With a single Conformer Block, the model achieves the highest classification accuracy, reaching 80%. As the number of Blocks increases, an initial improvement in Precision and F1 Score is noted, which then stabilizes or slightly declines with further increments. This trend may indicate that beyond a certain number of Blocks, adding more can provide limited benefits or even lead to overfitting, thus degrading performance. These findings suggest the necessity of finding an optimal balance between model complexity and performance in practical applications.

3.4 Impact of Different Input Features

Table 3 and Fig. 5g–i compare the impact of different input features (MFCC, Fbank, STFT Spectrogram, and their combinations) on the performance of the ConformerLSTM model. The results demonstrate that a combination of multiple features, particularly Fbank+STFT Spectrogram, offers the best performance across all primary indicators: Precision, Recall, and F1 Score. This indicates that the combination of diverse types of audio features provides the model with an enhanced capability to interpret data from multiple dimensions, thus more comprehensively capturing the complexities and subtle variations within speech signals, and improving the accuracy and robustness of recognition.

From the analysis above, it is evident that while a single feature or model structure may perform well on specific metrics, the integration of multiple features and the adjustment of model structures are key to enhancing the overall performance of speech recognition models. The ConformerLSTM model, when configured appropriately and combined with suitable features, is capable of achieving outstanding performance, making it particularly suitable for scenarios requiring high precision and balanced performance.

In this study, we utilized the ChatTTS voice synthesis model to convert and synthesize recognized throat speech signals. The ChatTTS model is an advanced text-to-speech technology capable of effectively transforming text information into clear, natural-sounding speech outputs. After accurately recognizing throat speech signals, we input these signals into the ChatTTS model to generate clear and natural speech. This process not only enhanced the intelligibility of the speech but also significantly increased the usability of the speech information. To demonstrate the effectiveness of the ChatTTS model in practical applications, we also generated a spectrogram of the processed speech. The resulting speech spectrogram, as shown in Fig. 6, illustrates that the synthesized speech retains the characteristics of the original signals while also displaying the fidelity and efficiency of the ChatTTS model in sound quality.

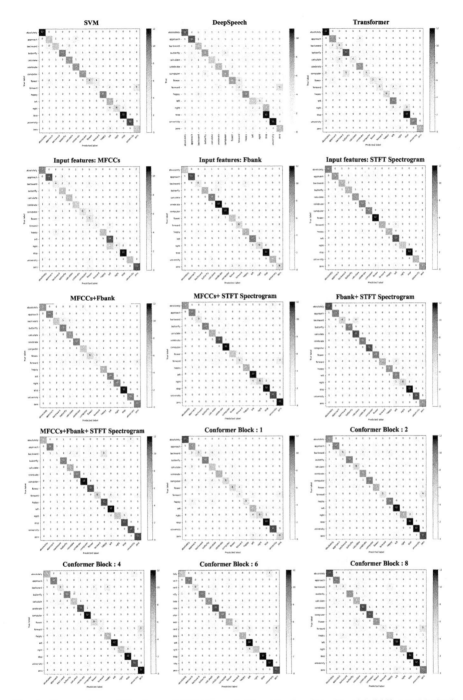

Fig. 4. Comparison of ConformerLSTM Speech Classification Results with Different Methods, Input Features and Different Numbers of Conformer Blocks.

Table 2. Comparison of Throat Speech Recognition Across ConformerLSTM Configurations.

Number of Conformer Blocks	Accuracy
1	80.00%
2	76.11%
4	74.44%
6	75.56%
8	76.11%

Table 3. Comparison of Throat Speech Recognition with Different Input Features.

No	Methods	Accurarcy
1	MFCCs	58.33%
2	Filter Banks	71.11%
3	STFT Spectrograms	77.22%
4	MFCCs+Filter Banks (MF)	72.78%
5	MFCCs+STFT Spectrograms (MS)	76.67%
6	Filter Banks+STFT Spectrograms (FS)	80.00%
7	MFCCs+Filter Banks+STFT Spectrograms (MFS)	77.22%

4 Discussion and Conclusion

We developed an intelligent wearable acoustic sensor capable of recognizing speech in complex and high-noise environments for human-machine interaction. The sensor is constructed from composite micro-nano materials into microstructured sensing units optimized for capturing speech signals and utilizes advanced speech recognition algorithms to ensure reliable voice recognition even under challenging acoustic conditions. This study conducted a comprehensive comparison and analysis of various speech recognition technologies, including Support Vector Machines (SVM), DeepSpeech, Transformer, and a model combining Conformer with LSTM. The results indicate that while SVM performs stably on small-scale datasets, it exhibits lower classification accuracy when dealing with complex throat speech signals and is unsuitable for processing high-dimensional and nonlinear features. DeepSpeech, a deep learning-based end-to-end method, performs well in environments with minimal noise but shows poor robustness to throat speech. Although the Transformer is capable of handling long-distance dependencies, it struggles with the complex characteristics of throat speech signals.

Advancing Human-Machine Interaction Using Intelligent Wearable Acoustic 419

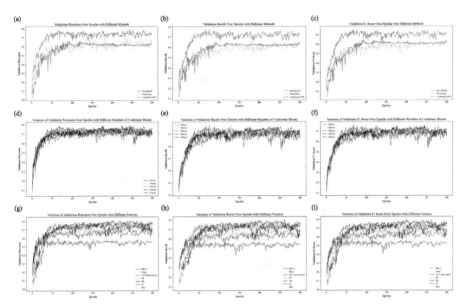

Fig. 5. Comparative Analysis of Speech Recognition Performance. (a)–(c) compares the Precision, Recall, and F1 Score results for three different speech classification methods: DeepSpeech, Transformer, and ConformerLSTM, using test data. (d)–(f) examines the effects of varying the number of Conformer Blocks (1, 2, 4, 6, 8) within the ConformerLSTM method on Precision, Recall, and F1 Score. (g)–(i) evaluates the impact of different input features—MFCC, Fbank, STFT Spectrogram, and their combinations—on the ConformerLSTM model, showing how each feature set influences the key metrics across the test data. This comprehensive view highlights the strengths and trade-offs of each method and configuration in terms of speech recognition accuracy and reliability.

Compared to the aforementioned methods, the ConformerLSTM model exhibited the best performance in this study. The Conformer structure integrates the advantages of the self-attention mechanism and convolutional neural networks, effectively extracting both temporal and frequency features from the speech signals. The inclusion of LSTM further enhanced the model's capability to process time series data. Additionally, our comparative experiments on the number of Conformer blocks demonstrated that the network already shows good performance with just one Conformer block. As the number of blocks increases, the model's recognition accuracy gradually improves. However, once the number of blocks exceeds a certain threshold, the gains level off, indicating that there is a need to balance performance with computational resource consumption in model design.

This study also explored the impact of different acoustic features on the effectiveness of speech recognition. When using MFCCs, Fbanks, or STFT Spectrogram as individual input features, each has its strengths and weaknesses. MFCCs excel in capturing timbre information, while Fbanks and STFT Spectrogram have advantages in preserving original acoustic information. By combining these three features, our ConformerLSTM

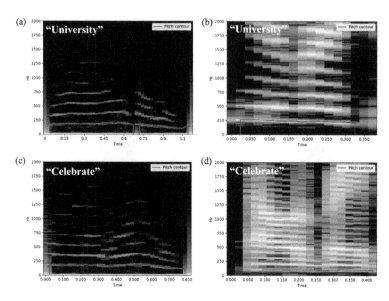

Fig. 6. Results of Recognizing Throat Vibration Signals Using Speech Recognition and Voice Synthesis with ChatTTS.

model achieved higher recognition accuracy, validating the effectiveness of a multi-feature fusion strategy. Furthermore, by integrating the classification results of throat speech signals into the ChatTTS voice synthesis model for speech generation, the study found that this method not only produces more natural-sounding voices but also effectively enhances the intelligibility and auditory quality of the speech. This approach particularly demonstrates unique value in applications requiring high levels of privacy protection.

Overall, this study not only advanced the processing technology for acoustic sensor speech signals but also significantly improved speech recognition accuracy in complex environments through the fusion of multiple features and advanced deep learning architectures. Additionally, both theoretically and practically, this research provides a solid foundation for further applications of throat speech signals, particularly demonstrating broad prospects in fields such as medical health, secure communication, and intelligent interaction.

Acknowledgments. This work was supported by the Hong Kong Research Grants Council (Project Number: 11216120), the University Grants Committee (Project Number: T42-717/20-R), the CRF-Collaborative Research Fund (Project Number: 8739045), and the InnoHK Project at the Hong Kong Centre for Cerebro-cardiovascular Health Engineering (COCHE).

Disclosure of Interests. The authors declare no conflict of interest.

References

1. Yu, D., Deng, L.: Automatic speech recognition. Springer (2016)
2. Chien, J.-T., Ku, Y.-C.: Bayesian recurrent neural network for language modeling. IEEE Trans. Neural Netw. Learn. Syst. **27**(2), 361–374 (2015)
3. Sundermeyer, M., Ney, H., Schlüter, R.: From feedforward to recurrent LSTM neural networks for language modeling. IEEE/ACM Trans. Audio Speech Lang. Process. **23**(3), 517–529 (2015)
4. Abdel-Hamid, O., Mohamed, A.-R., Jiang, H., Deng, L., Penn, G., Yu, D.: Convolutional neural networks for speech recognition. IEEE/ACM Trans. Audio Speech Lang. Process. **22**(10), 1533–1545 (2014)
5. https://github.com/2noise/ChatTTS
6. Suo, J., et al.: AI-enabled soft sensing array for simultaneous detection of muscle deformation and mechanomyography for metaverse somatosensory interaction. Adv. Sci. 2305025 (2024)
7. Suo, J., et al.: Enabling natural human-computer interaction through ai-powered nanocomposite IoT throat vibration sensor. IEEE Internet Things J. (2024)
8. Suo, J., et al.: Wide-bandwidth nanocomposite-sensor integrated smart mask for tracking multiphase respiratory activities. Adv. Sci. **9**(31), 2203565 (2022)
9. Wang, Q., Feng, C., Xu, Y., Zhong, H., Sheng, V.S.: A novel privacy-preserving speech recognition framework using bidirectional LSTM. J. Cloud Comput. **9**(1), 36 (2020)
10. Devi, K.J., Thongam, K.: Automatic speaker recognition from speech signal using bidirectional long-short-term memory recurrent neural network. Comput. Intell. **39**(2), 170–193 (2023)
11. Thiruvengatanadhan, R.: Speech recognition using SVM. Int. Res. J. Eng. Technol. **5**(9), 918–921 (2018)
12. Hannun, A., et al.: Deep speech: scaling up end-to-end speech recognition, arXiv preprint arXiv:1412.5567 (2014)
13. Dong, L., Xu, S., Xu, B.: Speech-transformer: a no-recurrence sequence-to-sequence model for speech recognition. In: 2018 IEEE International Conference on Acoustics, Speech and Signal Processing (ICASSP), pp. 5884–5888. IEEE (2018)

A Fast Online Adapting Algorithm for SEMG-Based Gesture Recognition in Non-Ideal Conditions

Shengli Zhou[1], Chuan Liu[2], Meibo Lv[1], Ruixing Yu[1], and Kuiying Yin[2(✉)]

[1] Northwestern Polytechnical University, Xi'an 710072, China
[2] Nanjing Research Institute of Electronic Technology, Nanjing 211100, China
yinkuiying77@outlook.com

Abstract. Gesture recognition based on sEMG signals has been studied for many years, but its practical applications are still limited due to the gap between laboratory study and practical applications. Among the many factors that influence the sEMG signals, the time factor and environmental noise was focused in this study. The data acquisition experiments were conducted for three consecutive days when seven electrodes were placed on the subject's forearm and hand. For each session, the subject was seated in a non-vibration environment and in a chair that vibrates in the vertical direction with vibration frequencies ranging from 0 Hz to 200 Hz randomly. Results of signal recognition with k-Nearest Neighbors (kNN) classifier show that the vibration will reduce the recognition accuracy, but the influence is limited when the test samples are from the same environment as the training samples. And the results of inter-session tests show that history sEMG signals is unreliable for new session sample recognition. When only one sample per movement was used as the training sample, the recognition accuracy was much higher than that with historical information. To solve such a problem, a fast online adapting algorithm based on training sample management and kd-tree was proposed. The results show that a much higher accuracy can be obtained when classifier is updated by using the samples that incorrectly recognized during calibration stage. The accuracies can be enhanced by 9.9% ± 8.2%, and 21.8% ± 10.7% respectively for the samples from non-vibration environment and vibration environment.

Keywords: sEMG · Vibration · Non-ideal · Inter-session

1 Introduction

As a non-invasive signal, surface electromyography (sEMG) signals have been broadly studied for applications like teleoperation for robotics, limb prostheses, games, and virtual reality in the past few years]. Among them, the most critical application is controlling prosthetic hands by motion classification with machine learning algorithms. High recognition accuracy has been reported in the literature. For example, a higher than 90% accuracy had been reported for the 10-class gesture recognition with four-channel sEMG signals almost twenty years ago [1]. When the number of gestures is increased to 52, the classification accuracy can reach 89% [2]. A 97% classification accuracy can be obtained when the number of gestures is eight [3].

Despite the high classification accuracy, the penetration rate of myoelectric control devices is still limited today. Among the factors that prevent the research from being applied to practical implementation, lack of robustness due to its inherent time-varying characteristic is essential [4, 5]. For long-term use, the shift of electrodes [6] is also inevitable due to the imperfect electrode doffing on and donning [7], which further reduces the robustness and reliability of classification results. The classifiers must be retrained with newly collected signals occasionally to obtain a usable recognition result. However, the new data collection and classifier retraining are both effort and time-consuming. It brings a burden to users and may prevent them from using them. Many efforts have been made to solve such a problem. Examples of these are transfer learning, multi-modality fusion, and post-processing [8].

Besides the lack of robustness due to the time-varying property of the sEMG signals, most of the current results are obtained in a controlled laboratory environment outside of vibration [9]. When the users with prosthetic hands are seated in a moving vehicle or work in a noisy vibration environment, the sEMG signals are easily influenced by the surrounding vibration, making the recognition even more difficult. Among the many studies on sEMG-based gesture recognition, the one on the sEMG-based hand gesture recognition in such a vibration environment is not too much. Most of previous studies focus on the influence of whole-body vibration on the sEMG signals of the lower limb. For example, [10] reported that the 30 Hz vibration frequency would result in a higher root-mean-square value of sEMG signals of vastus lateralis muscle during whole-body vibration in the half-squat position. The results in [11] also showed that the sEMG activity of calf muscle was much influenced by vibration frequencies of the platform, and the influence was not uniform for different frequencies. Besides the muscle activity level, the study in [12] showed that the sEMG signal collected during whole-body vibration contained motion artifacts and possibly reflex activity. The influence of various vibration frequencies on sEMG signals is studied in [9] by using LDA. It was shown that the classification accuracy was affected by the vibration frequency of the experimental test platform, where the 20 Hz vibration frequency leads to low accuracy, and the other 0 Hz, 40 Hz, and 50 Hz vibration frequencies lead to high classification accuracy. However, our experimental environment consists of vibration noise of different frequencies, so it is more similar to actual situation.

In this study, the non-ideal condition involves inter-session difference/electrode shift, and vibration of the experimental environment. It is believed that the result of this study will pave a way for those people who intends to apply the myoelectric prosthetic hand or myoelectric based recognition system to practical applications.

The rest of the paper is organized as follows. Section 2 introduces the experimental setup, signal processing and method for onset and offset detection. Section 3 introduces the online adapting algorithm. Section 4 shows the experimental results. And the conclusion in Sect. 5.

2 Data Description

2.1 Experimental Setup and Data Acquisition

The sEMG signals are weak biological signals, and are prone to be contaminated by environmental noises, so the Trigno EMG sensors from Delsys were utilized for data collection. The maximum sampling rate of sEMG signals were 2148 Hz. The data were transmitted to a computer via Bluetooth.

According to the muscle distribution of the human hand, the muscles related to the five-finger movement are located at the forearm and hand. So, the seven muscles selected in this study are flexor pollicis brevis (FPB), flexor digitorum superficialis (FDS), flexor carpi ulnaris (FCU), extensor indicis (EI), extensor digitorum (ED), extensor carpi ulnaris (ECU), and extensor carpi radialis longus (ECRL). Six of them are at the forearm, and one is at hand. The placement of the seven electrodes is shown in Fig. 1a and 1b. To simulate the vibration in the surrounding environment, the subject is seated in a chair on the top of a vibration platform that can vibrate at a frequency ranging from 0 Hz to 200 Hz randomly.

(a) Font view of electrode placement

(b) Back view of electrode placement

Fig. 1. Electrode placement and experimental platform.

The data collection experiment lasted for three days. For each day, a morning session and an afternoon session were conducted, so there are six experimental sessions in total. In each experimental session, the subject performed 20 repetitions of 10 hand movements according to the instruction on the cell phone in a laboratory environment. The movements conducted in the experiment are listed in Table 1. Between two same hand movements, the subject will have a rest for about 3 s, and there is a 10-s rest between two different movements. The experiments were conducted in non-vibration environment at first, and then the experiment was performed in the vibration environment after the subject took a rest for about 5 min.

The normalzied sEMG signals collected from the seven muscles when the subject performed the last five hand movements are shown in Fig. 2a and 2b. From these two figures, it can be found that the raw signals show much difference in different environments.

Table 1. Hand movements conducted in the experiment.

Number	Movement name	Number	Movement name
1	pronation	6	ulnar deviation
2	supination	7	index flexion
3	flexion	8	thumb flexion
4	extension	9	fingers spread
5	radial deviation	10	fist

The baseline noise level of sEMG signals in vibration environment is much higher than that in non-vibration environment, which should be considered during recognition.

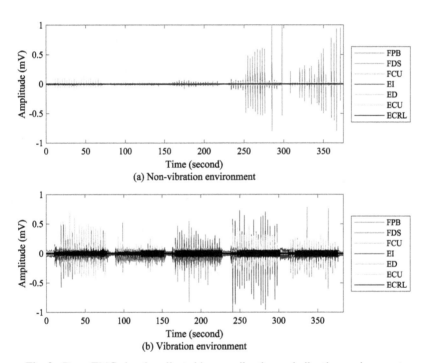

Fig. 2. Raw sEMG signals collected in non-vibration and vibration environment.

2.2 Onset and Offset Detection

The detection of the muscle contraction onset and offset is important for subsequent motion intention interpretation. In previous studies, single threshold, double threshold, and adaptive threshold methods are the three most commonly used methods [13]. Although some other algorithms, like visual inspection [14], and machine learning methods [15], have shown their capability offline, single threshold and adaptive threshold methods are the two that are fast and more appropriate for real-time applications. Due to its nonstationary property, the statistical model of sEMG signal is complex and not well known in advance. The single threshold method may fail when the noise level fluctuates with time. [16] proposed a modified adaptive linear energy detector (ALED) [17] based on order statistics (OM-ALED). The OM-ALED algorithm first improves the SNR by introducing Teager-Kaiser energy operator (TKEO) [18] for signal conditioning and then estimating the initial noise variance using order statistics. The algorithm can adapt its threshold according to noise levels, which greatly improves the detection accuracy compared with the other detection methods. The algorithm detects the onset and offset time in frame level. For the sEMG signal with small fluctuation in the middle, the algorithm will have a large chance separating it into two active segments, which would then be wrongly recognized as two movements by the classifier.

In this study, an improved sEMG active segmentation method was proposed. The method detects the onset and offset based on ALED [16] with a majority voting (VR-ALED). Similar to the study in [17], the raw sEMG signals are conditioned by TKEO first. And then the algorithm caches the activity status of each frame by using a 3-element buffer. The moments of onset and offset are determined by considering all the elements in this buffer. With this algorithm, the definition of onset and offset differs slightly from the one in [16]. The onset time is the time when an active frame follows two adjacent inactive frames. The offset time is defined as the time when two adjacent inactive frames follow the active frame. The status of the frame is determined by

$$\begin{cases} \text{If } median(|TKEO_i|) > \lambda Th, \text{ active} \\ \qquad \text{otherwise, inactive} \end{cases} \quad (1)$$

where $TKEO_i$ is the signals of the ith frame conditioned by TKEO; λ is a parameter to control false alarm probability; Th is the estimated noise level. For the frame that is detected as an inactive frame after the onset has been detected, its decision is made based on the status of the next frame. The pseudocode for determining the status of frame i-1 is shown below.

If frame *i* is active

    The frame i-1 is also active

else

    The frame *i* is inactive, the offset is detected

end

Finaly, the sEMG signal between onset and offset will be determined as active signal if its median TKEO is larger than $\gamma*Th$, where γ is the parameter to control signal-to-noise level. Since the algorithm is an extension of ALED, it can detect all the active segments that ALED can detect, but has the advantage of reducing the incorrect segmentation problem in ALED. To evaluate the performance of proposed algorithm, the miss segmentation rate (P_{ms}) is used, which is defined as follows.

$$P_{ms} = \frac{\text{number of detected segments - real number of segments}}{\text{real number of segments}} \times 100\% \quad (2)$$

2.3 Signal Processing

The raw sEMG signals are first filtered by using a six-order Butterwórth bandpass filter (20 Hz–45 0Hz). To extract the useful information of the sEMG signals, time domain, frequency domain, and time-frequency domain feature extraction methods have been commonly applied for sEMG-based gesture recognition. According to our previous study [2], time-domain features, especially root mean square (RMS) and mean absolute value (MAV) could help to achieve higher recognition accuracies than the other features. Therefore, the RMS was applied as a baseline feature extraction method. The RMS is calculated as follows.

$$\text{RMS} = \sqrt{\frac{1}{N}\sum_{i=1}^{N} x_i^2} \qquad (3)$$

where N is the number of data points in the current window; x_i is the ith data point.

3 Algorithm Description

The recognition accuracy of sEMG signal decreases when training sets and test sets are from different acquisitions [19]. The reasons are complex. Usually, they are the mixture of electrode shift, human physiological conditions, etc. To solve such a problem, an online learning system that learns new knowledge from the incoming signals should be adopted. As a classifier whose error rate is close to Bayesian rate as k goes to infinity, k-nearest neighbor (kNN) has proved its excellent performance in our previous studies [20]. Besides its simplicity, kNN was an excellent choice for the online learning problem because it does not need pretraining. It can directly be applied for test sample recognition whenever new training samples are available. However, the limitation is that the time cost for recognition will increase as the number of training samples increases. To enhance the efficiency and performance of the algorithm, we consider adopting method for training sample management and adopting an efficient searching algorithm.

Two training sample management strategies are proposed in this study. Both of these two strategies fix the number of training samples to N. The difference is that strategy 1 updates the training set using incorrectly recognized samples, while strategy 2 updates the training set by using correctly recognized samples. The procedures of these two strategies are shown in Tables 2 and 3.

As is known to all, kNN finds the best match by comparing the distance of the test data point to each data point of training samples. It takes a long time for prediction when the number of training samples is large. To enhance the searching efficiency, k-d tree was adopted in this study [21]. The k-d tree finds the best matches by partitioning the feature space and discarding the data points whose partition are further away than the k closest neighbors. Thus, the searching efficiency can be greatly improved.

For distance measure, our previous study [22] has shown that Mahalanobis distance helps to achieve higher recognition accuracy than Euclidean distance. Therefore, Mahalanobis distance is employed in this study. Different from Euclidean distance, the Mahalanobis distance transforms the features into uncorrelated features with variances

Table 2. The procedure of strategy 1.

Input: $X_i=\{x_1, x_2,\ldots, x_n\}$ of class C_i, and test sample x_t with true label C_i, i=1,2,..C
Prediction: the predicted label of x_t is C_j
If C_i is not equal to C_j and
   If n<N
      update $X_i=\{x_1, x_2,\ldots, x_n, x_t\}$
   else if n==N
      update $X_i=\{x_2,\ldots, x_n, x_t\}$
   end
end

Table 3. Procedure of strategy 2.

Input: $X_i=\{x_1, x_2,\ldots, x_n\}$ of class C_i, and test sample x_t with true label C_i
Prediction: the predicted label of x_t is C_j
If C_i is equal to C_j and n<N
   If n<N
      update $X_i=\{x_1, x_2,\ldots, x_n, x_t\}$
   else if n==N
      update $X_i=\{x_2,\ldots, x_n, x_t\}$
   end
end

---

equal to 1 by dividing the features with their covariance matrix. It takes into account the correlation of the data set and does not depend on the scale of measurement, which is more appropriate for our application. The Mahalanobis distance d between two points $\mathbf{x}$ and $\mathbf{y}$ can be calculated as

$$d = \sqrt{(\mathbf{x}-\mathbf{y})^T \Sigma^{-1}(\mathbf{x}-\mathbf{y})} \tag{4}$$

where Σ is the covariance matrix of all the training samples. As the number of training samples increase, the calculation of the distance for each pair of data points is time-consuming by using (4). To solve such a problem, we decompose Σ^{-1} with Cholesky decomposition so that

$$\Sigma^{-1} = \mathbf{R}^T \mathbf{R} \tag{5}$$

where R is a upper triangular matrix. Then (4) can be rewritten as

$$d = \sqrt{(\mathbf{Rx}-\mathbf{Ry})^T(\mathbf{Rx}-\mathbf{Ry})} \tag{6}$$

Thus, the calculation of Mahalanobis distance becomes calculation of Euclidean distance if all the data points are projected onto a new plane with the projection matrix **R**. Hence, given the training samples **X** in original space, the training samples **Z** in new space can be obtained by

$$\mathbf{Z} = \mathbf{RX} \tag{7}$$

And then the kd-tree can be applied for data point matching.

4 Experimental Results

4.1 Onset and Offset Detection with Proposed Algorithm

The P_{ms} of the proposed algorithm and OM-ALED evaluated for each hand gesture are shown in Figs. 3 and 4. From the figures, and it can be observed that the P_{ms} of VR-ALED is much lower than that of OM-ALED for the signals collected in non-vibration environment and in vibration environment. In the non-vibration environment, the P_{ms} is reduced by 86.5%, and in a vibration environment, the P_{ms} is reduced by 80.2%, proving the proposed effectiveness of the proposed algorithm.

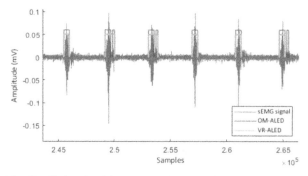

Fig. 3. The sEMG signal and its segmentation with OM-ALED and VR-ALED.

4.2 Cross-Evaluation of Recognition Results for Samples Collected in Different Environments

Figure 5 shows the recognition accuracies of the six sessions when the training sample and testing samples are from the same session. The horizontal tick labels are in the form of "training environment+test environment," representing the test environment of training samples and test samples. From Fig. 5, it can be found that the average recognition accuracies are much higher when training samples and testing samples are from the same environment (96.0 ± 2.1%, 95.4% ± 2.1%). When the training and test samples are from different environments, the recognition accuracy of training samples from non-vibration environment (93.5% ± 4.9%) is higher than that of training samples from vibration environment (91.9% ± 4.7%). It can also be observed that the standard deviations of the recognition results in the same environment are much smaller than those in different environments, suggesting the recognition system will suffer from accuracy loss when it is applied in different environments.

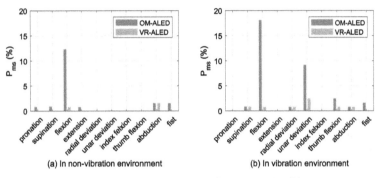

Fig. 4. Miss segmentation rate of proposed algorithms.

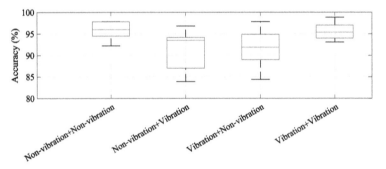

Fig. 5. Cross evaluation of recognition accuracies under alternate experimental environments.

4.3 Combined Effects of Inter-Day Difference and Electrode Doffing on Recognition Accuracy

The recognition accuracies of the system whose training samples are from the first session and test samples are from the six sessions are shown in Fig. 6. It can be seen that the recognition accuracies decrease when the time interval between the test session and training session increases. However, the decrease is not monotonic concerning session number.

The bars in Fig. 6 show the recognition accuracies of each session when different numbers of training samples from the same session are utilized for classifier training. It can be found from Fig. 6 that for most of the sessions, the accuracy of using one training sample is even better than the results of using the ten training samples from session 1. However, the results from the historical information are still much higher than those of random guesses. It can also be seen that increasing the number of training samples in the same session as test samples helps to improve recognition accuracies. If we combine the history information and a few current samples for classifier training, experimental results show that the accuracy will not be improved. The results discovered that for sEMG-based gesture recognition, the usage of history information for new task recognition may not be a good choice. Therefore, we suggest that inter-day usage of sEMG recognition should be calibrated with new training samples first. And the apply an online learning procedure to the classifier so that the classifier can adapt its parameters to the new test samples gradually.

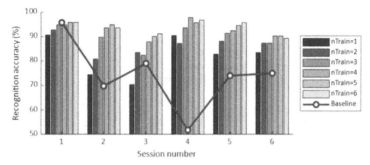

Fig. 6. Comparison of gesture recognition results when training samples are from the first session, and test samples are from each of the six sessions. The bars show the results when training samples and test samples are from the same session, and different numbers of training samples (nTrain) are used. The data were collected in a non-vibration environment.

4.4 Results of the Training Set Update Strategy

Figure 7 shows the experimental results on our database when the number of training samples was gradually increased from one to the maximum number 10. The red line was obtained when only one training sample of each class was utilized. The black one was obtained when the maximum number of training samples was fixed to 10, and strategy 1 is adopted, that is only the ones that were wrongly recognized were used to update the training set. The blue one was obtained similar to the black one, but only the correctly recognized samples were utilized for the training set update, which is strategy 2. The results show that when the training set is updated by using the correctly recognized samples, its recognition accuracies were not significantly improved. However, the recognition accuracies are much improved when the training set is updated by using the wrongly recognized samples. The improvement is 9.9% ± 8.2%, and 21.8% ± 10.7% respectively for signals collected from non-vibration environment and vibration environment.

Figure 8 shows that time cost for each movement recognition by using exhaustive method and the proposed method. It can be seen that the time cost of proposed method is much smaller compared with exhaustive method. The median time cost of exhaustive method is nearly 320 ms, which may not be appropriate for real-time applications, and not a good choice for classifier online adapting. But with the proposed method, the median time cost is only 6 ms. The classifier online adapting with this method will not cause a severe time delay to the recognition system. So, it can be used for real-time applications.

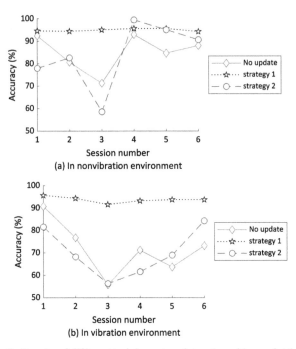

Fig. 7. Results of different training set update rules with our database.

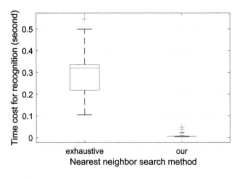

Fig. 8. Time cost for each movement recognition.

5 Conclusion

The paper studies the influence of experimental environment and time factor on the sEMG signal recognition. The results show that when training and test samples are from the same environment, the influence of the vibrating platform on the recognition accuracy is limited. Otherwise, a significant decrease in accuracy can be observed. The study on the inter-session sEMG signal recognition show that the accuracy decreased considerably when test samples are not collected on the same session as training samples, and the history sEMG signals is unreliable for new session sample recognition. The proposed fast online adapting algorithm based on training sample management and kd-tree for nearest neighbor search is able to solve such problems. The results show that the recognition accuracy can be much improved when incorrect recognized samples are utilized to update the training samples in calibration stage. The accuracies can be enhanced by 9.9% ± 8.2%, and 21.8% ± 10.7% respectively for the experiment conducted in non-vibration environment and vibration environment. It is believed that the result of this paper may provide information to researches on developing robust myoelectric control systems.

References

1. Hargrove, L., Englehart, K., Hudgins, B.: The effect of electrode displacements on pattern recognition based myoelectric control. In: International Conference of the IEEE Engineering in Medicine & Biology Society, pp. 2203–2206 (2006)
2. Zhou, S., Yin, K., Fei, F., Zhang, K.: Surface electromyography–based hand movement recognition using the gaussian mixture model, multilayer perceptron, and adaboost method. Int. J. Distrib. Sens. Netw. **15**(4), 1–13 (2019)
3. Zhang, X., Zhou, S., Yin, K., Fei, F., Zhang, K.: SEMG based wrist movement recognition with portable sensing device. In: The 1st IEEE International Conference on Micro/Nano Sensors for AI, Healthcare, and Robotics pp. 49–54. Shenzhen, China (2018)
4. Jiang, N., et al.: Bio-robotics research for non-invasive myoelectric neural interfaces for upper-limb prosthetic control: a 10-year perspective review. Natl. Sci. Rev. **10**(5), nwad048 (2023)
5. Jiang, N., Dosen, S., Muller, K., Farina, D.: Myoelectric control of artificial limbs-is there a need to change focus? IEEE Signal Process. Mag. **29**(5), 152–150 (2012)
6. Li, Z., Zhao, X., Liu, G., Zhang, B., Han, J.: Electrode shifts estimation and adaptive correction for improving robustness of sEMG-based recognition. IEEE J. Biomed. Health Inform. **25**(4), 1101–1110 (2020)
7. Zhu, B., Zhang, D., Chu, Y., Gu, Y., Zhao, X.: Senic: an open source dataset for sEMG-based gesture recognition in non-ideal conditions. IEEE Trans. Neural Syst. Rehabil. Eng. **30**, 1252–1260 (2022)
8. Bao, T., Xie, S.Q., Yang, P., Zhou, P., Zhang, Z.Q.: Toward robust, adaptive and reliable upper-limb motion estimation using machine learning and deep learning–a survey in myoelectric control. IEEE J. Biomed. Health Inform. **26**(8), 3822–3835 (2022)
9. Wang, Y., et al.: A study on the classification effect of sEMG signals in different vibration environments based on the LDA algorithm. Sensors **21**(18), 6234 (2021)
10. Cardinale, M., Leiper, J., Erskine, J., Milroy, M., Bell, S.: The acute effects of different whole body vibration amplitudes on the endocrine system of young healthy men: a preliminary study. Clin. Physiol. Funct. Imaging **26**(6), 380–384 (2006)

11. Di Giminiani, R., Masedu, F., Tihanyi, J., Scrimaglio, R., Valenti, M.: The interaction between body position and vibration frequency on acute response to whole body vibration. J. Electromyogr. Kinesiol. **23**(1), 245–251 (2013)
12. Lienhard, K., Cabasson, A., Meste, O., Colson, S.S.: SEMG during whole-body vibration contains motion artifacts and reflex activity. J. Sports Sci. Med. **14**(1), 54–61 (2015)
13. Carvalho, C.R., Fernández, J.M., del-Ama, A.J., Oliveira Barroso, F., Moreno, J.C.: Review of electromyography onset detection methods for real-time control of robotic exoskeletons. J. NeuroEng. Rehab. **20**(1), 141 (2023)
14. Kowalski, E., Catelli, D.S., Lamontagne, M.: Comparing the accuracy of visual and computerized onset detection methods on simulated electromyography signals with varying signal-to-noise ratios. J. Funct. Morphol. Kinesiol. **6**(70), 1–9 (2021)
15. Di Nardo, F., Nocera, A., Cucchiarelli, A., Fioretti, S., Morbidoni, C.: Machine learning for detection of muscular activity from surface EMG signals. Sensors **22**(9), 3393 (2022)
16. Bengacemi, H., Abed-Meraim, K., Buttelli, O., Ouldali, A., Mesloub, A.: A new detection method for EMG activity monitoring. Med. Biol. Eng. Compu. **58**(2), 319–334 (2020)
17. Bengacemi, H., Mesloub, A., Ouldali, A., Abed-Meraim, K.: Adaptive linear energy detector based on onset and offset electromyography activity detection. In: 2017 6th International Conference on Systems and Control (ICSC), pp. 409–413 (2017)
18. Li, X. Aruin, A.S.: Muscle activity onset time detection using teager-kaiser energy operator. In: Annual International Conference of the IEEE Engineering in Medicine and Biology Society, pp. 7549–7552 (2005)
19. Palermo, F., Cognolato, M., Gijsberts, A., Caputo, B., Müller, H., Atzori, M.: Repeatability of grasp recognition for robotic hand prosthesis control based on sEMG data. In: IEEE International Conference on Rehabilitation Robotics (2017)
20. Zhu, M., et al: Towards optimizing electrode configurations for silent speech recognition based on high-density surface electromyography. J. Neural Eng. **18**(1) (2021)
21. Freidman, J.H., Bentley, J.L., Finkel, R.A.: An algorithm for finding best matches in logarithmic expected time. ACM Trans. Math. Software (TOMS) (1977)
22. Zhou, S., Fei, F., Yin, K.: Toward improving the reliability of discrete movement recognition of sEMG signals. Appl. Sci. **12**(7), 3374 (2022)

Author Index

A
Aabloo, Alvo 360
An, Shunan 201

C
Cao, Baoshi 31, 123
Chang, Longfei 360
Chen, Chin-Yin 261
Chen, Han 261
Chen, Jun 336
Chen, Meng 388, 409
Chen, Wei 16
Chen, Xianbao 185
Chen, Zhu 138
Cheng, Zhongjiang 167
Chu, Hao 85
Cong, Qian 138

D
Dai, Junjie 261
Deng, Xiaomeng 45

F
Fan, Liting 167
Fang, Bin 275
Fang, Yuanyang 3
Fei, Fei 373
Feng, Weixing 352
Feng, Yu 388, 409
Fu, Min 85

G
Gao, Feng 185
Gerontiti, Dimitrios K. 111
Gong, Linan 45
Guo, Hongji 400

H
Han, Yu 167
He, Qingsong 286, 299
Hu, Guangyao 352
Hu, Jun 154
Hu, Ying 360
Huang, Anmin 60

J
Jiang, Boyu 167
Jiang, Lei 138
Jiang, Pei 311

L
Lei, Haiwei 336
Li, Bo 360
Li, Jiaxin 325
Li, Wen Jung 388, 409
Li, Xiaohu 3
Li, Xu 138
Li, Xueai 123
Li, Yingtian 311
Liang, Jiawen 400
Liu, Bao 325
Liu, Chuan 422
Liu, Enbo 60
Liu, Hong 31
Liu, Huaping 275
Liu, Shilong 201
Liu, Wen 336
Liu, Yang 31, 123
Lv, Meibo 422

M
Ma, Boyu 31
Mao, Jianliang 154

Mao, Lizhi 373
Mei, Dong 201, 211
Mei, Huan 235, 249
Mou, Chao 111

N
Ni, Fenglei 123
Ni, Shouyi 286
Niu, Dewen 352

P
Pang, Zaixiang 45, 73

Q
Qi, Le 123
Qin, Tao 85
Qiu, Rongcan 3
Qiu, Tianqi 96

R
Ren, Peng 85
Ru, Jie 352

S
Shang, Huiliang 16
Shen, Ziteng 138
Shi, Qiaowen 111
Shi, Yang 111
Shi, Ziyan 299
Song, Jian 138
Sun, Funchun 275
Sun, Hui 388, 409
Sun, Kui 123
Sun, Wandong 31
Sun, Yuhao 275
Sun, Zhongbo 73
Sun, Zhongyu 73

T
Tan, Kangning 201
Tang, Gangqiang 201, 211
Tang, Wei 60
Tian, Weijun 138
Tian, Xinze 123
Tu, Mingxi 400

W
Wan, Shaoke 3
Wang, Jia 85
Wang, Jianfeng 211
Wang, Liangyu 185
Wang, Lisheng 235, 249
Wang, Longlong 352
Wang, Nan 45
Wang, Ruicong 111
Wang, Ruizhi 138
Wang, Tao 360
Wang, Yanjie 201, 211
Wang, Yueming 96
Wang, Yunlong 3
Wang, Zhengpu 31
Wang, Zhihuan 235, 249
Wang, Zhirui 96
Wei, Xiaoxiang 336
Wu, Cong 388, 409
Wu, Xi 85
Wu, Yiqi 373

X
Xie, Lin 286, 299
Xie, Yuan 311
Xie, Zongwu 31, 123
Xu, Changguo 60
Xu, Changxian 73
Xu, Linsen 235, 249
Xu, Peng 96
Xu, Wei 96

Y
Yan, Tong 96
Yang, Canhui 223
Yang, Changli 286
Yang, Jin 336
Yang, Limin 185
Yang, Ruonan 373
Yang, Xiaomeng 409
Yang, Yang 311
Yang, Yiyong 275
Ye, Liangzhi 235, 249
Ye, Yuze 286
Yin, Kuiying 422
Yin, Yunpeng 185
Yu, Changlin 73
Yu, Haibo 400
Yu, Ruixing 422

Yu, Xiaodong 388
Yu, Xiaofeng 201
Yuan, Xuebing 60

Z

Zeng, Hui 336
Zhang, Chi 261
Zhang, Chuanlin 154
Zhang, Guanglie 388, 409
Zhang, Hailong 336
Zhang, Juchao 73
Zhang, Nan 352
Zhang, Qianru 373
Zhang, Renyuan 60
Zhang, Shixin 275

Zhang, Yachao 360
Zhang, Yang 167
Zhao, Chun 211
Zhao, Tianming 400
Zhao, Xin 211
Zhao, Xuan 16
Zhao, Yuncai 261
Zheng, Haozhe 311
Zhong, Qiyun 299
Zhong, Ying 261
Zhou, Jie 111
Zhou, Kuiyue 138
Zhou, Shengli 422
Zhou, Wu 336
Zhou, Xin 154

www.ingramcontent.com/pod-product-compliance
Lightning Source LLC
Chambersburg PA
CBHW050509100225
21662CB00007B/75